FRIENDS *of the*
Livingston Public Library

**Gratefully Acknowledges
the Contribution of**

**Judith Krafchick**

For the 2017-2018 Membership Year

ALSO BY KENNETH WHYTE

*The Uncrowned King:*
*The Sensational Rise of William Randolph Hearst*

# HOOVER

# HOOVER

## AN EXTRAORDINARY LIFE IN EXTRAORDINARY TIMES

### KENNETH WHYTE

ALFRED A. KNOPF

NEW YORK

2017

Library of Congress Cataloging-in-Publication Data
Names: Whyte, Kenneth, author.
Title: Hoover : an extraordinary life in extraordinary times / by Kenneth Whyte.
Description: First edition. | New York : Alfred A. Knopf, 2017. |
"A Borzoi Book." | Includes bibliographical references and index.
Identifiers: LCCN 2017015685 | ISBN 9780307597960 (hardcover) |
ISBN 9781524732462 (ebook)
Subjects: LCSH: Hoover, Herbert, 1874–1964. | Presidents—United States—
Biography. | United States—Politics and government—1929–1933. |
United States—Politics and government—1919–1933.
Classification: LCC E802.W49 2017 | DDC 973.916092 [B]—dc23
LC record available at https://lccn.loc.gov/2017015685

Jacket image: Future president Hoover, after his nomination
for the presidency, June 1928. Everett Collection, Inc. / Alamy
Jacket design by Carol Devine Carson

For Tina

# CONTENTS

# BOOK II

# BOOK III

# PREFACE

A contemporary once described Herbert Hoover as the sort of man "to whom the incredible was forever happening." Following a tragic childhood in which he was orphaned at the age of nine, he graduated (barely) with the inaugural class at Stanford University, made a name for himself in the rich goldfields of the Australian outback, and, still in his twenties, pulled off the biggest mining transaction in the history of China. The deal closed months after he had been given up for dead in the Boxer Rebellion. Settling later in London at the height of the Edwardian era, he raised a family, established himself as a global mining tycoon, and gained international acclaim as a humanitarian in the early years of the Great War. After almost single-handedly resurrecting the European economy during the Versailles peace talks, he returned to America, where he knew every president from Theodore Roosevelt to Richard Nixon, serving five of them in important roles in addition to fulfilling his own term in the White House. He remained a momentous and controversial figure through the New Deal, the Second World War, and into the Cold War, ending his days chasing bonefish in the Florida Keys and writing books, several at a time, in a luxurious suite in the Waldorf Towers with Cole Porter and the Duke of Windsor for neighbors.[1]

The challenge for Hoover biographers has never been a lack of exploit. Rather, it has been to find a coherent personality amid the nonstop action. As historical figures go, Hoover is a blur. He shielded himself from the scrutiny of journalists, independent biographers, and other strangers. Allergic to introspection, he rarely registered his thoughts and feelings in private conversation, let alone in diaries or journals. Wanting only to be remembered for his achievements, he destroyed an unknown quantity of his family's correspondence. His three volumes of autobiography reveal little of personal significance and what is divulged is often unreliable.

Fortunately, much of Hoover's life was lived in public, and he was often closely observed despite his reticence. Many of those working with him realized they were in the company of an extraordinary man and recorded honest and intimate impressions of him in their notes, letters, diaries, and memoirs. As well, important family correspondence escaped Hoover's purges. The portrait that emerges here is largely constructed from these sources, many of them not previously utilized.

Helpful as the sources are in locating elements of Hoover's personality, making sense of what is found is another matter. His capacities and achievements are obvious and awe-inspiring. Among the forty-four chief executives, he stands with the most intelligent and erudite, and none worked harder. He was the only president to have enjoyed two brilliant careers before the White House, and next to John Quincy Adams he was its most cosmopolitan inhabitant, having lived two decades abroad and circled the globe five times before the age of aviation. He was also a man of enormous goodwill, supporting with countless acts of charity his needy friends and relatives, not to mention the family of a colleague who was jailed for swindling him out of a large sum of money. The number of lives Hoover saved through his various humanitarian campaigns might exceed 100 million, a record of benevolence unlike anything in human history. Yet at the same time he bristled with more than the usual array of eccentricities, tics, tempers, neuroses, failings, and contradictions. He carried through his days the scars of his miserable boyhood, and he seems to have been determined in certain phases of his existence to prove points and settle scores of interest only to his bruised psyche. A man of force, quick-minded and brusque, he could be dangerous in pursuit of his interests, and he would rightly be concerned during his political years to obscure certain records from his business career. Tormented by guilt and paranoia, he twice broke down when his least honorable deeds came under public scrutiny.

The cracks and tensions in Hoover's personality expressed themselves in curious ways. When frustrated in pursuit of a righteous cause, he could fight with the heart of a saint and the conscience of a robber baron. He had a habit of crushing individuals and organizations who shared his objectives. Disliked, as a rule, by other politicians, including many Republicans, he disapproved of them in turn yet sought to lead them as head of state. Somehow he inspired fierce loyalty in chosen colleagues and employees without going to the trouble of forming normal human relationships with them. He knew thousands of eminent personages around the world yet related better to children. Genuinely modest, he had an almost biological compulsion to see his name in the papers. An introvert, he rarely ate a meal alone. A faithful family man, he was for decades almost a bystander in his family's life.

Hoover's political nature is also difficult to pin down. He does not fall neatly into any of the familiar political categories—Democrat or Republican, progressive or reactionary, populist or establishment, nationalist or internationalist. Pragmatic by temperament, he seldom thought in terms of labels or ideologies. He preferred to be true to himself and his thoughtful, in many ways commendable conception of America. This outlook, together with his perseverance, his unflagging willingness to serve, and the tumultuous years in which he lived, led him all over the political map. By his retirement, and despite his essential pragmatism, he had reasonable claims to paternity of the two main ideological currents of the American century: New Deal liberalism and the modern conservative movement born in opposition to it.[2]

If his reserve and his complexity make Hoover hard to know, the Great Depression, which began months after he was sworn in as America's thirty-first president (1929–33), and which stands as the worst domestic tragedy to befall the United States in the century and a half following the Civil War, adds enormously to the problem. Generations of historians and economists have been preoccupied with the questions of how the Depression started, how it ended, its consequences for domestic and international policy, and the relationship of Americans to their government, among much else. Naturally, they have studied Hoover for his contributions to the Depression, his efforts to fight it, and his failure to reverse it. His biographers have tended to adopt this same lens in treating him. One, for example, has prosecuted him as a man whose deficiencies of character and leadership rendered him insensitive and inept in his nation's hour of need, and another has defended him (the minority position) as a man of unexampled virtue whose life was an "almost unbroken record of success" and who did all that might reasonably have been done to

combat the Depression.* Either way, the Depression, or more particularly, Hoover's management of it, is the essence of the story, the trial
toward which everything in his life proceeds, and by which everything
is measured. Indictment and advocacy shape and often overwhelm the
story of the man.

I do not wish to diminish the contributions of any of these works
to an important debate on Hoover's role in a crucial historical event. I
have learned from them, and I join their conversation in parts of this
book. Hoover, as Anne O'Hare McCormick wrote, was "the pivot
of the dizziest turn of the wheel in this permanent revolution called
America," and it would be odd to avoid discussion of it. I nevertheless
find the Depression a problematic lens for the purposes of biography.[3]

For starters, it is only in the vast sweep of history that the Great
Depression appears as a single reference point. As Hoover knew it,
it was not a discrete event but a maddeningly unpredictable series of
emergencies of varied origin and severity—what he called "a battle
upon a thousand fronts." What's more, the Depression had political,
economic, social, and international dimensions, many of which had
histories of their own dating back decades, and many of which would
continue to haunt the nation through future decades. Hoover is a part
of the whole story, and, as we will see, his profile shifts markedly at
different points in the narrative.[4]

Not only is the Great Depression large and complicated, but
it is still in litigation. Its nature and its causes have been under dispute since its inception, not surprisingly given that it changed the
course of American history and raised questions of policy that are still
with us today. New facts and arguments are continually brought to
bear in its discussion as others are reordered, reinterpreted, or shot
to pieces. Our knowledge of the stock market crash and the Smoot-
Hawley Tariff, of the roles of fiscal and monetary policy and the gold
standard, have all been substantially revised over time. Great swaths
of the Depression story are reconsidered in these pages, including

---

* The two biographies mentioned, in order, are William E. Leuchtenburg's *Herbert
Hoover* and Glen Jeansonne's *Herbert Hoover: A Life*. A third, David Burner's *Herbert
Hoover: A Public Life*, ends abruptly at the nadir of the Depression as though there is
nothing left to say. There is also a six-volume official Hoover biography written by four
separate authors. It is in parts masterful, of uneven quality overall, and generally defensive about Hoover. All of these books are listed in the bibliography.

the Bonus Army episode, the Republican collapse of 1932, and the Hoover-Roosevelt interregnum. All this pleading is fair game. It is how we learn. Let it continue, recognizing that courtrooms are useful for testing evidence, scoring points, and rendering verdicts, but they are no place to learn someone's life story.

Notwithstanding my own contributions to the Great Depression debates, I have made a deliberate effort to privilege understanding over judgment in this narrative. It is the right approach for biography, and it seems only reasonable when one acknowledges that none of the policy makers, regardless of partisanship, ideology, or nationality, had a tight grip on what needed to be done with the economy after it crashed in 1929. It seems more reasonable still when we admit that our own expertise in managing such crises remains imperfect after ninety years of intensive study and additional practice.

My intention with this book is to spring Hoover from the Depression and present him in another context, that of his full life. This is not simply to say that he had a life beyond the Depression. It is to recognize that he was molded by a series of experiences stretching from the Gilded Age to the Cold War. His boyhood shaped his business experience, which informed his humanitarianism, which fashioned his approach to public service and his philosophy of American life, which in turn dictated certain attitudes to the challenges of his presidency, to the New Deal, to the next war, and so on. One thing leads to another and helps to make sense of the other, and it is only by following Hoover through his days as he lived them, one adventure at a time, without foreknowledge of outcomes or benefit of hindsight, that we can arrive at a faithful portrait of the man in his times.

His times are crucial because the United States was on a momentous journey of its own throughout Hoover's adulthood. The long road from Theodore Roosevelt to John F. Kennedy wound through booms, busts, cataclysmic wars, uneasy peace, and all manner of political and social upheaval. For the American people, as for Hoover, the Great Depression was not an island in time but one of a series of closely entwined events that combined to transform their nation in stunning and irreversible ways. These events are inexplicable without reference to one another: the Depression would not have happened as it happened, or at all, without the Great War, and the Second World War would not have happened as it happened, or at all, without the

Depression. I do not pretend that this is a revelation. I mention it only because we can get locked into reading history one episode at a time when, in many instances, as with a biographical subject, a longer view helps us to see things afresh. Indeed, by following the journeys of Hoover and the nation together through these decades, we gain a deeper appreciation for how each evolved, and how they affected each other. We notice the many ways in which they are mutually illuminative.

One of the wonders of Hoover is that he was incomparably a man of his times. He shows up not just at one dizzying turn of the wheel but at all of them in the most consequential half century in American history. He participated in and often embodied crucial national conflicts between traditional and modern, rural and urban, east and west, individual and collective, local and national, rich and poor, wet and dry, isolationist and interventionist. His involvement was consistently at a high level, and he always represented a strong point of view shared by some considerable portion of the American public. His prominence and ubiquity make him an invaluable guide to the epoch. This applies at a high level: he sharpens our insight into how the bucolic, wood-smoked America of his youth became the centralized, citified global powerhouse of his maturity. It also applies to particulars, for instance, the development of the nation's leadership. Through Hoover we see how a new class of professional managers emerged during and after the Great War, how the minds of these men (they were all men) were opened and haunted by that conflict, how they came to believe that they could manipulate the nation's economy for the betterment of its people, how they tentatively assumed stewardship of a broken system of international finance, how they laid years of groundwork for what in retrospect looks like a sudden leap from the austerities of the Coolidge era to the unbridled activism of the Roosevelt years.

The historian Eric Hobsbawm called the twentieth century "the age of extremes," and although he had world history in mind the phrase is appropriate to American experience. In Hoover's time, bloody international wars, unparalleled privation, and intellectual provocation lived in close quarters with massive economic expansion and social progress. He shared the extremes in his public and private lives, notching a range of achievement and failure unmatched by any American of his era, and perhaps any era. His highs, of which there were many, were wondrously high, his lows, also numerous, were unbearably low, and there were few points in his life at which reversal, in one direction or the other, did not beckon, whether by his own actions or by circumstances beyond his control. Any complete portrait of Hoover needs to embrace these ups and downs, volatility being a constant of the age.[5]

Despite the extremes, the welfare of most Americans improved strikingly between Hoover's youth and his old age. The same cannot be said for him. His presidency was more interesting and impressive than is generally acknowledged, but there is no getting around the fact that he was bounced from office in 1933 with the economy in pieces at his feet and one in four Americans unemployed. This inglorious political defeat at the pinnacle of his career is a fact, one it took him many years to absorb, and one from which he never entirely recovered. He would campaign doggedly for his vindication and adopt a brooding, obsessive animosity toward the political virtuoso who trounced him, Franklin Roosevelt. Both pursuits yielded modest results.[6]

To his enormous credit, Hoover did not allow his defeat and his enmity to destroy him. Nor did he let his battered prestige discourage him from pursuit of his admirable vision of American life, or interfere with his dedication to the service of the American people. He continued to work, to strive, to squeeze all he could from his existence, displaying toward his countrymen a magnanimity, not altogether reciprocated, that deserves to be considered among his greatest achievements.

# ★ BOOK I ★

# CHAPTER 1

# "A Pretty Stiff Time"

West Branch lay in the barely settled reaches of eastern Iowa at the intersection of two dirt roads. Downey Street, running north and south, was a crooked, rutted cart path that served as the main approach to town. Main Street stretched east to west for about ten blocks, ending in a mudhole.[1]

The community was two decades old in 1874, the year of Herbert Hoover's birth. Of its 350 citizens, most were Quakers, and all lived close to the land. The town fathers were proud of their amenities. A small schoolhouse. A livery stable. Several general stores and a restaurant. Two blacksmiths. A dollar-a-day hotel. A Friends meetinghouse. A forerunner of the Burlington, Cedar Rapids & Northern Railway had reached West Branch three years earlier, prompting the entire population to celebrate with a basket dinner. A two-plank sidewalk, the town's first, was laid from the depot to the corner of Downey and Main.

With all these refinements, West Branch was still more remarkable for its wants. It had no bankers or lawyers, no blacks or Native Americans, and few, if any, Roman Catholics or Democrats. It had no fairground, no sports field, no theater, music hall, or library. A saloon was out of the question, and a jail unnecessary. The local newspaper filled a single sheet once a month. What West Branch lacked in news it made up for in weather. In summer, an oppressive heat clung to the town, punctuated by howling black storms that stripped fruit from trees and reduced heavy cornfields to stubble. Winters were worse, and long.

Jesse Hoover was a West Branch blacksmith, a tall lean man with twinkling dark eyes, an easy smile, and a long dark beard, shaped like a diamond. He owned two lots on Downey Street just north of Wapsinonoc Creek. One lot held his shop and his forge, the other his home, a two-room cottage he had built with his own hands. It was a simple, sturdy wood-frame structure with walls of whitewashed barn board and a shake roof. The front door opened with a thumb latch. A man could walk in the front door and out the back in three strides. The parlor, dining area, and kitchen were one room, sparsely furnished. Jesse and his wife, Hulda, shared a tiny bedroom with their three-year-old son, Theodore, who slept in a trundle bed. The family's clothes hung from hooks on the wall. Off the back of the house was a porch shed used for summer cooking and, occasionally, as a sleeping quarters for Jesse's hired hand.

Late in the sweltering evening of August 10, 1874, Jesse tiptoed out to the porch and asked his assistant to run for help. Hulda was ready to give birth. Early the next morning, with the sun up and the temperature rising, Jesse slipped out of the house again and crossed the dusty street to tap on the window of his sister-in-law, Agnes Miles. "Well, we have another General Grant at our House," he said. "Hulda would like to see thee."[2]

There was nothing lofty or prophetic in the father announcing his son with an invocation of President Ulysses S. Grant. Jesse Hoover was a humble man. He possessed what passed for wit in the dour Quaker community. Agnes hurried over to see Hulda. The sisters, who were close, had spent the previous day visiting and sewing in the thick summer heat. Hulda had shown Agnes a bureau drawer full of handmade clothes prepared for the baby, all of them suited for a girl, to be named Laura. Several decades later Agnes recalled that the newborn, a boy, was "round and plump and looked about very cordial at every body."[3]

Naming the child was a problem as Laura, obviously, would not do, and the mother had no alternative in mind. Another sister reminded Hulda of a favorite book, *Pierre and His Family*, a Sunday school martyrology set among the Protestant Waldenses of Piedmont. The hero of the story is a spirited boy named Hubert who is dedicated to his Bible and longs to become a pastor. Hulda's sister remembered Hubert as Herbert, and the baby was called Herbert Clark Hoover. He shared his father's middle name.[4]

Apart from Aunt Agnes's belated recollections, there is almost no record of Herbert Hoover's birth. He arrived around midnight, but which side of that hour no one thought to mark, leading to a lifetime of confusion over his true birth date.* It appears that no one weighed him at birth, or measured his length, or jotted a note about his complexion, the shape of his face, the color of his eyes, the presence or absence of hair or teeth. We do not know if his delivery was difficult, if he entered the world with a howl or a whimper. There is no diary entry describing the blessed event, nor a contemporary letter to a friend or family member, nor a medical or legal certificate, nor a baptismal register or even a note in the family Bible.

The Hoovers were plain pioneer folk, and like most members of the Religious Society of Friends, as the Quakers are formally known, they lived independent of clergy and civil authority. They did not practice baptism, and they gave scant notice to Christmas, Easter, and birthdays. They were austere in almost every aspect of their lives, from their artless conversation, to their simple diet and drab clothing, to their record keeping.

During a winter cold snap when he was two years old, Herbert fell victim to the croup, a viral infection that inflames the larynx and obstructs breathing. He coughed his chubby face purple. His mother and aunts treated him with onion poultices, goose grease, and other household remedies, to no avail. When the attacks intensified, producing terrible strangling spells, Jesse fetched Dr. Henry John Minthorn, Hulda's brother and one of two physicians in West Branch. Minthorn ministered to his nephew by lamplight through most of an icy night as Hulda prayed and Jesse, under instructions to keep the temperature in the room constant, fed the wood stove. When the patient seemed better, Minthorn left to make an urgent call in

---

* As an adult, Herbert Hoover would switch his birthday between August 10 and 11 to suit his convenience. The earlier date is now taken as official, but it is an estimate. A certain imprecision around key points seems to have run in the Hoover family. Hulda not only named her son Herbert when she meant Hubert but sometimes spelled her own name Huldah. Herbert would sometimes write his own son's name as Allan, and other times as Allen.

the countryside. The attacks resumed while he was away, and Hulda's extended family crowded the little house and worried over "Bertie." No one could do anything to relieve his choking. He turned blue, stopped breathing entirely, and was given up for dead. Jesse held his wife as the women picked up the still child, stretched him on a pillow, straightened his tiny hands, wrapped his head in muslin, closed his eyes, and put a dime on each eyelid.

There are several accounts of what happened next. It seems a lookout had been established for the return of Dr. Minthorn. When, finally, in the full light of morning, he came flying up the snowy road behind two swift horses, he was alerted to the emergency at his sister's home. He threw his reins to the stable boy, ran to his own house to fetch warm blankets, and dashed back to his sister's, where he was greeted at the door with the cry "Bertie is gone!" The sitting room was icy cold, Jesse having finally let the fire die. By the light from the little home's east window, Minthorn, a tall, square-shouldered man with a stern face, picked up his nephew, wrapped him in blankets, and set to work. He used either mouth-to-mouth resuscitation or his finger, or some combination of both, to clear Bertie's throat and coax another coughing fit. The child's breath was restored, and the doctor handed him to his mother, saying "Here's your boy."[5]

The Hoovers were farm people of Swiss-German extraction. They had emigrated to North America in 1738, landing in Pennsylvania and exploding in number as they roamed south and west in search of cheap land. It was almost inevitable that some of their number would find their way to Iowa, with its abundance of rich soil. First mapped by the French explorers Joliet and Marquette in the late seventeenth century, the region had been acquired by the United States government from France as part of the Louisiana Purchase of 1803 and white settler families had begun trickling in during the 1830s, some from as far as Pennsylvania and New York, others from Ohio, Indiana, and Kentucky. They learned to adjust their eyes to the relatively bleak vistas of tall grass country, and to supplement scarce timber fuel with corn cobs and dried hay. They achieved statehood in 1846 with an unusually diverse population of German, Dutch, English, Swedish, and Danish settlers numbering just under half a million. Jesse Hoover had been eight years old and sturdy enough to lead an ox team when his extended family migrated from Miami County, Ohio, across the Mississippi to West Branch in 1854.[6]

Mechanically nimble, bored by farm life, Jesse tinkered with clocks and sewing machines and by age sixteen he had learned to assemble and operate the community's only thresher, making himself a figure of some importance in West Branch. At the first opportunity, he left his father's spread to set up shop as a blacksmith and mechanic. He was well liked and respected in the community, although some of the more devout Quakers, noting his commercial bent and the ornate harnesses on his span of sleek horses, considered him frivolous.

Jesse had known Hulda Minthorn since adolescence. She was born a loyal subject of Queen Victoria, raised in the town of Norwich, ninety miles southwest of Toronto in what was then known as the United Province of Canada. In 1859, when Hulda was eleven, the Minthorns had crossed the border by wagon team and landed on a farm three miles west of West Branch. They moved into town in 1866 with the unexpected passing of Hulda's father.[7]

To outward appearances, Hulda was a plucky personality. Family and friends described her as bright, kind, sociable, devout, and a born performer. She recited psalms at her mother's sewing bees and mimicked Quaker elders to the delight of her schoolmates. She was inordinately fond of sewing, sprucing up her hand-me-down dresses with colorful ribbons and bright buttons in mild defiance of Friends fashion. Notwithstanding these high spirits, she had something of a morbid streak. Seriously ill at least twice in her youth and plagued by chronic stomach ailments throughout her life, she wrote letters and quoted poetry that dwelled upon premonitions of an early demise:

> Remember me when death shall close
> my eyelids in their last repose

and

> O tell me if when I am pillowed in death
> When His pale seal is set on my brow,
> When lost is my feverish flickering breath,
> Thee will think of me kindly as now.[8]

Hulda, deeply affected by her father's passing, offended respectable opinion in West Branch by breaking out in song beside his casket. After the funeral, she abandoned her brief studies at the University of Iowa—that she was there at all was a rarity for a young woman—and announced that she would consecrate her life to God. As a sign of her seriousness, she purged her wardrobe of colors and flourishes. She taught Sunday school and spoke more frequently at First Day meetings, as Quakers called their Sabbath gatherings. A short, plump young woman, she had a square face, wide-set eyes, and a powerful jaw. In adulthood, no one considered her frivolous.[9]

In the absence of dances or theatrical performances, Jesse's courtship of Hulda consisted of family gatherings and the occasional visit to Iowa City for a debate or a lecture, followed by an oyster supper and a ten-mile buggy ride home. They were married on March 12, 1870, by their friend A. M. Smith, a Methodist pastor. That they eschewed the traditional Quaker ceremony of joining hands and acknowledging their union before their local meeting speaks to Hulda's independence of mind and spirit.

Herbert spent his early years in the neat little bungalow, rolling at his mother's feet on a bright rag carpet. He slept in a crib, probably until the birth of his sister Mary (called May) in 1876, at which point he would have joined his brother on the trundle bed. The family would gather after breakfast, everyone in chairs, the boys' legs dangling as Jesse read from the large black Bible. When he closed the book, they would all kneel with their elbows in the chair seats while Hulda prayed. Afterward the boys would scramble around the yard with its crab apple trees, chicken coop, and two-hole outhouse. Herbert would so frequently need to be pulled from the deep muck of Downey Street that Jesse called him "papa's little stick-in-the-mud."[10]

The young family had fond moments, picnics on the banks of the Cedar River, and Fourth of July celebrations with firecrackers and pink lemonade. Theodore remembered a trip to a fair in nearby West Liberty where they saw livestock, quilts, and pies. Like others of their faith, they steered clear of the horse races. They drove home at twilight, tired and quiet, the musky summer smells of goldenrod and ragweed floating on the air.

The boys spent a lot of time around Jesse's shop where Herbert's earliest recollection was of burning his bare foot on a hot iron chip on the clay floor of the smithy. On cold winter days, Jesse fixed a comfortable seat for his sons near his furnace so they could watch him work, moving tirelessly and efficiently amid ringing hammers and showers of sparks. One winter Jesse made the boys sleds. Theodore's was red with green stripes and had his nickname, Taddie, emblazoned on the front. Herbert found his slow and unsentimentally traded it for a faster, if dilapidated, store-bought model.[11]

West Branch, typical of small towns in the Midwest, was a tight community where traditional pioneer virtues of enterprise, fortitude, and self-reliance were preached in equal measure with collective responsibility. The families knew one another intimately, taking care of one another in times of sickness and hardship, raising each other's barns, building roads and collecting harvests together. Reverence was due those who gave the most and asked least of the whole.

The ethic of service was enhanced in West Branch by the self-sufficiency of the Quaker citizenry. Their desire to be independent of external institutions, whether governmental, judicial, financial, or clerical, could only be sustained by an unusual dedication to communal welfare. Faith, too, reinforced their collective orientation. Quakers believe that each individual, from the greatest to the least, has an "inner light" within, a direct experience of God that gives guidance and strength, diminishing the need for external authority. A world in which people are living with God is a world of equality, reasonableness, and harmony, a world in which the good of the whole stands before that of the individual.[12]

Herbert's introduction to community occurred among the Friends at the meetinghouse on First Days. The plain wooden hall was entirely functional in design; no steeples, stained glass, or pulpits. It was heated by a single stove that was insufficient to keep the faithful comfortable on cold days, so the women would heat stones and put them under their feet. Entering the room, which was parted down the middle by a wall four and a half feet high, Jesse and his sons would take seats on one side with the men, all of whom had arrived in broad-brimmed hats and dark suits, while Hulda and May settled into the opposite side among the women, who wore simple dresses and poke bonnets. At the front of the meeting, elders and distinguished visitors were perched on raised benches, facing the assembly.

The service was as spare as the surroundings. The West Branch Quakers did not go in for hymns or paid preachers, let alone bells or incense, nor did they set programs for their worship. All sat still and silent, clearing their minds in patient expectation of experiencing the presence of the Holy Spirit. Individuals moved by the spirit might speak or pray aloud. In a given session, several voices might be heard, or two hours might pass in total silence. Such speeches as did occur, Theodore remembered, were usually a compound of exhortation and scriptural quotation delivered in a cadenced oratorical style that varied from individual to individual. He fondly recalled one gentleman who employed a rising falsetto punctuated by squeaks. In rare instances a woman might break into hymn, an act that inevitably raised suspicions of vanity among the Quakers and sometimes prompted an elder to inquire into the sincerity of the singer's motives.[13]

For active young boys, hours of enforced physical and mental repose were excruciating. When finally released from their confinement, they would run around outside under the maples as their parents exchanged greetings, addressing one another in the traditional pronouns, *thee* and *thou*.

The Quaker community of West Branch was small and close, yet it still managed to blow itself apart during Herbert's childhood when an Indiana evangelist swept through the region preaching a more progressive path to sanctification. He convinced the younger Friends to tear down the partition in the meetinghouse, hire a preacher, and install an organ. The more conservative Friends moved to a new hall and carried on with the old ways. Hulda, distressed by the split but pleased with the organ, embraced the revivalists. Jesse teased his wife about her piety, yet he attended meetings with his family, more out of duty than out of spiritual engagement. His passion was his business, and business was improving.[14]

Herbert had been conceived during the panic of 1873, an international depression that produced an estimated 14 percent unemployment across the United States with eighteen thousand business failures

over two years, an ill tide that affected even subsistence farming communities like West Branch. Its tiny crop surpluses went unsold, cash
was scarce, and a blacksmith often had to settle for payment in eggs,
butter, or sausage. As the decade progressed and the economy slowly
turned, a steady stream of horses was brought for shoeing, along with
buggy wheels, pumps, and mowers for repairs, and by 1878, Jesse was
able to unload his business for $1,000 and open a farm equipment
store. He was an evangelist for the new arts of mechanized farming,
running the cheeriest advertisements in the West Branch *Times*: "Ho,
for Kansas! But if you do not go there go to J.C. Hoover and buy
your Farming Implements." Among the many agricultural innova-
tions championed by Jesse was barbed wire. He bought a fancy new
machine to aid in its production, and coated his reels of wire in tar to
prevent rust. Herbert, as a curious five-year-old, once tossed a burning stick into a cauldron of hot tar to see what would happen. When
the resulting conflagration threatened to consume both his father's
establishment and the butcher shop next door, the perpetrator left the
scene and did not confess his offense until middle age.[15]

Soon Jesse's budding prosperity enabled him to move his family south on Downey Street to a two-story, four-room house with a
parlor and an oil-burning stove, situated on an acre of land with five
large maples. Around this time Jesse was also chosen as a councilman
and the town assessor. That he was able to establish himself and his
young family in a relatively short period of time was testament to his
abilities and to the growing strength of the little community of which
he was an increasingly important part.[16]

They were all boosters, Jesse and the town leaders. The nature of
the frontier experience requires a bullish frame of mind, an ability to
envision a bounteous future while bravely absorbing the heavy costs
of the present. Raising West Branch from the Iowa dirt was a grueling
task. The townsfolk worked ceaselessly in every season, becoming far
more familiar with monotony and privation than with comfort and
mirth. They knew what it was like to scrape by after a disappointing
crop, to be cold for months on end, to endure sickness and injury and
grow old quickly. They knew loss. The routine scourges of pneumonia, typhus, diphtheria, and malaria would sweep their region and
thin their numbers with numbing regularity.

When Herbert was four or five, thirty members of the extended

Hoover clan gathered under a tree for a family photograph, probably at a picnic. They made a grim tableau. The men stood stiffly in
dark vested suits of coarse fabric and haphazard cut, squinting out
from weathered, bony faces, some stern, others sullen. The women,
in homemade high-collared dresses, looked haggard despite the odd
ruffle and bow, their hair parted in the middle and pulled back taut as
if to accentuate the tightness of their mouths and the pinch of their
cheeks.* While it was not customary in Victorian portrait photography for subjects to smile for the camera, a surprising number of these
faces were actually grimacing, as though the family were downwind
of a dump. The overwhelming impression is of a people habituated to
hardship, taught by faith and experience to temper their expectations
and take nothing for granted.[17]

One early December evening in 1880, Jesse came home with a
fever. His health had been weak for some time. Hulda packed the
boys off to the farm of their great-uncle Benajah to better concentrate
on her husband's care. She could do nothing for Jesse, however, and
late on December 13, a messenger arrived at Benajah's to bring Theodore and Herbert home to say their good-byes. They were roused
from bed, hurriedly dressed in their coats and mufflers, and hustled
outside to a horse-drawn cutter. They huddled under buffalo robes
and flew along the snowy road until their home came into sight, every
window yellow with light. The sitting room was crowded with family.
Hulda sat white-faced and quiet. Her husband was already gone.[18]

Jesse was thirty-four, the cause of his death uncertain. Neighbors
gave it as pneumonia and typhoid, while the death certificate cited
"rheumatism of the heart, complicated by gastritis." Dr. Minthorn,
who was in Kansas but remained close to his sister's family, declared
it heart disease.[19]

A relative wrote Jesse's obituary and with a bluntness characteristic of the West Branch Quakers chastised the deceased for neglecting
his spiritual calling. It was claimed that after suffering greatly during
the last days of his life he had, in his final hours, made peace with
his maker. Hulda, who sat on his bed singing "Happy Day" as he

---

* These are the ancestors of the sad, long-faced couple in Grant Wood's *American
Gothic*. A native Iowan, Wood also painted a more charming if less significant picture of
Hoover's hometown.

lay dying, once again startled the town elders by singing before her husband's coffin at his funeral. She ordered a tombstone to mark his grave only to be told by those same elders that it was too tall and ostentatious, and would have to be planted several inches deeper in the ground.[20]

Herbert, six years old at the time, would retain only a dim memory of his father. He would never speak publicly of him beyond a simple acknowledgment of his untimely death. It is tempting, when a child suffers so profound a loss at an early age, to read its influence into every aspect of his developing personality, and there can be no doubt that Herbert felt the impact of Jesse's passing, and that it altered the course of his life and the shape of his character, but aspects of his personality were already well formed. He had started school a year earlier and was described by his teacher as a "sturdy, independent fellow, not at all easy to approach at first." A visitor to Hulda's home in her time of grief found him chubby, busy, and "pretty much in the way." Of the three children, Herbert was "the hard one. He wallowed on his mother's lap and was always wanting something." These brief descriptions already hint at some of the adult Hoover's most salient characteristics: an aloof nature joined to, and somewhat at war with, a craving for attention, and an unusual amount of energy.[21]

Around this same time, the young Quaker girl who would grow up to marry Theodore Hoover noted another aspect of Herbert's character. While she was playing outdoors, her hoop skirt caught on a stick, and she was mortified to see the hoops exposed. Herbert solemnly walked over, removed the stick, pulled the fabric back over the hoops, and walked away. She was impressed that he had not giggled. "It was just like Bertie," she said. The same schoolteacher who had found him difficult eventually came to view Herbert, a flaxen-haired boy in bloomers and vest with his mother's square jaw and hazel eyes, as a favorite. While not particularly bright, according to the teacher, he was polite, well behaved, and industrious. He did as he was told, without enthusiasm. Asked years later to name his favorite subject, he answered, "None. They were something to race through so that I could get out of doors."[22]

The West Branch school was adequate, in large part due to the traditional Quaker encouragement of education. Herbert learned to read and write and count, and he had worked his way through most, if not all, of the Bible by the age of ten. Otherwise, the town was even more of a cultural wasteland than most pioneer settlements. The Hoover boys had little exposure to art or music and they seldom read. "Mine was a family," Herbert confessed in his memoirs, "unwilling to have youth corrupted with stronger reading than the Bible, the encyclopedia, or those great novels where the hero overcomes the demon rum." The anodyne *Youth's Companion* magazine was also out of bounds for the simple reason that it published fiction. The only community organizations Herbert joined were his church and the local prohibitionist chapter, temperance being a favorite cause of every branch of Protestantism at the time. He and his brother became acquainted with a local dentist who owned a collection of coins, fossils, meteorite fragments, and other curiosities. These impressed Herbert, who made his own collection of attractive stones, and another of crooked sticks. The latter, according to Theodore, was "saved from being commonplace by his genius for discovering sticks which were obtrusively or unnecessarily crooked."[3]

There was plenty of time to play and Herbert was said to be good on stilts. He built forts and tunnels along the creek bank with other boys his age and crawled through the storm sewers under Main Street. On winter evenings he would skate or join the hordes of children sledding on the local hill, lying flat on his belly and steering with his toes. In better weather he would wallow in the muddy swimming hole beneath the willows by the railroad bridge. He loved to fish, pulling suckers, catfish, and sunfish from Wapsinonoc Creek with a willow pole, a line of butcher's string, a one-cent hook, and an angleworm, spitting on the worm for luck and eating what he caught.

When they had nothing else to do, the West Branch boys would drown squirrels or dig for China with a hatchet or attempt to make a pet of a screech owl, an adventure that left an impressive scar on Herbert's scalp. Sometimes they would fence with willow branches or simply throw dirt at one another. Undeterred by Quaker devotion to nonviolence, Herbert initiated at least one fistfight with a boy who played pranks on him. Theodore recalled several tussles of his own, two of which, he claimed, were fought on behalf of his brother. Hulda

Hoover, on catching one of her boys swearing, beat him with a stick and washed his mouth out with soap.[24]


Hulda was now thirty-one years of age, a widow with three children and no regular income. With the help of her family, she sold Jesse's farm equipment business and auctioned his horses and cattle, thus raising money to put aside for the children's education. She took in sewing and a boarder, sold vegetables from her garden, and lived frugally. Her neighbors were generous with moral and material support and her brother picked up some of her bills, but the struggle wore on her. She was always short of money. To save on stamps, she wrote fewer letters, which heightened her loneliness. In addition to the loss of her husband, friends and family members were leaving West Branch, some driven away by the religious schism, others scattering farther west in search of fresh opportunities and cheaper land. One morning the summer after Jesse's death, Theodore, awakened at sunup by the chirping of birds, searched out his mother and found her crying softly in her bedroom. Without disturbing her, he went back to bed and pulled the covers over his head.[25]

The character of the Hoover home was changed without Jesse, who had been its jauntiest presence. Hulda, earnest and purposeful, now redoubled her commitment to God and his work. This involved an incredible amount of community service, teaching in the West Branch Sabbath school and serving as the leading spirit of the Young People's Prayer Meeting, an organization she had founded. She was secretary of the local chapter of the Women's Christian Temperance Union and an outspoken advocate of extending the franchise to women. "I have so much to do all the time," she wrote her sister, "considering I just keep my self ready first for service for my Master, then to work at whatever I can to earn a little to add to our living and then the care of my little ones every day is full and some times the nights."[26]

By 1882 she was speaking regularly at the West Branch meeting and in other communities as well. A council of ministers and elders conferred upon her the "gift of ministry" in 1883, and she was selected as a delegate to quarterly and annual meetings of Quakers throughout

Iowa and into Kansas. Her sermons on the subject of Christ's redeem-
ing love were fluid, graceful, and intellectually a cut above average.
She impressed her coreligionists with her self-possession and her
unhesitating convictions, as well as her devotion to her mission and
her community. She also sang beautifully. Her favorite hymn was a
missionary song, "From Greenland's Icy Mountains."[27]

Hulda was serious when she told her sister that her ministry took
precedence over her children. The work took her away from West
Branch for days and often weeks at a time, during which she would
leave her children in the care of her extended family. Over summers,
the boys were boarded farther afield. Herbert spent a season near
Sioux City with a homesteading uncle, living in a sod house and riding the lead horse on the plow team that broke the virgin soil. He
would remember the visit as a "Montessori school in stark reality."[28]

Another summer he boarded a train for Arkansas City, followed
by a long buggy ride to Pawhuska in present-day Oklahoma, where
his uncle Laban Miles was United States Indian Agent to the Osage
Nation. This was a common occupation for a Quaker, the faith's insistence on human equality and religious tolerance having long fostered
constructive relations with Native peoples. In 1869, Ulysses Grant
had effectively outsourced administration of the central and southern
Plains Indian territories to the Friends in what became known as the
President's Quaker Policy.[29]

Herbert and his cousins were the only white children on the
Osage reserve. They befriended Native boys who taught them how
to hunt with a bow and arrow, how to fish with a bent pin, and how to
cook on the lid of a tin can over a fire of their own making.[30]


Hulda was enjoying a rare spell of good health in the winter of 1884,
when Herbert was nine. She told her family she had never felt better in her life. Amid a February of furious blizzards and deep drifting snow, she traveled on foot to a meeting in the neighboring town
of Springdale; it would not have occurred to her to let the elements
interfere with her mission to preach. She trudged out of West Branch,
dodging ruts and drifts and following her visible breath straight east
for Springfield. It was a straight and lonely road, passing only a few

houses along the four-mile route. Cheeks stinging with cold, she looked up at the low gray sky and out over the white fields stubbled with straw and fence posts and rehearsed in her mind the talk she would deliver on arrival.[31]

At some point during the trip, Hulda fell ill. She was wrapped in blankets and brought home in a buggy by her hosts. Her sickness advanced quickly. She lasted little more than a week. In her final moments, she managed to draw herself up to her knees to pray for her children. She died at home on a Sunday morning, February 24, at age thirty-five. The official cause of death was pneumonia complicated by typhoid. Her sister Ann said she died of a broken heart. The funeral was well attended and her obituary, entirely laudatory, hailed her as "a worthy, useful, and exemplary Christian." She had been "tried and proved by service." She was "a builder; a lifter; and a doer of deeds."[32]

As an adult, Herbert Hoover gave the impression of remembering his mother only slightly more vividly than his father. All he would say of her was that she was the "sweet-faced woman" who held their family together for two years. He later used that same generic phrase— "sweet-faced"—to describe his West Branch teacher.[33]

He was no more helpful on the subject of his childhood. When it came time to write his memoirs, he would treat these years in brief and shallow fashion, not troubling to sort out the timing of his parents' deaths. He was all but mute on his emotional reaction to having been orphaned at the age of nine. Theodore would write that the loss of his mother filled him with "helplessness and despair, a dumb animal terror." There is no reason to believe his brother felt any different, whether or not he said anything: strong emotions would always render him inarticulate. Only time would suggest that his mother and the words spoken in tribute to her—"tried and proved by service," a "builder," a "lifter," a "doer of deeds"—made a lasting impression on him.[34]

The estate of Hulda Hoover was handled by the Circuit Court of the State of Iowa in Cedar County. The family's few assets were cataloged and liquidated, and the house was sold, along with its table and chairs and sink, the beds and bedding, the bright rag carpets, Hulda's sewing machine, her clothes, her shoes and underwear. The proceeds were dispersed to cover debts, including almost forty dollars in medical expenses submitted by the doctors who could do nothing for her, another twenty-five for the coffin and the funeral, and five more for the man who dug her grave.[35]

The court appointed the Quaker elder Lawrie Tatum, an esteemed resident of Springdale, as guardian of the children. He would also administer their joint estate, worth roughly $2,000 once Hulda's property was sold.* A council of relatives in consultation with Tatum decided that Theodore would live with an uncle in Harding County and May would remain with her grandmother. Herbert's school-teacher made a bid to adopt him but was rebuffed on the grounds that she was a spinster and not a relative. He would instead join the family of another uncle, Allen Hoover, who farmed just north of West Branch. The children were scattered to prevent them from becoming too much of a burden on any one household. Of the boys, Theodore received the more advantageous placement, presumably because his relations saw more potential in him.

Uncle Allen's farm was close enough to town that Herbert, or Bert, as most now called him, was able to continue school in West Branch, walking daily with his cousin, Walter, who was the same age. In bad weather, they rode double on a farm horse. Country living was an adjustment for the town-raised Bert. Years later, speaking in West Branch as a candidate for public office, he would be romantic about Uncle Allen's farm:

> We ground our own wheat and corn at the mill, we slaugh-tered our hogs for meat; we wove at least part of our own clothing; we repaired our own machinery; we got our own fuel from the woods; we erected our own buildings; we made our own soap; we preserved our own fruit and grew our own vegetables.[36]

In reality, Bert's lot was menial labor: cleaning the barn, cutting thistle, picking potato bugs. He did his chores dutifully, but like his

---

* Lawrie Tatum was a Quaker elder, a hero of the Underground Railroad, one of Presi-dent Grant's first Indian Agents, and the author of a book entitled *Our Red Brothers*. He would keep scrupulous records of the Hoover estate, accounts being one form of record keeping at which the Friends excelled.

father he had no taste for farm life. Aunt Millie, a wonderful cook, kept him chubby, and neighbors noticed that she treated Bert at least as well as her own brood. He did not speak of his grief to anyone in Uncle Allen's family. He scarcely spoke at all.

While Bert was not unhappy in Uncle Allen's care, the arrangement did not last. Hulda's brother, Dr. Henry John Minthorn, the same man who had saved Bert's life as an infant, had since settled in Newberg, Oregon. Easily the most accomplished member of the Hoover-Minthorn clan, he was a soldier, physician, missionary, and educator, married and the father of two girls. He had recently lost his only son and now wrote his West Branch relations asking that Bert be sent to live with him, offering as an inducement a free education for the boy at a new Quaker academy in Newberg, of which he was superintendent. Lawrie Tatum determined that it would be in Bert's interest to be raised in the home of so learned and capable a man.[37]

Two months after his eleventh birthday, Bert stood on a railway platform awaiting a westbound emigrant train. He was to travel in the care of a family named Hammell, with the cost of his ticket, thirty-three dollars, deducted from his share of his mother's estate. Aunt Millie had provided a bedroll for the bare wooden bunks of the second-class car and enough fried chicken, ham, and bread to feed Bert and the Hammells for a week. Bert said his solemn good-byes and boarded the train clutching Hulda's old telescope bag, which contained his clothes, his crooked sticks, and a prayer card she had left him: "Leave me not, neither forsake me, Oh God of my salvation." He had two dimes in his pocket.[38]

What was running through Bert's mind as the train pulled out of the town of his birth, taking him from his siblings, his adopted family, his friends, and the graves of his parents, is unknown. There can be little doubt of his pain. He would studiously avoid West Branch for the next three decades of his life, not spending a single night there despite crossing the country many times. Eyes wide open, he crossed the Missouri River and the sagebrush prairie and the Rocky Mountains before emerging in the thick cedar and hemlock forests of the Columbia River basin. Bert was among the first Americans to make the cross-country trip by rail to Oregon, the route having opened little more than a year before. He was captivated by the whole journey, and throughout his life he would run it through his mind like an old movie. He caught a glimpse of bustling Portland, with its tall-masted ships and taller buildings, unlike anything he had seen, before Dr. Minthorn gathered him up for a twenty-five-mile wagon ride up the Willamette Valley to his new home.

Newberg could not have made much of an impression on Bert. It was another tiny frontier village, raw and muddy even by the standard of West Branch. Every direction he looked he saw tree stumps poking up from freshly broken fields. The locals, most of them transplanted midwestern Quakers, lived and worked in a cluster of buildings along one main street. The Friends Pacific Academy, like so much of the town, was still under construction.

The Minthorns lived in a tall two-story house of modest Italianate design. The doctor's wife, Laura, and his daughters were in the backyard making pear butter over an open fire when Bert arrived. They saw a shy, awkward boy, short for his age and still chunky, his cheeks ruddy and his hair now light brown, his hands thrust in his pockets and his eyes averted. They offered him some pear butter from the kettle. It was warm, sweet, and delicious—a revelation for a boy who had never tasted the fruit. He ate nothing else for the next two days, fell ill, and waited many years before trying another pear.

Bert did manage to make two statements on his arrival. He took from his pocket a bottle of hive syrup, an expectorant used for the croup, and placed it on the Minthorns' mantel, declaring his hope to never have to take it again. Thanks to the salubrious coastal air, he never did. He also showed his uncle a pocket account book in which he recorded sums he had earned picking strawberries, as well as his expenditures, displaying pride in his understanding of the value of money. Frugal, as most Friends were, Minthorn was impressed.[39]

The doctor was a departure from homely Uncle Allen, who had been the main paternal figure in Bert's life since Jesse's death. Intelligent, industrious, versatile, and adventurous, Minthorn, as a youth, had run a wagon team in the Underground Railroad, a cause dear to the hearts of the Friends, and in 1864, weeks after his eighteenth birthday, he had joined the Union Army despite being a Quaker and a Canadian. He mustered out several months later with a low burning fever and chronic diarrhea, never having seen action (his regiment was assigned to guard supply trains).*

Desperate to escape a return to the family farm, he taught school in Iowa, Michigan, and Tennessee before settling on a career in medicine. He graduated from the State University of Iowa in 1874 and earned a second degree from Jefferson Medical College in Philadelphia with a thesis entitled, "Vaginal Touch as a Means of Exploration in Pregnancy."[40] Minthorn practiced in West Branch and among the Ponca in Indian Territory until a lingering bout of pneumonia convinced him to seek a different climate. In the two years before Bert arrived in Newberg, he had dragged his young family from Iowa to Oregon, south to Indian Territory, and back to Oregon again. He continued to practice medicine while establishing the Friends Pacific Academy, and in his spare hours he set up as a real estate developer.

Minthorn was as impressive in person as he was on paper. His mustache had a tendency to droop, as did the corners of his eyes, and the end of his nose, but everything else about him radiated vitality. Tall and square shouldered with a broad chest and thick arms, he wore stiff white shirts and tailored clothes. He was horse proud and always kept a half-wild team of some odd pinto or piebald color that he drove at reckless speeds. An adherent of the strenuous life long before Theodore Roosevelt took ownership of the phrase, he immediately appraised young Bert as soft and coddled, and set him on a remedial course.

It may be that Bert never stood a chance in his uncle's home, given the history of tension between Henry John Minthorn and his sister, Hulda. The eldest son in a family of seven children, Henry John, who went by his second name, had done a man's work on their father's farm from the age of thirteen, his chores piled so high that if he wanted to read, he tied a book to his plough. Hulda was relatively pampered. She was the only child in the family to be thrown a birth-

---

* In his memoirs, Hoover recalls his uncle speaking of his experiences fighting at Shiloh (a claim made by other Minthorn family members), but he signed up late for that particular battle. Minthorn does not seem like the type to exaggerate his service; perhaps his nephew got the story wrong. Or it may simply be that Shiloh loomed large in the doctor's mind and that he spoke of it with familiarity, owing to his time in Tennessee as a soldier and an educator.

day party, and she could always get away with shirking her household tasks to sew another pretty dress or play with friends. John would storm into the house and rail at her sinful ways. She would run out and hide in a cornfield rather than submit to his wrath. By adulthood, Hulda had grown more serious and they had put their differences aside, but John never entirely lost his impression of her as a spoiled child and he considered her an indulgent mother. He complained to his wife that Hulda had failed to break Bert with hard work when he was a suckling, leaving him unfit for a halter in his coltish years.

Bert was assigned school-day chores at the Minthorns': driving the two cows from pasture to the barn, milking them, feeding and watering the doctor's three ponies, cleaning the stable. Every night his aunt would issue commands—"It is time thee gets in the wood"— until Herbert hated the sound of her voice. Saturdays and some late afternoons during the week he was assigned to burn fir stumps as the men cleared fields. He would bore a deep hole in the stump for the fire and an adjoining hole for air. "It was sport," he later said, "the first few times." Sundays were more onerous still: worship and Bible study followed by youth temperance meetings.[41]

In summers, Bert was free to work for pay, and not for the last time he showed resourcefulness in finding the people and situations that answered his needs. Alva Cook and his father were tending a weed-choked onion field in the bottomlands north of town when Bert rode up on a calico pony and asked if they needed help. Alva said yes but they could not afford high wages. Bert negotiated fifty cents a day and board, strapped on a pair of leather kneepads, and immediately went to work stripping weeds, row after row, day after twelve-hour day, occasionally whistling and singing with Alva.[42]

Paid labor was a great improvement over being his uncle's chore boy. Bert liked the former and performed the latter with sullen resentment, a demeanor that annoyed Minthorn. The doctor came home one night and saw the horses pawing the ground, indicating that they had not been watered. He did the chore himself before rousting Bert from bed and making him haul buckets of water from the pump to the stables, emptying each one in the dirt. Bert would always consider his uncle the greatest disciplinarian he had ever met. (He would also come to loathe horses as much as the doctor loved them.)

In fairness to Minthorn, he did try, in his own taciturn way, to be avuncular. Bert often accompanied him on house calls, and they would travel for hours over rough and boggy forest roads with the nephew huddled under fleece-lined robes listening to his uncle discourse on religion, physiology, or the Battle of Shiloh. Minthorn, not much for conversation, did like to teach. His philosophy of life was expressed in maxims:

> The meanest thing a man can do is to do nothing.
> Go to school, first, last and all the time.
> Turn your other cheek once, but if he smites it, punch him.

It is likely that the doctor also told Bert something of his lost father, if only to encourage the boy's work ethic. Minthorn considered Jesse Hoover a kindred spirit, an entrepreneur and a striver "inspired by the strenuousness of life." He told stories of how Jessie, still in his teens, ran his thresher from sunrise until dark, moving from site to site overnight, sleeping on floors and living on chicken pot pie and rice pudding. Jesse, said Minthorn, was both a man of affairs and a student of science who had made his own way in the world by developing his talent for practical mechanics. All of this, his uncle believed, was Bert's inheritance.[43]

Minthorn also delivered on his promise of educating his nephew, who attended Friends Pacific Academy for two years, walking to class in the mornings with his uncle, assembling at nine for prayers and a twenty-minute lecture on morality, moving from classroom to classroom throughout the day in disciplined fashion at the tap of a bell. Although the youngest pupil at the academy when he started, and easily the smallest, he was strong in mathematics, which were taught by his aunt in an unusually pragmatic fashion. Students were given problems in compound interest, annuities, bank discount rates, duties and customs, foreign exchange rates, and partnerships. Another feature of the academy's pedagogy that left a mark on Bert was Minthorn's emphasis on self-reliance. He wanted students to solve their own problems, and would only help them after they had made their best efforts. Tenacity, he believed, was fundamental to achievement. As he had in West Branch, Bert attracted the motherly attentions of one of his teachers, Miss Evangeline "Vannie" Martin, who offered encouragement and had him to dinner on occasion.[44]

. . .

While Bert would remain in the Minthorns' care throughout his formative years, he never really felt a part of the family. He considered himself a "distant" relation, a "possession" that had been "traded off" from one uncle to another.[45] The doctor and his wife, busy people with beloved daughters to raise, did their duty by him without tenderness. Bert, through no fault of his own, was a poor substitute for the son they had lost. He was a useful member of the household but otherwise just one more face around a dinner table crowded with Minthorn's teachers, friends, relatives, patients, and students. The family's neighbors did not view Bert as a Minthorn: they looked upon him as an orphan, a lost boy with a "lonesome, wistful air." Said one classmate, "He was often in our home and because he was an orphan and seemed to be neglected in many ways, my mother did many things for him."[46]

Matilda Howard, who kept the restaurant in Newberg, remembered Bert as an object of pity, shy, forlorn, overworked, and obviously poor, his clothes tattered, his hands and neck grimy. She was always tempted to grab him and give him a scrubbing. She also remembers him as perpetually hungry. At first she gave him free meals, but having a regular charity case in her establishment grew irksome and she cut him off. "Bert had a pretty stiff time of it," she said.[47]

It was a confusing, degrading situation for a boy who had always wanted an unusual amount of parental attention and who had spent just enough time in the warm bosom of his mother's home to feel himself special and deserving. Generally, he kept his hurt to himself, although when provoked it would burst from him with force. On one occasion, toward the end of his three years in Newberg, he grew frustrated and resentful at what he believed to be Minthorn's excessive demands and showed mettle by going nose to nose with the doctor in a shouting match on the family's lawn. "I do not think he was very happy," Minthorn later admitted.[48]

Bert caught a measure of relief from the meager graces of the Minthorns in 1887 when brother Theodore moved to the home of another relative in Newberg. For a brief period, they roomed together at the academy boardinghouse and took meals at their uncle's home. Theodore remembered it as a time of plagues, with Bert suffering painful earaches most nights and both of them awaking in the mornings covered in flea bites. They were nonetheless grateful for one another's company. When time allowed, they headed outdoors through towering forests and jungles of ferns and berry bushes to stand for hours in rushing streams, alert to the splash of trout, communicating without words. They developed a closeness they would maintain deep into adulthood.

Further consolation came in the gentle form of Daisy Trueblood, a classmate at the academy who inspired Bert's most significant adolescent literary endeavor:

Friend Daisy

(and I hope you are more than my friend, although I do not dare to head it that way yet). You do not know the extent to which I am enthralled, an I am sure that no girl should be allowed such mastery over any person's heart, unless there are such feelings in her own heart. I could not have helped paying my attentions to you, if I had tried an I am sure I did not try very hard. I do not think you care. Do you?[49]

The letter shows a fair command of language for a boy of twelve. It also foreshadows a lifetime of insistence, insecurity, and poor spelling. It is not known if Daisy ever answered Bert's plaintive question, although she did keep his letter her whole life.

# CHAPTER 2

# "A Whole Jug Full of Experience"

In 1888, the restless Dr. Minthorn announced his resignation from the Friends Pacific Academy. He had taken a new position as partner and president of the Oregon Land Company in Salem, the state capital. The firm had raised $20,000 with which to convert wheat fields in the Willamette Valley into fruit orchards that it would peddle to newcomers from the Midwest.[1]

Inhabited by Native Americans for ten thousand years, and by European fur traders and fishermen since the sixteenth century, the Oregon Country had been slow to attract settlers and to develop agriculturally. The bountiful Willamette Valley had drawn a trickle of migrants over the Oregon Trail from the east in the middle decades of the nineteenth century, enough to establish Salem as a territorial capital in 1851, but it was only when the transcontinental rail link was formed that full-blown settlement occurred and land prices boomed, creating the opportunity on which Minthorn and his partners intended to capitalize.

The doctor built a handsome house for his family on the outskirts of Salem, as well as a cottage for his mother, who arrived from Iowa with Herbert's sister, May. Theodore and Bert drove the family's cow and horses thirty miles overland to their new home as the balance of the Minthorn possessions traveled upstream by riverboat. For the first time since their mother's death, the three Hoover children were reunited in one locale.

Salem was an opportunity for his fourteen-year-old nephew as well as for Minthorn. Bert chose to leave school and join the Oregon Land Company at a salary of twenty dollars a month, slightly more than he made weeding onions. He worked as an office boy in the firm's first-floor rooms at the busy corner of Commercial and Chemeketa, running errands, keeping the company stables, and sweeping up at night, and for the first time in his life he began to display some exceptional qualities.

According to a Mrs. Bickford who worked in the land company's office, Bert was "a funny looking little fellow, with a short neck, and a round head which was always surrounded by a funny little round hat." He took to his job immediately, applying himself with a diligence he could never muster in the classroom, starting every morning at seven and staying until well after dark. He read all of the company's correspondence and learned all of its files, organized the partners' meetings in the evenings, ensuring that all of them received proper notice and that the necessary documents were on hand at the appointed hour. He served as a resource at those same meetings, thanks to an encyclopedic grasp of administrative minutiae—dates, addresses, price points, deliverables. He also found time to pick up some typewriting and rudimentary accounting skills, and to learn the art of blueprinting roads and properties. He took charge of the company's advertisements, which were placed in a thousand newspapers through the prestigious agency of Lord and Thomas in Chicago. "He was on the jump when there was anything to do," said one of the company's partners. "Herbert Hoover," said Mrs. Bickford, "was the quietest, the most efficient and the most industrious boy I ever knew in an office. He even wore quiet shoes and you never knew he was around until you wanted something, and then he was right at your elbow. He knew everything about the office and the rest of us never tried to keep track of things. It was easier and quicker just to ask Bert about it."[2]

Among the investors in the Oregon Land Company were leading Salem politicians and bankers, men of solid connections and large ambitions who drew few distinctions between the public's interest and their own. The core of their business was their agricultural holdings, the heavenly groves of pears and prunes hyped by Bert's newspaper advertisements: "No Hot Nights in Summer—Grass Grows All Winter." The firm soon diversified into residential developments, building houses and outbuildings, a school, and municipal water systems.

It operated a hotel, a sawmill, and a flourmill, graded Salem's roads, and owned the Salem Street Railway. By 1890, its capital stock had swollen to an impressive $200,000.[3]

The more the company expanded, the more the partners relied upon Bert. As he hurried unnoticed in and out of the land office and along the raised boardwalks of Salem's commercial district, his attention seldom strayed from business. Once he had absorbed the details and the larger design of the company's affairs, his orderly mind began to seize on problems and inefficiencies. His newspaper advertisements, for instance, drew customers to Salem from all parts of the country, some of whom were intercepted by rival promoters, so Bert, on his own initiative, began plucking newcomers from the noisy bustle of the railway platform in order to keep them in his own clutches. He offered them cheap boarding in houses he had rented around town, saving the newcomers the expense of hotels, earning their goodwill, and keeping them out of lobbies crawling with hustlers. Bert also made a few dollars for himself by marking up the rentals. Minthorn was impressed that his nephew knew the importance of minimizing risk and closing a sale. "Bert enjoyed business," he said.[4]

Not all of Bert's initiatives succeeded. The company had been studying methods of preserving prunes and other fruits, a line of opportunity that fascinated Bert. He undertook some experiments of his own until one day the offices filled with sulfurous fumes, and employees, gasping for breath, traced the vapors below stairs to where he was absorbed with a pan, produce, and an alcohol lamp. The little laboratory was promptly shut down.

Bert spoke so infrequently that some acquaintances regarded him as "a trifle slow." The partners of the Oregon Land Company knew better. His uncle described Bert's role as critical. Another partner marveled at the boy's presence of mind, recalling a tense evening meeting at the company's offices where disgruntled investors were raising "a racket." As the men shouted and threatened blows, Bert slipped to the back of the building and shut off the gas, leaving the raging businessmen in total darkness. They had to light matches to find the door and make their way to the street, by which time they had cooled off. They went home without a fight.[5]

When he was fifteen years old, the land company upped Bert's salary to thirty-five dollars a month, a good wage for an office boy. He continued to record his income in his account book, along with his expenditures. His earnings meant a lot to him: they were the fruits of his hard labor and a measure of his growing self-sufficiency. Content as he was in his role at the land company, he still resented his dependence on Minthorn, and he was determined to work his way up and prove himself better than his circumstances. It was his ambition, he later said, "to be able to earn my own living without the help of anybody, anywhere."[6]

After some unsatisfactory experiences on a high-wheel bicycle, Bert committed several months' pay to a newfangled Victor safety bike with two equal-sized spoke wheels and cushioned tires. This single purchase expanded his freedom and independence immeasurably. He rode the bike all day long through Salem's soggy streets, on business and for pleasure. It became part of his identity, liberating him from four-legged transportation and distinguishing him from his horse-loving uncle. It also connected him with his father, a passionate advocate of machines over beasts.[7]

This was one of several echoes of Jesse Hoover. Bert attempted to make a business of repairing and selling abandoned sewing machines in Salem; while the local women did not trust the quality of his merchandise, his father would have applauded his enterprise. He also followed the paternal example in matters of faith. He believed in a "good, kind God," and he did what was expected of him, attending Sunday school, joining the Newberg and Highland Avenue (Salem) chapters of the Friends and participating in a Band of Hope debate on prohibition. He was honest, hardworking, and clean living, even by his uncle's exacting standards. Religion was not central to his life, however. Minthorn had a vague recollection of Bert falling under the influence of a traveling evangelist at age fifteen. If that was the case, the spell did not hold. Hulda's spiritual zeal appears to have bypassed all three children.[8]

After a year in Salem, Bert had yet to make a friend in town. Being passed as a chattel from household to household in his most impressionable years had done nothing to improve his sociability. Eventually, his Sunday school teacher noted his doleful air and introduced him to another solitary boy, Burt Brown Barker, who lived across the river on a vegetable farm with his mother and stepfather, his birth father having left after he was born. Burt's initial impression was that his classmate was not much interested in friendship. If only out of lack of alternatives, the boys eventually gave each other a chance. Bert would go to Burt's house in the country, where they would eat watermelons and play checkers without saying a word. Burt's mother, relieved that her son had found a companion, exasperated herself trying to get Bert to speak.[9]

Bert, remembered Burt, was aloof, "about as much excitement as a china egg." He was short and puffy, "what you would call fatty. Never interested in sports. . . . Even when he was playing with you he was not the boisterous, laughing kind—no, not at all. He was a very serious boy, and that's the reason he didn't get along with the kids. They didn't much like it."[10]

Over time, as Burt gained his new friend's trust, Bert revealed that he was acutely aware of the deterioration of his family life, and he spoke of having been passed from one uncle to another. Burt, also living with people who had their own natural children, was sympathetic. "We were on the outside looking in, and we knew it," he said. "Not that they intended that we should know, because they are not that kind of people, but we just knew it." Although Bert still had a room in the Minthorns' home, he chose to sleep many nights in a bed he made for himself in the back of the land office. Burt, too, called Bert's life "a pretty stiff" existence. "He was just facing life grimly. Very grimly."[11]

Smarter and shabbier than the other students in their class, Burt and Bert were both impressed by money and spent hours talking about who had it and what they did with it. Not having any, they saw it as an answer: money and success were antidotes to vulnerability, a means of escape, and necessary to controlling one's destiny.[12]

The teacher who introduced Bert and Burt was Miss Jennie Gray, a Presbyterian. She had waltzed into the land office one day, a tall woman in her early thirties with polished manners and a beautiful smile. Finding Bert by himself, she quizzed him about his education. He told her he was planning to take some business courses at a night school about to open in Salem. She asked if he read books and he replied that he sometimes read the morning paper after his boss was finished with it. The truth was that he seldom read. He had never been tempted by Dr. Minthorn's library of fiction, biography, and history.

Miss Gray invited Herbert to the Salem lending library, an adventure he readily embarked on. She withdrew Sir Walter Scott's *Ivanhoe* on his behalf. Herbert's time between office chores was soon filled with medieval battle scenes, chaste love stories, and the heroic deeds of the Black Knight. The experience must have been tolerable, for he soon returned to the library with Miss Gray and borrowed *David Copperfield*. Dickens's story of an orphan prevailing over his cruel stepfather and finding his way to love and happiness hit home with Bert. "I can still remember the harshness of Murdstone, the unceasing optimism of Micawber, and the wickedness of Uriah Heep," he recalled much later. He began to see literature as a living thing, and he would develop a serious lifelong reading habit, growing up to quote Milton: "A good book is the precious lifeblood of a master spirit, embalmed and treasured up on purpose to a life beyond life."[13]

Bert attended a Sunday school class taught by Miss Gray, perhaps because the Highland Avenue Friends Church was not yet open. She invited Herbert and Burt to Sunday dinners at her home, the only boys in her class so favored. They were astonished that this angelic woman would want to spend time with ragged, friendless nobodies. As Burt put it, they felt like pumpkins among the squashes. He developed a crush on his teacher that lingered into his nineties. Bert, he said, shared his feelings: "He worshipped her, that's all."[14]

The daughter of a wealthy banker, Miss Gray lived in the center of town in a splendid house surrounded by tall trees. The boys were overwhelmed at her table, not knowing how to use the silverware and unable to name the food they were eating. For dessert, she once served them strawberries and cream with confectioners' sugar, which Burt, mistaking for flour, refused. Bert, who had no better idea what was on offer, gamely accepted and was pleasantly surprised.

Over the meal, Miss Gray lectured her guests on self-reliance, urging them to take responsibility for their futures. She challenged some of their assumptions about money, advising them to develop their character more than their fortunes. She read stories and asked the boys to summarize them and comment. Bert would never volunteer for these exercises although he always responded when asked. "Anything that that woman asked or indicated to him that he should do, he did," said Burt.[15]

Miss Gray was another example of Bert's knack for finding and attaching himself to people who would nurture and take a paternal interest in him. Dinners at her home were a vital part of his education. She encouraged his intellect, bolstered his self-confidence, awakened him to social graces and conversational arts, and introduced him to a material mode of existence beyond Quaker austerities. Some of her lessons were lost on him. He never learned to appreciate a good table or to shine in conversation. He would not forget her kindness, however, and he would always be grateful to her for seeing in him special qualities that he knew himself to be there. In the years ahead, while studiously avoiding West Branch and Dr. Minthorn, Bert on several occasions traveled far out of his way for the purpose of visiting his teachers, Miss Gray and Newberg's Vannie Martin, women who had taken him up by choice, not out of obligation or need.[*]

Bert's family had emphasized education and put aside money for that purpose, but he made his own decision to attend university. Determined to rise out of his subservience, he had been taking evening business courses in Salem, early evidence of a strategic approach to fulfilling his ambitions. A chance meeting with a Quaker mining engineer who stopped by the Oregon Land Company's offices sharpened the direction of his future studies.

Engineering was an exciting profession in the late Victorian era, a time of railroads and steamships, heavy industry, transatlantic cables, man-made canals, steel skyscrapers, and an endless array of new patents and processes. Engineers, more than soldiers, thinkers, or politicians, were remaking the human experience, creating new sources of power, annihilating time and distance. They were simul-

---

* Miss Jennie Gray eventually married, unhappily, bore two children, and divorced. One night in 1913 she stepped off a streetcar in Salem and was struck by a meat truck. She died instantly. Burt Brown Barker, a graduate of the University of Chicago and Harvard Law, broke the news to his old friend. Evangeline Martin lived until 1928. Hoover bought her the first radio seen in Newberg and supported her financially in her later years.

taneously shrinking the world and building it up in heroic ways. As a field of academic pursuit, engineering was relatively new, the first American and European technical schools having emerged in the mid-nineteenth century, but what they lacked in stature against traditional arts and science programs they made up for in opportunity and ease of entry. Engineering required a sharp and disciplined mind, and nothing in the way of fortune, breeding, family connections, or social confidence, some combination of which was de rigueur at the leading eastern universities.

Learning from the visiting engineer that mining engineers were comparatively scarce and earned large fees, Bert began collecting college catalogs. With the major East Coast schools beyond his means and capacities, and the Quaker schools suggested by his uncle not to his taste, he set his sights on a new tuition-free college set to open in Palo Alto in October 1891. Over the summer, he traveled to Portland to take the entrance exams for Leland Stanford Junior University. Not surprisingly, given his aborted schooling, he struggled and came up short. He did, however, manage to impress yet another teacher. Joseph Swain, a Quaker and a professor in Stanford's inaugural math department, administered the Portland exams and admired the tenacity with which Bert attacked plane geometry. "I observed that he put his teeth together with great decision and his whole face and posture showed his determination to pass the examination at any cost. He was evidently summoning every pound of energy he possessed to answer correctly the questions before him. I was naturally interested in him."[16]

Stanford, in need of students to fill its dormitories, could afford to take a chance on an ill-prepared applicant who had just turned seventeen. Bert was admitted on condition that he bone up on geometry. He studied every night that summer, grimacing in concentration as he hunched over his books at a corner table in the land office or in the quiet loft of Minthorn's barn.

On August 29, 1891, a few weeks after his seventeenth birthday, he arrived at Salem station with a ticket for San Francisco. His departure was low key. He had not made a lasting impression during his three years in town. Outside of his own little circle, he had been a ghost on a bicycle. "It would be much easier to tell a great deal more interesting story about almost any other boy I knew," said one woman who worked at the Land Company. "Bert went his silent way and no one thought much about him." Bert was nonetheless confident of his prospects as he prepared to board the train. His luggage was light: two suits in a satchel and his bicycle. Grandmother Minthorn joined the doctor's family on the platform. "I think thy mother would like to see thee now," she told him. "Thee has always been a good boy, Bertie. I shall always pray that thee does a conscientious work."[17]

"Thee will have cause to be proud of me someday," he promised.[18]

Accompanying Herbert on his journey was another young man who had failed the entrance exams, Fred Williams, the son of a Salem banker. Williams's father had offered Hoover, as he would henceforth be known to classmates, modest financial assistance to coach Fred in geometry. The money was welcome. Between his savings and his share of his mother's estate, which had been carefully tended by Lawrie Tatum back in Iowa, Hoover had just under a thousand dollars to his name. Even at a tuition-free university, he would need an income to keep himself afloat for four years.

After two nights in their Pullman berth, the students alighted in Oakland and ferried across the gray-green bay to San Francisco. A policeman directed them past the wagons and cable cars to the Stanford train for the last leg of their journey, a short thirty-mile ride through the golden foothills of the Santa Cruz mountains. There were yellow poppies along the right-of-way and broad-limbed oaks scattered under the deep blue sky. The warm scents of summer filled the air.

Hoover and Williams got off at Menlo Park and took a hack down a dusty road back toward Palo Alto, which was not yet a station. They were dropped at a construction site that was not yet a university. Designed as a memorial to his late son and dedicated to preparing young men and women for practical lives and useful careers, Senator Leland Stanford's campus was laid out on eight thousand acres of what had formerly been a horse farm. At its heart was a mission-style quadrangle of intricately carved sandstone. Hordes of carpenters, masons, and painters were still crowding its Romanesque archways and arcades, all of which looked preposterous in the middle of the sun-burnt pasture. They would soon complete their work, however, and in the years ahead the senator's dream would be realized, raising the tone of the entire Santa Clara Valley.

Swain had given Hoover directions to a country house on the edge of campus where he would board and receive tutoring in his areas of deficiency. He studied hard, took his exams, and failed again, this time in English. Once more, he was waved through to admission on condition that he show effort and improvement. Hoover received the first room assignment under the red-tiled roof of Encina Hall, the men's dormitory, allowing him to claim throughout his life that he was Stanford's first student. He had no electricity or hot water until several weeks after classes began on October 1. He did not much care. He was happy. Among other delights, the dining hall offered alternatives to cornmeal and milk, his usual breakfast fare.[19]

Hoover began his studies in mechanical engineering and switched to geology at the start of his second year, doing the minimum of work in an array of science and humanities courses, and relying on an uncanny ability to absorb large amounts of information in short periods of time in order to pass exams. His career at Stanford was an unbroken four-year run of academic mediocrity. He dropped classes without proper notice or permission and received weak marks overall. Strictly speaking, he did not earn his degree. His conditional pass in English was only removed at the end of his senior year when a friendly professor rewrote one of his essays and submitted it on his behalf as evidence of his competence in the language. This bit of mischief does not appear to have troubled Hoover in the least, and he would always be weak in grammar, punctuation, and spelling.

His personal development occurred mostly outside of the classroom. With his savings and family bequest inadequate to the expense of his room and board, lab fees, and books, he sought employment and found plenty. Even before classes began, he was tending the livestock at his lodgings to pay his way, and for five dollars a week he registered his 558 classmates on their arrival at the university. He won a contract for distributing San Francisco newspapers at Stanford and wrangled a franchise for a San Jose laundry, performing weekly collections and deliveries on his bicycle. (He would eventually sell both of those businesses to other students.) "Am working awful hard," he wrote a friend. "Have considerable business worked up & 300000000000 schemes for making more."[20]

Hoover landed an important job at the start of his second semester when John Casper Branner, a charismatic teacher and chair of the department of geology at Stanford, arrived on campus. On the strength of his typing skills, Hoover earned twenty-five dollars a month as Branner's office assistant, a position he would hold until graduation. Aiming to impress Branner, he left nothing to chance. As he explained to a fellow student, "Do your work so that they notice it, and always be on the job." When assigned a task, Hoover would take off his coat, fix his whole attention on it, and work until it was finished, never repeating mistakes, and asking only necessary questions. Branner noticed:

> I'd always employed the working students of my classes as assistants or secretaries. Constantly we received Geological Survey reports and German scientific periodicals. These, as they accumulated, had to be bound. I'd hand them over to the ordinary assistant and he'd ask, "How and where?" "Send them to a binder in the city," I'd say, and he'd ask, "How?" I'd answer, "By express," and he'd ask, "How shall I pack them?"—and so on. But with Hoover I'd say, "Get these periodicals bound," and the next time I'd notice them they'd be back on the shelves and the bill for binding and shipping would lie on my desk.[21]

At the start of school, Hoover was one of the least prepossessing men on campus. A bout of measles in his second semester affected his eyesight and forced him to wear glasses. He was "very immature in appearance," said classmate Lester Hinsdale, "probably the youngest looking of us all. He seemed shy to the point of timidity—rarely spoke unless spoken to."[22]

Jackson Reynolds, a classmate who would become a leading New York banker, agreed Hoover was "backward." He would "always have his eyes down on the pavement. He would never look up. If you wanted to say anything to him you always had to speak first." Nobody, said Reynolds, "would ever slap him on the back." When students gathered for weekly receptions at Branner's home, Hoover would sit in a back corner and listen, always seeming ill at ease. On the rare occasions when he did open his mouth, things only got worse. He was blunt, said Mrs. Branner, "almost to the point of utter tactlessness."[23]

His maturity, at least in a physical sense, was hurried by the employment Branner arranged for him during his summer breaks. After his freshman year, Hoover was assigned to map a portion of the Ozarks, due south of his Iowa birthplace. He traveled on foot, with his surveying equipment over his shoulder and a rock hammer in his belt. Most nights were spent in the cabins of common mountain folk, farmers and moonshiners, who lived in unmitigated squalor. "Generations of sowbelly, sorghum molasses and cornmeal, of sleeping and living half a dozen in a room," Hoover later observed, "had fatally lowered their vitality and ambitions." His own vitality was increased by this adventure. On his return, Theodore noted that his chubby little brother had grown into a tall, slender sophomore, looking "very scholarly" in his glasses. He had also saved almost all of his salary.[24]

In his sophomore and junior years Hoover came out of his shell, in his own diffident way, making himself useful in student activities. Unable to make the baseball or football teams, he became their manager, scheduling games, collecting the gate, purchasing equipment and uniforms. Unwilling to perform onstage, he ran a lucrative lecture and concert series. Unconvincing as a student politician, he lent his administrative talents to more popular students such as Lester Hinsdale, the class president, and rode their slates to become treasurer of the students' association. The important point is that he saw himself as a student leader, even if his classmates did not take him that way.

Hoover was successful in most of these endeavors. He introduced new levels of financial controls in his capacity as class treasurer and swiftly cleared an inherited debt of $1,200, prompting the Stanford daily to laud him for his business acumen. The gate from one San Francisco football game against the University of California filled many grain bags with gold and silver coins and was sufficient to finance an entire season. He helped his friends draft a student constitution and wrestle control of campus politics from the fraternity set. Reynolds believed Hoover "acquired quite a phobia about fraternities." He was not bidden to join one. Instead, he connected with other nonfraternity students who self-identified as "barbarians," rallying them against the exclusive "frats." Having spent enough of his life feeling like an outsider and a second-class citizen, Hoover was determined to promote the political ascendancy of his circle.[25]

His extracurriculars were not without setbacks, such as a money-losing speech by a young congressman, William Jennings Bryan. Hoover nonetheless proved his competence and won the confidence of his peers. He reveled in the role of treasurer, which in his mind made him the general manager of student activities. He turned his pockets into card catalogs of the details of his various operations and took pride in his thrift and his ability to say no. When former United States president Benjamin Harrison attended a Stanford baseball game without a ticket, Hoover confronted him and quietly insisted he pay the admission price. He understood better than most of his classmates the power of purse strings: "I have vertually control of affairs," he boasted to a friend.[26]

When classmate Will Irwin, who would gain fame as a journalist, suffered a career-ending ankle injury playing center on Stanford's freshman football team, he was outfitted with a plaster cast and deposited in his dorm room. Hoover visited him to approve spending on the athlete's medical supplies. Although in considerable pain, Irwin was intrigued by the odd character of the student body treasurer, who was just under six feet tall, scrawny, at least compared to the men of the football squad, and who dressed in a double-breasted blue suit which was a kind of uniform for him. Said Irwin later:

> He had mouse-colored hair as stubbornly straight as an Indian's, and hazel eyes so contemplative that they seemed dreamy. His round but powerful face had not a straight line in it. . . . He stood with one foot thrust forward, jingling the keys in his trousers pocket; a little nervous trick which he has never overcome.[27]

Hoover carried his head to one side as he took in Irwin's cast and obvious discomfort. After consulting with the team masseur, who was acting as nurse, he dispatched Irwin's roommate to telegraph San Francisco for necessary supplies.

To make conversation and keep up his courage, Irwin tried to make light of his situation and watched as Hoover tried to laugh. A "deep, rich chuckle" originated far down in his chest, Irwin recalled, yet it was strangled "before it came to the surface," and it died without finding voice. Hoover did not offer the patient a single word of consolation or reassurance during his time in the room. Irwin assumed that Hoover's sympathies, for he did appear to be affected, were garroted and buried in the same internal graveyard as the chuckle. After a few minutes, Hoover headed for the door and, at the last instant, turned and blurted, "I'm sorry." Irwin recognized that this minimal expression of emotion was as traumatic for Hoover as a broken ankle.[28]

The visit with Irwin was characteristic of Hoover in several respects. The first is that he showed up at the hospital. He showed up everywhere, never missing an outing, a game, or a gala. "Went to every ball given," he told a friend, "in fact quite a social swell. Enjoyed myself better than ever before in my life." He believed it was "good in every way" for a man to be "a mixer." He was eventually known and accepted in most circles on campus, and he would make lifelong friends of the likes of Hinsdale and Irwin.[29]

Second, despite his appetite for company, he was hardly a swell. He could not hold another's eye, let alone his end of a relaxed conversation. He would have been the last person invited to light up a room.

Third, Hoover was deeply uncomfortable with his feelings. He would always do his best to throttle or otherwise repress them, a telltale sign of anxiety. The word *anxious* is derived from the Latin word *angere*, which means to strangle or choke, precisely what Irwin saw happen to Hoover's chuckle. Hoover succeeded in his repressions to the point where casual observers would wonder if he ever felt anything. It was rare for him to express any emotion beyond unease, and it would have been difficult to tell that young Hoover, at one of his galas, was actually having a good time. While physiology to some extent explains his grim, silent ways, they were exacerbated by his massive sense of vulnerability and his spiritual disquiet. Part of Hoover's identification with *David Copperfield* was likely rooted in what Dickens identified as that "old unhappy loss or want of something never to be realized."[30]

The truly mind-expanding, destiny-shaping part of Hoover's college experience occurred over two summers, before and after his senior year. On the strength of Branner's recommendation, he was hired as an assistant to the renowned geologist Waldemar Lindgren of the United States Geological Survey. Hoover almost missed the opportunity. He and a handful of other students were on a lark in the Yosemite Valley when he received notice to join Lindgren's party in the California Sierras. Unable to afford a stagecoach ticket, he walked eighty miles in three days to the Stockton riverboats and finally caught up with the survey camp. They were a small team including Lindgren, another geologist, a cook, and teamsters, all traveling on horseback with pack mules and specially built wagons. Hoover was by far the youngest.

A Swedish mining engineer trained in Germany, Lindgren was a vigorous man in his mid-thirties with short blond hair and pince-nez glasses. His specialty was economic geology, or the study of exploitable metals and minerals, a field in which he was a pioneer. He spent his winters in Washington and the rest of his year tramping through the western states in search of ore deposits. He led Hoover from mine to mine, lecturing all the way on engineering lore and practical geology. The seminars continued around the campfire in the evening, accompanied by ham and baked beans. At night, the party slept on the ground, which was crawling with black ants. For Hoover, it was bliss. "I have a fine man to work for and a favorite business to work in, and moreover a grand country to work over," he crowed.[31]

The attraction of Lindgren, for Hoover, was similar to that of Branner. The primary masculine influences to this point in his existence had been variations on the strenuous life, from his father to Minthorn. Lindgren was cut from similar cloth, only finer. He was hardworking, practical, and commercially astute. He preached the moral superiority of rigorous fieldwork and held those "damned bureaucrats" in Washington in contempt. At the same time, he operated on a high professional and intellectual plane, with important connections and a record of publication in prestigious journals dating back to his school days. Hoover took Lindgren as a role model and began thinking about graduate studies at Columbia or Johns Hopkins. "I am trying to make a specialty of mining geology for it offers the widest field," he wrote a friend. "I think it's invaluable to keep moving. I never stop anyway."[32]

Lindgren found his new disciple eager, organized, and capable:

"Never have I had a more satisfactory assistant." He wondered at Hoover's ability to get to the heart of a matter and solve problems in the simplest possible manner. Lindgren kept him in the field a month into his senior year. Indifferent as ever to his academic performance, Hoover skipped the month with alacrity. He knew he was getting "a whole jug full" of learning and experience, and he was honored when Lindgren included his name in the credits of his published surveys. Not incidentally, he also made enough money to settle his accounts with Stanford.[33]

Hoover so delighted in his summer adventures that he wrote a series of uncharacteristically exuberant letters to his sister and various female friends chronicling his adventures. Some of these dispatches, including the following hyperbolic description of a feast at a Yosemite hotel, managed to make him sound, for once, like a typical undergraduate:

> And even now you may hear of those 7 college boys who ate so valliently that day. For it is one of the legends of the valley. The proprietor is now bankrupt and at Stockton Insane Asylum you may now see a man, once a hotel clerk, who cries out at all times, "The dining room will now close!"[34]

And similarly:

> Had a ball in town last night. Two men were shot in royal mining style and the dancers danced on as if nothing had happened. The blood smeared over the floor became slippery, then sticky and finally brown again. I did not dance. I am timid about arguments on a six shooter basis. . . . As morning approached the whisky became worse in quality and more wicked in result until all were in the gutter.[35]

Other letters show a little-noticed but unmistakable romantic dimension of Hoover. The shy young man who was failing English, and whose literary style typically ranged from curt to brusque, rambled on for pages about the "almost intoxicating" beauty of his surroundings:

No prosaic description can portray the grandeur of forty miles of rugged mountains rising beyond a placid lake in which each shadowy precipice and each purple gorge is reflected with a vividness that rivals the original. Along their western summits gaunt peaks of similar strength and nobility, vast proportions combined with simplicity and grace, stand out like buttresses and turrets from a great wall, their sides splashed with snow, their passes and lateral ridges covered with a wealth of vegetation which gives the whole an air of solidity and affords a restful contrast from their rugged summits.[36]

Buttresses and turrets, of course, are not geological phenomena. Despite his empirical training and his talent for the technical aspects of his position, Hoover was seeing himself as the hero of his own Walter Scott novel, a knight of science in a brown duck suit and high-top boots, traversing the burning sands of Nevada and the snowcapped High Sierras in quest of useful knowledge. He was developing a professional swagger: "Don't worry about anything happening to me," he wrote his sister, "for we always leave definitely with hotel clerks the route we expect to travel during the day with explicit directions as to what use is to be made of the corpse." To another correspondent he bragged of a planned descent of the American River Canyon—"a thing people here say is impossible. But they are not geologists."[37]

Hoover never exposed much of his inner life to men, not even to his brother. All of the above letters are written to young women, and by his graduation he had quite an audience of female admirers: his younger sister, May; his cousin, Harriette Miles (with whose family he had boarded in Pawhuska); Nell May Hill, an Oregon girl who would also attend Stanford; Marion Dole, a classmate who organized women's athletics; a Miss Ordway with whom he had "quite a talk" on a football trip to Santa Cruz. Miss Miles also remembered a Miss Rose with whom Hoover appears to have been infatuated. He had a deep need for female comfort and approbation. A clear pattern runs from his mother's kitchen through Miss Gray's parlor to his undergraduate correspondence. He sought recognition from men as well, although not at the same pitch of intimacy. It was only these young women who were allowed glimpses of his full sense of self, of the rather dashing and ambitious soul beneath the hard, diffident shell. The letters ring with confidence in his abilities and prospects, however meager his circumstances. To Miss Hill: "Am much puzzled wherefrom I will derive the income to go on next semestr as my wad will last until just Xmas. But trust to my usual luck I suppose."[38]

Although well supplied with female companionship, Hoover was still looking for more on his return for his senior year. He informed Miss Hill of a new presence in Branner's department: "We have a young lady taking Geology as a specialty now, a very nice young lady, too."[39]

Lou Henry was a freshman from Monterey, the daughter of a banker who had given her a single name of a single syllable and raised her as a son. She could ride, climb trees, fish, and hunt with a rifle and a bow. At five foot six, she looked taller still, thanks to a pile of brown hair. She had blue eyes and a broad gap-toothed grin. Like Hoover, she was a Branner acolyte. Captivated by a guest lecture he had delivered in Monterey, she had convinced her parents to allow her to study geology at Stanford, thus becoming the only woman in the program.[40]

It was in Branner's presence, in a geology lab, that Lou Henry first laid eyes on Herbert Hoover. She knew of him already by reputation. As Branner's right hand and a two-time president of the Stanford geology club, his name often came up in conversation. What she had heard of his capacities did not match what she saw at their meeting. She had expected someone brawny and domineering, not the speechless young bumpkin before her. He was not altogether unattractive to her, despite the uncombed hair and careless dress. His summers had left him tanned and fit, his shoulders were broadening, and his restless eyes and twitchy manner were softened by the roundness of his face.

When Branner left the lab, the two students fell into conversation. Within a week Hoover accompanied Lou to her first party at the university, and from that point on they were frequently in one another's company. He learned that Lou could keep pace with the young men in the geology club, effortlessly climbing rocks and vaulting fences. He learned that she had been born in Waterloo, Iowa, seventy miles from West Branch, and that she was a lot of things he was not: friendly, playful, gracious, self-possessed. She could laugh and dance, and she belonged to a sorority. Everyone found it easy to talk with Lou.

With the help of a generous number of credits granted for his summer work, the same sort of leg up that had allowed him to gain admittance to the school in the first place, Hoover graduated in the spring of 1895 at the age of twenty with an AB in geology. It cannot be said that Stanford made a man of him. His most valuable qualities on walking out its doors were the same drive and intelligence he had brought from Oregon four years earlier. Stanford had nevertheless been good to him. He was fortunate to have landed at a new university with a pragmatic mandate and a relatively meritocratic ethic. The academic and social rigors of an established eastern college might have crushed him. As it was, he had received a decent grounding in his chosen science, a thorough introduction to the profession of mining geology courtesy of Branner, and the freedom to make his way outside of class. Most of all, the university gave him a sense of belonging that he had not really known since the destruction of his own family in West Branch. The community embraced him without regard for his quirks, his awkwardness, or his humble origins.

None of his classmates would have selected Hoover as the most likely among them to succeed. There were plenty of promising students on campus. The thin ranks of Stanford's football team alone produced an impressive number of lawyers, surgeons, politicians, and bankers. Hoover had gifts, including an orderly and retentive mind, implacable energy, a growing self-regard, resourcefulness bordering on wizardry, and the capacity to inspire trust in his superiors. Wrapped as all this was in a lusterless package, void of pedigree, magnetism, or conspicuous achievement, few gave him a second glance. "He was not the kind of a feller around whom stories stick," said a classmate.[41]

Even Branner, who knew his pupil as well as anyone at the moment of his launch from Stanford, demurred when asked decades later if he had appreciated Hoover's potential: "We can't see far around the corners of life."[42]

# CHAPTER 3

# "I Am the Devil"

Herbert Hoover, conceived in one economic depression, now graduated into another. The Panic of 1893 was like any other downturn—markets tumbled, banks called in loans, businesses failed, jobs disappeared—only more severe. Its depth was unprecedented in American history. A quarter of the workers in several major cities were unemployed, and a quarter of the nation's railways were bankrupt. Among the economic casualties was the Oregon Land Company. Dr. Henry John Minthorn was wiped out, forced to sell his home and household effects to pay his debts. His only option was to reestablish himself as a physician at the age of forty-eight.

Bert Hoover was another victim of the panic. He had been counting on full-time employment with the U.S. Geological Survey beginning in the fall of 1895 at a salary of $1,200 annually. "Owing to reductions in appropriations," he later wrote, "the staff of the survey was cut down . . . and I was put out." With forty dollars to his name, he headed for Nevada City and Grass Valley in the rugged green foothills of the Sierra Nevada, hoping to apply his education at a mine in some managerial capacity. He introduced himself to the locals, most of them Cornish, recruited from the failing tin mines in the United Kingdom and prized in California for their hard-rock technique and facility at draining water from deep shafts. The Cornish foremen were more interested in practical experience than diplomas, and Hoover's white-collar prospects soon ran out, along with his forty dollars.[1]

Needing to eat, he signed on as a mucker at the Reward Mine, shoveling wet dirt and rock into an ore car on ten-hour shifts for two dollars a day, seven days a week. The Cornishmen mocked his schooling and taught him the basics of their mole-like existence: how to breathe while the dust cleared from a blast; how to nap in a steel wheelbarrow heated from underneath by candles. The ceaseless grind of filling his car and pushing it up the slick rails of the Reward's dripping tunnels taxed Hoover's stamina. He was tortured in his sleep by muscle pain and neuralgia.[2]

Relief arrived in the form of a promotion to drill helper and then just as quickly disappeared. Management trimmed the payroll, and Hoover was expelled into harsh sunlight with his finances little improved. He tramped from mining office to mining office, enduring the humiliation of serial refusals before finally securing a graveyard shift at the Mayflower Mine for $2.50 a day. By Christmas of 1895, he had saved $100. He quit and joined Tad and May in the Oakland area, where his brother was working as a linotype operator and his sister was at school. They lived for a time in a little house on Twelfth Street, between Chestnut and Linden, along with May's goldfish.

Hoover's siblings were one attraction of Oakland. Another was opportunity. He knew in his aching bones that he was destined for something better than competing with a mule, as he described mine labor to a friend. A Nevada City engineer had suggested he seek a position with the legendary mining engineer Louis Janin across the bay in San Francisco.

A native of New Orleans, educated at Yale and Freiburg, Janin was in the midst of a spectacular sixty-year career that included associations with the mighty Comstock Lode and the Rothschilds. Hoover tripped over to San Francisco, found the Anglo-California Bank building at the corner of Pine and Sansome, and climbed the stairs to knock on the door marked "Janin." The plump and jovial proprietor welcomed him and took him to lunch.[3]

Hoover would later leave a charming, dubious account of their meal in which he and Janin arrived at the latter's club and were seated in its opulent dining room. He seized an opportune moment to request a tryout in Janin's office. Janin said he had no openings on staff, save for a copyist. Hoover revealed he could operate a typewriter and begged to fill the copyist's position. Janin declared him hired and signed for lunch, the expense of which would have fed Hoover for a week. After several days of office work, according to Hoover's account, employer sent employee on an engineering assignment to Colorado at $150 a month plus expenses. Employer was pleased with the results. Employee never looked back and never again wanted for work.[4]

However heartwarming that tale, the actual origins of the Janin-Hoover relationship appear to be grubbier. There is no reason to doubt that the two men shared lunch, likely at the Pacific Union Club on Nob Hill. Janin had recently been engaged as an expert witness in the North Star Mining Company's defense of a mammoth $825,000 lawsuit brought by the Carson City Gold & Silver Company. The dispute was over where one mine ended and another began or, more specifically, over whether geological breaks known as "crossings" represented immaterial interruptions in North Star's vein or the end of its claim and the start of a new mine belonging to Carson City Gold & Silver. Hoover had special knowledge of the mines in question. He appears to have intimated to Janin that he had visited them (it is not clear that he had). He certainly would have revealed to Janin that he was familiar with Waldemar Lindgren's work on the mines, not all of which had been published. It was on the basis of Hoover's utility to the North Star defense that he and Janin came to terms.[5]

The talents of Janin's new recruit were immediately applied to trial preparations with Curtis H. Lindley, North Star's lead defense attorney. Hoover published a technical essay on the geology of the mines in question in the *Mining & Scientific Press*. His supposedly objective opinions on crossings were in lockstep with North Star's defense and obviously intended to influence the proceedings. He dropped the estimable name of Waldemar Lindgren into the fray, quoting him liberally. Although Hoover acknowledged in the article that the crossings were brought to his attention by Janin, he did not mention an association with Janin, or the prospect of fees or employment with him. Immediately after the verdict fell for North Star, Hoover received his first engineering fee for his contributions to the defense. A Stanford newspaper promptly reported that Hoover, who had to have suggested the story, had been promoted to membership in the famous firm. While Janin's tactics were not unusual in the cut-throat world of western gold mining, it is understandable that Hoover would prefer his version of events on the record.[6]

Hoover did move fast in Janin's company. By spring of 1896, he was traversing the Southwest as a mine scout. He got a full education in commercial mining and grew familiar with the unique demands of operating on the outskirts of civilization, including parts of the future state of New Mexico, where the mine manager doubled as deputy sheriff and, having no jail, lowered his prisoners by rope into abandoned mine shafts. Hoover carried a sidearm, although he never drew it. Along the way he began referring to himself as assistant to the superintendent of his employer's southwestern properties. Whether the title was granted or assumed is unclear.[7]

In his spare time, Hoover followed the exciting election of 1896, with William Jennings Bryan and William McKinley battling over the use of rare metals as specie, an issue of enormous interest to gold and silver miners. He read Adam Smith, John Stuart Mill, and Walter Bagehot to improve his understanding of economics. He did not take the time to vote. Between mining assignments, he returned to the Bay Area and his family, which had expanded to include his favorite cousin, Harriette Miles, daughter of his Oklahoma uncle Laban Miles. Time permitting, he slipped up to Stanford to visit Lou Henry.

Janin, astonished at the capacities of his new hire, declared that he had never met a man who could survey a mine as speedily and thoroughly as Hoover, a lofty compliment from a master of the trade. The young man's salary was hiked to $2,000 annually before the end of his first year, almost double what Lindgren had promised him with the Geological Survey. Hoover was so pleased with his progress that when the promised offer of a position with the U.S. Geological Survey finally arrived, he turned it down, and not only because of the lower salary. He now had outstanding prospects with one of the preeminent mining financiers in North America. Professor Branner supported his choice. Branner, who had done research for Thomas Edison and had worked in Brazil for a Boston gold mining concern before turning to academic life, advised Hoover that a man who looked after his employer's interests in a large commercial mining company could expect to be promoted rapidly. Besides, a practicing engineer could keep his hand in the intellectual world by publishing occasional articles in trade and academic journals. Hoover would put just that plan into effect—not, however, from San Francisco.


Just short of a year into his career with Janin, an astounding opportunity fell into Hoover's lap. The London firm of Bewick, Moreing and Company cabled its connections in San Francisco in October 1896 seeking recommendations for experienced American mining engineers for service in its Australian goldfields. The salary was reported to be $5,000 per annum, more than double Hoover's pay. The minimum age requirement was thirty-five years. Janin, a generous soul, recommended this plum position to his prized employee, never mind that he was twenty-two years of age and a geologist rather than an engineer. Hoover, after a moment's stunned silence, accepted on the spot, never mind his age and lack of training, or that the high salary was in part danger pay—one of every nine Bewick, Moreing men returned from the outback in a box, most of them courtesy of typhoid.[8]

A flurry of activity followed. Hoover rushed to tell his Stanford friend Lester Hinsdale that he was sailing to London to meet his new employer before reporting for duty on the other side of the planet. Hinsdale dragged him to a Market Street tailor for a top hat, a frock coat, a couple of business suits, and a morning suit of noisy tweed, the latter insisted upon by Hinsdale, who was something of a dude. (It was returned to him by mail years later, unworn.) Hoover grew a mustache to hide his immaturity and wrote letters to friends trumpeting his news, rounding up his already impressive salary to $6,000, or $10,000 if one included expenses and fees. He spoke to a reporter and won notice of his appointment in a local paper. He bought an insurance policy that Hinsdale would administer and took the expedient of hiding from his insurer the health risks ahead of him.[9]

It was all coming together for Hoover: money, position, recognition, adventure, success. His pride in his new opportunity and the measure of control he had gained over his life were no doubt inflated by the hurt and powerlessness he had felt during his onion-picking years. A bright future and the promise of material plenty seemed a just payback for what he had endured, and for his faith in himself.

Seeing his progress in print lent a certain reality to the new identity he was fashioning.

That identity might have startled those who knew him back in Oregon. Hoover was a young man on the make, clawing his way up a pedestal, taking risks, cutting corners, and burying his Quaker humility beneath a pile of clippings and offer sheets. At the same time, however, he did not forget those closest to him. He arranged regular cash transfers through Hinsdale to support May, Harriette, and Theodore, who would follow his younger brother through Stanford's geology department. He also asked Hinsdale to provide funds to any of their friends who might be in genuine need. In this manner, and probably unconsciously, he placed himself at the head of a handpicked, makeshift family, and protected its members from the struggles and hardships he had known.

Hoover gathered for a farewell with the old Stanford gang at the Cafe Zinkand, a large, warmly lit room on the San Francisco waterfront. Oversized mirrors hung from mahogany-paneled walls. Thick smoke hung from the high ceilings. The boys drank five-cent beer from heavy stoneware mugs while Hoover sipped coffee and flashed a letter of credit for five hundred pounds sent to him by Bewick, Moreing to cover his expenses. It was the first time some of them had seen a letter of credit. They were shocked that an English firm more than five thousand miles away would put such confidence in their recently graduated classmate.[10]

Leaving San Francisco on March 24, 1897, Hoover crossed the country by rail, stopping in West Branch just long enough to share a meal with his remaining relatives, and to once more get his name in the newspaper as a local boy made good (in this instance he managed to leave the reporter with the inaccurate impression that he was connected to the Rothschilds). He reboarded his train, crossed the Mississippi for the first time in his life, suffered seasickness during a rough Atlantic passage on a White Star liner, and finally introduced himself to the uniformed footmen at the front doors of the resplendent London offices of Bewick, Moreing.[11]

Charles Algernon Moreing was a prominent man with a long nose and a thrusting jaw. He cut a hypnotic swath through London's financial community where gold and Western Australia were concerned. With several of the region's more promising mines under management, his firm was a darling of investors and a magnet for capital. Always in need of fresh properties to promote, he had hired Hoover as a mine scout, believing American engineers to be the world's best, which was indeed the consensus at the time. Moreing greeted Hoover in a booming voice and invited him for a weekend at his country place. Hoover's desire to see the sights of London lost out to his eagerness to impress his new employer. He agreed to the weekend and stood embarrassed on arrival at Moreing's estate as a footman named Buttons picked through Hoover's scant wardrobe and helped him to dress.

Hoover met the other partners of Bewick, Moreing and showed them his letters of reference from California, emphasizing his integrity. He was posing as thirty-six years old, commensurate to his job's requirements, and also the age he had given on the ship's register. The partners were not fooled. They professed astonishment at the ability of Americans to maintain their youthful appearances.

Beginning on April 16, Hoover rocked for fifty-three hours on the Australia-China mail train, reaching Brindisi, Italy, on time to board the steamship *Victoria*, bound for Australia via the Suez Canal. He wrote a "Dear People" letter, warning his family that with telegraph charges on the coming leg of his journey approaching a dollar a word, he would need to be brief in his communications. He would signal his safe arrival in ports of call and, ultimately, Australia, with the code word *revooh*, his name reversed. On receipt of that single word they were to assume the following:

> "I am here undrownded have not been seasick, have had all I could eat, have had plenty to smoke. My whiskers are doing well. I still have money. I am fairly happy. I convey to you my kindly affections and good wishes. I am still on top." Signed your cousin and brother, H.C. Hoover, Mining Engineer Supt.[*12]

---

* Like many a young man forging his own identity, Hoover experimented with a variety of signatures, including Bert Hoover, Herbert C. Hoover, and H. C. Hoover, before settling, more or less, on Herbert Hoover.

Notwithstanding his warning, Hoover proved a fluent correspondent, reverting in his letters to the wide-eyed style of his summers with Lindgren. He was struck by the heat and the perfect flatness of the white sand plains on the Egyptian shore. His geographer's eye saw skies the color of "molten lead" and a "metallic" sun on glassy seas. Port Said was "filthy and degenerate beyond anything in Chinatown," with naked children buzzing around in the heat like so many flies:

> As one goes up the street you are followed by a swarm of would be guides, dealers in all sorts of truck. Beer sellers with the tank on their backs and a glass in each hand, boys with watches, photographs, men with cigars, women with fruit. But being forwarned, [we] had heavy canes with which we protected ourselves.[13]

Hoover's contempt was not reserved for the Arabs. He came to abhor a collection of Englishmen on board the *Victoria*, public service recruits bound for India and their first employment even though, as Hoover noted, they were all approaching thirty. They "cling together like hornets," he wrote, and show "no more expression than a nail keg." All of them combined "could not show the intelligence of countenance of an American 10 year old." Hoover and another American traveler named Marion disparaged the English as "Willie Boys." Yet however sure he wanted to be of his own intelligence and abilities, Hoover was intimidated by the manners and social confidence of the Willie Boys, just as he had been unsettled in London by the silk hats and formal wear he saw in the streets and hotel lobbies. He knew that he suffered in the eyes of the Willies for the "supreme vulgarities" of being American and a man of commerce. He and Marion made themselves feel better by telling fabulous stories of each other within earshot of the Englishmen. At longer range, they invented effete nicknames for each of the Willies.[14]

Hoover further salved his social insecurity on shipboard by devouring Thackeray's satires of English life *Pendennis* and *The Newcomes*. He read on deck, dressed only in light white flannels and jacket, without shirt, socks, or underwear in concession to the heat. It is clear from his letters that he also smoked and swore and gambled, and somewhere around Ceylon he joined the Willie Boys in a fistfight.

Few of the Quaker strictures by which he had been raised were surviving to see Australia.[15]

In numerous letters over the next two years, Hoover would refer to Western Australia as hell, and he meant it. The landscape was hell, a flat, monotonous, dust-choked desert, barren but for low tangles of mulga and wattle bush as far as the eye could see, not a trout stream anywhere, in fact no water at all but for drops that could be dug up, condensed, or carried from the coast and sold at higher prices than beer.

The climate was hell, a dry broil for the most part, one hundred degrees at midnight for days on end, with brief diversions provided by Arctic cold spells in summer, dry thunderstorms accompanied by sand showers, and, worst of all, rare blasts of rain that raised a momentary, mocking verdure in the desert before the sun rebounded and burned everything back to drab.

The insects were hell: scorpions, tarantulas, snakelike centipedes, and disease-carrying airborne pests with an unerring aim for one's eyes and dinner plate.

The settlements were hell, overnight ramshackle boomtowns with names like Kalgoorie and Coolgardie, box-shaped lodgings with walls of corrugated iron that roared in the wind, beds with unwashed sheets, meals of beans, biscuits, canned potatoes, and "tinned dog" (probably mutton or ham), entertainment consisting of out-of-date copies of American magazines, the odd horse race, and drunks dodging camels on Main Street. "You cannot appreciate the real damnation of this country," wrote Hoover.[16]

Yet another level of hell in Western Australia was the business environment. The reporter Walter Liggett called the outback goldfields a hard, pitiless school where the world's sharks and sharpers congregated in ruthless pursuit of fortune. By the time Hoover arrived, the rush was almost clapped out. Hundreds of companies had been launched, tens of millions of dollars in speculative capital had been raised on the London exchange, and precious little of it had sifted through the pockets of promoters to actual operations. Frauds, swindles, and bribery were rampant. Just three of the hundreds of mines floated in Western Australia produced the vast majority of the region's dividends. Those rare successes were sufficient to draw money and keen-eyed men from around the world regardless of the risks.[17]

Hoover would blossom in this infernal environment. He arrived at Albany in May 1897, spent five days in quarantine due to an outbreak of smallpox on the ship, and made a quick stop in Perth before venturing 350 miles by rail through the endless bush to Coolgardie. The local press, such as it was, reported his arrival and gave an exaggerated account of his experience and expertise, likely with his active assistance.

Hoover was senior enough at Bewick, Moreing to be furnished with a bungalow, a cook, and a valet, although he rarely saw them. From his first week, he was always on the move, traveling sometimes by horse and trap, sometimes on the backs of the Afghan camels imported to cope with the arid expanse of the outback. Some treks took him three hundred miles beyond the nearest rail or telegraph line. He might evaluate four or five properties in a day. He learned to hate camels as much as horses. The furious pace of the lean young man with the pallid complexion and averted eyes captured the attention of mining journalists even without his encouragement. "No one I have ever met on the fields," one reported, "gets over ground so quickly and finishes what business he has so quietly and expeditiously. An early riser and tremendous worker, he flies from field to field with amazing rapidity." Others noticed that he missed nothing at the mines he visited—"every level, drive, stop and winze"—and that once implanted in his mind the information was there for good. "He could recall even minor details about ore bodies, methods of treatment, timbering and machinery which, perhaps the super-intendant had not observed."[18]

Although he was the most ubiquitous man in gold country, no one in Australia got to know Hoover well. He kept to himself, asking questions in his usual blunt and toneless style, answering in turn with *yep*s and *nope*s. In business meetings he seldom gave up much information, choosing to listen while doodling squares and figures with a pencil on paper. When he was in the mood to talk he would talk about work. A Perth lawyer who did work for Bewick, Moreing recalled nights camping with Hoover, who conversed in darkness about mining and the stock market until he realized that his listener was asleep.[19]

Hoover was also communicative with London. His reports began flowing in June, and it was immediately apparent that he considered himself much more than a scout. In addition to examining the geology and economic potential of new properties to guide the firm's investments, he stood in for vacationing mine managers and, without being asked, offered assessments of the absent managers' work. He had no compunctions about pushing himself forward at the expense of his new colleagues. He gave caustic reviews of what he understood as their overly generous labor practices and inefficient operations.

The harshness of the environment and Hoover's desperation to prove himself drew an element of savagery from him. He fired rafts of employees for laziness and incompetence and dumped two of his own assistants for being "damned noodle heads." When he fired a seventy-two-year-old bookkeeper, the man broke down in tears, having no means to support his wife in Perth. Moved by the bookkeeper's plight, Hoover raised an impressive $300 for him, and then dismissed him all the same. He formed a low opinion of all non-American talent in Australia and began to fill positions with his countrymen.[20]

Uncompromising in pursuit of better margins, Hoover haggled with camel dealers to save a few dollars on freight costs. He moved swiftly to shut losing properties that had been purchased at the heady height of the boom without sufficient regard to their intrinsic value. He lengthened shifts in the Coolgardie mines from forty-four to forty-eight hours. (His efforts to introduce labor-saving technology and practices at another mine would result in a job action, which Hoover answered by firing the strikers and hiring more pliable Italian labor.) He took cost per ton of ore as his key metric of success and posted remarkable improvements in a short period of time.

Hoover drove himself relentlessly as well, sleeping as little as four hours a night. His eyes and stomach gave him trouble. Months of roasting on the Western Australia grill left him with a chronic inflammation of the bladder. Sometimes he was so ill he could not sit up, but he refused to slow down, traveling on his back on a mattress on the bottom of a horse-drawn cart. His employers were so pleased with his performance that just two months after landing in Australia he was promoted to take on oversight of a second territory and granted a 10 percent share of the profits of the Coolgardie operations with a salary of $8,000. He now considered himself Bewick, Moreing's number-two man in the outback, and he would soon give the company more to be pleased about.

On June 16, 1897, Hoover journeyed north to Lawlers, a town as yet more famous for its barmaids than its gold finds. Hoover noticed the barmaids: "their personal beauty and their municipal influence is unquestioned," he wrote Theodore and May, but he does not appear to have been detained by them.* He camped overnight down the trail near the Sons of Gwalia lease and dropped in on the Welsh miners who were trying to make it pay. Awed at the prospects of their property, Hoover convinced London to secure an option on it. Late in August, he returned to the site, performed a careful examination of the claim, and in a series of memos told his employers that Sons of Gwalia was a valuable lease. He recommended its immediate purchase, there being half a million dollars in profit to be gained from the ore already in sight. He added that for the mine to reach its full potential it would need to be operated shrewdly with significant capital, modern equipment, and modern methods, and he left no doubt that he thought he was the man for the job.[21]

London committed a half million in cash to the property and installed Hoover to manage it. By the end of the year, he had produced 5,667 ounces of gold. Shares in the new company doubled in its first day of trading, and Sons of Gwalia was on its way to becoming one of the enduring sensations of the Western Australian gold belt. It made millions for Bewick, Moreing and subsequent investors before finally closing in 1963.

The firm was generous in crediting its new employee. Edward Hooper, head of operations Down Under, called Hoover "one of

---

* Hoover also noticed Australia's Aborigines. "Curiously," he wrote Burt Brown, "they have no religion. They have a devil-devil who is not a spirit but a real live nigger, who acts as executioner for the tribe and is therefore the medicine man's partner. His services can be secured on payment and he can be legitimately killed on sight, so he wears on his feet feathers pointing both ways, to prevent his being tracked." (David Burner, *Herbert Hoover: A Public Life*. Newton, MA: American Political Biography Press, 1978, p. 27.)

the most able mining engineers that ever came to this country." In November 1897, six months after stepping off the boat, Hoover received another raise to $10,000 a year and another promotion to junior partner, or "pardner," by his spelling.[22]

His letters home to brother Theodore show just how quickly Hoover got his feet under him in Australia. Three months after arriving, he was exploding with confidence: "I know I am equal to the job, not to be conceited, but I have made it go." After just a month more: "I have a grip here I am not bragging when I say I can put all the brains of these English gillies in two hairs of my own head. I twist them around my thumbs like thread."[23]

His fast start was perhaps not surprising. Hoover may have been new to Bewick, Moreing and new to Australia, but he had been engaged in business of one form or another for almost a decade, often carrying significant responsibilities, whether at the Oregon Land Company, or at Stanford with all his entrepreneurial and managerial endeavors, or managing mines for Janin. Still, the transformation of Hoover during his eighteen-month tour of Western Australia is something to behold.

To begin with, there was a startling physical change. Hoover had begun to have his picture taken on a fairly frequent basis, perhaps to convince himself and others of his progress. One photograph from this time shows him sitting casually under the bright antipodal sun, knees apart, hands resting on his thighs, fedora tipped back, a pipe clenched under his jaunty mustache. His hair is long and tousled. The baby fat is gone from his tanned face, although the boyishness remains. There is a hard glint in his eye and dirt caked on the pant legs of his rumpled tweed suit. He displays a confidence missing from all earlier photographs. For the first time he looks like a man who could reach into the guts of the earth and pull out a fortune in gold.[24]

His conduct was evolving, too. In his first few months in the outback, he was an aggressive, somewhat merciless manager doing his best for a demanding employer. He gave an account of his activities to Theodore:

> My predecessor was a rascal of the first water, mines were worked of no value, accounts all wrong, money short, rank staff and general hell. I have already laid at his door 63,000

pounds lost—$315,000 by our various companies, simple incompetency. He was only in office 7 months. I have fired every man on the staff but the clerks accountant and apprentices and have good men in now.[25]

By the time of his second promotion, his behavior had developed in alarming ways. Initially reluctant to recruit his Stanford friends in subordinate positions, in part because they were friends, also because he was unsure of their capacities, he now hurdled his misgivings. He hired several, letting them know that as a man responsible for businesses with expenditures of $5 million a year, he had a right to be exacting. He rode them with a ferocity that might have given Minthorn pause. His friend Deane Mitchell, who had been imported and promoted rapidly, at some point bridled at Hoover's direction. "I simply withdrew my backing to the board," Hoover wrote Theodore, "and after [Mitchell] gazed into the abyss beneath him he fairly crawled."[26]

Another friend, George Wilson, came over as Hoover's assistant and, after a swift promotion of his own, was assigned the job of sinking an eight-hundred-foot shaft at a Bewick, Moreing mine. "It is Wilsons job to get this shaft down quicker and cheaper than any shaft on the fields," Hoover wrote home. "He will and in doing so will make not only his reputation but my own as managing engineer. He must do it. If he fails he will arrive in San Francisco so broke he won't know where to eat. I have told all my California men this." His closing words to Theodore:

> It simply comes to this: men hate me more after they work for me than before. They don't need think they are coming to a snap. They're coming to a perfect hell and I am the devil.[27]

Charles Algernon Moreing appears to have appreciated Hoover's style. "I hear he is a slave driver," he is reported (by Hoover) to have said. "I would like to hire a few more slave drivers." Moreing also had to appreciate Hoover's results. Costs were down, margins were up, and new business was developed in magnificent fashion. The young devil was emerging as one of the leading mining engineers in Australia. George Wilson wrote Hinsdale that Hoover was making "a howling good reputation for himself. He is simply a wonder."[28]

Despite his rapid promotion and handsome pay increases, Hoover's attitude toward his employer began changing along with everything else. He grew imperious and turned on Bewick, Moreing before his first year was up. "Before you receive this," he wrote Theodore, "I shall have resigned from Bewick Moreing. Between ourselves they are a crowd of Sons of Bitches from stem to stern." He swore his brother to secrecy and reassured him that he had a big score lined up—"you'll hear something echo all over the mining world." He ranted about what he considered his ill treatment:

> I could tell you lots of things regarding mining finance that I don't want my name connected with nor do I think they treat a man right. I engineered the whole Sons of Gwalia deal out of which Moreing made $2,000,000 and never gave me a bean nor a share damn him. I'll fix his little game. It just happens that his business can't run without me and I will force him to make me managing director of Australia or tell him to the devil.[29]

Hoover's complaint with Bewick, Moreing was aggravated by the replacement of the company's managing director in Australia with an irascible Welshman named Ernest Williams. Hoover had been in Australia almost a year when Williams arrived, and he felt himself deserving of the position of managing director. He was not keen to cede authority to the new boss. He had learned in Salem and in Stanford that he liked power, and he was learning in Australia that control was almost as oxygen to him.

Rather than quit, he became paranoid about his boss and even attempted to organize the other engineers to stage a coup against their managing director. "[Williams] is quite the most complete scoundrel I have ever met," Hoover wrote Theodore, "and it's a question of fight or be done up behind my back. I'm giving him a damned merry chase I tell you and if I get the worst of it he can well say he has had a hard time." Hoover was prepared to lose his job in his battle with Williams, even if it meant putting his brother out of school for lack of financial support. Fortunately for Theodore, another solution to his problem presented itself. Bert resigned his staff position at Bewick, Moreing to take over management of its Sons of Gwalia property, a shift that put him at a distance from the despised managing director.[30]

The move did nothing to improve Hoover's demeanor. Indeed, his bullying ways now extended even to people dear to him. Lester Hinsdale, his close friend, and the former Stanford student body president, had been cheerfully helping Hoover manage his affairs stateside until he noticed that he was being treated like a junior office boy. Now a practicing lawyer and in no way beholden to Hoover, Hinsdale rebuked him. Hoover returned a groveling letter of apology, pleading the extremity of his circumstances. He also enlisted their mutual friend George Wilson to mollify Hinsdale. Things were eventually smoothed over, but judging by the tenor of future letters, their friendship never fully recovered.[31]

Hoover's sister, May, did not receive the same consideration as Hinsdale. Her first mistake was to take up with a young tradesman named Cornelius Van Ness Leavitt, of whom both Hoover brothers disapproved. "I wrote her pretty sternly about young Van," Hoover told Theodore. He claimed to regret his tone but guessed that it might have done his sister some good. She also appears to have been sharing her brother's financial assistance with relatives, a practice that did not meet his approval.[32]

May's biggest error, however, was to get involved in gossip that suggested a romantic affair between her brother and their cousin, Harriette, who had lived for a time with the three Hoovers in the Bay Area. Bert and Harriette corresponded frequently and intimately. Theodore alerted Bert that he was rumored to be involved with Harriette and, specifically, that he was thought to have arranged to meet her in Paris in 1900. "The worst Tommy-rot I have heard," Bert thundered in response. Harriette, he insisted, was "a good sister always, a thing I have never had. It is largely due to her kindly influence, encouragement and help that I kept up the battle and pulled through college. I love the girl dearly as a sister and have told her often that so long as I could afford it she should be treated as a sister hence her presence at Stanford."[33]

Bert attributed the rumors to a misreading of his financial support of his cousin, something he had hidden from Theodore. He was worried that the talk would reach California and, presumably, Lou Henry. He threatened that there would be "hell to pay" if it did. Harriette soon quit college, over Hoover's objections, and moved out of state. Bert told his brother that May was to blame for the mess:

> I have already said May has sufficiently alienated any regard I might have for her to place us entirely on a duty basis. On such basis she shall continue so far as I am concerned for the balance of her time. She shall have nothing to complain of from financial standpoint but must look to you entirely for other feeling or care. That's enough I shall not mention the subject again so long as I am able and I don't want to hear of it further.[34]

Bert also informed Theodore that his heart was committed to a different Stanford girl, one to whom he had proposed two years earlier, unsuccessfully. "Sufficient to say that as she has made other arrangements I have no intention of getting married," he writes. The girl to whom he proposed may have been Lou Henry, although he does not mention her by name, and she is not known to have had an arrangement with any other young man at Stanford. Hoover begged Theodore to keep this exchange secret from Harriette because he was "already worried to death with appeals, intrigue, and woes."[35]

Hoover would always insist that his relationship with Harriette was innocent, and that his conduct was impeccable. That may well be true. He and his cousin would remain on good terms and twenty-five years later, married and with children, she would say that Hoover's letters to her had compared Lou Henry favorably to the other young women he knew and showed that he was desperate at the thought of losing her. On the other hand, it is reasonable to wonder if there is not more to the story than has survived in the record given that Theodore considered the gossip serious enough to notify his brother; that Bert reacted violently and was anxious about the talk spreading; that he had hidden from Theodore that he was paying Harriette's way through school; that he asked Theodore not to discuss the matter with Harriette; that Harriette abruptly departed from California and later destroyed much of their correspondence; that Bert ostracized his only sister over the incident; and that he claimed the rumors were nothing yet confessed to being beset with "intrigues and woes."[36]

Many of the important bonds in Hoover's life were now frayed or broken. He seemed not to care. He heard that some of the old Stanford gang were saying uncharitable things about him and chalked it up to jealousy. He continued to plant news of his expanding responsibilities and salary increases in Palo Alto papers and instructed Theodore to broadcast his salary on his behalf.[37]

In addition to the habitual fibbing about his age and income, his boastfulness, his calculated cruelty to friends, and the fracturing of important relationships, Hoover was abandoning important personal disciplines. The careful financial habits that had served him so well in lean years were abandoned. "I am a damn fool in money matters," he admitted to his brother. "I'm paying my debts keep every body in world in college outside of the family. I am busted. I have been forced to overdraw like thunder but when my new agreement is fixed up I will be all o.k."[38]

He also monkeyed with numbers in his monthly reports and press releases for Bewick, Moreing to exaggerate the already stellar performance of his mines. He hired spies to work in competing mines and sent Theodore confidential mining documents in acknowledged violation of Bewick, Moreing policy. Hoover also continued to work for the company's "cussed crowd of damn rascals" despite knowledge of their shady financial practices, including manipulation of the market for short-term profit. This sort of stock jobbing Hoover knew to be disreputable, and he would later lambaste Moreing for it, all the while practicing it himself.[39]

Hoover's desperation to succeed was clearly affecting both his emotional balance and his behavior, and he was unraveling morally at almost the same pace as he was advancing in the company. He was determined to succeed by whatever means necessary, subordinating questions of right or wrong to the good of his career and driving himself crazy with his hunger for power and control, his hypersensitivity to perceived threats to his independence and stature, and his need to measure up. The fantastic promotions and pay increases were never enough: he felt unappreciated, indeed persecuted, by his company. The money and responsibilities he had been granted had gone straight to his head.

Of course, it would be easy for any twenty-three-year-old alone on the other side of the planet to lose his bearings, even before money and power and Hoover's deep-seated insecurities entered the equation. What is unusual in Hoover's case is that he continued to commit acts of extraordinary generosity while in Australia, granting or loaning up to $3,000 annually to keep various family members and friends in school. Some of the recipients were unaware of the source of their funds, in part because he did not wish to embarrass them, in part because he wanted to insulate himself against their expressions of gratitude. The strange way in which his better angels found accommodation in his breast alongside his demons is probably due to the fact that both had roots in his childhood pain.

He at least managed to stay on the right side of those dearest to him. Whatever happened with his cousin Harriette, they remained loyal and sympathetic friends. He had either continued or resumed a correspondence with Lou Henry while in Australia. And Bert's bonds with the Stanford community, while tested, were not broken. His relationship with Theodore also survived this run of personal carnage, although the nature of their attachment was altered. It had, in fact, been changing for years. The elder by three and a half years, Theodore was something of a lost soul, having rebelled in his teens against his Quaker upbringing without ever securing a foothold in the secular world. Aspiring to be a writer or an intellectual, he had drifted through a series of printing jobs in hopes of someday breaking into journalism. From the age of eighteen, he was conscious of gradually surrendering the role of big brother to Bert out of admiration for his judgment, dynamism, sturdiness of character, and "sheer capacity."[40]

By the time Bert joined Bewick, Moreing, their bond was less fraternal than paternal, with Bert in the lead role. He prodded Theodore to abandon his literary dreams, coldly and correctly advising that he did not have the talent to be another Jack London. He paid for Theodore to follow him through the Stanford geology department and dispensed advice to his elder on everything from the proper

use of summer vacations to physical conditioning. His plan was for
Theodore to graduate and hurry overseas to join him, solidifying his
dependence on his younger brother.

However green in some regards, Hoover was unusually adult in
others. Intense and purposeful, he was dedicated to fighting what to
him felt like a life-and-death battle to establish his place in the world
while most of his Stanford mates were enjoying their salad days. His
friend George Wilson, thrown into similar circumstances in Australia, albeit without the responsibilities or the high income, considered
it one great picaresque adventure. He filled his letters to Hinsdale
with details of his romantic hits and misses (he addressed Hinsdale as
"the chaplain" in honor of his dedicated attentions to fallen women).
He described his difficulty in getting his sea legs while crossing the
Pacific: "My voyage from SF to Honolulu was similar to the flight of
a meteor in that I left a wake of refuse behind in the first part of my
flight."

On arriving Down Under, the guitar-playing Wilson picked up a
few jig steps from Aboriginal war dances and happily allowed himself
to be detained by the barmaids:

> I must admit that they have a class of charmers in this coun-
> try that we haven't in the States and that we might do well
> to import and intergraft, -viz. Bar maids . . . they are all girls
> and good lookers in many instances. Now for instance, I have
> in mind a little, pretty, black haired Welsh girl at Kanowna,
> whose acquaintance I have cultivated on divers occasions with
> a fair degree of success.[41]

Hoover seems almost a generation apart from his carefree
schoolmate. One of the few occasions on which he shared Wilson's
high spirits was on the Fourth of July, 1898, which coincided with
America's emergence as a global power in the climactic battles of the
Spanish-American War. He marked the date by setting off four hundred pounds of dynamite at a remote mine, breaking most of the windows in the neighborhood.

A few months after that celebration, Hoover's career in Western
Australia blew up. His effort to organize his fellow engineers against
his boss, Ernest Williams, was discovered, resulting in an angry con-

frontation and suspicions that Hoover had burgled his boss's desk, an act he denied. While Hoover would always claim to have been promoted out of Australia, Williams was now calling for him to be dismissed.[42]

Luckily for Hoover, Charles Algernon Moreing, recently returned from a tour of China, had agreed to provide the imperial mining administrator at Tientsin with loans and engineering expertise. Moreing appreciated the young American's remarkable abilities, notwithstanding his insubordination: Hoover had a nose for ore, he understood his master's interests, and he was granted a second chance. His farewell at a Coolgardie club was hosted by friends and associates with no affiliation to Williams or Bewick, Moreing. He sailed for San Francisco to tie up a loose end before reporting to China.[43]

# CHAPTER 4

# The Adventures of Hu-hua and Hoo Loo

Photographs of Lou Henry as a young woman are not what one would expect of a Gilded Age banker's daughter. Lou posing with a rifle. Lou on horseback with a rifle. Lou in a Stanford sweater with a rifle. Lou posing with a rifle and a freshly killed deer. Lou balancing on a railing, jumping hurdles, and ice skating. Lou taking target practice with a bow. Lou perched with a fishing rod on a rock in the middle of a trout stream. She is frequently seen in male company, and she is plainly comfortable as one of the boys. Her dress is simple, long skirts and blouses, no jewelry. She wears her brown hair bundled high. She is not a beauty. She invariably looks cheerful and confident, with direct blue eyes and a crooked smile.[1]

The Henry family had migrated from Iowa to Texas, then to Kansas and Whittier, California, before settling in Monterey. Lou's father, Charles D. Henry, pursued a middling career in banking and lived for the outdoors. He raised his eldest daughter to consider herself the equal of any man. She and her younger sister, Jean, had been sleeping under the stars for as long as either could remember. A bright and popular girl, Lou was successful in school and active in literary and scientific clubs. She had an independent streak, not unlike Hulda Hoover, and chafed from an early age at her assigned gender role, writing letters on female equality and universal suffrage, protesting that "idiots, maniacs, and jailbirds" could cast ballots while women could not. In a high-school essay entitled "The Independent Girl," she expressed impatience with female conformity and stated a desire to marry "a spirit equally as independent as her own," someone with whom she would "unite forces and with combined strength go forth to meet the world."[2]

Life as an independent girl in the 1890s was difficult. After graduating from normal school, Lou worked briefly as a teacher and a cashier at her father's bank before convincing her parents to allow her to study geology at Stanford. Her college years were a satisfying whirl of sports, theater, study, and sorority life. She impressed her friends and professors with her sweet nature and her penetrating, skeptical intelligence. Her brains and competence, however, were not enough to gain her the professional footing she sought. She had hoped to succeed Hoover as Branner's assistant in the geology department, but the assignment went to a male student. Nor could she find a job in her field on graduation, despite Branner's assistance. She vented her frustration in a letter to a sorority sister, wondering if the "AB" in her degree stood for "A Boy":

> What wouldn't I give just about now to be one! They would not want me to stay meekly at home—I would not still have to face that old question of how far obedience is dutiful and I would have something to work for.[3]

By the autumn of 1898, Lou was killing time rolling bandages as a volunteer in the Spanish-American War effort and lamenting her lack of prospects. She had not seen Herbert Hoover for almost two years and his letters to Theodore suggest that she may have refused his proposal of marriage before he sailed for Australia. Just what was said in subsequent correspondence is only partially known, due to his destruction of a portion of their letters, but somewhere along the way they began to talk of marriage. It does not appear to have been a passionate courtship: in a letter from Stanford to Australia, Lou attempted to "bridge the physical distance" between them with an exhaustive account of the challenges of organizing a university athletics day. Neither was demonstrative in any sense of the word.[4]

More importantly, they were compatible, quite comfortable in each other's presence, and they shared many interests. They were the same age, twenty-four. Lou had always said that she wanted a man "who loves the mountains, the rocks, and the ocean like my father does." Her mother said she was so fond of travel that Hoover's life-style seemed ideal to her. Lou struck Bert as self-respecting, clear-headed, bold, and cheerful. She answered his profound need for companionship and female approval, and she was intelligent enough to understand his worlds of commerce and science, his drive and ambition. She was also a beacon of stability at a time when he was somewhat unhinged. It seems clear that they were each other's best option.[5]

On the occasion of his reassignment by Moreing, Hoover cabled Lou a brief message: "Going to China via San Francisco. Will you go with me?" She answered with a single word.[6]

Hoover could not escape the outback fast enough. "I am damned glad to get out of here," he wrote Theodore on November 2, 1898. "My whole stay here has been a nightmare in a dozen regards." He admitted to clashes with Williams and claimed to have resigned, although it is evident in the same correspondence that all was not right between Bert and Bewick, Moreing. Notwithstanding some brief noises about the lure of the Orient, he acknowledged that Tientsin was a hardship post, a "two-year siege in northern China." He was without salary until he started his new job. The company was only picking up his travel expenses. Times were tight, and Theodore, now a junior at Stanford, would have to be economical. Bert added that he was arranging to take the long route to Peking, via Suez, London, New York, and San Francisco, with the intention of marrying in Monterey. "Don't ever tell May," he insisted.[7]

Hoover left Australia on December 11, 1898, with an armload of books on China. He stopped long enough in London to see fog so thick that the street lamps were lit at noon, and long enough in San Francisco to smoke a fifty-cent cigar with a former classmate at the luxurious old Palace Hotel. He arrived at the end of January in Monterey with its green lawns and dazzling blue bay and met his in-laws for the first time in his capacity as prospective son-in-law. They appear to have met once before, although the circumstances are uncertain. Hoover had boasted to his friend Miss Hill of having spent a week changing from tennis flannels to full dress suit at the home of a lady friend, perhaps Miss Henry. Mrs. Henry had only the vague recollection of a single meal in his company.[8]

The Henrys were not prepared to like Hoover. They had forbidden their daughter to live on the fourth floor of her residence at Stanford out of fear for her safety, and now he was washing up in Monterey with the intention of whisking her halfway around the world. After a few days, they apparently warmed to him. "I think we all liked him about as much as Lou did," said Mrs. Henry by way of endorsement. The week before the wedding was a frantic muddle of last-minute preparations, introductions, fittings, dinners, travel bookings, and packing. The marriage license had to be fetched from Salinas, the county seat, a day's return journey from Monterey. The couple had no pastor; they were to be married by a Dr. Thoburn from Palo Alto, but he died six weeks short of the appointed date. The Henrys, nominally Episcopalian, could not find a replacement. There were no Quaker ministers nearby. The only man of the cloth available in Monterey was a Roman Catholic priest of Lou's acquaintance, Father Mestres. He agreed to preside.[9]

Shortly after noon on February 10, Herbert Hoover and Lou Henry were married at the Henry home in matching brown traveling clothes, a simple dress for Lou, cinched at the waist, and a three-piece suit for Bert, with a bowtie, sketchily assembled. Theodore was present. May, too, was permitted to attend. Bert and Mrs. Henry stood in the bay window of the living room as soft music played and Mr. Henry brought Lou through the little hallway and gave her to her man. The independent girl vowed to love and honor, and made no mention of obeying. Lunch was served, including two meat dishes that Father Mestres consumed to the horror of the Catholic serving staff (it was a Friday). The speeches were notable for their brevity. Pictures were taken outside amid the palms and pepper trees, Lou sometimes wearing a bowler hat, other times her father's Western hat.

When the fine horses and carriage that had been arranged to convey the newlyweds to the station failed to arrive on time, they rushed off in a hack to catch a two o'clock train that would carry them to San Francisco for their next day's voyage to China. It was an apt beginning to their lives together. The newlyweds would continue to scramble along at a breakneck pace for decades to come.

. . .

China at the turn of the twentieth century was a crippled empire of 300 million, its military weakness having been exposed five years earlier when the Japanese relieved it of Korea in a brief, one-sided conflict. That defeat had touched off a great and unscrupulous competition among Germany, Russia, France, Britain, and Japan for possession of China's vast resources. The prizes were land, ports, mines, railways, and cargoes of tea and silk, some of them purchased, others simply taken. At the start of the new century there were 672 foreign companies fattening themselves in China, half of them British, few of them alert to the increasingly volatile environment in which they operated. The young Chinese emperor Kuang Hsu had tried to brace China's sovereignty by embarking on a feverish program of modernization but his reforms were unpopular; the Chinese people were more anxious to see the foreigner driven into the sea than to adopt his ways, and the Empress Dowager, who had placed Kuang Hsu on his throne, shared their sentiments. China was on the verge of upheaval.[10]

A typical adventurer, Charles Algernon Moreing saw more opportunity than danger in China's distress. On his visit to the country in 1898 he made two crucial connections. One was Gustav Detring, a well-placed Chinese-speaking German who had formerly served as commissioner of the Maritime Customs of China in the city of Tientsin. Moreing and Detring struck an informal alliance to pursue commercial opportunities in China. Detring also introduced Moreing to Chang Yen-Mao, director-general of the Kaiping mines and director-general of mines for the provinces of Chihli and the district of Jehol. Chang's company had administrative control of the vast Kaiping coal mines northeast of Tientsin but had neither the capital nor the expertise to develop them fully.

Moreing, working through Detring, arranged a loan of £200,000 (US$1 million) to Chang and the Chinese Engineering and Mining Company to expand the Kaiping mines and build an ice-free harbor at Chinwangtao. The Englishman tried to negotiate himself a share of equity in the company but Chang would not bite, so Moreing settled instead for a steep 12 percent rate of interest on his loan. It was Chang who asked Moreing to recommend a mining engineer who could survey a number of gold mines in his realm, creating the opening for Hoover.

Strictly speaking, Hoover was to work as a technical adviser to Chang, who would pay his salary of $12,500. Hoover appears, however, to have joined Chang on questionable pretenses. Moreing, still coveting Chinese mining properties, wrote the British Foreign Office that Chang wanted to develop gold mines with British money and expertise, and that Hoover would manage the operations, suggesting that his young charge was intended for a role well beyond technical adviser. Moreing also granted Hoover a percentage of his profits in China, an arrangement likely unknown to Chang. Hoover told his brother that he would "have charge" of Bewick, Moreing's Chinese business. In all of his correspondence with friends and family, he presents himself as an agent of Moreing rather than of Chang. These conflicting understandings of his role would soon lead to immense problems for all concerned.[11]

The newlyweds signed the register on the SS *Coptic* as Mr. and Mrs. H. C. Hoover and sailed from San Francisco on February 11, 1899. Lou kept a travel diary and when she was not looking, her husband would fill it with playful imitations of her observations and emotions. She had her picture taken with leis in Honolulu and in a rickshaw in Kyoto. She did not much like Japan. Its pagodas and lantern shops and exotic costumes did not meet the romantic expectations raised by Gilbert and Sullivan. Lou found the people small, ugly, unkempt, and unhappy.[12]

Their mutual friend George Wilson, a casualty of Hoover's ill-fated Australian coup, was now following his classmate to China on the promise of a position. He arrived in Shanghai in mid-March. "I rushed up to the hotel register on arriving," he wrote Hinsdale, "and sure enough, my worst fears were soon realized—Mr H.C. Hoover and Wife—as large as life." Disturbed at the fall of a fellow bachelor, Wilson had no intention of following suit: "To bring a wife to China is far worse than to ship whole fleets of coal to Newcastle. You can buy them up here like sheep."[13]

The Hoovers proceeded from Shanghai to Tientsin, where

Bert required only two weeks to assemble his staff and organize a two-month inspection tour of mining properties. He left Lou at the Astor Hotel in the foreign compound on the outskirts of Tientsin to adapt to local customs and currencies and set up house. She found a stately fifteen-room blue brick residence on Racecourse Road, with a wide veranda, arched windows with bamboo curtains, and a grape trellis climbing almost to its gray-tiled roof. Lou could look out her front window and see rickshaws clattering up and down the elm-lined street. She decorated with paneled screens, rattan chairs, and her husband's collection of geographic photographs of the American West. She hired the usual multitude of Chinese servants, including a number-one boy, a number-two boy, three houseboys, a rickshaw boy, a cook, a groom, and a groom's assistant.

Bert, out in the field, was also surrounded by servants, much to his annoyance. Accustomed to traveling light, he had been brow-beaten by his Chinese handlers into outfitting an entourage befitting his station: a hundred Chinese cavalrymen and their officers, advance heralds, rear guards, grooms, cooks, interpreters, mules, ponies, and carts. The cooks were instructed to prepare him Western food so that Chang's investment in his salary would not be wasted by illness.

On this and subsequent journeys, Hoover drove his caravan from mine to mine through the interior of China, reaching north to Mongol camps little changed since Marco Polo's time. He saw the Great Wall and the Yellow River and the Gobi Desert but for the most part kept his nose in his books. He devoured Chinese history and in deference to his hosts sampled Confucius and Mencius. He heaped on Plato and Shakespeare, Goethe and Schiller, not to mention the French— Balzac, Dumas, Zola, and Montaigne. At each new mine, Hoover was greeted with banners and firecrackers. The mine works were typically walled and protected against marauding bandits by uniformed guards. He would descend into stopes and tunnels, appalling Chinese managers who believed it beneath their dignity to root around in the dirt.

He was disappointed at the scale of the mines, as well as their inefficiencies. The technology in use was primitive: hand pumps and bamboo buckets carried by throngs of laborers who were short on competence and expert at loafing. The amount of corruption and petty fraud, Hoover wrote Detring, was sickening. The Chinese were addicted to the squeeze, a complex system of graft they had come to view as a sacred right. Hoover was baffled at their lack of enthusiasm for mechanization and orderly administration. Lou reported that "the utter apathy of the Chinese to everything, their unconquerable dilatoriness" was almost heartbreaking to her energetic husband.[14]

Lou sometimes joined Bert's expeditions, and in remote locations she drew crowds of children curious to see a white woman. She followed him down into mines, again to the perturbation of the Chinese managers who, after she resurfaced, would exorcise with drums and firecrackers the demons she was believed to have left in the deep.* "China is great fun," she wrote to family friends. "Just as queer as it can be. . . . To us they are one great joke, from the time the 'boy' wakens us in the morning by bringing tea to our rooms, to the last thing we hear at night, which is the watchman's rattle or great gong which he sounds industriously to let thieves know where he is!"[15]

Bert, too, was amused by their setup: "Our No. I Boy is more jealous of my interests and more proud and insistent on my rank than I am - and our physical, mental and moral welfare are jealously guarded." He marveled at the resourcefulness of the staff. "All you need to do is wave your hand and anything you want will appear." He learned that his Chinese name was Hu-hua. His wife's was Hoo Loo.[16]

Although his domestic servants were an improvement over his mine laborers, Hoover shared the prevailing European conviction of Chinese racial inferiority. He would write of "the simply appalling and universal dishonesty of the working classes, the racial slowness, and the low average of intelligence." He initially joined Lou in practicing Chinese for two hours a day but gave it up before long and never advanced beyond rudimentary communications (she gained a basic competence in the language). His efforts to understand the Chinese and their culture were largely limited to his reading.[17]

George Wilson also complained of the rotten management of the Chinese, of gold thieving and bloated payrolls, of money wasted on celebrations and firecrackers. Still, unlike Hoover, he developed an affection for the country: "I like the place, the life, the people, the climate, the birds, the wondrous flowers, the grand sunrises, the novelty, the antiquity, in fact it all has a deep real interest for me."[18]

---

* Hoover's servants spread rumors that he could look into the ground and find gold because his eyes were green.

Lou, too, tried to appreciate and understand her surroundings. Her interest in the Chinese language was considered odd by Europeans in Tientsin (an unsurprising attitude for a community that built golf courses in Chinese graveyards). She bought Ming and early K'ang Hse blue and white porcelains, some of which were exquisite, and she collected macabre photographs of prisoners being tortured and executed in the streets of the city.[19]

The foreign compound where the Hoovers lived ran for a mile along the Peiho River, two miles outside the native city of Tientsin. It looked like a European theme park with its jumble of embassies, banks, shops, and residences in architectural styles representing more than a dozen nationalities. The British were the dominant community within and they kept up an active social scene into which the Hoovers plunged. Lou was popular, creating "her own atmosphere" at parties, according to her husband, who felt like a "wet crow" by comparison. They bought ponies to race at the local track and asked Theodore to send them a carriage from San Francisco, "a 'nobby' affair, as fully 'swell' as has been recently evolved." There were a sufficient number of Americans in China for the Hoovers to organize an alumni association of seven Stanford graduates.[20]

As in any marriage, there were accommodations to be made between husband and wife, and Lou, having taken a domineering mate, did much of the accommodating. She accepted the priorities of his business as the organizing principle of their life together. Never one to care about clothes in college—her parents had begged her to spend on her wardrobe—she now wrote her mother with orders for dresses, patterns, and materials to please her husband and make herself presentable in society:

> There are two things Bert likes that you may utilize. One is that he wants to see me in a black satin dress! But I can't think of any way to have it made that won't make me look too old—as tho' I were assuming too much dignity for my years. I think that will doubtless have to wait. But if you happen to run across a "youthful" style and trimmings for black satin—!

Bert also liked to see her in white and red, and she wore a lot of both her first summer in China. He wore his blue serge suits on every occasion. They went to bed in matching flannel pajamas with big sailor collars and silk cuffs.[21]

For his first meeting with his official employer, Chang Yen-Mao, Hoover was picked up in Chang's cart, with its silk-carpeted floors and mules in silver harness, and conveyed to a red brick mansion surrounded by a high wall. He was met in solemn greeting by the tall, impassive Chang, who wore a peacock-blue gown with rose, emerald, and purple trim, and tall black velvet boots embroidered in gold. The chain around his neck held a hundred amber beads and his crown-shaped winter hat of sable had a peacock feather and a ruby finial signifying his precise status as a mandarin. Chang took his blue-serged visitor inside and sat him amid teak tables where they engaged in the timeless ceremony of offering and refusing hospitality, and offering again, and finally accepting. They shared tea and cakes and lychee nuts.

During his stays in Tientsin, Hoover spent considerable time in Chang's company and, from the outset, he bombarded the mandarin with proposals for new ventures. He honed in on the Kaiping coalfields, among the world's largest, stretching for more than twenty miles northeast of Tientsin. Hoover considered them, by Western standards, the only successful mining venture in China. Nine thousand men worked three separate collieries, managed by the Chinese with assistance from European and American engineers. Thanks to Moreing's loan, a fourth colliery and an ice-free port were now under construction. Hoover, believing the current operations to be primitive and woefully inefficient, asked Chang to consider Moreing's offer to combine the four collieries and the new port into a joint Chinese-English venture, and offered as an inducement more of Moreing's capital, expecting in return control of any such enterprise. Without "absolute control," he had written Moreing, "the game is not worth the candle." Hoover realized that under Chinese law, the mines belonged to the emperor, and that Chang could not sell them to foreigners. He made additional proposals of comprehensive reforms to Chinese mining law, allowing foreigners expanded rights under government supervision.[22]

In the midst of these discussions, Hoover deliberately made his own murky position still murkier. He sent a letter in confidence to R. A. F. Penrose Jr., the American mining financier, describing his role in Tientsin as "consulting engineer, chief engineer, foreign advisor . . . I don't know exactly what, to Chang," and made no mention of Moreing. He said he has been "thinking on subjects intrigue-esque," and suggested that the rights to operate the mines could be transferred to an American-led syndicate if Penrose were interested. The Chinese, he said, would prefer U.S. interests over the British because of the latter's territorial ambitions. He described the opportunity as "unparalleled" and "worth the gamble." He frankly revealed that his own object was to secure his position as a leading mining figure in China and to make money. This breezy betrayal of his patron, Moreing, came to nothing. It did reveal, however, Hoover's capacity for duplicity, at least where Moreing was concerned.[23]

Unfortunately for all of his schemes, the tide of opinion in China was moving against further concessions to outsiders. Several months before Hoover had arrived in the country, the reforming young emperor was placed under house arrest and effectively dethroned by the Empress Dowager, who throttled his modernizations and moved to stop alien businessmen and diplomats from treating her realm as a complimentary buffet. New rules were introduced, unfriendly to foreign capital. Control and management of joint ventures was limited to the Chinese, with foreigners consigned to technical roles, and stiff royalties introduced on foreign profits.

Chang, reading the wind and enjoying control, was cooler than ever to Hoover's endless proposals for consolidations and mine modernization. He praised Hoover's abilities and character, raised his salary, expanded his role at the Chinese Engineering and Mining Company, and installed him as chief engineer at the newly created Mining Bureau for Chihli, but he would not be subordinated. Hoover pressed and complained and secretly wrote Moreing of his hopes that political unrest in China would overthrow the government and produce new opportunities for Western capital. He tried to nudge Chang by threatening to quit. The mandarin stood his ground as he would continue to do, until he had no choice.

·   ·   ·

June 1900 in Tientsin was an unbearable month of hot winds and high humidity. Banks of black and purple clouds rolled in from over the Pacific, drenching the foreign compound with lightning and torrential rains. Hoover was recovering from influenza and Lou from a sinus infection when all of northern China exploded.[24]

The Boxers were a populist, quasi-religious sect resentful of the rapacity and arrogance of "foreign devils," whether of the commercial, military, or missionary variety. Its adherents practiced magic and martial arts and believed that they held the powers to deflect gunfire and raise the spirits of dead soldiers to fight at their sides. The movement swept toward Peking and Tientsin like a whirlwind, offering hope to destitute and downtrodden Chinese.[25]

Traveling in great mobs, the Boxers were vicious with the foreigners and Christian Chinese in their paths. The famous *Times* of London correspondent George Morrison reported horrifying scenes of "women and children hacked to pieces, men trussed like fowls, with noses and ears cut off and eyes gouged out." His interpreter privately recorded much worse: "Many were found roasted alive, and so massacred and cut up as to be unrecognizable."[26]

The foreign settlement at Tientsin, backing onto the river and walled at one end, was dangerously exposed. Its defenses consisted of two small cannon, a dozen machine guns, and about two thousand foreign soldiers protecting seven hundred foreign civilians, including three hundred women and children, and thousands of Christian Chinese. On June 14, as Hoover helped build barriers at the entrances to the settlement out of sacks of sugar and grain, a howling, dancing horde of Boxers, twenty-five thousand strong, descended next door on Tientsin proper. They torched the French cathedral and turned the sky an ominous red. The mob attempted to light up the foreign compound as well until machine gun fire dispelled their delusions of invulnerability. The foreigners were not seriously challenged until five thousand imperial Chinese regulars sent to disperse the Boxers instead joined the rebellion and trained their artillery on the compound. By June 18, the Europeans were reeling under a constant barrage of shells. Bullets ricocheted off buildings and littered the streets. Fires were breaking out everywhere, choking the compound with smoke. Above it all was the ever-present threat of a mass attack by shrieking Boxers. "There must have been a million of them," Wilson wrote Hinsdale, "and they all carried firebrands." Demoralized Westerners began asking each other if they would shoot their wives to spare them worse when the hordes broke through.[27]

Hoover fought fires in the settlement and delivered food and medical supplies on his bicycle, hugging the brick walls along the street to avoid gunfire. Reporters on the scene observed that he seemed to be moving on the double quick, furiously jingling the change in his pockets and chewing nuts without shucking them. Lou, unwilling to join other women in the safety of the basement at city hall, ran bicycle errands of her own, a .38 Mauser strapped to her hip. She also stood night watch and volunteered at a makeshift hospital at the social club.

With the disruption of rail and telegraph service, Tientsin was cut off from the rest of the world throughout the siege. As reports of the Boxer frenzy spread overseas, American and European newspaper readers feared the worst for the tiny foreign settlement, and Stanford faculty and students read that several of their most talented alumni were probably dead: "It is almost certain that they have fallen victims to the savage ferocity of the Mongolian hosts, unless they managed to make their escape previous to the bloody massacre, which is not likely."[28]

In fact, casualties were light in the foreign compound. It was Hoover's employer, Chang Yen-Mao, who came closest to dying during the attacks. As a recognized ally of the Western devils, Chang was no friend to the Boxers. At the start of the uprising, he hunkered down at an estate in the foreign compound and waited for European troops and Chinese regulars to restore order. The defection of the imperial army unnerved him, however, in part because it stacked the odds against the foreigners, and also because it suggested that his patron, the xenophobic Dowager Empress, was encouraging the rebellion. Word soon spread in the foreign settlement that Chang was hedging his bets. He was believed to have entered negotiations with Chinese military officials to save his own skin and was said to have attempted a midnight escape from the foreign settlement by boat. Although there was no firm evidence against him, the harried Europeans were in no mood to sort fact from rumor: they arrested Chang on charges of communicating with the enemy and threatened him with execution.

On June 23, two thousand reinforcements reached the foreign settlement, temporarily lowering the threat level, although eighty thousand Chinese troops and several hundred thousand Boxers were now camped in the vicinity. Gustav Detring took advantage of the moment to visit Chang in his confinement. Hoover may have dropped by as well. Both men depended upon the mandarin for their livelihoods, and both had been arguing with his captors for his release.

As artillery boomed in the distance and shells burst randomly across the foreign concession, Detring and the imprisoned Chang worried over the future of the Kaiping mines. While reports from the field were incomplete, Detring was able to inform Chang that the Boxers had seriously disrupted their coal operations, scaring off miners, burning buildings, halting production and sales. The Chinese Engineering and Mining Company, already undercapitalized and heavily indebted, now faced a revenue collapse and its share price was plummeting. Worse, the most likely outcome of the Boxer uprising appeared to be an aggressive response by European armies, the collapse of the Chinese government, and the parceling out of Chinese assets to foreigners. Russian and Japanese troops were already said to be exploiting the chaos, planting their flags on the collieries and helping themselves to coal. Running out of options, Chang signed over his power of attorney to Detring and instructed him to seek protection for the company under the British flag on the best terms he could manage.[29]

Detring left Chang and called upon Hoover with the suggestion that they reorganize the Chinese Engineering and Mining Company into a joint Sino-British concern with a fresh injection of Moreing's capital. Hoover needed no convincing. They began plotting to deliver a piece of the greatest industrial venture in China from Hoover's employer, Chang, to his true boss, Moreing.

The preliminary deal they cobbled together would see the new company registered under British law, and its capital expanded to 1 million shares at a par value of one pound each. Existing Chinese shareholders would receive 375,000 of those shares in exchange for their equity. British investors would inject of development capital into the company within ninety days. There were, in addition to these terms, several understandings.

Detring and Hoover understood that Moreing and his fellow promoters would get roughly 200,000 shares to cover their expenses and services, although nothing to this effect was put in writing. They understood that the disposition of the remaining shares would raise the capital necessary to develop the company. Again, they put nothing in writing. They appear to have also understood that Detring and Chang would profit from the deal, yet once more, they put nothing in writing. And they discussed leaving Chang as director-general of the company, forming a board of directors in China and an advisory board in London, which would have suited the Chinese, but, of course, it was not written down.

Detring and Hoover backdated such paperwork as did exist to make it appear as though the reorganization of the Chinese Engineering and Mining Company had preceded the Boxer uprising. They feared that an agreement cooked up during the crisis, enabled by a power of attorney granted by an imprisoned Chang, would lack legitimacy in the eyes of other coal-hungry nations. They were undoubtedly right.

Hoover knew he had leverage over Detring and Chang, who could either accept hard terms with Moreing or risk losing the mines to the Russians or Japanese. He drove a hard bargain for his English master. Detring wanted a sale binding on Moreing; Hoover insisted on a nonbinding option to purchase. Hoover in turn bound Detring not to deal with anyone else while Moreing considered his option.

Hoover also took care of himself in the negotiations. Detring wanted to convey the deed for the Chinese Engineering and Mining Company directly to Moreing. Hoover said that he could not commit his employer and insisted the deed be made out to him as trustee. A welcome benefit of this arrangement was that Moreing would have to treat Hoover as a signatory and a responsible party to the deal, not as a mere courier of documents. This was crucial for a young man looking to secure his future. Detring worried that Hoover, given the trusteeship, might simply run off with the company. He may or may not have known about Hoover's earlier scheme to take over Chang's operations with American capital. An English lawyer involved in the negotiations observed, "neither of these men seemed to trust one another very much." In the end, Detring had no choice but to grant Hoover the trusteeship.[30]

Written in haste, the Detring-Hoover pact was seriously flawed. Leaving aside the backdating and violations of Chinese law restricting foreign ownership of assets, the negotiators had failed to address two crucial points. First, who, precisely, would manage the new joint enterprise: Chang and the Chinese, Moreing and his employees, or some joint administration? Chang expected that he would remain as director-general and that Moreing's involvement would be in an advisory rather than a managerial capacity. Detring and Hoover understood that Moreing and his designates would run everything.

Secondly, the deal stipulated that current shareholders in the Chinese Engineering and Mining Company would receive 375,000 of the million shares in the new company. It was silent on the disposition of the remaining 625,000 shares. Detring and Hoover assumed that Moreing would want 200,000 shares for himself and use the rest to raise capital, but there was enough uncertainty as to what would be required to finance the new company that they thought it best to leave London a free hand.

Detring and Hoover finished their negotiation on July 30, by which time the siege had lifted, not without causing a scene in the Hoover household. Lou, probably a better shot than most of the men in the compound, had refused to join an evacuation of women and children when the first relief troops arrived, leading to a heated exchange with her husband. Frederick Palmer, a *Collier's* correspondent who since reaching Tientsin with the relief contingent had been bunking with the Hoovers, thought that Lou reveled in the havoc. She posed for a photograph with one of the settlement's cannon. She did not flinch as shells landed in her garden and stable, and when one blasted through her second-story back window and exploded at the foot of her stairs, Palmer and another journalistic guest rushed through the smoke and lime to find Lou calmly finishing a game of solitaire in her parlor. Lou would afterward write a friend: "You missed one of the opportunities of your life by not coming to China in the summer of 1900 . . . you should have been here,—at the most interesting siege of the age."[31]

Bert had one last adventure of his own in the waning days of the siege, joining the five thousand foreign troops, including American regiments, who advanced under fire to liberate Tientsin's native city from Boxer control in the final days of the conflict. He was a guide, not a combatant. "I was completely scared, especially when some of the Marines next to me were hit," he later wrote. "I was unarmed and I could scarcely make my feet move forward. I asked the officer I was accompanying if I could have a rifle. He produced one from a wounded Marine, and at once I experienced a curious psychological change for I was no longer scared, although I never fired a shot."[32]

On August 4, 1900, Bert and Lou left the still smoking city of Tientsin for Shanghai, bound for London. He wired Moreing before departing the mainland: "Have obtained necessary agreement signed placing under offer to you Kaiping." He cabled a single word to Lou's father in Monterey: "Safe." The young couple spent six weeks on a German mail boat grinding over the Indian Ocean and the Red Sea. The food, the service, and the weather were all horrible. Hoover at least had the satisfaction at the end of the journey of delivering to Moreing a deed for the most coveted industrial prize in the Celestial Kingdom.[33]

Hoover was not long in London. He explained the documents to Moreing and relayed his unwritten understandings with Detring and Chang. Moreing professed delight at the deal, although his lawyers and his proposed investing syndicate studied its details and wanted "slight alterations." It was requested, for instance, that a phrase authorizing a reorganization of the Chinese Engineering and Mining Company by "such means and agencies as are ordinarily used and usually regarded as proper" be rewritten as permitting such terms and conditions as "Herbert C. Hoover may think expedient." Hoover was sent back to China to gain approvals for the alterations from Detring and Chang, armed with financial inducements should they resist.[34]

Stopping in New York on his return journey, Hoover, in an interview with local newspapermen, inadvertently revealed something of the mind-set he would take back to Tientsin to complete his work. Arguing for a forceful U.S. response to the disorder in China, he said: "Our whole policy has been to pat a rattlesnake on the head. Diplomacy with an Asiatic is of no use. If you are going to do business with him you must begin your talk with a gun in your hand, and let him know that you will use it."[35]

Back in Tientsin on January 10, 1901, he explained to Detring the changes requested by Moreing and the inducements on offer: fifty thousand shares in the new company for Detring and Chang each.

The German agreed without consulting the mandarin. Rather than call attention to the alterations and risk undoing their July 30 agreement, Hoover and Detring again resorted to backdating. They stealthily rewrote the July 30 document and had it certified at the British consulate as a copy of the original. They also decided that the transaction should be expanded to include not only the property of the Chinese Engineering and Mining Company but all the coal seams geologically connected with its mineshafts. In other words, Moreing and friends were to be granted an exclusive monopoly to the entire Kaiping basin, or about five times more coal than was originally contemplated.

By such methods, Hoover and Detring succeeded in protecting the Kaiping coal mines from other predatory powers. Brandishing their paperwork, they chased German soldiers off of their wharves, replaced Russian troops at Kaiping properties with British soldiers, and set about reorganizing the management of the coal works. Hoover meanwhile chased down one more significant detail to legitimize the transaction.

In an effort to pass muster under Chinese law, Moreing and his investors wanted Chang's official seal of approval on their agreement. Having been freed from confinement with help from Detring and Hoover, and having noticed that his assets were now under British guard and no longer in imminent danger of being swallowed by the Russians or Japanese, Chang balked at this step. He scrutinized the July 30 terms and protested that he had only authorized a joint Sino-English venture, not an outright sale of his company. He said that he had no right to alienate the mines from the Chinese crown. He also asked for more money for himself, assurance that he would be director-general for life, and that a Chinese board of directors would be installed to manage the mines. He was concerned for the income he and other Chinese parties received from the company. He told Detring that he was now deeply suspicious of the motives and character of Herbert C. Hoover. The stage was set for what would become known as the "four days' row."

On February 21, 1901, Detring, Hoover, various diplomats, and a Moreing lawyer began putting the screws to Chang in a series of all-night meetings. Chang's announcement that he would return to Shanghai on the 24th to be with his ailing wife lent a sense of urgency to the talks. According to a British consul, all involved "lost their tempers, fell out, fell in again, and generally made their lives miserable." Chang later testified that he was told by the Europeans that he would be crushed and his mines seized if he did not grant his seal.[36]

On the last day, Hoover, who had kept a low profile due to Chang's mistrust, brought his own interpreter into the room to ensure that the mandarin got the full force of his message. In a three-hour tirade, he accused Chang of reneging on their agreement and acting in bad faith, and he allegedly threatened to keep him from visiting his sick wife until they came to terms. Hoover, by his own admission, became "very heated" and displayed what one observer called a "dangerous" level of excitement. Chang complained that Hoover was insulting him and causing him to lose face. He received an apology and the discussion resumed.[37]

The impasse was finally broken when the Westerners agreed to give Chang more money and also to meet most of his demands. The new terms were embodied in a memorandum to be executed in concert with the transfer agreement. It declared that Chinese and foreign shareholders would have equal rights, that a board of directors in London would work cooperatively with another board in China, the latter bearing responsibility for managing the assets in China, with Chang secure as director-general of the company in China. These stipulations seemed to resolve the issue of Chang's alienating crown properties.

Hoover told Chang that the memorandum, and not the transfer agreement, would be the ruling document in the transaction, and that it would be binding upon the company. Taking heart from this explanation, Chang affixed his seal. Hoover, who privately considered the memorandum to be worthless, thanked the mandarin and, together with representatives of Belgian partners in Moreing's syndicate, used the seal to assert control over all of the assets of the Chinese Engineering and Mining Company. Ignoring their commitments in the memorandum, the Westerners pushed aside the Chinese and installed themselves as managers with what Hoover called "complete control" over operations. To get the property of the old company registered in the proper consulates as assets of the new company they needed the title deeds, which Hoover acquired, in his own words, by "main force." Angered by unauthorized disbursements, he seized "by violence" sums of cash in the company's possession.[38]

What exactly he meant by "violence" and "main force" is unclear. One report had him waving a revolver and threatening to shoot Chinese employees who failed to meet his demands. This is not wholly implausible given his earlier public comments about armed diplomacy with Asiatics.

While questions about his dealings in Tientsin would dog Hoover for the rest of his life, the context of his actions in these early months of 1902 is important, if not exculpatory. The Chinese throne was hiding in the interior of the country, and only the crudest pretense of civil authority remained in effect across the land. Russians and Japanese were raping and pillaging their way through the northern provinces while ruthlessly competing with Germany and France in a post-rebellion spoils scramble for mines and ports. Against the standards of these other powers, Hoover's actions were almost enlightened: he was at least preparing a legal gloss for his hustle, a precaution not obviously necessary at the time. And from a strictly commercial point of view, Hoover did succeed in securing the property of his Anglo-Belgian masters in a frightening and chaotic moment. He pulled off what has been called "the largest transfer of property to foreigners in the history of China," while at the same time introducing new financial disciplines at the company, sweeping out as many unproductive employees as he could, installing new managers where possible, and getting an industrial giant back on its feet regardless of the circumstances.[39]

As all of this transpired, Charles Algernon Moreing was back in London doing violence of his own to notions of fair play in international commerce. He registered the Chinese Engineering and Mining Company as an English limited liability company, excluding from its articles of association any mention of Chinese management and Chang's ongoing role. These omissions appear to have shocked Hoover, who had left London under the impression that Chang and the Chinese would be included, and who had assured Detring and the mandarin that they were.

Through a series of deft maneuvers, Moreing also distributed to himself and his mostly Belgian associates 625,000 of the new company's million shares at a par value of a pound each. This stock, more than three times the 200,000 shares that Detring and Hoover had agreed was fair promotional profit, and representing almost two-thirds of the firm's equity, was handed out for no cash consideration whatsoever. The net effect was to water down the 375,000 shares that had been dealt to the original Chinese shareholders in exchange for their equity in the old company. Having given away the 625,000 shares that might have been sold to raise capital, Moreing next saddled the new company with a £500,000 debenture at 6 percent to fund its expansion and to clear its debts (most of which were owed to Moreing and associates, and most of which were paid off with premiums).

Again, even Hoover was stunned. The new company, in his estimation, did not need anything like £500,000. The large sum would be a drag on its profits and the recovery of its operations. He wondered why Moreing would not sell shares to raise capital, considering that the company's stock was trading on the Chinese market at two or three times par. It was an excellent question.

In September 1901 twenty-seven-year-old Herbert Hoover and his wife sailed out of China together for the last time. If he was in any sense outraged at his master's ransacking of the Chinese Engineering and Mining Company, he did not move to stop it. Rather, he returned to London and strengthened his ties with Moreing, signing on as a "pardner" in the firm. He needed the position and the money. As he wrote his brother:

> I have carried one deal through and it may be two years
> before I realize anything from my shares. I hope for a moder-
> ate competence then. Meantime I am living on a pardnership
> that is all hopes and no cash so that I would be jolly hard up
> had I not made a few thousand dollars on a speculation here.[40]

In the same letter, Hoover asked Theodore to sign a promissory note for all of the money he had ever received from him. In another letter, he told Theodore that he was uncertain of his future income: "at present it is nil."[41]

On their way to London, the young couple stopped in San Francisco, where Bert sat for an interview with a former Stanford mate now on staff at the *Chronicle*. He made sufficient mention of his China earnings to get headlined as the "highest salaried man of his years in the world" at $33,000 per annum, an absurd assertion given his confessions to his brother. All that can be said in Hoover's defense is that his salary was indeed impressive on paper, but given the upheaval in China, he had collected little of it since the summer of 1900. The article also described Bert as "long, spare and squinty," much to Lou's amusement and his own annoyance.[42]

Hoover asked Theodore to ensure that the Stanford alumni network know he had attained a partnership in one of the world's great mining syndicates as a reward for winning the Kaiping mines, which he termed "a jolly good deal." He would not see it that way for long.[43]

# CHAPTER 5

# "The Late Jar Rather Smashed My Nerves"

Back in his California days, when Hoover was choosing between employment with the Geological Survey and an opportunity with a big mining concern, Professor Branner had advised him that "when one becomes connected with large interests of any kind nowadays, he has to live on the jump, as it were, for such interests, if they are successful, are well organized and run like big machines."[1]

"On the jump" is how Hoover now lived. In less than four years he had jumped from California to Australia, and from Australia to China, and from China to England. Starting in October 1901, using London as his base, he would in a series of short and long hops, by steamship and train, jump clear around the globe five times in five years. As his friend Will Irwin wrote, Hoover "boarded an ocean liner as casually as you or I take a trolley-car to our daily jobs." The Suez Canal became as familiar to him as Wapsinonoc Creek. He perfected the conduct of business afloat, receiving at each port a bag of reports and letters, sometimes responding with answers and instructions while the steamer coaled, other times taking them aboard and answering at the next wire head.[2]

The jumping was not always geographical. He jumped from one ambitious project to another, from unimpeachable success to gnawing failure, from high conceit to mental breakdown, from fortune to the brink of financial ruin, from personal controversy and highly publicized trials to Kensington dinner parties and his wife's café society. What Branner had got wrong was that almost none of this activity betrayed the least evidence of machine-like organization and precision. Lou was closer to the mark with a meteorological allusion. "The Hoover plans are like clouds," she wrote, "and come and go as rapidly."[3]

The Hoovers spent only a few weeks in London at the end of 1901, just long enough for Bert to finalize his agreement with Bewick, Moreing. He purchased his partnership for $40,000, a sum he had to borrow from the firm. Hoover would be the operating partner, spending most of his time in the field. There was a lot to operate at Bewick, Moreing. The firm was involved in some twenty mines around the world: coal in China and the Transvaal, tin in Cornwall, gold in South Africa and Western Australia; copper in Canada, silver in Nevada, and turquoise in the Sinai Peninsula. For his services he would receive 20 percent of all profits over a period of ten years.

Hoover's first stop on taking up his new duties was Western Australia. He arrived in Fremantle in mid-January 1902 and took Lou on a tour of his old haunts. Observant locals noticed small changes in Hoover's appearance since his last visit. He had added weight and lost his facial hair, and the squareness of his jaw had become more pronounced. His habits, however, were much the same. He stood with his legs apart and his hands deep in his trouser pockets, jingling his change. His hazel eyes still found his feet during conversation and they wrinkled at the corners on those rare occasions when he smiled.

The outback had not much improved in his absence, although his old nemesis Williams had departed. Hoover cleared out managers he considered loyal to the old regime and installed his own people in their stead. He consolidated properties and further reduced operating expenses by demanding more of his workers for the same salaries. Never short on audacity, he tried to sign up all of the major properties in the gold belt, aiming for a working monopoly in Western Australia. In the same manner as his old friends at the Oregon Land Company, he took control of ancillary lines of business—stores, foundries, and insurance companies—pushing aside middlemen and purchasing supplies in volume. The profits Bewick, Moreing made in these side businesses, together with the opportunities for insider trading open to a mine's managers, made the actual management fees paid the company by the property's owners almost incidental.

Back in London by spring, the Hoovers faced the problem of where to live. They already shared one property. On their way through California the previous autumn they had arranged through Lou's father to build a cottage in Monterey. It was something of a claim stake, a sign of their commitment to return to the United States once Bert had established his career. For their first summer in England, they leased a two-story cottage at Walton-on-Thames. Lou settled in and took up the violin. Bert scarcely noticed the place. His workdays were occupied with business; on weekends he charged over the English and Welsh countryside in his new automobile, a French Panhard with a massive ten-horsepower engine. In midseason he made a lightning-fast voyage to British Columbia and back, covering sixteen thousand miles in six weeks. He dropped in on his brother and sister along the way and found both of them married, Theodore satisfactorily, and May not, at least to Herbert's mind. She had wed her old beau, Cornelius Van Ness Leavitt. By autumn, the Hoovers had relocated to London, the center of the mining world and site of his firm's headquarters. They lived in a spacious apartment at 39 Hyde Park Gate, a fashionable cul-de-sac between Kensington Palace and the Royal Albert Hall. They got settled just on time for the roof to fall in at Bewick, Moreing.[4]

On Christmas Eve, 1902, the Hoovers had turkey with the Evanses, followed on Christmas Day by turkey and dancing with the Grays, followed on Boxing Day by a noon turkey dinner at the home of Mr. and Mrs. A. Stanley Rowe. After this last meal, the Hoovers joined the Rowes and several of the five Rowe children for a pantomime of Kingsley's *The Water Babies* at the Garrick.

Hoover, never the most perceptive of companions, thought his host seemed "highly nervous and filled with foreboding" throughout the afternoon. An accountant and a partner at Bewick, Moreing, Rowe asked Lou if she would raise his five children in the event that anything happened to him. On the way home, the Hoovers discussed what might be amiss and decided that Rowe was suffering from "the liver," as the English called mild depression.[5]

On December 29, Hoover arrived at his office and picked up a letter dated the previous evening. It was from Rowe, marked private and confidential. It said that he was leaving London. He was also resigning as a partner in Bewick, Moreing and as secretary of one of the mining properties it managed, the Great Fingall Consolidated. Rowe was in deep trouble: "I forebore telling you before Christmas so as to leave a few days of peace."[6]

Hoover picked up the telephone and learned from a hysterical Mrs. Rowe that her husband had told her the previous evening that he was ruined. He had said good-bye to the children, shaved his mustache, and vanished into the night from their home at Hyde Park Square with the additional disguise of an oversized pair of eyeglasses. He had left a second letter with instructions that it be conveyed to Hoover. This letter, written, like the first, in a hurried hand, explained that Rowe had suffered losses in stock market speculation and that he had tried to cover the shortfalls by forging and selling a quarter million dollars' worth of stock in the Great Fingall. His fraud had been detected. The mine's chairman had confronted Rowe on December 23, precipitating his flight. He claimed to have had "no dishonest intention" and to have suffered "the tortures of hell in my mind" over these affairs. "Dear Hoover," he concluded, "forgive me. I meant well."[7]

A dumbfounded Hoover wondered where to turn. Moreing, the man with the most at stake in the disaster, was out of town. Hoover would later write that Moreing was off hunting tigers in Manchuria when, in fact, he was in China smoothing over a lot of ill feelings in the wake of the Kaiping deal, and thus unavailable to Hoover in Bewick, Moreing's moment of crisis.[8]

Hoover called a meeting of Bewick, Moreing's lawyers and advisers, who gathered in the company's offices late in the afternoon. In his usual matter-of-fact voice, Hoover read excerpts from Rowe's letters, eliciting choruses of "I'll be damned!" with each successive disclosure. Hoover would later claim to have decided at that meeting on behalf of the firm, and at the risk of Moreing's wrath, to cover all losses suffered by outsiders due to Rowe's misdeeds. He would always insist that the company had no legal liability for the forgeries and that its generosity stemmed from concern for its reputation and a sense of moral responsibility. In a cable to Moreing in China, however, he mentioned that he had received advice that the partners were liable jointly and personally for Rowe's misdeeds, and that they were in danger of being "entirely ruined for the future and our firm destroyed." Bewick, Moreing had no choice but to make good the losses.[9]

A notice was sent to the press announcing the forgeries and embezzlements as well as Rowe's confession and Bewick, Moreing's commitment to restitution. Hoover spent several days on the phone nursing brokers, businesses, and individuals affected by the crimes, promising to make them whole out of the goodness of his heart. To his relief, Moreing eventually cabled approval of the plans to compensate victims. There is no question that Hoover was shaken by the Rowe revelations. His career was on the line, as was the survival of the company he had paid $40,000 to join. Yet even with angry brokers breathing down his neck and the eyes of London's financial community on him, he coolly suggested to Moreing that the Great Fingall was trading at an all-time low and that they might accumulate shares "with a view to recovering part of loss."[10]

The Rowe affair was a minor sensation in the British papers. Police searched high and low for the absconding accountant. Market scolds tut-tutted at yet another financial scandal courtesy of the Western Australian mining scene. These were "the most horrible events which could possibly have happened to us," said Hoover. Gloomy, exhausted, frustrated by the investigations and negotiations, Bert permitted Lou to drag him to Brighton for a weekend's rest. They stayed at the fashionable Metropole, expecting to walk on the downs one day and play in the sand another. It rained and blew a freezing gale all weekend. They returned home a day early.[11]

The storm at Bewick, Moreing meanwhile cleared, thanks in part to Hoover's efforts, the quick promise to cover all losses having played well in the press and in the mining fraternity. It was an expensive tactic, however, saddling the firm with financial burdens that would take years to clear. Hoover had to take on a share of the losses. His total indebtedness was now in the neighborhood of $300,000. A compensating benefit was that Rowe was written out of the partnership agreement, allowing Hoover a larger share in future profits. "I've still got position and opportunity to recoup," he wrote his brother.[12]

He spoke too soon. A London broker named Edgar Storey brought suit against Hoover claiming that Rowe and Hoover had reneged on a promise to buy $100,000 in shares from Storey on joint account. The accusation implicated Hoover in Rowe's crimes and threatened to sink his professional reputation. Hoover maintained that he knew nothing of Rowe's promises to Storey but a jury found for Storey and awarded him $30,000. Facing bankruptcy and disgrace, Hoover appealed.[13]

In the midst of this struggle, another bolt struck Hoover and his partners, this one from out of the East. Almost from the moment their deal was signed, Detring and Chang had been complaining that the terms under which the Chinese Engineering and Mining Company had been transferred to Moreing and his various partners and managers were being breached, with Chinese shareholders excluded from meetings of the new corporation. They had also discovered that the new company had been secretly and unnecessarily saddled with a huge debenture, that hundreds of thousands of shares in the company had been distributed to members of Moreing's syndicate for no cash consideration, and that the articles of association Moreing had registered in London made no provisions for Chinese management or other conditions of the memorandum negotiated by Hoover and Chang. During his visit to China, Moreing had tried and failed to assuage Detring and Chang with a promise of more shares.

Newspapers from Peking to London reported on the anger of the Chinese shareholders, with some opining that Moreing's antics reflected poorly on all British businesses in the East. The British Foreign Office looked into the matter and determined that the deal was rotten. The diplomats had no sympathy for Chang, whom they considered a "notorious" adventurer, or for Detring, whom they described as "a fearsome scallywag." One official wrote that in a fair world at least two of Chang, Detring, and Detring's son-in-law (who had a small role in the affair), would have been shot in the Boxer uprising. "What makes [them] wild is that they thought themselves rather smarter than most people, and yet got themselves fairly had by a Yankee man of straw acting for Moreing." The Foreign Office saw clearly that this man of straw, Hoover, had "fleeced" the Chinese shareholders. The whole thing, one envoy summarized, was "a case of rogues falling out."[14]

All of this attention on the Chinese Engineering and Mining Company was troublesome for Chang. He came under pressure from his imperial masters to recoup the mines, or at least to negotiate a better deal for the Chinese. On May 7, 1903, his lawyers brought suit in a British court against C. Algernon Moreing, the firm of Bewick, Moreing, and the newly incorporated Chinese Engineering and Mining Company. Chang asked that the British court either enforce the terms of the memorandum under which the original Chinese Engineering and Mining Company was transferred or declare that the mines had been fraudulently obtained and nullify the agreement. Hoover was not a named defendant in the suit. Nevertheless, he was now a partner in the company and his fingerprints were all over the disputed deal.[15]

From winter through the spring of 1903, Hoover rose early for breakfast and worked hard all day, not stopping to eat again until he returned home, edgy and morose, for supper. His mind ranged frantically over his troubles and debts and all that had happened since he had left Stanford. It had been eight years of the hardest work and worry, and he had nothing but debt to show for it. He rightly blamed Rowe for some of his misfortune. He also kicked himself for not having returned to America earlier. There was a point in 1901 when he could have sold his shares in the Chinese Engineering and Mining Company for $250,000 and waved off Bewick, Moreing. He did the math and figured that even with his shareholdings and an annual income of $60,000 it would be two or more years before he got his head above water. In the meantime, the Storey and Chang suits dragged through the courts. It was all too much.[16]

Hoover had an extraordinary constitution, able to withstand enormous strain and constant exertion, even when he was at his most pessimistic. He could focus like a laser for days and weeks on a single point or, if the situation demanded, juggle dozens of problems simultaneously. But his extraordinary constitution gave way in May or June of 1903. He dropped everything and took a monthlong vacation on the French Riviera, where Lou treated him with pastries and cigars. He informed his brother of his collapse with a single line in a July letter: "I was ordered away by the doctor as the late jar had rather smashed my nerves but I am allright again and though we are compelled to draw in our horns a little we have hopes of getting on our feet again someday."[17]

Lou continued to do her best to alleviate his troubles. At the end of a bad day, she would welcome him home, put his head on her lap, and apply ice to his fevered forehead. Ever practical, she fished out some of her scribblings from China and sent them around to magazines in hopes that an article would fetch a few extra dollars to lighten their financial load. She played bezique with him nightly in a vain effort to distract him. As she told her mother:

> He is so active, mentally, that it keeps me more than busy thinking of something new to give him entertainment for a few hours. And of course if he realized it was done for that special purpose he would cease to be "entertained" at once. Such long stretches of London are not good for him at one time. There are such a multitude of things that can be done at the office that of course he is never satisfied unless they are all going just as fast as possible, and that keeps up too high a tension. He reads three or four hours in bed nearly every night so I don't think it is good for him to spend the early part of the evening the same way. Consequently it is "up to me" to find the amusement—for he scarcely ever goes anywhere without me. He belongs to one of the nicest London clubs— and doesn't go inside it once in three months. Tonight he is going to an engineers dinner . . . where Ambassador Choate was one of the guests. Last night we had four Germans dining with us. Tomorrow one of our Italian friends who made our recent little trip so interesting is coming. So we manage to be almost as cosmopolitan here as in China.[18]

What Lou didn't tell her mother was that she was pregnant. She waited until she was almost due before breaking the news in order to keep her parents in Monterey. "It is too bad," she apologized, "that so many things had to come together—all Bert's troubles—the fact that he could not go to America now—that I could not possibly think of leaving him—that we will probably have to go away somewhere in the autumn so for economical reasons could not suggest your coming over for such a few weeks before then." Lou gave birth to Herbert Charles Hoover Jr. on the morning of August 4, 1903.[19]

Hoover received more welcome news in the fall when an appeals court dismissed the Storey verdict against him on grounds that the plaintiff had failed to prove an understanding between Rowe and the defendant. Storey would appeal in turn to the House of Lords, unsuccessfully. The Lord Chancellor found "not a particle of evidence" to implicate Hoover.[20]

Around the same time, Rowe was nabbed in Toronto, where he had been working under an alias at a brokerage house. Canada had been good to him: the arrest occurred shortly before he was to have been made a partner. He was shipped back to London and sentenced to ten years in prison. Hoover sent checks from time to time to help support the Rowe children, who were being raised by their aunt, Mrs. Rowe having apparently followed her husband's lead and disappeared.[21]

On his release after serving eight years, Rowe would write to thank Hoover and to suggest a meeting. He received the following response, along with a check for twenty pounds:

> My wife and myself have done the same for the children that we should have done for any other under similar circumstances and I think your real indebtedness is towards your sister, few people of whose loyalty exist in this world.
>
> I do not think any good could arise from a meeting between us for, when all is said and done, your actions caused me five years of absolutely fruitless work in the best portion of my life; nor do I see that we should have any further relations. I have no vindictive feeling in the matter and I shall be only too glad if by your future career you can reestablish your good name, and above all, give your children a proper position in the world.[22]

A month after he was born, Herbert Hoover Jr. was introduced to life on the jump. He was packed into a basket by his parents and hauled to Western Australia, along with his nurse. His father made a month-long inspection tour of Bewick, Moreing mines and caught up with his reading aboard ships and trains. In this manner, he devoured Carlyle's *French Revolution*, Gibbon's *The History of the Decline and Fall of the Roman Empire*, and countless detective stories. "At times it seemed to me that I would exhaust all the books on earth," he later said. "But the supply still holds out."[23]

On Christmas Day, the family sailed for California, where Herbert Jr. performed for his grandparents before returning to London in February. Circumnavigation was a rare experience for any individual at the dawn of the twentieth century. Herbert Jr. had completed his first by the age of six months. He would squeeze in a second as a one-year-old.

The child's father, meanwhile, had some success in repairing his firm's finances. His exceptional performance as a manager had increased dividends at existing Bewick, Moreing properties and won new contracts to operate other mines. He was known in the goldfields for doing rigorous financial reporting, hiring top talent, and producing ore at an unusually low cost per ton. There was some exaggeration of his gains; for instance, Hoover was more aggressive than most mining operators in eliminating from his operating budgets anything that might be construed as a capital cost. He also had his share of setbacks, deals that never produced a dividend, and mines that failed to yield metal; he would either refuse to acknowledge the failures or blame them on others. His success and his firm's progress were nonetheless indisputable. By 1904, Bewick, Moreing's share of gold production in Australia had more than doubled to 50 percent, taking it a long way toward Hoover's goal of monopolizing the goldfields. He estimated that the total market capitalization of the Australian mines under his control was more than $70 million.[24]

Now a major figure in one of the world's richest mineral plays, Hoover was routinely invited onto the boards of companies active in the region. Journalists sought him out as an authoritative voice from the mining sector, and he was becoming increasingly adept at working the press. He cultivated mining correspondents at trade journals, the *Economist*, and the *Financial Times*, using them both to boost his profile and promote his stocks. He also picked up a pen himself from time to time and wrote pseudonymous commentaries on such topics as organizational excellence and the regrettable proliferation of "titled non-entities" and "pompous dignitaries" on mining boards. He aired his views on the inferior racial characteristics of nonwhite labor forces. He liked to argue for the ethical superiority of firms

that did not speculate in shares, even though the Bewick, Moreing
partnership agreement had recently dropped its oft-breached pro-
hibitions on partners trading stock in the properties they managed.
He made great use of letters to the editor, sometimes anonymously
attacking his fellow directors, other times raising a straw argument
with a letter under an assumed name and then responding, vigorously
and righteously, in his own name.[25]

Not all of Hoover's journalistic efforts were self-serving. Some
were worthwhile contributions to professional issues—the training of
engineers, the causes of speculative bubbles, and so on. Whatever his
subject matter, Hoover's tone was always businesslike. He knew his
limits. He did not seek to be known as a personality. His intention was
that his achievements and his status be recognized.

There was another reason for Hoover to keep burnishing his
reputation, along with that of his firm: both remained under attack.
In the spring of 1904, with the dust still settling from the Rowe defal-
cations and the Storey trial, and with Chang's suit still hanging over
their heads, Hoover and Bewick, Moreing were hit by two fresh debacles in Australia.

On May 25, the governor of Western Australia announced a
Royal Commission that would investigate Hoover's practice of bidding down wages by importing workers from Italy—a "dago influx"
that had outraged newspapers and unions. And just as that commission was lining up some seventy witnesses, most of them hostile to
Bewick, Moreing, one of the company's major deals in the goldfields
was going horribly wrong. Hoover and Moreing had entered into an
agreement to manage the Great Boulder Perseverance Mine, one of
the legendary pits on Australia's Golden Mile. In order to get the
valuable management contract, they had agreed to a reckless kickback
scheme with the mine's chairman, and they were so anxious to close
that they did not commission an independent survey of the mine,
which turned out to contain a fifth of the recoverable gold claimed
for it. This shortfall and the financial chicanery were soon exposed,
the company's share value collapsed, and another Royal Commission
was launched. The cumulative effect of the mounting lawsuits, investigations, and financial calamities broke Hoover once again.[26]

. . .

"This finds me enroute to Johannesburg," he wrote his brother from the first-class saloon of the steamer *Carisbrook Castle* on July 21, 1904. He enumerated his burdens, including the rapid expansion of Bewick, Moreing's business, the Rowe frauds, and the Great Boulder misrepresentations. They had "all been too much for my nerves. I found myself slipping memory and unable at concentration of thought—and being able to sleep but 3 to 5 hours the Doctor ordered me off."[27]

It is difficult to say what was happening to Hoover in these break-downs. He was not forthcoming on the subject. He paid little attention to his physical well-being, and still less to his emotional life. He was not one for quiet hours in close examination of his feelings or his conscience, let alone for recording his observations in letters or diaries. He used work, reading, and ceaseless activity to keep from being trapped alone with his thoughts and emotions.

He seems even to have lacked the vocabulary to identify his problems. His language in his reports to his brother is stilted, even by Hooverian standards—"unable at concentration of thought." He does mention doctors, which suggests that he preferred to emphasize the physiological dimensions of his problems. There was no shame in a man's machinery giving out under the pressures of work. Yet he also attributes both crashes to "nerves." A case of nerves by plain definition meant that he was overcome by worries, anxieties, or depression. This is as close as Hoover would ever come to admitting emotional frailty. It is all he would ever say about it.[28]

Lou, knowing him well, encouraged him to keep busy and avoid introspection. She understood that inactivity threw him back upon his internal resources, with dark results. He would brood, find the worst in everything, and get lost in forebodings. "If you want to get the gloomiest view on any subject on earth," she once said, "ask Bert about it." Hoover did have much to brood about in the lead-up to these breakdowns. It seems likely that his mind was playing out all possible outcomes and that by dwelling upon the more catastrophic of them he had convinced himself that the world was crumbling beneath him.[29]

He spent most of the first twelve days of his voyage to Cape Town under the covers in his cabin. By the time the steamer docked, he appears to have largely recovered. He kept a busy schedule of visits to

South African mining properties, meetings, and dinners. He turned thirty along the way.

Hoover's problems, of course, were waiting for him on his return. The Royal Commission on Immigration of Non-British Labour reported in November that only one in twenty-five jobs went to an alien, although it did find concentrations of foreign workers in certain mines managed by Bewick, Moreing. The commission believed that they were hired for their servility in an effort by the company to evade government labor policies. The report recommended that the alien workforce at most mines be capped at one-seventh of the total. As the author and enforcer of Bewick, Moreing's Australian labor policies, Hoover bore the brunt of the implicit criticisms in the report. He was also ultimately responsible for safety levels in his properties. On several occasions between 1903 and 1905, Bewick, Moreing was cited for dangerous and unhealthy working conditions. Workers were said to be unduly exposed to dust and fumes and falling rock. A 1905 Royal Commission on the Ventilation and Sanitation of Mines was critical of most operators in the region, and it found that the air quality at the Sons of Gwalia was "notably bad." That the Western Australian parliament was launching six or eight royal commissions a year on subjects as trivial as whether to use stone or stucco in the building of new law courts takes some of the sting from these findings. They did, however, challenge the integrity of Hoover's operations and raise questions about how he obtained his stellar results.[30]

Tough as things were in Australia, it was the highly publicized Chang suit that posed the greatest ongoing threat to Hoover's reputation, and he knew it. Tortured by delays in the preliminaries, he let his distress show by complaining to the court that the plaintiff had made "the most serious allegations against myself personally" yet seemed in no hurry to bring them to trial.[31]

Chang Yen-Mao did finally engage Bewick, Moreing and Company, and Charles Algernon Moreing, before Mr. Justice Joyce of the Chancery division of the High Court of Justice on January 17, 1905. The trial ran sixteen days and captivated the London press. It involved the largest transfer of property in the history of China, including some $50 million worth of high-grade coal (Hoover's own estimate). Adding to the drama, as Hoover would later lament, was the colorful figure of Chang, a mandarin of the third button, parading in his dress silks and cap as "an innocent Asiatic."[32]

Chang, among the first witnesses called, did not take the oath usually administered by the courts but instead stood erect, held up his right hand, and made an affirmation of his own device. He was seated on a chair at the bench, with his interpreter in the witness box. According to press reports, Chang gave his evidence "with considerable animation and much gesture, and the fluency of his language constituted a thorough test of the capacity of the interpreter." He recounted his arrest at Tientsin and explained his motives in pursuing joint British-Chinese oversight for his mines. He described his heated meetings with Hoover and Detring, and the threats and insults made by Hoover, which he deemed too obscene to repeat at trial. He expressed disappointment that Moreing et al. had ignored the terms of their February 19 memorandum, the key issue at trial. He and Detring both objected to hundreds of thousands of shares having been given away and the company being burdened with a large debenture.[33]

Hoover was on the stand for two days of examination and cross-examination, speaking throughout in dull tones and clipped sentences, looking no one in the eye. He sang a new tune under oath, as did everyone in Moreing's circle. He acknowledged that the February 19 memorandum was binding, and claimed that he had done his best to uphold the document, including its joint-management provisions. When confronted with a later letter to Moreing detailing plans to free himself of "any interference from the Chinese board," he said that he was merely suggesting that the manager would have control of day-to-day operations subject to oversight by the Chinese board. Asked to explain a further reference to the Chinese board as a farce, he said he meant that the board might be improved. His testimony was disingenuous. The statements highlighted by the prosecutors were consistent with Hoover's earlier comments to Moreing that without absolute control of the Kaiping mines, the game was not worth the candle. Hoover also admitted on the stand to having harsh words with Chang. He excused his language on the grounds that the mandarin seemed at the time to be reneging on their deal.[34]

On March 1, Justice Joyce found for Chang, emphatically. The

February 19 memorandum, he said, was binding on both parties. The defendants had declined to recognize it as having any force or to abide by its provisions, yet they somehow believed themselves entitled to possession of the property. This amounted to "a flagrant breach of faith" that would not be tolerated under the laws of any country. The judge seemed appalled that Hoover "actually took possession of some of the title deeds of the property by main force." He saw plausible grounds for contending that the Chinese Engineering and Mining Company Ltd. had been defrauded of nearly 425,000 shares by the Europeans, and suggested the plaintiffs might have further recourse to the law on this point.[35]

Moreing and the defendants were ordered to either honor the February 19 memorandum or see the transfer of the company set aside on grounds that it had been fraudulently obtained. Costs were awarded to Chang. Joyce cleared the mandarin of any impropriety or bad faith, "which is more than I can say for some of the other parties concerned." Hoover would later obtain and apparently destroy every copy of the court minutes he could find (one set has survived).[36]


Hoover now began looking for the exit at Bewick, Moreing, prompted in part by the firm's bad odor. He had abided Moreing's sharp practices in the early years of his career, displaying a high tolerance for scoundrels: "God deliver me from a fool," he once wrote. "I would rather do business with a rogue any day if he has brains." But he was now in his thirties, a husband and a father, and his concern for his reputation was catching up to his hunger for money and position, and the blots on his record were increasingly difficult to hide. It was best to leave Moreing with the mess they had made and strike out on his own.[37]

Another reason to want out was Hoover's confidence in his ability to thrive outside Moreing's orbit. He knew how to make money in mining, and it had occurred to him that he could get by on his own without having to take orders from anyone. Hoover tried to sell his stake in Bewick, Moreing but finding that he was a year or two from getting the price he wanted, he continued with his life of toil and travel, and used his time aboard ships to undertake what he later called a thorough "re-education of myself," reading by his count thousands of volumes on history, economics, politics, government, and sociology. It took the company until early 1907 to clear its obligations from the Rowe embezzlements. Hoover opened a fine bottle of claret to celebrate.[38]

He had another opportunity for a toast on July 17, 1907, with the birth of his second son, Allan Henry. Within weeks, in fine Hoover tradition, the child was packed into a basket and carried off on his first transoceanic voyage.* Not long after the family's return to London, Hoover resumed his efforts to sell out of Bewick, Moreing, a project made difficult by the fact that he had signed a ten-year commitment to the firm in 1903. He asked Moreing to allow him to retire early for reasons of ill health attributable to continuous overwork. He gave his precise ailment as "consumption of the brain," a type of fever considered a legitimate cause of death at the time.[39]

Moreing did not believe for a moment that Hoover's brain was rotting or that he had any intention of retiring. Moreing knew that Hoover was an excellent engineer and a shrewd operator, relentless, ambitious, quick to exploit opportunities and adopt new technology, always hiring the best people, increasingly adept at finance, and well connected in London's capital markets. He had all the makings of a fierce competitor.

Hoover was told that he was welcome to sell his shares to another engineer, William Loring, provided that he sign a restrictive covenant. The covenant was a fat document with extensive clauses precluding Hoover from competing directly or indirectly in any mining or engineering activity in the British Empire or anywhere else Bewick, Moreing had interests without the express written consent of Bewick, Moreing. The covenant would apply for a period of ten years from the date of June 30, 1908. In case Hoover saw any wiggle room in the long paragraphs in which these restrictions were detailed, the document added:

> The Covenants in this Clause hereinbefore contained shall be
> read as repeated nine separate times with nine several periods
> of nine, eight, seven, six, five, four, three, two, and one years

---

* True to another family tradition, Allan was named after his father's favorite uncle, Allen, with the spelling confused. Hoover himself would use both spellings interchangeably.

respectively inserted in each of the said covenants instead of the period of ten years from the 30th June 1908.[40]

Moreing probably knew that Hoover liked to boast that no contract had yet been written that he could not escape.

Hoover signed the restrictive covenant, received $150,000 from Loring for his stake, and was permitted to stay as a director of various Bewick, Moreing firms. He almost immediately validated Moreing's caution. Freed from the partnership, Hoover retired for exactly three weeks to the resorts of Brighton in the company of his family before returning to the city and setting up offices at 62 London Wall, the same prestigious address as Bewick, Moreing. Throughout the autumn, he took on two new directorships and worked like a fiend to establish himself as an independent mining financier, organizing companies and directing capital flows, mainly although not exclusively in regions outside of those occupied by his old firm. Moreing watched him warily.[41]

# CHAPTER 6

# What Lies Beyond Wealth

Hoover's retirement may have been largely a charade, but his life did change significantly on his break with Bewick, Moreing. For the first time since Stanford, he was free to do as he pleased. His pace did not slacken—he still lived liked a man whose parents had died young—but his independence allowed him a greater variety of experience. Opportunities for new forms of work and the pursuit of personal interests multiplied. All this, together with the development of his family life, improved finances, and a secure and enviable standard of living, somewhat settled his soul. He would remember the period from 1908 to 1914 as perhaps the happiest of his existence:

> Pre-war England was the most comfortable place in which to live in the whole world. That is, if one had the means to take part in its upper life. The servants were the best trained and the most loyal of any nationality. The machinery for joy and for keeping busy doing nothing was the most perfect in the world. . . . To London came the greatest music, the greatest drama, the greatest art, and the best food in the world. The polite living in city and country breathed hospitality itself. Over our years of sojourning, we became greatly attached to our house on Campden Hill and to the stream of American and British friends with whom we came in contact. We spent many happy times there.[1]

The rented home on Hornton Street, Campden Hill, a respectable section of Kensington, was called Red House. It was a commodious early-nineteenth-century manor with eight rooms, including a morning room, a billiard room, and an oak-paneled library with a great fireplace and glassed-in bookcases. The walnut-paneled dining room had a small dais for speeches and performances. In the large garden, surrounded by a crumbling high wall, were an ancient mulberry tree and a fishpond with a fountain.[2]

The Hoovers filled the house with expensive furniture, Bert's mountain of books, Lou's Chinese ceramics, and a large dog, as well as a butler, a maid, a chauffeur, a cook, a nurse, and a governess. The dining room saw plenty of action. The Hoovers dressed for dinner and entertained most evenings, keeping an open-door policy for traveling Americans, notably Californians and Stanford alumni, many of whom Herbert would bring home unannounced.

"One met at their house," said Mary Austin, a literary friend of Lou's, "people from the ends of the earth—from China, Australia, and South Africa, from Russia and the Balkans, mining and engineering people. Their house was always open to these stray visitors and there was an immense amount of interesting and informative talk going on about their table, thoroughly American talk, and a great deal also that was rather boring."[3]

Hoover was an unlikely candidate for this manner of entertaining. He seldom took the time to enjoy his food, and was once clocked swallowing five courses in eleven minutes flat. His cellar was one of the best in Kensington, although he was not a big drinker. Lou would invite the renowned pianist Francis Grierson to play for guests, a pleasure lost on her husband's tin ear. Nor did Bert much care for conversation. His fund of small talk was perpetually overdrawn, and if he interacted with the guests at his elbows, it was typically in a series of grunts or nods. If he wanted to make a point, he made it in a flat voice and then stopped abruptly as if, as one friend noticed, someone had pulled his plug. If aroused, he would speak with force, sometimes veering into tactlessness, pursuing minor differences of opinion so harshly and indignantly that his victims nursed grudges for the rest of their natural lives. One acquaintance considered him the bluntest man in Europe, another "the rudest man in London."[4]

Hoover could work up a sort of loquacity when the mood struck him. Once, dining at another's home, he lost himself in descriptions of the military dimensions of the Boxer uprising. He grabbed knives, spoons, and forks to represent ports, mines, and fortifications. As the story progressed he brought glassware, saltcellars, and cruets into play, disrupting the entire table service, oblivious to the maid at his elbow waiting to serve him a plate of food. It was Lou who finally interrupted: "Bert, suppose we get on with dinner."[5]

She tried her best to make up for husband's social deficiencies, with mixed results. While one acquaintance said she could speak as long and as intelligently as the moment required to any given ear, others rated Lou's conversational arts only a modest improvement on Bert's and described her as "decidedly inept socially." The one point of agreement was that she always made an effort and, whatever her shortcomings, she was warm, utterly unpretentious, and as gracious as her husband was brusque. She dressed simply and elegantly, favoring beads of stone or metal ("bits of geology") over jewelry. She avoided high heels and cosmetics, and there was invariably a dog at her feet.[6]

A guest at the Hoover table would have been pardoned for wondering why Lou persevered with their entertainments when her husband seemed to find them agonizing. One answer may be that he believed it was the right thing to do. Consciously or not, he had created around his own dining room table a replica of the Minthorn home in Salem, with himself replacing his uncle as the reticent head of an extended family of friends, associates, investors, customers, travelers, and relatives.

Hoover also hated to eat alone. However annoying he found some of his guests, dining by himself was worse. An empty table upset his equilibrium. The unwanted ate alone, outsiders ate alone, friendless teenaged orphans in Salem ate alone. Lou understood this and surrounded him with other minds and voices to keep him occupied and out of his funks. Whenever possible, Hoover would live, eat, and travel in a flock, preferably one of his own making, and with himself as the center of attention.

Yet another impetus for heavy traffic at mealtime was ambition. The Hoovers' social climbing was primarily Bert's idea. He had no aristocratic pretensions, but he wanted the respect of the better classes, and he wanted connections. Anne Martin recalled him coming home from work while Lou was entertaining at tea. He "cast a supercilious eye about the room as though he were weighing the social importance of every guest—and was greatly dissatisfied with the result." Lou entreated her well-established friends to share their titled acquaintances, and Bert sought to have his wife presented at court. Neither effort was successful.[7]

Hoover held Lou responsible for their inability to make a splash, and Lou acknowledged to Mary Austin that she might not be the right woman to help him realize his social ambitions. Indeed, she was not blameless: her habit of inviting dull people who might like meeting someone interesting was kind to the former and vexing to the latter. All the same, she doubted that Bert could do better with anyone else, and she was right. Men of Hoover's profession, pedigree, and disposition were not in high demand at the better tables in London. Stanford friends who saw the Hoovers during this period noticed that Lou had been a positive influence on Bert's social development. She had "changed him a good deal," said Jackson Reynolds, who saw her offer tender instructions on how to handle situations. "Now Bertie," she would volunteer, "don't you think this would be better?"[8]

Another pleasure afforded Hoover in his new life were nights at the theater. Gilbert and Sullivan and Shaw were favorites, along with Shakespeare. He had more time to read, ending most evenings with a book in his hand. He ran through his growing collection of history, politics, and biography at the rate of a volume a day. Saturdays and Sundays were often spent with the children in Hyde Park and Kensington Gardens, tea on the grass under trees, model boats on the round pond. Hoover was fond of the zoo in Regent's Park. He liked to smoke a cigar under a California redwood in Kew Gardens.[9]

An additional weekend activity was the country picnic, with Bert piling everyone into an open car driven by his chauffeur and motoring out to pick beechnuts and wildflowers in the forest. He would find a brook, take off his shoes and socks, and spend the afternoon moving mud and stones and timber to divert the stream—an engineer even in repose.[10]

There was time for sightseeing, as well, with the Hoovers following the trail of William the Conqueror in 1066, and making a nighttime pilgrimage to observe a comet at Stonehenge, Britain's oldest engineering project. Bert's eyes watered at the sight of Wordsworth's Tintern Abbey at dusk, and he was similarly moved by the Speech House in the Forest of Dean, home to the Free Miner's Mine Law Court. He never lingered on these excursions. Once he had seen what there was to see, he was back in the car, ready to move on.[11]

Some of his discretionary travel took the Hoovers outside of Britain, often in the company of friends, most often Edgar Rickard, the lugubrious publisher of a mining magazine started with Hoover money. The two families pooled any windfalls that came their way into what they called a "Seeing Cairo Fund." A rule of the fund, which topped out around $5,000, was that once the date of departure had been settled, the destination would be decided only a few hours beforehand. The couples saw great swaths of Europe and Russia in this manner.[12]

One activity that had fallen off the Hoover calendar entirely was Sunday worship. Hoover does not appear to have frequented a Quaker meetinghouse after leaving Oregon, and no other church had taken its place. Neither he nor Lou was religious, and he admitted to intimates that he did not think much about his faith. He retained some of the Friends' ethics, including a distaste for display and ceremony, a horror of idleness, a neighborly sense of duty, a concern for the suffering of others, and a relatively tolerant attitude toward religious and racial differences. If he happened to be in town for Christmas he would dress up as Santa Claus and dole out books to the children and servants. He celebrated Easter with egg hunts. His adult life was secular to an extent that would have shocked his mother, although perhaps not his father or Dr. Minthorn.[13]

Despite Bert's complaints of having been passed around from relative to relative as a child, the Hoovers adopted the English custom of leaving the rearing of their children largely to nurses and governesses. Bert did love the boys. He taught them how to hammer gold quartz and pan it out like a forty-niner in their garden fishpond. He occasionally wrote them playful letters from distant locales. The boys were not in any sense a preoccupation, however.

Lou, too, kept a busy schedule, serving as an executive of the Society of American Women in London and playing an active role in the Lyceum Club, which organized lectures on such topics as Hilaire Belloc, Swinburne, and women's suffrage. She would sometimes leave the children with nannies in blue uniforms and white caps or with her parents in California so that she could travel with Bert. She even made side trips of her own, sprinting off to Tasmania or Egypt to collect rock samples for Dr. Branner. Regardless of how much time she spent out of the house, Lou was an alert and caring mother, and she doted on her husband. Each morning at the breakfast table, she would casually ask, "What do I do for you today, Daddy?"[14]

Lou kept a circle of friends separate from her husband's. His tended to be business associates and journalists, while she was attracted to characters. Her Stanford classmate Anne Martin showed up rather suddenly in London, seized with a passion for the women's suffrage movement. She bought a hammer and joined protests, smashing windows and policemen along the way. Bert, who had always considered Martin an "inoffensive pedantic nonentity," was baffled by her behavior. He bailed her out of jail twice, over her objections, and ultimately convinced her to buy a return ticket to the United States and seek martyrdom to the women's cause on familiar ground.[15]

Lou was also close to Mary Austin, the freethinking writer, clairvoyant, and compulsive namedropper. Austin had been a stalwart in the artists' colony at Carmel, with Jack London and Lincoln Steffens. By the time she reached England, she could (and did) boast of publications in the *Atlantic* and productions at the New Theatre in New York. She entertained Lou with gossip about the amorous adventures of her acquaintances Upton Sinclair and H. G. Wells. Bert was scandalized at Austin's familiarity with Wells, who had sired a child outside of marriage. "Herbert Hoover," Austin later wrote, "has the usual American man's prejudices against variation in conduct from the absolute norm of middle-class life."[16]

Whatever he thought of her morals, Hoover was fascinated by Austin's creative talent and myth-making capacities. It had occurred to him that he, or at least his kind, might be a worthy subject for the stage. The artist and the miner discussed his life and work and how it might be dramatized. "Seriously, I am interested in this matter," Hoover wrote her. "I've whiled away many idle hours constructing a drama to represent to the world a new intellectual type from a literary or stage view—the modern intellectual engineer—there're more possibilities than you think."[17]

Hoover mailed Austin a print of a copper mine furnace to serve as a backdrop for his prospective play. The front elevation, he envisioned, would fill the whole back of the stage. The furnace would be a noisy beast, spitting and blowing smoke like a ship's boilers. The plot would revolve around the efforts of a team of bold engineers attempting to construct a great copper mine where others had persistently failed. There would be resistance to their engineering genius, as well as sabotage and death:

> The equipment of these great copper mines has been in progress for two or more years. . . . A furnace has been built . . . and will treat 5,000 tons a day—employ 10,000 men. Their professional future and the financial success of the enterprise depends on this furnace. The criteria of success will be the actual flow of metal from the furnace. The day arrives when the smelter is to be "blown in." It has been charged some hours before. They stand by and moralize on their future and the probabilities of the monster chewing up metal. They evince proper stage anxiety. . . .
>
> Suddenly the foreman from up on the furnace stage (screams) announces she is ready (furnaces are also females). The chief engineer takes the honor (or delegates it to the ultimate victim) of the first tap. Everybody stands on one foot. He dashes along, opening the spouts (there are about 40 of them). The glowing metal ripples out, sparks; (water over red light). Everybody cheers, dance a minuet. But at the last hole a breastplate blows out. Great cloud of fumes, yellow smoke; victim dies either on or off the stage as you like.

Austin was unconvinced. A thoroughgoing primitivist, she had difficulty with his notion of a heroic engineer. He complained that she was "trying to make a villain out of [the engineer], which won't do." He insisted that the lead role be a martyr, and argued that the physical, intellectual, and educational passages of a successful man could never produce a bad person. If the play needed a "semi-civilized villain," a man who mistreated his wife, it would have to be the metal-lurgist or the foreman, he argued, not the engineer. He could never make Austin see it. Hoover so wanted the world to view this roman-tic portrayal of himself and his profession that he supported Austin financially for several years. She strung him along, warning on the one hand that genius could not survive "on a crust in an attic," and on the other that an artist's independent spirit could not be purchased. A good part of the money he gave her went to build an extension on her cabin.[18]

Years later, Austin would write that Hoover had fallen into a habit of crossing the Atlantic and telegraphing her to have breakfast with him and listen to him talk about his great plans for the future. He insisted that he did not want to be "just a rich man" but was otherwise unsure of what to do with himself. "Things came up in his mind and turned over, showing white bellies like fish in a net," wrote Austin. She answered him with flattery, suggesting that there would never be a ready-made position for a man of his enormous capacities, and that he would have to simply jump in somewhere and "elbow some small fry out of the way."[19]

Hoover's school-days habit of confiding to several women at a time seems to have carried into adulthood. Austin and Martin inde-pendently related that he would solicit their admiration by revealing his dreams and accomplishments. He does not seem to have been after anything more than approval. Austin doubted that his stiff sense of propriety "permitted him to play around much." She nevertheless wrote, in this period, the novel *A Woman of Genius*, in which an engi-neer, not unlike Hoover, achieves fulfillment by running away with an artist, not unlike Austin.[20]


Hoover could afford to indulge Austin and his theatrical dreams, for he was becoming rich. Early in his post-Moreing career, with his income approaching $100,000 annually, he had moved his office down the street to the still more respectable address of 1 London Wall. Sev-eral other, mostly American, mining engineers and executives, includ-ing brother Theodore, joined him there. They worked on friendly terms, without a partnership or formal organization—no direct ties that would contravene Hoover's restrictive covenants. Operating in every corner of the earth, Hoover and associates laid the foundations of a lasting fortune.

Theodore remembered his brother as the lodestar figure in the group, standing head and shoulders above the others, working the hardest, dominating by his intellectual powers and sound judgment. He also thought Herbert's uncompromising need to run the show was selfish. It was always "his team and his game," an attitude that sometimes drove off talented individuals with leadership capacities of their own, yet there was nothing anyone could do about it. Herbert built a community of loyalists, allowed himself few peers, and took orders from none. He would bicker, fight, and lose his temper at challenges to his absolute control.[21]

Hoover described his occupation in these years as an "engineering doctor to sick concerns," which was a deceptive phrase. He was doing little technical work or on-site mining. His activities were mostly financial. He had developed a specialty in rescuing distressed mines through corporate restructurings and consolidations with injections of new capital. Because of his reputation as a superb operator, he had no problem raising money or floating new ventures, and he worked with some of the most illustrious names in London mining circles. He claimed to find sheer joy in creating productive properties out of mines that other operators had failed to make pay. Much of the pleasure undoubtedly stemmed from the fact that he rarely risked his own money. He would receive for his services large fees and grants of shares that he would habitually sell early, at a premium.[22]

His colleagues were mesmerized at Hoover's facility in financial matters. "[He] would have the answer while the rest of us were trying to understand the problem," said one associate. "In the first place, he always came to a meeting thoroughly prepared and that gave him a big starting advantage. In the second place, he had an almost encyclopedic memory. And in the third place, his mind moved like chain lightning when his own financial interests were involved."[23]

Reported Walter Liggett, Hoover had a "gift of juggling corporate assets in such a manner that insiders almost always benefitted," whatever happened to the capital of the original shareholders. He was masterful at wielding write-offs and preference shares with multiple voting power on the grounds that new capital was required to avert bankruptcy. His favorite deals were those so complicated no one else could figure out how they worked.[24]

On top of this, Hoover could keep mental maps of dozens of mines in his mind and, by one account, follow the progress of each shaft like a blindfolded chess master. He liked to receive telegrams from these properties and, without opening them, noting only the date and address, predict the level of the mine and the cost per ton of ore. He was usually correct.[25]

His intellectual capacities and powerful will made Hoover a fearsome negotiator. Arriving at the table with shirtsleeves rolled up, abrupt and aggressive, he had a singular talent for stripping away nonessential information and getting directly to the root of things, and he knew how to close. He possessed what one businessman said was a curious dynamic force that could compel the most reluctant person to put signature to paper.[26]

In addition to his fees and share grants, Hoover made money in stock market speculation, using information gleaned from his own operations and from his vast network of connections in the mining world to buy and sell shares for personal profit. He shared offices in New York and London with the famous American miner A. Chester Beatty. They swapped inside information about mine performance and impending deals, often trading on joint account to their mutual benefit. Although insider trading was not illegal at the time, Hoover did not want to be seen gambling on the market. He would speak contemptuously of stock jobbers, the parasites and "idiots" who wagered on short-term swings in share prices, creating bubbles and market inefficiencies. His own speculations he considered sound and respectable transactions based on professional insight and judgment. In reality, the only difference between Hoover and the average punter was his earlier access to information. He traded in his own name, his wife's name, and in friends' names. Despite his privileged position, he once had to confess to Theodore that he had been speculating on his account without his knowledge and that all of his money was gone. As a result of the loss, Bert discharged all of Theodore's indebtedness to him.[27]

For all of his stock juggling and wagering, Hoover still made the bulk of his fortune the hard way, on a small number of long-term endeavors that required every ounce of his technical skill, financial wizardry, and strength of character before yielding fantastic wealth. He and his colleagues would examine hundreds of possible plays, thoroughly investigating dozens of them, before seizing the one or two opportunities on which to concentrate their efforts. A prime example of this approach was a zinc operation in Western Australia, begun while he was in the employ of Bewick, Moreing. It was well known that the silver mines at Broken Hill had, over the years, produced mountains of tailings rich in zinc. Alert to rising prices for zinc and new methods of separating it from ore, Hoover arranged to purchase 5 million tons of tailings and went to work. He raised capital to try new separation processes. He went through several cycles of investment and failure, all to the accompaniment of screaming shareholders, before generating regular dividends. It was a reckless adventure in all respects but one: the Zinc Corporation eventually became one of the longest-running and most financially successful operations of its kind in the world.[28]

Hoover first learned of the mine that would produce his biggest payoff from ancient Chinese manuscripts that told of fabulous silver deposits in Burma on the road to Mandalay. On his way home from investigating tin mines in Penang in 1904, still in the employ of Bewick, Moreing, he chanced to meet on board his steamer a railway contractor who knew Burma and spoke of gigantic abandoned works deep in the jungle. Hoover visited the site a year later, lodging in Hsipaw, the capital of the Shan state of the same name, whose structures were all built from bamboo. He traveled by rail and horseback over glistening green mountains to the lost mines. They were vast, extending over a three-mile area, with pits a thousand feet long and hundreds of feet deep. The Chinese had worked the site from 1400 to 1850, taking the most accessible silver. Hoover saw an opportunity to extract much more.

Burma would give Hoover some of the better stories from his mining years. On one plunge into the low, narrow tunnels dug by the Chinese, crawling through the mud with a candle in hand, he noticed fresh tiger tracks in a long shallow puddle ahead of him. His exit was as quiet as it was quick. The tiger, he said later, "was not of an inquisitive turn of mind and did not come out to greet us." He also succumbed to malaria in Burma. Bedridden for several weeks with chills and fever, he suffered delirium and began babbling incoherently in verse. His travel mates worried that he was losing his mind. Happily for poetry, the fever soon burned out.[29]

The Burma Mines, Railway, and Smelting Company was registered in 1906, with Bewick, Moreing as a leading shareholder. Within two years Hoover was managing director of the company and, for a change, he invested his own money, acquiring 18 percent of the mine. He built a smelter and a fifty-mile railroad and worked the ore from different directions and at various depths, overcoming caving ground and water seepage and labor shortages before, at last, a two-mile-long tunnel seven hundred feet below the old workings opened the most bountiful seams. Hoover called it the Tiger Tunnel. The mine was astonishingly rich. Over thirty years, it would produce 135 million ounces of silver and over a million tons of lead. A hundred thousand Shans and Chinese would find employment at the works, a source of pride to Hoover, who considered the Burmese the most cheerful people in Asia.[30]

Hoover's zinc and Burma projects were massive, long-term, multimillion-dollar undertakings requiring technical and managerial talents few industrialists in any field could match. As he approached the age of forty, Hoover was without question one of the great miners of his age. His path was littered with dry holes, lawsuits, and ruined investors, some of them the inevitable outcomes of an inherently risky business, others the special products of Hoover's ways. His capacities for action and accomplishment were nevertheless undisputed, and his services remained in high demand, earning him some of "the largest engineering fees known to man." He would take directors' fees up to $5,000 a year from eighteen separate companies with a total share capital of $55 million and 100,000 employees spread around the globe. He would soon estimate that he was in position to amass personal wealth of at least $30 million.[31]

No one watched Hoover's mounting good fortune with more chagrin than Charles Algernon Moreing, and it had not escaped his notice that his former partner was, on occasion, and without the express written consent of Bewick, Moreing, practicing as a miner and engineer well within the confines of the British Empire and other locales claimed by Bewick, Moreing as its own. Hoover had also been poaching top talent from Bewick, Moreing, and he was caught spying on the company through a disloyal corporate secretary who, on dismissal, was engaged by Hoover at 1 London Wall. Moreing brought suit against Hoover in 1910 for violating his restrictive covenants. It was settled out of court to Moreing's advantage.[32]

Hoover's decision to avoid an open trial was likely influenced by the weakness of his case, not to mention his concern for public relations. He had been working hard to put his Moreing-era scandals behind him and to establish himself as a respectable leader in the mining industry. As part of these efforts, he had published his first book in 1909.

Based on a series of lectures he had given at Stanford and Columbia, *Principles of Mining* is a technical treatise covering everything from machine drilling to cavage to stoping, valuation, bookkeeping, and risk management. By no means a leisurely read, it does offer insight into Hoover's professional mind through lectures on the necessity of efficiency, and on the business leader's need to keep firm control of his working environment. There are also modest political statements in the book, including a description of labor unions as a natural antidote to the concentration of capital in large firms: "The time when the employer could ride roughshod over his labor is disappearing with the doctrine of *'laissez faire'* on which it was founded." The latter statement is somewhat at odds with Hoover's union-busting in Australia, as well as his blasé attitude toward indentured labor, a practice he would introduce to Nicaragua in 1913. He generally believed in paying good wages, nevertheless.[33]

Among the book's idiosyncratic touches is Hoover's attempt to end discussion of the capacities of different races of workers, a common debating point in early twentieth-century mining, by quantifying a racial productivity gap. He deemed one white worker equal to two or three of the colored races in simple tasks like shoveling, and as high as one to eleven in the most complicated mechanical work.

Perhaps the largest statement made in *Principles of Mining* is that the supreme manifestation of professionalism in engineering in 1909 was an executive who operated much like Herbert Hoover: "The mining engineer is no longer the technician who concocts reports and blue prints. It is demanded of him that he devise the finance, construct and manage the works which he advises." The commercial aspects of the work "cannot be too strongly emphasized," Hoover insists. "The industry is conducted for commercial purposes, and leaves no room for the haughty intellectual superiority assumed by some professions over business callings."[34]

This was an important point for Hoover, though he was a geologist by training and a businessman by inclination. It would always please him to present himself as an engineer, a leading member of an expansive, upwardly mobile profession. Numbering seven thousand in his boyhood, the ranks of engineers in America would expand twentyfold by the middle of his life, and in this time they would claim such impressive feats as the Brooklyn Bridge and the Panama Canal. A broad definition of the profession emphasizing its commercial phases only enhanced Hoover's sense of belonging and his claim to leadership. Most prominent figures in the engineering community considered themselves a species of businessman, and they accepted Hoover wholeheartedly as one of their own.[35]

Not satisfied with positioning himself as the epitome of the modern engineer, Hoover also squeezed into the final pages of *Principles of Mining* a description of the "new intellectual type" he had wanted to bring to the stage with Mary Austin. The engineer is a creator, forsaking the comforts of civilization for the mountains and deserts where he works his art. He receives little public acclaim, because he does not advertise himself, yet year by year his profession rises in dignity and importance as the world learns the identity of the real brains behind industrial progress:

> To the engineer falls the work of creating from the dry bones of scientific fact the living body of industry. It is he whose intellect and direction bring to the world the comforts and necessities of daily need. Unlike the doctor, his is not the constant struggle to save the weak. Unlike the soldier, destruction is not his prime function. Unlike the lawyer, quarrels are not his daily bread. Engineering is the profession of creation and of construction, of stimulation of human effort and accomplishment.[36]

*Principles of Mining* did not much interest the press, apart from organs beholden to Hoover. It was a significant achievement nonetheless. It would become a standard text in many engineering schools and it remained in print throughout Hoover's lifetime, fulfilling his ambition to have an intellectual as well as a practical career in the manner of his mentors, Lindgren and Branner. It also kept him at his desk long enough to gain thirty pounds in the writing.

Hoover was as unlikely an author as he was host of the Red House dinner club. He had no respect for literary craftsmanship. Writers were just so many more specialists for hire: "You can get a man to write anything for five pounds a week," he told the author and diplomat Brand Whitlock. His own grammar and syntax were poor, his spelling remained abysmal, he was sloppy with dates and details, and he plagiarized without blinking. He wrote in a hurry, on top of all the other work in his life, so it is not surprising that *Principles of Mining* needed to be rewritten almost in its entirety by its publishers.[*][37]

Despite all of this, Hoover had begun chipping away at a still grander literary project while *Principles of Mining* was rolling off the press. He had long shared with his wife and brother an interest in the history of science. During their time together in London, Lou gave Theodore a copy of Robert Boyle's 1672 classic, *An Essay about the Origins and Virtues of Gems*, triggering a familial mania for collecting old and rare books on mineralogy, mining, alchemy, technology, and mathematics. The three of them spent many afternoons between 1908 and 1914 in London bookshops. Herbert and Lou alone assembled a library of 912 volumes, including Georgius Agricola's *De Re Metallica*, the first important attempt to gather between covers the world's knowledge on mining and metallurgy.[38]

The Hoovers knew the value and the lore of Agricola's masterwork, how it had been published in Latin in 1556 and chained to church altars in old South American mining camps, where priests translated it for workers. They also knew the book had never been

---

* Hoover appears to have had mixed feelings about his writing. He believed he deserved to be published, but his assessment of his literary talent can be gathered from a note attached to an article intended for the *North American Review:* "Enclosed some rot on China." (Hoover to Mr. Allan, 1901, Correspondence, Lou Henry Hoover Papers, Herbert Hoover Presidential Library and Museum.)

published in English. They decided to undertake the task themselves. Lou's proficiency in Latin and German (Agricola's native tongue), as well as her scientific training, made her an indispensable partner in the enterprise. A principal reason the book had never been translated was its difficulty: the author's Latin was riddled with medieval German vocabulary and forgotten technical terms. The Hoovers worked away at the translation in spare moments over five years, sitting on opposite sides of a desk in the Red House library, their reference works piled between them. In 1912, after four painstaking revisions, they were ready to publish.

The translation, hand-printed on sixteenth-century linen paper in the same fonts as the original, featured reproductions of Agricola's 289 woodcut illustrations. *The American Historical Review* called the book a "noteworthy monument of patient and intelligent scholarship." Their achievement won the Hoovers a special gold medal for distinguished service from the Mining and Metallurgical Society of America.[39]

The authors deserved accolades for the book, an honest labor of love, and a valentine to a profession they both held dear. Hoover would often quote Agricola on the subject of mining as "a calling of peculiar dignity" and he and Lou, with humility and respect, would take their places in its long traditions of knowledge and practice. At the same time, and less humbly, Hoover would complain incessantly of the lack of respect for engineers in Britain, where they were viewed as plumbers or carpenters, not high-minded achievers. He would never entirely lose his obsession with legitimating the profession and, by extension, himself.[40]

As early as 1907, before he had left Bewick, Moreing, Hoover was telling friends that as much as he loved mining he had taken what he could from the profession. The day-to-day challenges of the engineer had lost their novelty, and as the years passed, his dissatisfaction deepened. Money was not an issue. "If a man has not made a fortune by forty he is not worth much," he is reputed to have said. His point was that making money is not difficult if that is all one wants to do. By his late thirties, he was worth several million, with perhaps ten times that amount in sight. It was far more than he needed. He liked to live comfortably and he enjoyed the freedom and independence his wealth afforded him, but he was still enough of a Quaker to disdain diamonds and yachts and ostentatious display. As he had told Mary Austin, he wanted to be more than another rich man.[41]

He also wanted out of England, long having been ambivalent about the country. Its attractions were many, including the fact that many of his friends and associates were English. He himself was so thoroughly Anglicized that some in the mining world mistook him for a Brit, and his letters were idiomatically as English as they were American. From 1907 to 1910, Hoover had made only a single trip to his native land. Yet in his heart he was thoroughly American. He would gather his family and his English domestic staff on the Red House lawn every Fourth of July to sing "The Star-Spangled Banner," and as much as he wanted to be accepted in London, he knew he did not fit. He had no patience for the English social season, class distinctions, titles, and inherited wealth. He was sensitive to the underside of industrial England and the squalor in which the vast majority of its citizens lived. It also irked Hoover that the British condescended to Americans, and to engineers, treatment that he tended to answer with belligerence.[42]

Hoover had managed to stomach English ways while he was building his career. Now, with it built, he was fed up. "I am disgusted with myself," he wrote an American friend, "when I think how much better off you people are who stuck by your own country and place. When you walk down the street you meet a hundred men who have a genuine pleasure in greeting you. I am an alien who gets a grin once in nine months." This might have struck the British as rich coming from so saturnine a personality as Hoover.[43]

His preferred mode of escape from mining and England, he told his college chum Will Irwin, was to get into the "big game" somewhere. By the big game he meant public service. Newspapers were a possibility. Long fascinated by the business, Hoover had closely watched the progress of William Randolph Hearst, a fellow Californian, whose chain of dailies was leading the industrialization of the American press and gaining its owner an influence unprecedented for a private citizen in America. Hoover had an agent scout for newspapers in New York and Washington that might serve as a centerpiece for a chain of his own.[44]

A move to the academy was also a possibility. Thanks to his eminence in mining circles, Hoover's name routinely arose in searches for deans of mining and engineering schools at universities including Columbia. Politics, too, seemed open. He had been promoted by a friend as a candidate for governor of California, and Stanford president David Starr Jordan wrote letters of recommendation to the White House on his behalf. Jordan described him to President Taft as a millionaire retiring at age thirty-seven and looking to return to America:

> I would like to call your notice to a young man, available for executive service, and who possesses the greatest of talent for work in that line. . . . He is a very presentable man, of quiet, frank manner, but carrying conviction whenever he speaks. He has lately declined the deanship of the Columbia school of mines. . . . In short, should he enter public life in any capacity, he is a man who will make himself felt.[45]

Hoover's motives for this dramatic change of direction were several in addition to his stated reasons that he had run through his chosen field and desired to return to the United States. His noncompetition settlement with Moreing must have been on his mind, limiting as it did his prospects in mining. His rueful note in *Principles of Mining* that the public took scant notice of engineers was further argument for change: Hoover was hungry as ever for recognition and approbation. A move toward public service, like his earlier efforts to disentangle himself from Moreing and obscure the record of the Chang trial, would also help to burnish his reputation and to bury memories of the devil he had been. Hoover's acute sensitivity to criticism and personal attack, together with his two breakdowns at the height of his troubles, suggest that his conscience was bothering him. Although he rarely admitted to transgressions, he had to know that he was not living up to his professed moral code.

But above all of this was one other crucial factor: Hoover's genuine desire to do good. It is a sometimes difficult motive to credit, given his preoccupation over two decades of adulthood with his own advancement, yet his commitment to public service would prove so deep and enduring that it had to stem in large part from a sincere desire to be of useful service to his fellow man. It makes more sense when one considers the number of voices and examples from his formative years that encouraged Hoover to devote himself to the public good. Although he was no longer a practicing Quaker, the Friends' ethic of community service ran strong in his family. His father and his Uncle Minthorn had both been public servants and community leaders with a demonstrated concern for the welfare of others. His mother, especially, had put her dedication to her ministry above her children and her own health. He had heard her celebrated on her passing as a woman tried and proved by service, a builder and a doer of deeds who had lived a worthy and useful life. His grandmother had prayed on his departure for Stanford that he would do "a conscientious work." His beloved Sunday school teacher, Miss Gray, had urged him to find a purpose beyond accumulating wealth. That message had been echoed at Stanford, where President Jordan encouraged students to get into "the game" of useful service, a phrase Hoover adopted as his own.[46]

Service, moreover, was in the air. It was something of a mania in the first decades of twentieth-century America. Theodore Roosevelt, Woodrow Wilson, and every postprandial gasbag at the nation's multiplying lodges, clubs, and fraternal orders sang hosannas to the noble men and women who contributed to social betterment through community service. The Rotarian motto—"he profits most who serves best"—had become a national ethic. Everyone was expected to give and to belong.[47]

Under the combined weight of these influences, it is doubtful that Hoover could have been satisfied with the course of his life without at some point answering the call of service. There is, in fact, considerable evidence that Hoover was always headed for a career in public service, whether he realized it or not. His dedication to business and his sometime ruthless ways had never prevented him from looking after chosen others. Indeed, he gave more than most. While working his way through Stanford, he had found time for campus politics and student activities. As soon as he began making money he sent assistance to friends and family attending school or down on their luck. He had supported Rowe's widow and children, and he had secretly paid the salary of a favorite Stanford librarian for several years. He kept his home open to friends and strangers alike, running Red House almost as an unofficial American consulate in London. He maintained an

active presence in various trade associations, wrote articles on professional and educational themes not directly relevant to his commercial
interests, and made two fine book-length contributions to the sum
of industrial knowledge. He donated more than five hundred books
on China, including rare Jesuit publications, to Stanford and made a
major contribution to a fund-raising campaign for a students' union
building. Theodore would call his brother's benefactions "far beyond
liberal" and "unwisely lavish."[48]


Stanford won the honor of Hoover's first large-scale attempt at public
service as a post-mining career. He still considered the university "the
best place in the world," and it meant something to him to remain
a part of the Stanford community. He joined the Stanford board
of trustees in the autumn of 1912 in circumstances as cloudy as the
awarding of his geology degree seventeen years earlier. He escaped a
residency requirement by claiming immediate plans to relocate to San
Francisco, knowing full well he was at least a year away from leaving
London.[49]

Once installed on the board of trustees, he led a campaign to rein-
vigorate a campus that had been slumping after its initial years of
rapid progress. He thought it deficient "in a very great proportion
of the departments." He urged an upgrading of academic staff, too
many professors being "of the humdrum order," and to this end he
introduced some of the highest salaries in the country (he had been
surprised to learn that assistant professors could not afford domestic
help). He arranged for his friend and mentor David Starr Jordan, the
only president in the university's first two decades, to be kicked up to
chancellor and replaced with the geologist John C. Branner, another
Hoover mentor. That Branner was two years from retirement some
took as a signal that Hoover eventually wanted the presidency for
himself, which was true.[50]

Accustomed to years of command, Hoover had no compunctions
about ruffling feathers at Stanford, including those of his new president. He and Branner feuded publicly over the advisability of closing
their expensive medical school, with Hoover prevailing by coaxing
trustees to the "nay" side. Less successful was his attack on tenure,

which he considered a protection racket for the weak and lazy and an outrage on the sanctity of higher education. Tenure survived.[51]

In the midst of these reform initiatives at Stanford, Hoover elbowed his way into another opportunity to serve. Leading citizens of San Francisco, anxious to revive a local economy still prostrate from the calamitous earthquake of 1906, were organizing a Panama-Pacific International Exposition for 1915. The official occasions for the affair were the celebration of the opening of the Panama Canal and the commemoration of the discovery of the Pacific Ocean by Balboa in 1515. The city fathers were anxious that King George V and other European potentates attend the exposition.

Hoover invented a role for himself as leader of the charge overseas. He lobbied Arthur Balfour, leader of the Conservative opposition in Parliament, and lent his car on weekends to Sir Edward Grey, the Liberal foreign secretary. He courted this "noodle-headed" peer and that "empty-headed" peer, and countless European worthies. Hard as he worked, he could not overcome the simple fact that Congress had voted in 1912 to give preferential rates for U.S. shipping through the Panama Canal, an act of favoritism the British took as unfriendly and an insurmountable obstacle to a royal visit. Europe's other leading power, Germany, was also loath to celebrate the opening of a prejudicially priced tollway.[52]

By the summer of 1914, Hoover had gone down swinging on the exhibition bid. Eager to depart London, he had begun organizing the permanent relocation of his family and his business headquarters to San Francisco. He was shopping for a California newspaper and had hired an architect to build a posh house with an elevator in Presidio Heights when along came the worst calamity in the history of mankind and his plans once more scattered like clouds.

# ★ BOOK II ★

# CHAPTER 7

# "Hard to State Without Becoming Hysterical"

News that a Serbian nationalist had assassinated Archduke Franz Ferdinand in Sarajevo on June 28, 1914, made no impression on Herbert Hoover. "Just another Balkan lapse into barbarism," he told himself, and went about his business. Over the next several weeks, nothing he read in the London newspapers, nor anything he heard from his vast network of business and political contacts in England and Europe, urged a second thought.[1]

Austria-Hungary's bellicose ultimatum of July 23, accusing Serbia of complicity in the murder of the archduke, also failed to alarm Hoover. The conflict, he believed, was a regional affair, and the diplomatic mastery of the great powers would see that it remained so. He was aware of Europe's ancient animosities and imperial rivalries, not to mention its recent arms buildup, but a continental plunge into the madness of war was nevertheless inconceivable. He held the conventional view of Europe as the apex of civilization, the august repository of human achievement in arts, science, and politics, and the engine of global prosperity. Its peoples were enjoying what he regarded as the happiest moment in human history. Peace had reigned on the Continent for generations, and the increasing financial interdependence of the European capitals seemed to guarantee the minimum of cooperation required to prevent future hostilities.

Europe's spell of tranquility seemed all the stronger for the fact that it was a balmy, sunny summer, as glorious a season as anyone could remember. The kaiser was racing boats in the Norwegian

fjords. The czar was swimming at his summer home on the Baltic.
Sir Edward Grey, the British foreign secretary, slipped out of London
with his fishing tackle. Hordes of American tourists were debouch-
ing from steamships and trains, clutching their traveler's checks and
Baedekers, bound for castles, storied cities, the Riviera. Come what
may in the Balkans, the rest of Europe was a playground, open at its
unchecked borders to one and all. Hoover himself, who rarely holi-
dayed, was planning a short trip to the seaside with his children over
the August long weekend.

The continental markets sank on Saturday, July 25, the first
unmistakable sign of broader distress in Europe. Serbia had failed to
meet the impossible terms of the Austro-Hungarian ultimatum, and
troop movements were reported on each side of their mutual border.
The great powers began to declare allegiances. Serbia lined up with
Russia and France; Germany held with Austria-Hungary. England,
for the moment, played peacemaker.

U.S. stock exchanges joined the financial panic on July 28 when
Austria-Hungary finally declared war and crossed into Serbian territory. Hoover was now agitated. He paced his offices all day, devouring
headlines and vibrating "from small hope to great fear" as the diplomatic thunder rolled from capital to capital. He cabled his managers around the world to cut production and wondered how he would
provide for his key employees in the event of a prolonged conflict. He
clung to hopes that Sir Edward Grey would yet reel the continent in
from the brink, or at least contain the damage to the east.[2]

Hoover knew what he had at stake financially. He could do the
math in his head. He also understood that more than his wealth and
his pleasant mode of existence was threatened. He was days from his
fortieth birthday and on the cusp of realizing his ambitions of being
more than just another rich man. He had signed over his directorships and engineering responsibilities to his longtime associate, John
Agnew. He was deep in negotiations to purchase the *Sacramento Union*
when the markets tanked and filled his future with uncertainty. He
reluctantly suspended those talks.[3]

On Friday, July 31, the major European bourses went dark, and
Britain announced that its banks would close on Saturday in addition
to the Monday holiday. Hoover, who took pride in maintaining a sense
of normality in times of crisis, kept his promise to take his children

away for the weekend. On Saturday afternoon, the family drove out to Westgate, where his publishing friend, Edgar Rickard, had taken a cottage. The trip was a disaster. Hoover learned on arriving that Germany had declared war on Russia and that the French were mobilizing. Sunday morning, August 2, he heard that England's bank moratorium had been extended three days more and that Germany had sent an ultimatum to Belgium demanding passage for its army. The Hoovers and Rickards visited the local village inn for lunch, but the charms of Westgate were no match for the gloom across the Channel. Strain showed in every face. Hoover heard rumors that gasoline was in short supply and worried about his ability to return to the city. Relieved to learn that his driver had stocked up, he finally faced the futility of holidaying under a looming catastrophe and took his family back to London that same afternoon, driving by way of Portsmouth, where he could see the British fleet off Cowes, all "dark and sinister-looking."[4]

Monday morning Hoover was back in his office despite the holiday. Germany had declared war on France, and although England had yet to convey its intentions, troops were already passing on the street outside 1 London Wall. "It seemed like an earthquake," Hoover would later write. "The substance and bottom seemed to go out of everything." In a single weekend, the grandest of civilizations had sunk into an abyss of hatred and destruction.[5]

Hoover watched helplessly as his businesses crashed around his ears. Orders were canceled and production was suspended everywhere. His Russian workers were drawn from mines into armies, his ships with their cargoes of zinc, lead, and copper were ordered into port, banks were closed from Burma to South Africa, his managers were begging for direction and financial assistance. Hoover poured out his distress and amazement in a letter to a friend:

> I have a body of 100,000 men at work in various enterprises and this morning I do not see how we are to meet these payrolls by any human device possible. Our products are mostly base metals the market for which is paralyzed, shipping facilities are gone, and even exchange facilities to remit money— did we have it—are out of gear. Of still more importance is the fact that the moneys which we have in reserve in London

are unavailable, due to a [bank] moratorium. All of the wildest dreams of novelists as to what could happen in the case of a world war have already happened by way of anticipation, and as to what the realization of such a war may be one can only stutter at.[6]

Hoover had rented a house in Palo Alto and had booked passage for his family on the *Vaterland* for August 13. The ship was now pulled out of service. He booked another, the *Aquitania*, only to see it suffer the same fate. He had an inkling the crisis would not pass quickly. "If my judgment of the situation is right," he wrote that same day, "we are on the verge of seven years of considerable privation." At precisely that moment, with Europe's massed armies hurtling at one another with unprecedented force, and with his own fortunes gravely imperiled, Herbert Hoover did a remarkable thing.[7]

On the afternoon of August 4, a few hours after German troops had crossed into neutral Belgium on a dead run for Paris, he walked over to the offices of the U.S. consulate in search of Consul General Robert Skinner. It was a short walk, covering slightly more than a city block, but it would transform Hoover's life, launching him into the big game in a far larger way than he had ever imagined.

According to Lou Hoover, the consulate had called her husband and asked for his assistance. Skinner recalled that Hoover arrived at his own initiative and volunteered to help. Regardless, he was welcome. The U.S. consulate was under siege by its own citizens.[8]

Some 100,000 Americans were visiting Europe in the summer of 1914, and the call to arms had brought their happy adventures to a screeching halt. All were anxious to flee the Continent before the fighting began in earnest, but the amenities on which their travels depended had, without notice, ceased to exist. Banks were closed. Lines of credit, traveler's checks, and foreign currencies were worthless. Telegraph services were unavailable. Hotels were incapacitated as their employees rushed to enlist. Borders that days before had been unobstructed were blocked. Trains, ships, and horses were appropriated for troop carriage, and the few rail and steamship services still operating were overwhelmed by demand.

Most of the panicked tourists bolted for London, which despite its eventual declaration of war on Germany offered relative safety and the best odds on passage to America. Six thousand reached the city on August 3 alone. With their plans in chaos and the crowded London hotels refusing U.S. currency, they stampeded Skinner's consulate in the financial district and the U.S. embassy in the West End.

When Hoover arrived at the consulate, a thousand frightened and confused Americans were crowding the premises and milling in the street. Women were sobbing and fainting. Men were shouting at Skinner, wanting assurances that German aircraft were not about to bomb London. "Staunch and emphatic Americans were pounding the counter and demanding to know if their government was going to protect its citizens," recalled Hoover. "They insisted that Mr. Skinner had no right to allow solvent Americans to sleep in parks and go hungry like that. The American government should at once demand that the American banks in London be opened. . . . It was a disgrace."[9]

Hoover did not wait for Skinner to tell him what to do. After a brief conversation with a clutch of commercial men at the edge of the mob, he determined that the most urgent need was to provide short-term loans for the many Americans without any cash. He called his office and asked two associates to bring over the few hundred pounds he had on the premises and whatever other gold and currency they could muster. He called home to gather another hundred pounds from Lou. Hoover informed Skinner that his men would aid the travelers by exchanging small amounts of their U.S. funds for British cash; those who had no money would be offered loans at no interest in exchange for IOUs. The grateful Skinner organized the grumbling horde into five lines in front of five tables, behind which Hoover and his associates sat with papers, pens, and cash. Several hundred Americans were thus delivered from immediate distress.

By the following morning, Hoover had given thought to what more he could do for his fellow citizens. As his team continued to dispense funds at the consulate, he wrote a well-connected associate stateside to suggest that if Washington wanted a special commissioner for relief of American tourists in England, he was available. Without waiting for a reply (and none ever came), he convened twenty American businessmen resident in London, most of them fellow mining executives, and most associated with the American Society in London, of which Hoover was a stalwart. The meeting established the Committee of American Residents in London for the Assistance of American Travelers. Hoover was appointed chair. The committee members volunteered their own cash and raised money from other Americans in London, all of which was to be distributed as loans to individuals whose funds were temporarily frozen, or as charity to those who had nothing. Hoover gave about $6,000 personally, likely the largest single contribution.

Within twenty-four hours, Hoover's new committee had its own stationery, and within forty-eight hours it was operating from a booth in the ballroom of the Savoy Hotel as well as three other London locations. Through his business connections, Hoover managed to bypass restrictions on telegraphic service and open a transatlantic line to allow Americans to wire money to stranded friends and relatives. In a city suddenly flooded with refugees, he reserved for American travelers some two thousand rooms in hotels or boardinghouses. He issued a press release proclaiming that his Residents' Committee was assuming charge of all American relief work in the city, and that in doing so it had the blessings of its honorary chairman, Walter Hines Page, the U.S. ambassador to London.

Hoover's announcement was a surprise to Ambassador Page, who in any event was too beleaguered to object. It was also news to the leadership of another committee that had formed a day before Hoover's, for much the same purpose. The American Citizens' Committee had sprung out of a mob scene at the U.S. embassy. Led by the banker Fred I. Kent, it was comprised of American travelers rather than Americans who lived in London. It was operating out of the Savoy ballroom, posing a competitive threat that Hoover answered by opening his own branch there.

The initial efforts of these committees, along with the reopening of the American Express offices in London and the announcement of a U.S. congressional appropriation of $2.5 million for relief of stranded travelers, defused some of the early panic in London. The fundamental problems persisted, however. Each day, thousands more refugees from the Continent descended on the city, many without luggage, funds, or lodgings, and the small U.S. legation remained overwhelmed. Only $300,000 of Congress's $2.5 million was immediately available. Hoover and his resident volunteers worked around the clock to bring order to the situation and assist the travelers. Wearing badges and American flag pins, they met new arrivals at the station platform with refreshments and small loans of cash. They offered directions to hotels and boardinghouses. They arranged medical attention for those requiring it.

Some evenings, as late as midnight, Hoover himself could be found in the dim light of a near-empty platform, waiting to greet a train. Despite his badge and flag pin, he was easy to overlook, a nondescript man with a clean-shaven face and a slight stoop at the shoulder. His blue serge suit was in need of brushing and pressing. His shoes were scuffed, their laces broken and tied together in rough knots. He approached the arriving tourists directly, offering assistance and answering questions in single syllables, not a word or a minute wasted, before hurrying off toward home.

He might not have cut an inspiring figure, but Hoover's self-worth was as high as ever. He had always considered himself the most capable man in any room, and with rare exceptions he was right. He had supreme confidence in his ability to draw up a grand scheme, map it out to the smallest detail, and execute it in every dimension. He could improvise, bully, or bluff his way around any human or physical obstacle. He felt entirely competent to deliver 100,000 busted Americans safely home in the midst of a massive European conflagration. He was not so sure about the other parties to the relief effort.

Hoover resented the "Savoy bunch," as he called Fred Kent's Citizens' Committee. They had not had the sense to step aside when he announced in the press that his Residents' Committee was prepared to manage the entire relief effort. They had been unreceptive to his suggestion of cooperation, a magnanimous gesture from a man reluctant to share authority, and they had snubbed his advice on who did and did not deserve their assistance. The tension between the committees was further aggravated when Ambassador Page handed Kent the $300,000 in government funds at his disposal, despite the fact that they were providing mostly logistical support to the tourists while Hoover's group was doling out $10,000 a day in financial aid from its members' pockets.[10]

Hoover's frustration with Kent grew daily. He complained at

the embassy that it was inefficient to have two committees leading one relief project. When his various attempts to convince Ambassador Page to force a merger came to naught, Hoover set his sights on Henry Breckinridge, the U.S. assistant secretary of war. Breckinridge arrived in London from Washington on August 17 with two dozen army officers, a staff of functionaries, a large stock of gold, and a mandate to assist in the evacuation of American travelers. On landing, he was met by a Hoover emissary who brazenly suggested that Breckinridge subsume his mission under Hoover's Residents' Committee. Breckinridge answered that his instructions did not permit him to share his authority. He did note in his diary that he was impressed with Hoover's determination to be useful in the crisis.[11]

Hoover, for his part, could find no good in the Breckinridge delegation. He asked his colleagues how the War Department could think that dispatching a shipload of loafers and lackeys to London would help move hordes of stranded tourists. Breckinridge intended to occupy himself in traveling from one European capital to another aboard special trains, "calling on big potentates and explaining his great position in the United States" while practically ignoring the relief work. Given that the United States, as a neutral party, had no other business in the war, it made sense to Hoover that the assistant secretary would lend him a hand. Breckinridge's failure to do so was an "appalling travesty."[12]

Hoover did not have to suffer the Citizens' Committee or the Breckinridge delegation for long. The day after his arrival, the assistant secretary met with Ambassador Page to discuss solutions to their mutual problems. They noted that with the gradual resumption of transatlantic shipping, members of Kent's committee were packing for home, and that the U.S. legation had neither the manpower nor the expertise to handle the ongoing evacuation. Hoover's committee, alternatively, was conspicuously willing and able. On August 20, Breckinridge and Page formally asked the Residents' Committee to manage the organization and distribution of relief, including the $2.5 million allotted by Congress. Hoover was finally in charge.

Every day thousands more Americans poured into London, each group in worse shape than the previous one. All were met on the platform by Hoover's committee. Among the more picturesque newcomers were members of a Wild West circus that had worked its way back from Eastern Europe, arriving in London in full regalia of chaps and feathers but without its tent or livestock. Its ponies had been seized by armies in Poland. Its elephant, lion, and tiger had been abandoned for lack of food.

Settling in as chairman of the relief organization, Hoover saw no reason it should not be run as autocratically and efficiently as his mining businesses. He arranged that all authority over hiring, finances, organizational structure, and policy reside with him. He would take care of press and diplomatic relations and anything else requiring a decision. He assembled a volunteer staff of more than a hundred, including a team of accountants and auditors to ensure proper management of the funds entrusted to him. Irked at the Savoy bunch's policy of providing expedited service to its wealthier friends, Hoover insisted on uniform terms for all relief recipients. Among other rules, no one would return to America in a first- or second-class berth. All were booked in steerage.

Hoover's rules were put to the test when, early one morning, a wealthy but temporarily penniless American woman asked the committee for passage home and refused to take anything but a first-class ticket. When her histrionics failed to sway the clerks, she sat down in the ballroom of the Savoy and declared a hunger strike. Hoover ignored the woman through the morning and lunch hour. He waited until she appeared to wilt in the late afternoon, then brought her funds for supper and a steerage ticket. She accepted both.

Other complainants were received with less patience, including a hotheaded professor of history from the University of Michigan who wrote to accuse the Residents' Committee of mistreatment. Hoover refuted his charges indignantly and comprehensively, copying his response to the president of the university and its board of regents. After a meeting with his employer, the professor returned Hoover an abject retraction and apology.[13]

By early October, two months from the start of the war, 120,000 troubled Americans had passed through London to America, and the work of Hoover's Residents' Committee was finally winding down. More than forty-two thousand individuals had registered with his organization and many more besides had benefited from its work. In excess of $400,000 had been distributed, most of it in loans, including some $150,000 in government funds. All but a few hundred dollars of the loaned funds were eventually repaid. Hoover's administrative costs were negligible: he had relied upon volunteer labor, and his overhead, including offices and telegraph lines, was mostly donated.[14]

Ambassador Page, a balding, weak-eyed man with a bulbous nose, knew better than anyone the panic and confusion that had reigned when the first throngs of Americans descended on London. He wrote Hoover a personal note: "I count ourselves exceedingly fortunate in having your Committee at our service. . . . We couldn't have done the job without it." Not sure what to make of him at the outset, the ambassador now considered Hoover among the most trustworthy and devoted men he had ever known. Page's confidence would be critical to Hoover in the far greater and more desperate battles ahead.[15]

Throughout the two months of Hoover's relief work in London, competence of a different, entirely destructive character was blowing apart the Continent. The Great War was launched with frightening scale and force, reflecting years of weapons stockpiling and military strategizing by the great powers. The opening assaults were superbly engineered by a generation of officers educated in industrialized combat at Europe's proliferating staff colleges and war academies. They deployed their million-strong armies and awesome loads of artillery with mathematical precision and terrible speed. Germany alone scheduled eleven thousand trains in its mobilization.[16]

Berlin had demanded the right to pass through neutral Belgium to France on August 2. Its troops invaded two days later without having received a response. King Albert's valiant Belgian army, its cavalry in fur busbies and its infantry in feathered bonnets, was no match for Germany's new twelve- and sixteen-inch howitzers. It was like "laying a baby on the track before a locomotive," said one diplomat in Brussels. Albert retreated all the way to Antwerp and clung to that corner of his kingdom for the remainder of the war.[17]

Rolling south, Germany blasted the French infantry off the beet fields of the Sambre and routed the British Expeditionary Force at Mons. The whole Allied army backed up to the Marne Valley, just short of Paris, and regrouped for a savage war of position in the last week of August. Under a blazing sun, 2 million men clashed in open fields without benefit of fortification or strong defensive holds. More than half a million were left dead or wounded before the armies began digging into protective trenches along a 450-mile line from the North Sea to the Swiss frontier. While the Somme Offensive and the Battle of Verdun loom larger in the popular imagination, the bloodiest fighting and the highest kill rates of the First World War were seen in those first two months of mobile combat.[18]

While the bloodletting was generally restricted to the battlefield, the collateral damage was profound in Europe and around the world. By the time Hoover looked up from his work on the American evacuation he found his diverse business interests "shot to pieces" by the war. Mining, shipping, smelting, refining, and the system of international finance that supported his enterprises had all "gone to smash." The fortune anticipated from his mining investments had evaporated.[19]

There was no longer any question of decamping to California. Hoover needed to salvage something of his holdings, and short on cash, he needed the income from his fees for attending and chairing various directors' meetings in London. On October 3, he stayed behind as Lou, Allan, and Herbert Jr. boarded the *Lusitania*, headed ultimately for Palo Alto. They would be safe in the United States, sheltered from Europe's strife by the Atlantic Ocean and the sentiments of the American people, who were unanimously determined to remain neutral in the conflict.[20]

Even by his own doleful standards, Hoover's outlook in October of 1914 was bleak. The Europe he had known was dead, and it was never coming back. He thought it would take him five to ten years to make money again, and he had no interest in trying. He told a friend that his reversal of fortune had left him "stunned and unstrung," and for the first time in his life he lacked a clear sense of direction. It was hard, he said, to become accustomed to world wars.[21]

Dark as things appeared, Hoover never stopped working. For each ounce of pessimism in his character, there were at least two of physical and mental vitality. Running at full capacity was his natural state, and he saw no reason to change because of the war. He also admitted to a psychological need to feel useful in the maelstrom of horrible events. "The troubles of American tourists served to reduce the feeling of helplessness," he said.[22]

It was perhaps inevitable, then, that as the war progressed Hoover would find another opportunity to serve. It appeared in the first week in October, in the days between his waving good-bye to his family and his receiving a cable from Lou announcing that they had arrived safely in New York, and that Herbert Jr. had eaten seven cream puffs in one day. At first blush, the new opportunity did not look like a life changer. It looked more like a chore. Hoover had been introduced to an American engineer named Millard Shaler, who needed help shipping 1,500 tons of cereals to Belgium.

Prior to the war, Belgium had been a thriving nation of 7.5 million, the sixth-largest economy in the world. Its capital, Brussels, was one of the most charming cities in Europe, an urban paradise of fine restaurants, stately homes, drowsy boulevards, and beautiful high-walled formal gardens. Diplomats considered it the ideal posting. "Nothing can happen in Brussels," they said, and they continued to say it, amid dances at the palace and rounds of golf in the suburbs, right up until the first weekend of August 1914.[23]

The simple fact of Germany's violation of Belgian neutrality had been sufficient to overcome antiwar sentiment and bring Great Britain into the war. The manner of the invasion outraged the international community. In Tamines, 383 civilians, including women and children, had been herded into the square and shot by German execution squads, the survivors bayoneted. Large-scale massacres, along with lootings and torching, had been repeated in town after undefended town in what came to be known as the Rape of Belgium. The worst brutality occurred in Louvain, the Oxford of the Low Countries, where German troops had shot the mayor, the university rector, and hundreds of civilians before forcing the evacuation of the entire population of forty-two thousand. Some 1,100 buildings had been destroyed, including the magnificent university library with its irreplaceable collection of Gothic and Renaissance manuscripts. Despite all the carnage to come in the Great War, the reputation of the German army never recovered from the barbaric assault on Louvain.[24]

From high on the terrace of Saint Gudula church, Brand Whitlock, the American ambassador in Brussels, had watched a "gray, grim horde, a thing of steel, that came thundering on with shrill fifes and throbbing drums . . . and wild song." German soldiers paraded into the city past sullen crowds of Belgians. Whitlock listened in the glinting sunlight to boots beating on paving stones, the clatter of the wagons bearing heavy guns, the pounding drums, and the proclamation of occupation. He decided that the old Brussels was already lost.[25]

"All the big factories are closed," wrote a secretary in Whitlock's legation. "Most of the shops have their shutters up and the streets are filled with idle people. Importations of foodstuffs even from the outlying districts have stopped dead."[26]

The stoppage of food transport would prove more consequential to the average Belgian than the fact of military defeat. Densely populated, Belgium produced only 20 percent of what it ate and traded for the rest. The German army had helped itself to the nation's fall harvest, as well as to all the livestock it could round up. The British had meanwhile imposed a naval blockade to prevent shipments of food, arms, and other items to Germany and its occupied territories, including Belgium. With nothing coming in from field or port, shelves in stores from Bruges to Liège quickly emptied.

The Germans disavowed all responsibility for feeding an occupied people, and under international law they indeed had the right to provision themselves at the expense of their hosts. They blamed the British blockade for the specter of mass hunger in Belgium. The British countered that they could not be expected to feed German captives. Caught between these warring powers, 7.5 million Belgians worried about their next meal. By early September, Brand Whitlock had noticed a new phenomenon: women begging in the streets of Brussels.[27]

That same month, a group of Belgian businessmen calling itself the Comité Central de Secours et d'Alimentation received permission from the Germans to send one of its members, Millard Shaler, across the Channel to buy $100,000 worth of food for distribution in Brussels. Shaler arrived in London on September 26 and made his purchase. He then sought an export permit, no sure thing given that he was intending to transport his food behind enemy lines in violation of the British blockade. After much negotiation, British trade officials declared that a permit would be granted if the U.S. government, as a neutral party, would supervise Shaler's payload. That stipulation led Shaler to Ambassador Page, who asked permission of the State

Department in Washington, which thought it advisable to request explicit approval of the shipment from the German government. It all took a great deal of precious time.[28]

Hoover met Shaler on or about October 6 and was as galvanized by Belgium's distress as he was furious at Washington's foot dragging. It was obvious to him that his government had a moral obligation to help. "The French, German, Austrian, English and Russian people are quite well able to take care of their own," he said. The Belgians, on the other hand, were blameless and "the most acutely tried." Through his friend Ben S. Allen, London bureau chief of the Associated Press, Hoover fired a salvo at the State Department under Shaler's name on October 13. The article depicted Brussels as a starving city on the verge of food riots thanks to Washington's inaction. Thousands of lives were in the balance. "The American government," he declared, "owes it from reasons of pure humanity to insist that Germany take favorable action or to make shipments through American diplomats, whether Germany agrees or not." The story appeared under the headline U.S. RED TAPE STARVES BRUSSELS. The State Department was unmoved.[29]

Hoover continued to fret about Belgium as Shaler's 1,500 tons of cereals wasted on the docks. News reports indicated that Liège, Charleroi, and other Belgian cities were at least as desperate as Brussels, their populations resorting to miserable diets of potato soup and black bread. With the Allies and the Central Powers digging in on the Western Front, it was clear that the predicament of the Belgians would end no time soon, and it was obvious to Hoover that Shaler's single purchase of food would be nowhere near sufficient to the nation's needs. A much larger effort would be required.


On October 10, Hoover announced to Ambassador Page that he was considering various schemes for provisioning the Belgians. He asked if he might count on the embassy for diplomatic support. Page readily assented, and within forty-eight hours Hoover returned to his office with a comprehensive plan for the relief of Belgium. Page convened a meeting to discuss Hoover's proposal, inviting Emile Francqui, chairman of the Comité Central in Brussels, among other officials. Francqui was one of the richest men in Belgium and a former lieutenant for King Leopold II in the Congo. Stout, round, with fine dark features set off by glowing brown eyes, he was "sociable and genial," according to Whitlock, "but with dignified reserve. He is one of those men who . . . feel it as a necessity of their natures to rule, to dominate."[30]

Francqui was known to Hoover. They had overlapped for six months in China, with Francqui representing Moreing's Belgian partners in the Chinese Engineering and Mining Company. They had not gotten along but now put aside their differences in the ambassador's presence. They spent four days discussing the situation in Belgium, the dietary requirements of its people, the soaring costs of purchasing large quantities of food, the supreme difficulties of cargo shipping in wartime, the reluctance of the British to lift their blockade, and the German army's tendency to requisition all consumables in occupied territories.

Page was impressed with the performance of Hoover, who was at his best in small meetings. Clear-headed and focused, he spoke sparingly but powerfully, offering a thorough and lucid answer to each problem that arose. Surprisingly, given the state of the world, the logistics of acquiring and distributing enough food to sustain a country of 7.5 million people were of little concern to Hoover. A certain broker in Chicago would handle the wheat futures. A friendly agent in Rotterdam would arrange shipping. The greater challenge, he guessed, would be to convince the British to allow relief shipments through the blockade to enemy territory, and then to keep the Germans from stealing the provisions once they had landed in Belgium. Lord Kitchener in the War Office was of the opinion that if the Belgians were allowed to starve, German troops would need to be diverted from the front to put down revolts, strengthening the military prospects for the Allies. A Prussian finance minister had already summed up the German position, saying in September, "it's better that the Belgians starve than we do." Relieving Belgium, as one observer said, was "like trying to feed a lamb trapped in a cage with a lion and a tiger."[31]

Hoover knew that the great powers were sensitive to international opinion, and to American sentiment in particular. The British relied on the United States for arms and money. Germany wanted Washington to remain neutral and an ocean away from the Western Front. Hoover thus proposed a monumental international public relations campaign to stoke sympathy for the starving Belgians. His hope was that public pressure from the U.S. would persuade the British to ease the blockade and prevent the Germans from confiscating provisions.

In the midst of Page's meetings, unbeknownst to its participants, Brand Whitlock cabled President Wilson from Brussels that the situation in Belgium was now critical. Families, rich and poor alike, had run out of food. Winter was coming and they had nowhere to turn. "In two weeks," he wrote, "the civil population of Belgium, already in misery, will face starvation."[32]

Page's summit at the embassy culminated in the founding of the Committee for the Relief of Belgium (CRB). Hoover wrote a long letter to the ambassador dated October 20 that laid out an informal charter for the committee. It would be a private, neutral, volunteer organization based in London. It would raise money from governments and private individuals and purchase food from around the world, shipping it to the neutral port of Rotterdam and from there by canal boat to Belgium. Hoover would chair the CRB, working in concert with Francqui's Comité Central, which would handle the distribution of food on its arrival in Belgium.

The letter bore several Hoover watermarks, beginning with its heavy load of facts and figures organized in point form. It noted that myriad relief committees were springing up both inside and outside of Belgium and urged consolidation. "It is impossible to handle the situation except with the strongest centralization and effective monopoly, and therefore the two organizations will refuse to recognize any element except themselves alone." The letter also contained Hoover's usual autocratic and slightly paranoid demands for "absolute command" of his part of the enterprise, which, in this instance, would ultimately prove to be sound strategy. He also wanted the relief effort to reflect his philanthropic ideals, by which he meant that it "couldn't be run like a knitting bee." He might permit honorary chairs, but there would be no drones or dilettantes, no "titled non-entities" or "decorative personalities" cluttering his hallways. The CRB's officers would be men of commercial experience working for free, covering their own expenses entirely so that every penny raised would go to purchasing food for Belgians.[33]

The CRB was not the world's first international relief effort. There are many examples throughout history of private and public aid programs for peoples afflicted by hunger and natural disaster. The Irish potato famine of the 1840s, the Russian famines of the 1890s, the volcanic eruptions in St. Vincent and Martinique in 1902 all prompted gifts of cash and goods from the United States and other nations. Nor was there anything novel about a nongovernmental agency stepping up in the face of crisis. Private aid, in fact, was far more common than governmental aid at the time. The Red Cross and innumerable sectarian and nationalist organizations were well established by 1914. What separated the CRB from all previous efforts was its preposterous ambition.[34]

Hoover was not contemplating a one-time shipment of food or money to a troubled land, nor was he proposing to supplement the meager diet of a people in lean times. The aim of the CRB was to provide almost the entire food supply for a nation of 7.5 million people, indefinitely. Hoover, representing a neutral country, intended to move massive supplies of food from the capital of one belligerent country (London) to the capital of a captive country (Brussels) occupied by their mutual enemy (Berlin). He would manage all of this in an atmosphere of war-bred suspicion and hate, and despite the disruption of conventional transportation and commercial activity in what was already shaping up as the most destructive war in history.

No humanitarian venture, public or private, had ever approached Hoover's initiative in scale or audacity. Whitlock admired the initiative but worried that the CRB had set itself goals impossible even for peacetime. In wartime, it was "a piece of temerity that no one but a set of God's own fools would ever have undertaken."[35]

Hoover did have some inkling of the scope of his project and the extreme demands it would make upon him, and the consequences for his business career. Will Irwin, a Stanford friend and war correspondent for the *Saturday Evening Post*, was living at Red House through the week of Page's meetings. He heard his host pacing upstairs long into the nights. One morning, Hoover came down to breakfast without having slept, looked his guest in the eye, and said, "Let the fortune go to hell."[36]


The CRB set up shop at No. 3 London Wall Buildings, two doors from Hoover's business offices. Even before he had hired a secretary,

Hoover was orchestrating what he called his campaign of "enormous propaganda." He browbeat newspapers and governors in the United States to raise money and collect food on the CRB's behalf, playing the politicians off against each other by dropping hints in one state that another had done more. He urged reporters to investigate the famine conditions in Belgium and play up the "detailed personal horror stuff." He personally arranged for a motion picture crew to capture footage of food lines in Brussels, and he hired famous authors, including Thomas Hardy and George Bernard Shaw, to plead for public support of the rescue effort. Wrote Shaw, if "one Belgian goes without a full meal whilst thousands of lapdogs are living in luxury from Canterbury to San Francisco . . . there is really nothing more to be said for mankind."[37]

Hoover wrote Lou, now in Palo Alto with her sons, with orders to promote relief in California.

> Over one million people on bread line in Belgium at present moment with supplies estimated to last from one to three weeks. While we are securing some supplies here for emergency purposes real situation cannot be met without direct exports from States and we shall require upwards of twenty thousand tons foodstuffs monthly. Can you interest . . . prominent San Franciscans to present shipload food from California . . . I can think of no greater contribution to this occasion of world's stress than a food ship from California and if possible one from Oregon and another from Washington. It might be pointed out that our Commission is largely Californian and that we should have support of our own state. Could also make some claim as to Oregon in my connection.[38]

He signed this cable to his wife, as he often did, with his whole name, "Herbert Hoover."[39]

It was one of several insistent messages Hoover sent to Lou in these weeks urging her to work for the cause and to return to London as soon as possible: "It is the greatest work to which we could be devoted." She sent him an exasperated reply:

You may think I am not busy building fences over here, but I just am. I believe it has been worth my coming, even if there were no boys in the problem. And the more this war goes on and the more I see the boys in California—the more glad I am I brought them over.

I should have been worried beyond endurance if I had stayed in England with them—but I am sorry you think I am foolish![40]

Softening somewhat, she added that everyone at Stanford was proud of her husband for answering "the call of humanity," and that the boys were flourishing. She then signed off using her own full name, Lou Henry Hoover.[41]

The American people were predisposed to sympathize with the Belgians, having read for weeks of the neutral nation's plucky but doomed effort to repel the Germans. The first shipload of gift food— 3,500 tons of beans, bacon, flour, and rice—arrived in Holland on November 21. More would follow. Hoover succeeded in making short work of many of the CRB's logistical problems. Emphasizing the voluntary nature of the relief, he convinced two of the largest British shipping concerns to provide transport free of charge, and arranged for telegraph and railroad services and New York piers at no cost. He soon had at his disposal a global supply network of warehouses, docks, barges, and ships with remarkably low overhead, as well as a back-office staff to receive and distribute funds and keep audited records of each transaction. Francqui did a masterful job of organizing the distribution of food to his country's 2,633 self-governing municipalities, or communes, at a time when the normal machinery of life inside Belgium had ground to a halt.[42]

To Hoover's dismay, his early announcement that the CRB and Francqui's Comité would monopolize the relief of Belgium had not stopped thousands of committees of philanthropists and do-gooders around the world from independently adopting the popular cause. Some of these, like the multimillion-dollar Rockefeller Foundation, Hoover took as mortal threats. He tried, unsuccessfully, to coopt the Rockefellers to his committee. He next charged them, privately and in the press, with compromising his ability to raise funds by waving their money around and giving potential donors the impression that no more was needed. He said they were trying to monopolize the Belgian issue and acting with jealousy and malice, which, of course, was not unlike what he was doing.[43]

By pressuring his political connections and Ambassador Page in London on the need for efficiency and a single line of communication with the belligerents, Hoover was eventually able to get written confirmation that his was the only gate into Belgium. The other agencies backed away, including the Rockefellers.

Its early success notwithstanding, the CRB soon ran into serious difficulties. Hoover had estimated that he would need to ship "upwards of twenty thousand tons" of wheat, maize, rice, and dried peas into Belgium each month. By late October the breadlines had lengthened and Francqui was cabling to say that at least 80,000 tons would be required to meet minimum monthly requirements. And Francqui meant "minimum": Belgium had imported about 250,000 tons of grain per month before the war. Hoover began purchasing food on credit even before he had figured out how to pay for it. His original calculation had been that $1 million a month would sustain his organization, an amount he would raise through charitable gifts, assistance from the Belgian government-in-exile, as well as Belgian banks with holdings abroad, and proceeds from the sale of food to those Belgians who could afford to buy it. It was now clear he would need to raise at least $4 million, far more than these sources could supply. He needed what he called "a substratum of government subvention," which was geologist-speak for a massive government subsidy.[44]

He first turned to Sir Edward Grey at the Foreign Office. Grey had been quick to encourage Shaler's initial efforts, and he had mused aloud about a monthly subsidy for the CRB, but his cabinet colleagues were sharply divided on the issue. A large faction, including Prime Minister Asquith, Kitchener at the War Office, Winston Churchill at the Admiralty, and David Lloyd George at the Exchequer, objected to supporting a civilian population in enemy territory. The Belgians, they maintained, were the responsibility of the German army. If the Allies did attempt to ship food into Belgium, the occupiers would confiscate every scrap of it for themselves. Either that, or they would let the Allies feed their captives and help themselves to the next Belgian harvest. Hoover's activities, they insisted, would have the net effect of strengthening the enemy and prolonging the war. They cut Grey's suggestion of a monthly subsidy to a one-time grant of $500,000. The CRB's chairman was disappointed, but he was not finished with the Asquith government.[45]

While plotting a new approach, Hoover decided to see for himself the condition of the Belgian people. Booking passage on a ship for Rotterdam, he was strip-searched and made to stand in line for three hours on leaving England, and he received the same treatment from German soldiers at the Dutch-Belgian frontier. Passing the barbed-wire fences of the German border controls, he felt the cold reality of Europe's war. It was like entering "a land of imprisonment." The Belgians were "surrounded by a ring of steel and utterly unable by any conceivable effort of their own to save themselves." On each lifeless street corner, Hoover saw a German soldier in a steel helmet and black hobnailed boots. He toured the remains of the Louvain library, and block after block of destroyed homes and buildings in Antwerp.[46]

The night before Hoover arrived in Brussels, Brand Whitlock sat before the great fireplace in Emile Francqui's drawing room on Avenue Louise in Brussels. Francqui gave the ambassador a lengthy description of Hoover's character, summing it up by tracing an arc with his finger below his own double chin: *"Une mâchoire, vous savez."* A jaw, you know.[47]

Whitlock, a literary man who prior to the outbreak of war had expected to write four novels during his quiet posting in Belgium, had trouble reconciling Francqui's gesture with the anxious figure in blue serge who arrived in his office the next day and sank into a chair. Apart from the strong jaw, he saw nothing else that might distinguish Hoover as a man of force. His hands and feet were unusually small. His smooth-shaven face had a youthful air. It was "not at all the face of the sanguine type of business man, but a face sensitive, with a delicate mouth, thin lips, a face that wore a weary expression, as of one who dispensed too much nervous force and was always tired." His eyes were dark and scowling when he spoke of the problems of relief; they turned soft and pitying when he spoke of the plight of the Belgians. His voice was dull whatever the subject. Hoover also seemed to have lost his comb. Whitlock decided he was a splendid type of American businessman: able, positive, direct, and uncouth.[48]

A third of Brussels's population was receiving free food at more than a hundred canteens set up by the Comité Central and supplied by the CRB. Ration cards entitled the bearer to coffee, soup, and bread. On the cold, wet morning of December 1, Whitlock took Hoover to the street outside a theater that had been converted to a canteen in the Quartier des Marolles. They saw hundreds of Belgians shivering silently in the breadline, some of them wearing wooden shoes, all of them holding bowls or pitchers, not a smile among them. Hoover noted how the recipients whispered *"Merci"* as they took their food and shuffled off into the rain.[49]

Whitlock kept his eyes on Hoover throughout the visit and saw him turn away and stare off down the street rather than share his feelings. Whitlock understood Hoover's reaction as simple reticence. Others witnessing the same sort of behavior found it disturbing. They noticed how Hoover obsessed over the logistics of food distribution while avoiding interaction with recipients of relief and thought him a bloodless man. "He told of the work in Belgium as coldly as if he were giving statistics of production," said a U.S. official. "From his words and his manner he seemed to regard human beings as so many numbers. Not once did he show the slightest feeling."[50]

Hoover's reticence was chronic. He was the sort of man who could sit for three hours on a train with his closest colleagues and not utter a single word, or bid farewell to his wife, not expecting to see her again for several months, in a curt telegram: "Goodbye. Love, Bert." It was often difficult to know if his behavior was due to bad manners, callousness, anxiety, or an effort to manage powerful emotions, because he was capable of all of these things. Indeed, a few days after he averted his eyes from the breadline, he wrote, "It is difficult to state the position of the civil population of Belgium without becoming hysterical." The sight of ragged and hungry children had especially bothered him, and he soon inaugurated a program of daily hot meals of bread and cocoa at Belgian schools.[51]

Returning to London on December 3 with visions of breadlines fresh in his mind, Hoover worked his cabinet contacts with new vigor. To his surprise, he gained an appointment with Prime Minister Asquith the very next day.

# CHAPTER 8

# A Pirate State
# Organized for Benevolence

Herbert Henry Asquith was an urbane man of sixty-two with messy white hair and a well-earned reputation for decency and caution in politics. He liked to transact his official business with great speed, leaving plenty of time for reading, his mistress, and bridge. He opened his meeting with Herbert Hoover by saying that he was unsympathetic to the CRB and that he felt no moral or legal obligation to feed the Belgians. The duty was Germany's, and he considered it a "monstrous idea" that Britain should "simply fill the vacuum created by German requisitions."[1]

Hoover was not surprised by Asquith's position. He had spent his whole journey to and from Belgium formulating his response. He lunged at the prime minister without preliminaries. He lectured him on the condition of the Belgian people and leveled accusations and warnings at his government:

> I pointed out that the civil population had been brought to this pass through the action of the British [blockade]; that if the British claim that they were fighting the war on behalf of Belgium were true, they would be unable to substantiate this claim in history if they prevented others from saving the Belgian population from decimation by starvation or through slaughter arising out of starvation riots; that although the British Government refuses to give us assistance, it dare not put an end to our shipment of foodstuffs from America into

Belgium if it wished to hold one atom of American public esteem. . . . I was convinced that the Germans would not feed the Belgians, and that they must certainly starve unless the activities of our Commission continued.[2]

By Whitlock's account, Hoover went further still, cautioning the prime minister that the American people sympathized with the Allies only out of pity for the suffering Belgians, and threatening to send a letter to the American press damning England for letting Belgium starve.[3]

Asquith, taken aback, told his visitor that he was unaccustomed to being addressed in such tones. Hoover gave a halfhearted apology, explaining that his concern for the Belgians and the dire future that awaited them if the prime minister offered no assistance more than justified his manner and emotion. Asquith turned conciliatory, perhaps only to escape the meeting. "You told me you were no diplomat," he said to his guest, "but I think you are an excellent one, only your methods are not diplomatic."[4]

Hoover left Asquith's office empty-handed. The prime minister may have softened his position, but the cabinet was still opposed to relieving its enemy of the burden of feeding an occupied people. As the year 1914 came to a close, the CRB was spending over $6 million a month in food and transportation, and running a monthly deficit of more than $2 million. A sharp increase in global food prices was driving up costs, and the proliferation of mines and submarines was scaring off shipowners. Hoover was working from early morning until late at night in his London headquarters, eating meals at his desk. "How long I can go on building up this financial air-castle I do not know," he wrote a friend, fearing it was all about to collapse. He began pledging the remains of his personal wealth as security against food purchases, a move his colleagues told him was reckless.[5]

When he signed up for the Belgian relief, Hoover had asked his wife if she supported his decision. She knew the question was a formality and gave her approval, although she often wondered afterward what he would have done if she had told him that adequate care of his wife and children was his first duty. Hoover did not see Herbert Jr. and

Allan for eleven months after October 1914. Once Lou had the boys settled in California, she herself returned to London and did not see them for half a year, an eternity in their young lives.

Before leaving America, Lou did a remarkable thing of her own. Aware of the risks of transatlantic travel in wartime, and understanding that London was a more dangerous place than neutral America, she took measures to provide for her children in the event that something happened to their parents, and she did so without consulting her husband. Jackson Reynolds had been a classmate of both Hoovers, although he was closer to Lou, whom he always considered one of the most brilliant women he had ever met. A former star halfback of the Stanford football team, he had paid his way through college working at the library during the school year and summers on a ranch where he gained a reputation for being able to pitch more hay than any other two men in the county. He had gone on to teach law at Columbia University and was now a New York railway lawyer. Lou wrote him the day before she sailed for England:

> I am doing the very inconsiderate thing of leaving you a present of my boys, if anything should "happen" to Bert and me, that we could not go on assuming our responsibility for them ourselves—and of doing it without first asking your permission.
>
> That is because I don't really expect anything to happen.
>
> But of course if there should, I want them to have the best care and guidance that is possible for them, - and I don't know anyone whose judgment I would trust as far in those matters as yours. Bert, I am sure, would agree with me. For while we have not discussed you in this relation, - we have in others— and we come to the same opinion.
>
> Of course I do not ask you to take them into your home and father and mother them. That is too much to ask of anyone. But do direct their education and let them see enough of you to get your ideals of the world.[6]

Lou explained that her own father was too old to take care of her children, that her sister had married a thoroughly impractical man, and that while brother-in-law Theodore was acceptable, his wife, owing to certain "negative tendencies," was not. Reynolds, she believed, was her best shot at raising "brave, true, honest boys." She wanted them to have a few years of outdoor life in the West and a few years at a big school in the East. She gave Reynolds a list of family friends and suggested ways in which they might be useful. She recommended Herbert's cousin, Harriette Miles, as "the sanest and best influence over boys of our folk," adding that her health was not strong.[7]

Lou was not sure how much money would be available to her sons—perhaps a great deal, and in any event she had put aside enough in accounts in New York and California to ensure their education. She asked Reynolds not to let them get "a money measure" for all the affairs of life. "The ambition to do, to accomplish, irrespective of its measure in money or fame, is what should be inculcated," she declared.*[8]

Reynolds must have found it odd that his friend would offer up her children without consulting her husband, and Lou did not explain why she was acting unilaterally. There is nothing in her instructions on how to raise the boys that Bert would have found objectionable. (Indeed, he might have made a personal motto out of "the ambition to do.") Perhaps he did not share her opinion of Reynolds, or her doubts about his own family. It may be that she wrote the letter on an impulse before leaving port and did not have time to inform Bert of her intentions, or that she was simply exercising her independent mind.

Obviously concerned about her impending journey, Lou also wrote Herbert Jr. a long middle-of-the-night letter telling him that while she expected to return, "one never can tell in this world of ours when it is going to be time for us to stop being as we are, and to begin in another way." This ominous sentiment was followed with twenty pages of spiritual guidance. Lou told her son that while she believed in the existence of God, it was foolish to spend time trying to know him: "If he had wanted us to know he would have made it quite plain and simple." She believed in praying for strength, and in an immortal soul. She held that each individual soul has a different fate: the souls of lazy,

---

* Jackson Eli Reynolds, who counted Franklin Roosevelt among his least esteemed law students, would go on to argue the famous Reading antitrust suit before the Supreme Court. Still later, according to *Time* magazine (November 5, 1934), he cut "an awesome figure astride the highest peak in the mountain range of Morgan banks."

useless people would probably sleep through the afterlife. The souls of helpful people would go on being helpful. And if at any time in his life Herbert Jr. needed help, he had only to pray and his mother's soul would be available to him. "And that's what I want you to be perfectly sure about me. I know that if I should die, I can pray my soul to go over to my two dear little boys and help and comfort their souls."[9]

Lou did not once mention the boy's father amid all this spiritual reassurance. This omission, together with her recruitment of Reynolds as guardian, suggests another explanation for her letters: her solitary experience of parenting. While Lou might have preferred a different balance of priorities in Bert, she nevertheless understood his nature, and she remained loyal to him. In this same flurry of prevoyage letters, she wrote her "dear darling little Allan" that "you and I both said it was right for me to go and take care of our dear Daddy, who is so kind to us, and who has to stay over there in England and work so hard. And so I am going to be very cheerful about it even if I am very unhappy about it inside me."[10]

Allan wrote back, "Tell Daddy I want to see him again soon and live with him too."[11]


Bert and Lou were together amid the Gothic spires of Brussels for Christmas. Passing the German ministry in the company of Whitlock, Bert noticed trees in the windows and suggested wryly that they should be decorated with bayonets.

"I admire this man Hoover," Whitlock told his journal, "who has a genius for organization and for getting things done, and beneath all, with his great intelligence, he has a wonderful human heart." Whitlock wrote his new friend in early January:

> I am sorry you were not here on that New Year's Day for something very beautiful occurred. Spontaneously, quietly, all day long, a stream of Belgians poured into the Legation leaving cards and signing names in a little book that Baron Lambert provided. Over three thousand in all, to express their thanks for what America has done, all sorts and conditions of men, from noblemen whose cards bore high titles, down to the poorest woman from the slums, who had carefully writ-

ten her name on a bit of pasteboard, the edges of which still showed the traces of the scissors. It was very touching, very moving, and I want you to know of it, for you have done so much more than any of us to help them.[12]

Pleased as he would have been by this story from Whitlock, Hoover knew that unless he could relieve the financial pressures on the CRB, its efforts to relieve Belgium would soon be at an end. He refocused his attentions on the Asquith government. If a subsidy was out of the question, perhaps some other form of support was available. He scheduled a January 21 meeting with Lloyd George. He wanted the Chancellor of the Exchequer to permit people outside of Belgium to send money to individuals inside the country so that they could pay for their food, lightening the burden on the CRB. Even this small maneuver would require an exception to the blockade, and Lloyd George initially did not bite. Hopes of a short war had faded, he said, and the conflict was now bound to be decided in the long term by economic attrition. Britain wanted to starve the enemy into submission, and any food or money flowing into Belgium could find its way to Germany, increasing its economic stamina. The minister was not concerned that Belgians might starve. If that were to happen, he said, Germany would have no choice but to feed them.

Hoover was prepared for Lloyd George's objections. Having failed to bully the prime minister, he tried reason on the Exchequer. For fifteen minutes, Hoover spoke flawlessly, not a word out of place, one hand gesturing and the other jingling change in his pocket. He reminded Lloyd George that Great Britain had entered the war with the "avowed purpose of protecting the existence of small nations," and suggested that it would be a hollow victory over Germany if Belgium were "extinguished in the process." He denied that the Germans had seized or would seize any CRB food (when in fact he knew they had taken much). He pointed to reports of starvation in German-occupied Northern France as evidence that Berlin would be indifferent to suffering Belgians. He raised again the support of Americans for the Belgians.[13]

Hoover also told Lloyd George that the CRB's work was of significant strategic advantage to the Allies. The Belgians were as yet refusing to operate their mines, factories, and railways, or to collaborate in any other way with their occupiers. They would continue to assert their independence so long as there was food on the table. Supporting the CRB was thus the smartest military expenditure the Allies could make. Lloyd George's reaction startled Hoover. "I am convinced," he said. "You have my permission." He instructed his staff to work out the details and told Hoover that "the world will yet be indebted to the American people for the most magnanimous action which neutrality has yet given way to." Lloyd George was later quoted as saying that Hoover's presentation was the clearest he had heard on any subject. While there is no reason to doubt this, the Exchequer's change of heart was likely influenced as well by his government's dependence on American money and arms, which was deepening as the war dragged on.[14]

Hoover was relieved to win this narrow exception to the blockade but there were two problems with it. He still required a gigantic subsidy if he was going to balance the CRB's books, and he also knew that the exception could be pulled from him at any time. Indeed, he worried that it might be pulled immediately. Coincidental with his triumph, Berlin, anxious about its own economic stamina, imposed a war indemnity on Belgium of 40 million francs a month. The captors were now milking the captives to subsidize their military, as Lloyd George had suspected would happen. Hoover's first thought was that he would not get another farthing from the British. How could they justify pumping resources into Belgium when the Germans were pumping them out? Berlin's move, however, had an unanticipated effect on the Asquith government.

Shortly after his conversation with Lloyd George, Hoover was pulled aside by Sir Edward Grey, who suggested that if the CRB could persuade Berlin to change its mind about the war indemnity, the cabinet would consider itself "under the obligation of supporting the Commission" by way of a subsidy. The British feared that the German money grab was the first stroke in a larger initiative to integrate Belgium into its war effort. They were coming to believe that the power of the Belgians to resist the Germans was directly related to their food supply, the very point Hoover had made to Lloyd George. Taking up Grey's challenge, Hoover packed his bags for Berlin.[15]

·  ·  ·

Hoover left London on January 26 intending to cross the channel to Holland but changed his mind on the train and returned to the city to inform U.S. secretary of state William Jennings Bryan by cable that he was headed for Berlin on CRB business. Despite having no diplomatic standing, Hoover brazenly instructed the secretary to speak with the German ambassador to the United States about the importance of the CRB's work. Specifically, he wanted Bryan to tell the ambassador that the CRB was conferring "a vast advantage" to Berlin by preventing an uprising of starving Belgians and by convincing the Allies to absorb the expense of feeding the population. This, of course, was opposite to what Hoover had told Lloyd George. It also ran contrary to official American policy, which was to regard the CRB as a neutral humanitarian operation.[16]

It is difficult to say which side Hoover honestly believed was benefiting from the CRB's activities in Belgium.* It is clear from his actions that he did not much care. While his letters indicate that his private sympathies were with the Allies, his only loyalty as a neutral American was to Belgium; his job, as he saw it, was to keep 7.5 million people from being crushed between the German and British war machines. To accomplish that, he needed a subsidy, and he would wield whatever arguments were necessary to obtain one. Questions of military strategy and good faith in negotiations were secondary.

Hoover arrived in Berlin intending to "besiege the German government at the top directly and on all fronts," and he succeeded in meeting countless officials, including the finance minister, the foreign minister, and, ultimately, Theobald von Bethmann Hollweg, chancellor of the German Empire. At each opportunity, he repeated his contention that the CRB's efforts gave Germany a military advantage worth a great deal more than the 40 million francs a month that the occupier was squeezing from Belgium. He not only asked the government to drop the indemnity, he wanted Berlin to publicly state that it would do so only if the British financed the relief. He led the German officials to believe that aid to Belgium was so unpopular within

---

* His brother, Theodore, tended to side with the British Admiralty on the military impact of the CRB: "As a cold-blooded proposition in the strategy of the World War the Belgian Relief Commission may have been a mistake." (Theodore Hoover, "Statement of an Engineer," Herbert Hoover Presidential Library and Museum.)

the Asquith government that the CRB might be compelled to cease operations any day, leaving Berlin to deal with a nation of starving Belgians.[17]

Sadly for Hoover, the fate of his mission was to be decided by the tall, dashing figure of His Excellency von Bethmann Hollweg, the same man who at the outset of the war had famously dismissed Germany's guarantee of Belgian neutrality as "a scrap of paper." They met at 6 p.m. on February 7. Bethmann Hollweg told Hoover that he was grateful for the CRB's work but said "at once with emphasis" that German public opinion demanded the indemnity, and international law allowed for such measures in support of an occupying army. With a hint of desperation, Hoover reminded the chancellor that Germany benefited from Washington's neutrality and could not afford to have these issues tried in the court of American public opinion. Bethmann Hollweg snorted that the United States was already selling arms to the Allies and that it would continue to do so, ensuring a protracted war. He had nothing to fear from American opinion. Hoover tried a last-ditch appeal to Bethmann Hollweg's humanity, but that only brought more complaints about the barbarity of the British blockade. The Germans did discuss with Hoover the notion of a large loan to the Belgians on complicated and unattractive terms. That, and a headful of disagreeable impressions of wartime Berlin, was all the CRB chairman took back to London.[18]

On his return, Hoover brooded over what he had seen in Germany. All of the officials and many of the civilians had been in uniform, and he could remember one instance of laughter during the whole of his ten-day trip. He had felt himself amid "the Spartans of Europe." Any lingering hopes of a short war, he believed, were folly. As each month passed, the combatants had dug deeper into their trenches, reinforcing their positions with concrete, steel, and wire, supplementing their machine guns and mortars with flamethrowers, chemical weapons, and massive howitzers capable of lobbing powerful shells with fearsome accuracy. They were stockpiling enough artillery at certain battle sites to pound each other with 100 shells a minute for six months on end. Worse, the conflict was spreading in every direction, to the Mediterranean, the Middle East, Africa, Asia, and the Pacific. It was being fought on land, at sea, underwater, and in the air. Sixty-five million Europeans would wear uniforms, and their blood would mingle in the mud and water with that of young men from four other continents.[19]

Hoover knew the war was unusual in historical terms. It was not army meeting army in columns and squares on some distant plain. Entire economies had been redirected to military aims, entire populations were mobilized to arm, feed, and otherwise supply their warriors, and entire societies were living under siege. The Allied blockade, by denying food to the Central Powers, projected hatred into German homes with every meal. Germany, with its submarine attacks on merchant ships and its Zeppelin raids on British cities, was indiscriminately killing women and children. There was mass privation and extreme animus on both sides. Total war, he realized, engendered total hate. Negotiation and compromise were out of the question: too much had been lost on both sides, and nothing short of total victory could justify the horrible sacrifices made by the combatants.[20]

Hoover got a firsthand glimpse of some of those sacrifices on a later visit to German general staff headquarters in Northern France:

> We motored for several hours to a point near a hilltop observation post in the forest, a distance back from the forward trenches and a mile or two away from the main roads. During the last few miles an occasional shell cracked nearby but the ingenious camouflage of the road . . . seemed to give protection to our route. At the post the constant rumble of artillery seemed to pulverize the air. Seen through powerful glasses, in the distant view laid the unending blur of trenches, of volcanic explosions of dust which filled the air where over a length of sixty miles a million and a half men were fighting and dying. Once in a while, like ants, the lines of men seemed to show through the clouds of dust. Here, under the thunder and belching volcanoes of 10,000 guns, over the months of this battle, the lives of Germans and Englishmen were thrown away. On the nearby road unending lines of Germans plodding along the right side of the front, not with drums and bands, but in the silence of sodden resignation. Down the left side came the unending lines of wounded men, the "walking cases," staggering among cavalcades of ambulances. A quarter of a million men died, and it was but one battle in that war.

The horror of it all did not in the least effect the German officers in the post. To them it was pure mechanics. . . . They said that the British were losing two to one—butting their heads against a stone wall. That was true. It was all a horrible, devastating reality, no romance, no glory.[21]

The barbarism he saw in Europe left Hoover wondering if civilization "has yet accomplished anything but enlarged ruthlessness in destruction of human life."[22]

Disheartening as it was to have his humane entreaties for Belgian relief rejected in the highest offices of the great warring nations, Hoover gained clarity from the encounters. He returned to London in a different frame of mind. He had a new measure of the fear and desperation that gripped the leadership on both sides, and he saw plainly that appealing to the better natures of the governments would only try their patience. Henceforth, he would downplay the humanitarian dimensions of his mission and manipulate the fears of the great powers to force their hands.

On February 15, Hoover reported to the British Foreign Office on his meeting with Bethmann Hollweg. He exaggerated the generosity and workability of Berlin's offer of a loan to the Belgians. As he expected, the British were immediately concerned that the desperate captives might throw themselves into the arms of the enemy. It would be a diplomatic coup for Bethmann Hollweg to be seen as the savior of a country he had so recently sacked. It would raise Germany in the eyes of neutral nations, especially America, while the Asquith government, having failed to act, would lose international prestige. This was a risk Britain could not afford to take as its dependence on America escalated.

Two days after his meeting at the Foreign Office, on a Wednesday afternoon, Hoover received a call from Lloyd George who said that the cabinet would meet at noon the next day to consider feeding the Belgians, and that while Churchill and Kitchener remained "very much opposed, on military grounds," the Exchequer was now agreeable. He wanted Hoover to write him a comprehensive memo to use against his fellow ministers. "He stated that I should make it as vigorous and as strong as possible, and to approach the subject as though our work were about to be suppressed, and to put any arguments in which would meet such a proposal," wrote Hoover in a CRB memorandum.[23]

Three hours later, Lloyd George had in his hands a powerfully worded document containing all of the arguments in Hoover's arsenal. Without a continuation of relief, he had written, the Belgians would be decimated: "Except for the breadstuffs imported by the Commission there is not one ounce of bread in Belgium today." The Germans had refused to feed its occupied peoples before, and "it was perfectly clear and confirmed" that they would do so again. The British people had embarked upon "the greatest war of their history" to defend Belgian neutrality, which entailed protecting its citizens from starvation. Relief was of no military advantage to Germany; rather, it assisted the Allies by encouraging the passive resistance of Belgium. Finally, "I cannot too strongly emphasize the fact that should this relief work fail to receive the sympathy and support of the English people, it would have a most serious bearing on the whole attitude of public sentiment in the United States."[24]

The cabinet met on February 18, after which Lloyd George cheerfully informed Hoover that His Majesty's Government had agreed to recommend to its French ally a joint subvention of almost $5 million per month in the form of nominal loans to the exiled Belgian government, with the money intended for support of the CRB. "You have made a good fight," Lloyd George told Hoover, "and deserve to win out."[25]

Interestingly, the cabinet had decided against directly subsidizing the CRB. Loaning the money to the Belgian government-in-exile rather than granting it to Hoover allowed Lloyd George to bypass the House of Commons and keep the whole matter under wraps. The government was not keen on a public debate on the advisability of diverting scarce resources to German-occupied territory. That was fine with Hoover, who did not want Berlin to think that the English were anxious about the Belgians, which would only result in rougher treatment for the captives. He and Lord Grey went so far as to pretend in publicly released correspondence that the cabinet had rejected a subsidy.[26]

With five months of work, Hoover had secured the immediate

financial future of what was by then the largest relief organization the world had known. Roughly $1.8 million worth of food was being purchased weekly from America, Australia, and the Argentine. Hoover had a fleet of several dozen cargo vessels skimming back and forth over the oceans, in addition to six hundred tugs and barges operating on the canals of Holland and Belgium. He oversaw a hundred volunteers in his London office and tens of thousands of volunteer fund-raisers from Spain to Canada, and the monies collected were distributed equitably in shattered Belgium by another forty thousand volunteers. In 1915, at the request of desperate French citizens caught behind the Western Front, Hoover expanded the CRB's operations to include 2 million people of Northern France, bringing his total client base above 9 million, spread over twenty thousand square miles.[27]

The scope and powers of the CRB were mindboggling. Its shipping fleet flew its own flag. Its members carried special documents that served as CRB passports. Hoover himself, after his first round of strip searches, was granted a form of diplomatic immunity by all belligerents, with the British permitting him to cross the Channel at will and the Germans providing him a document stating: "This man is not to be stopped anywhere under any circumstances." Perhaps no other individual in the world moved so easily across enemy lines during the Great War. Hoover had privileged access to generals, diplomats, and ministers. He enjoyed personal contacts with the heads of warring governments. He negotiated treaties with the belligerents, advised them on policy, wrote letters that they released under their own signatures, and delivered private messages among them. Great Britain, France, and Belgium would soon be turning over to him $150 million a year, enough to run a small country, and taking nothing for it beyond his receipt. He did all this as a sovereign agent, with minimal input from the State Department. As one British official observed, Hoover was running "a piratical state organized for benevolence." Whitlock, in Brussels, put it another way: the CRB "is one of the modern wonders of the world, if there are any more wonders in this world."[28]

Hoover's accomplishments naturally attracted the attention of newspapermen, exciting his usual ambivalence about the press. He wanted the attention. He reveled in public approbation, and he relied on coverage to promote his fund-raising efforts and to pressure the belligerents into cooperating with his relief plans, but he also wanted to be noticed on his own terms. He was furious when a CRB publicity release mentioned his past business associations: "I see no occasion to advertise Bewick, Moreing at my expense." He was mortified when stories exaggerated his adventures in the Boxer uprising and tried to present him as a warm and folksy character. Fearing for his dignity and reputation, he insisted that Lou give interviews to set the record straight. She gamely informed a reporter for the *San Francisco Bulletin* that her husband, in fact, had not been a war hero in China.[29]

Washington was also interested in this new man, Hoover. The State Department began to compile a dossier on him, a development his suspicious mind worked up into an effort to discredit him. He managed to pack a jumble of wounded, contemptuous, humble, and arrogant sentiments into a short letter of response to a government contact:

> It is really difficult for me to take the matter seriously for I want nothing from the President or anyone else in this World except my good name amongst men. As to my social standing, I have broken bread with lawyers, engineers, Earls, Viscounts, plain Knights, Chevaliers, Prime Ministers and ex-Prime ministers, Members of Parliament, United States Senators, Congressmen, Editors of Newspapers, miners, porters, and sundry other persons. I regret that I have never organized these efforts into that Social Status which of course can only be evolved by close attention to the feminine side, shoots, hunts, balls, dinners and so forth. As you know, on the contrary, I have preferred a modest existence and with my off-time devoted to literary work.[30]

He added that with an income of $100,000 a year, he could pay his bills.

Proud as he was of the launch of the CRB and much as he enjoyed his growing international stature, Hoover knew that it was still hanging by a thread. The winning of a subsidy in no way guaranteed the future of the organization. Hardly a week went by without him feeling that the whole edifice was about to crash.

One major threat came in the person of His Excellency, Baron von Bissing, a seventy-year-old Prussian with a hard, leathery face, piercing dark eyes, and a long saber banging against his thin legs. He was governor general of Belgium, and it irked him to see American relief workers dashing around Brussels receiving salutes and cheers from the same Belgian people who treated their occupiers with open contempt. Von Bissing believed that the CRB permitted the Belgians to avoid work, leaving it to the German army to operate civil services and keep order in the country. Just as Hoover was getting his finances sorted out, the governor general decided to assert his authority. He would bring the Belgians to heel by seizing control of Hoover's relief effort.[31]

Von Bissing demanded that the number of CRB delegates in Belgium be reduced and that they be replaced with his own appointees. Hoover protested that the British only permitted his food purchases through the blockade because they trusted the CRB to ensure its distribution to qualified recipients. Regardless, Von Bissing began to impose restrictions on CRB operatives. An enraged Hoover went over the governor general's head to Berlin, threatening to withdraw from Belgium if his freedom of movement was not reinstated. Calculating the cost in international standing and the expense of provisioning the Belgians itself, Germany relented, and Hoover kept control of his organization, something the Red Cross was not able to do in Belgium.[32]

The ruthless von Bissing would soon find another way around his problem, one that Hoover was powerless to prevent. He rounded up and forcibly deported 58,432 Belgians to German factories and munitions plants. He press-ganged another 62,155 to work in France and Belgium, some of them building trenches and roads at the front lines.[33]

Elements of the British government also continued to take a dim view of the CRB. Hardly a month went by without the Foreign Office raising objections to Hoover's operations. He was instructed to stop shipping emergency clothing to Belgium when the British learned that Germany was seizing all raw or manufactured wool in occupied lands, and his shipments of canned condensed milk were protested on the grounds that they provided tin to the enemy. Charges that Germany was sneaking food out of Belgium were constant, and often accurate. Hoover had knowledge, for instance, that Belgian peasants

were growing oats instead of wheat because the Germans would pay
more for oats.[34]

It was the Admiralty, however, that most wanted the CRB out
of business. Hoover had blown a hole in the blockade of German-
controlled ports that its officers were at pains to close. After several
failed attempts to stop the relief shipments, and an aborted effort to
convince the CRB to gather intelligence of German military operations on its behalf, the Admiralty hit on a new line of attack: it would
investigate and attempt to discredit Herbert Hoover. Allegations
were brought that Hoover had an unsavory background, and that
he was aiding the enemy through his German business connections.
The Foreign Office was compelled to launch an inquiry, a judge was
appointed, and Hoover, outraged and humiliated, was compelled to
testify. The scrutiny triggered his paranoia. Convinced that his opponents were being fed information by a former employee, Hoover
hired a spy in New York to follow the man, whom he insisted was
mentally unstable, an accusation he would throw at enemies, real or
imagined, with regularity. The judge cleared Hoover of any wrongdoing, but the Admiralty would continue to be an obstacle throughout his thirty-month run at the CRB.[35]

Hoover's ability to maintain the Belgian relief in the face of
powerful adversaries, under the ever-darkening clouds of suspicion
and enmity, is testament to the soundness of his initial strategy. The
massive scale of the CRB and its monopoly over the flow of food
into Belgium shielded it from the bullying and manipulation of the
great powers. Messing with the CRB's chairman meant messing with
the fate of 7.5 million Belgians, something Hoover had understood
intuitively when he insisted on consolidating all relief efforts at the
outset. The neutrality of the CRB and its high public profile—two
other features insisted upon by Hoover—afforded further protections. Although the structure of the CRB was improvised in the early
weeks of the war, and suggested (or at least encouraged) by his personal quirks and imperious management style, it was built to last. The
credit is due Hoover, whose vision and experience enabled him to
foresee the demands of industrial-scale humanitarianism in an age of
industrialized global war.

.   .   .

Perversely, given the might of his external opponents, it was his partners in the Belgian relief who frustrated Hoover the most. Not long after he had stabilized the CRB's finances, the once coopera-tive Comité Central in Brussels decided it was competent to run the relief without American involvement. For the better part of a year, Hoover and Emile Francqui engaged in a near-psychotic quarrel for preeminence in the relief cause. They accused each other of ambition, corruption, and deceit, and both of them threatened to resign if they did not get their way. Hoover at one point talked of laying a train of powder to blow up Francqui, and at another threatened to train a machine gun on the "glory hunting Belgian pinheads." The infight-ing drove Ambassador Whitlock to despair. It was a needless distrac-tion at a time when the Germans were menacing the independence of the CRB and conducting slave raids on the Belgian population.[36]

Eustace Percy, the Foreign Office staffer with responsibility for policy toward Belgium, shared Whitlock's dismay. An incredibly adept young diplomat, Percy happened to believe in the relief, unlike many of his colleagues. He made a personal project of trying to resolve mat-ters between Hoover, whom he liked and admired, and Francqui. In late November 1916 he offered Hoover a friendly warning:

> If, by any action of yours, you make it more difficult at this eleventh hour for America to act a part in preventing the destruction which threatens to follow upon the growth of German despair, you will lessen, instead of save, the dignity of America. Every sign points to a new campaign of frightfulness on the part of Germany: a campaign which is going to bring upon Belgium sufferings all the more bitter and overwhelm-ing because they come at the very moment of reviving hope; and I ask you all with confidence to make greater sacrifices than ever in order that you may not be drawn into the great-est sacrifice of all, namely the sacrifice of your position as the advance guard and symbol of the sense of responsibility of the American people towards Europe.[37]

It was a brilliant note, appealing all at once to Hoover's good nature, self-interest, fears, dignity, and patriotism. It was as though Percy had studied every aspect of the man's vanity and vulnerability and crafted the best possible paragraph to pull him from the brink of self-destruction. He played Hoover as well as Hoover had ever been played, and failed.

The battle between Hoover and Francqui raged on until the end of December, when the Belgian finally relented. The warring champions of relief met at the Savoy in London and aired their differences. They came to terms, but not before Francqui had accused Hoover of using a sledgehammer to kill gnats, and Hoover had replied that he would "use a pile driver to kill a malarial mosquito." They agreed to maintain relations between the CRB and Francqui's Comité much as they were before their dispute.[38]

Before long, yet another internal fracas came dangerously close to ending Hoover's reign at the CRB and ruining his standing in American public life. Lindon Bates was an engineer and a close personal friend of Hoover employed as vice chairman in the CRB's New York office. He had been making speeches on the noble cause of Belgium, saying nothing that Hoover himself had not said but neglecting to mention his chairman by name in his remarks. Reporters were left with the impression that Bates and the New York office were largely responsible for the commission's success. Hoover seized upon a *Saturday Evening Post* story of August 1915 and fired a long and intemperate letter to Bates enumerating "46 absolute untruths and 36 half-truths" in the article. He accused his colleague of being an attention seeker and prohibited the New York office from doing further publicity. The wounded Bates marched off to the U.S. State Department and the Justice Department to charge Hoover with criminal transgression of the Logan Act, a piece of legislation prohibiting American citizens from engaging in unauthorized negotiations with foreign governments.[39]

The charge of violating the Logan Act was not easily answered given the scope of Hoover's activities, his interventions in the affairs of Britain, Germany, France, and the Belgian government-in-exile, and specifically his efforts to establish work-for-food programs in Belgium, all of which might be viewed as breaches of American neutrality. Hoover first attempted to dismiss the complaint by using a pile driver on Bates personally. He claimed that his friend was an unreliable source and jealous of his authority. Relying again on ad hominem attacks, he said that Bates was deranged by the loss of his son, who had gone down with the *Lusitania* the previous May. The

Justice Department, however, was disinclined to reject the complaint on Hoover's testimony alone. He was forced to return to the United States in October to defend himself.

Lou Hoover was summering in California with her sons when the Bates controversy arose. She received an urgent cable from her husband asking her to come east while he crossed from London: "Developments make it absolutely necessary for me proceed New York. Expect leave here Sixteenth . . . Do not wish anyone to know of journey as do not wish to be bothered exterior interests. Expect remain one week."[40]

Although this message came three days after another informing Lou that Bert had no plans to visit America and wanted her to return to London as soon as possible, she dutifully rushed to New York with the boys to meet their father, whom they had not seen in almost a year. They caught up to him in Manhattan, with disappointing results. "New York was such a jumble," Lou told a secretary. "[Bert] spent his entire time on Belgium Commission business. I scarcely saw him, and never had time for a word or any other subject. The hotel sitting room always had 3 or 4 men there discussing that."[41]

After several days in New York, Hoover traveled to Washington and began a lobby in his own defense. His two most important contacts were Wilson confidant Colonel Edward House and Franklin Lane, secretary of the interior. Hoover relied primarily on an indignant plea that he was serving a noble cause, the Logan Act be damned. To that end, he coaxed his reliable London booster, Ambassador Page, to cable a personal reference describing him to the secretary of state, whose department was giving Hoover the most grief, as "the soul of intellectual integrity." Said Page:

> The Commission for the Relief of Belgium is Hoover and absolutely depends on Hoover who has personally made arrangements with the governments concerned and has carried these delicate negotiations through only because of his high character and standing and unusual ability. If he is driven to resign the Commission will instantly fall to pieces.[42]

Through Franklin Lane, Hoover gained a meeting with Woodrow Wilson on November 3, 1915. He was not unknown to the president. In the opening weeks of the war, Wilson had written to thank Hoover for his aid in the evacuation of Americans stranded overseas. Around the same time, Wilson had asked Lane for a dossier on the humanitarian engineer. Lane obliged, misinforming the president as to Hoover's age, his college education, the title of his Agricola book, and the name of his wife before confidently concluding: "There is no American sojourning abroad who has a higher financial, mining or social status than Mr. Herbert C. Hoover."[43]

It was a good time to visit the White House. The president was in the sweet spot of his tumultuous first term. He had been elected unexpectedly in 1912, the first Democratic president since Cleveland and the prime beneficiary of a cleavage in the Republican base caused by Theodore Roosevelt's launch of the Progressive Party, also known as the Bull Moose Party. Wilson's first year was impressive, producing tariff reforms, a federal farm loan act, a workman's compensation system, a ban on child labor, and the Federal Reserve System, among other measures. His wife of twenty-nine years, Ellen, died in the summer of 1914, and with her went much of the administration's momentum. The president admitted to Colonel House that he was broken in spirit and no longer fit to hold office. He wandered for six months in blind grief until giddily rebounding into the arms of the voluptuous widow Edith Galt. House soon came to believe his friend unworthy of office for entirely different reasons: "It seems the President is wholly absorbed in this love affair and is neglecting practically everything else."[44]

Wilson was ill cast in the role of lothario, looking and acting, as Roosevelt said, "like an apothecary's clerk."* Fifty-eight years old, thin and prissy, the president admitted to a "vague, conjectural personality" and a lack of "human traits and red corpuscles." He was nevertheless in love with Mrs. Galt, dancing little jigs and whistling "Oh, You Beautiful Doll" when he had her in mind, which was often. Cabinet officers and senior congressional figures complained of the besotted president's inaccessibility. He wrote her three times a day and eventually married her.[45]

---

* Roosevelt made a fetish of insulting Wilson, also calling him a "damned Presbyterian hypocrite" and a "Byzantine logothlete." (David Pietrusza, *1920: The Year of the Six Presidents.* New York: Basic Books, 2008, p. 61.)

By the fall of 1915, when Hoover and Bates were at odds, Wilson was clinging to the notion that the war was a European matter "whose causes cannot touch us." It was a precarious position, given that the fight had crashed American markets, upset American trade, and inflamed American citizens, who were providing funds and arms to the belligerents. Still, Wilson sought to keep his distance and assert the rights of neutral nations. Consistent with this pose, he was sympathetic to the predicament of the Belgians, victims of German aggression. Hoover had no problem convincing the president of the importance of the relief. After their meeting, Wilson wrote his fiancée:

> My most interesting interview to-day . . . has been with Mr. Herbert Hoover, the Chairman of the Belgian Relief Commission. I wish you could meet him. He is a real man. . . . He is an American mining engineer living in London—one of the very ablest men we have sent over there, and has devoted his great organizing gifts and a large part of his fortune, too, to keeping nine million people alive . . . so that he has become a great international figure. Such men stir me deeply and make me in love with duty![46]

Wilson issued a public statement of support for Hoover and the CRB, and the Bates controversy died. While it is likely true that Bates was disturbed by the loss of his son, Hoover's counterattack on his erstwhile colleague was vicious. His habit of resorting to discreditable measures to defend his actions and integrity had carried over from private affairs to public life.

It does not excuse his handling of the Bates matter to note that Hoover was not at his best in these months. He was working endless hours. He took no holidays or breaks. The intellectual and emotional loads of the relief were tremendous, and they took their toll. When Lou rejoined him in London toward the end of 1915, she noticed that he had developed a wheeze, accompanied by severe headaches, chronic ear abscesses, and throat problems. She also noticed changes in her husband's personality. She had always appreciated in him capacities for happiness—a "quaint whimsicality," a certain "sparkling spontaneity"—that no one else would ever claim to see. The previous

winter she had watched him stop on his way to work amid a heavy
London snowfall and roll a snowman. That part of him was now lost,
or at least buried deep beneath the surface by the strain of war and
command.[47]

Bates's defection was an anomaly in Hoover's administration. He
worked primarily with a small, handpicked circle of associates, most
of them younger men, many of them engineers or Americans. It was a
loose organization, surprisingly so for a man obsessed with efficiency.
"An organization isn't a chart," he liked to say, "it's a body of men."[48]

Although aloof from his associates at a personal level, he
impressed them with the integrity of his work and his passion for his
cause, and he commanded a high degree of loyalty. One journalist
credited Hoover with exercising a strange, mesmerizing, low-voltage
magnetism. A diplomat, after meeting him, said: "Somehow I feel like
doing what that man asked me to do."[49]

No one was more impressed with Hoover than Ambassador Page,
who wrote unprompted to President Wilson:

> Life is worth more, too, for knowing Hoover. But for him
> Belgium would now be starved, however generously people
> may have given food. He is gathering together and transport-
> ing and getting distributed $5,000,000 worth a month, with a
> perfect organization of volunteers, chiefly American. He has
> a fleet of thirty-five ships, flying the Commission's flag—the
> only flag that all belligerents have entered into an agreement
> to respect and to defend. He came to me the other day and
> said, "You must know the Commission is $600,000 in debt.
> But don't be uneasy. I've given my personal note for it. . . ."
> He's a simple, modest energetic little man who began his
> career in California and will end it in Heaven; and he doesn't
> want anybody's thanks.[50]

An equally high recommendation came from an unlikely source.
Lord Kitchener was a determined opponent of the CRB throughout the war, but in the spring of 1915 he summoned its chairman to
a meeting at the War Office. He asked if Hoover would renounce

his American citizenship and become a British subject. Hoover asked why. Kitchener replied that he wanted him to do a "great service" for the war effort. The Asquith government had been damaged by reports of a shortage of shells at the Western Front, a scandal that would soon shorten Kitchener's career. It was now proposing to give Hoover charge of its munitions production, perhaps as minister of munitions in a new cabinet department. The War Office thought he could fix the greatest industrial crisis Great Britain had ever faced. Hoover answered that he would like to help but would not renounce his citizenship: "I should soon lose my Yankee energy," he said. The conversation went no further. When Hoover mentioned the offer at the U.S. embassy, an astonished Ambassador Page told him he had thrown away a peerage, a notion that Hoover dismissed with a grunt.[51]

Hoover was capable of answering almost any proffered honor with a grunt, but it was always an eloquent grunt, far more so than Page could have known. It spoke for the welter of conflicting impulses that tortured Hoover: it reflected his altruistic belief that good works were their own reward; his ingrained Quaker conviction that the pursuit of personal glory was sinful; his acquired sense of noblesse oblige that required him to at least appear to work selflessly for the public good. At war with all this was his psychological need to collect his measure of acknowledgment and validation; his compulsion to advertise his deeds and rank and salary; his pride in belonging in the company of senators and chevaliers; his desire to reap the opportunities that flowed from making a difference. Complicating matters still more was Hoover's practical understanding that the first rule of self-promotion was to hide one's self-promotions.

The battle in Hoover's breast between humility and the desire for recognition, always a close fight, may have been tipped toward a grunt of refusal in the case of Kitchener's offer by another factor entirely. The British had always made Hoover feel inferior as an individual and a professional. He shielded himself with a sense of superiority as a free-born American and a self-made man. He held the British honors system, wasted on "noodle-headed" nonentities and other ornamental personages, in contempt.[52]

Over the years he would accept his share of honors, including a bushel of honorary degrees from the likes of Harvard, Princeton, Yale, and Oxford. When he rejected an accolade, as with Kitchener, he tended to let others know, thereby brokering a compromise between his warring parts.[53]

Over a mantel in the lunchroom of the CRB's London office was a placard reading THIS CANNOT GO ON FOR EVER. It ended for Hoover in early 1917 with Wilson's decision to enter the Great War. With his status as a neutral compromised, Hoover reluctantly handed the CRB over to Dutch and Spanish authorities.[54]

In thirty months, the CRB had spent $200 million and shipped 2.5 million tons of food. By the peace, the total relief distributed would amount to $865 million (the U.S. government eventually kicked in as much as $20 million a month), with only $4 million of the total going to administrative overhead, a detail in which Hoover took great pride. It was, as Lord Curzon remarked, "an absolute miracle of scientific organization. Every pound of food and supplies is accounted for."[55]

It is impossible to say what would have happened to the Belgian people under German occupation if Hoover had not founded and led the CRB. There would have been other relief efforts, certainly, but it is doubtful any of them would have had the scale and strength of Hoover's commission. It is possible that Germany might have decided to feed the Belgians if they began to starve. Its own population, however, was living on meager rations, averaging less than one thousand calories a day toward the end of the war, and there is no chance Berlin would have given Belgium food without demanding that its people commit to the German war effort. It is conceivable that the twentieth century's horrific string of man-made famines might have run through Belgium had the CRB not intervened.[56]

As Hoover made his exit from his commission, the *New York Times* surveyed the "machinery, the orderly plan, the large, wise humanity of the distribution of relief among the ruined populations of Northern France and Belgium" and proclaimed Hoover's leadership "the most splendid American achievement of the last two years." This was precisely the sort of acclaim Hoover needed as he now set his sights on President Wilson and his next move in the big game.[57]

# CHAPTER 9

# Make Way for the Almoner
# of Starving Belgium

Woodrow Wilson was not Herbert Hoover's type. Once, amid a search for a new Stanford president, Hoover had moaned about the candidacy of a classicist known to him as that "loud-mouthed Princetown [*sic*] professor." There were three strikes built into that short phrase. Hoover had never shaken his Quaker mistrust of loquacity. He was skeptical of the administrative capacities of career academics. And he loathed Princeton as a bastion of Eastern privilege and everything detestable in American college life. Wilson, orotund and patrician, a career professor and former president of Princeton, failed on all counts.[1]

Yet Hoover admired Wilson's intelligence and accomplishments, and was flattered by his attentions. The president's initial letter congratulating him on aiding Americans stranded in Europe had given Hoover a foot in the White House door, and he'd kept it there ever since, asking Wilson for occasional assistance with the Belgian relief and commenting, with or without invitation, on the conduct of U.S. foreign policy. Like most Americans, Hoover supported the president's early efforts to keep the nation out of war. He agreed that the proper international role of Americans was to avoid European entanglements, vindicate the rights of neutral nations, and do what they might to mitigate the barbarism of the belligerents.

Hoover and Wilson would form a long and productive relationship, and they would always be a curious pair. In some ways they were alike: both erudite and ambitious sons of ministers, hungry for power, tireless in its pursuit, jealous of their prestige, and difficult to know. In other ways they were not: East Coast versus West Coast, mining tunnels versus ivory towers, Wilson's long, lordly face against Hoover's flat block. All of this like and unlike produced a strange sort of harmony between them. Hoover was a hardened man of action who craved intellectual respectability. Wilson was a respected intellectual who admired "men on the make" and surprised opponents with his ruthlessness. Wilson wrote an important book about governance before taking up its practice; Hoover wrote an important book about mining after fifteen years in the field. Wilson was renowned for battling privilege and improving the quality of education at one of the country's oldest universities; Hoover had fought to promote academic excellence and to prevent privilege from rooting at a new institution.[2]

Generally they got along, but the one important limit to their compatibility was Hoover's reluctance to scale the higher reaches of Wilson's idealism. Hoover had nothing against high-mindedness, as any one of his sermons on the engineer as agent of social progress might demonstrate. He had ideals, and he admired ideals. Ideals, however, only took one so far. Their attraction intensified for Hoover in proportion to their attainability. Achievement was his highest good.

He understood this about himself. He laid out his philosophy of life in a brief, unpublished autobiographical fragment in 1916. "There is little importance to men's lives except the accomplishment they leave to posterity," he said. "When all is said and done, record of accomplishment is all that counts." This was not to say that the ends justified the means for Hoover: it mattered to him *how* things were done, and he would demonstrate more integrity in public life than he had in business. His point was that he wanted something to show for his efforts, something demonstrable and measurable. He held "the organization or administration of tangible institutions or constructed works" in highest regard. These were hard outcomes. Moral influence and thought leadership, he believed, were soft outcomes, always of "indeterminate" effect.[3]

Wilson, although occasionally pragmatic in pursuit of personal and political agendas, was a true idealist, genuinely believing that he could achieve "the destruction of every arbitrary power everywhere" and establish the "reality of equal rights between nations great and small." Like many idealists, Wilson lacked the executive temperament. He admitted to Lincoln Steffens that he preferred talking, listening, and thinking to making decisions, and that he often struggled to shut down his mind in order to act. These tendencies struck Hoover as problematic, even dangerous. He thought Wilson was lost in the clouds at critical moments on America's path to war.[4]

One of those moments had come on May 7, 1915, when Germany sank the unarmed ocean liner *Lusitania* off the coast of Ireland. The dead numbered 1,198, including 128 Americans. An outraged Hoover wanted a forthright response from the White House. He bombarded Ambassador Page and the president with what he admitted were "mighty long and possibly pretty crude" instructions on how to rally the neutral nations to answer the barbaric German "violations against life." Instead came Wilson's troubling address at Convention Hall in Philadelphia: "There is such a thing as a man too proud to fight. There is such a thing as a nation being so right that it does not need to convince others by force that it is right." The speech was savaged in the London press as an indulgence of cold-blooded murder.[5]

Hoover wrote the president that Americans in England were "filled with humiliation" at the interpretation of his remarks. While he did not believe the United States should go to war over the *Lusitania*, he begged that Wilson articulate a policy "which will not necessarily lead to war but which in its vigor might bring to an end at least some phases of these violations of international law and humanity." Wilson responded dismissively, thanking Hoover for his patriotism.[6]

It would require several months and several more attacks on unarmed ships before Wilson took a harder line with Germany. In the meantime, Berlin, anxious to keep the United States out of the conflict, halted U-boat attacks on unarmed passenger vessels. The president's patient approach seemed to have brought the desired result. While their differences remained, Hoover congratulated Wilson on his management of the crisis, showed him support and respect, and played the role of courtier with aplomb. He never betrayed impatience with Wilson in public or in person, and he privately flattered the president on his oratory and ideals. The task was no doubt eased by Hoover's conviction that Wilson was a great man. It also helped, in moments when his faith was tested, that Hoover needed Wilson. The more likely it became that the United States would go to war, the more Hoover wanted a role in the administration.

. . .

Hoover's many accomplishments as a miner, engineer, financier, author, and humanitarian had done nothing to slake his ambition. Nor had married life, fatherhood, or middle age. He continued to fret about his place in the world. His promise to his grandmother on leaving for college—"Thee will have cause to be proud of me someday"—still rang in his own ears.[7]

Like many a careerist, he kept in the back of his mind a well-thumbed book of prospects ranked by desirability and probability. Early in his CRB tenure, the presidency of Stanford had caught his eye. As he gloried in the warm glow of international recognition conferred by the Belgian relief, he reset his sites, imagining himself as material for high public office. His friends began picturing him in the White House. *Harper's Weekly* mentioned him as a potential vice-presidential nominee in 1916. Although Hoover dismissed the speculation, he had probably already weighed the presidency as a long-term goal. Again, audacity came easily to him.[8]

He began his campaign for a role in the U.S. war effort at an unseemly moment. In the fading weeks of 1916, Wilson was still determined to forge a peace. He had just won reelection on the slogan "He Kept Us Out of War." Hoover wished the president well but felt the odds on eventual U.S. mobilization were strong enough to warrant some preparedness on his own part. He signaled to associates to lobby on his behalf in Washington. Letters were dispatched to key figures in the administration noting Hoover's availability in the event that matters escalated. Articles began to appear in the press celebrating Hoover and the CRB's achievements, implicitly advertising his services.[9]

At the same time, the extended Hoover clan packed for home. Theodore and his wife returned to California at the end of 1916 after ten years in London. Lou and the children, who had returned to England as their father's work dragged on, followed several weeks later. It seemed the sensible thing to do with Zeppelins bombing London and, perhaps more alarming, the boys developing accents and behaving like proper English gentlemen. Bert, too, began spending more time stateside. He spent January and February of 1917 in Washington and New York. Officially, he was on a fund-raising tour for the CRB; unofficially, he was trying to insinuate himself further into national affairs and Wilson's circle. He used a well-publicized address to the New York Chamber of Commerce on February 1 to make his first serious effort to exert leadership in American political life.

Hoover's speech confronted one of the uncomfortable truths about the United States and the Great War: American business was getting rich off of Europe's woes. Firms were selling food and war materials to the combatants, loaning them money, and replacing the belligerents in foreign markets. The U.S. economy was booming and Europeans were bitter. America's "profits from misfortune" would only be justified, Hoover said, if the nation assumed "its burden towards the helpless in Europe." He closed with a fund-raising pitch for the CRB, calling it "the greatest work which America has ever undertaken in the name of humanity." The argument for American generosity toward Europe for reasons of humanitarianism and for the protection of American economic interests abroad was one Hoover would make repeatedly in the years ahead.[10]

He did not have to wait long for his chance to serve. The very day he spoke to the Chamber of Commerce, newspapers blared that Germany had answered Wilson's latest peace proposals with a declaration of unrestricted submarine warfare, promising to sink any vessel, belligerent or neutral, armed or not, in British waters and the Mediterranean. Berlin's wager was that its subs could starve England into submission before the United States could mobilize. So far as the press was concerned, the fight was on. Wilson, said to be "staggered" and "amazed" at Berlin's treachery in resuming submarine attacks, handed the German ambassador his passports on February 3 and spent the next eight weeks in what the press called "a twilight zone" between peace and war, hoping for some last-ditch opportunity to avoid the inevitable while watching helplessly as U-boats picked off U.S. and Allied merchant ships with ease and regularity.*[11]

---

* The public was ahead of Wilson on the war. Theater audiences, it was reported, were cheering "The Star-Spangled Banner" after this diplomatic break. The nation was "aflame with patriotism and joy," wrote the *New York Herald*. Added the *Tribune*: "At last, the United States of America is about to throw its might upon the side of the great

It was during this period that Colonel House asked Hoover to reflect on his observations of European mobilization and prepare a memorandum for the White House on the economic and logistical challenges facing a U.S. war effort. Hoover turned it around in less than a day. The memorandum was cool to the notion of raising a large American expeditionary force for deployment in Europe. Hoover recommended instead that the United States answer the Allies' real needs by sending them food, money, and ships. One of his more startling proposals was that the British blockade of Germany, which he had previously decried as inhumane and militarily counterproductive, be strengthened for reasons of military necessity. Hoover did not explain his change of heart beyond the claim of necessity. He told House that his revulsion at the policy remained intact. Hoover's boldest proposal was that a man of cabinet rank be appointed to run the U.S. war in Europe on President Wilson's behalf, operating for efficiency's sake outside of the usual ambassadorial and bureaucratic channels. He made it clear that he saw himself in this exalted role.[12]

House forwarded the memo to the president. "I think you will agree with most of his suggestions," he wrote, adding that if Wilson wanted a European war chief, Hoover was the best man available. Wilson forwarded the memo to Secretary of War Newton Baker, describing it as worthy of consideration. Hoover was summoned to the White House four days later for a private conference with Wilson. They discussed the needs of the Allies. Hoover ventured that food would be second only to military action as a factor in the outcome of the Great War. Wilson asked Hoover to return to Europe and study the economic organization and food policies on both sides of the lines. This conversation, together with a further talk with Secretary Lane, left Hoover convinced that the United States was going to fight and that he would be invited to oversee the nation's food supplies when the moment came.[13]

With passenger service suspended because of the U-boat campaign, Hoover returned to Europe on the *Antonio Lopez*, an ancient, reeking Spanish cargo steamer with a full sailing rig and livestock pens on its forward deck. By the time the vessel docked in Cadiz on

democracies of the world which are fighting a military autocracy." (*New York Tribune*, February 1, 1917; *New York Herald*, February 4, 1917.)

March 25, the world had convulsed again. Czar Nicholas II, Emperor and Autocrat of all the Russias, had abdicated after losing the support of his army. In Washington, Woodrow Wilson had been informed of the infamous Zimmerman Telegram—Germany's attempt to lure Mexico to its side with the promise of American territory. Hoover had just made his way from Cadiz through Paris to London when Wilson appeared before a special session of Congress to ask for a declaration of war.

It was an extraordinary address. Wilson, in his rich baritone, opened with a clear denunciation of Germany's unrestricted submarine warfare and an assertion of America's right to neutrality, and promptly ran away with himself. By the end of his 3,400 words, he had proclaimed that his people were entering "the most terrible and disastrous of all wars" with the monumental objective of liberating the world for all time from militarism and autocracy. The United States would fight "for democracy, for the right of those who submit to authority to have a voice in their own governments, for the rights and liberties of small nations, for a universal dominion of right by such a concert of free peoples as shall bring peace and safety to all nations and make the world itself at last free."[14]

While Congress voted overwhelmingly to give the president his war, some notable voices bridled at his grandiose aims. "I want especially to say that I am not voting for war in the name of democracy," said Ohio senator Warren Harding. "It is my deliberate judgment that it is none of our business what type of government any nation on this earth may choose to have. I am voting for war tonight for the maintenance of just American rights."[15]


As the Wilson and Harding statements suggest, America was not clear on its purpose in embarking for Europe. The president's holy war for democracy was an improvisation. Only a few weeks earlier, one of his allies would have been Nicholas II. A fight to end autocracy in partnership with the Czar would have been problematic for a leader of Wilson's stamp. The establishment of a republic in Russia had given him an opening to proclaim his mission in ideological terms.

Hoover articulated his own position on war aims in a congratulatory telegram he sent Wilson after his address: "[Your] message enunciates our conviction, born of our intimate experience and contact, that there is no hope for democracy or liberalism and consequently for real peace or the safety of our country unless the system which has brought the world into this unfathomable misery can be stamped out once and for all." A lot of care went into the note. Hoover tethered his thoughts to "experience," as well as to specifics: the democracy of "our country," and the German "system" he held responsible for the war. He was doing his best to convince the president that he was on board with his war message without endorsing the full scope of his crusade. He had also dropped his resistance to an American expeditionary force. Within days of Congress's war declaration, Hoover learned from Ambassador Page that he was wanted at home with respect to U.S. food supplies.[16]

The opportunity was smaller than expected. The Council of National Defense, a temporary body established by Wilson to advise on war policy, was asking Hoover to chair its committee on food supply and prices. The position had no staff, budget, authority, or defined responsibilities. Hoover took it with the intention of leveraging it into something more. He hired his friend Ben Allen as his press agent and began filling American newspapers and magazines with stories on the importance of food to the war effort. After less than a week in London, he prepared to recross the Atlantic.[17]

On April 21, 1917, a party of a dozen CRB men headed by Hoover fought its way through the noisy jumble of bicycles, horses, omnibuses, and automobiles on London's Drummond Street. They hustled under the magnificent Doric arch that served as the gateway to Euston Station, climbed down the wide staircases into the Great Hall, and there amid the din and tobacco smoke they encountered still more traffic, this of the human variety: porters, hawkers, civilian travelers, soldiers shipping out, soldiers on leave, soldiers wearing the white lapels of the invalid. Finding their platform, Hoover shook hands with the CRB men who were staying behind. Years later he would say he was touched by their little send-off. At the time, he simply stepped onto his train, took a seat at a window, and began dictating a letter to his secretary. His devotees on the platform waved as the wheels turned. Hoover paid them no notice.

Not only did Hoover leave the station without a wave, the whole Hoover family had forsaken England without looking back. London had been the family's seat for the better part of two decades. It had been the backdrop to almost the whole of the Hoover marriage, and the stage on which Bert had built his career and made himself wealthy. Red House had been the hearth at which the children were raised, at which the Hoovers' extended families and hundreds of friends had been entertained. All of it was abandoned, along with the family automobile, the piano, the pianola, most of their heavy Victorian furniture, and the domestic staff. It was the sort of thing that happened in the Great War. Tens of millions were dislocated and dispossessed. It mattered less for the Hoovers because they had a choice, and because England had always been something of a hotel for them.

The SS *Philadelphia*, Hoover's ride home, was a stately old passenger liner painted camouflage gray and outfitted with antisubmarine guns fore and aft. U-boat fears kept her bottled up at Liverpool for three days awaiting clearance to sail. While pacing the decks of the near-empty ship, Hoover shared with his companions his premonition that they would be torpedoed at sea. He had recently spoken to Rear Admiral William Sims, the U.S. naval representative in England, who confided that Germany was sinking more tonnage than published figures indicated.

On April 25, the *Philadelphia* was finally escorted by the British navy through a maze of mines to the open sea. In its first twenty-four hours out of port, the ship's radio received a flurry of SOS calls from stricken vessels along its route, victims of German subs. Unable to respond without endangering itself, the *Philadelphia* held to its course as its crew and passengers held their collective breath. They had been assigned life preservers for the voyage, an unusual precaution even in wartime. Preferring icy weather and turbulent seas to the threat of torpedoes, the captain of the *Philadelphia* steered a high northern arc that took eight days to complete. Hoover had plenty of time to lie in his berth and ponder the job ahead.

He knew as well as anyone that the war had created a global food crisis. Mass strikes and food riots in Petrograd had been instrumental in the fall of the Romanovs. Shortages in France and Italy were reaching the critical point: five hundred would die in a Turin food uprising before long. The English were struggling. The brutal effectiveness of the U-boats, sinking four or five British ships a day, had left the island with just six weeks' supply of wheat. Lloyd George, now prime minister, thought his people could not last a year. He would soon resort to rationing, banning even the throwing of rice at weddings.

Germany, too, was desperate, having just suffered through what was ruefully known as the Turnip Winter. Scarcity and high prices had sparked bread riots in major cities. The Austrian foreign minister doubted the Central Powers had sustenance to fight another year. Hoover, perhaps overestimating the enemy's strength, believed Germany could hold out indefinitely, barring a disastrous harvest.

Wholesale food prices in America had jumped 21 percent in the early months of 1917, demonstrating that not even neutrals were immune to the food panic. Wheat, eggs, oranges, sugar, and milk were expensive. Through February, while Hoover was still in the city, New York dailies reported that angry homemakers had overturned peddlers' carts in the Bronx and Harlem. Five thousand women had marched on Madison Square crying for bread. Boycotts were organized, commissions struck, and protesters were arrested by the hundreds. It seemed an open question whether food would decide the war or start another.

While the president had not mentioned food in his war message, he had at least described a policy framework in which Hoover could operate. Wilson had promised to draw abundantly and efficiently on the material resources of the country for the war effort. Hoover understood that to mean that the first duty of the United States was to supply the Allies with food. Failure to do so, he had told the press before sailing, "may possibly result in the collapse of everything we hold dear in civilization."[18]

Having declared a food emergency, Hoover faced the question of how the United States should organize to meet it. He had witnessed England's early efforts to muddle through the war without any special food controls and its subsequent race to catch up with Germany in the wholesale militarization of its economy. The productivity of the German state was the talk of the war, and all of the combatants were now more or less following its lead. The influential *New York Times* reporter Oscar King Davis had lived in Berlin through the Turnip Winter and come away impressed by the possibilities of an authoritarian economy. Two days after Wilson's war message, King published the first in a series of articles praising German advances in centralized planning and industrial organization. He quoted economists on the efficiencies to be gained by abolishing trifles and luxuries and directing the nation's full resources to the production of essentials:

> We do not need a drug store or a cigar shop and a bakery and that sort of thing in every block as we have now. That must be stopped, and we must have those men and women working at lines of industry which will produce something not only for their profit but also for the benefit of Germany as a whole.[19]

To Hoover and many of the American intellectuals concerned with state organization, Berlin's scientific approach made the United States, with its own abundance of cigar shops and bakeries, seem woefully inefficient. Hoover's business experience, moreover, had left him with a taste for centralized control. He had discussed with Wilson the extraordinary powers necessary to stabilize prices and reduce speculative profits in wartime markets. The reins of command, he had said, would need to be placed in the hands of America's best industrial brains, men of affairs, not bureaucrats who, in Hoover's view, were barely tolerable even in peace. Wilson, his cabinet secretaries, and his agency heads would need to forgo peacetime modes of operating and move with the speed and ruthlessness of dictators.

They must not become dictators, however. Hoover's years in Europe had also sharpened his appreciation for traditional American liberties. He knew his countrymen were accustomed to a loose system of minimal, decentralized government. He had to balance the organizational demands of total war with the democratic character of the American people. He would use public opinion to ignite "the spirit of self-denial and self-sacrifice" across the land and encourage a self-governing people to voluntarily bind themselves to the state's objectives. If they could be persuaded to cut their consumption and waste, and to produce and export more food, prices could be held at reasonable levels without the government setting the market. The power of the state would be more a threat than a reality, used only in emergencies, or to chasten uncooperative hoarders, speculators, and profiteers.[20]

This, Hoover believed, was how a truly democratic society went to war: organized and unified, depending upon the goodwill and honest efforts of its citizenry rather than a coercive state. It was consistent with the administration's approach to mobilization. In his second inaugural, Wilson had expressed his hope that the heat of battle would purge the country of faction and division, of party and private interest, and let it "stand forth in the days to come with a new dignity of national pride and spirit."[21]

The SS *Philadelphia* cruised into foggy New York Harbor in the early morning of May 3 without having spotted a single German submarine on its voyage. It docked at Chelsea Piers, where Hoover was greeted by a large contingent of CRB men and a troop of Boy Scouts who in response to his public requests for increased agricultural production were cultivating bean fields to feed American soldiers. Lou had wanted to meet him, but unspecified concerns for the health of her boys kept her in California. "We are so terribly glad to get you back," she wired.[22]

A quick scan of the papers would have told Hoover he was lucky to be alive. U-boats were now destroying Allied merchant ships, fighting ships, and fishing vessels at a rate of almost ten a day. Secretary of the Navy Josephus Daniels had admitted the damage wreaked by subs was far worse than his experts had thought possible.[23]

Hoover also learned on landing that Wilson was asking Congress that very day for absolute authority to regulate food and other essentials for the duration of the war. This vast expansion of presidential powers was embodied in the Food and Fuel Control Act, introduced with administration approval by chairman Asbury Lever of the House Committee on Agriculture. The Lever Act, as it became known, would grant the president a free hand to fix prices, seize factories, ban uneconomical practices, regulate exchanges, interfere in railways, and do whatever else he felt necessary to ensure sufficient food supplies and fair prices for producers and consumers.[24]

The bill's sponsors soft-peddled this eye-popping expansion of presidential authority. "It is hoped," said Lever, "that the mere conferring of the more extreme new powers will be sufficient without its becoming necessary to exercise them." There was speculation that the president's new powers would be delegated to Hoover in the capacity of United States food commissioner, or as some phrased it, the nation's "food dictator."[25]

Entertaining the press at the CRB offices in New York the afternoon of his landing, Hoover explained that the administration's new powers were essential. The situation was "grave," he said, "extremely grave," and one of "extreme gravity." His manner, reporters noticed, was as heavy as his language. He saw no quit in the enemy. Germany had the will, the industrial strength, and the material resources to sustain a long fight: "If the Hohenzollerns and the militarist Government are to be destroyed—and nothing short of the destruction of these mad dogs will give hope of permanent peace—the war must go on at least a year more, or probably two years."[26]

The press gave Hoover coverage on the assumption that he was set to serve as food dictator, but he remained nothing more than a committee chair and adviser. He caught up with Colonel House at half past four that afternoon and put on a show in hopes of winning the powers he was already reputed to hold.

Hoover employed with House his favorite job-seeking tactic of pretending to be unavailable. He presented himself as a humble mining engineer, indifferent to title, accolades, or power, yearning only to escape the burdens of war relief for the comforts of his California hearth. Washington could offer him only headaches. He allowed that any man of duty would feel compelled to sacrifice himself in service to his country if called upon to do so by the president in a time of emergency. And he permitted the conversation to turn to the role of food dictator. It would be a dreadful task, he said, one that only a man of force and experience could manage. Such a man would need to be granted broad powers. Such a man would also need complete autonomy in order to give all that was in him to give and to make his enormous personal sacrifice worthwhile. Such a man could not accept any compensation for his services. This last provision emphasized his selflessness while underscoring his independence. He would not be beholden to his masters for his pay.[27]

House was a veteran campaigner. Born to affluence and a politically connected family, he had elected a string of Texas governors before latching on to Wilson as confidant and fixer. The title of Colonel was honorary, and he did not look of the rank: he was a pale, balding little man, a habitual hand-wringer with a gift for intimacy and a sixth sense for the ways of powerful men. House listened to Hoover with his famously friendly eyes and replied to him in confidential tones. His analytic mind, at the same time, found Hoover an easy read. His principal worry was "what authority he would be given" over food policy, House wrote in his diary. "He has a well thought out and comprehensive plan if he can only put it into execution."[28]

It occurred to House that Hoover was on a collision course with Secretary of Agriculture David Houston, who quite reasonably saw himself as responsible for what Americans grew and ate. House thought Houston had better judgment—Hoover's pessimism wore on the cheerful colonel—but that was Houston's only edge. "Hoover knows the question of food control as no other man does, and he has the energy and driving force which Houston lacks."[29]

Before going to bed, House sent a note to Wilson describing his chat with Hoover: "He has some facts that you should know. He can tell you the whole story in about forty minutes, for I timed him." Hoover's expertise and reputation would inspire confidence in Europe and America, the colonel continued, and unless "Houston does give him full control I am afraid he will be unwilling to undertake the job, for he is the kind of man that has to have complete control in order to do the thing well."[30]

Just before midnight, Hoover rushed to Pennsylvania Station and boarded a red-eye to Washington.


The rush to mobilize had thrown the capital, a comfortable little town, home to a small and inefficient national government, into turmoil. The local population jumped by almost a hundred thousand people as volunteers, job seekers, and businessmen descended on the Mall. Traffic was suddenly jammed. Restaurants had lines down the sidewalk. Office space was at a premium and office supplies were sold out. It seemed everyone in D.C. wanted an appointment with everyone else, and through it all the administration continued to launch new boards and agencies, each claiming authority over some huge swatch of the public business. Despite the chaos and confusion, Hoover managed an impressive entrance to Washington. He wrangled a suite at the city's best hotel, the new Willard, and found offices at the Department of the Interior courtesy of his friend Franklin Lane. While waiting to see Wilson, he lobbied cabinet secretaries and congressional connections and appeared before two congressional agricultural committees.

At 2 p.m. on the afternoon of May 9, Hoover had his appointment at the White House. The president was cool to the idea of a one-man food controller precisely because it would appear to be a dictatorship. He had already alarmed Congress with his request for sweeping presidential powers. He proposed instead to form a board or commission, his preferred approach to all questions of war management. Hoover, by his own account, protested that committees were inefficient, indecisive, and contrary to the spirit of American leadership, which had always preferred a single executive head. He argued that an individual leader would be more effective in rallying the citizenry to sacrifice and voluntary effort. While insisting on dictatorial powers, he agreed that the title of "dictator" was dangerous: he preferred "administrator." Wilson closed the meeting without a commitment.[31]

Hoover walked out of the White House and told reporters he had no intention of becoming "food dictator of the American people." The man who accepts such a position, he said, would "die on the barbed wire of the first line entrenchments." He followed up the next day with a press release stating that he did not want any public office, and that all public service he had ever rendered had been forced upon him. He reached a pitch of sanctimony that might have made Wilson blush: "My only desire is to see the proper instrumentality set up to meet this, one of our greatest emergencies, and a man of courage, resource and experience at its head who is willing to sacrifice himself on the altar of the inarticulate masses whom he must protect."[32]

Secretary Houston, a North Carolinian who, like Wilson, had entered politics through the academy, knew exactly the threat the newcomer posed to his Agriculture Department. He thought Hoover shifty: "he could not look you in the face." He complained to Josephus Daniels that separating the management of wartime food supplies from Agriculture would be like putting all battleships in a bureau separate from the navy. Daniels advised him to brace for the inevitable:

The food commission must do a work that will not appeal to people, for they will not wish to deny themselves wheat or sugar. If you or any other member of the Cabinet should ask people to give up food to which they are accustomed, they would resent it. But if the Almoner of starving Belgium, crowned with world praise, makes the request, people will respond.[33]

For all the gamesmanship in Hoover's demands for power and independence, he was prepared to walk away if they were not met. "Matters are very uncertain here as to organization," he wrote Lou, "and unless it is put on footing that gives some promise of success I certainly do not intend become connected with it. It may be some time before situation becomes definite."[34]

Lou replied: "Have written and wired my plans absolutely dependent on yours could leave at any time for short time but do not think I should leave the boys for all summer and they cannot go east till cold weather do you think it advisable build fifty thousand dollar house or five thousand or none at all."[35]

Before dealing with his wife's telegram, Hoover answered a return summons to the White House on the warm and sunny evening of Sunday, May 13. While the details of their conversation are unrecorded, the president apparently told the almoner of starving Belgium that he was getting his way. Hoover wired Lou that he felt secure enough to rent a home in Washington and that she could get on with her plans in California:

> I want you to do whatever you consider in the best interest and pleasure of yourself and the children I shall remain here throughout the summer and I must have a house to live in which I am trying in odd moments to find you can build any sort of house you wish but if it is to be the ultimate family headquarters it should be substantial and roomy. The cost is secondary.[36]

Within a week, Wilson announced that he would create an emergency food administration under the auspices of the Lever Act, with Hoover at its helm. He claimed that the experience of the belligerents had proven the necessity of placing unexampled powers in the hands of one man. He hoped that Hoover could engage the voluntary cooperation of the American people and supply all wants without exercising the powers at his disposal. Secretary Houston surrendered, telling reporters that he and Hoover were entirely in accord on food matters, that Hoover was the best man for the job. He went so far as to claim that he had been instrumental in Hoover's rise to prominence in Washington.[37]

With Wilson's endorsement, Hoover had cleared an important hurdle in his bid to return to America in a top job. He was still not official, however. The Lever Act required congressional approval.

# CHAPTER 10

# A Hero in the House of Truth

Not everyone on the Hill was pleased to allow a single individual, and a Washington outsider, no less, to waltz into town and rule supreme over the American kitchen. Hoover was not merely new to Washington: he and America were almost strangers in 1917. He had left California as a young man in the late Victorian era, returning in modern times, at age forty-two, having only occasionally flashed across the surface of the country in the interim. America had changed. The Spanish-American War had made the country a global power, its economy was now without peer, and Europe was heavily in its debt. Its population had swollen by a third to more than 100 million. Streams of immigrants from southern and Eastern Europe were changing the voice and character of the nation. The era of the frontier had been declared over and the age of rapid urbanization had dawned. The small communities in which Hoover and his cohort were raised were being overwhelmed by automobiles, airplanes, the Panama Canal, the telephone, motion pictures, and professional baseball.

Hoover did not find these changes alienating. As an international businessman, he considered himself an agent of America's material progress, not a victim of it. His lifestyle as a leading figure in a pioneering generation of transatlantic business elites was as cosmopolitan as it was privileged. It had accustomed him to most of the new modes and amenities. He believed he had kept up and, more than that, he believed he belonged in the United States. He *needed* to belong in the

United States. The difficulties of his formative years had left Hoover sensitive to issues of identity, desperate to be accepted in all of the communities to which he became attached, and the United States of America was the biggest and most important community of all.

Yet he was undoubtedly an outsider to America in 1917 where politics were concerned. Hoover had avoided local and national affairs before going abroad. He had missed a generation of political experience, from McKinley's assassination through the tumultuous Roosevelt years to the surprising Democratic interregnum in 1912. His education in the rise of progressivism and its attendant chapters on trust busting, labor unrest, suffrage, and prohibition was acquired, like most of his American political knowledge, at a distance of 3,500 miles, often through the filter of a foreign press. This left him at a disadvantage in Washington.

Certainly nothing in Hoover's life, not even his quarrels with Prussian generals, had prepared him for the likes of Senator James A. Reed, the "silver-topped sycamore," a cigar-chewing master of vituperation representing the state of Missouri. Reed was one of a minority of legislators disconcerted by the sweep of the Lever bill now making its way through the House and Senate. Although a Democrat, he was no friend of Wilson. He sniffed at the president's vaunted idealism, viewing it as a cheap Calvinist camouflage for political opportunism. The Lever bill struck him as a White House power grab and a crime against liberty, the victims being more than 30 million Americans engaged in the production of agriculture. When Hoover appeared in a crowded room before the Senate Committee on Agriculture, Reed was all teeth. Would Hoover please explain how his dictatorship would work, and why he required the power to commandeer corn from a farmer's crib and to dictate to Americans whether they might eat steak or slop on a given day?[1]

No slouch at one-to-one combat, Hoover responded that the Lever bill was necessary to support the Allies. Failure to supply food to Britain and France would leave America alone to fight Germany. The administration was not trying to manage the entire food chain, only key commodities where prices were volatile. It would not regulate menus in private homes, only hotels and restaurants, and regulation would only be employed as a last resort. "If democracy is worth anything," Hoover lectured Senator Reed, "we can do these things by cooperation. If it cannot be done, it is better that we accept German domination and confess the failure of our political ideals."[2]

Reporters judged that Hoover had gotten the better of the senator in the exchange, responding to Reed's barrage with "perfect sang froid" and altogether "routing his antagonist." The senator was undeterred. All he had heard from Hoover was his admission to seeking absolute control over flour and sugar, and to infringing on the right of any freeborn American to walk into a restaurant and order a steak dinner. Unless he was granted unprecedented powers, Hoover seemed to be saying, the price of food would skyrocket, millions would starve, Germany would win the war, and America itself would fail. Reed called him "the greatest calamity howler" since Jeremiah.[3]

That Hoover had survived their first encounter only whetted Reed's appetite. Standing on the Senate floor, head high, shoulders back, eyes flashing, he dug into Hoover's career in Belgium and accused him of driving up the price of wheat in America with his multimillion-dollar relief purchases. Hoover was a hypocrite, personally responsible for the price instability he and Lever now proposed to address with their "despotic and unconstitutional" power play. Hoover wanted "a power such as no Caesar ever employed over a conquered province in the bloodiest days of Rome's bloody despotism." Leaving no analogy unturned, Reed also likened Hoover to J. Rufus Wallingford, the notorious motion-picture conman played by Oliver Hardy.[4]

Hoover suffered the Senator's attacks through the month of June and watched in horror as the Lever bill was dissected and redrafted by legions of legislators. He ran to Wilson's office complaining of interminable discussion and delays, unfair attacks, and special-interest meddling—i.e., politics. The president counseled patience and told Hoover to concentrate on those aspects of his duties not requiring new law, such as the appeal to Americans to voluntarily save food and eliminate waste. It was sound advice.

After several weeks at the Willard Hotel, Hoover had moved to a rented house on Sixteenth Street and filled it with a dozen friends and associates, many of them veterans of the CRB. He fleshed out his ranks with new recruits, once again avoiding bureaucrats and professors. He also broke with the current fashion for decorating new agencies with bluebloods, Spanish-American War veterans—what he called "costume jewelry." He valued readiness as well as intelligence.[5]

Lewis Strauss was a typical Hoover recruit, albeit the sort of man who might never have caught the eye of conventional Washington. He was a twenty-one-year-old traveling shoe salesman, Jewish, with one good eye, the other having been lost in a rock fight in his native West Virginia. Strauss had been saving money to study physics at the University of Virginia when the United States declared war. Determined to serve, and having read coverage of Hoover's speeches, he tracked the prospective food dictator to the Willard and hovered on the carpet outside of his room until he emerged. Strauss hurriedly introduced himself and volunteered to work without salary for two months. Hoover sized him up in a glance and told him to take off his coat and get to work. Strauss did as he was told.[6]

Hoover's team, or the Firm, as it had taken to calling itself, huddled for breakfast every morning at seven and spent an hour or more shaping plans and talking over the problems of the day. They proceeded to the office as a group at half past eight or nine, talking all the way. They would return to the house at the end of the day, sometimes joined by members of other agencies or visiting delegations, to talk through dinner and continue over digestifs or walks in the garden. Hoover would retire around midnight, reserving the right to telephone his staff at any hour of the night or morning to talk some more.

The first product of these discussions was a valiant campaign to enlist the women of America in the cause of food conservation. Never one for half measures, Hoover aimed to recruit from across the country thousands of volunteers who in turn would attempt to sign every housewife in 22 million American households as a member of the United States Food Administration. By signing a pledge card, the housewives would commit to carrying out the directions and advice of the Food Administration in the conduct of their homes. They were to serve smaller portions and, to prevent waste, abide "the gospel of the clean plate." They were given recipe cards for Meatless Tuesdays and Wheatless Wednesdays. They were instructed to think scientifically about meals and the efficient provision of the minimum necessary calories.[7]

The Food Administration's pledge drive was backed by a stupendous public relations blitz. More than 200,000 letters were sent to American religious leaders and another twenty-one thousand to newspaper editors enlisting their support. Hoover drew on artistic talent from top-flight advertising firms to produce posters and slogans. Some encouraged vegetable gardening: "Let no backyard be a slacker!" Some promoted conservation: "Food is Ammunition— Don't Waste It!" Most famous of all: "Food Will Win the War!"[8]

That Hoover had begun his administration without legislative approval astonished Washington. Supreme Court justice Louis Brandeis rated his progress "the strongest argument of recent years for the needlessness of law." An unabashed fan of Hoover, Brandeis called him "the biggest figure injected into Washington life by the war."[9]

James A. Reed, seeing less to admire, entertained the Senate by mocking the dictator-in-waiting for hours at a time. He seized upon Hoover's long absence from America. Did it make sense to hand control over the necessaries of life to a man "of whom this country knows but little," a man "who lived in England all his grown-up life, whose house and whose home are in England, whose business associates are Englishmen, in the interest of England." He brandished an English newspaper report in which Hoover had declared himself a "Liberal" in politics. Not a Democrat or a Republican or a Populist, thundered Reed, but an English Liberal ignorant of American public policy. Who was this "stranger," this "Sir Herbert Hoover," and how could he be trusted with the regulation of America's diet, an extravagant power denied even the kaiser in Germany?[10]

Week after week, Reed showed Hoover what one congressman called the deference due a chicken thief. He read into the record quotations from the Food Administration's official instructions for voluntary conservation. "Cut their bread on the table and only as required" was one of his favorites. "How," asked Reed, "have we gotten along all of these years without that knowledge? How does it occur that in the flight of time and the mutation of life the human race has blundered on and on without some Hoover to tell them to cut their bread on the table only as required?" The senator asked that the Senate investigate Hoover's past (it declined). He demanded Hoover be replaced by a three- or five-man board (he was not). He urged Americans to refuse to comply with the Food Administration (most complied).[11]

Had Hoover been more experienced or more politically adept he might have eased his progress through Congress by inviting key Senate figures to participate in his work, or by soliciting their suggestions for appointments to organizations affiliated with his own. He might have been more disciplined in his alarmist communications. He might have approached the whole project with a touch more humility. His supporters were busily publishing articles celebrating him as the "genius" from West Branch, all but inviting the back of Senator Reed's hand. Hoover had proved, as a California friend admitted, that he was "as far away from the mechanics of American political life as the Gaekwar of Baroda."[12]

Hurt, embarrassed, discouraged by the delays and attacks, and still without an official role, Hoover grew paranoid and desperate. He made empty threats in the press to expose his congressional opponents: "Nobody knows what I am up against here. Nobody knows the forces I have to fight. . . . If [this bill] isn't passed soon I'll go to the country and tell the people the truth. They shall know the men who are holding me back—and when the people know, heaven help those men."[13]

He muttered about quitting and returning to his mining career, and even drafted a letter purporting to be from his staffers advising that they would resign en masse if the Food Administration were to be headed by a committee and not an individual (he thought better of releasing it). He poured out his troubles to Colonel House on a July 4 visit, lamenting that the president would not smooth things along. House's view was that the White House was merely unaware of Hoover's problems. He believed that if the president and his food administrator were to sit down and talk, they could clear things up in no time.[14]

Hoover was learning that Wilson was not the most fastidious of war managers. In truth, he was not the most diligent of chief executives. On a typical day, the president and his new bride would golf together in the morning, eat their meals together throughout the day, sit together as he answered his correspondence, and go for a car ride together in the evening. Wilson seldom broke his banker's hours and rarely worked weekends. He delegated heavily to an uneven range of cabinet talents and rarely met with them. He answered the demands of the war reluctantly. House thought him "too refined, too civilized, too intellectual, too cultivated" to be a war president.[15]

Nonetheless, Wilson did answer Hoover's concerns, writing the Senate majority leader on the need to pass the unamended Lever bill. He also offered Hoover another piece of sound counsel. The outrageous statements by Senator Reed, like the "tedious and vexatious process" of congressional approval, must simply be endured. Wilson promised that the end result would be a satisfactory bill, and it was.[16]

On August 8, after a nasty two-month battle in the Senate, by far the longest engendered by any of the new war legislation, a compromise draft of the Lever bill was passed with only seven dissenting votes, Reed's included. The president, beneficiary of an unprecedented expansion of executive powers, signed it into law two days later, on Hoover's forty-third birthday. The United States Food Administration was finally an official body, with Hoover as its official head. He reported directly to the president. Ambassador Page congratulated him from London: "It's an awful job you have; but you are a man made for awful jobs."[17]

Once officially installed, Hoover flexed his muscle. Shifting emphasis from dampening demand for food to encouraging supply, he elaborated his plans for stimulating production and restraining prices of key commodities. He called to Washington representatives from every link in the food chain, from "soil to stomach," as he liked to say, for two hundred separate conferences. They negotiated self-governing rules and regulations for their various industries.[18]

Recognizing that businessmen were uneasy with his assertion of control over their livelihoods, Hoover attempted to reassure them with his language. He would guide and coordinate markets—what he called "constructive regulation"—rather than dictate to them. He would help to stabilize rather than set prices. He expressed confidence that farmers were rational and cooperative enough to take his direction, eliminating the need for him to employ the "drastic force" at his disposal.[19]

His faith in volunteerism was not an absolute faith, however. Hoover knew that he had an awful job and that his Food Administration would be blamed for any instances of price inflation or short supply. There was a grain of realism in his comment about the food dictator dying on the barbed wire of the first-line entrenchments, so he hedged his bets. The wheat market prompted the first of several aggressive interventions. Unstable prices and uncertainty over the government's plans for grain markets in the summer of 1917 had led farmers to withhold wheat from market and millers to cut production. Facing a national flour shortage, Hoover licensed all wheat elevators and flour mills in the country, thus lending himself the ability to put out of business those operators who hoarded or set unreasonable prices. He launched the Food Administration Grain Corporation, the first U.S. government corporation created by executive fiat, with a mandate to buy, store, and sell wheat in domestic and international markets. It dictated the fair price at $2.20 a bushel, substantially less than wheat had been commanding throughout the summer. The price was set primarily to satisfy consumers.

Grain growers, of course, were furious to find Hoover choking prices for their crops when demand was high and the costs of machinery, fertilizer, and other inputs were rising. Protest rallies were organized from the Dakotas to New Mexico. Farmers continued to withhold their wheat from market, hoping that shortages would make the food dictator sweat and reconsider $2.20. Hoover called the protesters "skunks" and malcontents and hired thousands of public speakers to spread the food administrator's word throughout the West. He imported wheat from Canada to keep U.S. mills running full out. This last maneuver prevented shortages and broke the protests as farmers reluctantly delivered their wheat and complied with his pricing, but they would never forgive Hoover his intervention.[20]

By October 1917, the food administrator had boldly asserted federal dominion over the entire food chain in America. He licensed all persons and businesses engaged in the production of food, from packers, canners, and bakers to distributers, wholesalers, and retailers, requiring them to refrain from "unjust exorbitant, unreasonable, discriminatory or unfair commission, profit, or storage charge." Failure to meet the terms of the license would result in shutdowns and possibly criminal prosecution.[21]

The fears of Hoover's critics were thus realized. In a matter of weeks, the man of whom the country knew but little had stepped between Americans and the necessaries of life, and between farmers, who represented roughly half of the American economy, and their markets.

. . .

It was no small job, overseeing the food supply for 100 million people. Hoover spent the long hours between breakfast meetings and
late-night conferences gathering and processing mountains of data
about the global food trade: current U.S. stocks of fish and apples;
the bushels of corn required to produce one hundred pounds of live
hog; the minimum human requirements of calories, proteins, carbo-
hydrates, and fats; the rightful percentages of revenue owed to ship-
pers, wholesalers, and retailers. "To Hoover's brain," said presidential
adviser Bernard Baruch, "facts are water to a sponge." In addition to
its ability to absorb data, Hoover's mind impressed with its unusual
depth of field. He could see the full sweep of the market as clearly as
the minutiae. This is what Henry Stimson, whose illustrious career in
Washington spanned both world wars, meant when he said Hoover
had "the greatest capacity for assimilating and organizing material of
any man I ever knew."[22]

Those new to his orbit also marveled at Hoover's stamina and
powers of concentration. Wrote Mark Requa, a Food Administration
volunteer:

> I remember upon one occasion riding downtown with him in
> the winter of 1917–1918, when the streets were sheets of ice,
> and the automobile skidded and crashed into the curbstone
> in front of the Army, Navy and State Building. [Hoover] was
> deeply engaged in expounding certain fundamentals, his con-
> centration faculties were going full speed ahead, when the
> automobile struck the curb and the rear wheel collapsed. I
> opened the door and got out, he following me, and we walked
> on down the street without, I think, his skipping a word or for
> an instant breaking his train of thought . . . he said nothing to
> the chauffeur about it but simply left the machine and walked
> on down the street continuing his discussion.[23]

This sort of behavior was familiar to those who knew Hoover.
His fixed habits, good and bad, from twenty years of executive work
were all on display in his management of the Food Administration.
He preached the mantras of measurement, efficiency, and standard-

ization. He continued to view other administrators as potential rivals who needed to be subordinated or sidelined. Thanks in part to the jurisdictional chaos caused by the explosion of wartime departments, agencies, and commissions, he had his elbows up all the time with Agriculture, the navy, and the army. He went over the head of General John J. Pershing, commander of the American Expeditionary Force, to ask Wilson to exempt skilled agricultural workers from the draft. Wilson sided with Pershing.[24]

Hoover's biggest battle was with William G. McAdoo, secretary of the Treasury, director general of railroads, and Wilson's son-in-law. A tall southerner with aquiline features and a dandy's wardrobe, McAdoo had married Miss Eleanor Wilson in a quiet ceremony amid a sea of white lilies in the Blue Room of the White House during her father's first term. At the end of 1917, the president had handed the "Crown Prince," as McAdoo was known, responsibility for sorting out America's congested and newly nationalized railways. This placed him directly in the path of Hoover, most of whose food traveled by rail. Through the months of January and February 1918, Hoover complained incessantly and sometimes publicly that shortages of rail-cars were playing havoc with the movement of food. Breweries and piano manufacturers were finding freight capacity while his essentials sat on sidings.[25]

Hoover brought the conflict to a head on February 22, 1918, by telling the press that the incompetence of the railway director was about to visit an unprecedented crisis on the United States. McAdoo had already complained to his father-in-law that Hoover's statements were exaggerated; now he blasted the food administrator in the press for failing to appreciate the difficulties caused by winter storms and the competing demands for rail access. Newspapers reveled in the spat. Hoover, the aggressor, lost support among his senior colleagues for embarrassing the administration and was forced to back down. McAdoo recorded a visit to his office by Hoover and William Glasgow, a Food Administration lawyer:

> Glasgow did all the talking. Hoover sat with downcast eyes, like a diffident schoolboy. . . . Glasgow told me, on Hoover's behalf, that the Food Administration wanted to cooperate with me in every possible way; that Mr. Hoover regretted his

statement that had appeared in the "Times" . . . and he hoped it would not interfere with our cordial relations.[26]

McAdoo and Hoover would never reconcile. Aside from his resentment at having been publicly attacked, the Crown Prince, an arch-Democrat, suspected Hoover of being a closet Republican, and he sneered at Hoover's Belgian acclaim as "celebrity easily won." The task of giving away free food "requires very little wear and tear on one's ability." Hoover nursed a hatred of McAdoo for decades, deriding him in an unpublished section of his memoirs as a "complete phoney," "the most arrogant person in Washington," and a man unloved even by his wife.[27]

Hoover's sensitivity to criticism seems to have been heightened during the war by his conviction that he was doing God's work. Intellectually, he knew he would come under fire as food administrator; emotionally, he succumbed to his furies. No one got under his skin more than the Missouri senator, Reed, who continued to rail against the food dictator's perceived excesses throughout 1918. Hoover reliably rose to the bait. Failing to silence Reed with facts and counterargument, he consulted lawyers to see if he might charge the senator with sedition, and when that did not work he arranged for a private detective to scour Reed's past for embarrassing or scandalous revelations. The man spent months traveling across several states retracing Reed's legal and political careers, as well as his personal life, to no avail.[28]

Wilson, while leaning more than ever on his food administrator, taking his advice on such crucial matters as the structure of the war cabinet and the contents of presidential addresses to Congress, grew impatient with his histrionics. He complained to House that Hoover's relentless pessimism made their meetings oppressive: it was as though "nothing was ever being done right."[29]

The colonel seconded the president's complaints and added a few of his own. "I find with Hoover," he told his diary, "that the matter he is working on is the most important in the world. . . . I find this characteristic in nearly all self-centered individuals having a particular specialty."[30]

Those working under Hoover in the Food Administration had an entirely different sense of him. Mostly younger men of high ideals and good education, they found Hoover open and collaborative. He involved them in every aspect of his toils and openly discussed his options with them before making decisions. "In these conferences," said one staffer, "he has no pride of opinion, and he expects the most searching scrutiny of the facts by everybody present."[31]

Hoover's men actually enjoyed his company. Conscious of working with an extraordinary individual, they took pains to record their observations in letters and diaries. They delighted in his human qualities, how he would arrive bleary-eyed for breakfast every morning in his usual blue suit and tie to wolf down his usual order of bacon and eggs. How he would stop most evenings at the Belgian embassy for a cocktail, chew through an entire unlit cigar while listening to a speech, regale a dinner party with tales of dastardly German generals, blush like a schoolboy on being teased, and swear up a storm at bureaucratic imbecility. "He does not often let his feelings get away with him," said one friend, "but when he does it is worth coming miles to hear."[32]

Sundays he would take the Firm to the country in a caravan of automobiles. They ate out of doors. "It isn't a picnic unless the Chief scrambles eggs over a hot fire in a short-handled frying pan, burning his hands and [getting] his eyes filled with smoke," wrote Hugh Gibson. Afterwards, they would set to work on "a great engineering feat, which carried a mountain stream along the side of a hill on beams and sluices and turned it into a quarry. We all labored for about three hours and were glad to climb into our cars and come on home. It was bitter cold."[33]

The men of the Food Administration were not blind. They noted their leader's callous disregard of niceties and his stubborn refusals of reasonable compromise. They saw him bully officials and politicians he ought to have courted, and they recognized that his busyness and his reticence were poor excuses for rude behavior. They thought all of these things insignificant next to his sincere and unselfish desire to help people. "It is a joy," Gibson wrote his mother, "to be with a man who really thinks as he does and who feels as intensely about things that ought to be done without smelling of the reformer or the uplifter."[34]

Hoover's gloominess did not strike Gibson as a character defect. It was evidence of a noble heart and high aspirations. "Had a good dinner with Hoover last night," he wrote his mother, "and a long talk over the state of things in general. He is depressed almost as much as I am and that is saying a good deal. We went over the troubles of the race in detail and broke up almost in tears."[35]

Hoover's magnetism extended beyond the men in his own ranks. He had quickly established himself in the press as a strong, humane, and impassioned leader. He was seen to be calling Americans to follow him into public service. Businessmen were being urged to give more to America than the price of their goods; women were being called to share the sacrifices of their men in uniform. Hoover was insisting that every individual could and should be of service to the nation, its allies, and the hundreds of millions of innocent people suffering because of war. He was gaining support from some of the leading activists of the times, including suffragist and pacifist Jane Addams and the editor and civil rights activist Oswald Garrison Villard.

Hoover's greatest appeal was to Americans of a progressive mindset. Always the loosest of coalitions, progressivism in the early twentieth century was a flag of convenience for all kinds of meliorists and social justice advocates. It drew from the Democratic and Republican parties as well as Theodore Roosevelt's short-lived Progressive Party. The common conviction of its adherents, wrote Felix Frankfurter, a young Harvard law professor and one of the movement's brightest lights, was that the country had given itself over for far too long to mere money making: "the time had come for social movements, social reforms, putting an end to glaring and garish ruthlessness and inequalities" of American life.[36]

The progressives had enjoyed a heyday before the war, forcing minimum-wage laws and restrictions on hours of work, new rights for female workers, and improved access to education. Roosevelt had carried their hopes with his promise of a New Nationalism in the failed Bull Moose campaign of 1912. Wilson, early in his first term, had delighted progressives with antitrust measures, the Federal Reserve System, the income tax, and direct election of U.S. senators. By 1917, however, Roosevelt was in the wilderness and Wilson was adrift domestically. New leadership was needed if the progressives were to complete their project of guiding America into a more benevolent and collectivist future. To many, Hoover looked like the answer. Progressives were enemies of machine politics and ward-heeling politicians; he had burst on the scene with no political baggage and no discernible partisan taint, his long absence seeming more an asset than a detriment. Progressives railed against cutthroat capitalism and corporate greed; Hoover demonstrated daily his confidence in cooperative action, his belief in a positive role for the state, and his willingness to stamp out predatory business practices. Progressives were in thrall to expert administrators promising a more rational, efficient, and scientific approach to government; Hoover was the great engineer, rationalizing an entire sector of the economy and teaching Americans to live more efficiently for their own good.

Hoover was progressivism incarnate, and he was pleased to carry the movement's banner. He was conscious of leading a noble experiment in social engineering, one that he hoped would outlast the war. All he had learned in business and all he had seen in wartime Europe had convinced him that the postwar world would belong to the most efficient, the least wasteful, the most economically competitive nations. He considered his Food Administration to be laying a foundation for America's future.[37]

If the progressive movement had a brain trust in 1917 it was the cluster of young, mostly single men domiciled in a red brick townhouse on Nineteenth Street, near Dupont Circle. Felix Frankfurter, on loan from Harvard to Secretary of War Newton Baker, was among the boarders, as were Walter Lippmann, a founding editor of the four-year-old *New Republic*, and Eustace Percy, Hoover's Foreign Office confidant, now with the British embassy in Washington.

Justice Oliver Wendell Holmes, a frequent guest, described them as the "fastest talkers, the quickest thinkers" in town, bound by convivial habits and aggressively liberal politics. They entertained nightly in comfortable bohemian fashion with a handful of servants, a well-stocked bar, and a sprinkling of attractive women. Their dinner table debates were so animated and their opinions so earnest that Holmes dubbed them "The House of Truth."[38]

Hoover was a favorite at the House of Truth. Accomplished, cosmopolitan, bathed in the glory of the Belgian relief, he dazzled Lippmann, who thought him "bold and brilliant," an "entrancing talker" with a gift for exposition. "Many felt, as I did," Lippmann would later write, "that they had never met a more interesting man, anyone who knew so much of the world and could expound so clearly what to almost all Americans in 1917 were the inscrutable mysteries of European politics." The ideas Hoover had imbibed during his time in London watching the Liberal Party of Asquith and Lloyd George launch social welfare programs, including unemployment, health insurance, and old-age pensions, were far beyond the dreams of American progressives. He seemed to the Lippmann crowd marked by destiny as the man to lead America from a laissez-faire past to a more cooperative or collectivist future through the medium of public service. The *New Republic* was among the staunchest supporters of the Food Administration.[39]

The attention Hoover received in magazines, newspapers, and his agency's propaganda made him a popular national figure. He was not only a household name: he was a household verb. To "Hoover-ize" meant to clean one's plate, endure a meatless meal, or otherwise consume food in an economical matter. Newspapermen came calling at the Food Administration offices expecting to find a figure large enough to justify the hype. They were surprised to find that Hoover in the flesh cut so ordinary a figure, an "unobtrusive man" working day by day at his desk in a sparsely furnished office. They also found an unexpected lightness to him. He almost always had "a little, quizzical crease in one corner of his mouth, and amused eyes that are always smiling."[40]

Mrs. Hoover, too, gained a higher profile in Washington. She organized the Food Administration Club for Women, made speeches and gave interviews on food conservation, and encouraged women to pick up their own groceries to save manpower on deliveries. Not all of the attention she received was helpful. There were grumblings in the press about the fine chef she had hired for her home, and both Hoovers were embarrassed when her plans for a $50,000, twenty-one-room Stanford mansion were leaked to California papers. There was a whiff of untimely extravagance to the story. Lou fired the architect, put her plans on ice, and took an existing home in Palo Alto.[41]

The mansion clamor was a symptom of a general domestic disorder in the Hoovers' busy lives. Bert's managerial talents were almost comically absent from his own household. His family and its possessions were scattered over multiple dwellings, three cities, and 5,500 miles. In addition to the home in Palo Alto, the family lived in three separate houses in their first two years in Washington, not to mention a summer home near Chevy Chase. Wherever they were situated, people would arrive unexpectedly for meals or stays. Hoover kept as many as three jitneys in service for family and guests, and the household was forever outspending whatever Lou had left on account. On top of all this, the Hoovers had yet to properly close Red House in London.[42]

On leaving England, Hoover had asked his wife's friend Mrs. Alice Dickson to pack up the family's personal effects and move them to the basement until he decided how best to dispose of the property. His primary concern had been for his library. He asked Mrs. Dickson to paste bookplates in each volume and pack the rare books according to British Museum methods in zinc-lined boxes. They were to be insured for $25,000 and placed in storage. His engineering books and files were packed in cases and stored in his bombproof wine cellar, along with two trunks of private papers. His only other instruction had been to deal with a man named Agnew in the dismantling of the household. He neglected to introduce Mrs. Dickson to Agnew. "So," Mrs. Dickson wrote Lou, "I scurried around to find who and where Mr. Agnew might be."[43]

It was the start of a long journey for Mrs. Dickson. She walked into Red House and found a handful of CRB men using it as a dormitory. One of them, Mr. Poland, fought her for control of the incoming mail. Mrs. Dickson learned that the Hoovers' automobile had been loaned to the Red Cross and their carpets to the American Women's Club. Various milkmen and other services were charging the household accounts on behalf of people who no longer lived there. There was an iron safe in the morning room; no one knew the combination or what it contained. Sheaves of licenses, insurance policies, club memberships, registration cards, tickets, and vouchers sat neglected. Gilbert, Hoover's chauffeur, was attempting to sell the piano and automobile for personal gain.

John Agnew was overseer of Hoover's remaining business ventures in London, and of no assistance to Mrs. Dickson. Nor, to her surprise, was Lou Hoover of any help. Letters to California reporting the state of affairs at Red House went unanswered. Mrs. Dickson began addressing her friend as "Dear Lady of the Perfect Silence." She charitably attributed Lou's lack of interest to the pressures of work and gamely decided on behalf of the absent family what should be shipped, what stored, what sold.*[44]

Both Hoovers accepted disarray as an inevitable byproduct of busy lives and the disruptions of war. They were still living on the jump, too focused on the future to be sentimental about the past. They had a high tolerance, personally and financially, for loose ends, broken plans, abandoned residences, overdrawn household accounts. Bert seemed oblivious to his living arrangements so long as his address was respectable, things were in working order, and the furniture was sensibly arranged.

There is no evidence that the tumult caused strain in their marriage. Together now for nineteen years, the Hoovers had grown accustomed to change and long periods of separation. Lou understood her husband's ambition and sense of duty. When in Washington, she helped him entertain his nightly parade of guests, including Marshal Joffre of France, Arthur Balfour of England, and the young assistant secretary of the navy, Franklin Roosevelt, and his wife, Eleanor. Bert accepted Lou's independence and her attachment to California, where her sister and parents resided. They lived under the same roof when mutually convenient and otherwise called on each other when necessary. Their letters contained few terms of endearment as before. His colleagues heard Bert say he "ought to be hanged" for the way he treated his family, and he meant it, although having uttered the sentiment he would never follow up with a visit or a long letter. Public life took clear precedence over family among the Hoovers.[45]

After spending the winter of 1918 together in Washington, they

---

* Mrs. Dickson received from the Hoovers as compensation for these heroic services a comfortable sweater.

scattered. The boys, who attended the local Sidwell Friends School, traveled west for the summer with their mother. Their father prepared for an overseas tour.

The reasons for Hoover's tour were revealed in a visit to Colonel House in June. Hoover reported with some excitement that all indications pointed to a bountiful crop in 1918, which would leave the United States and the Allies with ample food for the next twelve months. House was delighted by the news: "I suggested that this fact should be used as propaganda to stimulate the morale amongst the Allies, and to depress that of the Germans." To the colonel's dismay, Hoover announced that he intended to travel to Europe himself and spread the word among political leaders and other dignitaries. It sounded less like a morale-building exercise and more like an adventure in self-promotion by "the greatest living advertiser," House wrote in his diary. "I have never known a man with a less sympathetic personality." He nonetheless jotted thoughts in his diary about how he might run a Hoover presidential campaign.[46]

There was something strange, dreamy, almost delirious about Hoover's journey. He shared a midnight train to New York with Mrs. Hoover and her attendants, one of whom carried a noisy Maltese cat in a wicker basket. They parted amid the warships on the pier where he boarded the RMS *Olympic*, sister ship to the *Titanic*, along with six thousand American servicemen. In a bath of yellow light, the monstrous vessel was accompanied to sea by an airplane, a dirigible, and a destroyer until reaching open water, where the guard turned back and the *Olympic* crossed solo.[47]

Hoover and his men were berthed in cabins decorated in high Victorian style with real beds, imitation coal fireplaces, and enough gold, plush, and mahogany to outfit a mortuary. They rose every morning to pass a medicine ball in the gymnasium, Hoover's first honest attempt at exercise. On a Sunday night he appeared on deck to address two thousand rambunctious troops at a religious service. He lectured them on food and service and war. "Feed us seagulls," they cried. "We're tired of tripe!"[48]

A special train whisked Hoover from Southampton to London's Waterloo station, where he was smothered by reporters and dignitaries. Three military cars dropped his party at the sumptuous Savoy, where he was treated to ration cards for beef, sugar, and butter. He requested somewhere to work, and a three-story office replete with furniture and telephones was arranged for his pleasure in a matter of hours. Rather than enjoy the consideration shown him, Hoover chose to exaggerate past slights: "It's different from the time I used to slink through here like a hunted dog."[49]

As he had anticipated, Hoover was a center of attention in London. Between meetings with the Allied food controllers, he was received in top hat and cutaway coat at Buckingham Palace by King George and Queen Mary. He was feted before a swarm of dukes, earls, and ambassadors at Mansion House by the Lord Mayor of London. An amused Lewis Strauss wondered if the tiny portions served at Mansion House undermined Hoover's declaration that the worst of the food crisis had passed. At a gala dinner, Prime Minister Lloyd George, rude and disinterested through most of the evening, ultimately rose to toast Hoover as the savior of Europe: "It seems to me that you represent not only the United States, but also Providence."[50]

His ears throbbing with applause, Hoover crossed the Channel with an escort of destroyers. "I do not think I have seen him look better," a member of the Firm wrote Lou. Hoover and his entourage were just settling into their Boulogne hotel when they heard three shots followed by a bugle call, the alert for a German air raid. As searchlights and antiaircraft guns swept the black skies, most of the hotel's guests, men and women in various stages of dress, rushed to the lower floors. Hoover walked out onto a balcony. "Let's watch the show," he said. "We might be better off here than going down in the cellar and battling with the rats." Strauss set up a camera and attempted to take a time-exposure photograph of the air raid. A munitions dump on the waterfront one or two blocks from the hotel blew up, sending flames hundreds of feet high and blasting out the French doors in Hoover's room. The picture was ruined, and a fragment of glass cut Hoover's hand. The men continued to watch the fireworks through their broken windows.[51]

From Boulogne, Hoover moved to Paris, where he received the homage of the city. "He went with his usual grunt," wrote Gibson, and he "came home grunting still more heavily." He went on a walk through the streets of the city and came back to his rooms with a smoking-hot souvenir fragment from a long-range German shell that had blown the doors off the Hôtel de Calais and killed fourteen people.[52]

Despite his tight schedule, Hoover managed a significant side trip during his tour, motoring out to the Belgian coastal town of De Panne, where, in a little villa among the sand dunes, he found Albert, king of the Belgians, in full military dress. Stripped of his possessions, cornered in the westernmost tip of his occupied kingdom, four miles from the horrors of the front, Albert was doing his best to preserve the dignity of his office and the morale of his people by sharing their jeopardy. Hoover stayed for lunch. It was a simple meal prepared by the queen and served informally around an oval table. Hoover sat between the queen and Marie Jose, the twelve-year-old Princess Royal, with her magnificent pile of frizzy hair (she would later be the last queen of Italy). Always at his best with children, Hoover learned that the girl had herself been collecting shell fragments from the small garden behind the royal cottage. She offered one of her largest pieces for eleven-year-old Allan Hoover. She spoke of how the aerial bombardments "make you feel small in your bed."[53]

Amid discussions of Belgian relief and walks on the beach, Albert's foreign minister mentioned to Hoover that the king wanted to confer upon him the Grand Cordon of the Order of Leopold, his country's highest honor. Hoover gave the usual grunt, aware that as an American government official he could not accept a foreign title without the consent of Congress. When it was noted that he had already accepted the French title of Commander of the National Order of the Legion of Honor, he quibbled that it had been bestowed upon him without consultation. He told the foreign minister that he would be pleased to be known simply as a friend of the Belgian people.

Hoover stayed on for dinner with Albert and his prime minister, and toward the end of the evening, guns booming in the distance, the monarch announced that he wished to show his gratitude to their benefactor by making Hoover the sole member of a newly created order, an *"Ami de la nation belge."* Overcome, Hoover tried, and for the most part failed, to articulate his appreciation. Albert and his staff accompanied him to his car and saluted as he drove away.[54]

# CHAPTER 11

# Inconsolable in the Hall of Mirrors

Hoover deserved the acclaim he received in Europe. Americans, their army, and the Allies were fed. Agricultural production was increased substantially without use of quotas. Millions of Americans were convinced to conserve food without resort to rations. Inflation was held at a tolerable level. Twenty-three million metric tons of food were shipped overseas, and with the Europeans paying for their sustenance, Hoover was able to return to the Treasury his agency's $10 million appropriation and $150 million of working capital with a net surplus at the end of the day.[1]

His execution was not flawless. The degree of voluntarism was less than Hoover had wished, with only half of the nation's housewives signing their pledge cards. He had levied eight hundred penalties for breaches of his directorate's rules and closed 150 businesses for violations. By the summer of 1918, he had even taken to policing the nation's grocery stores to enforce his prescribed prices. This was consistent with the broader experience of the administration. It grew increasingly repressive as its commitment to the war deepened, even jailing and deporting citizens for expressions of dissent under the notorious Sedition Act of 1918. The government's message of volunteerism, intentionally or not, provided cover for its unexampled interference in private lives.

There were awkward consequences to Hoover's interventions in the market. His incentives to the hog trade resulted in a billion pounds of surplus pork. He asked Americans to curb their consumption of sugar to forestall looming shortages and was chagrined as anxious shoppers cleared grocery shelves of every last pound. Hoover glossed over these outcomes in his speeches and reports.

On the political front, he left more bruises in Washington than were necessary, standing out even in an administration noted for excusing sharp elbows with high purpose. Members of Congress, the Wilson cabinet, and the military felt they had been roughed up by Hoover's methods, and he was fortunate not to have alienated the president. When Wilson directed scarce shipping resources to the military ahead of the food relief, Hoover complained in the press and secretly lobbied Lloyd George to intervene on his behalf with the White House.[2]

Still, all in all, it was a bravura performance. Hoover had taken an awful job, with an unprecedented mandate, in a climate of fear and panic, with inflation spiraling and food shortages breaking out at home and overseas, and with dire consequences in the event of failure. There were no guarantees that the people of America would respond to his dictates. War can bring discipline to a nation. It can also stoke mistrust and unrest. The year 1917 saw a record 4,450 labor strikes in the United States, all of them in consequence of the same wartime economic dislocations that Hoover confronted daily. His administration struck a balance of self-regulation and authority palatable to the American people. It amounted to an American way of war, and Hoover emerged as an inspiring leader to millions.[3]

Toward the end of his European victory lap, a string of Panhard touring cars took Hoover and his entourage north from Paris to the Western Front. They passed villages flattened by heavy artillery and treeless fields littered with rusted barbed wire, abandoned tanks, the debris of battle. Rifles were planted upright in the mud, marking human remains that had been buried deep enough to escape the eye but not the nose. Near Reims, they mounted a camouflaged observation tower and watched through a telescope the soldiers crawling behind barbed wire and the barrages of shellfire boiling the earth between the trenches. They were unwittingly witnessing a climactic moment of the Great War. Through the spring and early summer of 1918, the German army had pushed within seventy-five miles of Paris with a series of brilliant thrusts, culminating in the Second Battle of the Marne, fought to the immediate east and west of Reims.

It took the combined weight of French, British, and American forces to finally grind the Germans to a halt. On August 8, three days after Hoover's visit, the Allies launched their Hundred Days Offensive and kept Germany on its heels until the Armistice.[4]


Hoover waited out the autumn of 1918 in Washington, watching from a distance as the Europe he had known for so many years died with the war. England and France, victorious, were battered beyond recognition, their industry and their treasuries exhausted, their people demoralized by the staggering human cost of the conflict. The ancient dynasties that had upheld Central Europe's political and social order for centuries were carried away with the smoke of battle. Kaiser Wilhelm II vamoosed to the Netherlands in an ignominious close to the Hohenzollern saga. The last Hapsburgs slunk off to Switzerland at the demise of Austria-Hungary. Farther east, the Ottomans were completing their long slide from the glories of Suleiman the Magnificent to a bloody oblivion of genocide and revolt. From this detritus rose dozens of new nations with feeble governments, disputed borders, and embittered populaces. There also emerged another awful job for Hoover.

He returned to Paris in December of 1918 to find the skies, the Seine, and the entire city of light bathed in gray. The street lamps along the city's wintry thoroughfares burned faintly for want of coal. There were sandbags piled in front of Notre Dame Cathedral and boards on its windows, its famous stained glass having been placed in storage for protection. The grand hotels, at least, were filling up as thousands of eminent statesmen, diplomats, lawyers, economists, and generals gathered from around the world for the Paris Peace Conference. They bustled in and out of salons and meeting rooms by day and in the evenings brought some wanted luster back to Paris's restaurants and dance halls. Hoover was not a part of the official American delegation. He was in Paris reprising on a colossal scale his performances as relief agent and food czar, serving, in Lloyd George's bitter words, as "food dictator to the world."[5]

Wilson had made up his mind about the roles and responsibilities of Americans in Paris over the objections of Colonel House and Hoover, both of whom thought the president was best off exerting moral authority from home, far from the haggles and intrigues of the negotiating table. Instead, Wilson swept into Paris at the head of a regal procession to take personal charge of the American delegation. He had declared "a Peoples' War for freedom and self-government among all nations of the world," and he wanted his vision to undergird the Peace.[6]

Together with Lloyd George, Georges Clemenceau of France, and Vittorio Orlando of Italy, Wilson settled the terms to be offered Germany, redrew the maps of Europe and the Middle East, wrote a charter for the League of Nations, and dealt with the innumerable demands of the many parties to the talks. Hoover was assigned responsibility for what he called "the gaunt realities which prowled outside" the conference.[7]

Those realities were that Europe was a smoldering wreck. The abrupt cessation of fighting had left tens of millions of people unemployed as armies demobilized and munitions factories shut down. Commerce and transportation were at a standstill, with many mines, railways, and bridges destroyed. Food supplies were dangerously low, prices were extremely high, and most nations lacked the financial resources to import provisions. Entire villages across Central Europe were surviving on beets and cabbage soup. Millions of children had no milk. With winter coming on and the next harvest ten months away, Hoover estimated that as many as 400 million people faced starvation.[8]

Anticipating the havoc that would attend the peace, Wilson had dispatched Hoover to Europe in the ill-defined position of special representative for relief and economic rehabilitation. Hoover had accepted the assignment with the usual claim that he had no interest in the job, simultaneously seeking for himself the broadest possible mandate and absolute control. The broad mandate, he said, was essential because he could not hope to deliver food without refurnishing Europe's broken finance, trade, communications, and transportation systems. Full control was necessary because France and Britain were seeking to jointly administer the relief, the granting or withholding of which would gain them more leverage at the conference, and in the shaping of the postwar world. Hoover had a hundred ships filled with food bound for neutral and newly liberated parts of the Continent before the peace conference was even under way. He formalized his power in January 1919 by drafting for Wilson a post-facto executive order authorizing the creation of the American Relief Administration (ARA), with Hoover as its executive director, authorized to feed Europe by practically any means he deemed necessary. He addressed the order to himself and passed it to the president for his signature.

Hoover kept his former titles as U.S. Food Administrator, chair of the U.S. Grain Corporation, and alternate chair of the Inter-Allied Food Council. He also sat as economic director of the Supreme Economic Council, chair of the European Coal Council, and head of the European Children's Fund. There were some sixty commissions, agencies, and boards involved in the rehabilitation of Europe that winter; Hoover, operating primarily through the ARA, which in time gained a $100 million congressional appropriation, sat on twenty and held sway over all of them.[9]

In addition to serving as virtual ruler of the European economy, Hoover had unusual access to his president. Wilson, anxious and temperamental as the pressures mounted in Paris, shrank his inner circle, shunning his chosen delegates and advisers, including to a large extent Colonel House. Hoover was indispensable for his vast working knowledge of Europe and his extraordinary ability to register and process every twitch in political, military, and economic affairs from Ireland to Ukraine. The president's direct experience of the Continent was limited to a three-week tour in his twenties. ("What ignorance of Europe," Clemenceau would complain of Wilson, "and how difficult all understandings were with him.") The president sat Hoover at his elbow for significant moments during the talks and took his advice on matters from the U.S. position on Bolshevism to the recognition of Finland.[10]

The actual delivery of relief was ingeniously improvised. Only Hoover, with his keen grasp of the mechanics of civilization, could have made the logistics of rehabilitating a war-ravaged continent look easy. He arranged to extend the tours of thousands of U.S. army officers already on the scene and deployed them as ARA agents in thirty-two different countries. Finding Europe's telegraph and telephone services a shambles, he used U.S. Navy vessels and Army Signal Corps experts to devise the best-functioning and most secure wireless system on the continent. Needing transportation, Hoover took charge of ports and canals and rebuilt railroads in Central and

Eastern Europe. The ARA was for a time the only agency that could reliably arrange shipping between nations. Where currency shortages made cross-border transactions difficult, Hoover's men bartered. Two locomotives in Austria were traded for 2 million eggs from Galicia. The price seemed fair because neither party to the transaction could vouch for the age of its goods.[11]

All of this, Hugh Gibson wrote another member of the Firm, was accompanied by a lot of "rumbling and growling of the exact tone you are accustomed to, with an occasional flare-up and a good deal of bad language sprinkled along the line, but, in spite of the fact that no member of The Firm in good standing will admit that anything is all right, there has been a lot of progress."[12]

Hoover gathered more intelligence than any nation or commission represented in Paris. In addition to ARA agents traveling across Europe on fact-finding missions, he had a labyrinth of far-flung contacts that gained him confidential information on the progress of crops in Tunisia and the rise of Bolshevism in Stockholm. What did not come in by wire was transmitted in person. His office drew steady streams of callers from nations great and small, all bearing problems and valuable local knowledge. Hoover recorded their intelligence on napkins and menus and stuffed them into his pockets. It was part of Lewis Strauss's job to fish through his boss's pockets every morning and salvage the crumpled paper. Hoover's up-to-the-minute reports made him the leading expert in a city loaded with expertise. Frequently called to the conference's councils and committees, he was at one point seen patiently explaining the diet of Italians to Italy's delegates. An Allied official sputtered that he was "damned tired" of having all decisions held in abeyance until this man Hoover's opinion could be ascertained.[13]

Information was power in Paris, and Hoover, like everyone else in the city, was using all the leverage he could muster to advance his nation's priorities. Naturally, some American initiatives were better received than others. Wilson and Hoover had decided in war cabinet meetings well before the Armistice to ship food across the lines and feed the enemy, in part as a humanitarian gesture. America, Hoover said, was not at war with German women and children. He either forgot, or wanted the world to forget, that the United States had tolerated the blockade of Germany in 1917–18. Wilson and Hoover also believed that their policy was rooted in their country's civilizing mission to the world. They saw the end of the war as an opportunity to redress centuries of tyranny and inequity in Europe, and they considered the political and social institutions of the United States as models for reform. They aimed to support fledgling republican governments rising in place of former tyrannies by alleviating their hunger, knowing that failure to do so might botch the transition and invite a return of the old guard, or leave Central Europe a playground for radical agitators, notably the Bolsheviks, who claimed to offer a solution to postwar problems. "Populations engulfed in starvation and misery," said Hoover, "are easily misled."[14]

Hoover had two more practical reasons for wanting to ship food to Central Europe. First, he envisioned legions of Yankee capitalists riding in behind his aid cargoes to share in the bounty of European reconstruction and postwar prosperity. The Wilsonians considered it a happy coincidence that U.S. economic interests were perfectly aligned with the good of humanity. Second, Hoover was desperate to unload a sudden surplus of food. Britain and France had used the Armistice as an excuse to back out of contracts to purchase American meat and grains at wartime prices, leaving Hoover with an enormous unsold inventory, including a billion pounds of pork, much of it sitting in ports under personal obligations amounting to more than $500 million. He needed to pierce the British blockade and unload his excess stock on Germany and Austria or suffer financial ruin and the wrath of millions of American farmers who had expanded production at his urging.[15]

Britain and France, in no mood to help, kept the blockade in force throughout the Peace Conference. They held that the enemy should be fed only after it had submitted to a treaty and arranged to pay a massive war reparations bill. The American people, having lost 120,000 of their finest in combat with Germany, were also in opposition to Hoover. The slogan "Make the Hun Pay" was current on both sides of the Atlantic. The Senate had expressly prohibited the ARA from using its $100 million appropriation for aid to enemy states.[16]

Hoover persisted, undeterred by the law, the mood at home, and Allied intransigence. He was concerned for the future of Europe, and he worried about the condition of his perishables. He engaged in a series of transactions so byzantine that it was impossible for outsiders to see exactly what he was up to. Orders flew at a dizzying pace, food moved from dock to ship, from agent to agent, from country to country, and money flowed from private banks and national treasuries through the various agencies and corporations Hoover oversaw and among the intermediaries he had arranged. In the end, 42 percent of the 1.7 million tons of food delivered by the ARA during the Armistice found its way to the former German and Austro-Hungarian empires.[17]

Aware that he was sometimes operating outside the law, Hoover assuaged his conscience with the conviction that he was doing what was best for all concerned. Unless food was delivered and stability established in Central Europe, there would be nobody left for the Allies to make peace with, and nobody to pay reparations. While he had the president's tacit support, he nevertheless felt exposed. To forestall the possibility of congressional investigation, he produced a blizzard of reports attesting to his impeccable administration of the relief.

They were unnecessary in the end. Those who had watched his work in Paris were, on the whole, impressed. John Maynard Keynes, representing the British Treasury at the peace conference, described Hoover as "a complex personality, with his habitual air of weary Titan . . . his eyes steadily fixed on the true and essential facts of the European situation." He had "imported into the Councils of Paris, when he took part in them, precisely that atmosphere of reality, knowledge, magnanimity, and disinterestedness which, if they had been found in other quarters also, would have given us the Good Peace."[18]

Those who did criticize Hoover objected to his manner more than his methods. Lloyd George found him brusque and tactless, and blamed tension between the United States and the Allies on the relief administrator's lack of diplomacy: his "surliness of mien and peremptoriness of speech" tended to provoke negative answers to his requests. These comments were echoed by a British diplomat who decried Hoover's lack of "parliamentary arts." Colonel House heard the British and French complaints and told his diary that Hoover's "besetting fault" was a propensity to dictate rather than collaborate. Nevertheless, he added: "I like Hoover and admire him the more I see of him. He is one of the few big men at the Conference."[19]

. . .

Hoover lived throughout the talks on Rue de Lubeck in a white and gold palace rented from a French countess who had abandoned Paris during the air raids. It had rich carpets on its marble stairs and a magnificent crystal chandelier in the dining room that every evening cast dazzling light on Hoover's brooding mug. As was its habit, the Firm gathered evenings for group meals at which conversation revolved around whatever was uppermost in Hoover's mind. On occasion there were entertainments at the palace. An eight-piece combo comprised of demobilized American soldiers set up one night to play the new jazz music. "They played on every kind of thing you ever saw and made a row like nothing on earth," Gibson reported to Lou. "The Chief sat through dinner with a look of acute misery on his face which those who understand his inner soul were compelled to explain was his customary way of expressing rapture and appreciation of the beautiful."[20]

A Stanford friend, Adaline Fuller, recalled a livelier time with Hoover involving gambling in Deauville, races at Longchamp, drinks at the Inn of William the Conqueror, and an evening on which, full of wine, he took the baton from the conductor of a hotel orchestra and led it through a song. These would appear to have been exceptional moments. At around ten o'clock on most nights, Hoover would claim pressing business, grab one of his murder mystery novels, and sneak off to bed. If his guests lingered within sight of the staircase, he would climb up the back way, looking, said Gibson, "as though he had been robbing a hen roost."[21]

Toward the end of every week, Hoover's energy would flag, the rims of his eyes growing redder, his shoulders slumping. Residents of the palace would pile into a convoy of two or three motorcars for a Sunday drive to some portion of the battlefront where they would stumble for hours through the shell-pocked fields, dodging barbed wire and prowling trenches. By the end of the conference they had seen almost every mile of the front from the sea to Verdun. These strenuous hikes somehow restored Hoover. He came back each week, said Gibson, like an elastic band.

. . .

At 4 a.m. on May 7, Hoover was roused from sleep by a member of his household staff who told him that a messenger was waiting downstairs with an important document requiring his personal attention. Hoover dragged himself from bed and received a copy of the first draft of the Treaty of Versailles. It was to be presented to the Germans for signature in a matter of days. He immediately sat down and read the document. His heart fell with each succeeding paragraph. "Hate and revenge," he later said, ran through every political and economic passage of the draft. He believed its punitive terms would reduce Germany to such poverty and political degradation that its new representative government would fail. The document seemed to him to invite another war.

> I arose at early daylight and went for a walk in the deserted streets. Within a few blocks I met General Smuts and John Maynard Keynes of the British Delegation. We seemed to have come together by some sort of telepathy. It flashed into all our minds why each was walking about at that time of morning. Each was greatly disturbed. We agreed that the consequences of many parts of the proposed Treaty would ultimately bring destruction. We also agreed that we would do what we could among our own nationals to point out the dangers.[22]

The president, aware that members of his team in Paris objected to the terms of the draft, called everyone together for an airing of views. Hoover said that he thought it absurd that Berlin should be asked to accept an open-ended reparations bill. He attacked the partitioning of Germany, arguing that the loss of coal-producing regions would leave the country with insufficient fuel to run its factories. How would Berlin pay its reparations and rebuild its economy without industrial recovery? How would America and the rest of Europe ever recover economically with a swamp of instability and insolvency at its center?

Hoover, still valuing his association with Wilson, did not intend to antagonize him. He generally approved of the president's approach to the conference. He applauded Wilson's intention of forging a treaty on the basis of an end to tyranny and the self-determination of peoples. He shared the president's skepticism of Europe's traditional reliance for security upon a balance of force among the great powers. He bought into the new collective approach to international security represented by the Covenant of the League of Nations, which Wilson had lovingly and at the cost of other priorities embodied in the treaty. He hoped that the creation of the League would prove a basis for a lasting peace and allow the United States to back away from any long-term commitments to the Allies, for whom the realist in him predicted an ugly future. "The social wrongs in these countries," Hoover told Wilson, "are far from solution and the tempest must blow itself out, probably with enormous violence." Better for America to stand apart as "the one great moral reserve in the world," and to exert such influence as it could through the League.[23]

All this notwithstanding, Hoover felt strongly about his objections to the treaty as drafted, and he spoke with force at Wilson's meeting. The president was not in a receptive mood, suffering ill health, violent coughing fits, fevers, and diarrhea. The sheer volume of insoluble issues was wearing on him, and the slipperiness of Lloyd George and the cynicism of Clemenceau exasperated him: he called them "mad men." The combination of pressures and ill health left him pale and grim, and he developed a facial tic. Hoover noticed Wilson groping for ideas, struggling to recall "previous decisions and precedents in even minor matters." Regardless, he began criticizing the draft with specific attention to the partitioning of Germany. Wilson listened for a time with clenched teeth and his eyes flashing angrily. He snapped at Hoover that he saw no injustice in Germany's loss of territory.[24]

Hoover followed up the next day with a memo that could only have compounded Wilson's irritation, attributing their differences of opinion on the treaty to the fact that he was better informed and more objective than the president, having not been a party to the negotiations. He doubted that Germany would sign so punitive a peace, and even if it did, the result would be resentment, political instability, and further upheaval at the heart of Europe. He pledged to stand with Wilson whatever the outcome but asked him to soften the terms of the peace in the interests of getting Europe back on its feet. There was no use in attempting to punish Germany, Hoover added, as no penance could possibly answer for her crimes.[25]

Hoover later admitted to having used in their conversation "over-vigorous words" that Wilson took as personal accusations. Their relationship deteriorated, and Hoover soon found himself in the ranks of Wilson's marginalized advisers. Germany eventually accepted the Allied terms.[26]

On June 28, the Allied commissioners and two German plenipotentiaries gathered in the Hall of Mirrors at Versailles to solemnly sign the four documents that comprised the peace. Hoover sat uneasily in their midst. He had been surprised that his attendance was welcome. "A great man with a child's modesty," said the U.S. official who had handed him the invitation.[27]

When at 3:50 p.m. the last signatures were appended to the documents, guns began to boom in the battery near the Orangerie. "The great fountains of the park were turned on," wrote an American reporter, "and the water marvels of Le Notre began to play in the mellow sunshine throughout one of the most impressive playgrounds of the world."[28]

The Germans left immediately, climbing into their cars to return to their hotel. Clemenceau invited Wilson and Lloyd George to view the fountains with him and the moment they appeared, "a great wave of wildly cheering humanity rushed toward them . . . men slapped them on the back in their exuberance, strangers shouted hoarse greetings into their ears." Amid the merriment and mellow sunshine, Hoover was inconsolable. Members of the American delegation had been telling him that he was too pessimistic. "Just wait about five years and see," he said.[29]

Hoover remained in Paris through the summer as the grand hotels emptied, cleaning up his ARA business and unloading his forebodings on Colonel House:

> Hoover fairly wallowed in gloom last night. He talked to me steadily from seven o'clock until ten and there was not a ray of light to be seen in any direction. Europe is to be in chaos, according to him, within thirty days. I tried to get him to make it thirty-one but he refused.[30]

Whatever his despair, Hoover never stopped working. The official mandate of the ARA expired July 1, by which time it had distributed $1.1 billion in food and aid. Still running an international coal commission and using ARA resources to support four European governments, Hoover was free to give more of his attention to the hordes of European children who, as they said in Oregon, were having a pretty stiff time of it. He secured Wilson's approval to use his ARA surplus to endow the European Children's Fund as a new private charity. Over the next five years it would provide clothing, hot meals, and medicine to 15 million children living in pitiable conditions in fourteen different countries.[31]

His final split with Wilson occurred over the League of Nations charter. The president returned to the United States determined to ram the treaty and the charter through the Senate, without amendments or reservations. Objections to the charter were raised from both sides of the aisle, many of them fixing on Article X, which obliged members of the League to protect one another against external aggression. This requirement was seen to undermine Congress's powers to declare war and also appeared to commit the United States to guaranteeing the security of Europe in perpetuity. Rather than strike a deal with the skeptics, Wilson, the gray and creaking autocrat, beset by twitches and blinding headaches, took his case to the people in a cross-country campaign.

Hoover realized that Wilson's only hope of gaining the necessary two-thirds majority in the Senate was to cut a deal, particularly on Article X. He wrote the president that some of the reservations were reasonable and should be accepted. Once established, the League would gain a measure of control over its own destiny and "develop such measures as will make it effective." Holding out for "a few percent more ideal structure," he warned, would only destroy the "great constructive effort" of the treaty, imperiling the economic recovery of Europe and America's foreign trade. He received no response. He would never hear from Wilson again.[32]

Seldom one to acknowledge the hard work of his men, Hoover now took the time to pen letters of gratitude to leading members of the Firm. To the one-eyed shoe salesman who had volunteered for two months, stayed for two years, and who would go on to a remarkable public service career of his own, he wrote:

My dear Strauss:

Letters are poor expressions of one's feelings. If I could write
a letter that conveyed the sense of affection I have and the
appreciation I have, I would do it.

    You have given from slender means two years of
voluntary service to the American people. At my request you
refused a commission in the Army. While you make the best
private secretary that any public man has had during this
war your attributes are too great to remain in that groove
except during a period of national distress where every red
blooded man must make sacrifice—we both go out of service
together and if you ever need a commendation from me
write it yourself and I will strengthen it up for I never trust
you to do yourself justice. But I am indeed promising a poor
return for the obligation I am under.

This is at least genuine, Herbert Hoover[*33]

For the second consecutive summer, Hoover left Europe to great
applause. The *New York Times* said that it was only becoming apparent in retrospect how much power he had wielded during the peace
talks: "He has been the nearest approach to a dictator Europe has had
since Napoleon." The *Manchester Guardian* reported that the "nominal powers" of Europe had needed to go through Hoover to get their
voices heard in the Central and Eastern regions of the continent.
Keynes, whose pessimism toward the peace settlement had matched
Hoover's, called him "the only man who emerged from the ordeal of
Paris with an enhanced reputation." He showered praise on the ARA:

Never was a nobler work of disinterested goodwill carried
through with more tenacity and sincerity and skill, and with

---

* Lewis Strauss served as a partner in the New York investment bank Kuhn Loeb and as
a financial adviser to the Rockefeller brothers before President Truman appointed him
the first civilian chair of the Atomic Energy Commission. In that capacity he championed
the development of the hydrogen bomb and played a leading role in revoking the security
clearance of J. Robert Oppenheimer, director of the Manhattan Project. He accepted the
Presidential Medal of Freedom in the Eisenhower era.

less thanks either asked or given. The ungrateful Governments of Europe owe much more to the statesmanship and
insight of Mr. Hoover and his band of American workers than
they have yet appreciated or will ever acknowledge. . . . It was
their efforts, their energy, and the American resources placed
by the President at their disposal, often acting in the teeth
of European obstruction, which not only saved an immense
amount of human suffering, but averted a widespread breakdown of the European system.[34]

Keynes's perspective was widely shared in Europe. When Woodrow Wilson won the 1919 Nobel Peace Prize for his work in Paris, a
leading Austrian newspaper wrote that it would more appropriately
have been awarded to Hoover, "who has earned the gratitude of mankind as no one else has done."[35]

Back in 1914, at the very start of his humanitarian venture in Europe,
Hoover had gathered his volunteers together and told them: "When
this war is over, the thing that will stand out will not be the number
of dead and wounded, but the record of those efforts which went to
save life." Over the years, he had taken pains to collect the files of the
CRB, the ARA, and other agencies, believing they would someday
stand as a monument in American history. It was a reasonable expectation. At a time when the world had lost its mind to hate and turned
all of its genius, technological prowess, and prodigious resources to
the task of destroying young lives by the millions in the abattoir of the
Western Front, Hoover and his men had applied their own considerable powers to sustaining millions of lives near the heart of the battle.
They had stood firm against the century's currents of destruction and
stemmed an enormous amount of suffering and loss.[36]

Yet Hoover was wrong. There is now an enormous literature on
the political, economic, and military dimensions of the Great War,
and extensive work on themes of violence, brutality, and revolt in the
artistic and literary culture of the age. The literature on humanitarian
relief is thin. Hoover himself is remembered almost exclusively for
the new career he would begin immediately upon returning home in
the early autumn of 1919.

# ★ BOOK III ★

# CHAPTER 12

# An Engineer at the Opera

It was September 16, 1919—a strange night in the Grand Ballroom of the Waldorf Astoria, with writhing flesh on the ceiling, half-naked dancers and musicians painted there in a celebration of the classical arts by the muralist Edwin Blashfield, and far below in stiff-backed chairs some twelve hundred starched-collared men of science representing the American Institute of Mining and Metallurgical Engineers. W. J. Saunders, past president of the Institute, stood to welcome home Herbert Hoover, an "eminent American citizen, a successful engineer, a genius of constructive administration, a practical economist, and a statesman of worldwide vision."[1]

Before concluding his remarks, Saunders asked the crowd if their special guest was not fit to guide America's ship of state. The engineers rose with a roar that rippled two thousand American flags suspended in the ballroom for the occasion. The hooting and applause continued for thirty seconds until overwhelmed by a lusty chant: "One, two, three four, Who are we for? Hoover!" Through it all, the man of the hour sat at the head table blushing behind candelabras, so affected by the reception that he would have difficulty beginning his speech.[2]

Although he would have denied it, that evening at the Waldorf was Hoover's political coming-out party. After being introduced as a contender by Saunders, he delivered a long, carefully crafted, and intensely political speech. He said little about his past work with the ARA beyond telling his audience that the organization had saved European civilization. He trained his attention instead on important issues facing the nation at war's end and treated the engineers to an exposition of his core political beliefs.

The first of the crucial issues addressed by Hoover was the role of the state in human affairs. The fall of the Old World's tyrannies, he said, had raised the question of how best to secure for the civilized world a greater measure of equality of opportunity and a better distribution of the fruits of industry. The choice, he said, was between U.S.-style democratic capitalism and Europe's rampant postwar experiments with socialism. The latter were of considerable interest to American intellectuals.

Socialism, insisted Hoover, was a wasteland, whether in its milder form of state-directed organization or in its more virulent strain, Bolshevism:

> The whole of the various sorts of socialism are based on one primary conception. That is that the productivity of the human being can be maintained under the impulse of altruism, and the selection of the particular human for his most productive performance can be made by some superimposed bureaucracy. My conclusion is that socialism, as a philosophy of human application, has already bankrupted itself. It has proved itself, with rivers of blood and suffering, to be an economic and spiritual fallacy. I believe it was necessary for the world to have this demonstration. But it is not necessary that we of the United States, now that we have witnessed the results, plunge our own population into these miseries and into a laboratory for experiment in foreign social diseases.[3]

The alternative, said Hoover, was an American-style system of democracy with limited government and open markets. He called it the best political organization that the world had evolved over thousands of years. Yet it contained imperfections that he believed required attention. The American system would be improved, he argued, by greater distance from the economic doctrine of laissez faire, under which all considerations of social good were left to private interests. He saw a positive role for the state in encouraging productivity and economic justice. Government must ensure that industrialists, professionals, farmers, laborers, bureaucrats, and politicians recognized their interdependence and worked together for the national good. Government must give each sector of the community a voice in the administration of production without permitting any one element to dominate the others. The state must also address the inequities of an economic system that allowed some to become grossly overpaid and immensely rich while too many others were poor.

Hoover saw nothing revolutionary in the improvements he sought to the American way. They could be managed within existing economic and political frameworks, and they would meet the approval of a majority of Americans because they were consistent with the "normal development of our national institutions." Ideals of justice, equality of opportunity, neighborliness, and concern for the greater welfare had always been fundamental to the American experience.[4]

The other important issue Hoover took up with the engineers was the role of the United States in the international community. He wanted Americans to inspire the struggling nations of postwar Europe with high ideals and democratic commitment. "We alone have the economic and moral reserve with which to carry our neighbor back to strength," he said. "To do this also is true Americanism." The United States needed to ratify the Treaty of Versailles and the League of Nations charter, for nothing else would bring peace to Europe, and peace was a necessary precondition of European recovery and North American prosperity. The rejection of the League by the Senate would mean chaos and anarchy on the Continent, said Hoover, and America's intervention in the Great War would be for naught.[5]

As he stepped out of the Waldorf that night into the cool evening air, reporters asked him if the White House was a tempting prospect. Hoover said that he had no interest in a presidential bid and that he would not be a candidate in 1920. Nevertheless, the final edition of at least one newspaper played the political angle on page one: "Toastmaster Kicks Hat of Food Boss in Ring and Diners Sing." The veteran Washington correspondent David Lawrence admired Hoover's "straightforward statement that he wasn't a candidate" as the most effective way "to start people thinking about him for President."[6]

Lawrence did not see Hoover entertain the tailcoats that night. He was out west, logging thousands of miles in a railcar as Woodrow

Wilson rallied his public to the cause of the League. Although the president had yet to declare his intentions for the election of 1920, his health and his political support were weak enough that the likes of Lawrence were privately wondering about his Democratic successor. A week after the Waldorf dinner, when the president collapsed from exhaustion in Colorado and cut short his tour, Lawrence took his speculations public. He was interested in Hoover, whom he shrewdly described as a popular "California progressive with a tendency to be as radical as the times demand."[7]

Lawrence did not waste much space discussing Hoover's virtues, which were understood. He was a businessman, a symbol of the modern, progressive, technologically driven world, yet he had reassuring small-town roots and a humanitarian's heart. He had seen the world and returned home more patriotic than ever. He was not afraid of big ideas, and he could be counted on to deliver what he promised. He was popular with the general public and a darling of the intellectually respectable (the faculties of Cornell and Harvard, the president of Yale, the journalists William Allen White and H. L. Mencken would all line up behind him in 1920). There was a strong sense that Americans were "weary" of the familiar Republican and Democratic politicians and that Hoover, a "practical man" of "straightforward accomplishments," represented something fresh.[8]

Lawrence was more interested in Hoover's electability than his credentials or merits, and it took him one short paragraph to expose the problems that would doom Hoover's campaign. He had no organization. He had no roots in the Democratic or Republican parties. He was a poor speaker and campaigner, and he knew "nothing of the art of political mixing." Moreover, said Lawrence, Hoover hated "the processes by which men get delegations to support them at political conventions." In short, he was no politician.[9]

It was true that Hoover had never really had a party. He had served Wilson's war administration as a nonpartisan, campaigning for the Democrats only once, and then more or less at gunpoint. Wilson, fearing that a looming Republican triumph in the 1918 midterm elections would undermine his influence at home and abroad, had asked his food director to publicly endorse a Democratic majority in both Houses. Understanding that his career with the arch-partisan Wilson would end if he failed to comply, Hoover called for Americans to show "united support to the President" in the conduct of war and in the negotiation of the peace. Those words helped him with neither party. The Republican National Committee denounced him as a Democrat, while Democratic regulars continued to suspect him of being a closet Republican.[10]

Hoover's natural home was the Republican Party, the party of business, the party of the West Branch Quakers, and the party of Uncle Henry John Minthorn and his Salem cronies. Yet Hoover had never worked for the Republicans or paid them much notice. When he first registered to vote, in Oakland on his twenty-second birthday, he registered as a Republican without bothering to vote. He joined the Republican Club of New York in 1909 and then bolted for Theodore Roosevelt's Bull Moose Progressives in 1912. He formally renounced his membership in the Republican Club before joining Wilson's administration in 1917.

Hoover's stump skills, as Lawrence noted, were feeble, and he knew that he did not possess the "mental attitude or the politician's manner." He feared crowds. He abhorred glad-handing and small talk with strangers. He squirmed under the scrutiny of the press corps. He wrote his own earnest, closely argued speeches, through which reporters had a difficult time following his ideas and figuring out where he stood on issues.[11]

His elocution was dreadful, even before a friendly group such as the engineers at the Waldorf. On an occasion that called for a touch of Blashfield's artistry, he stood motionless and expressionless, chin buried in his already unfashionable Prince of Wales collars, eyes fixed on his text. His voice was bereft of grace and energy. He hit the same note over and over again, word after word, page after page, like a dripping faucet. He had a single oratorical trick, often employed near the end of a speech when he felt a need for grandiloquence. He would speak most of a long sentence at his usual metronomic pace and deliver the final few syllables with a flourish: *Dum dum dum dum, dum dum dum dum, dum da dee dee dum.* He would then repeat the trick, sentence after sentence, like a stuck record.

Lawrence was also right that Hoover did not want to abide the usual processes by which candidates sought delegates. He had the amateur's disdain for political practice, as though it were beneath his dignity to ask for a vote, as though he preferred to be hired to the presidency rather than to campaign for it.

Hoover's initial strategy was to make the process and its keepers come to him. He planned to remain on the sidelines without a partisan commitment throughout the primary season, loudly proclaiming his unavailability until one party or the other gathered for its convention, recognized him as the best available man, and drafted him as its nominee. The wily Texan Colonel House knew exactly what Hoover was up to. Discarded by the enfeebled Wilson, House kept his hand in the political game by acting as a freelance adviser to prospective candidates of both parties. He had noticed how Hoover's every claim of noncandidacy was followed a few days later "by a letter or a statement apropos of nothing unless he is a candidate." Indeed, from the time he returned to the United States until the conventions, not a week went by without Hoover delivering a speech or making a press statement or being featured in a magazine. He cooperated with a worshipful biography by the author Rose Wilder Lane and testified at nine congressional hearings.[12]

He knew better than to hide his ambitions from the colonel in their regular private meetings. They had candid conversations about tactics, issues, and the pros and cons of each party. House warned Hoover that he risked appearing insincere with his long run of coy statements and his partisan aloofness.

The best that could be said for Hoover's strategy of noncommitment in 1920 was that it was a good year for an unorthodox campaign. The postwar environment did seem to argue for a new approach to politics. With the country painfully readjusting to civilian life and the Democratic administration and the Republican Senate fighting a noisy new war over the League of Nations, there was something appealing about a practical, sensible man of business, free of partisan baggage. Wrote another aspirant to a national political career, young Franklin Roosevelt:

> People are more and more seeming to get away from the old political stuff, and to be insisting upon a practical busi-

ness administration of their governmental affairs. Of course, Hoover, of all candidates, is more ideally fitted for this particular line of administrative work than any other, and I am especially gratified to see the apparent interest in Hoover's candidacy in the solid South.[13]

Novel as it may have been, Hoover's campaign was inept. He could not hold a strategy. After saying for months that he would wait to see the party platforms before choosing sides, he decided at the end of March, months before the conventions, that he needed to declare. His best shot was with the Democrats. McAdoo, himself a candidate, viewed Hoover as a serious threat. Roosevelt and his friends promoted the notion of a Hoover-FDR ticket, which Colonel House blessed as the party's best chance for victory. Hoover liked Roosevelt—they were by now regular dinner companions—but he was not interested in the nomination. The Democrats, he decided, could not win, "and I did not see myself as a sacrifice."[14]

He came out for the Republicans at the end of March, far too late, and a week later won the Michigan Democratic primary without having entered it. He took a halfhearted approach to the Republican primaries, skipping most of them, committing himself wholeheartedly to only one, in his home state of California, where Senator Hiram Johnson cleaned his clock. The Republican establishment could not have been less interested in him.

Political life was every bit as revolting as Hoover had expected. His opponents accused him of British loyalties and doubted that he was sufficiently American for the presidency. He was reduced to producing legal proof that he had resided in the United States for fourteen consecutive years as required by the Constitution. The Chinese Engineering and Mining Company scandal that he had been so desperate to bury was resurrected in the press. He protested that he was not a defendant in the case, which was true, and laid the entire blame on Moreing, which was misleading. He showed a thin skin by having his attorney threaten civil and criminal action against anyone who challenged his version of events. Hugh Gibson saw Hoover less than a month into his campaign and found him already looking "tired and harassed and bored." He was disgusted by opposition mudslinging, but having entered the contest, "he has got his teeth set and is going to fight it through."[15]

Lou Hoover, also upset by the attacks, wrote her son Allan that the newspapers were telling "so many perfect lies" about his father that the public had no idea of his true nature. "And that makes one perfectly furious,—that there are no laws to punish one for telling horrible lies about another person. That is something which we will have to change."[16]

Even distant members of the candidate's family were burned by the limelight. A profile serialized in *Everybody's Magazine* by his friend Vernon Kellogg gave an inaccurate and melodramatic picture of Hoover's childhood. Intent on portraying Hoover as a sympathetic and self-made man, Kellogg overstated the abuse and neglect he had suffered as a child. Uncle Minthorn, now living in Alaska, was furious. He believed the article was unjust to Hulda and Jesse Hoover, who had raised their son to the best of their abilities and had provided for his education. The old doctor also thought it unfair to Bert's Oregon relatives who had taken him in, furthered his education, and given him a start in business. Minthorn had not been a part of his nephew's life since they were together in Salem, and they had not kept in touch, but he was moved now to write Theodore with his complaints about Kellogg's work, a choice of addressee that tacitly acknowledged his estrangement from Bert. He was careful to blame Kellogg rather than Bert for the article's slights and mistakes, although he had to know that the author was reflecting his subject's points of view. Minthorn asked that in future his nephew not be celebrated at the expense of others: "The pinnacle that Bert is on has room a plenty."[17]

Despite all this, Hoover's popularity held up reasonably well through the spring, as surveys of Republican voters ranked him third or fourth in a crowded field, behind frontrunners General Leonard Wood and Governor Frank Lowden of Illinois. Many of the better writers who traveled to the Chicago Coliseum for the party's convention in June held candles for Hoover: Heywood Broun, William Allen White, and Edna Ferber among them. The same could not be said for the delegates. Through endless rounds of balloting, Hoover fluttered between totals of four and six votes. He showed thirteenth out of fifteen candidates on the first ballot and peaked at nine and a half votes on the tenth ballot, when Warren Harding broke the deadlocked convention with a winning total of 692.2.*[18]

Hoover, who had not attended the convention, in accord with the customs of the time, had failed miserably in his first political contest. "We know that the intelligent are all for him," said the devoted Edgar Rickard, "but we are the rankest sort of politicians and do not know how to get at the men without a white-collar."[19]

Several weeks after the convention, another member of the Firm, the young mining executive Ralph Arnold, visited Hoover in New York at the rented Park Avenue apartment where he had waited out the balloting. They had a long and frank discussion about Chicago and the nomination race. Arnold sat in an armchair near Lou, who followed the conversation while knitting under a floor lamp. Hoover strode back and forth, running his hands through his hair, bristling with nervous energy. His loss had obviously galvanized him. He had expected to show better than nine votes, and he needed to know what had gone wrong. As the evening wore on, it became clear to Arnold that whatever tentativeness Hoover had once felt toward the presidency had evaporated. It was replaced by a crystal-clear focus on dominating the Republican Party and gaining the White House. Arnold quoted Hoover as saying:

Well, son, I have had about all the experience that a human being can have. I have known all of the principal crowned heads of Europe, and have had acquaintance with great men of the world as it is today, and I feel that I have had about all of the honors that can be bestowed on a human being. However, the Presidency of the United States is the most powerful position in the world. Anyone in that position, if so inclined, can do more good than in any other position. For that reason and for that reason alone, I will leave my hat in the ring.[20]

* For arcane reasons, some convention votes were represented by two or more delegates, resulting in fractions.

Those words sound like a stage version of Hoover rather than the man himself (Arnold wrote his account of the meeting years after the fact, evidently from memory). Nonetheless, Hoover and the Firm did, from this point, abandon the notion that fate would sweep them into office. They worked to establish themselves as Republican regulars, building a base in the party's California ranks and ardently supporting the Chicago ticket of Warren Harding and Calvin Coolidge. They would learn the game and patiently await their next chance at the big prize.

Hoover's challenge in the meantime was to keep busy and stay relevant in national politics until the next electoral opportunity came along. There was never any serious question of him returning to his business life. He would muse about it from time to time, but his heart was no longer in his ledgers. The absence of commercial affairs from his daily routine had only made him fonder of service and politics, and he had all the money he required. The Hoover fortune had never quite gone to hell, as he had feared it might back in 1914. He had kept several of his directorships during the early years of the war in order to collect fees, and he had held on to some of his investments, knowing that the conflict would increase the demand for metals and raise prices for mining stocks. He finally resigned his board positions in 1916 when Moreing sued him once again for violating the terms of his restrictive covenant (they settled out of court). He liquidated most of his stock holdings that same year. Thanks to depressed wartime markets and soaring wartime taxes, he realized less than a million of what he had once anticipated would be a $30 million nest egg. He held on to his Burmese silver shares, however, which brought another $3 million five months before the Armistice. At a time of negligible taxation and relatively enormous purchasing power, that was more than enough to secure his family's future. Hoover was rich by almost any standard.[21]

Publishing was a well-trodden path for men of means seeking political relevance, and one that had always appealed to Hoover. At the end of 1919, before his campaign was launched, he had purchased a share of the *Washington Herald*. He was at pains to avoid the impression that the acquisition was a signal of his political ambitions, even though the *Herald* blew his horn throughout the election season. He also helped his friend Ben Allen overpay for the *Sacramento Union*, which sang his praises on the opposite coast. Neither venture was successful, both were short-lived, and the *Union* was a financial disaster. Hoover was not going to maintain his profile as a press baron.[22]

Some of his friends thought he should forget about politics and return full-time to what they considered his highest and best use: humanitarian endeavors. Hoover had remained active in European relief and child welfare causes even through the election season of 1920. He had traveled the country hosting fund-raising dinners, sitting grimly at head tables in dinner jacket and white tie, always next to an empty chair representing his "invisible guest," a starving European child. The New York dinner sold tickets at $1,000 apiece. The European Children's Relief fed 3 million children in the first year of its leader's return to America.[23]

Hoover's commitment to the welfare of European innocents was admirable given the national mood. The high spirits of mobilization had given way to an inevitable postwar spiral of disillusionment and despondency. Wilson's promised global "dominion of right" had never materialized. Rather, the international scene looked as unruly and dangerous as ever. The Continent seethed with hunger, injustice, ancient rivalries, and disturbing new radicalisms. There was a fresh appreciation of the Founding Fathers' warnings about the incorrigible corruption of Europe.[24]

Hoover fought the tide of insularity, preaching humanitarian duty and lecturing his countrymen on the economic necessity of European recovery, an exhausting and thankless task. He complained to friends of the strain of his fund-raising activities, and he was always on the lookout for some businessman who might be convinced to take over his duties at the European Children's Relief. Failing to find a suitable replacement, he stuck with the cause.[25]

Hoover's own sense was that his political relevance required proximity to the seat of power: he wanted to live in or near Washington, a desire that had implications for his family. While Ralph Arnold did not record Lou's reaction to Bert announcing his long-term objective of reaching the presidency, she could not have been overjoyed.

His politicking, since returning from Europe, had kept him shut-
tling between New York and Washington. She preferred to resettle
the family on the West Coast. California was Lou's home, her husband's adopted home, and her parents' home. She wanted it to be
her children's home as well. As the wartime mood of frugality and
sacrifice lifted, she dipped into the family purse to build the dream
house in Palo Alto that she had abandoned when Bert headed the
Food Administration. She chose an attractive site on San Juan Hill,
overlooking the Stanford campus. She drew the plans herself, with
assistance from several architects and designers, taking strong cues
from the California Mission Revival school and tossing in ideas from
English country cottages as well as Algerian homes she had admired.
She hid the size of the house from street view: only two stories were
visible at the front while fifty-seven rooms rolled down the hillside at
the back to cover 12,500 square feet.

The finished product was a bit of a jumble, although not without
charm, and very much in Lou's image. She spent $170,000, nearly
three times her initial high-end estimate. Her husband could not have
been less interested in her project, despite the expense. His only contributions were to insist on fireproof building materials and a reinforced concrete structure. He seemed to have considered the house
a vast storage vault. She thanked him for her liberty by giving him a
study with a spectacular view of the Santa Clara Valley all the way to
San Francisco.

Although it was intended as the family home, it would be rare
to find all four Hoovers under the roof at San Juan Hill once it was
raised. Their scattered lifestyle showed no sign of abating, with Lou
and one or two of the boys and a menagerie of dogs, birds, and reptiles
spending long stretches of time in California to escape the weather in
Washington. Guests, expected or not, would come and go with great
frequency. Bert made only occasional visits, most of them brief.

The boys, now in their teens, were increasingly independent.
Herbert Jr., earnest, aloof, much like his father in his interests and
appearance, enrolled at Stanford to study engineering. A bout of
influenza in the pandemic of 1918 had affected his hearing, although
not enough to prevent him from developing a passion for amateur
radio. Allan was something of a black sheep among Hoover men:
jovial, carefree, easy to be around.

Both boys had grown accustomed to parental absences and absorbed them without apparent harm. Active and intelligent, they bonded with their father, when they had his attention, over record players, radio sets, and automobiles (Herbert Jr. tried to build a car in the family's basement). Their mother was more intimately involved in the boys' lives, dispensing advice on how to manage their studies, diets, and social lives. Some of this advice was delivered in person; much of it came through the mails.

Lou was acutely aware of the centrifugal forces tugging at the family, and she struggled against them. The first challenge was to simply keep track of her husband's movements. She and her staff needed allies on Bert's staff to learn of his travels and dinner companions. When things were working smoothly, Lou received daily reports. Even from the opposite coast, she would worry about her husband's state of mind and arrange, through friends, to see that he was appropriately distracted with weekend motoring trips and other recreations. "I feel we want to keep his interests as varied as possible," she told Edgar Rickard.[26]

Bert, needing help with some domestic muddle, would think nothing of calling on Lou cross-country as though she were in the next room. When he could not find his honorary diplomas, she led the search from Palo Alto. "Please hunt all likely places for Daddy's diplomas," she telegraphed. "Some are in Dutch cupboard drawers other in large round paper parcel sent by Dare [Stark McMullin, her assistant] weeks ago and other perhaps in my desk drawers and hall closet near Allan's room." While expecting immediate responses to his own needs, Bert was as unreliable as ever. He was forever telegraphing Lou to announce new duties, commitments, and plans, often canceling or putting off vacations and family time, or requesting her and the family to adjust their schedules to meet his.[27]

It all wore on Lou, who needed more communication and emotional connection with her men than she was receiving. She constantly pleaded for more letters, worrying that they had forgotten her. One feels for her in learning through correspondence, often written by staff, of Bert's triumphant speeches, of changes in Allan's voice as he emerged from puberty, of school dances and holidays, earaches and lost dogs. At the same time, Lou was often the cause of dislocations, making last-minute scheduling adjustments to extend visits or to balance her many personal interests. She was aware that her own affairs and her independent nature complicated her family life, yet she was not prepared to settle for life as a typical Washington homemaker. Bert, appreciating her spirit, consumed with his own interests, did not stand in her way. It was an enlightened attitude for the time, although it did not amount to active spousal support.

One feels for the children as well, especially the younger Allan, who, left alone in Washington for Christmas in 1920, decorated the house with the assistance of domestic staff. An apologetic letter was a poor substitute for his absent father:

> This is to convey the love that I cannot give to you in person by being with you on Christmas Day. I feel the separation more than you will ever appreciate but I know that you will understand that it is entirely in the interest of other children and that you will have a happy Christmas with mother. Daddy.[28]

A typical letter from his mother:

> It seems that you will have to be fearfully brave again, - and do something that you will not at all want to. And that is to start to school without your dear old Mum being on hand to see you off, or to hear all the stories there are to tell when you get back! However I think it is much harder on me than on you.[29]

From his mother, again, explaining why Allan must remain in Washington with his preoccupied father:

> This world is full of duties, if one is not perfectly selfish. And your duty seems to be to cheer up Daddy all you can.[30]

In the summer of 1920, it was Senator Warren Harding, not young Allan Hoover, who had the wherewithal to cheer Daddy. Bert had decided that keeping a high profile in Washington and winning a seat in the cabinet were the best means to serve his country and ensure his presidential prospects. He wrote Harding after the Republican convention to say that he would be refusing "offers which I have received to enter into business." He wanted instead to devote himself to the public good and was "open to any suggestion as to how I can be of service."[31]

Harding answered Hoover's letter warmly and they kept up a correspondence throughout the campaign, much of it focused on the League of Nations, which Hoover favored and which Harding pretended not to oppose. Hoover made a series of speeches on behalf of the Republican ticket and tried to convince his pro-League friends that Harding's speeches bashing Wilson's handiwork at Versailles did not reflect his true feelings. He was determined to make the relationship work.

Warren Gamaliel Harding had a gift for relationships and a genius for politics. He had gone to Chicago as a long shot and meticulously executed a strategy to make himself the second choice of every delegate. His organizers met each arriving Republican at the train station, and he sent a Harding glee club from his native Ohio to serenade workers in competing candidates' headquarters. He brought fellowship and a conciliatory spirit to a party still reeling from the great Roosevelt-Taft split of 1912. When the various frontrunners failed to knock each other out, they turned, exhausted and grateful, to the "great harmonizer."[32]

Harmony was Harding's métier. He was middle of the country and middle of the road. He preferred making friends to making arguments or decisions. He rarely pushed a cause unless it was unanimous, and he rarely opposed one until it was dead. He had a fetish for fences—mending them, sitting on them. His only accomplishment in six years of service in the U.S. Senate was to rack up an attendance record abysmal even by that chamber's sorry standards. He once distinguished himself by calling the Prohibition amendment to the Constitution "unwise, imprudent, and inconsiderate," and then voting for its approval. But he seldom missed a senatorial poker game, and he was on great terms with all of his colleagues.[33]

Harding's first meeting with Hoover was illustrative of his style. Like many a congressional figure, he had made his way to the Food Administration offices during the war but unlike other visitors seeking preferment or favors, Harding simply shook Hoover's hand and said: "I haven't come to get anything. I just want you to know that if you wish the help of a friend, telephone me what you want. I am here to serve and to help."[34]

Harding was precisely what the Republicans needed in the campaign of 1920. President Wilson had left the nation a shambles, socially, politically, and economically. Demobilization had been bungled, with some $35 billion in government contracts and commitments canceled without plans for economic reconstruction, and 13 million workers and servicemen dumped onto the job market without a plan for their reintegration. A brief postwar economic boom was running out of oxygen and unemployment was high; those who could find jobs were paid low wages in a time of high inflation and soaring corporate profits. The cost of living had almost doubled since the prewar years with food and clothing leading the way, and people were fed up. Four million workers took part in labor actions in 1919. Boston descended into hooliganism and chaos when its police force walked off the job, and the general strike emerged as a fearsome weapon of protest in Seattle. Both of those events were portrayed in local and national press accounts as the dawn of Bolshevism in the New World. None of the hatreds and suspicions stirred by war had dissipated with peace: fear of Germany had mutated into fear of Reds, revolution, and anarchism. It was a time of reactionary immigration restrictions and Attorney General A. Mitchell Palmer's deplorable mass deportations of suspected foreign radicals. Even those who could rise above the pervasive hysteria could not help but wonder what the future held: with communism on the rise, with Europe's dynasties destroyed, with much of the world sunk in economic distress and civil wars, there were legitimate questions as to what kind of order would prevail.

Wilson had been a shadow of his former self over his last eighteen months in office, and his illness had become a symbol of the nation's health. Shattered, wasted, bedridden, obsessed with his treaty, he had no answers to the problems of the day, indeed, he was barely aware of them. The Republican-dominated Congress, obsessed with thwarting Wilson and his internationalism, was equally ineffectual.[35]

"We are at the dead season of our fortunes," wrote Keynes in an estimation of the international mood that applied equally to America. "Our power of feeling or caring beyond the immediate questions of our own direct experience and the most dreadful anticipations cannot move us. . . . We have already been moved beyond endurance, and need rest."[36]

Harding, a veteran of two decades in the Ohio and United States senates, caught the moment perfectly: "America's present need is not heroics, but healing; not nostrums, but normalcy; not revolution, but restoration . . . not surgery but serenity." He campaigned from his front porch in Marion, Ohio, appearing daily to wave his straw hat in greeting to his public. He looked presidential, tall and power-fully built, with a chiseled face and thick black eyebrows over sympa-thetic eyes. His blue-gray hair was carefully brushed and pomaded. His dark coat and white trousers were pressed and creased. Harding's demeanor struck one reporter as "the calm, gracious, assured manner of the delegate from some grand lodge exemplifying the work of the local chapter." His oratory was puerile: William McAdoo heard "an army of pompous phrases moving over the landscape in search of an idea"; Harding himself admitted to "bloviating"; Mencken called his butchery of the language "Gamalielese." Regardless, Harding's voice was strong and soothing and his presence reassuring, and the people loved him.[37]

The great irony of Harding's life was that he shared none of the confidence in himself that he inspired in others. He was a troubled man, constantly doubting his abilities and thinking himself a fraud, tormented by suspicions of miscegenation in the Harding line. As an adult, he suffered a series of nervous collapses, checking himself into Dr. Kellogg's famous Battle Creek Sanitarium on five occasions in twelve years. His ambition and his powerful need to conform led him to marry a socially prominent woman he did not love, to publish a boosterish local newspaper, to join the Elks and the Rotarians and the Chamber of Commerce, and to answer the rest of his needs in a double life. He pursued a long and passionate extramarital affair with his best friend's wife and spent the war years gamboling with a recent high-school graduate who secretly bore his child. He continued in these reckless ways despite close calls with Mrs. Harding and police detectives.

His affairs were one of many forms of self-soothing. He ate heart-ily: waffles and chipped beef for breakfast. He liked a couple of drinks in the evening along with his cigars, his cigarettes, his pipe, and the occasional plug of Piper Heidsieck champagne–flavored chewing tobacco—"the height of good taste." He relaxed at the poker table with his Ohio and senatorial cronies and on the golf course with his Airedale, Laddie Boy, trained to retrieve his practice balls. By these means, he was able to maintain his splendid facade.[38]

On November 2, 1920, Harding demolished the Democratic candidate, James Cox, another Ohio newspaper publisher, with the largest popular majority (60.3 percent) to that point in U.S. history. He carried thirty-seven of forty-eight states, including every one in which he had campaigned. Six days after his election victory, Harding invited Hoover to visit Marion, Ohio, to confer on international relations and to exchange views on what Harding called "the best proposal on which we may hope to unite American sentiments." It was a summons for Hoover to interview for a cabinet post.[39]

Expected early on the morning of December 12, Hoover kept the president-elect waiting, arriving by automobile at 10:45 a.m. He nodded to reporters and disappeared into the Harding home, a stately two-story with a large colonnaded veranda. Two hours later, Hoover emerged, nodded again, and hopped into his car for the return to Columbus. Somewhere along the way he let reporters know that he had discussed with Harding his future and "the whole gamut of international and national troubles without arriving at any definite conclusions." Specifically, he mentioned that he had treated his host to another recitation of his views on the League of Nations.[40]

It was somewhat baffling to the general public that the League remained a live topic. The Republican-controlled Senate led by Henry Cabot Lodge had voted to kill Wilson's treaty in November 1919 and again in March 1920 but with an election upcoming, and in the absence of an official peace between the United States and Germany, supporters of the League had managed to resurrect the issue. Hoover had joined former president William Howard Taft and former secretary of state Elihu Root as unofficial co-captains of Republican pro-League forces. They were influential enough to force a compromise in the Chicago platform: the party rejected the League as embodied in Wilson's treaty while remaining open to some sort of international association. Throughout the campaign, Hoover and what he called the "thinking progressive" wing of the party convinced themselves that the League might yet live with minor reservations. The Lodge faction meanwhile did its best to reseal the grave.[41]

Harding managed the situation in his inimitable manner, telling Hoover that once the American people were unified he would attempt to "get the nations of the world to a friendlier understanding of a workable world league." Hoover would seize upon these vague words as pro-League promises and publicize them to the chagrin of Lodge and the isolationist senator William Borah. Lodge and Borah would in turn request and receive from their leader earnest although not quite definitive support of their own positions.

On occasion, Harding would flirt with compromises, suggesting, for instance, that the treaty might be reopened and renegotiated. Hoover would explode, writing to express his "overwhelming shock" at the proposal. Rewriting the treaty was a nonstarter, he said, given that it was a signed agreement that had asked and answered "ten thousand questions" in "documents already executed." The twenty-three nations involved in its negotiation, he continued, could not be reassembled without causing "complete chaos" and irreparable harm to American trade and diplomacy with Europe. Harding's choices, according to Hoover, were to succumb to Lodge and Borah ("the worst forces in American public life") and scrap the entire treaty, or to accept the pact with minor reservations.[42]

Like most Republicans, Hoover vacillated between elation and outrage during the League discussions, never knowing for certain where his leader stood. In fact, Harding stood amused. He read newspaper reports of the various interpretations of his enigmatic remarks with pride and delight. His exclusive concern was unity: he juggled the interests of all factions—pro-League, mild-reservationists, strong-reservationists, and irreconcilables—with the simple goal of keeping them all in the Republican tent, and he would succeed in doing so.

Ten days after their meeting in Marion, the mutual courtship of Hoover and Harding entered its operatic phase. Without having received an offer of a position, Hoover wrote the president-elect to take himself out of contention. He said that opposition to him from Republican stalwarts would hamper his ability to serve effectively. "I cannot enter public office except as an insistent call to public service, and not as a matter of political adjustment," he wrote. "Nor do I wish to be an embarrassment to you in the great task that lies before you. I will, of course, give every support to constructive policies of the administration and the party, without public office. . . . I hope you will fully realize that I am always personally at your service, and that you will dismiss from your mind all thought of my appointment."[43]

Hoover was right about opposition to him among establishment Republicans. News coverage of his visit to Marion had prompted howls of protest from the old guard in the Senate, who detested him as a progressive, an internationalist, and a League stalwart. "Hoover gives most of us gooseflesh," said Senator Frank Brandegee of Connecticut.[44]

Even the Republican new guard, more sympathetic to Hoover's progressivism, mistrusted him as an ambitious publicity hound with a Democratic résumé. Indeed, suspicion of Hoover was one of few things elected Republicans could agree upon at the end of 1920, yet none could do anything to stop him so long as Harding coveted him.

Hoover did not intend his letter to take him out of consideration. It was a plea for Harding to call the Republican senators to heel, and it was also a negotiating tactic. Hoover, wanting into the cabinet, and wanting a good seat, hoped that his reticence would convince Harding to up the ante and offer him secretary of state. He was slow to accept that his views on the League made his confirmation in so crucial a role by a Republican-led Senate unthinkable. State would go to Charles Evans Hughes, the former governor of New York and Supreme Court justice.

Hoover's demurrals did nothing to dissuade Harding, a man who enjoyed a chase. He wanted Hoover for Interior or Commerce, and the wailing of his former Senate colleagues seemed only to whet his appetite. He was impressed at Hoover's "super eminent ability as an organizer and director of large affairs." He liked his reputation in the business community and his popularity with Republican voters, and he appreciated that having Hoover on board would placate the small but influential pro-League Republican faction. Most importantly, Harding believed that bringing Hoover into the cabinet in the right role would increase American prosperity.[45]

"Taking Herbert Hoover up one side and down the other," Harding told a friend, "and taking into consideration the knowledge he has of things generally, I believe he's the smartest gink I know."[46]

Over the holiday season, the president-elect sent emissaries to gauge Hoover's state of mind and to keep their conversation running. By early February, Harding was fishing and golfing in St. Augustine while Hoover was in New York telling reporters that he could not decide on his availability until presented with an official offer directly from Harding. He told Edward House in confidence that an unofficial offer had already been made. The colonel, still believing Hoover ill-suited for political life, urged him to concentrate on international humanitarianism, knowing all the while that he ached to join the "official family."[47]

With time running out before his inauguration, Harding neatly removed an important obstacle to Hoover's ascent by telling Lodge that Senate Republicans would only get their candidate for Treasury secretary, the Pittsburgh financial wizard Andrew Mellon, if they accepted someone they disliked in Commerce. With the chorus of opposition silenced, Harding prepared to offer Hoover a seat. On the morning of February 22, 1921, Hoover received a telegram from St. Augustine: "Please advise me by wire where I can get in touch with you by telephone at six o'clock Tuesday Feb twenty second."[48]

Rather than rejoice in the moment, Hoover, working out of offices in the Financial District on lower Broadway, issued a balky statement through his press agent on the afternoon of the 22nd. He announced that he had been advised by friends to refuse a cabinet spot on grounds that the Department of Commerce offered little scope for the sort of "constructive national service" he liked to do. What's more, said the agent, "Mr. Hoover had hoped that as soon as the funds for child relief were secured he would turn some of his attention toward his own profession of engineering, as he is not a rich man and he does not feel he can continue indefinitely to give his entire time to public service. In fact, I know that he has had negotiations to this end."[49]

The offers to enter into business were another bluff, although perhaps not a fabrication. Paul Warburg, one of the leading figures in international finance and a father of the Federal Reserve System, was then organizing the International Acceptance Bank of New York to promote the financing of European reconstruction. He reportedly asked Hoover to join on whatever terms he wished. A similarly attractive pitch is said to have come from the Guggenheim brothers, owners of the world's leading mining and metallurgy concern. They offered Hoover leadership of their business, full partnership, and guaranteed earnings of at least $500,000 a year. Neither proposal dampened Hoover's appetite for public office.[50]

His last-minute demurral raised eyebrows on the shaded verandas of St. Augustine. After a closer read, however, Harding and his advisers noticed that Hoover had stopped short of saying he would decline an offer: he had merely stated a preference. Assuming that the candidate could still be persuaded to answer the call of duty, Harding telephoned at the appointed hour. Hoover answered and after hanging up rushed through Manhattan's evening throngs to the Metropolitan Opera House for a gala performance of *Carmen* on behalf of the European Relief Fund.

"It is true that Senator Harding and I have had a conversation over the telephone this evening as to my accepting a post in the cabinet," he told reporters on the steps of the opera house. "Naturally these are matters requiring consideration, and equally they are not matters for me to discuss now."[51]

It was the first gala performance of *Carmen* at the Metropolitan in a decade, with Giovanni Martinelli and Geraldine Farrar in the lead roles. Regular box holders had bought their own seats for the evening for $1,000, contributing to a net haul of $50,000 for the relief fund. There was the usual complement of Whitneys, Vanderbilts, Astors, and Potters in attendance. The women had left their jewels at home in deference to the occasion; they wore brightly colored gowns to compensate. Debutantes roamed the aisles selling souvenir programs at a dollar apiece. Hoover entered late. Oblivious as Carmen threw her flower at the feet of Don José, he found his way to J. P. Morgan's box, where he buttonholed Edward House. He drew the colonel back into the shadows at the rear of the box in order to be heard over the music.[52]

Hoover was excited as he relayed the details of his phone call. "We talked it over during a large part of the evening," House wrote in his diary. Harding had officially offered secretary of commerce, and Hoover had accepted on condition that he could reorganize the department and expand its purview to the field of foreign commerce. He also wanted to play a leading role in all government activities that affected domestic and foreign commerce, and in the structure of government generally. Harding promised that he would have a free hand. It crossed the colonel's mind as he sat in the back of the box that his friend had "started in for the Presidency, was afterward mentioned for Secretary of State," and was now jockeying for "practically the lowest position in the Cabinet." It was nonetheless apparent long before Carmen stabbed Don José that nothing would keep Hoover from his goal of joining the official family.[53]

Not that he was ready to announce his acceptance. Like a diva on his ninth encore, Hoover arrived at 42 Broadway the bright, cold morning after the fund-raising gala and told reporters that nothing had been concluded. He was not sure that Commerce was the right role for him. He outlined for reporters the "enormous field" of responsibility he had requested of Harding. He made it clear that he intended to continue his humanitarian relief and children's aid while serving in the cabinet.[54]

Harding called again that evening, reiterating to Hoover that he would have a free hand, and the deal was finally consummated. Hoover issued a release suggesting that the ardor was all on the other side:

> President-elect Harding this evening asked me to state that he has included myself in his nominations for the Cabinet as Secretary of Commerce. Senator Harding enters whole-heartedly into plans for upbuilding this department, and wishes that I continue to direct the policies of European relief.[55]

A week later, Hoover heard from an old friend, Franklin Lane, freshly loosed from public service in a role similar to the one Hoover had agreed to assume. Through seven years in Wilson's cabinet, Lane had known his share of achievement, satisfaction, trouble, anxiety, insult, and humiliation, and now, like so much else from the Wilson administration, he was in ruins: out of a job, his bank accounts empty after two decades of low-paying public service, his health failing. He wrote Hoover from a doctor's cot with a "half mile" of red tube down his throat draining an infected gallbladder. He was dying of heart disease. "I am weary," he said. "So damn weary."[56]

A wise and erudite man who lifted his spirits in the pages of Gibbon, Lane looked from his cot to the world around him and scratched
his bald head with dismay. He hardly recognized the country and the
people he had served. Everything looked "awry, distorted and altogether perverse." He recalled the hopes and ambitions with which
he had begun his career and struggled to reconcile them with what
the Wilsonians had wrought. He was staggered by the gap between
intent and effect. His letter to Hoover conveyed impotence and futility without a hint of self-pity. He offered his cautious congratulations:

> I hope that you will find political life possible. That is my
> only doubt as to you and your new place. They are hungry
> these politicians—and they are blind to a lot of things that
> you & I see. They will be brutal. They think there is no one
> thing as important as to satisfy some constituent. . . . Good
> luck old man. I should like to be near you but Heaven knows
> when I shall see you.[57]

Hoover responded within the week with a warm letter that
revealed his disdain for large parts of the political world he was about
to enter:

> My dear Lane:
>
> I am indeed greatly touched by your note of March 1st and
> I feel everything you say. I pursued every alley in endeavor
> to find an excuse for refusing this position and each one of
> them became a blind alley to my own conscience.
>      I realize that the surrounding forces in and out of the
> Government are such that any one man can do but little. In
> these times I doubt whether any man has the right to refuse
> to take service lest he could accuse himself of something that
> he could have, at least partially, mitigated.
>      I do recognize that I am not intellectually constituted for
> this kind of job and that bold diagnosis and strong action are
> not consonant with our political institution except in times
> of emergency.[58]

# CHAPTER 13

# Meddling with God's Economy

In his letters to Hoover during the campaign, Harding had left no doubt as to what would be the primary ambition of his presidency. He wanted to unite and lift the national spirit. This, he intuited, required normalcy, by which Harding meant relief from the addling effects of war and demobilization, and respite from two hectic decades of progressivism and the upheaval and uncertainty it had inspired.

Harding diligently worked the knots of America's body politic from the moment he took office, soothing conservatives by resizing the federal government for peacetime and adopting a pro-business outlook, soothing his Republican base by raising tariffs and lowering taxes, soothing the left by releasing from prison the socialist icon Eugene Debs and other radicals rounded up during Palmer's Red Scare, soothing the battered farm belt with an emergency tariff and federal protection for farm cooperatives, soothing labor with public works programs to ease unemployment and by cajoling the steel industry into abandoning its inhumane practice of twelve-hour shifts. Harding soothed the isolationist and nativist majority in America with tighter immigration policies and a foreign policy emphasizing legitimate national interests over crusading idealism. He soothed international tensions by normalizing relations with Germany and other former enemy states, and by convincing the world's leading naval powers to reduce tonnage at his Washington Disarmament Conference, the first gathering of its kind and a remarkable, unexpected success.

Normalcy did not allow much scope for large ideas and grand ambitions. It was unclear at the launch of the administration how Hoover's penchant for "bold diagnosis and strong action" could be satisfied within the president's limited framework of political objectives. That Hoover oversaw a minor department made his hopes seem faintly ridiculous. Oscar Straus, who had managed a combined labor and commerce portfolio in Roosevelt's cabinet, told Hoover that Commerce was a "dignified and agreeable" department of no consequence whatsoever. The new secretary was advised to satisfy himself working only two or three hours a day, "putting the fish to bed at night and turning on the lights around the coast."[1]

Hoover got his first taste of his insignificance on the morning of March 8, 1921, when Harding first gathered his official family in the buff-colored cabinet room of the White House executive offices. The president stood majestically at one end of a long mahogany table to welcome his new colleagues; he faced his tiny, tight-lipped vice president, Calvin Coolidge, sitting at the other end beneath a portrait of Lincoln. After laying his ground rules, stressing collegiality and confidentiality, Harding asked each of his executives for a report on issues and policies. Hoover, whose department had been proclaimed as an independent entity in 1913 on the last day of the Taft administration, ranked lowest in seniority and reported last of ten. At age forty-six, he was also the second-youngest man in the room.[2]

Yet Hoover did not view his fief as low or menial. He had studied the Commerce Department's enabling act, which gave him authority to "foster, promote and develop the foreign and domestic commerce, the mining, manufacturing, shipping and fishing industries, and the transportation facilities of the United States." It was plain to him that he had oversight of the entire U.S. economy, and he was not about to ease up, whatever the public mood. He arrived in his office with a self-assigned mission to improve the business of America to the benefit of all its citizens.[3]

Like so many of the economic managers who had operated on a vast scale during the Great War, Hoover had come to understand the national economy as a single gigantic plant, rather than as a collection of local or regional markets and industries. He had been impressed at how the productive resources of a nation could be rationalized and organized to meet important public objectives. He wondered at the potential strength of an economy unencumbered by such wasteful phenomena as unemployment, labor conflict, and the dreary ebb and flow of business cycles, and what might be accomplished if some of the old wartime spirit and efficiency could be carried into peace. Bernard Baruch, the Democratic financier who had sat alongside Hoover in Wilson's war cabinet as head of the War Industries Board, had come to many of the same conclusions. Their mutual experience, he said, pointed "to the desirability of investing some Government agency [with powers] to encourage, under strict Government supervision, such cooperation and coordination in industry as should tend to increase production, eliminate waste, conserve natural resources, improve the quality of products, promote efficiency in operation, and thus reduce costs to the ultimate consumer."[4]

These were radical thoughts to conservative Republicans in Washington, who wished to erase every trace of governmental expansion from the Wilson years. Yet facts on the ground were providing momentum to the new thinking. The early decades of the twentieth century were remarkable for the emergence of a national consumer economy. American enterprise was becoming dependent on mass production and mass communication and on national distribution to national chains. The economy's problems, whether coal shortages or rail strikes, had national consequences. "We have reached a stage of national development of such complexity and interdependence of economic life that we must have a national planning of industry and commerce," said Hoover on taking up his post. "Government has a definite relationship to it, not as an agency for production and distribution of commodities nor as an economic dictator, but as the greatest contributor in the determination of fact and of cooperation with industry and commerce in the solution of its problems."[5]

Commerce operated out of a blockish yellow building at Nineteenth Street and Pennsylvania Avenue. Hoover took an office on the top floor. He sat at an uncluttered desk with a battery of secretaries and aides-de-camp outside the door. They scheduled his appointments and telephone calls in half-hour slots from nine in the morning until early evening. His days continued to be bracketed by informal meetings over breakfast and dinner.

Hoover pulled as many of Commerce's scattered bureaus into the building as would fit. He undertook what would over time prove to be a wildly successful bid to wring funds from Congress for departmental growth. With merit-based hiring still something of a novelty in Washington, he took a broom to political hacks in every corner of his dominion. He began recruiting administrative talent from the commercial world, most of them college-educated professionals. Responding to their leader's call of service, these recruits worked at a fraction of the salaries available to them in the private sector. Hoover also assembled a panel of twenty-five distinguished leaders from industry, labor, and agriculture to help guide the department's policy, the first time a brain trust had been applied to peacetime administration in Washington.[6]

The professionalization of his staff was a necessary first step in making Commerce the leader and facilitator of American business. It would show firms how to adopt a more scientific, data-based approach to management and supply them with up-to-date information on market activity, commodity inventories, employment, and other information critical to better business planning. This would allow for lower costs, improved quality, higher margins, and other elements of what we would now refer to as increased productivity. Working through industry representatives and trade associations, Commerce would encourage the adoption of common standards to conserve resources, reap the benefits of scale, and eliminate unnecessary competition. (The Germans may have lost the war, but their economic critique of the cigar shop and bakery on every corner had conquered important minds.) Additionally, Commerce would lead the charge to strengthen the national infrastructure: upgrading domestic waterways, reorganizing railroads, and vastly expanding regional electrical systems to lower the costs of business and increase the speed and efficiency with which it was consummated.

Hoover's plan amounted to a complete refit of America's single gigantic plant, and a radical shift in Washington's economic priorities. Newsmen were fascinated by his talk of a "third alternative" between the "unrestrained capitalism of Adam Smith" and the new strains of socialism rooting in Europe. Laissez-faire was finished, Hoover declared, pointing to antitrust laws and the growth of public utilities as evidence. Socialism, on the other hand, was a dead end, providing no stimulus to individual initiative, the engine of progress. The new Commerce Department was seeking what one reporter summarized as a balance between fairly intelligent business and intelligently fair government. If that were achieved, said Hoover, "We should have given a priceless gift to the twentieth century."[7]

Hoover repeatedly framed his objectives in high-flown terms, a habit that culminated in his declaration of "a new era in the organization of industry and commerce in which . . . lie forces pregnant with infinite possibilities of moral progress." A bold vision, boldly expressed: Hoover had learned something from Woodrow Wilson.[8]

He nevertheless proceeded in a practical manner, moving swiftly to attack one of the biggest obstacles to his plans, the federal government's profound ignorance of the American economy. Reliable data on employment rates, industrial output, and net financial reserves were nowhere to be had in Washington. A consumer price index had been launched only a year earlier. Politicians had a weak grasp of market economics and the real effects of their decisions. Businessmen had little sense of what was happening in the commercial world beyond their own operations.[9]

Knowing that he could not manage what he could not measure, Hoover made Commerce both a producer and a clearinghouse of relevant information on the U.S. economy. Once again, he turned to like-minded experts, this time primarily in the academic community. Hoover announced the Advisory Committee on Statistics and recruited to it such luminaries as Edwin Gay, the first dean of the new Harvard Business School; Edwin Seligman, the Columbia economist and a founder and past president of the American Economic Association; and Cornell's Walter Willcox, a past president of the American Statistical Association and a former co-director of the U.S. Census. Another eminence, Julius Klein, the Harvard economist and historian, was recruited to head Hoover's Bureau of Foreign and Domestic Commerce and allowed to increase its budget by a factor of six and its personnel by a factor of five. In short time, these and other initiatives turned Commerce into a vast reservoir of information on every aspect of economic life from steel to motion pictures. Its specialists sucked in information from across the country, analyzed it, and published an endless stream of reports intended to improve the economic intelligence of governments and business. The bet was that more accurate information would take emotion and guesswork out of planning, prevent overexpansion and speculation, and produce a more perfect market.

While the data managers at Commerce were careful to present their findings in an objective, scientific manner, it was never difficult to identify the guiding hand of Hoover behind their work. His obsession with productivity was manifest in data demonstrating the woeful inefficiency of the U.S. economy. Commerce's Bureau of Standards was appalled to learn that there were sixty-six sizes of paving bricks on the market, and thirty-two discrete ways to measure a one-inch board. Hoover's experts turned up endless examples of needless variation in shapes, sizes, and specifications of thousands of products, from auto tires to men's suits to baby bottle nipples. This rampant diversity raised costs on manufacturers and prohibited them from operating at scale. It was also deemed an inconvenience to consumers: who would not benefit from a standard electric light socket? While Commerce insisted that its standardization efforts were voluntary, Hoover used government purchasing power to hurry things along. He also organized more than a hundred conferences and commissions in Washington where industry leaders and trade associations discussed mutual problems, shared economic intelligence, and enlarged their sense of responsibility. They were advised of the interdependence of business, labor, and government and the need for all sectors of society to pull together in the common interest as they had done in wartime. They were lectured on the social and economic costs of nonstandardized practices and urged to introduce uniformity to their goods and processes, right down to the documents on which they worked. While the effect of the standardization blitz was unquantifiable, Hoover claimed it would save consumers $600 million a year, a huge sum at the time.[10]

He had barely started on these and many other initiatives in the Department of Commerce when, like virtually every other time in his life Hoover had launched an important (at least to him) venture, disaster struck.

The American economy has crashed at the rate of once or twice a decade since the early seventeenth century. Some crashes originate in commodity markets, some in stock markets, others in the banking sector, or foreign exchange. All of the crashes share a sudden shift from optimism to pessimism, from greed to fear and panic, with investors liquidating their assets into a failing market, losses mounting, lending seizing, business activity declining, and people suffering.[11]

The depression of 1921 began on Woodrow Wilson's watch as the economy struggled to adjust to a postwar footing. A short burst of growth after Armistice Day was followed by a rapid decline. The nascent Federal Reserve noticed the burst, raised its discount rate to stifle the inflation it expected would follow, and failed to register the downturn. Its rate hike hit just when lower rates were needed to stoke a recovery. The combination of high rates and dwindling demand caused agricultural markets to plummet and the economy to choke in the weeks after Harding's inauguration. GNP would soon be down 16 percent from an end-of-war high. Prices and wages began falling precipitously, as did employment, leaving a third of industrial workers on the street within a year.[12]

Orthodox opinion in both parties dictated that a government beset by economic storms batten the hatches and wait them out. That is what Roosevelt had done in the Panic of 1907, and that is what every president had done before him. Cyclical fluctuations in income and output were viewed as inevitable and inescapable forces of nature; to challenge this perspective was to doubt the universal laws of economic and natural life. Treasury Secretary Andrew Mellon was as orthodox as they came, insisting on a minimal role for government generally: it was responsible for national defense, the currency, customs and excise, and little else. Washington spent roughly 3 percent of gross national product before the war, and Mellon aimed to return to that level from wartime highs of 23 percent by keeping spending tight and taxes low. This approach was just fine with Harding, whose economic philosophy was encapsulated in the headline of an article he wrote for a popular magazine: "Less Government in Business and More Business in Government." He did not see it as Washington's job to eradicate unemployment or bail out bankers or calm markets. He was predisposed to let the downturn do its worst. Prices and wages would eventually fall and good times would inevitably follow.[13]

A new school of economists with whom Hoover was aligned were inclined to challenge natural law. Impressed by Washington's ability to manipulate the economy in wartime, they believed that with proper leadership and cooperation from industry and lower levels of government they could mitigate the effects of the business cycle, if not eliminate them entirely.

As 1921 progressed and bad news accumulated, the old orthodoxies became increasingly difficult to sustain, even for conservatives like Harding. The downturn was so stunningly swift and steep as to shake faith in the future of capitalism. Free-market nations, their credibility already weakened by the Great War, now faced aggressive new challenges to their legitimacy from the Bolshevik Revolution, socialist experiments in Europe, and radical agitation in the United States. Even within capitalist circles, there was a growing recognition that governments, having dislocated their economies to fight the war, had a responsibility to help pick up the pieces. It was noted that many of the newly unemployed were ex-servicemen; also that agricultural overproduction had been encouraged by the state.

Hoover toed the administration line in the initial months of the crisis, making positive speeches he would later describe as "whistling while passing the economic graveyard so as to keep up public courage." The United States was fundamentally sound, he said. The economy had "turned the corner." In fact, industrial activity remained prostrate and unemployment deepened. By August 20, 1921, he was ready to goad Harding into action. He suggested a presidential commission on unemployment comprised of men and women "representative of all sections, predominantly those who can influence the action of employing forces and who can influence public opinion." The aim would be to properly determine "the facts and needs of the [unemployment] situation." Harding was uneasy enough to agree.[14]

The Interior Building, the most modern of federal buildings, was chosen as the venue for what would become known as the President's Conference on Unemployment. Sixty handpicked delegates from cross-sections of industry, labor, and government passed under the huge carved stone eagle at its entrance on the morning of September 26, 1921. Among them were Charles M. Schwab of Bethlehem Steel, Samuel Gompers of the American Federation of Labor,

Detroit mayor James Couzens, and Ida Tarbell, the journalist and social reformer. The president welcomed them with a brief address in the auditorium at 10:15 sharp. His short, hackneyed speech made plain his ambivalence toward the conference. His office had been telling reporters for days that he doubted anything could be done to relieve unemployment. He had agreed to host the event only because Hoover wanted it, and he had confidence in Hoover.

The president ventured that simply measuring the size of the problem might be a good start to solving it (jobless estimates ranged from 2 million to 8 million at the time). He cautioned the delegates against tampering with America's social, political, economic, and industrial systems: "the temple requires no remaking." Depressions were natural and unstoppable forces, coming and going "as surely as the tides ebb and flow." He warned against seeking "either palliation or tonic from the public treasury." More government spending would be "a new cause of trouble rather than a source of cure," as European experience had amply demonstrated. At the same time, Harding acknowledged that all Americans wanted to know "the way to speediest and dependable convalescence." And lest anyone think him defeatist, he contradicted everything he had just said by asserting that there were no problems known to man "which we can not and will not solve."[15]

Hoover took the podium next and offered some equivocations of his own. He echoed Harding's claim that the depression was one of the "bitter fruits" of readjustment from war, and shielded the public purse: "It is not consonant with the spirit or institutions of the American people that a demand should be made upon the public treasury for the solution of every difficulty." With this duty of presidential solidarity fulfilled, Hoover charged ahead with his own intrepid agenda for the conference:

> There is no economic failure so terrible in its import as that of a country possessing a surplus of every necessity of life in which numbers, willing and anxious to work, are deprived of these necessities. It simply can not be if our moral and economic system is to survive. It is the duty of this Conference to find definite and organized remedy for this emergency and

I hope also that you may be able to outline for public consideration such plans as will in the long view tend to mitigate its recurrence."[16]

Unlike his president, Hoover, the trained geologist, the practicing engineer, had no doubt that the business cycle, a "natural" phenomena, was susceptible to human ingenuity. He told the delegates that downturns could be "modified and possibly controlled by practical remedies available through cooperative service on the part of those abundantly able and doubtless eager to render it." It was their job to mobilize the assembled "intelligence of the country" to prevent the miseries and losses of future depressions and eliminate unemployment.[17]

If the delegates needed any further evidence that the president's conference was a Hoover production, the schedule itself provided it. There was no reception, no opportunity to mingle or chat. The two opening speeches and all other preliminaries were crammed into twenty minutes. By 10:45 a.m., the delegates broke into groups to begin committee work. By 11 a.m. the committee on organization was in session. At 2 p.m. the advisory committee had gathered. At 3 p.m., the entire conference met again, and by 3:30 it was divided back into ten committees, three of which worked late into the evening. The committee on public hearings began deliberations at 11 p.m. The *New York Times* remarked that Washington was unaccustomed to "promptitude, thoughtful preparation and absence of loquacity," and ventured that if unemployment were attacked across the country in the same manner, the problem would soon cease to exist.[18]

For three weeks the delegates holed up in committee rooms, windows shut against the autumn rains. They studied data and analyses provided by the National Bureau of Economic Research, a new private think tank Hoover had contracted to handle the conference's empirical work. The rest of Washington, wrote David Lawrence, looked on with "the usual skepticism that attends every endeavor of an experimental nature." What could the conference actually accomplish, Lawrence asked: "Can it alter the laws of supply and demand?" He allowed that a better understanding of the causes of unemployment might suggest ways to alleviate the problem. Facts could replace fear and uncertainty and buttress public confidence. Merely getting the mortal enemies labor and business to agree upon a set of facts after the discords of 1919 and 1920 might put the nation on the path to healing. But would any of this find jobs for workers?[19]

The conference's answers were rolled out at its close on October 13. Hoover's experts had estimated the number of idle at between 3.5 and 5.5 million. They proposed emergency measures to help the country through the coming winter: shorter hours and job sharing in manufacturing; the creation of local employment agencies; the coordination of local charitable relief. They recommended the novel idea of moving public works projects scheduled for spring ahead to fall or winter to stimulate the construction industry, providing jobs and income that would in turn increase demand for other goods and services, helping the economy as a whole. Construction costs, it was noted, were lower in a downturn and governments should take advantage. Because municipalities and counties, responsible for streets and schools and water systems, were the largest public works spenders, most of the remedying would necessarily occur at the local level. The federal government, limited to interstate projects such as national defense and the postal system, represented only 10 percent of public-sector construction. That suited both Hoover's and the public's bottom-up ideals of federalism. Local governments were closer to the people, and without the power to coin new money they would never be tempted to inflate their way out of any debts incurred.[20]

Those recommendations, innovative, practical, achievable, were sufficient to exceed most expectations for the conference. The final report made positive headlines in major newspapers, and was mailed to three hundred mayors across the country as the Commerce Department publicity machine ramped up to convince governments, business, and the general public to take action on its proposals. To Hoover's frustration, the conference produced none of the desired legislative results. Specifically, he wanted something permitting the countercyclical phasing of public works, an idea too advanced even for so progressive a senator as Nebraska's George Norris, who said, "We had better let God run [the economy] as in the past." Hoover's partisans nonetheless declared victory: bond issues for local public works hit record highs within months of the gathering, and several federal departments advanced spending projects that had been lingering on drawing boards. The seasonal increase in unemployment through the winter of 1921–22 was less than usual, and by the second half of 1922 joblessness was on the decline. Hoover drafted a letter of self-congratulation that was released under Harding's signature:

> We have passed the winter of the greatest unemployment in the history of our country. Through the fine coordination and cooperation among federal and state officials, mayors and their committees of employers, relief organizations and citizens, we have come through with much less suffering than in previous years, when unemployment was very much less.[21]

In his own speeches, Hoover boasted that as many as a million and a half people had been put back to work without any wasteful public spending. This, he said, was a direct result of the comprehensive and effective initiatives of his administration. In fact, Hoover and his experts, along with virtually all other economists and politicians, misread cause and effect in the depression of 1921. Monetary policy had been instrumental in sinking the economy, and monetary policy was the primary factor in its improvement. Benjamin Strong, governor of the Federal Reserve Bank of New York, had reduced discount rates over the summer prior to Hoover's conference, fueling recovery. Hoover's program was too limited to produce the results claimed for it. He would emerge from the downturn with undue confidence in the economic benefits of voluntary measures.[*]

Misapprehensions were not the only legacy of the 1921 conference. Hoover, more than Harding appreciated, had saddled the federal government with a greater share of responsibility for the condition of the national economy. Once an administration had claimed to cure a depression, there could be no going back to the old practice of patiently waiting for ill economic winds to blow themselves out. All subsequent downturns would need to be met with a fight. Hoover would have counted this new attitude as progress. The larger purpose of the unemployment conference had always been, as per his opening

---

[*] Another misconception: Harding's tax cuts and spending restraints, believed by some Republicans to have spurred the recovery, were neither steep nor timely enough to have made much difference.

remarks, to develop "such plans as will in the long view tend to mitigate" the recurrence of depressions.[22]

Hoover's progress on the long view was not well recognized at
the time but a large section of his final report was devoted to solving the business cycle. Four times since 1894, the delegates declared,
peak periods of economic activity, featuring speculation, overexpansion, and extravagance, were followed by stagnation, unemployment,
and suffering. "Both of these extremes are vicious, and the vices of
the one beget the vices of the other. It is the wastes, the miscalcu-
lations, and the maladjustments grown rampant during booms that
make inevitable the painful process of liquidation." The report called
for "exhaustive investigation" and a permanent research committee
into downturns and counterbalancing policy solutions. Said Hoover
in a speech to the Academy of Political Science weeks later: "There is
a solution somewhere and its working out will be the greatest blessing
yet given to our economic system."[23]

The business cycle would remain an obsession for Hoover
throughout his time in Commerce. He extended the work of the
unemployment conference by founding a permanent research committee comprised of representatives from the Wharton School, the
Harvard Business School, banks, trade associations, and the National
Chamber of Commerce. It produced an elaborate study on business
cycles and unemployment in 1923, complete with twenty-one supporting economic studies examining the government's responsibility
for the economy, the role of the Federal Reserve, and the possibilities
of alleviating slumps. It was well circulated in government and the
economics community.

While light in immediate impact, the 1921 conference was nonetheless a watershed in American history. In addition to inaugurating a
century's worth of struggle against the business cycle, it further legiti-
mated the idea that public policy should be guided by experts working
in the public interest and not left to politicians and other amateurs.
Economists now migrated from the margins to the mainstream of
public life; Hoover's actions helped open the door to the central position they hold in our political dialogue today.

The conference was also a milestone in the acceptance of a data-
driven approach to decision making in government. Hoover was
hardly the only evangelist for scientific management in the early

decades of the twentieth century. It was colonizing great swaths of American life. The intellectual godfather of the movement was Frederick Winslow Taylor, a trained engineer who published *The Principles of Scientific Management* in 1911 and went on to found the practice of management consulting. The leading industrial practitioner of scientific management was another trained engineer, Henry Ford, whose Highland Park assembly line had been launched in 1913.* Hoover's contribution was to advance scientific management in the public sector. His faith that better data would lead to better decisions spread to every field of policy and every level of government work, as did his practice of hiring experts to define and quantify public problems and achieve practical solutions. Within a generation, it would be taken for granted that policy decisions needed to be informed by comprehensive analysis of economic and social data, or at least packaged in the language of empirical validity.

It did occur to some of the reporters covering the 1921 unemployment conference that the lead role ought to have been played by someone other than Herbert Hoover—James J. Davis, the labor secretary, for instance. A union man and national leader of the Loyal Order of Moose, Davis oversaw a department created to "foster, develop, and promote the welfare of working people . . . and to advance their opportunities for profitable employment." Yet he had been slow to tackle the jobs problem, at least compared to Hoover. "At the conference on unemployment," one observer said, "the best and only example of the unemployed present was the Secretary of Labor."[24]

---

* Hoover and Ford met briefly in Europe during the war. The substance of their conversation was not recorded, but they apparently had an intense meeting of minds on the subject of industrial efficiency.

# CHAPTER 14

# Hoover Versus a Botched Civilization

During his time at Commerce, Hoover would prove himself expert at the boarding house reach, gobbling up new assignments, responsibilities, and offices, often directly from the plates of his cabinet colleagues. He considered all things involving markets, transportation, the workplace, and statistics within his domain. He proposed to transfer at least sixteen agencies from other departments to his own, including Treasury's Bureau of Customs Statistics and the War Department's Panama Canal. Most of these grabs were repulsed, including a brassy lunge at the new Bureau of the Budget (later the Office of Management and Budget), which Harding rightly kept for himself. Hoover would eventually succeed in moving a small number of agencies to Commerce: the Bureau of Mines and the Patent Office, both from Interior. Others that he was unable to acquire and still felt he needed, he simply replicated.

His rapacity did not endear him to other members of the cabinet. Agriculture Secretary Henry C. Wallace railed against "that man" in Commerce. The farm sector accounted for roughly half of the U.S. economy and for decades after the war it would suffer from an excess of supply and weak demand. Hoover felt a personal stake in these problems, having stoked production during the war in response to looming shortages. He wanted Wallace to content himself with managing food production in the narrowest sense, allowing Commerce to oversee distribution, marketing, and anything else that did not occur directly on the soil. He opposed a Wallace scheme to introduce marketing cooperatives to manage farm surpluses as too bureaucratic and championed an array of policy alternatives, none of which got off the ground.[1]

Hoover tackled two other crippled industries, coal and railroads, with similar zeal. Overexpansion in both sectors had resulted in ruthless competition and nationwide labor strife. He proposed conferences, panels, studies, negotiations, pacts, and legislation. He generally acted as though the Interior, Labor, and Justice departments were not competent to carry their files.

Much to the annoyance of the State Department, Hoover fielded his own foreign service, a corps of commercial attachés who roamed the globe in aid of American business. The attachés were proficient in such fields as foreign law and international transportation. They acted as guides and consultants for manufacturers and producers seeking to expand their markets. They could do anything for an expanding merchant short of closing his sales.

Hoover loved his attachés, fitting as they did his favorite narrative of the trained expert as public-spirited superhero. He cooperated with a friendly series of articles in the *Saturday Evening Post*, later published as a book by Isaac Marcosson, that celebrated the derring-do and "real romance" of the Commerce attachés: they "have risked the glaciers of the Andes, and braved the fevers of Ecuador; they have been wrecked on the headwaters of the Amazon; they have encountered bandits beyond the Great Wall of China, all to the end that fresh fields be opened up for the products of American farm and factory."[2]

Beneath this storybook rhetoric was a serious purpose. Hoover understood that the American way of life was dependent on foreign markets for rubber, tin, coffee, and other materials it could not produce itself. "The quantity of such products that we can import," he said, "depends in turn upon the volume of goods we can export and exchange." Foreign trade secured vital imports, opened export markets, and improved the quality of life of Americans. At a deeper level, Hoover was attempting to accomplish through trade what he had been unable to manage through the Versailles Treaty and League of Nations. He wanted America to engage with the world and help lead Europe back to prosperity. He continued to fret about economic and political instability on the Continent and the mounting isolationism of his countrymen. He preached the virtues of a global outlook: not only did the modern economic system depend upon trade, but open markets and international cooperation also provided "the incalculable social values of an enlarged national mind, opportunity and development of world unity and mutual interest, and thus peace."[3]

That his reaching aggravated his cabinet mates never seemed to bother Hoover. Rather, he complained of the strain their protests caused him: "The main trouble is too much effort to conciliate my political colleagues by giving them ideas which they exploit and spoil instead of definitely taking the headship myself."[4]

Harding welcomed Hoover's active participation and constructive approach to the economic problems facing his administration and remained true to his promise of allowing his commerce secretary an expanded scope of duties, notwithstanding the awkward dynamics in the cabinet. At times the two men freelanced together, to notable effect.

The American steel industry's refusal to abandon the twelve-hour workday had become a national embarrassment by the early 1920s. Hoover led the administration's campaign to convince steel companies to adopt eight-hour shifts. He commissioned professional studies and held meetings with steel executives. His triumphant blow was a public letter challenging Elbert Gary, chairman of U.S. Steel, America's first billion-dollar corporation, to show leadership by reducing hours and giving the American people "pride and confidence in the ability of our industries themselves to solve matters which are so conclusively advocated by the public." The letter was written by Hoover and issued under Harding's signature. Gary was sufficiently embarrassed to announce the change within weeks.[5]

As with the unemployment conference, Harding several times abandoned convention and imposed Hoover on the business of other departments. He brushed aside Interior Secretary Albert Bacon Fall to appoint Hoover chair of an interstate commission to decide the fate of the Colorado River. Harding felt that Hoover was the right man for the job, and indeed he was. He had been captivated by waterways since boyhood. There is no other way to explain the endless hours of leisure he had spent splashing about in creek beds, moving mud and rocks to create channels, pools, and waterfalls to no real purpose other than his happiness. He was fascinated by America's great rivers—the St. Lawrence, the Tennessee, the Mississippi, the Columbia—and their potential for transportation and hydroelectric development. He developed an ambitious plan for nine thousand miles of navigable river corridors running to every point of the compass and drastically reducing the distance between America's producers and consumers. He was devoted to his vision for a St. Lawrence seaway linking the Great Lakes to the Atlantic that would relieve the strain on west-to-east rail traffic at harvest time. The seaway meant "more to me than almost anything else in the world," he would say, but it was decades ahead of its time and went nowhere in the twenties. He would have more luck in the Southwest.[6]

Almost 1,500 miles long, the Colorado River flows from the Rocky Mountains through the arid lands of Arizona, draining seven states before spilling into the Gulf of California. At the time, it ranked third in water volume among American rivers, and it had a nasty habit of flooding. The governments of the Colorado's basin states could agree that it needed to be controlled for safety, hydroelectric power, and irrigation needs. There was tension, however, between the upstream states that wanted the power dam and the downstream states, led by California, seeking a steady flow of water for agriculture. State leaders managed to agree to a regional compact that would locate the dam and allocate water rights under federal supervision. Hoover was applied to the project in part because he was the only member of the cabinet, aside from Hughes in State, capable of delivering an agreement, and also because Interior's Fall considered it a lost cause and Agriculture's Wallace thought America already had more agricultural land than it needed.

Leading negotiations among the affected states, Hoover focused the discussion on a Bureau of Reclamation report that favored a dam in Nevada's Boulder Canyon. He untangled a thicket of riparian rights stretching from Wyoming to Mexico and arranged for the protection of native land rights. It was taxing work. The governors of the seven states reminded him of the combatant governments at Versailles: the stakes were smaller, but the mistrust was similar. A solution emerged based on the principle of dividing the water fifty-fifty between upper basin states and lower basin states. In less than a year, Hoover collected seven signatures and was able to announce that the Colorado had been "freed from a generation of litigation, strikes and arrested development."[7]

The Colorado River Compact was a critical step in the development of the Southwest, a region that would lead America in growth in the twentieth century. It was also a gratifying accomplishment for a man who had begun his career pushing carts beneath the arid surface of those same states.

His emphasis on development, combined with successes like the Colorado deal, allowed Hoover to claim ownership of the word *progress* in Washington throughout the Harding era. He became the administration's point man for distinctly modern problems. When the millions of automobiles spit out from Detroit's production lines at a rate of one every ten seconds produced a disturbing increase in highway carnage, Hoover stepped forward with a plan to coordinate national traffic safety standards. When a nascent airline industry suffered from a lack of public confidence in the safety of air travel—entirely warranted given the early attrition rate of airborne postal workers—Hoover asserted a broad federal authority to improve navigation systems and runways, inspect planes, and license pilots. His Aeronautics Branch would produce dependable commercial aviation by the end of the decade and evolve over time into the Federal Aviation Administration (FAA). When an explosion of new radio stations including 790 commercial stations and almost seventeen thousand amateur broadcasters created anarchy in the airwaves, Hoover granted himself authority to issue licenses and assign frequencies. Federal control of commercial broadcasting was by no means a certainty at the dawn of the industry. His Federal Radio Commission (later the Federal Communications Commission, or FCC) made it so.[8]

Harding embraced Hoover as the necessary leavening agent in an otherwise cautious administration. He understood the limits of his own call for normalcy. A purely reactionary approach to governance would not sit well with business interests in his own party, and it would not play with boosters anywhere, and Harding knew boosters, having joined every service club in Marion. America still liked a builder. People wanted a vision of growth and prosperity and an exciting future, and Hoover brought that to the Harding team. The president was so indulgent of his commerce secretary that he sometimes supported his projects outside of government, even when they conflicted with the spirit of administration policy.

Taking Wilson's lead, Harding had refused to recognize the Soviet Union, stating among his reasons that the Soviets had refused to assume the czar's debts and responsibilities, and that they could not be counted on to protect American life or property. As a practical matter, nonrecognition meant a refusal to engage the Soviet Union on any matter. In the summer of 1921, however, reports reached America of crop failures and imminent famine in the Volga River region.

Hoover had some experience of Russia as a miner and an investor. He had sold his holdings in the country months before the 1917 revolution, narrowly escaping the nationalization of his assets. During the Versailles talks, he had written an influential memo in response to President Wilson's request for advice on how to manage the new Bolshevik regime. He had advised Wilson to offer food in return for an end to Soviet aggression against other nations, a proposal accepted by the Council of Four.* His familiarity with Russia and its food situation allowed him to be quick off the mark when the famine reports reached Washington, along with requests for aid. Hoover recommended to Harding and Secretary of State Hughes that the United States send food to Russia under the auspices of the American Relief Administration, which Hoover still headed. Hughes was reluctant. He wanted to kill Bolshevism through strict quarantine. Pounding his fist and conjuring images of starving children, Hoover convinced Harding to ask for $10 million to purchase grains for Russia.[9]

ARA representatives negotiated terms of engagement with the Soviets on August 19, 1921, and within ten days an advance guard of relief men arrived in Moscow. By the end of year their number would swell to two hundred, overseeing eighteen thousand aid stations. The House Republicans did bring forward a bill authorizing a $10 million purchase of corn and seed grain. Although exactly what Harding had

---

* Opinion at the time ranged from the liberal position that Lenin deserved a chance to Churchill's call for military action against the Bolsheviks. Hoover denounced the Soviet regime for its wholesale slaughter of its own people yet opposed armed intervention on grounds that it would result in a long and bloody conflict with uncertain political outcomes. He believed the Soviet economy, having throttled individual initiative, would soon collapse under the weight of idleness and hunger, an optimistic prediction, as it turned out.

requested, Hoover thought it insufficient. He appeared before the Senate Foreign Affairs Committee and browbeat it into doubling the amount: "We feed milk to hogs and burn corn under our boilers while there are millions of children who will starve unless we help. The American people spend $1,000,000,000 a year for tobacco, cosmetics, and like un-essentials. Twenty millions would not be a great drain on a nation that can afford to do that."[10]

Russian relief would prove less popular than the Belgian variety, with the left accusing Hoover of seeking to undermine communism with capitalist aid and of being primarily concerned with unloading surplus U.S. grains overseas, and the right charging him with rescuing and legitimating the shaky Soviet regime. Hoover gave the same answer to all critics: "Twenty million people are starving. Whatever their politics, they shall be fed."[11]

Maxim Gorky, in Italy nursing his tuberculosis, wrote Hoover personally: "In the past year you have saved from death three and one-half million children, five and one-half million adults. In the history of practical humanitarianism I know of no accomplishment which in . . . magnitude and generosity can be compared to the relief you have actually accomplished."[12]


The scope of Hoover's activities in Commerce was stupendous. Singlehandedly doing enough work for an entire cabinet, he was said to be "Secretary of Commerce and Undersecretary of everything else." The range of his interests at any given moment could make him look scattered and undisciplined, a victim of his own administrative gluttony. Even friends wondered if he was trying to do too much. Was it really the place of government, the journalist Mark Sullivan asked, to tell people which variety of screw to use?[13]

Yet there was a certain coherence to Hoover's activities. Long days of reading on steamships and trains, and many hours of reflection on the similarities and differences between the cultures and economies he had experienced, had left him with a comprehensive view of the kind of America he wanted to effect. His vision considered the discrete roles of the individual, the community, and government, the Constitution, and the unique problems and opportunities of modern American life. It was informed by a deep concern for the social and economic welfare of the average worker. It was a surprisingly elegant vision of America, and it can be observed close to the surface of every project Hoover undertook at Commerce, even his niggling obsession with standardization.

To Hoover's understanding, standardization of screws and bricks was not about efficiency for its own sake. Standardization was a means to several ends: lowering the costs of manufactures, providing consumers with less expensive goods, allowing Americans to more easily satisfy their basic requirements, and, by doing so, opening doors to new worlds of progress and human expression.

His vision was explicit in Hoover's attempts to standardize the American hearth. Home ownership had dropped slightly between 1900 and 1920, due in part to scarce construction during the war. As many as one-third of Americans lived in crowded and ill-equipped rental properties. Hoover worked with the American Institute of Architects to produce plans for standardized houses made of standardized building materials with the aim of reducing the cost of building by a third. He backed the Better Homes Movement as it embarked on a nationwide celebration of home ownership: its demonstration models of the new standard homes with modern plumbing and the latest electrical appliances were shown in more than a thousand towns and cities. Hoover also succeeded in promoting improved mortgage terms for consumers. He produced model zoning ordinances and municipal building codes to support best practices among developers and local administrators, literally shaping the houses and neighborhoods that generations of twentieth-century Americans would dream about and live in.[14]

Literature produced by the Commerce Department explained its higher purpose: standardized homes satisfied the basic needs of families efficiently and inexpensively, allowing them greater freedom to pursue happiness as they saw fit, in fulfillment of the promise of the founders. The owner of a standard home, stated one pamphlet, "works harder outside the home; he spends his leisure more profitably, and he and his family live a finer life and enjoy more of the comforts and cultivating influences of our modern civilization."[15]

This was the vision behind every standardization initiative Hoover pushed: "The man who has a standard automobile, a standard telephone, a standard bathtub, a standard electric light, a standard radio, and one and one-half hours less average daily labor is more of a man and has a fuller life and more individuality than he has without them."[16]

Consistent with this line of thinking was Hoover's mission to standardize the American child, which was not as horrifying a project as it might sound. The aim was not to homogenize the young and erase their individuality but to provide for the basic needs of children so they could develop to their full capacities, a strategy Hoover believed would produce as rich a variety of healthy human types as might be found in the plant kingdom. Hoover knew that many children suffered physical, psychological, and educational deficiencies as a result of their environments. He had witnessed in Belgium and as head of the European Children's Fund how hunger and destitution stunted the growth of young bodies. He was aghast at U.S. government reports that 80 percent of American draftees had carried some manner of mental or physical defect, which to him seemed a horrifying waste of human potential.[17]

The question of how he, as commerce secretary, could address issues of child welfare was delicate. Hoover wanted to advise parents and health officers on minimum standards of health and well-being for children, and to establish benchmarks for their normal or natural development, but he had no mandate for this sort of work. To the extent that any department of the Harding administration could claim an interest in child welfare it was Labor, home to the U.S. Children's Bureau. Further complicating matters was Hoover's belief that these issues were best managed locally. Parents, volunteer organizations, and community health authorities needed to retain frontline responsibility for children, taking guidance and encouragement from the national level. He maneuvered himself around these obstacles by assuming the presidency of the volunteer American Child Health Association (ACHA).

The ACHA was a loose association of sixty-odd private organizations scattered across the country. Hoover, in a by now familiar pattern, centralized it into a single national organization firmly under his thumb. He staffed it with "scientifically trained men and women," many of them recruited from the American Relief Administration. He used his stature and fund-raising abilities to absorb or sideline rival groups in the child welfare space and soon came to dominate the field.

He used his flair for publicity to create a sense of urgency around the state of America's children and to shame officials into building local health clinics and hospitals, using variations on his oft-stated argument that a country that spent a "billion dollars on ice cream, cosmetics, and chewing gum" could afford to support this worthwhile cause.[18]

Although Hoover's concern for the well-being of children was often dressed in data and analysis and presented as an efficiency issue, it went deeper than economics. There was a personal motive. Here, as in Belgium, Germany, and Russia, he was identifying in some visceral way with deprived children. He made impassioned pleas for attention to their emotional as well as their physical requirements: "the need for wise love and understanding, for protection against such psychic blights as fear, and the abuse of primitive emotions such as anger."[19]

Child welfare went to the heart of Hoover's vision of social progress and his hopes for a more compassionate America. Minimal standards of physical and emotional care for children allowed them a fair chance to realize their full capacities. "If," he said, "we want this civilization to march forward toward higher economic standards, to moral and spiritual ideals, it will march only on the feet of healthy children."[20]

Hoover's conviction that civilization advanced through standardized living did not meet universal approval. It was attacked on economic grounds: some, like his friend Mark Sullivan, saw standardization as an unwarranted imposition on the normal operations of free markets. It was attacked on legal grounds: the antitrust division of Harding's Justice Department saw Commerce's promotion of industry-wide cooperation on standards and practices as anticompetitive and an invitation to collusion at the expense of consumers. Most searchingly, it was challenged on philosophical grounds: there was something incongruent, even faintly absurd, in these postwar years about the notion of civilization marching on to higher ideals and new summits of achievement by any means.

Intellectuals were keenly aware that Western civilization had just finished marching ten million souls to their death and that the destruction had occurred in spite of, indeed partially because of, the West's technological prowess, economic might, and soaring ideals. The lost promise of Wilson's peace and the continuing economic and political crises of Europe mocked every hope of a better world throughout the Harding years. Disillusionment and pessimism were the drugs of the moment. "The dead season," said Keynes. "A botched civilization," said Pound. "All Gods dead," added Fitzgerald, "all wars fought, all faiths in man shaken."[21]

These minds were profoundly distrustful of political and social institutions, the men who ran them, and the masses they served. The year 1922, the midpoint of Harding's term, was the nadir of postwar pessimism, producing monumental expressions of lost hope and cultural ruin, the most magnificent, of course, being Eliot's *The Wasteland*. A more prosaic effort was Harold E. Stearns's *Civilization in the United States*, a collection of essays by leading American intellectuals— Lewis Mumford, H. L. Mencken, Van Wyck Brooks—all competing to offer the bleakest assessment of the times. Their collective conclusion was that America did not have a civilization worth the name. Its heritage and its traditions had "withered in our hands and turned to dust," wrote Stearns in a deliberate echo of Eliot. He complained of the "emotional and aesthetic starvation" of postwar America, the mania for regulation and material organization, the spiritual impoverishment that was robbing the citizenry of "true art and true religion and true personality."[22]

If Stearns's book levels indirect criticisms at elements of Hoover's managed and standardized society, Sinclair Lewis's *Babbitt*, also published in 1922, is an uproarious full-on assault. The hero of Lewis's novel, George Babbitt, is a midwestern realtor in a "standard suit" who worships the god of progress. He lives in a standard house decorated to "the best standard designs," and he keeps a standard book beside his standard electric bedside lamp: "These standard advertised wares—toothpastes, socks, tires, cameras, instantaneous hot-water heaters—were his symbols and proofs of excellence; at first the signs, then the substitutes, for joy and passion and wisdom."[23]

This became the standard intellectual view of the modern middle-class American: a soulless consumer with poor taste and a lazy mind, reveling in the materialism of a rapidly improving economy, imbibing philosophy at Rotarian lunches and experiencing literature in *Reader's Digest* (which also debuted in 1922). Rather than think for himself, the average American was content with doing whatever was "the thing to do," turning his back on creativity, liberty, and the traditions of American individualism. As Mencken famously put it that same year, "The American people, taking one with another, constitute the most timorous, sniveling, poltroonish, ignominious mob of serfs and goose-steppers ever gathered under one flag in Christendom since the end of the Middle Ages."[24]

Hoover, too, published a book in 1922. *American Individualism* is a short work, not quite a classic of political philosophy, yet one of the more thoughtful efforts ever to come from the pen of a practicing American politician. Rather than scorning the masses, he addresses them directly. His subtitle is "A Timely Message to the American People."[25]

The author is determined from the first page to answer the prevailing mood of alienation and despair with optimism and commitment. Where others find no heritage on which to rebuild their lost civilization, he lays out the glory of the national character and makes a compelling case for why its best days are still ahead. *American Individualism* is an attempt to hold a moral center in a demoralized world, written by a man who had experienced as much of the Great War's devastation as any other American author.

The greatness of America, Hoover argues, resides in its singular conception of individualism. It holds that human progress stems from the intelligence, character, and courage of individuals. Individual yearnings for self-expression, individual desires for achievement and creation, represent the constructive instincts of mankind. Because civilization is based upon the attainments of the individual, and because every person contains the divine spark of the human soul and thus the potential to make a worthy contribution to life, it follows that it is in the best interests of society to ensure equality of opportunity for all. Every citizen should have the liberty to give all that is in him to give. Every individual should be free "to take that position in the community to which his intelligence, character, ability, and ambition entitle him."[26]

It is emphatically not a philosophy of every man for himself. "No doubt," he wrote, "individualism run riot, with no tempering principle, would provide a long category of inequalities, of tyrannies, dominations, and injustices." The tendency of big business, big government, or entrenched social classes to crush individual initiative must be curbed.[27]

Hoover offered two primary ways of protecting individualism. The first and most important was organizing for social mobility. Governments and communities must conduct themselves to provide a decent standard of living for all, not for a single class. "Education, food, clothing, housing, and the spreading use of what we so often term nonessentials, are the real fertilizers of the soil from which spring the finer flowers of life," he wrote. The powers of the state needed to be extended and tuned to keep pace with the growing complexity of American life and to ensure that the many benefited and were not dominated by the few. Every practical problem of government, every new piece of legislation, needed to meet two tests: "Does this act safeguard an equality of opportunity? Does it maintain the initiative of our people?"[28]

The other means of protecting individualism was to "glorify service as part of our national character." The American people, Hoover asserted, have always recognized that individualism needed to be tempered by a sense of community. They have looked beyond their own needs and venerated public service. Hoover wanted to cultivate that "enlarging sense of responsibility and understanding" that comes with service. He was encouraged by the proliferation in the early decades of the twentieth century of chambers of commerce, service clubs, trade associations, and labor unions. He recognized that these organizations contained variable mixes of altruism and self-interest. They nevertheless encouraged connections and reciprocity among individuals, the growth of community, and the accumulation of social capital. They offered individuals an opportunity for self-expression and participation in things larger than themselves, and they trained the leaders of tomorrow.[29]

In one of the most widely excerpted sections of *American Individualism*, Hoover noted that of the twelve-man executive, comprising the president, the vice president, and the cabinet, nine had earned their own way in life and eight had begun their careers with manual labor. All of them had lived to see a world in which the vast majority of Americans had far higher standards of living than their forefathers. That proved to his satisfaction that America still worked and that Americans could look forward to a better future. Hoover took umbrage at the notion that America's best days were behind it, directly challenging the belief of the pessimists that the nation's dynamism had died with the closing of the frontier at the end of the nineteenth century:

> There will always be a frontier to conquer or to hold as long as men think, plan, and dare. . . . There are continents of human welfare of which we have penetrated only the coastal plain. The great continent of science is as yet explored only on its borders, and it is only the pioneer who will penetrate the frontier in the quest for new worlds to conquer.[30]

The ideas in Hoover's book are not original. His notion of brotherly individualism traces back to the Founding Fathers. Thomas Paine had posited that individuals were innately sociable and that given their liberty they would construct a world where cooperation and harmony were the norms. Great achievements would follow. Brotherly individualism had been the working ethos in generations of Quaker and Protestant communities in America, including West Branch, where it was practiced with aplomb by Jesse and Hulda Hoover. Hoover's conception of equality of opportunity deliberately echoes and expands upon Lincoln's call for every man to have "an open field and a fair chance." His emphasis on community service is true to the principles of Benjamin Franklin, who celebrated volunteer firehouses and police forces as examples of individuals pulling together to provide for the practical public good, and to those of Thomas Jefferson, who said, "There is a debt of service due from every man to his country, proportioned to the boundaries which his nature and fortune have measured to him."[31]

The idea of a limited but essential role for government also has deep roots in American thought. Paine held that individuals and local communities were capable of solving most of their own problems. God had granted them reason, innate decency, and the gift of practical decision making to do so. They would resort to government only as a sad necessity, when some powerful individual or group interfered with the natural flow of harmony and benevolence. At that point it was entirely legitimate for government to step in and secure for individuals their inalienable rights to life, liberty, and the pursuit of happiness.

Hoover added equality of opportunity to those inalienable rights and maintained that the complexity of modern society, specifically in the economic realm, required government to occasionally step in with a regretful foot.

Although well received, *American Individualism* would never gain the intellectual currency enjoyed by more defeatist views of American life, which would hold sway even as the nation regained its social equilibrium relative to the immediate postwar years, and as the economy turned from broken to booming in the second half of Harding's term.

On a drizzly July Fourth, to the accompaniment of a navy band playing "Yes! We Have No Bananas," Herbert and Lou Hoover boarded the USS *Henderson* in the small Pacific Northwest port town of Tacoma for the second leg of Warren Harding's great American tour of 1923, a thousand-mile cruise up the Inside Passage to Alaska. Harding had already been on the road for two weeks aboard the *Superb*, a private Pullman car that was part of a special ten-car train with a presidential portrait fastened above its cowcatcher. He had delivered an important address on foreign policy in St. Louis, operated a wheat binder in Kansas, fed a bear in Yellowstone Park, and joined a Native American powwow in Meacham, Oregon. He had bloviated bareheaded at so many sunbaked stops along the way that his face was burned and his voice strained.[32]

While Hoover was not aboard the train for the cross-country portion of the trip, his influence had been felt along the way. Harding delivered a speech in Denver on the need for the United States to accept its dominant position in the world and exert leadership in international affairs. It was straight from the Hoover songbook, objecting on moral and strategic grounds to the notion of America "as a hermit nation." The alternative to engagement, said the president, was a selfish insularity. Americans were in danger of becoming a "sordid people," reveling in their material existence at home while turning their collective back to their neighbors. The way forward was to commit "to something more of international helpfulness, so that [we] may be ready to play [our] part in the uplift of the world and in the movement to prevent in the future conflict among the nations."[33]

Gratifying as it was for Hoover to have helped the president to a more internationalist position, it was to no avail. The whistle-stop tour had been designed in part to crack the determined mood of isolationism in the country, yet even Harding's cautious suggestion that the United States consider membership in the Permanent Court of International Justice, or World Court, outside the control of the League of Nations, was unacceptable to Senate Republicans and, likely, to the majority of Americans.

The winding waters of the Inside Passage afford some of the most beautiful scenery on the planet, but Hoover saw little of it in the president's company. As the *Henderson* glided through blue fjords, past misty rain forests and gigantic glaciers, the two men sat for hand after monotonous hand of bridge, playing as many as ten hours a day, a schedule Hoover found excruciating but that the president found tranquilizing. Hoover understood that Harding needed rest. Even before the tour, his energy was sapped to the point where he could no longer make it through eighteen holes of golf. He had difficulty sleeping, and his blood pressure, never low at the best of times, was elevated. High office had taken its toll, so Hoover endured the bridge.[34]

Harding's term had not been without satisfaction. He had weathered the worst of the 1921 depression, restored business confidence, set Washington back on a sustainable fiscal track, and at least partially met his objective of restoring a sense of normalcy to the country. He had also maintained his hold on both houses of Congress in the 1922 midterm elections, and he was positioned for renomination in 1924. His troubles, however, had been mounting. The Republican Party, and primarily its Senate caucus, remained fractured and multifariously mutinous. The coal industry and the railways remained crippled, agriculture remained depressed, and labor strife seemed endless. On top of this, adding immeasurably to Harding's burdens, were the misdeeds of some of his closest colleagues.

In February, he had demanded the resignation of his friend Charles Forbes, director of the Veterans Bureau, who had been selling government supplies to associates on the cheap and otherwise plundering his office. In March, Charles Cramer, Forbes's accomplice and the general counsel of the Veterans Bureau, had shot himself in the head after the launch of a Senate investigation into their activities. In April, the *Wall Street Journal* had raised concerns about Interior Secretary

Albert Fall's favorable leases of naval oil reserves to friendly parties. Teapot Dome, an obscure Wyoming geological formation marking one of the oilfields, was on its way to infamy. May brought still more trouble, this time in the domain of Attorney General Harry Daugherty, Harding's chief political adviser and poker pal. Harding had demanded that Daugherty distance himself from his aide-de-camp, a shady character named Jesse Smith who was suspected of influence peddling and pillaging government property. Smith committed suicide on May 30, two weeks before the president set off on his tour. "My God, this is a hell of a job! I have no trouble with my enemies. I can take care of my enemies all right," Harding complained to William Allen White. "But my friends, my God-damn friends . . . they're the ones that keep me walking the floor nights."[35]

Hoover would later recall a quiet moment aboard the *Henderson* in the privacy of the president's quarters when a worried Harding asked him what he would do if he were president and learned of a scandal on his watch. "Publish it," Hoover replied, "and at least get the credit for integrity on your side." Harding told Hoover that he had uncovered irregularities in the Justice Department involving the late Jesse Smith. Hoover probed, but the president would say no more.[36]

That Harding took Hoover into his confidence, even to that limited extent, is testament to the bond between them, as is the very fact that the Hoovers were invited on the Alaska voyage. None of the president's poker circle had made the *Henderson*'s passenger list. It seems that Harding was belatedly sorting good friends from bad and leaning more on his strongest secretaries. The only member of the cabinet who matched Hoover's stature in the president's eyes was the Secretary of State. Harding had trusted Hughes to stay behind in Washington and "sit on the lid."[37]

The purpose of the Alaskan swing was to sort out an administrative tangle: no fewer than five cabinet officers and at least two dozen bureaus were bickering over management of the land and its rich resources. Hoover saw a meaty role for Commerce in Alaska. He would also discharge a personal burden while there. Henry John Minthorn was dead. He had passed in the fall of 1922 at age seventy-six, having lived a full life until the very end. His financial reversals in 1893 had done nothing to undermine his phenomenal energy and curiosity. He had rebuilt his medical career in Iowa, returned to Oregon for new business opportunities, and ventured to Alaska to join a community of Quakers ministering to the native community. Widowed at a late age, he had taken a second wife, herself a Quaker missionary in the northern territory. At the age of seventy, suffering from the cancer that would eventually kill him, Minthorn had enrolled in an optometry course at the University of Kansas.[38]

The good doctor's relationship with his nephew had never improved, and contact between them had been rare. In the spring of 1922, Minthorn had written a "Dear Bert" letter lobbying on behalf of Alaska fishermen who were having trouble getting their product to market. There was not a single personal note in the full-page letter. Hoover's return was only slightly warmer: "Glad to know that you are still able to produce such well thought out documents. . . . I hope you are well and happy."[39]

It was only with his uncle on his deathbed that Hoover reconsidered his hard feelings. The bitterness he felt at having been a chore-laden outsider in his uncle's home, the resentment he had nursed over the great taskmaster's discipline, simply melted away. "Will you convey to Dr. Minthorn," he wrote an intermediary, "my great solicitude for his recovery and ask him if there is any wish that I could fulfill for him." The reply was brief: "Dr. Minthorn sends his thanks for your kind communication and his loving regards, with his blessing."[40]

Hoover could not leave it at that. His uncle's impending demise seems to have forced him to reflect upon their relationship. He was at last prepared to admit that Minthorn, for all his flaws, had exerted a tremendous influence upon him, had fostered his interests in business and community service, had taught him the appeal of a strenuous life, and the meaning of achievement. Hoover's habits of intellectual curiosity, constant motion, and a communal table are all traceable to his uncle. Hoover's mature life reflected more of the doctor than any other man. It was of little matter that Minthorn had raised him out of duty and necessity rather than out of tender love. He had raised him and made a man of him, and Hoover now rushed to acknowledge that fact.

A day after the above exchange of correspondence, informed that Dr. Minthorn was failing fast, Hoover took the unusual step of preparing a declaration to the press on a personal matter. The relations and affections between uncle and nephew, he said, were deeply founded: "He was, in fact, my second father." When Minthorn finally died on October 11, Hoover admitted in another public statement that he owed his uncle "the greatest of affection and obligation."[41]

He met his uncle's widow in Metlakatla, his first stop in Alaska. She joined him for part of the three-week tour by ship and train around the state. Harding golfed, no more than one round a day, and made brief speeches. Hoover fished and attended public meetings. Everyone benefited from the bright, long days and from being far from Washington.

It was only when the *Henderson* turned back to the mainland that the president's mood darkened noticeably. He appeared so weak during stops in Victoria and Seattle that his party told the press he had eaten tainted shellfish and rushed him down the coast to San Francisco by rail. Hoover wired ahead to his friend Ray Lyman Wilbur, president of Stanford University and a medical doctor, asking him to meet the train with a heart specialist.[42]

On July 29, Harding made it up the front staircase of the Palace Hotel without assistance and immediately retired to his room. He was seen by a succession of doctors over the next several days. He swung back and forth from lucid and cheerful to desperately ill. Hoover joined the small crowd wearing out the hotel's carpets outside the president's room. He was worried for Harding's health. He was worried for the future of the administration. He was worried that the president might be incapable of delivering a foreign policy address on July 31 that was to be a powerful statement of support for U.S. membership in the World Court. Hoover, who had high hopes for the speech, and who had been informed by Wilbur that statistically Harding's chances of surviving were not one in ten, made sure that the text was released to the press. We have only his word that the president authorized the release.[43]

On the afternoon of August 2, Hoover visited the anteroom of Harding's bedchamber and found it empty. He stepped out to the hall and asked the Secret Service if there were physicians in with the president. There were. Hoover returned to the anteroom and stood outside the partly open door and listened as the doctors tried to revive Harding with stimulants. Fifteen minutes later, Wilbur emerged from the bedchamber and pronounced the president dead. Doctors on the scene believed he died of a cerebral hemorrhage. The death certificate would say apoplexy. Mrs. Harding refused an autopsy.

Hoover quickly released a statement that would stand as one of the best tributes to his fallen leader:

> When he came into responsibility as President he faced unprecedented problems of domestic rehabilitation. It was a time when war-stirred emotions had created bitter prejudices and conflict in thought. Kindly and genial, but inflexible in his devotion to duty, he was strong in his determination to restore confidence and secure progress. All this he accomplished through patient conciliation and friendly good will for he felt deeply that hard driving might open unhealable breaches among our people. We have all benefited by the success of his efforts.[44]

He accompanied the president's body back to Washington, and prepared himself for a new leader.

# CHAPTER 15

# Scandal, Embarrassment,
# and the Little Feller

Herbert Hoover had kept his presidential ambitions closeted as he carried out his duties in the Harding administration, hoping to patiently position himself as his leader's obvious successor. It was a reasonable plan. A *Collier's* magazine poll published in July 1923, at the start of Harding's cross-country tour, showed Hoover, Secretary of State Hughes, and California senator Hiram Johnson as the most popular Republicans next to the president.* Hughes had failed as the nominee against Wilson in 1916. Johnson was a regional candidate and too progressive for mainstream Republicans. The road seemed reasonably clear for the man in Commerce.[1]

One month after the *Collier's* poll was released, Harding's body lay in state at the Capitol. Calvin Coolidge, who had clung to the bottom-most rungs in the *Collier's* poll, who had been known to Harding as "the little feller," and who was memorably described by William Allen White as a "runty, aloof, little man, who quacks through his nose when he speaks," was now president. Although Coolidge initially positioned himself as a caretaker, all bets on the 1924 Republican nomination were now off.[2]

Worse than Coolidge's ascent for Hoover's ambitions were the scandals. Harding was only a few months in the ground before the

---

* The man most Americans wanted to see as president was auto magnate Henry Ford, who attracted almost twice the support of the second-place Harding. Ford's party affiliation was never clear. Nor was he ever a serious candidate.

Republicans were sunk in mire deep and dark enough to threaten
the careers of everyone associated with his administration. Warren
Harding's magnificent tomb offers the best vantage point from which
to view his reputation's implosion. The fund-raising for its construction began immediately upon his death, while the nation's newspapers
were brimming with laudatory eulogies. More than a million people
donated just under a million dollars, including twenty-five dollars in
the name of Harding's faithful Laddie Boy. An architect was hired to
design the tomb. A ten-acre site was selected in Marion, Ohio. White
Georgia marble was hauled in by the ton to erect a circle of simple
Doric columns vaguely resembling a Greek temple. It would stand
103 feet in diameter and 53 feet high. Then came the revelations.[3]

Two Senate investigations began almost concurrently two months
after the funeral. The first, in the Veterans Bureau, yielded a sordid tale of greed, bribery, and corruption that brought its director,
Charles Forbes, a sentence of two years in Leavenworth for conspiracy to defraud the government. The second targeted Secretary of the
Interior Albert Fall and his crooked disposition of naval oil reserves.
After six years of trials and retrials, Fall was found to have raked in
close to $400,000 directly or indirectly and clearly illegally through
secret deals with the oilmen who had gained access to the reserves.
He was sentenced to a year in jail for his part in the Teapot Dome
affair, becoming the first former U.S. cabinet officer locked up for
malfeasance in office.[4]

By January 1924, four months after Harding's death, the conduct of Attorney General Harry Daugherty was being assailed for six
hours a day in the Senate. He was accused of mishandling both the
oil lease investigation and the Veterans Bureau case. In time, he and
his department were further suspected of corruption, bribery, illegal transfers of property, and destruction of evidence, among other
offenses. Although never convicted, Daugherty would earn as much
infamy as either Forbes or Fall.[5]

Well before construction of his tomb was complete, Harding's
name was so toxic that Coolidge, who owed his elevation to the man
lying within, would refuse to participate in its dedication. Harding
was not directly touched by the scandals, but his death permitted stories of his unseemly private life to surface. Flossie Harding did everything she could to bury her dear Warren's past, gathering up all the

letters she knew him to have written and putting them to the torch. She could not silence every source, however, least of all the mother of her husband's illegitimate child. Nan Britton published a book detailing her intimate relations with Harding, from teenage flirtations to assignations in the White House. Her story was steamy, breathless, and a hot seller. Harding's family denied his paternity of Britton's child, although the book contained pictures of a little girl with Warren's eyes, eyebrows, nose, sturdy jaw, and, no doubt, his volubility.*6

Through the first half of 1924, the height of the scandals, eleven committees of the Senate, comprising more than half its members, were engaged in corruption investigations. The House was similarly active. Among the targets were the Justice Department, the Treasury Department, the Attorney General's Office, the Interior Department, the Veterans Bureau, and Agriculture. Every significant member of Coolidge's cabinet (he had kept the Harding team intact) was under attack. Reputable newspapers were devoting three or four pages a day to the latest revelations. Teapot Dome, involving resources worth hundreds of millions of dollars, was singularly dangerous. Coolidge claimed ignorance of any wrongdoing. Hoover and Hughes insisted that the oil leases arranged by Fall had never been discussed at the cabinet table.7

Lewis Strauss wrote a fellow member of the Firm of his "absolute nausea and disgust" at the news pouring out of Washington. "I have never overheard such cynical comment on the processes or personnel of government as is now common in subway, barber-shop, smoking car or wherever an impromptu forum comes to exist." Strauss had advised Hoover to step out of public life around the time of the 1922 midterm elections. If he had done so, Strauss lamented, "the conscience of the entire country would have crystallized into a tidal wave for our great friend." Instead, Hoover was one of many Republican grandees scurrying for cover.8

Touchy as ever about reputational threats, Hoover found the scandals excruciating. He was hoping no one would remember his

---

* Nan Britton was accused of lying for money and condemned as a "pervert" for her claim to have had Harding's love child. On August 12, 2015, the *New York Times* reported that DNA tests confirmed her daughter, Elizabeth Ann Blaesing, was indeed sired by Harding.

comment that Interior had never had "so constructive and legal a headship" as Secretary Fall, and praying that people would forget that he had been "undersecretary of everything" in the now notorious cabinet. Of course, they did remember. The disposition of federal oil leases was the sort of issue that Hoover might have claimed as Commerce's legitimate purview. How could he not have known about Fall's deals? How could he plead ignorance about everything going on at the Veterans Bureau?[9]

The Republican old guard, never friendly to the commerce secretary, joined the Democrats in trying to implicate him in the known scandals. Lou was sufficiently concerned to write one of her long exegetical letters to her sons lest they worry about their father. The Teapot Dome scandal was overblown, she insisted, a result of political gamesmanship and personal animosities on Capitol Hill. Senators were behaving in "a perfectly inexcusable manner" and holding up the legitimate work of the government. She nevertheless admitted that Secretary Fall was "at least criminally careless" in his actions, and that his lies about his conduct had destroyed her faith in his honesty. While Lou told her boys that their father had done nothing wrong and that nothing would stick to him, her actions suggest that she was not so confident as she let on.[10]

On January 18, 1924, two days after one of the leaders of the Democratic assault, Thaddeus Caraway of Arkansas, stood in the Senate to compare former Interior Secretary Albert Fall to Benedict Arnold for having betrayed the public trust by selling national oil assets for corrupt consideration, Lou contacted a lawyer. William C. Mullendore was a chubby Kansas-born attorney who had served as a flying cadet in the Great War. He joined the Firm as a member of the American Relief Administration and afterward worked briefly as assistant secretary of the Commerce Department before returning to private practice. Brilliant and discreet, he had earned the trust of both Hoovers.[11]

The stated motivation of Lou's writing to Mullendore was to arrange for a will but by the midpoint of the letter it is clear that she is primarily concerned with separating approximately $100,000 in Henry family assets from the Hoover family trust. It would be one thing for congressional investigators to ensnare her husband: the

Hoovers had faced down disaster before, in Tientsin and London, and she was certain that they could do so again. She was less sanguine about her dependent father and sister (her mother had died in 1921). She suggested to Mullendore that the Henry assets, which had been signed over to her for safekeeping, be shifted to a new trust under her sister's name.[12]

In subsequent weeks, Lou and Mullendore worked through the mails to return the Henrys their properties. Mullendore alerted Lou to tax complications and the difficulty of transferring to her sister assets that under California's community property law belonged in half to her husband. They had an understanding that Bert was not to be informed of their discussions. From time to time they communicated in code: Mullendore was supposedly tendering "legal advice on the matter of Mrs. Hoover's water-softener." Nothing was resolved until late June when, with the scandals still boiling, Lou informed Mullendore that her husband had taken it upon himself to restructure the family trusts.[13]

The gales of obloquy lashing Washington had prompted Bert to rummage through his own dealings and identify his points of vulnerability. He was concerned that the use of a trust to divide his wealth among his family members might be viewed as an attempt to evade taxes or death duties. He proposed a restructuring with Lou as the sole trustee, a measure to which she had no objection, but at the same time he wanted "uncontrolled discretion" to manage the trust as he saw fit. Lou did not want personal responsibility for her husband's decisions. What if he were to "make mistakes or bad investments," she asked Mullendore. They devised a plan for her to escape liability for Bert's choices, using her own words so as not to alert him to her resort to legal counsel.[14]

Fortunately for the Hoovers, interest in the Harding scandals abated in the late summer of 1924. A lack of new revelations and a preoccupation with the 1924 national elections pushed the investigations off the front pages. It was reasonably certain that Bert would not be implicated. Lou's anxiety for the family estates evaporated. It would be several years before she returned her attention to the Henry family assets.

Hoover escaped the Harding-era inquisitions without a dent to his reputation, and he would always insist upon his rectitude. There is no definite reason to doubt him. Nor is there reason to be convinced of his absolute innocence.

Hoover was not above living with dark secrets, professional and personal. He had remained in the cabinet alongside Daugherty even after Harding's confidences aboard the *Henderson*. He was perturbed enough about the attorney general to advise a freshly sworn-in Coolidge to relieve him of his responsibilities, yet when Coolidge refused, Hoover continued to serve. Years later, Hoover would tell a friend a story of being aboard the presidential yacht *Mayflower* with Harding, who broke out a bottle and a deck of cards. "Harding got so drunk that night he did not know what he was doing," said Hoover. "I am not a prig, but I was so disgusted that I was fully determined to resign from the Cabinet upon my return to Washington. It was difficult indeed for me to reconsider my decision." Given all this, it is not inconceivable that Hoover knew some or most of the dirt on the Harding regime before it became public, that he had weighed the risk of association with scoundrels against the benefits to his career of staying in the cabinet, and took his chances.[15]

Hoover also practiced his own variety of the cronyism that had enabled the Harding scandals. His personal affairs were entwined with those of Edgar Rickard, his close friend from mining days, and a number of friends from his relief career, including Julius H. Barnes and Prentiss Gray. In fact, their dealings were so tangled that it was difficult to say where one's interests started and another's stopped. Rickard managed Hoover's personal accounts and investments. Rickard, Hoover, and Barnes jointly owned a farming operation near Bakersfield, California. Barnes and Hoover were each among the owners of the *Washington Herald*. Barnes and Rickard shared offices in New York and had interests in the Penobscot Paper Company. Gray and Barnes were officers of the J. Henry Schroder Banking Company and the Manati Sugar Corporation, among other commodity-based businesses. And on and on. Their web of interrelated operations and investments in corresponding fields of endeavor resembles those of the London mining group Hoover set up after departing Bewick, Moreing in part to evade his noncompete agreement.[16]

Hoover had been careful to turn over his affairs to Rickard for management, creating the appearance of an arm's-length relationship between himself and his money, yet Rickard's diary makes it clear that

he regularly took direction from Hoover about their business interests. Prentiss and Barnes made money during the twenties in industries in which Hoover, as commerce secretary, had oversight. Rickard
was actively involved in the Hazeltine Corporation, a leader in radio
receiver technology, while Hoover was trying to wrap his arms around
the radio industry. Rickard reportedly acquired a basketful of patent
businesses while his friend sat atop the Patent Bureau.[17]

It is not difficult to imagine subtle and untraceable advantages
falling to Hoover associates somewhere along the blurry line between
business and government. With a more sophisticated mind than most
in Harding's orbit, and a better class of friend, Hoover would not
have needed to resort to the gross transgressions of Forbes and Fall
to serve private interests.

All that said, there is no evidence that Hoover committed any
clear transgressions, or that he and Lou were anxious about anything
other than overzealous congressional investigators. He was undoubtedly more mature and far more scrupulous about his conduct in public
service than he had been in his early business career, and his ambitions for still higher office would have urged him to walk the straight
and narrow.

The one scandal of 1924 that did succeed in implicating Hoover had
nothing to do with politics and existed almost entirely in his head.
Belle Livingstone was an aging American courtesan known for her
"poetic legs" and opulent figure. Her memoir was excerpted in the
June issue of *Hearst's International-Cosmopolitan* magazine under the
title "They Called Me the Most Dangerous Woman in Europe." It
recounted her time in London, where she was popular among the
city's millionaire miners. Having charmed her way to a share in a Sinai
turquoise concession managed by Bewick, Moreing, she determined
in 1900 to travel to Arabia with the company's engineering team.
Bewick, Moreing refused to take her. "I did not find much difficulty
in satisfying myself that Mr. [Herbert] Hoover was the nigger in my
woodpile," she wrote, "and that it was he who was putting obstacles
in the way of my carrying out my cherished idea."[18]

Livingstone says that she telephoned Hoover and invited him to
dinner at her Walsingham flat. He arrived and she saw at a glance, as

he entered, "how he was hating himself" for having agreed to the rendezvous. She would recognize the same look "twenty years later when I saw him at the Hotel Crillon, during the Peace Conference in Paris; only then he had more reason as he had accumulated an exceptionally admiring following."[19]

She claims to have found Hoover "easier to tame" than she had expected:

> I was wearing a very lovely dress, marked "Paris" all over; . . . I turned my best side towards him. . . . The fun I directed at myself melted him into smiles, and he not only withdrew his objections but expressed the intention of accompanying the expedition himself. This change of attitude was so marked, indeed, that I thought it just as well to ring the bell for dinner to be served at once, and thus brought to an end what looked as though it might become an embarrassing tete-a-tete.[20]

Just as dinner arrived, Livingstone's doorbell rang and a well-known businessman was announced as waiting in her drawing room. Hoover, she says, was flustered. He did not want to be seen alone with a notorious woman. Annoyed at his attitude, she shut him in a broom closet, where he stood for three hours while the other man ate his dinner.

So her story goes. Edgar Rickard had the pleasure of breaking news of the excerpt to his best friend. Hoover denied ever having met Livingstone, and he doubted that he had even been in London during 1900 (he was, briefly). The article, he insisted, was libelous. Rickard telegraphed the ARA public relations chief in New York, George Barr Baker: "Chief says it is dirty libel intended make public man ridiculous and unless redress afforded action should be taken."[21]

Lawyers were retained, facts were investigated and challenged, strategy was discussed by cablegram, sometimes in code, and demands for retractions were made of author and publisher. The Hoover team tried to convince Livingstone's agent to turn on her. They volunteered that their man had been mistaken for another Bewick, Moreing partner named Hooper, who also denied being locked in Livingstone's closet, although he allowed that he had met with her at her apartment on business. This admission prompted the team to hunt down Livingstone's address in order to stage a face-to-face confrontation with Hooper in front of witnesses. The idea was abandoned when it was pointed out that Hooper, possessing a minimum of dignity, might be reluctant to cooperate.[22]

The Hoover fixers, resting their case on their chief's integrity, his infallible memory, the unlikelihood of his being in London in that season, as well as Hooper's quasi-admission, forced a retraction from the publisher, but try as they might, they could never shake the author from her insistence that the man she had bedazzled and closeted was Herbert Hoover. She had seen what she had seen, and she had seen it again in his face twenty years later at the Crillon in Paris.

Whether or not the incident actually occurred is of no consequence. Either way, the only injured party was Hoover's vanity. The excerpt was ignored by other media and by Hoover's political opponents. The nature of his response was more interesting than the story itself. He kept his team on the barricades for the better part of two months and heightened the frenzy in his circle by postulating a "conspiracy" on the part of William Randolph Hearst to disgrace him politically. He would not be talked down from this view despite an utter lack of evidence of any political intent. The story did not even refer to his role in Harding's cabinet.[23]

Hoover's behavior follows a pattern that stretches through his response to the taunting of Senator Reed to his overreaction to the Bates matter during the Belgian relief, to his paranoid squabbling with his boss in Australia. His anxieties and hypersensitivity had not been diminished by time and success. He would keep in his employ until old age a shadowy former Secret Service agent named Larry Richey, who, as Hoover's confidential secretary, worked in an office with a safe and drawn blinds. Popularly known as Hoover's "private sleuth" or "official snooper," Richey was entrusted with a range of missions including the investigations of leaks, hostile journalists, and political enemies.[24]

Hoover's new leader shared his old leader's impeccable timing. Calvin Coolidge was the right man at the right hour, at least for Republicans, and at this even Republicans were surprised. He had been a nonentity in his two years as vice president: those who met him could never figure out if he was cagey or slow. There was talk before Harding's death that Coolidge might be dumped from the ticket in 1924.

That Coolidge had been so little noticed as vice president turned out to be a blessing upon Harding's death: the moment he moved into the White House, he passed for a breath of fresh air. It also helped that in many ways he was the antithesis of his discredited predecessor. He did not look like a waxwork president. He was slight, hatchet-faced, ginger-haired, stern, and graceless, the first farm boy to occupy the White House since Benjamin Harrison. He knew nothing of blo-viating. It was said that he could be silent in five languages. He did not drink to excess, run a poker table, or chase teenagers. Coolidge lived in half of a rented two-family home in Massachusetts and shared a party line with his neighbors. He had no time for books, and he had never traveled farther than a brief honeymoon trip to Montreal, the closest international destination to his hometown. William Allen White captured Coolidge in his famous phrase "a puritan in Babylon"—dutiful, upstanding, and ungenerous.[25]

Most importantly, Coolidge was a seasoned, tough-minded political operator who had doggedly worked his way from Massachusetts state assemblyman to president of the state senate to lieutenant governor and two-term governor. He gained a modest national profile with his firm handling of the Boston police strike of 1919. Two years as vice president and keeper of the U.S. Senate had introduced him to Washington's plumbing and personalities, completing a thorough preparation for highest office. From his first days as president he went solemnly and steadily about his duties, exhibiting a sort of crabbed nobility. He pledged himself to continue with Harding's priorities while sweeping all traces of his predecessor's political demimonde out of the White House. Coolidge refused to be ruffled by the scandals in the Capitol, neither obstructing investigations nor permitting them oxygen. He played his party well, refusing to dump Daugherty, a powerful force in the swing state of Ohio, until all but the dimmest Republicans viewed him as a liability. These moves bought the new administration time and allowed a rapidly improving economy to work its magic on the public mood.[26]

The Coolidge-Hoover rapport had been friendly and respectful through the Harding years. As vice president, Coolidge had liked

Hoover well enough to permit him use of his offices in the Capitol. Their wives maintained a friendly correspondence. After Coolidge's swearing-in, Hoover went out of his way to ease his transition, becoming the new president's best source of information and advice on the current state of governmental affairs. "I can not tell you how many things I feel we are dependent on you about," wrote Coolidge's secretary, Bascom Slemp, in a note to Hoover ten weeks after the changeover.[27]

Although public conjecture about the next Republican nomination had begun two days after Harding's death, it was not immediately clear to Hoover or anyone else in Washington whether the new boss was a stopgap or an impediment to other presidential aspirants in 1924. Coolidge shrewdly squelched the speculation at the earliest appropriate moment by announcing along with his December 1923 address to Congress that he intended to keep his job. He won the support of the cabinet and Republican regulars and took the 1924 convention in a landslide. The speed with which he had moved let no other candidacy get off the ground, minimizing damage to the ever-fractious party.[28]

With his presidential hopes dashed again, Hoover's attention turned to other opportunities for promotion. Whatever he had accomplished in Commerce, it was still a junior portfolio. His name surfaced at the Cleveland Republican convention as a serious challenger for the junior spot on the ticket. He seems to have had no hand in this development, and in any event, the position went to General Charles Dawes, Harding's inaugural director of the Bureau of the Budget.[29]

Hoover campaigned enthusiastically for Coolidge in California, a key Republican state in 1924, making an important contribution to his party's landslide. The "little feller" took 54 percent of the popular vote nationally, leaving 29 percent for the weak Democratic candidate, John W. Davis. Senator Robert La Follette of Wisconsin, scraping up the remains of the Progressive vote in America, registered 17 percent. Hoover sent a congratulatory telegram to the president-elect and was pleased to receive a fond reply. Coolidge was "deeply grateful to you for all that you have done in behalf of the cause for which we both stand." Hoover hoped to convert this gratitude into an appointment as secretary of state. Press chatter seemed to confirm him as the natural candidate to replace Secretary Hughes, who had recently announced his retirement, but Hoover was thwarted again. Coolidge tapped Frank Kellogg, U.S. Ambassador Extraordinary and Plenipotentiary to Great Britain, for State. Hoover was offered Agriculture, a department vacated ten days before the election by the unexpected death of Henry C. Wallace.[30]

Coolidge's motives were likely mixed. He and Hoover were aligned on agriculture: both opposed the McNary-Haugen Farm Relief Bill, a proposal by farmers and their friends in Congress to have the U.S. government buy surplus crops at a set price and dump them abroad at whatever they would bring, letting the taxpayer eat the difference. They saw it as an unwarranted peacetime intervention in the grain business. Hoover advocated instead a system of farmer-run marketing cooperatives supported by a federal marketing board. Strictly from a policy perspective, Hoover fit Coolidge's plans for Agriculture. At the same time, Coolidge, wary of potential rivals, knew that Agriculture was a toxic portfolio, and it had to have occurred to him that a few years of grappling with the intractable problems of oversupply on the American farm would wear on Hoover's popularity. Hoover, familiar with the challenges of the portfolio, told Coolidge he did not think he could be effective in Agriculture given that its bureaucrats were in favor of McNary-Haugen and he opposed it. They compromised on his return to Commerce.[31]

Coolidge became Hoover's third president since his return to the United States in 1917, and another with whom he would forge a close working relationship, an unusual feat in any era of Washington politics. Each somewhat leery of the other, they nonetheless proceeded in good faith, and it seemed for a time that Hoover would be able to continue the success he had experienced under Harding straight through the new president's term. Coolidge's reasonably vigorous inaugural hit many of the notes Hoover wanted to hear. Reduction of the size of government to an appropriate peacetime level, with an attendant decrease in tax burdens. The application of "science" to government. Development of continental waterways and natural resources. The promotion of peace in Europe with a corresponding emphasis on disarmament and the encouragement of economic recovery. The most restrictive immigration controls in U.S. history, a popular move that the commerce secretary supported on "biological and cultural grounds."[32]

Hoover continued to interpret his mandate as broadly as possible, designating Commerce "the economic and business laboratory of the nation." His preaching on waste and efficiency, his faith in individualism and equality of opportunity, were unabated. Coolidge blessed his work by sparing Commerce the ax in his first budget, one of two departments so favored, and by formally liberating aviation from War and Navy and settling it in Commerce. He followed Harding's habit of involving Hoover in matters that might more properly have been handled by other departments, including coal strikes, railway and shipping policy, and European debt negotiations. Coolidge also listened carefully to his secretary's policy advice. Three months after receiving a long memo from Hoover on the depletion of American oil reserves and the consequences for American security and industry, Coolidge announced the creation of the Federal Oil Conservation Board and gave his commerce secretary a seat at its table.[33]

Hoover kept to his now-familiar working routines, still operating out of Nineteenth Street offices in the old Commerce building. He arrived early in the morning, walking in the long, swift, purposeful strides of the field engineer, usually accompanied by some part of the retinue that had joined him at home for breakfast. His uniform of double-breasted suits was unvaried, except perhaps for richer neckties, an indulgence reminiscent of the bright ribbons his mother had sewn into her plain Quaker garb. He sat much of the day at his desk in a straight-backed chair, either alone with his papers or entertaining visitors, usually one at a time and seldom longer than half an hour. He saluted callers with his regular greeting, "What can I do for you?" He would lean back and listen, drawing on a light Corona cigar or stuffing tobacco into the bowl of his plain briar pipe.[34]

He smoked constantly. When restless he would doodle on a notepad, mostly triangles or spider webs that suggest nothing more than impatience. He would start rubbing his knee as though it were sore, or he would stand and pace the floor, jangling the coins in his pocket. On his desk was a cradle telephone. It rang constantly. Hoover had also set up a new intercom system that allowed him to summon a secretary at the press of a button. A peephole had been installed in his door, not so that he could look out but so that his staff could glance in to see if he might be interrupted.[35]

Outside of Hoover's door were his usual bevy of aides and a steady stream of visitors who, collectively, had taken on Hoover's personality. Staff, said one of their number, tended to be "extremely grave in appearance and unsmiling and almost taciturn." Conversation was kept to a minimum and much of it was done over the telephone rather than in person. Staff meetings were rare. Indeed, the various aides hardly knew one another. Their relations and loyalties were almost exclusively with the chief.[36]

To many on the outside, it appeared as though Hoover's role in Coolidge's cabinet was indeed unchanged from Harding's day. Six months into the new administration, the press he attracted was, if anything, more laudatory than what he had garnered under the old regime. Hoover, reported the *Minneapolis Tribune*, "is Mr Coolidge's most trusted and most highly valued adviser." *Time* magazine found it "amazing the number of pies in which [Hoover] has his fingers. There are those who say he practically represents the brains of the Administration." The *New York Times* said that Hoover had so successfully expanded his cabinet position that he had emerged "as a cabinet" in his own right, one dedicated to leading the material development of the nation.[37]

The *New Republic*, in the process of crediting Hoover for moving Coolidge from lukewarm to aggressive on the World Court, described the division of authority in Washington as follows. The president made appointments, occupied center stage, dealt with the press, and called in Hoover when there was real work to be done:

> The plain fact is that no vital problem, whether in the foreign or the domestic field, arises in this administration in the handling of which Mr. Hoover does not have a real—and very often a leading—part. There is more Hoover in the administration than anyone else.[38]

Hoover's omnipresence through a second Republican administration left the press stretching for historical antecedents. The *Des Moines Capital* said Hoover was regarded in Washington as the most

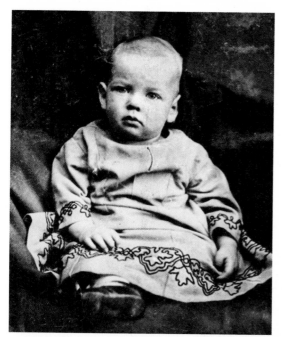

Herbert Hoover as a baby, 1875: "He looked about very cordial at every body."

Main and Downey, 1878: The local newspaper was one page, once a month.

Jesse and Hulda Hoover, 1879:
They courted at oyster suppers and buggy rides.

A people habituated to hardship: the extended Hoover-Minthorn family, 1878. Those pictured include: 1: Herbert Hoover as a baby, in the arms of 2: his father, Jesse Hoover; 3: his mother, Hulda Hoover; 4: his brother, Theodore Hoover; 5: his sister, Mary Hoover.

The three orphaned siblings: Theodore, Herbert, and Mary Hoover at Salem, circa 1888.

Young Lou Henry with a rifle, as per usual, August 22, 1891.

An unbroken record of academic mediocrity: Hoover (bottom left) and a surveying squad at Stanford University, 1893.

Herbert Hoover at age twenty-two, passing himself off as thirty-five, 1897.

Lou Henry, a nominal Episcopalian, and Herbert Hoover, a nominal Quaker, were wed by a Catholic priest in Monterey, 1899. Mrs. Henry (bottom step, right) and Jean and Mr. Henry (higher step), 1899.

"I am the devil." Herbert Hoover in the Australian goldfields, 1900.

Mr. and Mrs. Hoover with Mr. and Mrs. Rickard, enjoying Piazza San Marco
and their unusually cosmopolitan lifestyle, February 15, 1912.

The Hoovers were so thoroughly anglicized that they were sometimes mistaken for British. Traveling with Allan (left) and Herbert Jr. (right), 1917.

"The nearest approach to a dictator Europe has had since Napoleon." Herbert Hoover, on the eve of the Paris Peace Conference.

"The biggest figure injected into Washington life by the war."
Hoover (top left) with Woodrow Wilson and the U.S. World War Council, 1918.

"Many," said Walter Lippmann, "felt that they had never met a more interesting man." Hoover works a crowd, date unknown.

An independent woman and an unusual political wife:
Lou Henry Hoover with two Girl Scouts, 1925.

"When the United States of America is sick they call for Herbert Hoover."
With children rescued from the great Mississippi flood,
Natchez, Mississippi, 1927.

Hoover with friends at "the greatest men's party in the world,"
Bohemian Grove, 1927.

Hoover was careful not to break Calvin Coolidge's spell of supremacy. Aboard the presidential yacht *Mayflower*, 1928.

"We are nearer today to the ideal of the abolition of poverty . . . than ever before." Hoover campaigning on Republican prosperity, 1928.

"He could hardly take his eyes off [granddaughter Peggy Ann] whenever she was about him." The Hoovers in Palo Alto at the end of the election trail, 1928. Left to right: Herbert Hoover Jr.; Mrs. Herbert Hoover Jr.; Mrs. Herbert Hoover, holding Herbert III; Herbert Hoover, holding Peggy Ann; and Allan Hoover.

"I ask the help of Almighty God in this service to my country to which you have called me." President Herbert Hoover is given the oath of office by Chief Justice William Howard Taft in Washington, D.C., March 4, 1929.

"In violent defiance of the law and the public authorities." Veterans stage bonus demonstration as Congress struggles with the deficit, April 8, 1932.

Hoover and his circle were convinced his odds of reelection would be best if Franklin Roosevelt were the Democratic nominee. At FDR's inauguration, March 4, 1933.

A Hooverville in Bakersfield, California, April 1936. Even through the Roosevelt era, every shantytown was known as a Hooverville.

top: Hitler, said Hoover, was "an extraordinarily emotional character" whose mind
"gets to mysticism at a jump." The former
president meets the Reich Chancellor in
Berlin on March 8, 1938.

middle: "Yours has been a friendship which
has reached deeper into my life than you
know." President Harry S. Truman and
former president Hoover at the White
House, February 7, 1951.

right: John F. Kennedy would have been
Hoover's sixth president, but Hoover
declined the offer to serve. With then-
senator JFK, January 1956.

capable of modern Americans and that one needed to go back to Benjamin Franklin to find a man who had been so active in so many fields and had made such a broad contribution to public life. The *Chicago Tribune* thought Alexander Hamilton a more appropriate comparison. Like Hamilton, the most able man in Washington's first cabinet, Hoover not only dominated the administration of his day by talent and force of personality but also shaped the administration of the United States government for generations to come.[39]

The truth was more nuanced. Hoover did play a mighty role in the new administration, yet Coolidge was his own man with his own ideas about the role of government. He had his liberal impulses: he had admired Teddy Roosevelt's progressivism and Wilson's antiwar idealism. These views, however, struggled for sunlight in the shadow of Coolidge's fundamentally conservative view of government.

To Coolidge's mind, the pursuit of ideals, Wilson's example notwithstanding, was more an individual than a state affair. He believed that government existed to prevent harm, not to do good, and certainly not to spend. It should be small and frugal, dedicated to facilitating trade and avoiding war. Intervention in private affairs was always a bad idea. Abuses might exist in the private sector, but it was not "the concern of the federal government to attempt their reform." Inequities would work themselves out over time. His administrative advice to Hoover was to let problems sit: nine out of ten would "run into the ditch before they reach you." Coolidge's genius for passivity extended even to his dealings with individuals. He told Hoover of his method for handling the special pleaders who crowded his office: "If you keep dead still, they will run down in three or four minutes." His attitude toward public statements was similar. "If you don't say anything," he told Hoover, "you won't be called upon to repeat it." For a man known as Silent Cal, he was eminently quotable.[40]

Hoover thought Coolidge's political outlook the most laissez-faire of any president since the aforementioned Harrison. He also thought it dangerous. Nine out of ten problems may indeed hit the ditch, but the tenth, by the time it reached the White House, would be formidable.[41]

What generous and constructive elements there were to Coolidge's nature were further dampened in office by personal tragedy. In the summer of 1924, his son Calvin Jr. developed a blister on the middle toe of his right foot after playing tennis on the White House courts. Within a week he had died of an infection. Coolidge grew distracted and listless, sleeping more than twelve hours a day. He was given to bouts of rage and irascibility aimed at his wife, his cabinet secretaries, even his barber. Grace Coolidge said that after Calvin Jr.'s death her husband never regained his "zest for living." He would never regain his zest for leadership, either.[42]

Valuable as Hoover was to the administration, he did not retain the favored-son status he had known with Harding. If Coolidge looked to anyone in his cabinet with awe and admiration, it was his secretary of the Treasury. Andrew Mellon was the most important adviser and cabinet member in the new administration. His economics, not Hoover's, set its tone.

Andrew Mellon was one of the more curious figures ever to grace a federal cabinet. He was sixty-eight years old, a hollow-eyed, hollow-cheeked ghost of a man, weighing a mere 145 pounds. He dressed like an undertaker, smoked thin black cigarettes, and had an air of being in perpetual retreat: one journalist said he looked like "a tired double-entry book keeper who was afraid of losing his job."[43]

Yet Mellon owned the second-largest fortune in the United States, $80 million at the time he took office, spread over an unusually diverse portfolio: oil, coal, steel, banking, railroads, manufacturing, distilling, and chemicals. He invested carefully and was a master of stock manipulation, trading heavily on his insider's knowledge. He deftly skirted the Sherman Antitrust Act to build sturdy monopolies in his chosen industries. He benefited enormously from the preferences he expected and received as a principal bankroller of the Republican Party in Pennsylvania. His appointment to Treasury violated the spirit if not the letter of a 1789 statute prohibiting its secretary from engagement in trade or commerce. Mellon resigned his directorships but continued to hold most of his stock, and his income and wealth increased enormously during his Treasury years. He and his companies would be under congressional investigation throughout most of that time.[44]

Mellon's personal life was sad. In middle age, the emotionally stunted millionaire had married a twenty-year-old British brewing heiress who gave him two children and, after twelve years together, a messy public divorce involving serial adultery on her part. He afterward lived in an apartment occupying the entire top floor of a new luxury Beaux Arts building near Dupont Circle, surrounded by an impeccable selection of Gainsboroughs. His daughter Ailsa served as his official hostess.[45]

While Hoover and Mellon might be mistaken on first glance for a matching pair of pro-business Republicans, they in fact represented opposite poles of mainstream opinion within the party (leaving aside a rabidly progressive faction of insurgent Republicans well to the left of Hoover). Mellon, like Coolidge, preferred a national government so small that most citizens would not notice if it went out of business. He liked low taxes, low interest rates, and sound money. He believed progressive taxes penalized the rich and discouraged enterprise. He was comfortable with monopolies, which he viewed as the fruit of diligence, and he hated labor unions. He was also a committed isolationist, anti-Versailles and anti-League.[46]

Hoover could agree with Mellon on overall tax reduction and the need for free markets, economy in government, and little else. One of the issues that put their differences in sharpest relief was the estate tax. Mellon had an almost religious commitment to the sanctity of massive intergenerational fortunes. He believed Americans had a moral right to accumulate and safeguard money without penalties for success. He opposed efforts to redistribute wealth, and monkeying with the estate tax was to his mind the worst method of all.[47]

Hoover, the champion of equal opportunity, thought it fair that the wealthy should accept a greater burden of taxation, and he was comfortable with using taxes to limit the political and social influence of wealth and to prevent the formation of large intergenerational estates. It annoyed him that the rich could evade taxation by investing in tax-free municipal bonds, a dodge that shifted the burden unduly to corporations and lower-income Americans. Understanding that there were reasonable arguments for the tax-exempt status of government bonds, Hoover aimed to make the rich pay their share through inheritance taxes.

Their debate on these issues bubbled throughout the Harding and Coolidge administrations. Both Hoover and Mellon claimed to be looking out for the greater good of the economy. Mellon argued that progressive taxes and estate taxes would stunt growth, leaving all of America poorer. Hoover felt that the government's reliance on corporate taxes was taking productive money out of the market. He also believed that innovation and economic growth came from the bottom up; therefore, tax relief was more important at the lower end of the earning scale. Each man was arguing in part from personal experience: Mellon was born to wealth; Hoover was not.

Mellon's position held sway in the Coolidge years, and he chipped away at both estate taxes and assessments on high earners, while leaving the overall tax regime lower and less progressive than he had found it. Revenues by 1926 were strong enough to effectively exempt every household's first $4,000 of income, which dropped the number of people on the tax rolls by a third.[48]

Tax relief was one of several important battles Hoover lost to Mellon. Coolidge also sided with his Treasury secretary against Hoover's bid to restrain what became a deluge of high-interest loans to unsteady European governments, some of which were using the funds to finance fiscal deficits and arms purchases. The administration was reluctant to interfere with private lending.

Mellon's press through the Coolidge years was as adulatory as Hoover's. He, too, attracted comparisons to Hamilton.* He, too, was seen as a man of the moment, an ideal representative of American mastery and expertise. He claimed that his tax regime was "scientific," designed to maximize revenue while minimizing the burden on individuals. His view of bankers was as grand as Hoover's view of engineers: "No one is in a better position than the banker to know the pulse of the nation's business and, what is of more importance, to regulate in some degree that pulse."[49]

Happily for the administration, prosperity popped like a champagne cork in the mid-1920s. The economy was so spectacularly buoyant that Coolidge, Mellon, and Hoover could all claim credit.

Never mind that most of the heavy lifting had been done during Harding's time, Coolidge could boast of a real gross domestic product

---

* William G. McAdoo, Wilson's Treasury secretary, had also been compared to Hamilton, which suggests that Hamilton is the gold standard and that no one else has really come close. (Geoffrey Perrett, *America in the Twenties: A History*. New York: Touchstone Books, 1983, p. 130.)

that grew 5 percent a year between 1922 and 1929, one of the better runs in U.S. history. Corporate profits soared 75 percent from 1922 to 1927. Unemployment sat at a healthy low of 4 percent from 1922 to 1929. From a global perspective, the U.S. economy was a colossus. By 1925, it was producing almost half of the planet's economic output and, by 1926, 42 percent of its manufactured goods. All of this with 6 percent of the world's population.[50]

Mellon took pride in cutting government spending by half and reducing the federal debt by $6 billion. He believed, counterintuitively, that his tax cuts were responsible for increasing government revenues by freeing up more cash for productive purposes. Surprisingly large fiscal surpluses allowed him to dismantle wartime surtaxes on high incomes.

Even if he would have chosen different priorities, Hoover, too, reveled in the administration's feats of economy. He took pleasure in how America's economic surge was affecting the lives of average citizens. Signs of improved quality of life were everywhere: annual incomes increased by 30 percent from 1922 to 1929; increasing numbers of workers kept a more leisurely forty-eight-hour week; electric lighting, indoor plumbing, and the automobile, known only to the affluent at the beginning of the decade, were commonplace by its end; medical costs were dropping; more young men and women could afford to stay in school, and record numbers were graduating and heading to college.[51]

The national-scale, consumer-driven economy of which Hoover was both herald and shepherd was a crucial element of the boom. Against the umbrage of Sinclair Lewis, shoppers were rushing to Kresge's and S&P chains to stock their shelves with the new standard products: nationally advertised food and household brands such as Quaker Oats, Heinz Pickles, Old Dutch Cleaner, Ivory Soap, and Gillette Safety Razors. They filled their homes with refrigerators, radio receivers, electric mixers, toasters, and sewing machines, often employing new consumer credit vehicles such as the layaway plan to finance their purchases.

The economy was by no means perfect. Farm incomes continued to falter. Relief continued to elude the distressed coal sector. Urban centers benefited more from growth than rural areas, most notably in the South. Whites saw more improvement than blacks. High incomes grew faster than lower incomes, a trend that by decade's end would produce a historic peak in income inequality. Nevertheless, most Americans savored the unusually broad economic gains delivered in the twenties. With the advance of prosperity came the luxury of time and the expansion of leisure and freedom, as well as a new mobility and independence, granted by the automobile, to migrate, travel, and escape parental and community authority. Prosperity, leisure, and independence, along with the burgeoning popular culture inspired by these gifts, would come to define the Jazz Age.[52]

With Commerce under control, his relief work subsiding, and years to pass before another shot at the presidency, Hoover, too, found himself with time on his hands. In the past he had filled these gaps with self-improvement or self-advancement projects, whether binges of learning and reading, authorship, money-making ventures, or public service. He was now at another stage in life. He had turned fifty shortly before Coolidge's election. This placed him far beyond the longevity afforded either of his parents. His hair was gray at the temples, his face fleshy, and a paunch stretched his belt. In worldly terms, he was as successful, prosperous, admired, and influential as a man could reasonably hope to be, and he had a thick catalog of achievements to his credit with a likelihood of more to come. Whether conscious of it or not, he appeared satisfied, for the first time in his life, with the mark he was making in the world. His gnawing need to prove himself at every hour of the day occasionally abated slightly, permitting him to take a cue from the broader culture and relax on occasion, live a little, even to the point of taking honest vacations.

# CHAPTER 16

# Sleepless in Good Times

Hoover had always loved to fish. The happiest days of his youth had been spent chasing suckers in Wapsinonoc Creek with a cheap hook attached to butcher string and a willow pole. In his Oregon years, he had become an accomplished fly fisherman, battling steelhead in cold fast rivers. Since those days, life had afforded few opportunities for his favorite sport. He had picked up a rod in South Africa while mending his shattered psyche in 1904. He had snuck in the odd camping trip to California, favoring the High Sierras and Yosemite National Park. His brother Theodore, who after the war had joined the new Department of Mining and Metallurgy at Stanford, owned a piece of property along the coast of Central California where the brothers occasionally fished from the beach. Hoover's return to the sport in middle age was encouraged by his responsibilities in Commerce where he had oversight of the Bureau of Fisheries, which kept a number of boats including the *Kilkenny*, a coastal survey vessel that Hoover would commandeer from time to time to chase rock bass and perch in the innumerable bays and inlets of the Chesapeake. It was a trip to Florida in 1924, however, that deserves most of the credit for reigniting the passion of his youth and launching Hoover into the piscatorial big leagues.[1]

The Long Key Fishing Club was built in 1908 by Henry M. Flagler's Florida East Coast Railway Company to encourage use of the line and shore up tourism in the region. Sitting halfway between the mainland and Key West, with a two-story guesthouse and a scattering of cottages, Long Key immediately attracted one of the world's most famous sportsmen, the author Zane Grey. He became a regular at Long Key and the first president of the club in 1917. It was Grey who established the club's high-minded statement of purpose: "To Develop the Best and Finest Traits of Sport, To Restrict the Killing of Fish, To Educate the Inexperienced Angler by Helping Him, And To Promote Good Fellowship." Grey organized competitions with prizes—gold, silver, and bronze buttons—for fish of various weights caught with specific tackle. More importantly, he invented and popularized the sport of sailfishing.[2]

The sailfish had long been regarded as a saltwater pest, stealing bait intended for prized tarpon or kingfish. Grey thought it might be fun to pursue the fast-swimming, high-leaping sailfish with light tackle. And it was. As the twenties progressed, as the economy boomed and Americans felt flush, the author had plenty of company at Long Key. The idea of a winter vacation in warmer climes, previously the prerogative of the rich, was catching on with the gentry. Mounted sailfish, with their long bills and graceful dorsal fins, began to fill the offices and dens of doctors and business executives throughout the northern states and the Midwest.[3]

Hoover first visited Long Key in 1924 and quickly became a regular, spending his days floating under the tropical sun, dressed in jacket and tie, wrestling marlin and tarpon for hours before hauling them into the boat. In the evenings he grilled his catch for dinner and retired to the porch to smoke his pipe, listen to the breeze rustling through the canopy of coconut palms, and talk of the day's fishing. If it had been a good day, he would tell stories of his adventures in China and Australia. Altogether, he enjoyed himself immensely and was in a good mood throughout the trip, rising early every day, pouring himself a strong cup of coffee, and greeting everyone with a cheerful "Isn't it a beautiful morning?"[4]

Hoover failed to snare a sailfish on that initial trip and so returned to Long Key again in the winter of 1925, this time with Lou, Attorney General and Mrs. Harlan Stone, and Mark Sullivan and his wife. They spent eight glorious days drifting and trolling in perfect weather from Miami to Key West. While the *Kilkenny* served as their base, most of their fishing was done from a smaller thirty-foot boat hired for the occasion. Its captain was a diminutive fellow who, according to Lou, jumped around his deck like a fox terrier. Hoover and Stone fished from wicker camp chairs on the open aft deck, protected from the intense sun by a canvas awning. Sullivan perched on a rail.[5]

Lou herself picked up a rod from time to time and fished from the top of the cabin. When the trip was almost over she unpacked her Corona typewriter and composed a letter to her boys that attempted to do justice to the beauty of the Keys:

> You never dreamed there were such queer colors on sea
> or sky. I won't say I have never seen more beautiful,—but
> certainly I have never seen anything like them, nor any
> more variegated than we had one day. Inside the reef there
> was all sorts of bright thick colors. Sometimes the whole
> of the water in sight would be . . . not clear at all, quite as
> thick as the Potomac but a real milky jade instead of brown.
> And there were all other shades, it seemed, of pale greens
> and blues and pinky grays and browns and mauves. Then
> we went through the reefs out into the Atlantic, and there
> were all those colors again, but now crystalline clear, - the
> jade became the glimmery clear jade that you could see right
> through, and you could see the bottom of the sea as plainly
> at forty, or they said a hundred feet as you could at five.[6]

Lou's husband was less inspired by the grandeur of the Keys than the activity of fishing. His enthusiasm for it was deep enough to qualify as spiritual. He spoke in public of the soul-nourishing effects of standing in a trout stream, or trailing a nine-thread line in deep waters, of the peace that came from contemplating the eternal movement of water and the mysteries beneath its surface, the respite from modern civilization with its office towers, cement pavement, radios, telephone bells, office boys, and columnists. He grew fond of drawing political and moral lessons from his experiences with rod and reel. "All men are equal before fishes," was one of his favorite lines. Angling, he said, mocked ambition and taught humility. To be skunked on an afternoon, or to be outwitted or outmuscled by a gilled competitor, was a fine way to reduce egotism, soothe troubles, and shame wickedness.[7]

As much as he fished for his soul, Hoover, a man of achievement, always fished with a goal. On every trip, he wanted the most impressive catch. If someone else won the honors, a gloom would envelop his party even under the brilliant cloudless skies of Southern Florida. His goal on the 1925 trip was the elusive sailfish, preferably a big one, eight to ten feet long. He was shut out for a second straight year. Fortunately, wrote Lou to their sons, Bert had otherwise "caught much the most and the biggest fish."[8]

Biggest of all was an amberjack, eighty-seven pounds. Hoover had been trolling just off Key West toward the end of the trip when the fish struck his line with force. It leapt high out of the clear green water and took an hour to reel in. It was heavy enough to win him a medal from the Long Key Fishing Club. Key West and Miami reporters wrote brief stories about the catch, and he had his picture taken, smiling broadly beside the hanging fish. No one else in the party caught anything comparable, although Lou pulled in two good-sized barracudas. The amberjack allowed Hoover to leave Florida happy. His party boarded the train home to Washington. Time passed. Trout season opened. He put the deep-sea fishing and the amberjack out of his mind, until 6:07 p.m. on the evening of June 5.[9]

At that moment a telegraph arrived at Hoover's doorstep in Washington with a request from the *Key West Daily News*. The paper wanted Hoover to confirm that his catch of the eighty-seven-pound amberjack was made in Key West waters. No sooner had this appeal been delivered than a second telegraph landed. The *Miami Herald* begged Hoover to wire a statement COD as to where he caught his monstrous fish.

Unbeknownst to Hoover, the picture of him with his amberjack had made its way into land promotion advertisements. Florida was in the midst of a boom, and Miami, its epicenter, had been growing ferociously. Its city limits had expanded a clear twenty-five miles to the south, and real estate promoters and the Miami Chamber of Commerce were inflating their pitches by alleging that Hoover's fish had been caught in Miami's suburbs. Key Westers were alarmed at Miami's imperialism and offended by the city's claim to a celebrated fish caught off its own shores. Hence the first two telegraphs.

Any chance of dismissing the messages as a spat between two boosterish newspapers evaporated at 6:30 p.m. when a third telegraph arrived. Jacob Rosengrowen, president of the Miami Chamber of Commerce, demanded that the commerce secretary confirm his fish was caught in annexed Miami territory. Any suggestion to the contrary, he warned, would cause "irreparable damage to hundreds of millions of dollars of property and would invalidate investment in advertising and selling campaign now organized."[10]

Proof positive that the story had spiraled out of control came in the form of a fourth telegraph at 6:45 p.m. The sender was none other than William Jennings Bryan, "the Great Commoner," the "Silver Knight of the West," the leather-lunged orator of the Platte, and four-time loser in presidential contests as head of the Democratic ticket. Bryan was now working as a public relations flack for the South Miami Realtors Association. He did not ask Hoover to alter his story or to confirm any one version of it. Bryan merely informed Hoover that the cash offer from the Miami real estate tycoons was being made with his knowledge and support. Hoover was not yet aware of any cash offer. That came five minutes later, at 6:50 p.m., in a fifth telegraph. Rosengrowen was offering $5,000 for a statement from Hoover that his fish was pulled from Miami waters.[11]

At 7:30 p.m. the Izaak Walton League, a new organization of avid fishermen dedicated to natural resource conservation, telegraphed the welcome news that regardless of where the amberjack had been caught, it weighed enough to qualify for another prize button.[12]

The Los Angeles Chamber of Commerce saw the humor in the whole affair and wired Hoover at 7:56 p.m. asking him to hold off on any determination until "final action on legislation extending easterly city limits of Los Angeles to Gulf Stream." Sadly for Los Angeles, the commandant of the Navy Yard Key West settled matters at that exact same moment. He informed Hoover that his fish had been caught fifteen knots and eight furlongs northwest of Key West, or about two miles south of Miami waters.[13]


Fishing and camping once again became a significant part of Hoover's life in the twenties. There were regular weekend trips to trout streams with friends and business associates. There were longer vacations in California and Nevada with Lou and the boys. They would drive to the Sierras in the family Cadillac, proceed to higher ground on horseback, find a nice camping spot by a lake or stream, catch some fish, cook them over a fire, watching for bears and swatting mosquitoes, and then move on to another spot.[14]

By all appearances, the Hoovers continued to appreciate one another's company despite looser ties than ever. Five or six years after the guns had been silenced, they could no longer attribute their scattered existence to the exigencies of war. The Hoover version of a cosmopolitan lifestyle had become habitual for all of them.

Herbert Jr. graduated from Stanford in 1925 with an engineering degree. Stubborn like his father, he disregarded his parents' suggestion of a career in mining and instead struck out for the aviation industry via Harvard Business School. Before leaving Stanford, he announced to his parents his intention of marrying his girlfriend, Margaret Watson. Lou, noting his determination, wrote Bert that opposition would be futile and that pushing for a long engagement would be a better strategy (their grounds for interfering at all are not clear). The couple wed in June 1925.[15]

Allan would that same year set out to become the fourth Hoover with a Stanford degree (fifth counting his Uncle Theodore). He and Lou were close. They could go months without writing, Allan forgetting his letters in his golf clothes, Lou pleading the pressure of events, but they were the two Hoovers who most seemed to need each other. Allan welcomed his mother's advice on everything from how to treat his girlfriends to how to use the family's connections at Stanford to get himself released from academic probation. They bonded over the quirks of the rest of the family. Allan told his mother, "You know, Herb's gotten a terrible lot like Daddy. I just noticed it these last few days. He laughs exactly like him, has the same kind of a chuckle, and really looks more like him. It tickled me no fooling."[16]

When Allan was out of touch with Lou for a length of time, she would accuse him of joining "Daddy's telegraphing club," a reference to Bert's habit of communicating, infrequently and succinctly, over the wires. Bert and Lou continued to live apart as much as they lived together: she stayed for months at a time in Palo Alto, while he kept up a heavy travel schedule from his base in Washington. When together, they picked up as though they had never been apart, sharing meals, attending ceremonies, and, if time permitted, talking through the day's events.[17]

They had finally settled in an old brick Colonial home at 2300 S Street, a fashionable address near Dupont Circle. It had an acre of gardens, twenty-two rooms, and a black and gold color scheme introduced by Lou. Like every other Hoover dwelling, it made room for innumerable guests, some expected, some showing up in the middle of the night or when the Hoovers were out of town. The house required Lou's regular attention and a large staff whether she was on the East Coast or the West. Someone once counted eight butlers roaming the halls. If anyone had bothered to keep a tally, there may have been an equal number of dogs, several of whom were fed by the commerce secretary off of his own plate.

Mrs. Hoover hired and managed the servants and made apologies to them when bills went unpaid. She trained the staff in the ways of her husband, telling them not to mind when he disappeared for days on a last-minute business trip, or arrived home just as suddenly in a whirlwind of telephone calls and telegrams, trailing an entourage that needed to be fed. They were taught not to let him touch invitations, which he would invariably make disappear, unanswered, in the leaves of books or pockets of coats.

The staff managed quite well with the Chief but had less luck with the dogs. One, Tut, made a sport of spoiling the Hoover carpets, and also bit one of three neighborhood children who had climbed over the fence to explore the Hoover fishpond. The boy's father, the police, the pound, and a veterinarian descended on the house. The staff, with help from a Commerce Department aide, resolved the situation and won Tut a pardon without anyone alerting either the master or mistress of the house.[18]

That the Hoover household was the usual bedlam does not mean that nothing had changed. Bert and Lou did not share each other's lives to the extent they had in prewar times. There were no months-long journeys together, no absorbing literary partnerships, and she did not share his fascination with politics; he did not feel her attachment to Palo Alto.

Despite Lou's sadness about the telegraphing club, she simply moved forward with her own life, as her husband had done. In middle age, Lou Henry Hoover was a capable, confident, tough-minded woman. She demonstrated her self-sufficiency upon her mother's death in 1921 when, instead of a period of formal mourning, which was not the Henry family way, she piled her father, his Filipino houseboy, and her seven-year-old nephew, Delano Large, into a Cadillac and drove from Palo Alto to Washington, D.C., camping along the way. It was an impressive feat in an era when few women drove automobiles, and paved interstate highways were still far in the future. There were no reliable maps or road signs along the route. Over some stretches through the Rockies and Utah, there was nothing that could properly be called a road. Lou crept along twisting wagon trails, dodging stumps and boulders and treacherous drops. Apart from the odd flat tire and some food poisoning in Iowa, the journey was smooth and cathartic. She made it to Washington in just over a month.[19]

Lou's love of the outdoors and her commitment to public service found full expression in the twenties through the Girl Scouts of the United States of America. Founded in 1912 by Juliette Low, the organization introduced young women to the culture of the local service club so much in vogue among their parents. Lou joined as a vice president of the seventy-thousand-strong tribe in 1921 and served two terms as president. She raised more than half a million dollars, tapping into Bert's web of charitable agencies, most notably the America Relief Administration Children's Fund.[20]

The Girl Scouts struck a balance of progressive and wholesome views that appealed to Lou. Her charges were told that they should chart their own destinies, embrace the outdoors, apply themselves to their studies, contribute to their communities, and ready themselves for careers, as well as their natural roles in the home. The time had ended when a woman could expect nothing beyond the "tedious routine of household duties." An "evenly balanced life" was now possible and desirable.[21]

Her executive responsibilities made Lou an impressive figure in her own right. She turned fifty in 1924, and her hair, short, white, and fluffy, now contrasted with her dark eyebrows and brought out the blue in her eyes. Under the hard-brimmed hat of her scouting outfit, she could look almost masculine. In evening clothes, she displayed a comfortable, unfussy elegance, allowing herself one or two pieces of simple ornamentation, usually beads. There was a sturdy confidence behind her crooked smile.

Whatever her accomplishments outside the home, Lou's highest profile was as a political wife, a role about which she was ambivalent.

She believed in Bert's mission and wanted to support and protect him, yet she did not want to be defined or confined by his endeavors. She was hurt in 1923 when her old friend Mary Austin told the author of an anonymous book entitled *Boudoir Mirrors of Washington* that Lou's ambition in life was to be "a background for Bertie." The author gave Lou credit for character and ability and for being equally at home in the social seasons of Washington as in the wilds. At the same time, it presented her, undoubtedly with Austin's help, as a failed writer, a dull hostess, and a timid supporter of women's rights. Lou denied ever having presented herself as a background for Bertie. Regardless of whether or not she had, it was clear that she was in an unwinnable situation, never sufficiently traditional or sufficiently progressive to please her critics.[22]

With his embrace of recreation, his secure position in the Coolidge cabinet, and his appreciation for America's fair economic weather, Hoover savored the midtwenties more than most periods of his life. He would later look back on these years as a happy time of constructive toil and significant achievement. Happy times for Hoover, however, did not meet any common or popular standards of happiness.

He was perpetually anxious, not least because he did not trust America's new prosperity. In his public voice, he was its cheerleader, but the voice in his head told him the luminous blue skies could fall at any moment. He was forever on the lookout for signs of disaster, agonizing over the slightest indications of economic trouble. Probably no cabinet member in any administration ever lost as much sleep in good times as Hoover. Almost from the moment prosperity began he was warning that the moment of low prices and high wages was unlikely to last. He wagged his finger at the Chamber of Commerce in a widely reported 1923 speech, advising that business needed to be vigilant against the dangers of overconfidence because there was always a reckoning, the inevitable bust. As a countercyclical measure, he succeeded in getting a handful of federal construction projects shelved until the economy went off the boil.[23]

Hoover also worried about the international scene, with good reason. The Continent, he had warned Harding as early as 1922, had made "remarkable progress in recuperation from the war," but the finances of the combatant states were a mess and threatened not only their futures but "world commerce as a whole." Europe was struggling with enormous debts, rampant inflation, unbalanced budgets, violent currency fluctuations, and widespread unemployment. Running through it all was the curse of Versailles: Berlin resisted what it considered the unjust reparations due its former enemies and effectively defaulted by printing money and letting the mark inflate to the point of worthlessness; France and Belgium occupied Germany's Ruhr valley and, together with England, announced that so long as Germany was failing to make its reparation payments, they could not be expected to make payments on their war debts to the United States. These tensions and suspicions frustrated all talk of European economic renewal.[24]

The United States was uncertain what role to play in Europe. With their high degree of economic self-sufficiency and their suspicion of imperialism, Americans did not feel the same responsibility toward the global financial system accepted by Great Britain, its chief architect and a trade-dependent imperial nation. Many observers, like Hoover, thought it only a matter of time before Britain regained its bearings and rose to dominate world markets once more. At the same time, Hoover understood that long-term American prosperity required stable currencies and a resumption of global trade. He promoted loans to Germany, as well as adjustments to the reparations settlement, and the reestablishment of the gold standard, hallowed symbol of international financial security. On all of these larger points, he was aligned with his cabinet colleagues and most American economic experts. There was no agreement, however, on the details.

Take foreign lending, for instance. Throughout the twenties, U.S. banks were tripping over one another to lend in Europe, where interest rates were relatively high. Hoover saw this practice as good and necessary for European recovery, although as early as 1921 he called for the terms of lending to be scrutinized in Washington to ensure that borrowed funds would be used for productive purposes. He opposed loans that supported military spending, deficit financing, and currency inflation. European renewal, said Hoover, would remain elusive without productive investments that generated foreign exchange, and without balanced budgets.[25]

His call for supervision of European loans put him in conflict with his friend Benjamin Strong, president of the Federal Reserve Bank of New York. Strong, a key player in the creation of the Federal Reserve, was a dominant force in American monetary policy. He was a tall, handsome man, confident and intelligent, with careful judgment. He held that government interference in the lending market was unfeasible and likely only to leave Washington holding the bag for failed loans. Mellon and Secretary of State Hughes agreed. Hughes, in fact, was so disturbed by Hoover's meddling in State affairs that he cut his access to official correspondence on European reparations.[26]

Hoover countered that as a practical matter the government was implicated in lending to Germany whether it wanted to be or not: banks would have no recourse beyond diplomatic channels if their borrowers defaulted. He managed to swing Strong and Hughes in favor of an informal agreement whereby U.S. bankers would keep the State Department informed of loan negotiations with foreign governments, but it had a negligible effect on the volume or the quality of loans.

Despite his bickering with Hughes and Mellon, Hoover managed to keep himself in the reparations discussions, and the United States made progress. A committee headed by Hoover's nominee, Illinois banker (and imminent U.S. vice president) Charles Dawes, crossed to Europe in 1924 to negotiate a new international agreement on war payments. Hughes, having given the committee its instructions, was exasperated to learn that Hoover had ordered three of his European commercial attachés to Paris to provide expertise to the Dawes party. Hughes cabled instructions that Hoover's men were not to be permitted any formal standing or to be placed on any committees or subcommittees. The men remained in Paris, exerting influence from the sidelines and keeping Hoover informed of the negotiations.[27]

The Dawes committee was a triumph, producing a plan that reduced Germany's annual reparation payment, imposed foreign supervision on its currency, and supplied Germany with $200 million in loans, while pushing France and Belgium back from the Ruhr. Hoover boasted in his 1924 report on business conditions that the Dawes Plan, assisted by technical experts from the Department of Commerce, would "bring about a revival in world trade and increased consumption of commodities, in which the United States [would] have its share."[28]

Welcome as it was, the Dawes Plan did not fix the European economy. It set the reparations issue aside so that leading countries could concentrate on a larger and more intractable problem, one that once again set Hoover in opposition to Benjamin Strong.

For generations before the war, the spine of the international financial system had been the gold standard. All national and international monetary relations, all ultimate settlements of balances of trade between countries, were based on the understanding that currencies were convertible into gold at fixed rates of exchange. The prewar pound, for instance, had been pegged at 123 grains of standard gold, which amounted to US$4.86.[29]

The gold standard meant order and smooth operations among the treasuries of the world. Governments would do whatever was necessary in the management of their monetary policy to maintain established rates of exchange and to buttress confidence in the system. If a country's gold supplies were reduced, it would raise interest rates to replenish its stocks, even at the risk of an economic slowdown and unemployment at home. The war, however, smashed the gold standard along with so much else. Countries abandoned monetary discipline, borrowed billions, spent far beyond their means, and let inflation run amok. The sea of paper money they created made a return to the gold standard at prewar rates next to impossible.

Hoover, Strong, and virtually every monetary expert of note agreed that a return to gold was critical to stabilizing exchange, balancing prices, and curbing inflation throughout Europe and the United States. Only cranks and irresponsible politicians felt otherwise, said Montagu Norman, governor of the Bank of England. The trouble was that three-quarters of the world's $6 billion in bullion now resided in the United States. Before the Great War, it had been equitably shared with France, England, and Germany. Somehow gold had to be made to flow back across the Atlantic.[30]

Hoover was among the first to voice misgivings over the accumulation of gold in America. As early as 1923, he had warned of the enormous temptation to use the excess bullion to create "a castle of credit and currency" in the United States. The result would be "the greatest era of inflation and speculation in our history." Americans would import like mad, price themselves out of export markets, and produce an adverse balance of trade that would someday "cause this gold to flow abroad with a rush from under our castle of credit and we should have an unparalleled financial crash." He wondered aloud if the excess gold might be taken out of circulation or somehow transferred back to Europe. Anything that could be done to make it easier for major trading partners to return to the gold standard, he reasoned, would stabilize the foreign scene and lend security to his domestic economy.[31]

Benjamin Strong also wanted to help Europe. Where he broke with Hoover was on the use of interest rates to benefit trading partners. Strong brought rates at the New York Federal Reserve Bank down to 3.5 percent in June 1924, a policy that encouraged capital and gold to flow out of the United States toward the higher interest rates in the United Kingdom. At home, the low rates had the additional benefit of refueling the Coolidge boom, as it was now called, after a brief slowdown over the previous winter. By 1925, corporate earnings were double what they had been in 1913. The Dow Jones Industrial Average had leapt to 150 points by October 1925, from a bottom of 67 in August 1921.[32]

Hoover believed Strong's low rate policy was doing more than maintaining the Coolidge boom. He was convinced that low rates were overheating the U.S. economy, setting the stage for a spectacular bust. He was particularly disturbed that much of the new money in the New York Exchange was borrowed, indicating a speculative frenzy. Hoover believed the economy needed a sobering jolt of tight credit from the Federal Reserve, but unfortunately for him, the Federal Reserve operated independent of the administration. Hoover would need to work through others to have his way.

On a wet and windy Sunday afternoon in November 1925, Hoover bounded from his Washington home a half block up S Street to the front door of his friend Adolph Miller, a member of the Federal Reserve Board since its inception in 1914. Without waiting for the butler to answer, Hoover let himself in, took the stairs two at a time, and burst into Miller's study to find that his neighbor, too, was fretting over monetary issues. The two men agreed that Strong's policy of assisting Europe with low interest rates, while laudable in principle, had been taken too far. The domestic economy was their first priority

and it was swimming in cheap credit, which was encouraging speculation and inflation. It could only end badly. They hatched a plan
to pressure Strong and the New York Federal Reserve Bank to raise
rates.[33]

Miller, like Hoover, was obliged to work indirectly. While the
Washington-based Federal Reserve Board had supervisory author-
ity over the twelve member banks, including Strong's New York
branch, it refrained from interfering in their credit decisions. Miller
and Hoover chose as their instrument Irvine Lenroot, a like-minded
Wisconsin senator and a member of the Senate Banking Committee.
Wound up by Hoover and Miller, Lenroot began bombarding D. R.
Crissinger, chairman of the Federal Reserve Board and a Strong confidant, with warnings of the "steady increase of speculation" on the
New York exchange. In paragraphs ghostwritten by Hoover, Lenroot
predicted that the "gambling" mentality on Wall Street would soon
spread to commodities, "which will bring the greatest calamities upon
our farmers, our workers, and legitimate business."[34]

The concerns of the Hoover gang were amplified in important
elements of the financial press. The *Commercial and Financial Chronicle* argued that low rates were inciting "gigantic speculation" in both
grain and stocks. "No more reckless speculation has ever been carried on in stocks on the Stock Exchange than which has been spread
before our eyes during the last three or four months."[35]

Crissinger and Strong were quick to recognize Hoover's voice
behind this campaign. They also knew that certain data in Lenroot's
letters could only have come from someone on the Reserve Board,
obviously Miller, the only member to object to New York's low rate
policy. With Strong's assistance, Crissinger answered Lenroot that
low U.S. rates were helping Britain's effort to remain on the gold
standard, a priority for the Federal Reserve. What's more, he said,
American prices were stable. There was no sign of inflation in the
broader economy. Stock market valuations merely reflected strong
corporate profits. A rate hike might chill the broader economy as well
as the stock market, causing the whole nation to suffer for the isolated
sins of speculators in New York. It was best for America that the Fed
stand aside, letting the majority revel in their boom, and letting the
gamblers meet their inevitable end in good time.[36]

Both Strong and Hoover understood that it was difficult to distinguish between a bubble and a justifiable rise in prices. Their aggressive, unyielding personalities made them seem further apart than they were. While he publicly attributed stock market valuations to rapid economic growth, Strong, in private correspondence, admitted that the United States seemed to be enduring "a speculative orgy." Americans, he lamented, were of an exuberant temperament. He had already begun hinting to markets that rates would soon rise.[37]

The exuberance of Americans was not limited to the stock market. Hoover had witnessed firsthand the 1925 land bubble in Florida, where tennis pros were moonlighting as realtors and valuations in Miami property had increased sevenfold since 1922. Meanwhile, in Chicago, New York, and Detroit, investors were riding a high-rise boom. All of this activity was fueled by the same cheap credit, the same rapidly escalating valuations, the same seductive promise of quick returns that was intoxicating Wall Street.[38]

Strong's concerns about speculation prompted him to finally push his rediscount rate from 3.5 percent to 4 percent on January 8, 1926. The economy and the Dow Jones Industrial Average cooled through the year, and the speculators were chastened. Florida real estate prices crashed, leaving the usual post-bubble rubble of broken fortunes, bankrupt municipalities, and failed banks. A category four hurricane swept through Miami as if to confirm the folly of the boom. Hoover's monetary concerns slackened along with the economy, but his relationship with Strong would never recover, and their debates over the Fed's handling of speculative bubbles and the amount of risk the domestic economy should carry in support of Europe were left dangerously unresolved.[39]

Not only was Hoover failing to enjoy America's burgeoning economy in the twenties, he was failing to profit from it personally. His investments were a mess. Some of his wealth had been sunk into industrial firms, including Klearflax Linen Looms of Duluth and the paper company Pitney Bowes, and some had been poured into his large produce farm near Bakersfield, which employed as many as three hundred workers at peak season. Edgar Rickard was nominally responsible for these investments, none of which performed to expectations. Rickard noted in his diary a long string of hasty and depressing conversations about their failing mutual ventures, but Hoover had neither the time nor the inclination to see to them. Nor would he give Rickard a clear mandate to do what he thought necessary. The boom would continue to pass them by.[40]

Hoover's inattention to personal matters extended to his former philanthropic activities, including the American Relief Administration and the American Child Health Association. These were left in the hands of Rickard and other members of the Firm. "He has been more and more absorbed in affairs in Washington," Rickard told his diary on December 31, 1925. "I seem to detect a desire on his part to weigh almost all matters first from the standpoint of political significance."[41]

Rickard tended to idealize Hoover and was slow to admit the potency of his friend's presidential ambitions, not for an absence of clues. Hoover stopped at every train station along the routes he traveled, meeting with chambers of commerce, submitting to interviews with local press, and having his picture taken with local officials. Rickard understood these activities as a manifestation of Hoover's dedication to public service, but outside observers read the situation more clearly. A mere nine months after Coolidge's inauguration, a Boston newspaper published an article entitled "Hoover's Eyes on White House." It anointed the commerce secretary the most ambitious person in the capital: he was "going after the presidency in the same systematic and methodical way he runs the Department of Commerce."[42]

While Hoover and his political advisers had no doubts about their goal, they also had no doubt that any hint of disloyalty to Coolidge, let alone a show of gunning for his job, would be fatal. Calvin Coolidge was not a man to be overlooked. Runty and unprepossessing, underestimated from his school days straight through to the 1924 election, Coolidge was proud of his attainments and his office. The stature of the presidency, manifest in pomp and ceremony, never lost its sweetness for him. He liked to stroll on the deck of the presidential yacht *Mayflower* as it cruised up and down the Potomac. He delighted in the goodwill of the five hundred or more strangers who arrived daily at the White House to shake his hand. His fellow Republicans knew better than to break the spell of his supremacy.[43]

Coolidge was also popular. Rural folk might be troubled by rapid social and economic change, and urbanites might be neck deep in the indulgence and extravagance of the new era, but nothing seemed too far gone so long as Silent Cal was at the helm. His stolid persona and old-fashioned rural virtues made him a reassuring beacon of stability in a fast-changing world.

The problem for Republican presidential aspirants was that no one knew how long the president intended to remain at the helm. Chief Justice Taft, one of few White House intimates, had no doubt that Coolidge wanted to be renominated in 1928. Henry Mencken, who thought Coolidge's great accomplishment was to "sleep more than any other president," agreed. Hoover was unsure. Probably Coolidge himself was not yet sure.[44]

In their stealth campaign, Hoover and company covered their tracks, regularly professed fealty to Coolidge, and kept relations with the White House smooth for the first half of the president's mandate. It was not until the approach of the midterm elections of 1926 that Hoover began voicing to the Firm misgivings about Coolidge. Amid clouds of cigar smoke on warm Washington nights, Hoover would complain in a relaxed monotone of his leader's passivity. He could not understand why the president refused to draft a constructive alternative to the radical price-fixing schemes sought by the farm bloc as cures for what ailed agriculture, or why he refused to take advice on the need to restructure or cancel British and French wartime debt to America. Hoover wondered aloud if he would be better off resigning from the cabinet and moving out of Washington to put distance between himself and the administration.[45]

It was after the midterms that Hoover's ambitions became an issue within the administration. With the conventions eighteen months away, the press corps began thinking ahead to the campaign of 1928. Speculation as to who would compete for the nominations was rife, and several aspirants aside from Hoover had launched low profile campaigns. Coolidge hoped to discourage this jockeying by refusing to speak about his future, a tactic that only increased the frustrations of his potential successors and fueled more speculation. Throughout these months, Hoover's agents kept tabs on the preferred candidates of newspaper publishers and party power brokers, and the organizational efforts of the presumptive Republican candidates, Vice President Dawes and Illinois governor Frank Lowden. Senators and congressmen were already rumored to be choosing sides.[46]

The imminence of a nomination battle and the anticipation of strong competition brought changes to Hoover's inner circle. George Akerson was hired to manage publicity, and he began traveling with Hoover everywhere. A bluff, hulking Harvard man who had covered Washington for the *Minneapolis Tribune*, Akerson possessed the sodden bonhomie of the press gallery raconteur. A large part of his job was to increase Hoover's personal appeal. The team was worried that its candidate commanded the respect, rather than the hearts, of the Republican base, that he was too much the bloodless engineer. He had no affecting anecdotes to tell, no endearing frailties to expose, no humor, no whimsy, no charm. There was no faulting the team's diagnosis of Hoover's weaknesses. More questionable were its assumptions that more publicity would make Hoover seem more human and that he could enhance his already oversized public profile while remaining in Coolidge's good graces. In just the first two weeks of April 1927, Hoover made national headlines with his views on international trade, child health, decency in movies, railroad policy, the passenger airline business, the unrest in China, the decline of sport fishing, the tenth anniversary of America's entry into the Great War, and whether or not the cabinet required an education secretary (he thought not). In the middle of this run came one of the biggest headlines of his tenure in Commerce, front page of the *New York Times*, lead position: "Far-Off Speakers Seen as Well as Heard Here in a Test of Television." The first sentence of the story read: "Herbert Hoover made a speech in Washington yesterday afternoon. An audience in New York heard him and saw him."[47]

Association with the great technological advances and human achievements of the modern age was a carefully constructed pillar of Hoover's political identity. To that end he had sat at 2:15 p.m. on April 7 in a small, crowded studio to read a brief statement into a new "television apparatus." It captured his words and image and transmitted them at eighteen frames a second over two hundred miles of wire to a demonstration room of the Bell Telephone Laboratories on Bethune Street in New York. It was the first public demonstration of AT&T's television technology. Viewers rated Hoover's likeness, displayed on a screen two by three inches, as excellent. "It was as if a photograph had suddenly come to life and begun to talk, smile, nod its head and look this way and that," wrote the *Times*. The newspaper was awed by what it had seen:

> The demonstration of combined telephone and television, in fact, is one that outruns the imagination of all the wizards of prophecy. It is one of the few things that Leonardo da Vinci, Roger Bacon, Jules Verne and other masters of forecasting failed utterly to anticipate. Even interpreters of the Bible are having trouble in finding a passage which forecast television. H. G. Wells did not rise to it in his earlier crystal-gazing. . . . Science has moved ahead so rapidly in this particular line that one of the men, who played a major part in developing the television apparatus shown yesterday, was of the opinion four years ago that research on this subject was hopeless.[48]

A week after the television demonstration, Hoover arrived in New York and met Edgar Rickard in the grand-palazzo confines of the University Club on Fifth Avenue. Flush with the attention of the nation's press, he was in good humor, and he confided to Rickard that he might be on the verge of a promotion to secretary of state, something that had been whispered in the papers as far back as Christmas.[49]

The next morning, newspapermen in the capital, having asked a White House spokesman about a supposed split in the cabinet over how to handle an ongoing conflict in China, were handed a prepared statement denying any rift. The note went on to say that Secretary of State Frank Kellogg, who had replaced the retiring Hughes, would not be resigning from the cabinet and that in the unlikely event that he should ever resign, the commerce secretary would not succeed him.[50]

The Washington press corps was dumbfounded. The White House almost never commented on internal cabinet affairs, and it certainly was not in the habit of ruling out future candidates for theoretical vacancies. That the target should be Hoover, believed to be the closest thing Coolidge had to a handpicked successor, was still more mystifying. Stunned to be the subject of a presidential rebuke, Hoover was visibly upset when Rickard next saw him. Rickard believed his friend had been double-crossed: "[Hoover] wouldn't have said he was getting [State] without some kind of assurance."[51]

Coolidge's motives immediately came under scrutiny. There was general agreement in the press that Hoover had dissented from Kellogg's handling of China policy. An attack on the American consulate at Nanking had resulted in the death of an academic, and the secretary of state had wanted to respond in concert with other nations. Hoover thought the United States should make a unilateral demand of the Chinese, yet even if he had pressed his views, the White House response was highly irregular. "Throughout three years and eight months that Mr. Coolidge has been President he has leaned heavily on Mr. Hoover for guidance and action," wrote the veteran correspondent Richard V. Oulahan. Rather than accuse Coolidge of petulance, most reporters chose to profess themselves mystified by his actions.[52]

The White House attempted to bury the story by extending a short-notice invitation to Hoover for breakfast with the president and several other cabinet secretaries on Easter morning, April 17. Hoover took the train back to the capital from New York and sat to the left of the president in a room brimming with lilies and roses. Breakfast was served. Although conversation was polite, Coolidge made no attempt to explain or apologize for his controversial words. It was "one of the strangest Easter feasts on record," said one Washington reporter. "The guests came away in even greater bewilderment over the conduct of the President."[53]

Hoover chose not to confront Coolidge about his statement, perhaps expecting that the president would wave him off, saying that no insult was intended, or perhaps fearing that Coolidge would call him on his ambitions. He took his usual course of delivering messages through surrogates, who let reporters know that the White House had left Hoover "dangling" in a "mortifying position," and that "only his dignity prevents him from withdrawing from Cabinet."[54]

Lou gave further insight into her husband's thinking in another long letter to Allan and Bert Jr. She opened with what would become the family line on their father's ambitions:

> Daddy is playing ball in a team, and whether anyone ever
> persuaded him to run for the Presidency or not, he certainly

would not do it, directly or indirectly while Calvin Coolidge was still apparently thinking of it. For of course he would never plot against the man who was captain of his team.[55]

Lou went on to complain that Coolidge had not given Bert any idea of his plans. If he planned to retire, "he's being selfish because he's making it difficult for whoever is going to follow him." His friends, she said, have their hands tied while his enemies are organizing. Regarding Coolidge's "queer and irrelevant remark about Daddy," Lou said it was "quite uncalled for . . . and naturally made us perfectly boiling with rage." Coolidge was upset because "there has been such a lot of publicity about Daddy recently, and much of it too complimentary . . . that the President thought Daddy had instigated it himself and was really annoyed at it and at Daddy." Lou, clearly reflecting her husband's opinion, considered Coolidge ungrateful.[56]

There was obvious sulking on both sides of the contretemps. On the question of whether or not Coolidge's words were warranted, the press sided with Hoover. It was well known, wrote the *Times*, that the commerce secretary's admirers had aroused "suspicion that they were planning to bring his name before the Republican National Convention next year," yet it was also understood that Hoover was intensely loyal to his boss, both politically and personally. Two days after Easter, the White House was forced to announce that Hoover was fully competent to fill any position in the cabinet he might desire, and that "nobody stands higher than Mr. Hoover in the President's respect and affection."[57]

If Coolidge's hope in slighting Hoover had been to fire a warning shot over his head, he had failed utterly, and if he had hoped that his subsequent gesture of support would close the matter, he failed again. It led directly to a round of press stories on whether or not Coolidge *should* seek another term, and who might replace him if he stepped down. Worse still for the president, it was raining hard in the Mississippi River basin and he was about to need Herbert Hoover more than ever.[58]

The Mississippi River basin drains roughly 40 percent of the U.S. mainland, an enormous area of 1.24 million square miles stretching in an arc from the Alleghenies to Canada to the Rocky Mountains. Several weeks of massive rains and snows at the end of 1926 had brought the river to flood levels at its head in Cairo, Illinois, on the first day of the New Year, the earliest date on record. The storms continued and intensified through February and March. The air over the heartland was unusually cold. More lightning than sunshine lit the skies. Gales toppled brick smokestacks and tornadoes hit four states, killing more than thirty people. By early April, the crest of the flood was pounding with waves five to ten feet high the levees designed to keep the Mississippi within its banks. The list of overflowing tributaries included the Missouri, the St. Francis, the Black, the Arkansas, and the Yazoo. A million acres were under water, and the rain kept coming.[59]

Carefully built of clay and concrete, the Mississippi's levees represented a half century of work and a $229 million investment by Congress to control the unpredictable forces of the continent's mightiest stream. They were an impressive engineering feat, standing at least three feet higher than the highest flood line on every bank, yet they were no match for water churning at 3 million cubic feet per second. The levees began to crumble on Good Friday, April 15, in Missouri, and six days later a mile-wide crevasse burst open at Mounds Landing, Mississippi. A wall of turbid water one hundred feet high surged into the surrounding delta, sweeping up trees, livestock, homes, and buildings before forming a lake approximately one hundred miles long and fifty miles wide. The levees would be breached at 140 points in six weeks, and still the rains fell.[60]

"The roaring Mississippi river, bank and levee full from St. Louis to New Orleans is believed to be on its mightiest rampage," reported the *Memphis Commercial Appeal*. Inhabitants of the lower states were terrified by the volumes of water headed their way. "For God's sake, send us boats," cried Mississippi governor Dennis Murphree.[61]

By the time the levee burst at Mounds Landing, six governors, including Murphree, had begged Calvin Coolidge for federal assistance. To their minds, a massive flood of the nation's most important waterway, the inundation of myriad interstate highways and railroads, and the dislocation of hundreds of thousands of people qualified as a national emergency. Specifically, the governors had asked that Herbert Hoover be assigned to lead a federal rescue effort. Hoover, cabinet secretary, engineer, and disaster relief specialist, was the obvious choice. He had made a series of speeches across the region just months before the flood on the need for a comprehensive federal plan for the nation's river systems, one that considered transportation, power generation, and flood control, among other factors. Talking up monumental waterway improvements around the country was a key element in Hoover's plans to broaden his political base. His proposal for a six-year, $120 million project to realize the potential of the Mississippi Valley had caught the governors' attention.[62]

Even as editorialists, broadcasters, mayors, community leaders, and senators and congressmen of both parties joined the chorus urging federal action, Coolidge had sat perfectly still. His understanding of the role of the national government did not extend to shielding local citizens from the weather, and precedent was on his side. Natural disasters had historically been managed at a state and local level. The Constitution, as Grover Cleveland said, did not provide for the national government to indulge "benevolent and charitable sentiment through the appropriation of public funds" to alleviate individual suffering. Coolidge turned back requests for a special session of Congress to deal with the flood on the grounds that extra sessions were excuses for the creation of new federal obligations and raids on the Treasury, and he considered Hoover's ambitious plans for development of the nation's waterways ridiculously expensive. Hoping that if he sat still for long enough, the sun would break through and mop up the Mississippi Valley without any help from Washington, he refused even to visit the stricken region.[63]

It was the Mounds Landing break that finally forced the president's hand. With the death toll approaching three hundred, with a million people on the move and a refugee crisis brewing, he drafted a statement. On April 22, two days after retreating from his rebuke of Hoover, Coolidge appointed him chair of a special cabinet committee to relieve the stricken areas. The commerce secretary was once again front and center on a stage he could dominate better than anyone alive. "When a man is sick he calls a doctor," said Will Rogers, "but when the United States of America is sick they call for Herbert Hoover."[64]

.   .   .

Although it had been six years since he stood face-to-face with a
large-scale emergency, Hoover's skills were intact. He chaired the
first meeting of his new committee within two hours of his appointment, hit the ground in Memphis at 7 a.m. the next morning, and by
the end of his first week bestrode the Mississippi like a dripping colossus. He opened direct lines of communication and transportation corridors to all of the affected states. He kept two homicide detectives
from the Memphis police force at his disposal to seek out and bring to
him anyone he needed. He put local sawmills to work building skiffs
and rented outboards from manufacturers downstream, and assembled a fleet of eight hundred borrowed barges and boats, not to mention two dozen aircraft. He directed tens of thousands of volunteers
and U.S. servicemen to collect victims of the deluge from roofs and
treetops and distribute them, along with hundreds of thousands of
refugees, the majority of them poor and black, in camps built on high
ground by the Red Cross under Hoover's supervision. More than 150
of these kerosene-lit tent cities sprang up, complete with water and
sewer lines, electric lights, and communal dining halls. Some held as
many as twenty thousand people, all receiving food, shelter, clothing,
and, in most cases, medical supervision.[65]

Coolidge had given Hoover access to all the federal resources he
required with the exception of cash. Fund-raising thus became a preoccupation of the relief effort. Hoover used the trainload of press
that had been invited to follow him through the flood zone to beat
the drum for donations to the Red Cross, his relief agency of choice.
Articles and newsreels captured him slogging under black skies from
Memphis to Baton Rouge, posing uncomfortably on muddy dock-
sides with downcast eyes and hands thrust deep in his pockets, bark-
ing orders to his entourage and reciting practiced jeremiads: "There
has never in our history been such a calamity as this flood. It is impossible to exaggerate the problem of relief."[66]

In this emergency, as in others he had faced, Hoover talked up
the importance of volunteerism and "the cooperative spirit of Main
Street" in restoring order. This emphasis is often mistaken as evidence
of a hidebound commitment to small government and laissez-faire.
Hoover did firmly believe that local agencies should be the first line
of defense in emergency situations, and he saw it as his duty to show
Americans what they were capable of accomplishing as self-governing

communities. He was also conscious of serving a president and a party resistant to creating in the populace an expectation of federal aid in every emergency. Notwithstanding these restraints, Hoover separated himself from Coolidge throughout the flood with regular assertions of a federal role in disaster relief, as well as in the development of American waterways. On his first trip to New Orleans he pointed out that thirty states had contributed water to the flood, and that no part of the nation "can suffer a loss without that loss reflecting on every other part. The people in this vast region who contribute so much to national wealth and prosperity should be relieved of this anxiety and terror. It is a national problem and must be solved nationally and vigorously."[67]

Hoover's emphasis on volunteerism was not intended to minimize the national government but to make its expansion, within limits, palatable to his party and the public. It was the same approach he had employed in the Food Administration and at the unemployment conference, committing Washington in times of distress to new responsibilities from which it could never entirely back away.

Apart from the river itself, Hoover emerged as the main character in the story of the Mississippi flood. That he did not cooperate in any coverage of a personal nature satisfied him that the immense publicity he received was in service of the Red Cross financial drive and not his political ambitions. The highlight of his performance, the splendid demonstration of his ability to command a moment, came on April 30 when he took to the airwaves for his second momentous broadcast in a month. He became the first major U.S. politician to directly address a national audience in a time of crisis, appealing to Americans across the NBC radio network to give to the Red Cross:

> I am speaking from Memphis, the temporary headquarters
> which we have established for the national fight against
> the most dangerous flood our country has ever known in
> its history. We, here, in the midst of the scene, are humble
> before such an outburst of the forces of nature and the
> futility of man in their control, but we have the obligation to
> fight its invasion and to relieve its destruction. . . .
>      It is difficult to picture in words the might of the
> Mississippi in flood. To say that two blocks from where I

stand it is at this minute flowing at a rate ten times that
of Niagara seems unimpressive. Perhaps it becomes more
impressive to say that at Vicksburg the flood is 6,000 feet
wide and 50 feet deep, rushing on at the rate of six miles
an hour. A week ago when it broke the levees at Mounds
Landing, only a quarter of the river went through the hole.
Yet in a week it poured water up to twenty feet deep over
several counties . . . flooding out 150,000 people.[68]

He spoke with professional pride of the heroic work done by the
U.S. Army Corps of Engineers, "men of magnificent courage and
skill." He used the language of battle, describing the water as the
"enemy," an effort to create the sense of urgency and sacrifice that
had helped him accomplish so much during the Great War.[69]

It was an unusual speech for Hoover in that while replete with facts
and figures and delivered in a familiar monotone, it spoke directly to
the hearts of his audience, imploring them to rise above their own
interests and give in service of their flood-stricken neighbors who had
not only to endure a calamity but face the ordeal of rebuilding their
lives in some of the poorest regions of the country.

The people of the South are demonstrating daily their courage and their abilities. No man can charge the fate of these
unfortunate people to any failure upon their own part. Our
country has been greatly blessed by Almighty God. More
millions of our homes tonight rest without fear of the health
and life of our little ones than in any nation in the world. But
a catastrophe has come to the people of our South.[70]

Having fulfilled his own two-year-old prophecy that nothing
could "so effectually weld this country into a unit in thought and
action as radio," Hoover next passed the microphone to the great Al
Jolson for a rendition of "April Showers."[71]

The broadcast brought the Red Cross's fund-raising total to $17
million, more than three times the initial target. Of Hoover's radio
performances, the *New York Times* wrote that the medium's "possibilities have often been discussed, but never before had it been asked to
tap this field and exploit its possibilities to [this] extent."[72]

As the water finally receded, Hoover basked in another round of adoring headlines. The newsmen who had watched him work tirelessly for sixty days in the flood zone, sleeping most nights in makeshift quarters on ships and trains, were deeply impressed. The great Kentucky journalist Silas Bent wrote in *Scribner's* that "miracles are the meat this Caesar feeds on." Following him in Mississippi was "like watching a master play billiards: even though you didn't understand the game you could recognize supreme skill."[73]

Calvin Coolidge was gracious in his praise of his secretary: "Your work in the South has been of great service to that region and thereby to the whole nation. I do not think of any one else that was equipped to handle it as you have done." He extended an invitation for the Hoovers to visit him in the Black Hills, where he was vacationing with Mrs. Coolidge.[74]

The collegiality of his note was not indicative of the president's true feelings. Hoover had been as omnipresent in the greatest domestic crisis of the administration as Coolidge had been absent. William Allen White believed the president held "a subconscious, unformed wish that the Secretary of Commerce would fall in the floods and choke."[75]

# CHAPTER 17

# "The Wonder Boy"

Hoover had every reason to be satisfied with his Mississippi rescue: it would stand for decades as the model of how to deal with a national emergency. The medical attention received by refugees, including an antimalarial campaign and vaccinations against typhoid and smallpox, was the best many of them would see in their lifetimes. Hoover had made his case for a national role in the management of American waterways. Coolidge would shortly sign off on the most expensive single public works projects authorized by Congress, the landmark 1928 Flood Control Act, which reengineered levees, diversion works, and outlets along both the Mississippi and Sacramento rivers.

Still, Hoover could not refrain from habitual exaggeration in his claims for the effectiveness of the relief, maintaining that there had been no more than half a dozen deaths in the basin since he was assigned to the crisis. He certainly deserves credit for a great reduction in the death rate and for preventing any catastrophic spread of disease, but it appears that more than eighty lives were lost under his supervision. He also overemphasized the voluntary nature of the relief as he had done in his previous career as food czar. The public's response was impressive: more than thirty thousand people lent a hand, and fund-raising events were held in almost every theater in America, but much of what had been accomplished was due to the federal contribution of boats and aircraft, guardsmen, food, and provisions.[1]

Another set of mixed results never fully acknowledged by Hoover flowed from his encounter with southern poverty and racism. He had little experience of the South. He was touched by the penury of the region, the squalid primitive lives of poor whites and black sharecroppers. He at first disbelieved and then grew offended at reports that African Americans were being mistreated by white leaders in refugee camps and in several instances being forced to work on the levees at gunpoint. As his mind inevitably turned from crisis management to rehabilitation of the flooded states, he envisioned an opportunity to use the crisis to reengineer the delta along more equitable lines. Hoover arranged for the distribution of vegetable seeds in the tent cities to give the mostly black refugees something besides cotton to grow on their return. He had agriculturalists provide instruction on how to improve their self-sufficiency by raising chickens and preserving fruit. He spoke with African American leaders about using relief funds to purchase unused lands for sharecroppers to become individual farmers, and he browbeat northern business leaders into funding a reconstruction corporation that would lend money to southern planters wiped out by the floods. Sincere in these initiatives and tending to give people the benefit of the doubt, Hoover underestimated the obstinacy of southern ways and overestimated the interest of the rest of the country in helping out. The South's economy was little altered by the disaster. White planters, dependent on cheap black labor, frustrated change. Most of the pledges of northern industrialists were never realized. When the Colored Advisory Commission formed by Hoover to investigate conditions in refugee camps found substantial evidence of racial abuse, he kept its report out of the newspapers with further and largely unmet promises of reform.

It remained one of the perversities of Hoover's personality, rooted in his lifelong insecurities and constant need to prove his worth, that he could not admit setbacks even when the sum total of his efforts was a resounding success.


Hoover took a well-deserved break in the summer of 1927, starting with a shopping trip for fishing tackle with Edgar Rickard, who noted that his friend was in a fine mood and very pleased with himself. Toward the end of July, three Hoovers, Bert, Lou and Allan, were once again traveling along single-lane back roads through the hills of

California and Nevada in their Cadillac. They fished by day, cooked meals at the water's edge, and spent most nights at inns and road-houses. As usual, wrote Lou, "they got so many more mosquito bites than trout bites." From this welcome family time, Hoover headed at the beginning of August to what was becoming for him an annual retreat at Bohemian Grove amid the California redwoods.[2]

The Coolidges were meanwhile lodged high among the pines of the Black Hills in a rustic chalet that served as the summer White House. It was an unpleasant time for the president. Restless and irri-table, he fished without joy or success, and visited a Sioux commu-nity in nearby Deadwood to pose scowling under a ceremonial war bonnet. He caused a scene by forcing the transfer of a Secret Ser-vice agent who had disappeared for a long walk in the woods with Mrs. Coolidge. On August 2, the fourth anniversary of his ascent to the presidency, he rode in a short motorcade to a small schoolhouse in Rapid City that served as his executive office and at 11:40 a.m. asked members of the presidential press corps to line up single file. He handed each a small slip of paper reading, "I do not choose to run for President in nineteen twenty eight." With no further comment, he drove back up into the hills.[3]

Bohemian Grove was a ruling-class campground on the Russian River amid 2,700 acres of California redwoods. Founded in the late nineteenth century by genuine bohemians, mostly writers and musi-cians, the males-only club invited its members to "shake off your sor-rows with the City's dust and scatter to the winds the cares of life." It adopted as its motto a line from *A Midsummer Night's Dream:* "Weav-ing Spiders, come not here." The camp opened every year with an elaborate torchlight parade through the forest, men in red hoods and robes carrying a large wooden coffin containing the body of Worldly Care to the water's edge for cremation in a giant bonfire.[4]

By Hoover's time, the bohemians had given way to a mostly Republican commercial and cultural elite, but the ceremonies endured. Members set themselves up in encampments, many of them built at considerable expense, and spent their days fishing, hiking, and listening to speeches, while in the evenings they attended skits and concerts. Hoover passed his time in Caveman Camp, a neighborhood dominated by members of Stanford's inaugural class. He relished his time at the Grove. He found it in equal parts restful and stimulating. On inviting Mark Sullivan to join him there in 1925, he wrote, "I do not believe you have ever attended the encampment of the Bohemian Club. . . . This has now become the greatest men's party in the world."[5]

He had scarcely arrived under the redwoods in August 1927 when an AP wire report was handed him in the middle of an afternoon. He and his intimates were shocked and confused by news of Coolidge's apparent resignation. Like so many weaving spiders, they gathered in camp to spin out theories as to what Coolidge meant by his statement. Was he through with politics? Was he putting the onus on his party to enlist him for another term? Was there some connotation to the phrase "I do not choose" that only New Englanders understood?[6]

Whatever the intended message, it was agreed in the shade of the Grove that a new political dynamic was afoot. Hoover was soon on his way back east, and in the days following Coolidge's announcement, his name was high on the slate of potential Republican leaders bruited in the press. Perennial candidate Charles Evans Hughes was also mentioned, along with Illinois favorite Frank Lowden and Vice President Dawes. Unsure of Coolidge's intentions, Hoover moved cautiously. He professed loyalty to the president and remained at his cabinet post, refusing to declare a candidacy or hire a campaign team. True to form, he admitted no interest in the job he so desperately wanted.

Behind the scenes, often at his apartment in New York, he met with his stealth campaign team. Its members had started rounding up endorsements and delegates across the country in the event that Coolidge was indeed finished. Hoover's choice of lieutenants was shrewd and surprisingly strong given his otherwise weak connections to the Republican machine. Hubert Work, his de facto campaign chair, had served in the Harding and Coolidge cabinets and was a respected party elder. Will H. Hayes, a lobbyist for the motion picture industry and a powerful figure on the West Coast, was a former chair of the Republican National Committee. Senator Reed Smoot was a veteran of five Republican conventions and chair of the Senate Finance Committee. The team's deep roots in the mainstream of the party helped their man overcome pockets of opposition to his candidacy: the old-guard Republicans who remembered Hoover's connections to Wilson and every instance when, as an advocate of a professionalized public service, he had failed to appoint a loyal partisan as a steamboat inspector or radio commissioner; also the insurgent Republicans from agricultural states who remembered Hoover's hostility to the McNary-Haugen Farm Relief Act.

There was also concern in some quarters that Hoover was not the most magnetic figure available for the nomination, although few regarded this as fatal to his chances. The Republicans had come to see themselves as the natural governing party of the United States. Leaving aside the Cleveland and Wilson accidents, they had been in power since Grant's day. If Republican delegates declared an uncharismatic Hoover worthy of the presidency, voters were unlikely to argue. Coolidge, after all, had won in a landslide.

On the whole, Hoover was an easy sale within the party. His stellar performance in the cabinet, his outsized media profile, his relentless travel and speech making, his deep connections with chambers of commerce and professional organizations across the land, not to mention his recent triumph in the South, had gained him a stature none but the president could match. He was the picture of competence, progress, and prosperity. He continued to use his Commerce pulpit to burnish his reputation, going so far in December 1927 as to preempt Coolidge's State of the Union with his own year-end report on the nation's outstanding economic growth.[7]

The front-runner from the very outset of the nomination race, Hoover held that position over the eleven months between Coolidge's Black Hills announcement and the GOP convention of 1928. Hughes declared himself unavailable early in the contest. Lowden failed to register as anything more than a regional force. Dawes, unimpressive in his term as vice president, never got off the ground. Although he remained an undeclared candidate through most of this time, Hoover worked relentlessly on his campaign. Rickard would drop by 2300 S Street for breakfast or dinner and find the house crawling with political men and even more chaotic than usual: "[Hoover] is so completely absorbed in winning the nomination. . . . I am sorry to see how completely this dominates his every action."[8]

Rickard's disappointment was due to his lingering sense of his friend as a disinterested public servant. Part of him wanted to believe

Hoover's claims that he was without ambition, that he was being pulled by forces beyond his control up Washington's greasy pole. Lou, too, seems to have believed in her husband's immaculate ascent or, at least, she wanted the rest of the family to believe in it. She wrote her sons that "affairs are going with uncanny rapidity towards making your Daddy President. Even he is perfectly amazed at it, and sometimes says it just does not seem possible that this can all be happening on its own impetus, and practically without any effort on his part." This delusion was facilitated by Bert's abruptly moving the conversation away from politics when Lou entered the room.[9]

As the nomination contest advanced, the only man who retained the power to unsettle the Hoover organization was Calvin Coolidge. Was he really out of the race? If the party were to draft him before or during the convention, would he accept renomination? Hoover knew that he could not win a fight with a popular sitting president. He visited Coolidge twice in the fall of 1927 asking for direction, both times saying that he was being urged by supporters to seek the nomination, and both times professing that he would prefer to direct his efforts to renominating Coolidge if the president would give some indication of his receptivity to a draft. Both times Coolidge told Hoover not to discourage his friends. As for his own intentions, the president was silent.[10]

It was Coolidge's turn to play the diva. He made a speech on December 6 to the Republican National Committee in which he encouraged the party to seek a new leader. While most observers took his words as evidence that he was retiring, some noticed that he did not say that he was certain the party would find a new leader, or that he would refuse a draft. This kept the curtain up on his own career.[11]

Hoover, keenly studying Coolidge's remarks, and unable to satisfy himself that anything conclusive had been said in the President's December speech, made an anxious return to the White House in February. He plotted his approach carefully. He did not want to ask the obvious question: Would Coolidge refuse renomination in any circumstance? That might have cleared the air, but any hesitation, any dodge, any answer short of a definitive "yes" would have obliged Hoover to shelve his ambitions. He instead informed the president that Hoover supporters in Ohio wanted to draft him into the crucial state primary which by law required a nominee's permission. He asked if Coolidge had any intentions of entering the race. On hearing a no, Hoover asked if the president had any objections to his answering the call of his friends in Ohio. "Why not?" said Coolidge. This gave Hoover the permission he wanted to take his candidacy public. He entered Ohio. Still uncertain as to Coolidge's game, he hastened to add he would not participate in the campaign to see himself nominated, preoccupied as he was with "the great objectives of President Coolidge's policies."[12]

The president was in a miserable state of mind as the convention approached. His bouts of rage were more frequent. His doctor saw signs of "mental disturbance" and diagnosed a "temperamental derangement." While his unhappiness undoubtedly owed more to the loss of his son than any other factor, it did not help that Hoover was elbowing him toward the wing. The Coolidge cruel streak, customarily expressed in public ridicule of his wife's cooking or practical jokes on White House staff, now targeted the commerce secretary. He began scorning Hoover as "the wonder boy." That man, he complained to a friend, "has offered me unsolicited advice every day for six years, all of it bad." How can you like someone, he asked another, "who is always trying to get your job?" He relished the fact that his enigmatic statements were keeping Hoover off balance.[13]

Always susceptible to catastrophic possibilities, Hoover could not keep his mind from the president. He invented scenarios that would invite Coolidge to another term: if, for instance, Hoover failed to win on the first ballot, an anybody-but-Hoover alliance could deadlock the convention and push delegates toward the tidy solution of begging Coolidge's return. The prospect of failing so tortured Hoover that with a month to go before delegates arrived in Kansas City he played the supplicant one final time, visiting the president and reporting that he had already signed up 400 of an expected 1,100 delegates. He offered to pull his own name from consideration and throw all of his support to a Coolidge candidacy. It was a short conversation. Coolidge rebuffed the offer and, quite aware what Hoover really wanted to know, once more refused to categorically rule himself out and relieve his secretary's torment.[14]

Notwithstanding the great Coolidge question, which loomed

larger in his own mind than anywhere else, Hoover's candidacy had gained an air of inevitability by the time delegates boarded trains for Kansas City and the convention's opening day, June 12. Crucial Republican constituencies, including corporate America and a growing women's vote, were lined up behind him. The *Saturday Evening Post* hailed him as a man to whom "the incredible is forever happening," the kind of man whom the fates like to challenge in order to watch him answer. "It is no wonder that the big, broad-gauged men of the country . . . are his staunchest supporters."[15]

Hoover entered eleven primaries in all, winning Maryland, Massachusetts, New Jersey, Michigan, California, and Oregon. As if to confirm the Hoover narrative of predestination, Senator Frank Willis, who as a native son was his most dangerous opponent in Ohio, died at a fund-raising event days before the state primary.

It suited the Hooverites to feel their candidate's triumph was written in the stars, as opposed to admitting that it was due, in part, to the bare-knuckled tactics they would swear were beneath him. Just how much the Firm had learned since the debacle of 1920 was evident in Hoover's southern campaign. The Mississippi flood had aligned Hoover with reformers who sought through such political channels as the Republican Party to improve the lot of African Americans. Hoover had made elaborate promises about a redistribution of power in the region and an end to black peonage. But when it came time to collect delegates, Hoover organizers stormed the southern states looking for support wherever they could buy it by generously defraying the travel expenses of delegates. With a third of the ballots required to elect a nominee at the convention cast by southerners, they left nothing to chance. Common cause was found with racist "lily-white" organizers in some states and with racially tolerant organizers in others. Taking for granted that both parties played dirty in the lowest states, the *Baltimore Sun* nonetheless cited Hoover's organization for an "extremely smelly" southern campaign.*[16]

The candidate chose not to travel to Kansas City. It would have

---

* It may have been true, as his loyalists claimed, that Hoover was not aware of the tactics employed on his behalf. His managers kept him in the dark about certain payments to delegates while he went around insisting that none of his support had been bought. It may also be that Hoover knew enough to not want to know more.

been unbecoming of a man who had refused to campaign for the nomination to suddenly appear interested on the eve of victory. Rickard wandered over to 2300 S Street early on June 8 to find Hoover shaving, dressing, and obsessing over Coolidge. The scenario racking him that morning was that an initiative to draft Coolidge would rise from the floor and stampede delegates to the president. It would be very difficult, thought Hoover, to get his supporters back on board even if Coolidge were to decline.[17]

Hoover bunked out for the duration of the convention in his Commerce offices, which had been wired at his expense with extra telephones so that twenty to thirty people could take calls and record voting results at any given time. The lines sizzled all week with intelligence from the floor and backrooms of Kansas City. Hoover smoked his pipe and paced the floors uneasily, Coolidge still haunting his thoughts. What might the president do to foil him? Another nightmare scenario: Coolidge would at the last minute throw his might behind Charles Curtis, a conservative senator from Kansas. That might steal just enough Hoover support to deadlock the nomination and invite Coolidge back to center stage.

The Hoover headquarters was in Kansas City's St. Francis Hotel, where all the carpets and furniture had been removed from a stately ballroom, and supporters and delegates milled beneath the enormous posters of Mr. and Mrs. Hoover that draped the walls. Speechmakers and a brass band kept the energy high until late in the evenings. On the sidewalks outside, delegates wore elephant pins and elephant costumes and took pamphlets from Hoover boosters sweating between sandwich boards.[18]

Events at Convention Hall, the main venue, opened every morning with a prayer. The hall was crowded and overheated throughout the proceedings, so much so that many delegates preferred to stand outside in the shade and listen to the speeches over radio amplifiers. Hoover's organization manhandled events on the floor, seating all of its delegates, winning the chairmanship of the Republican National Convention for Hubert Work and directing the construction of the party platform. John McNab of San Francisco made a relatively short nominating speech for Hoover. At the first mention of the candidate's name, an ovation erupted and held for thirty-one minutes. The roll call began with Alabama casting fifteen votes for Hoover, followed by nine from Arizona, and all the way through the alphabet to victory.[19]

Hoover had always been confident that 1928 was a Republican year, meaning that whoever took the party's nomination was more or less assured the White House regardless of who the Democrats put forth. By his logic, news arriving over the radio that he had gathered 837 votes for an easy first-ballot win in Kansas City was cause for celebration. Yet Hoover, alone among the crowd of friends and family at his Commerce offices, was not visibly affected by the outcome. He calmly shook hands all around and at the earliest available moment sat down at a table with a handful of staffers and began analyzing delegate totals and potential electoral votes in the farm states.[20]

Later in the day, he posed for photographers on the front steps at 2300 S Street and waved to the carloads of beholders who jammed his street until well past midnight. Otherwise it was a quiet day, as was the next, spent answering congratulatory messages and exchanging pleasantries with Coolidge. The president was vacationing in Wisconsin. When told by his Secret Service agent of Hoover's triumph, his face went hard and he ordered a bottle of whiskey.[21]

Hoover's restraint at his nomination set the tone for the Republican campaign of 1928. It was a Republican year in a Republican country, with prosperity a fact, the stock market soaring, and even farm prices, for the first time since 1920, rising to respectable levels. There were no acute domestic or international issues. Hoover's task was to carry his party to November 6 without distracting voters from the appreciation of their good fortune, and without alerting them to the deep concerns he had about certain aspects of the nation's economic performance.[22]

This approach suited Hoover, who had many aversions to campaigns and elections. Some of these were political. It was part of his appeal to appear above the partisan fray, and he was so weak an electoral horse that it made sense to keep him in the barn for long stretches of time. Other aversions were customary. Notwithstanding the cross-country antics of William Jennings Bryan in successive Democratic campaigns, it was still considered proper form for

an American presidential candidate to delegate his promotion. And
then there were Hoover's high-minded aversions. Hoover retained
the progressive's distaste for the clubby and sometimes corrupt dealings of party grandees and regional bosses with their systems of vote
pledging and patronage. He viewed intense partisanship as an unpro-
fessional waste of resources unlikely to lead to optimal managerial
outcomes, and he thought the theater of retail politics foolish and
inherently dishonest, a notion that permitted him to make a principle
of having no skill at it.

The deepest of Hoover's aversions to campaigning were psychological. He was too diffident, too uncertain of how to put himself
across, and too afraid of rejection to push himself as a candidate.
Much better to be courted, he felt, than to court, and much better to
pretend the whole process of office getting was an irritation forced
upon him by an admiring public rather than his life's ambition. Of
the many rules he laid down for the conduct of his campaign, the best
honored were those protecting his dignity. "I'll not kiss any babies,"
he insisted. Nor would he dress in local costume: he had been disgusted at photographs of Coolidge in cowboy outfits and war bonnets. He would make a minimum of speeches, and he would write
them all in his own dense, careful, pallid prose.[23]

With Hoover striking his pose of Olympian indifference, the
chore of vote chasing was undertaken on his behalf by Hubert Work,
members of the now captive Republican National Committee,
friendly senators such as George Moses and William Borah, and the
party's vice-presidential nominee, Kansas senator Charles Curtis.

Hoover's opponent in 1928, Democratic nominee Alfred E. Smith,
was something new in the annals of U.S. presidential races. He was
of German, Italian, and Irish blood, up from a murky bottom, Manhattan's Lower East Side. With a long, unhandsome face and a short
rubescent wife, he spoke nonstop through his prominent nose in an
accent—*woik, raddio, youse people*—alien to most of the country. A
failed amateur actor, he wore the brown derby and flashy waistcoats
of a Broadway star. He boasted of never having read a book, giving as
his alma mater the Fulton Fish Market, where he had worked in his
teens to support his fatherless family. He was faithful to the Catholic

Church and the notorious Society of St. Tammany. He loathed Prohibition, delighting in nothing more than an afternoon with his foot on the saloon rail, blowing foam off his beer and swapping stories.[24]

Smith was in many respects an anti-Hoover: gregarious, combative, and never embarrassed. He lived in public and loved it, reveling in the experience of his own charisma. He typically spoke extemporaneously, using emotion more than speechcraft to hold and move a crowd. He had deep political experience, serving four terms as governor of New York despite the general Republican ascendancy in that state, and despite the opposition of the mighty Hearst, whom he mocked and outmaneuvered at every turn. On the strength of his public appeal, and despite legislative minorities, Smith had wrestled from the Albany statehouse an impressive array of educational and health reforms and improved working conditions for women and children. He was as effective as any working politician in America.[25]

Smith, like Hoover, had a relatively easy ride to his party's nomination, winning on the second ballot at the Democratic convention in Houston. To balance the ticket, Arkansas senator Joseph T. Robinson, a dry Protestant, was chosen as his running mate. The fact that the two parties devised platforms that, as Lippmann said, "contain no difference which would be called an issue," let the campaign focus on the personal qualities of the candidates. Each represented an important force in twenties politics.[26]

Smith was of a new strain of charismatic Democrat. Like William Jennings Bryan before him, he led by force of personality, but the Great Commoner had been *for* the people, while Smith, along with Louisiana's mesmerizing new governor Huey Long, was *of* the people in speech, manner, and tastes. Both men had powerful local bases and national aspirations.

Hoover typified the technocrats, a new breed of public-spirited professional. Like Vice President Dawes, a lawyer, banker, and diplomat, and Owen D. Young, founder of RCA and future presidential aspirant, he had a global outlook, broad experience, policy expertise, a way of moving effortlessly between the public and private sectors, and a difficult time putting himself across to ordinary people.

The inevitable contrasts with Smith were dangerous to Hoover, who seemed more stooped, sullen, and mechanical next to the "happy warrior," as Franklin Roosevelt christened his fellow Democrat. Some reporters claimed Hoover had overcome his tendencies to look a man in the vest buttons and to scowl his way through interviews, but the writer Henry Pringle was closer to the mark when he described him as "abnormally shy, abnormally sensitive, [and] filled with an impassioned pride in his personal integrity." Before a podium, Hoover could still strike a phrase "in so prosaic, so uninspired, and so mumbling a fashion that it is completely lost on nine out of ten of his auditors."[27]

Smith's charisma joined Hoover's political aversions as another reason for his team to run a low-availability campaign. There were doubts, in some circles, that the approach would work. Theodore Roosevelt may have avoided the stump in 1904, but at all other times he had done everything in his power to forge a personal bond with the American public, making of himself, he admitted, a kind of circus performer to encourage among people the "feeling that the President was their man and symbolized their government, and that they had a proprietary interest in him . . . and that they hoped he embodied their aspirations and their best thought." A president, Roosevelt said on another occasion, needs to know "how to play the popular hero and shoot a bear."[28]

In place of a bear hunter in 1928, the Republicans were selling a conception. Hoover was the omnicompetent engineer, humanitarian, and public servant, the "most useful American citizen now alive," according to his clippings. He was an almost supernatural figure, said Charles Michelson, a Democratic journalist, "whose wisdom encompassed all branches, whose judgment was never at fault, who knew the answers to all questions, and who could see in the dark."[29]

*Time* magazine was incredulous at the Hoover campaign's reliance on its candidate's résumé: "In a society of temperate, industrious, unspectacular beavers, such a beaver-man would make an ideal King-beaver. But humans are different." What gave confidence to the Hoover team was its knowledge that his candidacy would be produced, packaged, and advertised like no other in history. George Akerson had lined up leading minds on Madison Avenue to sell Hoover to the masses. Bruce Barton of BBDO, already celebrated in communications circles for naming General Motors and inventing Betty Crocker, would help with public relations. Henry Sell, a leading practitioner of the nascent art of polling, would probe the wants and responses of the people. Hoover's college chum, the author Will Irwin, was writing a book and making a film about Hoover's achievements to supplement the bales of promotional literature set to land on every main street in America. So long as the candidate could stand as the embodiment of a Republican prosperity that had supplied "A Chicken for Every Pot," his personal shortcomings were surmountable.[30]

While the methods of Madison Avenue had never before been tried in a national campaign, most observers were willing to give them the benefit of the doubt. It was, after all, an age of packaging. A society that found innumerable uses for such new materials as Bakelite, cellophane, and aluminum could surely employ slogans, billboards, newsreels, and radio spots to make Hoover presentable.

Smith started a distant second and failed to close the gap at any point in the race. He could not make his geniality and charisma work at scale. The stories and mannerisms that had slayed them in the five boroughs seemed oddly foreign to a national audience. With endearing allegiance but questionable political judgment, he played "The Sidewalks of New York" as an anthem at every campaign stop. What's more, the few issues that arose during the campaign tended to work against Smith, starting with Prohibition.[31]

Since the 1919 ratification of the Eighteenth Amendment to the Constitution of the United States, forbidding the manufacture, sale, or transportation of intoxicating liquors, national leaders of the major parties had sidestepped the Prohibition issue in campaigns. The teetotalers had won their epic fight to banish the saloon. The Volstead Act, setting out guidelines for enforcement of Prohibition, was the law of the land. The dry faith that a new age of reduced drunkenness, crime, poverty, and disease was dawning in America remained reasonably firm through the midtwenties. Except in the wettest states, any politician voicing misgivings about Prohibition or its enforceability could expect a merciless challenge come voting time from the well-drilled troops of the Anti-Saloon League. Most leaders, including limited-government zealots like Calvin Coolidge, found it advisable to at least pay lip service to the law.[32]

Dodging the issue had become more difficult by 1928, however. It was obvious to all that something was amiss in America's war on booze. However popular the dry laws, they had not stopped people from drinking. A great market had developed for illegal alcohol, and enterprising smugglers were competing to fill it. A high-proof flood of bootleg liquor was flowing over the long and mostly unguarded U.S. border with Canada. Rum runners were dumping small mountains of kegs and casks at myriad select points along the East and West Coasts. These imports competed with the abundant beer, moonshine, and bathtub gin produced by illicit domestic operations. Customers who recoiled from traffic with criminals could usually find a sympathetic doctor willing to write a prescription for whatever libation good health required. In backrooms, speakeasies, private homes, and private clubs, on campuses, in small towns, and in big cities, wets were having their way. "It was absolutely impossible to get a drink in Detroit," wrote one newspaperman, "unless you walked at least ten feet and told the busy bartender what you wanted in a voice loud enough for him to hear you above the uproar."[33]

People were able to keep drinking not only because they were thirsty but because enforcement of the dry laws was poor. Federal responsibility rested in the Treasury Department, overseen by Secretary Andrew Mellon, a former distillery owner and unapologetic wet who considered the Volstead Act a gross infringement on personal liberties. His Prohibition Bureau, underfunded and indifferently staffed, was woefully inadequate to policing an entire nation with thousands of miles of borders and coastlines.

Coolidge, who had said so little about the Eighteenth Amendment, publicly and privately, that Hoover could not be certain where he stood, was as averse to spending money on enforcement as he was on everything else. The states, given concurrent responsibility for enforcement under the Eighteenth Amendment, were doing no better. An overwhelming majority of governors professed to be dry, yet more than two-thirds of them, whether out of fiscal rectitude or indifference to the law, had refused to provide a nickel for enforcement. In all, the states spent six times more upholding fish and game laws than they did on Prohibition. Many municipal police forces had meanwhile succumbed, in whole or in part, to the millions of dollars in kickbacks and bribes available to officials willing to abet the illegal trade or at least to look the other way. Sixty percent of Chicago's police squad was estimated to be active in the liquor business.[34]

In this disorderly atmosphere, with billions of untaxed dollars at stake, law breaking flourished. Criminal syndicates sprang up across the land and in a short period of time acquired a scale and sophistication that corporate America might envy. Lines of supply were secured. Territories were carved up. Logistics were streamlined. Profits were reinvested in new lines of vice. Risk was managed through the systematic corruption of cops, judges, and politicians. The likes of Meyer Lansky, Al Capone, Lucky Luciano, Longie Zwillman, and Detroit's Purple Gang were applying techniques of scientific management to the lucrative market for contraband spirits. With each passing year they grew bolder and richer, and more violent. Chicago saw two hundred gang-style murders in a three-year period, a shocking total at the time. The criminals operated with such impunity and contempt for authority that Washington was shamed into rousing itself lest the entire legal system fall into disrepute. Both party platforms called for more rigorous enforcement of Prohibition in 1928.

Hoover had no objection to the Republican plank on the Eighteenth Amendment. He had no passion for it, either. Moral crusades were not his thing. Lippmann was probably right in saying that Hoover regarded "both Wets and Drys as substantially insane." He was a moderate drinker who had built a decent wine cellar before Prohibition, purchasing part of the late Senator Stanford's collection. It has often been claimed that Lou drained the cellar when the Volstead Act went into effect, but a decade later, on instructing Allan to look for some papers in a cupboard under the stairs of their Palo Alto home, she gave flimsy alibis for the port and champagne he might find there, showing her household to be as hypocritical as any other in America.[35]

Hoover's ambivalence about Prohibition permitted him to drink occasionally in Washington. He did not keep liquor at 2300 S Street, but he had a habit of stopping by the exempted Belgian embassy for cocktails after work. At the same time, he supported the notion, common in Washington, that Prohibition was good for other people, liable to improve the health, welfare, and personal finances of the masses, not to mention the productivity of the economy. He was genuinely concerned about escalating crime rates and what he perceived as popular indifference to the rule of law. If pushed, he identified more closely with the God-fearing dry tribe, a hangover from several generations of temperance activists in his maternal line. He would not want to be the man who crushed their abstemious vision of America, yet politically, he saw no reason to alienate either side by taking a firm stand. He delayed saying anything substantive on the subject for as long as possible.

It was William Borah, the influential dry senator from Idaho, who forced Hoover's hand during the nomination process. Borah demanded a written statement on Prohibition of the various candidates clamoring for his support. Hoover agonized for weeks over what to say before settling on a Hardingesque straddle that declared the Eighteenth Amendment "a great social and economic experiment, noble in motive and far-reaching in purpose." It worked. Wets took encouragement from his use of the equivocal word *experiment*. Drys did not like that word but were pleased with everything else. Borah accepted Hoover as a suitable champion of temperance and gave his endorsement.[36]

Al Smith had fewer options. Whatever the Democratic platform said, there was no shaking his wet reputation. He had openly served highballs at the executive mansion in Albany, and he had repealed New York State's Prohibition enforcement statute. He considered the great experiment crazy and doomed to fail, as did most voters in New York City and other major urban centers. That was sufficient to make Smith anathema to drys in the Democratic Party, many of whom, especially in the South and Midwest, were driven into Republican arms.

Smith's problems were further aggravated by his ethnicity. It was not an accident that the exclusionary Immigration Act of 1924 had come hard on the heels of the Eighteenth Amendment; Prohibition and nativism were fellow travelers. A cocktail of anti-Catholic, anti-Semitic, anti-immigrant, and anti-saloon sentiment had helped the Ku Klux Klan break out of its southern confines in the twenties, finding support in every corner of the land. Even with the Klan now in remission, a victim of its own excesses and internal corruption, the prejudices that had sustained it survived.

Smith, as the first Roman Catholic nominated for the presidency by a major party, ran headlong into a virulent strain of anti-Catholic sentiment in American life. There were at least a hundred anti-Catholic journals in publication in 1928, including the Klan's *Fellowship Forum*, as well as the Rail Splitter, America's "oldest, most resourceful, and most reliable Anti-Papal publishing house." The latter was chief promulgator of the charge that Jesuits had assassinated Abraham Lincoln. Anti-Catholicism in these years cut across regional lines, the urban-rural divide, income and educational levels, and party lines. Serious men in Smith's own party worried that a Catholic president would owe allegiance to Rome ahead of the Constitution and the United States. Religion joined liquor as a major factor behind the growth of a Democrats-for-Hoover movement across the country.[37]

As the Quaker son of German immigrants who traced their American roots to prerevolutionary times, Hoover was spared the indignities faced by Smith. At the outset, at least, he was offended on his opponent's behalf. He viewed freedom of conscience as fundamental to the American experience. At the first opportunity, in his acceptance speech to a lively crowd in the Stanford Stadium on August 11, he made an unambiguous and eloquent appeal to his party and the American people to disregard faith in the campaign:

> I come of Quaker stock. My ancestors were persecuted for their beliefs. Here they sought and found religious freedom. By blood and conviction I stand for religious tolerance both in act and in spirit. The glory of our American ideals is the right of every man to worship God according to the dictates of his own conscience.[38]

This statement was consistent with Hoover's oft-repeated message on equality of opportunity as the foundation of American life and "the right of every American—rich or poor, foreign or native-born, irrespective of faith or color." He presented himself to voters as the beneficiary of this same right: "In no other land, could a boy from a country village, without inheritance or influential friends, look forward with un-bounded hope."[39]

Hoover and his official campaign team were reasonably successful in avoiding religion throughout the contest of 1928. Inevitably, given the virulence of anti-Catholic sentiment, not all in his party followed his example. Pockets of Republican activists, including at least one attached to the national committee, were caught in the act of papal scaremongering. The flow of anti-Catholic literature increased markedly throughout the country as the race intensified. Shown evidence of a Virginia campaign manager prophesying Rum and Romanism in America if Smith was elected, Hoover publicly denounced the speaker, and toward the end of the campaign he reiterated his call for tolerance.⁴⁰

As far as Smith and the Democrats were concerned, Hoover's response to the prejudice unleashed in his service was wanting. In an emotional address in Oklahoma City on September 20, Smith accused "Republicans high in the councils of the party" of having countenanced bigotry. They may not have actively promoted it, he said, but "a sin of omission is some times as grievous as a sin of commission."⁴¹

Hoover believed he had said his piece at the start of the campaign, and as a practical matter, he had nothing to gain by addressing religion and authenticating Smith's victimhood. Republicans were campaigning on prosperity, and it was a winning issue. Intolerance was a Democratic theme, used by Smith to raise money and rally his vote. The Democrat nevertheless had a point about sins of omission. Hoover, despite his calls for religious tolerance, told reporters that Smith's Oklahoma speech would only fan the flames of intolerance and that reticence was the best policy. The notion that Hoover might have been inclined to take his points in the Electoral College instead of heaven would have offended his followers, but his contempt for political opportunism was not absolute. He knew where his interest lay in the campaign against Smith. The acerbic journalist Oswald Garrison Villard was correct in saying that Hoover had all the qualities one required of a presidential candidate: "the ability to play politics, to compromise, at times to deceive oneself and the general public . . . to defend the Golden Rule and the Commandments against all comers . . . and then to keep silent in the presence of national sin."⁴²

The oddest aspect of Hoover's response to the religious issue was his conviction that he suffered as much as, if not more than, Smith from mudslinging. He was heard to give slur-by-slur accounts of all the malicious rumors and personal attacks aimed at him during the campaign: that he had been a war profiteer, that he was implicated in the Harding scandals, that he was racist, or too friendly with African Americans. He was especially aggrieved that the Democrats tried to challenge his eligibility for the presidency on the grounds that he had been absent from the United States for most of his adult life. He was so touchy on the subject that, far in advance of the campaign, he had commissioned a legal opinion in support of his eligibility using unnecessarily exaggerated and distorted facts to strengthen his case.*[43]

Hoover drew large and admiring crowds everywhere he appeared during the campaign, apart from Boston, where Catholics threw rocks at his car. His few phlegmatic, fact-choked speeches were safe and predictable. He located himself rather robotically as the son of pioneering Americans in West Branch, as a supporter of labor in New Jersey, a friend of manufacturers in New England, a champion of financiers in New York, and the best hope of southern voters in Elizabethton, Tennessee.

The narrative of Republican prosperity was the unifying factor in all of his addresses. It went like this: Republicans had in seven years taken a war-ravaged national economy and through far-sighted management built it into a marvel that grew the national income from $30 billion a year to more than $45 billion, that built 3.5 million new homes, that equipped 9 million more homes with electricity, 6 million with telephones, 7 million with radio sets, and put into service another 14 million automobiles. Every region of the country had seen the development of new office buildings, highways, parks, and medical facilities. The number of students enrolled in high schools had increased 66 percent, the number in institutions of higher learning 75 percent. Wise government policies, including the protective tariff, restrictive immigration, fiscal responsibility, and the pursuit of peace had permitted spending on social goods unknown to most of the rest of the world. "Fear of poverty has been reduced," said Hoover. "Fear of loss of employment has been lessened by stability. Fear of old age and for the future of the family has been lessened."[44]

Hoover tried not to push the story too far. His rosy pictures were almost always qualified. His comment that "we are nearer today to the ideal of the abolition of poverty and fear from the lives of men and women than ever before" was placed "in the context of 150 years

---

* Among other misleading statements, the opinion asserts that the candidate had "maintained his base of operations" in the United States from the time he graduated from college until the outbreak of the Great War. At best, he had merely owned property in the United States through most of that period. Regardless, Hoover did meet the constitutional requirement of having been a resident within the United States for fourteen years.

of American history." While the statement was true, he was tempting fate, given his own private misgivings about the economy.[45]

Hoover was perhaps the only participant in the election of 1928 capable of refuting or at least challenging the Republican prosperity message. He had doubts about its sustainability, and the stock market was once again the focus of his concern. Share prices had held steady throughout 1926 and the first half of 1927 until Benjamin Strong, his health terminally ravaged by tuberculosis, his policy still preoccupied with Great Britain's struggles to return to gold, dropped the New York Federal Reserve Bank's rediscount rate back down to 3.5 percent. The broader U.S. economy, he believed, was not so hot that looser credit would create problems, and, in any event, he was willing to live with the risk of a stock market bubble. The activities of gamblers, he insisted once again, should not stand in the way of the needs of the broader economy.

Hoover had been wrestling the Mississippi when Strong made this move. On his return from the flood, noting a substantial increase in the volume of brokers' loans on Wall Street, a measure of speculative activity, he shot a missive to the Federal Reserve Board arguing that "inflation of credit is not the answer" to Europe's troubles and that an increase in speculation "can only land us on the shores of depression." He tried, unsuccessfully, to rally Coolidge and Mellon to step in on the matter. Indeed, Coolidge told the press that the volume of brokers' loans merely reflected the economic health of the country. Hoover, shown the president's statement, had to read it twice. "Did that man say that?" he gasped.[46]

Coolidge and Mellon continued to make optimistic statements on the conditions of business and the reasonableness of stock prices through the last months of the year, tacitly endorsing Strong's direction and sending share prices higher. By the end of 1928, Hoover's fears were realized. The Fed rate cut had triggered a massive speculation: money was flowing in amounts large and small from every corner of the nation to Wall Street. Share prices hit dizzying levels. The Dow Jones Industrial Average leapt almost 20 percent in the last quarter without any corresponding increase in fundamental values. All this despite Strong belatedly lifting the Fed rate, in stages, back up to 5 percent in the course of the year. When the NYSE confirmed that an increase in brokers' loans was fueling price rises, Coolidge reassured the nation that brokerage lending was no cause for alarm, and the market careened ahead. Veteran traders could not recall any chief executive ever pronouncing on technical trading matters.[47]

The stock market was the greatest but not the only economic problem that weighed on Hoover in the course of the campaign. The now higher interest rates at home were repatriating money from overseas loans, freezing large parts of the European economy. Spending on home construction in the United States had been dropping since 1926, as had auto production, indicating that purchasing power was under pressure. These facts, combined with Hoover's predisposition to pessimism, were more than sufficient to start him worrying that the economy was headed down a primrose path to disaster. Still, he soldiered on with his promise of a new era of Republican prosperity.[48]

While Hoover never came close to relinquishing his lead in the campaign of 1928, he could not be convinced that his team had matters in hand. He fretted over every move by the Smith camp. He was compulsive in his attentions to the temper of editorial opinion. It was his anxieties, his talent for taking the gloomiest view of things, which led him in the final days to make his most questionable and consequential decision of the contest.

William Borah, the powerful Idaho senator who had blessed Hoover's prohibition stance, was a man of great personal magnetism, political cunning, and independent spirit. He owed his vast influence in the Senate in large part to his oratorical gifts, which were once described as "something between the technique of Cicero and the Swiss bell ringers." A champion of agricultural issues and a leading dry, he had been instrumental in shaping the Republican platform despite the fact that he qualified as an insurgent. Borah, said Lippmann, was "about as warmly attached to the Republican Party as the Irish Free State is to the United Kingdom." As an insurgent, Borah's relations with Republican presidents had been antagonistic and, for his chief executives, painful. Coolidge, hearing talk of Borah on horseback, expressed surprise that the senator and his mount could ride in the same direction.[49]

Nevertheless, in this electoral season Borah had been among the first leading Republicans to fall in behind Herbert Hoover. Before and after the Kansas City convention, he had been in close contact with the commerce secretary. They were aligned on important matters of policy, including Prohibition, farm relief via the protective tariff, and the pursuit of international peace. Hoover accepted Charles Curtis on his ticket largely at Borah's insistence. The senator helped Hoover keep the expensive McNary-Haugen agricultural price-support initiative out of the platform and after the convention defended his nominee not only as a friend of the farmer, but as someone who could actually cure what ailed agriculture. To an audience of twelve thousand in Minneapolis:

> Bear in mind that Mr. Hoover stated in his acceptance speech that it is the most imminent problem before the American people today. Bear in mind that he pledges himself to the solution of the problem. Then bear in mind that Herbert Hoover has never set himself to the solution of any kind of an economic problem that he has not made good.[50]

Borah emerged as Hoover's leading supporter and as the most effective voice for either party in the campaign. He stumped the Midwest ridiculing Smith's views on Prohibition. He insulated the Hoover camp from accusations of intolerance by canceling a speech at a Methodist conference in Peoria after a minister said that Smith's candidacy should be denounced on religious grounds from every Methodist pulpit in America. He took his show to the South, where his views on states' rights had made him a popular figure and sold Hoover to great crowds in Nashville, Tulsa, Chattanooga, and Richmond.

Some observers wondered if Hoover's alliance with Borah, a man known to serve "only that he may later betray," would last the campaign. In fact, Borah was entirely sincere in his admiration of the nominee, telling friends that he was not at all uneasy about the kind of administration Hoover would bring. He viewed Hoover as the man who would make Republicanism safe again for progressives, reuniting the insurgents with the flock.[51]

Hoover was thrilled at Borah's unexpected warmth and dedication to the mainstream Republican cause. On October 20, he encouraged the senator by wire to tour Baltimore and the Northeast. The following day, speaking in Tennessee, Borah suggested that Hoover, if elected, should call an extraordinary session of Congress in the spring to pass legislation for agricultural relief. As a statement of policy, this comment was consistent with the Republican platform: farmers needed urgent assistance. However, the idea that the agricultural situation was too desperate to wait a year for the next regular session of Congress was Borah's improvisation.

That it was not a fleeting inspiration became apparent on October 26 when the senator stopped in Washington to discuss over lunch with Hoover his touring schedule and the progress of the campaign. Borah brought welcome news of unexpected Republican strength in such Democratic strongholds as Texas and Tennessee, and he offered to make a second trip to North Carolina, where he saw promise of a Hoover breakthrough. He warned the candidate that the declaration for Al Smith by another contrary-minded Republican insurgent, Nebraska senator George Norris, threatened their campaign in the farm belt. He suggested that Hoover blunt Norris by announcing a special session to pass agricultural aid. Borah walked out of the meeting and told reporters that while nothing had been firmly decided, he himself was "thoroughly in favor of an extra session."[52]

There were obvious attractions to Borah's proposal. Hoover was averse to leaving votes on the table, and he understood that his relationship with farmers and the insurgents could make or break his success with Congress in the years ahead. There were also reasons to balk. The race was almost over and Hoover's victory was reasonably assured. Extra sessions had a way of running away on a president, and the idea that meeting Borah's demand would buy any degree of loyalty from the insurgents ran contrary to all congressional experience. "Turmoil," said William Allen White, "was their meat and drink."[53]

Hoover announced the extra session the next day: "There are a number of questions, particularly agricultural relief, which urgently require solution and should not be delayed for a whole year. It is our most urgent economic problem." Borah bolted off to shake the rafters in Baltimore, Boston, and Utica.[54]

At 1:45 p.m. on November 5, five thousand people, including a delegation of Stanford alumni, the Stanford marching band, and schoolchildren from as far away as San Jose, yelled and cheered and waved tiny American flags behind cordons of uniformed policemen who moments before had cleared them to either side of the tracks at Southern Pacific Station so that a special presidential train could roll on schedule to a grinding, jerking, belching halt and deliver from its caboose on the eve of the 1928 election a bare-headed Herbert Hoover, wearing an unaccustomed smile.

It was not much of a smile. His head was tilted down and his eyes barely lifted to meet the surge of beaming faces that blocked his view in every direction. Yet it was enough of a smile to show a warm and genuine appreciation and reciprocation of his public's affection. Lou followed him off the train and said with a wide gap-tooth grin what her husband felt and could not express.

That he had learned something in the ten-week campaign was evident in Hoover's next move. He took Lou's arm with purpose, marched a few quick steps up the platform, stopped, squared up, and presented the Republican Party's first couple in a distinguished pose for the convenience of those photographers and newsreel cameras able to keep their balance in the melee.

A motorcycle escort helped the Hoover party to its vehicles and guided them down Palm Drive toward campus. The route was lined with still more rejoicing Californians. Classes had been suspended for the day. Flags billowed out of fraternity houses and classrooms. An informal convoy of students formed behind the Hoover fleet. They leaned out of car windows wearing red Stanford caps, or rode on fenders and radiators, or ran alongside. Overhead, an airplane wrote "Welcome Home" in the sky.[55]

Before disappearing into their hilltop home, the Hoovers, all seven of them, gathered for more pictures on their front step with the strong sun in their eyes. Lou, giddy, beamed under her cloche hat. Her tall and slender sons stood as bookends to the party, Herbert Jr. with his right hand in his suit jacket pocket like a proper English gentleman, Allan, genial and relaxed, holding his father's hat. Daughter-in-law Margaret wrestled with a squirming Herbert III. The candidate carried his beloved granddaughter Peggy Ann in the crook of his right arm like a bag of groceries, another smile, less bashful than the last, crossing his face.

Hoover gave his last campaign address that night from his study, a simple, nonpolitical message carried across the nation by radio, urging Americans to get out and vote. It was considered a superb performance. Wrote the *New York Times*:

> Mr. Hoover, it was found, had a splendid radio voice, and, as he remained immobile during the delivery of his speeches, he always talked directly into the microphone. Radio listeners thus heard a clear, even voice that always made a favorable impression. The restraint of his delivery, the absence of gestures and flights of eloquence and rhetoric did not serve as handicaps.[56]

The next morning at 10 a.m. Hoover voted at a polling station in the Stanford University Women's Club building. He spent most of the rest of the day in his study, reading telegrams and smoking cigars. He got down on the floor to amuse his grandson with an empty cigar box and a pet kitten. Late in the afternoon he took a yardstick and on two large blackboards that Allan and some Stanford friends had erected in the living room calmly listed the states alphabetically and drew beside them columns for electoral votes and total precincts. He assigned the boys to fill in the blanks. At the far right of the boards were columns reserved for Republican and Democratic totals. Six telegraph lines had been rigged into the basement to provide the newswire returns that would fill these spaces.

Hoover sat down to dinner with Lou at his customary hour of 7 p.m. while the Stanford boys bolted up and down the stairs with the early returns. By the time he stood up from the table, around 7:20 p.m., the numbers indicated that all was unfolding as expected. Just before 8 p.m. he was standing with one hand in his pocket, a sheaf of returns in the other, watching the boards and nodding to the 150 guests who had been invited for an evening of fruit punch, sandwiches, and vote counting. At the top of the hour, the *New York Times* declared Virginia and Smith's home state of New York for Hoover, virtually deciding the election. A large cheer went up in the living room, and a quizzical smile crossed the victor's face. "I am happy," he said, before quickly retreating to his study.[57]

He came back into the living room not long afterward as a series of moving pictures from the campaign were played for his visitors.

He sat embarrassed, puffing his pipe, rubbing his forehead, eyes to the floor, as the projector whirred. He endured more applause around 10 p.m. when Al Smith's telegram of concession and congratulations was read aloud. Hoover sat still and smiled and tried not to look too pleased. A voice called for a speech. "No speeches," said Hoover, too self-conscious even to thank his supporters. A woman sat down at his piano and played "America." They all stood and sang in tones more reverent than jubilant.[58]

As the piano played in the Hoover living room, a torchlight parade was advancing up the hill toward the house. Thousands of students were marching and singing in the cool night air behind the baton of the old bandmaster John Philip Sousa. On reaching the Hoover home, they stopped under the motion picture klieg lights erected on the street, unleashed their college yells, and demanded the appearance of the president-elect.[59]

He came out to his balcony with Lou and the rest of the family and treated the students to a wave. Sousa responded with a series of patriotic numbers, after which the students requested something livelier and a dance party broke out on Hoover's lawn. At a break in the action, Hoover said, "I thank you for coming up tonight and giving us this greeting. I do appreciate it from the bottom of my heart." Sousa closed with the Stanford hymn, "Hail, Stanford, Hail." Hoover's eyes glistened as he joined the singing.[60]

They would all wake up in the morning to learn that Hoover had won resoundingly, taking 444 Electoral College votes to Smith's 87, and 58 percent of the popular vote to the Democrat's 41 percent. He carried forty states, including five in the formerly solid Democratic South.

# ★ BOOK IV ★

# BOOK III

# CHAPTER 18

# "Giving Genius Its Chance"

Despite winning election in November 1928, Hoover would not take office until his inauguration in March 1929, a torturous delay for an impatient man accustomed to a heavy schedule. There was no question of lounging around Washington through the interregnum. Coolidge did not want him there, and Hoover, irritated by political ritual, wanted no part of the legions of congressmen, party officers, job seekers, and advice givers clamoring for his attention. He resorted instead to his old device of living on the jump, commandeering a battleship for a ten-week, ten-country tour of Central and South America. It was a longer voyage than any president or president-elect had taken to that time, featuring twenty-five speeches from Honduras to Argentina. There were promises of renewed trade, promises to remove Coolidge's marines from Nicaragua, and the enunciation of what he dubbed a "good neighbor" policy in the Americas. A hundred thousand people threw confetti as he rode through the streets of Rio de Janeiro with President Washington Luís. It was an unambiguous success.[1]

Back in Washington, Hoover gave two weeks to desk work, preparing cabinet appointments and cementing priorities with the Republican legislative leadership, before bolting south again, this time to Florida for fishing and bridge. He socialized with a deaf Thomas Edison, with Edison's neighbor, Henry Ford, and, warmly and unexpectedly, with a vacationing Al Smith. The Hoover party was impressed at the heavy drinking and scant bathing costumes in a rebounding and garish Miami.[2]

Cabinet making was a wearisome task for Hoover, involving as it did myriad human and political considerations. He felt for the many friends and followers who would not make the cut. He understood, as one colleague said, that for every ten names on his list of prospects, nine would become enemies, and the tenth an ingrate. His instincts impelled a nonpolitical approach to appointments, with preference to men of merit and administrative ability, yet there were important constituencies that needed to be served.[3]

He kept Mellon in Treasury to appease Wall Street and old-guard Republicans. James J. "Puddler Jim" Davis, a man of the people and a former Pennsylvania steelworker, first appointed by Harding, remained in Labor. To smooth his relations on the Hill, Hoover appointed James Good of Iowa, a pragmatic politician and former chair of the House Appropriations Committee, as secretary of war. Another intermediary with Congress would be Walter F. Brown of Ohio, who filled the postmaster's office with its generous patronage opportunities.[4]

More in his own image, Hoover selected as his secretary of agriculture Arthur M. Hyde, a successful lawyer who as the one-term governor of Missouri had reconfigured and rationalized his government while setting it on a progressive course. Robert P. Lamont of Illinois, succeeding the president in Commerce, was an engineer and steel executive. He had been chief of the ordnance division of the army during the Great War as well as a partner to Hoover in flood relief. Ray Lyman Wilbur, medical doctor, third president of Stanford University, and a former classmate of the president, was named secretary of the interior. Charles Francis Adams III of Massachusetts was an unexpected choice for secretary of the navy: a glittering figure, graduate of Harvard Law, America's Cup champion yachtsman, successful businessman, descendant of two U.S. presidents, he had no experience of public office beyond two years as mayor of Quincy, Massachusetts. All four of these appointees were professional men, seldom exposed to politics. William Mitchell, the new attorney general, was picked from the same litter. A prosperous midwestern lawyer and railroad administrator who had also studied engineering for two years at Yale, he had served as Coolidge's solicitor general. To the extent that he had a political profile, he was a Democrat.

Secretary of state was the most difficult office to fill. Charles Evans Hughes, Hoover's first choice, maintained that four years in the position under Harding and Coolidge had been sufficient. Hugh Gibson, Hoover's friend from the Belgium years and a career diplomat, also refused, probably because of financial considerations (a lofty social profile was expected of the secretary). Harlan Fiske Stone, another possibility, would have added spice to the cabinet—as Coolidge's attorney general, he had prosecuted Mellon's Aluminum Company of America for antitrust violations—but he did not want to leave the Supreme Court for State. Out of a sense of political obligation, Hoover offered the office to Senator Borah, who recognized it for the halfhearted gesture it was and declined. The president-elect turned finally to Henry Stimson, who was serving as governor of the Philippines after a career as a Wall Street lawyer and Taft's secretary of war. He accepted.

It is a measure of Hoover's suspicion of career politicians that only Good had served more than one term in elected office. The cabinet looked more like a business council than a political body, and an elite one, at that. The eight members, not including the president and vice president, had sixteen degrees among them. All had professional degrees. Four were Ivy Leaguers. Most had been born to privilege, sons of lawyers, politicians, or millionaires. Everyone in the cabinet beyond Davis was affluent, rich, or very rich. Industrial and Protestant America were overrepresented. There was not a Catholic, a Jew, a southerner, or a woman in the fold. Nor was there a journalist, a soldier, a small businessman, or an academic. Hyde and Hoover owned agricultural operations, and Stimson liked to ride, but none could be called a farmer. The average age was sixty, older than any of the previous three cabinets. Hoover was content to sacrifice regional and demographic balance on the altar of administrative competence. He wanted strong and compatible departmental managers to whom he could delegate authority, leaving him free to concentrate on major policy initiatives. He also wanted safe hands. It no doubt crossed his mind that the political animals had been the weakest links in Harding's cabinet.

Prior to the election, in one of his speeches on equality of opportunity, Hoover had spoken of the value of self-made men, the type who began life close to the soil and who through talent and application assumed positions of leadership in business or government:

> Our leadership rises, as if in capillary tubes, from the great underground river of unceasing human capacity and integrity, latent and recessive in some one generation of a family, let us say, but then out-breaking and triumphant in the next.[5]

He still believed in this archetype, described at length in *American Individualism*. To relinquish it would be to undermine his personal story and abandon his view of himself as an American ideal, but as a practical matter he was drifting from it. Privileged individuals filled his cabinet, and many of his senior non-cabinet appointments, as well. Probably more than any other president, Hoover favored scions of great American families. Charles Hughes Jr., son of the former presidential candidate, would be Hoover's solicitor general. Robert Taft, son of the former president, had been his lawyer at the American Relief Administration and a member of the Firm. William R. Castle, whose father dominated the Territory of Hawaii, would become Hoover's undersecretary of state. Theodore Roosevelt Jr. would be his choice as governor of Puerto Rico. Ogden J. Mills, heir to the fabulous, multigenerational Mills fortune, divorced from a Vanderbilt, would be his undersecretary of the Treasury, eventually replacing Mellon.

It was difficult to fault any individual appointment, and public reaction to Hoover's cabinet was reasonably positive. The strategy, however, contained risk: he failed to appreciate how education, affluence, and several decades of viewing life from the boardroom had separated his ilk from the everyday concerns of the farm, the ward, and the average voter. He failed to appreciate how meritocracy, in practice, can slide into elitism.

While Hoover's supposed lack of humanity is exaggerated, it is true that the American people could become an abstraction for him, as evidenced by his comment that American leaders routinely emerge from a great underground river. This Styxian metaphor relegated the citizenry, the people among whom he had been raised, to the benighted borders of Hades. He would have found this interpretation of his remark appalling and insisted on his sensitivity to the common man and his positive view of human nature, but by surrounding himself with like-minded administrators, he was setting himself up to be insulated from the voice of the people.[6]

Hoover returned from his fishing trip to Washington for two final weeks of preparations. Politics had not rested in his absence. Republican speaker of the House Nicholas Longworth had been trying to convince the lame-duck session of Congress to address agricultural relief so as to relieve Hoover of his commitment to an extra session in the spring. Combating Longworth at every step was Senator Borah, seemingly convinced that he and not Hoover had earned the great Republican electoral mandate of 1928, and with it the right to schedule an extra session. A spring session was inevitable, said Borah, "unless we propose to disregard the promises we made to the voters in the last campaign."[7]

Hoover might have backed out of his commitment to Borah. A new president was allowed a window of time to get his feet under him in the White House before having to deal with legislative matters. It was also well understood that extra sessions of Congress were for extraordinary purposes, and none but farmers believed agriculture was in crisis. Coolidge had refused to call Congress back to deal with the Mississippi flood, and his popularity had survived. Hoover could nudge his commitment back to autumn, by which time other issues might supplant agriculture as a priority, providing an escape. But he made no attempt to delay, scheduling the extra session for mid-April. His reasons were a muddle of good intentions and political delusion: he thought the business of the extra session worthwhile, and he wanted to maintain the support of Borah and the farm states; he was invested in his identity as a man of integrity and reluctant to betray a campaign pledge in the plain light of day; he also convinced himself that Congress would act reasonably and affirm his request to limit the extra session to farm aid and the revision of agricultural tariff items, leaving manufacturing rates alone. The latter he believed despite the hordes of lobbyists and congressmen already beating down the doors of the House Ways and Means Committee in anticipation of an opportunity to raise protective duties on items of interest to their clients or constituents.


Presidential inaugurations had been held outdoors on March 4 on the Capitol's East Portico since Andrew Jackson's time. The weather usually cooperated. In fact, any expert, any scientist, or any committee or conference of experts or scientists, asked on the date of Hoover's election to forecast the weather on the date of his inauguration, would have called for a fair and comfortable day, with sunshine or light clouds and a noontime high of about fifty degrees Fahrenheit. It was the rational expectation for early spring in Washington, but Hoover's inauguration would be an exception.[8]

At dawn on March 4, 1929, the Pennsylvania Avenue parade route waited cold, wet, and empty under heavy banks of dark clouds. Rain dripped from fresh lumber on the vacant grandstands, and from every statue and monument in sight. Over on S Street, Secret Service officers stood sentry under the sheltered entrance to Number 2300 and kept a watchful eye on a huddle of newspapermen across the street. The reporters smoked cigarettes and spoke in low voices under their umbrellas, their damp feet slowly turning numb. They glanced regularly through the feeble light to the rain-streaked upstairs windows of 2300, looking for signs of life. They saw none, despite a record number of Hoovers under the steep-pitched roof. Lou, Allan, and Herbert Jr. were at home, along with daughter-in-law Margaret and both grandchildren. Two rare visitors, May Hoover Leavitt and her son, had arrived from Long Beach.

The only member of the household on his feet at that early hour, unbeknownst to the contingent outside, was the president-elect. Hoover had risen discreetly before his usual time and now found himself uncharacteristically alone with his ham and eggs at the big kitchen table. He sipped his coffee and flipped through newspapers filled with details of the ceremonies that would in several hours make him a working politician for the first time in his life.

Although Hoover left no record of what he was thinking as he sat alone at his breakfast table on that rainy morning, he had to be conscious of the monumental expectations he was carrying into the White House. No one would let him forget them, least of all the reporters outside on the sidewalk. By one tally of 900 newspaper endorsements, he had received 720. WORLD'S BIGGEST MAN CHOSEN TO FILL WORLD'S BIGGEST JOB, read one headline. The *San Francisco Chronicle* had already granted him a second term, predicting "he will drive so forcefully at the tasks now before the Nation that the end of his eight years as President will find us looking back on an era of pro-digious achievement." The great Anne O'Hare McCormick, the first woman to earn a Pulitzer Prize, wrote in the *New York Times*:

> We were in a mood for magic . . . and the whole country was a vast, expectant gallery, its eyes focused on Washington. We had summoned a great engineer to solve our problems for us; now we sat back comfortably and confidently to watch the problems being solved. The modern technical mind was for the first time at the head of a government. Relieved and grati-fied, we turned over to that mind all the complications and difficulties no other had been able to settle. Almost with the air of giving genius its chance, we waited for the performance to begin.[9]

While Hoover had confidence and high expectations of himself, the prognostications were nonetheless daunting. "My friends," he said in a private letter, "have made the American people think me a sort of superman, able to cope successfully with the most difficult and com-plicated problems. They expect the impossible from me and should there arise in the land conditions with which the political machinery is unable to cope, I will be the one to suffer."[10]

He seemed in no hurry that morning, his usual impatience to get on with his day checked by his apprehension for what it held. The cer-emonial aspects of his new position were largely repugnant to him; that much had been apparent throughout inaugural weekend. He had avoided the press and the locals and some 200,000 visitors who had filled Washington to bursting for the affair, and he had skipped all but the most essential receptions and events, including a reunion for veterans of his various relief operations. The previous morning, a Sunday, he and Lou had attended the Friends Meeting House at

Thirteenth and Irving Street, where they would be regulars during his term. The plain little building, lucky to hold forty attendees on a typical Sunday, was packed with two hundred in anticipation of his appearance. Another five hundred waited outside to watch him come and go. They raised a ripple of applause when he stepped from his car. Rather than ignoring it, or subtly, or politely, or cheerfully acknowledging it, Hoover had squelched the ovation with a definite frown.[11]

By 8 a.m. the phone was ringing, the morning mail had arrived in two bursting bags, and the bevy of Hoovers had made its way downstairs, chattering excitedly about preparations for the day. Hoover disappeared to his study for a few more minutes of quiet. It would have suited him to spend the rest of his day there, executing his oath of office through the mails.[12]

At 10:30 a.m., Mr. and Mrs. Hoover, in formal morning attire, left 2300 for the White House. Twenty minutes later they were ushered into the Blue Room to await Calvin Coolidge, who had spent his last hours in the executive mansion wandering through his vacant offices and saying curt farewells to his staff and associates of six years. In no hurry to greet his successor, the president came downstairs at the last moment and after the briefest of receptions escorted Hoover through the North Portico into the gray midmorning. They stood elbow to elbow awaiting their car, each in a black overcoat, Hoover's plain, the president's with a regal fur collar. As they waited, Coolidge gave a friendly tip of his silk hat to the photographers and spectators across the street. Hoover watched and imitated him like a tourist adopting a foreign custom.[13]

A bugle corps sounded the president's call as their open black limousine, the lead car in what would be a twenty-four-vehicle procession, swung out of the driveway behind a guard of United States cavalrymen. Hoover and Coolidge shared a blanket over their knees and continued to tip their hats to onlookers. At the Capitol they were swept into the Senate wing and on up to the president's room, where Coolidge signed last-minute legislation. Hoover pretended to be calm and patient as the new vice president and the junior senators took their oaths inside the Senate chamber.

Shortly before 1 p.m., Coolidge and Hoover made their way to the East Portico's open-air pavilion and found their seats in the front row, where they shook hands and nodded to the congressmen, justices, diplomats, and dignitaries seated behind them. On the plaza below, a mass of umbrellas, tight as paving stones, obscured a crowd of fifty thousand. To the right and left of the pavilion, reporters scribbled and cameras whirred. The inauguration was being captured for the first time on talking newsreels. Among the last people into position were Lou Hoover and Grace Coolidge, who had somehow gotten lost in the crowd. The rites were delayed a moment as they rushed down the steps to their seats, out of breath and giggling. Hoover, feeling each second's delay as an eternity, stood snapping his fingers.

Finally, at 1:07 p.m., the president-elect turned in front of a battery of microphones to face the walrus-like figure of Chief Justice William Howard Taft. By some failure of design, they were the only two individuals on the platform not protected from the elements as Taft raised his right hand and in emphatic voice, with the rain blowing directly into his eyes, asked Herbert Hoover if he did solemnly swear to faithfully execute the office of the presidency. Hoover, motionless, hand on a new Bible, answered a forthright "I do."[14]

With that, the thirty-first president of the United States, the first Quaker president, the first president born west of the Mississippi, and the first surveyor or engineer to sit as president since Washington, bent to kiss the Book. It was open to his favorite verse of Proverbs: "Where there is no vision the people perish, but he that keepeth the law, happy is he." As Hoover straightened, Coolidge, with joy and the relief of newfound freedom on his face, leapt to offer congratulations.[15]


As the cheering subsided, Hoover drew from an inside breast pocket his speech and with bare head and grave face turned to the microphones. Without preliminaries, he fastened his eyes on the yellow pages in his hands and began reading into the rain. His only acknowledgment of his enormous audience was a curt "My Countrymen."[16]

He had written his speech with great care over several weeks. It was solemn and businesslike. It held to the inaugural tradition of describing the problems facing the nation and proposing their solution, yet there were personal touches. At the outset he expressed his sense of the grandeur of the moment and the hallowed nature of his public service:

> This occasion is not alone the administration of the most sacred oath which can be assumed by an American citizen. It is dedication and consecration under God to the highest office in service of our people. I assume this trust in the humility of knowledge that only through the guidance of Almighty Providence can I hope to discharge its ever-increasing burdens.[17]

Hoover's read of the situation of the United States at home and abroad was brief and optimistic. He spoke of how the nation had emerged from the Great War, the conflict that had changed everything, with higher degrees of comfort, security, and individual freedom than any country had ever known. Surprisingly, in view of the profile he had built in Commerce, he touched lightly on economic issues. The bulk of his domestic comments were devoted to issues he had assiduously avoided throughout the campaign and, indeed, throughout his entire time in Washington: Prohibition and its enforcement.

Rather than take a clear side on the Eighteenth Amendment, Hoover reminded Americans that it was the law of the land. Those who dissented were welcome to attempt its repeal, but in the meantime, they were obliged to obey the law, just as his government was obliged to enforce it. With rain dripping from his forehead and chin, he acknowledged that dry enforcement was failing and that America had suffered a "dangerous expansion in the criminal elements who have found enlarged opportunities in dealing with illegal liquor." He scattered blame among the citizenry, who created a market for bootleggers, and the states, for not doing their part in enforcement of the Volstead Act. He announced the transfer of federal oversight from Treasury to the Department of Justice, and, more significantly, he promised a review of the entire federal machinery of justice, from investigation to appeals. A bold and unexpected move, the judicial review served several purposes. It removed the liquor issue from the quasi-religious war of wet versus dry and subjected it to the sort of expert analysis Hoover preferred. It broadened the debate, implicating the entire justice system, while sparing Prohibitionists liability for a nationwide boom in organized crime. It also answered the real need for a judicial review, something bar associations and politicians had been advocating for years. Finally, and not least importantly, the review bought Hoover time to find a way out of the Prohibition debacle before the next election.[18]

Reaching the halfway mark of his address, eyes still glued to his wet yellow pages, Hoover read on with what one reporter described as "the methodical efficiency of a well-oiled machine, hardly stopping for bursts of cheering," of which there were many during the Prohibition section. He next resurrected and dwelt upon another issue that had been largely absent from his campaign: the cause of world peace.[19]

From the Washington Naval Treaty of 1922 to the Kellogg-Briand Pact of 1928, peace had become almost as core to Republicanism as the protective tariff. It was a clever, sanctimonious, and somewhat disingenuous way for an isolationist party to express an interest in international affairs—lobbying for a blissful global quietude that would preserve the status quo, preclude foreign entanglements, and leave the world safe for Americans to trade from a position of unprecedented dominance.

While Hoover shared his party's conviction that the American way was an indubitable blessing to the world, he was more sincere than most in his attachment to peace and internationalism. He bid to make the issues his own with an atypical resort to emotive language. "I covet," he said, "for this administration a record of having further contributed to advance the cause of peace." He raised the specter of millions of "vacant chairs" in homes of soldiers across America and Europe, and attributed his "passion for peace" to the fact that he had experienced "as much of the horror and suffering of war as any other American." Categorically renouncing imperialism and calling for greater limits on armaments, he sang, in his plodding monotone, verses from Wilson's hymnal:

Surely civilization is old enough, surely mankind is
   mature enough so that we ought in our own lifetime
   to find a way to permanent peace . . .

We wish to advance the reign of justice and reason
   toward the extinction of force.[20]

In deference to the isolationist mood of his party and the country, Hoover freighted his exhortations with qualifiers. He ruled out membership in the League of Nations. He called the Permanent Court of International Justice a uniquely American inspiration and the most potent instrument for peaceful settlement of disputes among nations, yet begged the world not to take offense at the U.S. Senate's many reservations about participating in it.

At 1:40 p.m., his hands red with cold and his overcoat soaked through, Hoover ended his address as he had begun, praying for the public servant and insisting that forces beyond his control had brought him to this juncture: "I ask the help of Almighty God in this service to my country to which you have called me."[21]

The crowd roared from under its umbrellas, the Marine Band played "The Star-Spangled Banner," the Coolidges headed for Union Station and a 2:30 train to Northampton, and the Hoovers piled into yet another open car for the procession down Pennsylvania Avenue, now so black and slick with rain that a quarter million onlookers could see the parade both above the pavement and mirrored in it. Entering the portals of the White House for the first time as president, Hoover was greeted by friends and family shouting "Chief! Chief!" He answered with a boyish, bashful grin.[22]

For the rest of the afternoon, he watched his splashy parade from the shelter of the White House reviewing stand with his grandchildren at his feet. He evinced no enthusiasm for the pageant. He ignored the five hundred people, including diplomats, government officials, and visiting delegations, who had been invited to lunch, choosing to eat alone with Lou.

The *Washington Post* wrote the next morning that "Herbert Hoover's long, world-wide search for the most in life culminated yesterday in the White House." He appeared at his new offices, comfortable and bullish, at 8:55 a.m., before his staff had arrived. Determined to be the hardest-working chief executive ever to serve the American people, he plunged directly into a full day of meetings, beginning with his first press conference.[23]

Much as Hoover liked his good press, he did not like reporters, who made him feel "like a microbe on a needle under a microscope."

Determined, nevertheless, to extend the good rapport he had known with them while serving as secretary of commerce and get off on the right foot, he met with correspondents on the White House beat prior even to sitting down with his cabinet, a gesture designed to flatter them. He solicited from the leaders of the press gallery suggestions as to how his office might serve them better:

> I generally wish to see us develop a relationship between the press and the President that will be helpful and feasible in the proper conduct of affairs and at the same time of maximum assistance to you. I have no revolutions to propose, but I think, out of experience, we can accomplish something from time to time and probably in the course of 50 years develop it to perfection.[24]

Two days later Hoover declared the special session of Congress for April 15, and in the weeks that followed made a series of announcements that clearly distanced his administration from those of his predecessors.

He swept the stage clear of Coolidge's props, most notably the *Mayflower.* There was a touch of spite in his public release of a report that the presidential yacht and its complement of 157 officers and enlisted men had cost $300,000 a year to maintain. He also closed the White House stables, a predictable move considering his contempt for horseflesh, and he began filling the executive mansion with modern accoutrements. Whereas Harding and Coolidge had taken calls in a booth down the hall, Hoover installed a telephone on his desk. He expanded the presidential garage to accommodate a fleet of more than twenty vehicles, including Cadillacs, Lincolns, Fords, and Pierce Arrows, most of them provided to the White House free of charge by manufacturers.[25]

He threw more dirt on the graves of Harding and Teapot Dome by calling an immediate halt to the issuance of oil drilling permits on federal properties: "There will be no leases or disposal of Government oil lands. . . . There will be complete conservation of government oil in this administration." This act did more than bury the past: it established conservation as a priority for the administration and signaled Hoover's intention to be a responsible steward of America's natural bounty. It was an agreeable role for a trained geologist who understood commodity markets and loved the outdoors. He had been appalled to see some thirty-four thousand permits for drilling on public lands issued during the twenties. With the economy increasingly dependent on fossil fuels, he worried for the security of U.S. supplies. He lectured oil companies on how higher levels of extraction were resulting in weaker margins, and he negotiated a deal with them to cap production in 1929 at the previous year's level.[*][26]

As the financial community had feared, Hoover was also quick to turn his attention to Wall Street, where wild optimism and rampant speculation showed no signs of abating. Untethered from actual commercial performance, shares had yielded a preposterous 44 percent in 1928 and were promising to top that in 1929. Despite a Fed rate holding at 5 percent, money continued to pour into the market, much of it financed by increasing volumes of brokers' loans. Hoover launched an unprecedented presidential campaign against stock speculation. Agreeing with the Federal Reserve Board that further increases in its discount rate would put undue burden on farmers and legitimate business borrowers, he worked with the board to put direct pressure on New York City banks. They were told to choose between lending to brokers and retaining access to the Fed's discount window. Hoover also sent his friend Henry Robinson, head of Security First National Bank in Los Angeles, to lecture Wall Street on the dangers of speculation, and he called Richard Whitney, president of the New York Stock Exchange, on the White House carpet and sent him away with presidential warnings about brokers' loans ringing in his ears. Editors and publishers of major newspapers were lobbied to lecture their readers on market risks. Hoover wrote a statement that was released under Treasury Secretary Mellon's name recommending that investors turn from overpriced stocks to undervalued bonds.

There was no question of the sincerity of Hoover's market worries. Edgar Rickard was staying at the White House one busy Sunday in April that saw the Hoovers attend a Quaker meeting in the

---

* On the heels of the drilling permit freeze, Hoover introduced restrictions on hunting of migratory game birds. He would also move to control reckless timber harvesting and expand the National Park System, among other measures. He saw a clear link between conservation and his obsessions about efficiency and waste reduction.

morning, a lunch with Colonel McCormick of the *Chicago Tribune*, and a large dinner with various bankers and senators. At a break in the action, the president instructed his friend to sell their shares in Pitney Bowes and to settle their bank loans in anticipation of "possible hard times coming." This was several weeks after Rickard had followed Hoover's order to pull his money from the loan market, and several weeks before he said that he wanted his funds in cash and low-risk bonds. The pair would repeatedly discuss the liquidation of their investment fund in the months ahead, a move that had been under almost constant consideration throughout five years of disappointing returns.[27]

The president's interest in markets was one of several signals to Wall Street that its relationship with Washington was changing. Another was a March 14 executive order directing the commissioner of internal revenue to expose any refund or abatement of income taxes or estate taxes in excess of $20,000. This was a measure Andrew Mellon and the financial community had mightily resisted throughout the Coolidge years, pleading the right of wealth to privacy. Hoover compounded his Treasury secretary's embarrassment by again using him as a puppet, demanding that he formally request the executive order of the president by public letter, stating as his reason for recommending the new policy the public's need to know that "there is nothing which the Treasury desires to hide." It was obvious to the press that the measure had been imposed on Mellon, notwithstanding Hoover's insistence that the secretary had made the proposal himself.[28]

If there was any lingering doubts that the permissive Coolidge-Mellon approach to the moneyed classes was finished, Hoover declared: "Excessive fortunes are a menace to true liberty by the accumulation and inheritance of economic power."[29]

Wall Street was not Hoover's only target in these early days. The American people, too, came in for a scolding. They seemed to have adopted the "extraordinary notion," Hoover told the Associated Press, that obedience to the law is a matter of choice rather than a necessary precondition for self-government. In addition to illegal liquor traffic, and in part to underline his point that the problem of lawlessness in the United States was broader than Prohibition, he cited an array of rising felony rates, including nine thousand killings in America each year. This was twenty times the rate in Great Britain, with only a small percentage of the perpetrators brought to justice. "In many of our great cities," he lamented, "murder can apparently be committed with impunity." In May, Hoover appointed George Wickersham, Taft's attorney general, to chair an eleven-member National Commission on Law Observance and Enforcement charged with conducting the first comprehensive national study of crime and policing in U.S. history.[30]

Another set of early Hoover initiatives aimed to address problems held over from his Commerce years. He undertook to reorganize and rationalize federal government departments, a muddle never addressed under Harding or Coolidge. He laid plans for the rebuilding of the Republican Party in the South to eliminate the noxious practice of trading postal and judicial appointments for political support. He proclaimed May 1 as National Child Health Day, inviting the people of the United States "to make every reasonable effort to bring about a nation-wide understanding of the fundamental significance of healthy childhood, and of the importance of the conservation of the health and physical vigor of our boys and girls throughout every day of the year." This was followed by the announcement of a massive conference of experts on child welfare.[31]

Most ambitiously, Hoover applied the scientific, data-driven approach that had guided his work on the American economy to the whole of American society by drafting the country's preeminent social scientists, including William Ogburn of Chicago, Howard Odum of North Carolina, and Alice Hamilton of Harvard Medical School, to investigate the actual living conditions of people in every corner of the land. His hope was that the review would provide the basis for "the formulation of large national policies looking to the next phase in the nation's development."[32]

Hoover was using neither Coolidge nor Harding as a model in establishing his administration, notwithstanding his dependence on their legacy of Republican prosperity. He took more guidance from another party icon, a man he seldom mentioned, had hardly known, and whose day had come and gone while Hoover was overseas. It had been Theodore Roosevelt's 1912 campaign that had first quickened Hoover's political pulse, and now almost every domestic note the new president hit was an echo of the late Rough Rider's progressivism: the bias for vigorous action, the courting of the media, the insistence on honesty and merit in public service, conservationism, protection of the less fortunate, insistence on law enforcement, reliance on experts, campaigns against waste and inefficiency, and, finally, fist shaking at what Roosevelt had called "the malefactors of great wealth."[33]

Hoover's debt to Roosevelt was noticed occasionally and approvingly in the press. That it did not receive more attention was due in part to dissimilar personal styles. It was difficult to see reflections of the beloved Teddy in a successor so averse to playing the hero and shooting the bear. Hoover was determined to professionalize the presidency, by which he meant adopting a businesslike style of leadership, low key and collaborative as opposed to charismatic and combative.[34]

Professionalization was what Hoover meant when he advised the press corps not to expect any headline-making bombast of him. He stuck primarily to facts and figures in his public statements and press conferences, and less than a month into his administration was arriving empty handed at his regular press briefings: no news, no confidences, no affability, just another "famine morning," he would grunt to the disappointed gallery.[35]

His notion of professionalism permitted Hoover to evade those chores of leadership requiring him to expend energy on human interaction. He cut the daily ritual of shaking hands with visitors to the White House to two days a week. While Roosevelt had found these sessions invigorating, Hoover, unable to drop his guard and act freely and naturally around strangers, afraid of contracting colds or fevers, considered them a drain on his time and vitality. Professionalism applied as well to relations with Congress. "It is much less heroic," Hoover acknowledged, "for the President to cooperate than to carry the banner of the people against the bastions of Congress," but more could be accomplished by showing legislators respect and meeting them on common ground.[36]

Undergirding his commitment to a professional style of leadership were, of course, Hoover's familiar anxieties and apprehensions. Professionalism was an alibi for his diffidence and insecurities, his fears of error and ridicule, and his discomfort with human emotion. He seems to have been so firmly convinced of the rightness of his approach, or perhaps so repulsed by the alternatives, as to never have second-guessed his motives.

None of this was as idiosyncratic as it might seem. Leaders almost always define their job in terms of their own capacities and inclinations. Confronted with any new problem, Roosevelt's first impulse was to cry "bear" and fire away. Hoover preferred to gather facts and manage a problem into submission, free from the demands of public performance, with time and space to concentrate on what he perceived as the substantive aspects of his role.


Once visiting hours were reduced and all traces of Coolidge removed, Hoover settled easily into life at the White House. The physical setting suited him. He was accustomed to large residences crowded with family, staff, and guests. "We are beginning to feel perfectly at home," Lou wrote Allan in May. "Daddy has moved all the upstairs furniture once, and most of it twice." She had shipped in a small pile of heirlooms and photographs from Palo Alto, where their home, in typical Hoover fashion, had been abandoned in haste, with check stubs and personal papers strewn around studies and bedrooms, and no plans made for its occupancy.[37]

Hoover took as his study a room on the second floor of the executive mansion that had been used by Coolidge to the same purpose. He positioned his desk to allow a side view of the White House grounds and the Washington Monument. He kept his office hours in the Oval Office in the West Wing. That his office hours routinely numbered twelve, fourteen, even sixteen a day fascinated a Washington accustomed to Wilson's banker's hours, Harding's tee times, and Coolidge's somnolence. Hoover would emerge from the rounded course of Georgian pillars at the rear of the White House at about half past eight each morning and stride to his office. His first hour was devoted to correspondence and newspapers, after which he cleared his desk and launched into a series of eight-minute appointments that ended on schedule with him pressing a button to summon a secretary. His staff, under these time constraints, learned to bring him solutions to approve rather than problems to solve.

Tuesdays and Fridays the morning routine was broken for ninety-minute cabinet sessions. He would walk back to the residence for lunch and be "back to the mines," as he said, in as little as fifteen minutes. The afternoon passed in longer conferences on issues at the top of his agenda. Around 6:30, his face gray, his shoulders sagging, his tie askew, his jacket sprinkled with cigar ash, he would clear his desk for a second time and walk back from his office, often with Lou at his side, her arm linked in his, past the saluting guards and through the rear doors of the old mansion. He would often retire to his bedroom, disrobe, and lie down for fifteen minutes, all the refreshment he required, before working on a speech or reading documents and dressing hurriedly for dinner, which began promptly at eight.[38]

It was his dedication to his desk that led a journalist to call Hoover America's first "presidential industrialist." He and his friends thought this a helpful positioning. Wrote Vernon Kellogg, in words Hoover would himself echo:

> The difference between Mr. Hoover and most other Presidents is that he expends practically all of his time in his overalls down in the roundhouse, working desperately to repair the engines of civilization; a less conscientious man in his position would put on a high hat and take his post in front of the railroad station where he could be pleasant to the customers and assure them that he would like to give them all a free pass on the train.[39]

Dinners at the White House were crowded and stimulating, the table packed with friends, colleagues, and visitors, sitting without precedence. "[Hoover] not only sees but converses with more people than any one in Washington," said Anne O'Hare McCormick. "With the possible exception of Roosevelt, he is the most gregarious President we have ever had." Alice Roosevelt Longworth, Washington's leading social arbiter, also approved of the Hoovers' entertaining, although like McCormick she overestimated the degree to which Hoover was interested in his guests: he was more a presence than a participant in many of his functions. Lou kept things moving at the table, communicating with servants by such simple tricks as turning her eyeglasses in her hand. After the last course, the men would retire to the Lincoln Study on the second floor for cigars and conversation. It was generally for others to talk, impart information, and tell stories, and the president to listen. After an hour, Hoover would suggest they rejoin the ladies in the Blue Room on the main floor. After another fifteen minutes, good-nights were said and Hoover would return upstairs to read mysteries or history for an hour or so before falling asleep around midnight. It was common for him to wake in the night and read or work for another hour before dozing off again. He would arise in the morning at six, without exception.[40]

The interval between waking at six and walking to the office at half past eight each morning was as jam-packed as every other part of the presidential day, albeit with activity of another sort. A new influence had come into Hoover's life when he moved into the executive mansion.

Joel Boone, the White House physician, was a natty naval surgeon who had been assigned to the *Mayflower* during the Harding and Coolidge years. He met Hoover for their first official appointment in the president's dressing room several days after the inauguration. The doctor examined a plump man slightly less than six feet tall and slightly more than 190 pounds. He had a forty-three-inch chest, short legs, small feet, powerful hands, a weak pulse, poor teeth, and enough wax impacted in his ears to affect his hearing. He also had difficulty breathing after two minutes of moderate exertion. He admitted to doing little exercise beyond calisthenics on ships or trains and occasional visits to a masseur. He excused his personal neglect on the grounds of busyness, and he was palpably reluctant to change his habits.[41]

Dr. Boone was not the sort of man to be daunted by a show of presidential recalcitrance. He had been awarded the Medal of Honor, America's highest military decoration, for repeatedly exposing himself to heavy barrages of shellfire and poison gas while tending to wounded Marines on the battlefields of France. He had been at bedside for the final breaths of President Harding in San Francisco and Calvin Coolidge Jr. in the White House. He wanted no more losses on his watch.

Boone also believed there was a danger that Hoover would push himself too hard in office, and while he found the president's "powers of concentration . . . amazing," and his capacity for work "astounding" and "beyond his associates' comprehensions," he thought the workload would crush him without changes to his lifestyle. He fixed his large brown eyes on Hoover and told him that he was going on a diet to bring his weight under 180 pounds and that he would be taking regular exercise, preferably outdoors. Hoover listened carefully, asked a few questions, and, satisfied with the answers, nodded assent.[42]

The question remained, what type of exercise? Hoover, no athlete, had a single suggestion: he mentioned to the doctor that occasionally on shipboard he had tossed a medicine ball with friends and sailors—a good and strenuous exercise, he thought. Within the week, Boone had arranged for a collection of the president's friends and associates to gather every day at 7 a.m. on the White House's south lawn for a game of their own invention. It called for two to four players a side. It used the rules of tennis with a six-pound medicine ball heaved back and forth over an eight-foot volleyball net. Victory went to the team with the most points when a factory whistle down by the Potomac blew at seven thirty. Eventually they would call the game Hooverball.[43]

They played six days a week, in the heat, rain, and snow, missing a day only if the president was out of town. Hoover arrived for action in casual clothes: old trousers, a flannel shirt, crepe-soled high-top shoes, and a leather bomber jacket if it was cool. The most regular attendees were Boone, the journalist Mark Sullivan, White House aide Lawrence Richey, Interior Secretary Wilbur, Attorney General Mitchell, and Supreme Court justice Harlan Fiske Stone. The Hoover kennel, which at different points included an Irish wolfhound, an Irish setter, an English setter, a Norwegian husky, a German shepherd, an elkhound pup, and a Scotch terrier, roamed the sidelines.

The game was by all accounts a vigorous workout. Stone, a former stand-out guard for the Amherst University football squad, threw the ball with enough heat to knock opponents backward. Hoover also threw with force, although he tended to get spun around on his catches, which Boone attributed to his small feet. He was roughed up from time to time, as they all were, by balls to the face or other points of vulnerability. Still, he would get upset if he suspected his opponents were taking it easy on him.

. . .

With this exercise and a diet heavy on nuts and fruits, Hoover did not take long to make Boone's prescribed weight. His strength and fitness improved noticeably. The doctor, having demonstrated his worth, was presented with additional presidential infirmities. There was an extensive dermatological situation, wrote Boone, in a part of the anatomy not usually exposed to other observers, that Hoover out of modesty had been hesitant to mention. The condition was treated with the help of a specialist. Another problem was found under the president's jaw. He thought it was a gland, but Boone, suspecting a dental issue, ordered X-rays that turned up an infected molar. While examining the president's mouth, Boone made further inventory of bleeding gums, cavities, and leukoplakia (thick white and gray blotches) of the palate, tongue, and cheek, which he attributed to Hoover's heavy cigar smoking. He arranged extensive dental work that would stretch over his patient's first year in office. The leukoplakia seemed to recede once the molar was removed.[44]

Soon adopted as one of the family, Boone routinely joined the Hoover family for breakfast after medicine ball, as did Justice Stone, Secretary Wilbur, and Mark Sullivan, with whom the president was especially close. Florid, funny, and exceedingly well informed, Sullivan was great company, and Hoover, said Boone, particularly enjoyed having him around. The mode of conversation at table was light and unstructured. Topics ranged from sports to politics to whatever the president happened to be reading at the time. Hoover's dogs climbed over him. His attention would flag only if granddaughter Peggy Ann happened to be present. He could "hardly take his eyes off her whenever she was about him," said Boone.[45]

The doctor approved of the First Lady's habit of filling her table with guests morning and night, and of the informality of the gatherings. Among friends and associates, the president was talkative, even voluble by his standards. With strangers he tended to lapse into grunts and silences. Boone became a great admirer of Lou, a person of "unusual alertness," he said, with beautiful eyes and a striking appearance.[46]

Boone's intimacy with Hoover allowed him to continue a study of presidential moods and idiosyncrasies begun during the previous administration. He had watched with empathy and concern Coolidge's deterioration, his black rages, his stomach ailments exacerbated by eating binges that afterward required enemas or purgatives. He was mesmerized by Coolidge's evening practice of dressing for dinner, mounting a mechanical horse that had been presented him as a gift, and arriving at dinner covered in sweat. Hoover's quirks were milder. He ate like a starving man, bolting his food with hardly a chew. He always finished before anyone else (sometimes before others had been served), and as soon as he had finished he popped a cigar into his mouth.[47]

Hoover was not fussy, as his scant attention to food, grooming, attire, and his surroundings would attest, but he was extremely fastidious about his tools, from his first-rate fishing tackle and top-of-the-line automobiles to his cigars. He loved his cigars, and only his cigars. If another were offered him, no matter the brand, he would accept it, prepare it for lighting, and surreptitiously reach into his pocket and exchange it for one of his own.

He would chew through as many as ten cigars a day. He appealed to the Department of Commerce's commercial attaché in Cuba for help in finding brands to his taste. "I am having difficulty finding a good Cuban cigar that is mild enough not to corrupt my soul," he wrote, requesting three or four hundred different samples. The White House also corresponded with the Ritz-Carlton in Havana, which eventually provided from its humidor a quantity of La Corona Del Ritz "especially manufactured and selected to his liking." Hoover ordered five hundred at a cost of $290 (the price of a Ford Runabout). They did not meet expectations. A dealer in New York introduced Hoover to Ramon Allones Havana Cigars, Grovnicos de Luxe, No. 2-25, English Market Selection, which were delightful until the annual variation in the taste of cigars due to harvest quality frustrated the president and the hunt was resumed. Fortunately for the productivity of the administration, Hoover's taste in pipe tobacco was easily satisfied by a single variety available at the University Club in New York.[48]

That his long-standing pursuit of a better smoke blossomed into an obsession in the White House is undoubtedly a measure of the stress the president was under. He was fortunate to have Boone at hand to whip him into shape and attend to matters of health that he would otherwise have ignored. The long ordeal of his presidency was about to begin in earnest.

# CHAPTER 19

# "He Didn't Know
# Where the Votes Came From"

The Seventy-First Congress was called into extraordinary session on April 15, 1929, with Hoover and his congressional leadership determined to push through his top priorities, farm aid and limited tariff revisions, before summer brought its worst. "I speak from experience," said Speaker Longworth, "when I say that legislation framed in a temperature of 90 degrees is not apt to be good legislation."[1]

From some angles, Hoover's odds of success looked favorable. He carried the prestige of an overwhelming electoral triumph into the extra session and he was stunning the Capitol with his pace of activity. Washington, wrote McCormick, recently returned from Europe, was "preoccupied with one man and one question as no capital has been since Rome gathered on street corners to wonder about Mussolini and where he was going." Journalists, she said, were agog at the pace at which Hoover drove his administrative machine, how he kept four secretaries busier than two had been under his predecessors. The press gallery's "almost unanimous admiration for this brisk and rational mind," she added, "is a real tribute, since their romanticism makes the gentlemen of the press as hard to please as does their cynicism."[2]

Congress, meanwhile, seemed deflated and submissive. The champions of high manufacturing tariffs appeared to be acquiescing to Hoover's instructions to limit rate increases largely to farm items. Even the high-tariff torchbearer, Joseph Grundy, president of the Pennsylvania Manufacturing Association and a leading Republican donor, had been quoted as supporting limited manufacturing reform on his way out of a White House meeting with Hoover.[3]

In addition to his overwhelming majority in the House, the president was believed to have a working majority of Republican regulars in the Senate. The insurgents, those nominal Republicans so nettlesome to Coolidge, seemed in retreat. Nebraska's Norris, their recognized leader, had endorsed Smith for president only to see Hoover take his state by a whopping margin. The same fate had befallen both of Wisconsin's Smith-happy insurgents, Senators Robert La Follette Jr. and John Blaine.

The White House's strategy for the extra session, in keeping with Hoover's professional, nonheroic style, was to let a sleeping Congress lie. He declared his respect for the constitutional division of powers between the legislative and the executive branches, believing the Republican platform and his campaign speeches had offered all the guidance lawmakers needed to do their job. Congressional leaders could work out the details of the proposed bills, and he would make himself available for conferences should they get stuck. He hoped that his momentum and the rightness of his cause would ensure best behavior among all parties. Mainstream editorial opinion considered this approach shrewd of Hoover. The president's congressional allies, John Q. Tilson, House majority floor leader, and Senator Reed Smoot, chair of the Senate Finance Committee, assured him that they could pass the necessary legislation and put a bow on the extra session before summer.[4]

From other angles, Hoover's odds were less promising. While respect for Congress was to an extent admirable in a chief executive, some wondered if Hoover was not drawing too literal a line between lawmakers and the White House. Had any president accomplished much in the way of legislation without making his presence felt on the Hill? As for the insurgents, was it reasonable to consider them housebroken on the results of a single election? Could they be trusted to abandon their fratricidal ways and do Hoover's bidding? An impressive mandate had not won Coolidge the insurgents' loyalty.

And then there was the nature of the tariff itself. Experienced hands knew that debates on rate schedules had a way of teasing out every greedy, stubborn, and otherwise pernicious impulse known to Congress, bringing to its chambers the aspect of a hot day in the souk. A tariff bill was any federal politician's best shot at delivering the goods for businesses back home. He or she could plausibly claim to be an author of rate hikes and protections for industries important to constituents or, alternatively, be blamed for failing to deliver for those same constituents. It was the district-by-district, state-by-state impact of tariff reform that made it such a powerful and volatile exercise. It was fair to wonder if the president's call for restraint was realistic with so much on the line. If Hoover were to succeed in effecting a limited revision, said the *New York World*, he would stand alone among presidents in living memory: "The stage has been set for as fine an exhibit of log-rolling as the country has ever seen."[5]

Whatever one considered a likely outcome, it was clear from the outset that the extra session would be read as a test of presidential authority and leadership.


"I have called this special session," Hoover told Congress on April 16, "to redeem two pledges given in the last election—farm relief and limited changes in tariff." The two items would be taken in that order. The president said that he wanted to lift the farm question out of the political realm and reestablish it "on more economic lines," a sincere statement that sounded odd coming from a man who had got himself stuck with an extra session on farm aid in pursuit of political advantage in the heat of an election campaign.[6]

The Republican House leadership promptly produced a bill, the Agricultural Marketing Act, which called for the creation of a federal farm board of eight appointed members and the secretary of agriculture. It provided for a revolving fund of $500 million to be administered by the farmers themselves, organized into cooperatives. The cooperative approach would permit the farmers to market their products and purchase supplies at scale, drawing on the fund to store surpluses in weak markets and selling at periods of high demand. The act was easily the most comprehensive legislative initiative ever introduced on behalf of the farm community. It met only token opposition on the floor of the House—"the greatest gold brick ever handed to the American farmer by any Congress," shouted one Democrat—before Republicans, with their vastly superior numbers, voted its approval.[7]

The reception of the bill in the Senate was cooler. What appeared to be a narrow Republican advantage in that assembly evaporated as the western insurgents awoke and decided the Act required an enhancement of cash payouts to farmers. With cheerful assistance from the Democratic minority, a complicated debenture scheme was amended to the bill. It was designed to keep domestic prices steady by dumping agricultural surpluses overseas: farmers would be compensated from the public purse for the losses on their exports, a prospect anathema to Hoover.

A joint conference of the House and Senate was called to resolve differences over the bill. Senate representatives were compelled to give up the debenture. When the consensus report was returned to their chamber, however, it was stubbornly defeated. The insurgents, knowing they did not have the votes to force the debenture over a presidential veto, contented themselves with another round of showboating before allowing the act to pass, satisfied that they had made their presence felt.

"After many years of contention," said Hoover on signing the Agricultural Marketing Act on June 15, "we have at last made a constructive start at agricultural relief with the most important measure ever passed by Congress in aid of a single industry."[8]

The bill as passed was indeed a victory for the administration. It was shaped to Hoover's stated wishes and it fulfilled an important campaign promise. He had also dodged the debenture, which would only have exacerbated the fundamental farm problem of overproduction. At the same time, he had paid a price. The insurgents had shown the president that his working majority in the Senate was illusory, and his erstwhile champion, Senator Borah, who throughout the election campaign had accepted Hoover's definition of farm relief, now broke ranks to support the debenture. The "sons of the wild jackass," as New Hampshire senator George Moses called the insurgents, were emboldened on the eve of the tariff initiative.[9]

If Hoover had been approximate in his instructions for the Agricultural Marketing Act, he was positively vague on what he wanted in the way of tariff reform. This might have been expected: there was no real economic rationale to revisit the tariff in 1929. In place of fact-based arguments for higher agricultural duties, he appealed for equity between hard-pressed farmers and relatively prosperous manufacturers. Agricultural rates would be raised while manufacturing rates would be restrained except in industries that had suffered "a substantial slackening of activity . . . and a consequent decrease of employment." One of few specifics he requested was a flexible-tariff provision that would allow the president more scope in adjusting individual rates between once-a-decade rewrites of the law.[10]

Republican congressional leaders listened carefully to Hoover's instructions but came away confused at the meaning of such vague terms as "limited" and equitable reform, and a "substantial slackening" of business. The task of rendering the president's pointers as a draft bill fell to Representative Willis C. Hawley, chairman of the Committee on Ways and Means, a genial career educator with five degrees and a passion for the tariff. He was said to be "the only living man who ever really knew what the defunct equalization fee really meant." He had been holding preparatory hearings since January to review the tariff code and its fifteen schedules covering chemicals, sugar, tobacco, silk, metals, and onward to sundries. The detail was mind-numbing: chemicals, for instance, included the subcategory of salts, which covered aluminum salts, antimony salts, manganese salts, cobalt salts, Rochelle salts, Epsom salts, Glauber salts, aniline salts, cocaine salts, strychnine salts, opium alkaloids and salts, bath salts, salt peter, salts of cerium, and thorium salts. The committee heard from 1,100 individuals, almost all of them demanding upward revisions in tariffs.[11]

On May 7, 1929, as the farm act was working its way through the Senate, Hawley presented an eighty-five-thousand-word tariff bill to the House of Representatives. It contained Hoover's provision for a nonpartisan, mildly enhanced tariff commission. It went further than Hoover had suggested in raising rates: almost a third of the 2,683 items captured in the 1922 tariff act were raised. Manufacturing rates received more attention than agricultural rates, creating greater inequities where more equity had been requested by the president. As for the necessity of the manufacturing increases, the committee report blithely asserted that the adjustments were "justified by existing differences in competitive conditions."[12]

Hoover was unhappy with Hawley's bill and said so, to no avail.

Special-interest advocates, some hired, some elected, some self-appointed, had overrun the House at the introduction of the legislation. Even after imposing limits on debate, Republican leaders could do nothing to halt the stampede. As the proposed tariff schedules filled whole sections of newspapers, the public learned that rates were set to rise for chickens and tobacco as well as for such non-farm items as glassware, cement, surgical instruments, doll clothes, baseballs, and window blinds. This brought new demands for increases on still more items. New Jersey representatives requested higher rates on imported canned tomatoes. A California delegation including nine Republicans declared that it would henceforth vote Democratic if protections were not extended to figs and dates. In every instance, the requested increases were deemed essential to protecting jobs in challenged industries.[13]

As the California fig example suggests, it was soon difficult to follow the battle lines on the floor. In general, Democrats were opposed to manufacturing increases on grounds of equity to farmers. Western Republicans tended to side with Democrats. Northeastern Republicans were mostly heedless of the West's concerns, doubting that agricultural tariffs would solve the basic problem of agricultural overproduction. Almost all Republicans professed to back the president's call for limited revisions, excepting the handful of items affecting their own constituents. The trouble was that these exceptions, in aggregate, covered much of the tariff field. Logrolling, by which congressmen of every stripe struck deals to support one another's pet tariffs, further blurred partisan lines.

Outside of the House, Pennsylvania's Grundy, so recently sworn to respect the president's wish for limited reform, announced that if Congress would not go further in raising manufacturing rates he would take his fight to the Senate Committee on Finance, the next stop on the legislative trail. Meanwhile, foreign governments, led by Canada, America's largest trading partner, were aghast at the proposed rate hikes. Letters of protest flew into the State Department from every corner of the globe. London's *Economist* magazine called U.S. trade policies "deplorably crude" and said that if all countries were to follow America's lead, global commerce would grind to a halt.[14]

More disquieting for Hoover was an attack on his sacred flexible tariff provision. The Texan John Nance Garner, House minority leader, led a bid to strip the president and the tariff commission of the powers to raise or lower rates. He wanted final decisions on tariffs back in the hands of Congress. In a close escape for Hoover, Garner could not muster the necessary votes.

The president was conspicuously quiet through the rest of May as delegations pressed their tariff claims on Congress. He had been keeping close tabs on press coverage of the bill, hiring two new monitoring firms to supplement the usual White House service. He was pleased that sentiment in news stories and editorial opinion was heavily against the Hawley act, and he was galled that congressional Republicans were often first movers in the orgy of logrolling that pushed manufacturing rates to new heights. He met privately with Hawley and other House stewards to remind them of his guidance and their campaign promises, and to advise them that excessive protectionism would disrupt the State Department's efforts to maintain cordial international relations and negotiate an agreement on naval reductions. The conversation did nothing to improve Hoover's confidence in the loyalty of his troops, or the governability of Congress. Tilson told the president that he was not optimistic that high industrial rates could be reversed, even with a Republican majority, while Longworth, privately a high-tariff man, doubted that they should be reversed.[15]

A final House vote on the Hawley act was called for May 29. More than 90 percent of the 435 representatives were in their seats for the first time in three sessions of Congress. The bill passed easily, 264–147, with the vote falling roughly along party lines. When Speaker Longworth announced the tally, there were none of the huzzahs that traditionally accompany the success of a notable piece of legislation; newspapermen heard "a feeble cheer" from the floor. It was obvious to members on both sides of the House that the bill had failed the broader interests of the American people. Republicans dreaded to think what would happen to the bill when the Senate got hold of it.[16]

Just six weeks into Hoover's extra session, wrote McCormick, something had happened in Congress to break the neatly outlined pattern expected of it—"the same something that always happens to rationalized plans for human government."[17]

. . .

It was customary during summer congressional recesses, when soupy air and hordes of insects chased legislators home to their electors and all work in the capital ceased, for a president to establish a Summer White House in some less ghastly corner of the country. Teddy Roosevelt spent summers at his twenty-three-room mansion, Sagamore Hill, luxuriating in cool Long Island breezes and taking vigorous rides on horseback. Wilson had preferred Cornish, New Hampshire, a small inland town clinging to its late-Victorian reputation as an artists' colony. Coolidge had tried a new spot every year, from his family homestead in Vermont to Wisconsin to the Dakotas. Hoover, never having seen the point in long vacations, and unwilling to waste precious months of presidential working time, stayed in Washington clear through the dog days. He organized his leisure in an efficient, businesslike fashion, over the weekends.

Well before his inauguration, Hoover had been asking around about possible locations for a fishing camp on the eastern slope of the Blue Ridge Mountains. A Shenandoah Park official recommended a site along the Rapidan River in Madison County, eighty miles southwest of Washington. The Hoovers took their first trip to the region days after moving into the White House, driving along mostly gravel roads before switching to horseback and impressing Dr. Boone and the Secret Service with their riding skills on a steep uphill climb over the final miles. Arriving at a brooding, peaceful wooded plateau where Laurel Prong and Mill Prong met to form the Rapidan, some 2,500 feet above sea level, Hoover looked up at the blue peaks of the mountains and down into the clear turbulent waters, filled with silver trout and lichened boulders, and declared himself satisfied. He spent a couple of hours roaming among the oaks and hemlocks, explaining how the camp would be laid out.

Marine engineers were dispatched from the nearby Quantico base to improve the road to Rapidan. Brush was cleared, trees felled, and an encampment was built to the president's specifications. A cluster of cabins surrounded a main hall sixty feet long with a great stone fireplace and a screened sleeping porch. Hoover stripped Coolidge's *Mayflower* of its rugs, china, linen, furniture, and cooking equipment as well as a complement of its cooks, stewards, and mess boys to furnish the retreat. Lou insisted on dressing rooms, a bathroom, and indoor sleeping options in the family's quarters, as well as a sitting room for herself. A porcelain bathtub, hot water heater, electricity, telephones, and twice-daily newspaper delivery relieved the site's rusticity. "No accessories of beauty," said Lou, "but fairly comfortable." The Hoover lodgings were close enough to the water that the president could go to bed with it burbling in his ears.[*18]

From early spring through autumn, the Hoovers piled into separate cars on Saturday mornings—she liked to drive, he liked to be driven—bound for Camp Rapidan. They traveled at unconscionable speeds, even along the last eight miles of rough mountain road with its uncharted rocks and mud holes. Lou had trouble convincing wives of cabinet ministers to ride with her. Her husband, at eighty-five miles an hour, was known to ask a driver "What's holding you back?" Among the usual guests were Dr. Boone, staffers Richey and Akerson, two stenographers, a selection of cabinet members and congressmen, and a friendly journalist or two.[19]

They fished. Military engineers had cleared low-hanging tree limbs to facilitate presidential fly-casting. Hoover, in waders, jacket, and tie, would enter the stream with a group before wandering off on his own to appreciate in solitude the crisp mountain air and the rush of water around his knees. The subtle work of teasing trout to the end of his line cleared his mind and refreshed his spirit. He often fished to his limit. At the end of the day, he would gather with the party, lay their catch on a table, and determine who had caught the largest.

As an alternative to fishing, the president would sometimes decide that his company needed to wade into the stream and move boulders to create pools in which to trap fish. From time to time, he would pick up a crowbar and with red-faced exertion help to dislodge rocks, but more often he would play the role of architect, directing others in the exhausting work from a grassy bank. Lou, who liked to ride on weekends, often led expeditions over a summit of the Blue Ridge Mountains that provided a vast and beautiful view of the Shenandoah Valley. After dinner, Hoover would sit in the main hall near the fireplace with his male guests, smoking and casually talking until past sundown. "He has never really relaxed completely in his lifetime for

* Hoover bought the property and paid for most of the building materials himself, with the intention (later fulfilled) of donating the entire camp to Shenandoah National Park.

more than a few hours at a time," said Rickard. Mountain evenings were among those rare moments.[20]

The two most interesting guests at Rapidan in its first summer of operation appeared on the same weekend, which happened to coincide with the president's fifty-fifth birthday. The aviator Charles Lindbergh, easily the most famous man in the nation, hauled boulders in the stream before winning a horseshoe contest over Allan Hoover, Secretary Hyde, and William Allen White. Lou, meanwhile, had met an eleven-year-old country boy named Ray while out riding. He arrived in camp with a baby possum in a soapbox that he offered to Hoover as a birthday gift. Ray entertained the party with an account of how his father had been surprised by Hoover's victory: "My paw was such a bum guesser that he had to climb a big hickory tree after the election because he said he would if Hoover won." The president eventually pulled Ray aside for a long, quiet personal chat, Hoover in a camp chair, the boy leaning against a tree. Before leaving, Ray was introduced to Lindbergh, who was delighted to finally meet someone who had never heard of him. The president would later intervene and pay to have a school built for the local mountain children, and he and Lou would hire and cover the salary of the schoolteacher until 1938 when the responsibility was assumed by local government.[21]

Hoover's decision to summer in Washington forced some adjustments on others in the capital. While Congress took its recess, diplomats and government officials opened their windows, turned on their fans, and remained at their desks through the sweaty season. As a result, the city's streets, stores, and hotels were busier than usual. Cabinet members appeared for their weekly meetings in light-colored Palm Beach suits while Hoover, continuing with his dark favorites, seemed hardly to notice the heat or the discomfort of his colleagues.

Staying in Washington while Congress vacationed permitted the president to meet emerging problems with a prompt hand. On August 1, prisoners at the federal institution in Leavenworth, suffering from overcrowding, intense summer heat, and one too many meals of red rice, hurled their bowls at guards and began a demonstration that led to a riot. Knives, forks, and table legs were used as weapons against the guards, who opened fire, killing one inmate and wounding others.[22]

Five days later, Hoover, interested in penal reform, appointed the noted expert Sanford Bates as superintendent of the Federal Bureau of Prisons in the Department of Justice and announced a $5 million program to relieve overcrowding at the four existing federal institutions, as well as plans to build a new prison in the Northeast. In the interim, he used military prisons to alleviate the state of "infinite demoralization" in federal jailhouses. Leavenworth had been 87 percent over capacity at the time of the riot, and Atlanta 120 percent, largely due to violations of both the Volstead Act and the Harrison Anti-Narcotics Act of 1915. What began as a spontaneous reaction to a specific event soon evolved into one of the more impressive dimensions of the president's law-and-order agenda. Bates would oversee the passage of eight bills dealing not only with overcrowding but proper training of prison guards, improved health benefits and educational opportunities for inmates, and parole reform as well.[23]

Notwithstanding the prison situation, it was the fate of his tariff initiative that preoccupied Hoover through the summer. He worried about the damage the Senate might do to his intentions. It was of some solace that Republican members of the Senate Finance Committee, not least the chair, Reed Smoot of Utah, appeared to appreciate his criticisms of the Hawley bill passed by the House. They were promising to "scientifically" revise the heavy increases on manufacturing items, by which they meant downward and significantly. This was generous of Smoot, an apostle of the Mormon Church and an evangelist of protection looking to cap his career by leaving his name on a major piece of tariff legislation.[24]

The Finance Committee's fealty to the president's vision would be sorely tested. Its mostly white-haired members worked through the summer in their wrinkled suits in a small hearing room choked with cigar smoke and expert talk. They heard from a thousand witnesses, almost all of them making the same impassioned pleas for rate increases that had been so well rehearsed in the House. To add to their difficulties, Senator Borah had devoted his last days before the recess to principled troublemaking. He introduced a resolution on the Senate floor to confine revisions of the tariff strictly to agricultural products. On its face, Borah's resolution might have seemed helpful to Hoover, bringing Congress closer to the farm-friendly tariff he favored and closing the gap between agricultural and manufacturing rates. The intention of Borah's maneuver, however, was not to help the president but to expose the hypocrisy at the heart of the House bill. He knew that Republicans, on the whole, were more interested in industry than farming, and that they were using agricultural relief as a cover to deliver tariff increases to their friends in manufacturing. Borah called their bluff. If they were so interested in helping farmers, why not forgo the manufacturing elements of the bill?

Borah's gambit failed by a single vote, with Republican regulars and a handful of Democrats from industrial states insisting on higher manufacturing rates. The consequences of the resolution were nonetheless profound. The Senate was seen to be in favor of general and not limited revision of rates. Many began to wonder if Hoover, on the tariff issue, was not closer to the Democrats and insurgents than to his own party. What's more, Borah, by forcing senators to declare their positions without opportunity for equivocating or straddling, destroyed what meager appetite for compromise had existed in the chamber. All this while Smoot's bill was still being drafted.[25]

Smoot and his fellow Republicans emerged in late August with a revision of the Hawley act that increased farm rates while lowering select industrial rates. Here, finally, was a bill Hoover could accept. It seemed to him to give the farm bloc enough of a victory that the still sizable gap between agricultural and manufacturing tariff levels could be tolerated. Unfortunately for the president, the time for compromise had passed. Borah and the Democratic Senate leadership signaled that they believed the gap between agriculture and manufacturing still too large, and still more dissent came from Republican regulars who grumbled at the loss of Hawley's rich bounty of manufacturing increases.[26]

Hoover had a moment, as the Senate was returning from recess, to reconsider his legislative strategy in light of the mounting opposition. The extra session had already dragged on much longer than anticipated, and the prospect of success on tariffs seemed only to wane as the months ticked by. Congress was polarized with high-tariff Republican regulars at one end and the coalition of insurgents and

Democrats at the other. The latter group remained determined to revive the detested farm debenture and to strangle the flexible tariff provision that Hoover was counting on as the means to correct whatever inequities he found in the final draft. Borah's mischievous resolution in favor of strictly agricultural revisions had demonstrated that the coalition was only a vote or two from having the strength to rewrite the bill to suit itself. It was an opportune moment for a new plan, a brokered compromise, or perhaps an assertion of presidential leadership—anything to shake the intransigence of one or both camps and lead to a quick and reasonable solution.

Hoover chose to stay his course. His office merely reminded Republican senators once more of their campaign promises and offered no further guidance. All that can be said for his approach is that Hoover, a few months removed from launching the extra session with goodwill and high hopes, did not give the appearance of being rattled by opposition to his program.[27]

Smoot came out aggressively before the full Senate after Labor Day, trumpeting the merits of what was officially entitled "An Act to Provide Revenue, to Regulate Commerce with Foreign Countries, to Encourage the Industries of the United States and to Protect American Labor." He painted Borah and the farm-only brigade as internationalists unsympathetic to the needs of American business. He reminded the assembly that Hoover had taken forty states and received an unexampled mandate from the American people less than a year before, and intimated that his was the only version of tariff reform capable of commanding presidential support and avoiding a presidential veto.[28]

Smoot's opponents were not intimidated by the president's mandate or his veto power. Democratic senator Harrison of Mississippi called the bill "a legislative monstrosity" and suggested a more appropriate title would have been "An Act to Destroy Revenue, to Stifle Commerce with Foreign Countries, to Discourage Industries of the United States, to Flim-Flam American Labor and to Fleece the American Farmer." Borah, determined to drag Hoover, the man he had fought so hard to elect, into the debate on agriculture's side, joined his fellow insurgents in leaping on the one issue dear enough to the president to draw him from the shadows. Together they recommended that the flexible tariff provision be eliminated from Smoot's bill as an unwarranted expansion of presidential powers. This was a direct hit.[29]

Late on the afternoon of September 24, three days after a statement insisting that no presidential comment on the tariff was required, Hoover made his first on-the-record remarks on the subject since the start of the extra session. He spoke of the importance of allowing the Executive to increase or decrease a duty by 50 percent if recommended by the Tariff Commission; it was "a necessity in protection of the public interest." The pace of commerce, he said, was such that timely adjustments to individual rates could not wait for a once-a-decade opening of the full tariff schedule. Nor could Congress be trusted to expeditiously address a problematic individual rate without provoking "discussion all along the tariff line."[30]

The president had fallen headlong into a Borah trap. Two days later, the senator stood on the floor of his chamber, jowls shaking, and demanded to know why Hoover was sticking his nose into congressional business. He reminded his audience of the constitutional division of powers, lamenting an extensive history of presidential meddling in legislative affairs dating back to the Civil War. Having fully vented his outrage at the intervention he had invited, Borah niftily changed pace and asked the president, now that he had put himself on speaking terms with Congress, to extend his remarks beyond his defense of the flexible tariff provision. Hoover, said Borah, should declare his approval or lack thereof on industrial tariffs: "The President has put his hand to the plow. He cannot turn aside because of rough furrows."[31]

Hoover now had two choices, neither palatable: he could drop his strategy, take up Borah's challenge, and pronounce on tariff rates; or he could slink back into the shadows, never to be heard from again on tariff policy, at least not without making a larger issue of his leadership. He remained mum.


On October 2, the Senate voted 47–42 in favor of an amendment to remove the president's flexible tariff provision. Down went what Hoover had called "one of the most progressive steps taken in tariff making in all our history." Two weeks later, the coalition added to Hoover's embarrassment by attaching the agricultural debenture scheme to Smoot's bill in a 42–34 vote.[32]

The extra session was for all intents and purposes over. Opposed to the House bill and divided against itself, the Senate ran out the remaining seven weeks in a debauch of taunts, accusations, recriminations, and procedural argument. While nominally responsible for the chamber, the Republican regulars were in truth an impotent minority. They threw up their hands and forfeited any semblance of control to the insurgents, who in turn accepted no responsibility for outcomes and behaved as irregularly as their party affiliations. They spent endless hours squabbling over rates on metal-filament light bulbs as opposed to rates on light bulbs with nonmetallic filaments. They prosecuted a rhetorical war of the agricultural west against the industrial east, and another of the Senate against the House, and another of the insurgents against their Democratic coalition partners. On November 22, having spent ten fruitless weeks on Smoot's act, the extra session closed shop. Only eleven senators bothered to attend the adjournment. As per tradition, a congressional delegation knocked at the door of the White House to inform the president in language customary and risible that the body was retiring, having "completed its work."[33]

With the failure of the extra session came doubts. How had the Republican Party, that supposed bastion of efficiency and business-like practice, so quickly, and with a president in the White House, rendered itself unable to legislate on a critical issue in the glare of the national spotlight? Might this be the beginning of the end for what many still presumed to be America's natural governing party?[34]

Hoover's performance came under scrutiny. He had in fact made repeated efforts, behind the scenes, late in the session, to pull his party together. In a twenty-four-hour period in mid-October, he had met privately and individually with an array of Senate leaders in hopes of landing on a workable compromise. None was forthcoming. He met Borah, too, and engaged him in a conversation of mutual assurance that had no evident effect on the senator's conduct.

The president's inept public intervention in the Senate debacle had torched his cloak of invincibility, and emboldened Democrats began to attack him directly. Hoover's sole contribution to the tariff debate, jeered Senator Harrison, had been to reduce the rates on fishing tackle. Harrison blamed the chaos in Congress entirely on Hoover's leniency: "If the President would pluck up courage at this psychological time and let one group or the other in the Republican party know where he stands then we could either proceed with consideration of the bill or take other action."[35]

The lack of presidential leadership became a favorite theme of a resurgent Democratic National Committee. The committee had been overhauled in the wake of the Smith disaster of 1928, with a new national headquarters opened in Washington and a publicity bureau that issued daily attacks on Hoover and the tariff. "What sort of chief executive," asked Jouette Shouse, chair of the DNC's executive committee, "would sit back and permit his own Congress to make a larcenous hash of its whole session?"[36]

Other criticisms of Hoover were launched from closer to home, not least by Joseph Grundy, the manufacturers' lobbyist, newly appointed by Pennsylvania's governor, John Fisher, to fill a Republican Senate vacancy. He called Hoover an amateur. The president had never before held "even the office of dog catcher," said Grundy. "He doesn't know anything at all, from experience, of what legislation means."[37]

The question of where precisely Hoover had erred on the tariff issue became a debating topic in Washington. Some blamed his decision to open the tariff in the first place, others his choice to open it in a special session, others his misplaced faith in the erratic Borah. While there was some merit to all of these opinions, as there was in the Democratic charge that Hoover had failed to lead, it was Grundy's blatantly hostile comment that landed closest to the mark. Hoover's inability to manage Congress was rooted in a fundamental and amateurish misapprehension of his job. He had overestimated the degree to which the Executive could concentrate on administrative matters and delegate leadership of important political affairs.

To his credit, Hoover had come a long way in politics for a man with a stubborn distaste for most things political. His ascension to the presidency without benefit of the usual Republican machinery had duped him into thinking that he had little need of his party's congressional potentates. He had never adequately studied the maelstrom of competing interests on the Hill and the discord in Republican ranks. His relatively easy relations with Congress during his Commerce years had lulled him into complacency about legislative processes. "He didn't know where the votes came from," said one astonished Republican congressman. He was constantly surprised by the myriad motives, noble or otherwise, of political animals. Having foresworn the use of such valuable management tools as patronage and the presidential touch, he had few means of keeping legislators in line. Harding had possessed strong political talents and a far clearer sense of congressional relations than Hoover and still during his presidency had suffered spiky relations with the Senate.[38]

Lacking the broad sense of what it meant to be the duly elected executive head of the national government, having disdained to make the requisite personal investment in the success of his tariff initiative, and having delegated its management to a handful of knowledgeable but ineffectual congressional office holders, Hoover had invited failure. He had left a leadership vacuum that "the sons of the wild jackass" were glad to exploit. The question, now, was whether or not he could learn fast enough to recover his momentum.

# CHAPTER 20

# Nothing to Fear but Fear Itself

By midsummer of 1929, it was clear that Hoover's efforts to wrangle a runaway stock market had been no more successful than his bid for a short extra session. Secretary Mellon's advice to investors to favor bonds, recognized by the press as a highly unusual and significant intervention for a Treasury secretary, had nonetheless been ignored. Henry Robinson reported to the president that bankers in New York had scoffed at the notion that the markets were unsound: stock prices, they insisted, were warranted by the potency of a more technologically advanced economy. The NYSE's Whitney, who answered not to Hoover but to New York governor Franklin Roosevelt, had turned a blind eye to speculation. Editorial cautions against the risks of the stock exchange were meanwhile futile against the lure of massive returns.

Only one measure sponsored by Hoover met with even modest success: this was the wise and unparalleled effort of the Federal Reserve to directly pressure major New York banks to quit financing the brokers' loans that were stoking speculation in stocks. As the majors stepped aside, however, smaller banks, foreign banks, investment trusts, insurance companies, and corporations, all of them beyond the reach of the Federal Reserve System, were delighted to walk in and offer demand loans to speculators at 20 percent interest. The majors soon broke ranks and resumed lending for stock purchases. That their interest rates were fantastically high made no impression on investors. "When the public becomes mad with greed," lamented Hoover, "and is rubbing the Aladdin's lamp of sudden fortune, no little matter of interest rates is effective." He considered the New York bankers "iniquitous" for underwriting the speculation.[1]

The Federal Reserve, seeing share prices now almost double their mid-1927 level, and seeing brokers' loans up 50 percent to $8.5 billion since mid-1928, was by early August forced to admit that its direct pressure tactics had failed to halt speculation. It raised its discount rate from 5 to 6 percent. Hoover, by now despairing that anything short of disaster would rein in speculators, did not support the move. He worried for the effect of the rate hike on legitimate business activity, with good reason. The nation's business was reasonably stable: auto and machinery production had hit new highs in August, as did the iron and lumber industries. In retrospect, this would be identified as the peak of the business cycle, although policy makers had no way of knowing it at the time, lacking the tools to properly read the economic moment, let alone predict the economic future.[2]

There were almost immediate signs that the Fed had pushed too far with its rate hike. Interest-sensitive spending by companies and individuals stalled, and real output in the United States dropped almost 2 percent from August to October. Another unintended consequence of the increase was that foreign central banks raised their own interest rates in order to protect their gold supplies. These tight money policies helped push much of Central Europe further into depression.[3]

At first, the New York stock market seemed unfazed by the Fed's turn of the credit screw. Share indexes continued to advance through August: Radio Corporation of America, General Electric, and other darlings of the new economy led the charge. Businessmen riding their suburban club cars back to the city after a sweltering Labor Day weekend read newspaper stories about Wall Street's big winners, the fortunes they had made, and their foolproof methods of market forecasting. Everyone in the summer of 1929 was bullish on the markets, and bullish on America. The Dow Jones Industrial Average would close that very day, September 3, 1929, at a new high of 381.2, representing a stunning ascent of 500 percent from the start of the bull market in 1921.[4]

Prices would not hold that peak. They drifted lower in the coming weeks, with sudden plunges of as much as 5 percent, sufficient to rough up margin traders. Whether this retreat represented the correction that Hoover and other skeptics had expected, or whether there was more trouble to come, was anyone's guess. On October 19, Thomas Lamont, acting head of J. P. Morgan and the leading financier in the nation, wrote Hoover a twenty-page letter advising faith in the markets and proclaiming it wonderful that small investors were continuing to put their life savings into stocks, allowing them to own pieces of America's greatest companies. "This document is fairly amazing," Hoover scrawled on the letter.[5]

Irving Fisher of Yale University, considered by some the greatest economist America has ever produced, declared in a New York speech of October 21 that share prices were not inflated, that stocks were not yet reflecting their real underlying values, and that history was a poor guide to the performance of the market:

> During the past six years there have been pronounced changes in the tempo of production and trade, due to the vast increment of scientific research and application of inventions. Virtually every line of manufacture witnesses daily technical development that results in a greater total of products, at reduced costs, greater profits and lower prices to consumers.[6]

Within a couple of days, Fisher was proved wrong.

Hoover was out of town when it happened, traveling to Dearborn, Michigan, for the dedication of the Edison Institute and a celebration of the fiftieth anniversary of its namesake's invention of the incandescent light bulb. The event had been organized by Henry Ford, patron of the institute. Hoover admired both Ford and the eighty-two-year-old Edison, and he appeared to be in a good mood at a glittering dinner with the likes of Marie Curie and Orville Wright. In a broadcast speech, he gave America a glimpse of that rare phenomenon, the droll Hoover. He enumerated the benefits of electric light:

> It enables us to postpone our spectacles for a few years longer; it has made reading in bed infinitely more comfortable; by merely pushing a button we have introduced the element

of surprise in dealing with burglars; the goblins that lived in dark corners and under the bed have now been driven to the outdoors; evil deeds which inhabit the dark have been driven back into the farthest retreats of the night; it enables our cities and towns to clothe themselves in gaiety by night, no matter how sad their appearance by day. And by all its multiple uses it has lengthened the hours of our active lives, decreased our toil, and enabled us to read the type in the telephone book.[7]

The next day, Wednesday, October 23, the Dow Jones Industrial Average gave up 6.33 percent of its value in a wrenching trading session on Wall Street. Reactions to the Wednesday decline are perhaps the best measure of the severity of the stock market collapse we know as the Great Crash of 1929, which did not start until the following day, Black Thursday, October 24. Wednesday's losses on the New York exchange, where trading volume exceeded 6 million shares, reached a sickening $4 billion, more than the annual federal budget. "The market crumbled," wrote the *New York Times*. "Fear and apprehension swept feeble support aside and dropped prices lower and lower with practically each succeeding sale. . . . In the last hour of trading, values fairly melted away." Traders and the financial press spoke of a once-in-a-generation rout destined to rank among "the most tragic hours in the stock market's history." And they had only heard the overture.[8]

In Black Thursday's sell-off, shares changed hands at a rate of 2.6 million an hour. A thousand brokers shouted and sweated at their posts on the littered trading floor. Newsreel cameras captured a massive crowd milling anxiously on the street in front of the NYSE's noble white façade. Extra police and ambulances were called in answer to wild rumors of riots (nonexistent) and suicides (several but later in the week). Records were broken for shares traded, for price drops, for money lost, for telegraphs delivered and telephone calls made.

Late in the afternoon Thomas Lamont of J. P. Morgan emerged to say that he and other leading financiers had confidence in the market and the broader economy. This momentarily stemmed the panic, but in succeeding days the declines continued in almost ritualistic fashion. Unbridled fear brought more panic selling, brought more havoc on the trading floor, brought more smashed records, brought more sickening losses, brought increasingly dubious reassurances from financiers and public officials that the system was merely purging speculators and gamblers, that the session's violent convulsions represented a market bottom, and that normalization was only a sunrise away.

So it went for a long and devastating week. Buyers of shares were knocked from tentative to frightened to scarce. The deluge of selling swept everything before it. Victims ranged from the humblest punters to chairmen of blue-chip boards. Losses totaled $30 billion, a sum nearly twice the national debt, a sum almost equivalent to what America spent in the Great War. Finally there was no last line of investors or bankers to offer reassurance, just surrender all around. The clerks and brokers who had spent long nights at their desks desperate to salvage something of their holdings finally gave up and went home, leaving the canyons of Wall Street in still and eerie silence.[9]

Wall Street's periodic panics had always occurred offstage so far as Washington was concerned. The two hundred miles of coastline between D.C. and Lower Manhattan tangibly supported the laissez-faire attitude of political leaders toward the financial community, as well as money's desire to be left to its own devices. Many in both capitals continued to believe that mutual aloofness desirable even as automobiles, air travel, radio, newsreels, and telephony were making the distance less relevant. Walter Lippmann thought it foolhardy of the administration to interfere with the natural laws of economics and try to guide business through its crisis. Hoover's own Treasury secretary agreed. "Mr. Mellon had only one formula," wrote Hoover years later. "Liquidate labor, liquidate stocks, liquidate the farmers, liquidate real estate. . . . It will purge the rottenness out of the system. High costs of living and high living will come down. People will work harder, live a more moral life."[10]

Hoover had been arguing for more interaction between power and money since his first days as commerce secretary. He had no doubt that the growth of a national economy, the creation of the Federal Reserve System, and the expectations of the style of activist government he embodied warranted Washington's intercession in an economic crisis.

Hoover viewed the Wall Street crash as an opportunity to implement the countercyclical policies he had advocated from his skunk works in the Harding administration during the downturn of 1920–21. He could distinguish himself from the inert Coolidge and win respite from the frustrations of the tariff debacle by launching himself directly and constructively into the path of an urgent problem. It was just the sort of emergency the American people had with so much confidence elected him to meet.

With no other means of measuring the depth of the damage, Hoover ordered staff to produce studies of previous market debacles, with emphasis on the Panic of 1907. In that instance, a market crash had led immediately to runs on banks and trust companies, a spike in interest rates, a liquidity crisis, and a litter of financial failures. This precedent convinced Hoover that the crisis needed to be contained to the stock market. During and immediately following the crash, he reassured Americans that the underlying U.S. economy was sturdy. He reminded them that the Federal Reserve System had been created after the Panic of 1907 in part to give policymakers the tools to prevent a stock market crisis from extending to broader industrial activities.[11]

The Federal Reserve Bank of New York did rise to the occasion in 1929, making capital available by purchasing government securities on the open market, expediting lending through its discount window, and quickly lowering its discount rate back down to 5 percent, and to 4.5 percent by mid-November. These measures helped to keep commercial banks open for business and limited the damage. The president rightly credited the Fed with prompt and effective action.[12]

With the banks steady, Hoover identified panic as America's next major threat. "We are dealing here with a psychological situation to a very considerable degree," he said. "It is a question of fear." Ordinary citizens were worried about their savings, their jobs, and how to pay their bills. If nothing was done, consumption would fall, production would slow, unemployment would creep up. Hoover determined to "disabuse the public mind" of the notion that there had been "any serious or vital interruption in our economic system."[13]

He spent the first two weeks of November in private consultation with financiers, his cabinet, and other administration officials, devising a program to buoy public confidence. By November 14, with Wall Street still face down in the gutter, he was ready for action. As an initial step, Secretary Mellon and a bipartisan group of congressional leaders committed themselves to a 1 percent cut in personal and corporate taxes in the December session as proof of their faith in the economy and as an aid to recovery. These measures, together with the Fed rate cuts, seemed to have the desired effect. The Dow promptly picked itself up, dusted itself off, improving on its previous day's close of 198.7 points (roughly half of the early September peak). This suggested a floor had been reached.[14]

The following day, Hoover summoned business, farm, and labor leaders to Washington to enlist their support in shifting the economy's attention from stock speculation to constructive capital investment. "The postponement of construction during the past months," said the president, "including not only buildings, railways, merchant marine and public utilities, but also Federal, State and municipal public works, provides a substantial reserve for prompt and expanded action." The coordination of business and government, he promised, would ensure the construction trades were activated at scale and with dispatch. Hoover made it explicit that his initiatives were designed to boost confidence. In market booms, he said, a climate of excessive optimism prevails, to be followed in the inevitable bust by a reverse into excessive pessimism:

> They are equally unjustified but the sad thing is that many unfortunate people are drawn into the vortex of these movements with tragic loss of savings and reserves. Any lack of confidence in the economic future or the basic strength of business in the United States is foolish. Our national capacity for hard work and intelligent cooperation is ample guarantee of the future.[15]

Hoover's intention was to teach the public that downturns were regularly recurring economic phenomena better answered with rational plans than with pandemonium. "The problems with which we are confronted," he said, "are the problems of growth and of progress. In their solution we have to determine the facts, to develop the relative importance to be assigned to such facts, to formulate a common judgment upon them, and to realize solutions in a spirit of conciliation." To further demonstrate his composure, Hoover would speak of a "depression" rather than use the customary terms "crisis" or "panic."[16]

On November 19, Hoover sat at the head of his cabinet table in front of eight railway leaders whom he hounded into agreeing to spend a billion dollars on capital projects in 1930. The next day, the same table saw an all-star gathering of business leaders, the greatest show of corporate muscle in the capital since the Great War. Henry Ford, Pierre du Pont, Julius Rosenwald of Sears Roebuck, Walter Teagle of Standard Oil, Owen D. Young of General Electric, and Alfred P. Sloan of General Motors heard Hoover ask for restraint from application of the usual corporate responses to economic storms, namely retrenchment, layoffs, and wage cuts. He wanted them to maintain wages in order to sustain consumption, at least until the cost of living fell. He told them that if they would forgo layoffs he would request that labor forgo the sort of strike actions that had unsettled the country in the depression of 1921. The tycoons agreed and turned the cabinet table over to a caucus of union chieftains led by William Green of the American Federation of Labor. They, too, fell into line and promised labor peace. Hoover insisted that all of these agreements were voluntary and, but for the full weight of his office, they were.[17]

Hoover did not dwell on the stock market crash in his State of the Union address of December 3. He invited legislators and the public to take the market meltdown in stride. There was no cause for panic or fear. In the past year the nation had grown in strength, advanced in comfort, gained in knowledge, maintained its moral and spiritual foundations, and worked harder than ever before to establish peace in the world. The rational expectation for the year ahead, he said, was more of the same.[18]

Two days later he told members of the U.S. Chamber of Commerce that while there would necessarily be some unemployment as a result of the market crash, it was their responsibility to ensure that the first shock of adjustment fell as much as possible on profits and not on wages. This would contribute to the dampening of "undue pessimism" in the economy. It was also the right thing to do: "The very fact that you gentlemen come together for these broad purposes represents an advance in the whole conception of the relationship of business to public welfare. This is a far cry from the arbitrary and dog-eat-dog attitude of the business world some thirty or forty years ago."[19]

The Seventy-First Congress immediately delivered to Hoover his requested reduction in corporate and income taxes. The administration announced an increase in the federal building program and the granting of seagoing mail contracts to encourage shipbuilding. It continued to urge businesses and lower levels of government to take advantage of low interest rates and idle labor and ramp up capital investment. By the end of the year, business and government at all levels were reported to have pledged more than $4 billion in new building to keep the economy moving.[20]

The sweep and speed of Washington's response to the crash, which gave the impression that Hoover had "thoroughly anticipated the debacle and mapped out the shortest road to recovery," was hailed in the press as an entirely new approach to management of the nation's economic affairs. Said the *Herald-Tribune* in its year-end summary:

> President Hoover's prompt action to prevent the depression extending to business and industry saved the situation. The "panic" was checked in a few days. Wages were left unaffected; stabilization was insured; production was encouraged to continue as usual. This leadership was all the more notable, since it was practically the first of the sort ever to originate in the White House.[21]

The *Evening Post* believed none of the president's remedies were as important as his leadership. He had succeeded in "imparting to the business of the country the idea that it was possible for it to avert the consequences of the Wall Street crash and that it was its duty and privilege to do so. What business entered upon with some misgivings when it was summoned to Washington, it will carry out with enthusiasm in somewhat the spirit with which it cooperated with the Government to win the Great War."[22]

The *Evening Post* had a point. Some of Hoover's moves were largely symbolic. Tax rates were so low at the time that a cut of one point, while proportionately impressive, made a small difference in a worker's discretionary income. Hoover's federal public works expenditures, even including $140 million pledged by Congress in the

New Year, were piddling next to $2 billion spent at the state level and $9 billion in private construction. The fact was that the federal government, spending just 3 percent of GDP, was too small to influence business activity on its own. Nor did it have the capacity to suddenly ramp up billions in new spending, hence Hoover's frequent encouragements to state and local governments to undertake public works. Providing leadership and inspiration to the investments of others was the most constructive thing he could do at that point in the crisis.[23]

It was the psychological dimension of Hoover's approach to righting the economy that struck editorialists as radical, so much so that they struggled to articulate it. The *Times* said Hoover had attempted to work "a sort of mental transformation," a change in "the mental attitude of a whole people," substituting confidence and hope for fear and apprehension:

> It is little to say that no President but Mr. Hoover would have gone about the business in the way chosen by him. No other President would have had the necessary knowledge or aptitude, born of practice, even if he had possessed the inclination. With extraordinary promptness and skill President Hoover made up his lists of railroad men, bankers, captains of industry, representatives of organized labor, whom he brought together at the White House day after day, not to lecture them, or impose his will upon them, but to elicit from them in friendly conference opinions and judgments which could be given out in summary to the whole country. It has been a fine piece of work, and there can be no doubt that a helpful spirit of reassurance has gone out from the White House to permeate the whole land.[24]

Economists joined journalists in congratulating Hoover on what was easily the most sophisticated response to a major economic event by any administration. "For the first time in our history," wrote Keynesian forerunners William Trufant Foster and Waddill Catchings, "a President of the United States is taking aggressive leadership in guiding private business through a crisis."[25]

At year's end, just two months after what Keynes himself would call "one of the greatest economic catastrophes in modern history," just two months after Wall Street was written off as a land of "vanished hopes, of curiously silent apprehension, and of a paralyzed hypnosis," the country, while still cautious, appeared firm on its feet. There had been no bank runs or significant bank failures, no massive layoffs by leading employers, no unusual labor unrest, and no aftermath of public hysteria.[26]

Opinion was divided on the question of whether or not America was headed for a general recession. Professor Fisher did not believe so, and even among the bears, the consensus was that any downturn would be brief. All other corrections since the founding of the Federal Reserve had been short, however sharp, and they had not been met with the bold leadership of the Hoover administration.[27]

Handsomely as Hoover came through the crash, there was no question that it was a stroke of bad luck for his presidency. The Coolidge bull market was over, and it soon became clear that even if the havoc was contained, the economy was in a swoon. Industrial activity fell 9 percent in the last quarter of the year. Consumer demand slowed and commodity prices, too, were slipping.[28]

Shortly after lighting Washington's community Christmas tree and making a national radio address, Hoover joined Lou for a families' dinner party in the state dining room in the White House. The Marine Band played songs of the season while children played games. In the basement below, a switchboard operator noticed smoke curling into his room. He notified the duty policeman. By the time they located the source of the problem, smoke and flames were pouring out of the West Wing's windows. Hoover was about to share his dessert with Susanne Boone, the physician's daughter, when a staffer interrupted him with the news. He instructed the band to keep playing, grabbed his overcoat, and rushed out onto the frozen south lawn. He was preparing to direct the firefighting himself when Secret Service men reminded him of his eminence and hustled him off the scene. He reappeared moments later on the roof of the West Terrace, which connected the White House and the West Wing and afforded a premium view. He lit a cigar and watched calmly as Allan Hoover and members of the presidential staff pulled his personal files out of danger. Nineteen fire engines, representing practically the whole of the Washington brigade, arrived to battle the blaze. An unruffled Lou, seeing no reason to break off the party, distributed Christmas gifts to the children as the sirens wailed.

The fire was not declared out until 7:27 a.m. Fifteen firemen were injured in the fight. The cause was eventually traced to the overheated flue of an open fireplace in Secretary Newton's office. The West Wing was gutted.[29]


Any hopes that the young Hoover administration could bury the ashes of 1929 and start afresh in the New Year were dashed by a glance at the legislative calendar, promising as it did the resumption of the tariff debate that had been left hanging at the end of the extra session. Hoover's State of the Union address had failed to give Congress any new direction in the matter beyond asking that the legislation be expedited. Senators therefore contented themselves through January and February with sitting on their hard leather seats reading newspapers while colleagues stood one after another to beg a few more points of protection for camphor, bread, lard, lumber, etcetera. Hoover held himself as still as Coolidge ever had.

It was still more logrolling that finally broke the Senate deadlock. Grundy and an army of lobbyists struck enough deals for higher rates with enough insurgents and Democratic senators to win the advantage for protectionist Republicans. Smoot's bill was approved in the Senate on March 25, 1930. A House-Senate conference returned the president's flexibility provision to the legislation and removed the agricultural debenture. The unified bill put rates closer to the House version than the Senate version. It remained to be seen if the president would approve.[30]

Despite having passed both chambers, what would come to be known as the Smoot-Hawley tariff bill was less popular than ever. Borah and the Democrats continued to attack it as a betrayal of agriculture. Republicans disliked it, although they could not agree why: committed protectionists believed that the industrial rates were too low while administration loyalists thought they were too high and a violation of their campaign promises to farmers. The general public agreed with Lippmann that the act was "a wretched and mischievous product of stupidity and greed." Hoover's correspondence secretary told him "there has seldom been in this country such a rising tide of protest as has been aroused by the tariff bill." Editorial opinion in forty-three states opposed the bill and more than thirty foreign nations were bombarding the State Department with protests.[31]

Piling on to this dissent was a coalition of 1,028 economists, representing the very discipline that Hoover had piloted to the main stage of political discourse over the previous decade. It called the bill a mistake and urged that the president, Washington's foremost promoter of expert opinion, veto it. The economists had strong arguments: tariffs were already high, and international relations would be embittered by new American barriers to trade.[32]

But Hoover had no intention of vetoing the bill. He had engaged in tariff reform for political rather than economic reasons, and politics urged his signature. To reject the bill at this late stage would be to repudiate the work of his congressional colleagues, and to frustrate the many Republican congressmen planning to run on the fruits of their high-tariff efforts. It would mean an ignoble capitulation to the insurgents and the Democrats who had been determined to thwart and embarrass the administration. It would mean that Hoover cared more about tariff rates, on which he had been silent, than he did about the flexible tariff and the removal of the debenture, both of which he had promoted, and both of which were reflected in the final bill. It would also mean that he had wasted much of the first half of his term on a great legislative misadventure. In a quiet White House ceremony at 1 p.m. on June 17, Hoover signed the Tariff Act of 1930 and made the following statement:

It contains many compromises between sectional interests and between different industries. No tariff bill has ever been enacted or ever will be enacted under the present system that will be perfect. A large portion of the items are always adjusted with good judgment, but it is bound to contain some inequalities and inequitable compromises. . . .

I believe that the flexible provisions can within reasonable time remedy inequalities, and that this provision is a progressive advance and gives great hope of taking the tariff away from politics, lobbying, and logrolling.[33]

·  ·  ·

Despite the hubbub, the economic impact of Smoot-Hawley was negligible. It moved the average tariff on dutiable imports in the U.S.
from already high to slightly higher. The legislation was responsible
for a 5 percent decline in American imports, an insignificant amount
when dutiable imports represented just 4 percent of GDP in 1929. It
did spread discriminatory trade policies internationally, most notably
in the British Commonwealth, although by the spring of 1930 the
depression itself was responsible for most of the damage to global
trade volumes. Farmers received no real benefit from the bill, not
surprisingly, in that they faced almost no foreign competition.[34]

The real impact of Smoot-Hawley was political, and it was
Hoover who paid the price. He had started off talking about taking
the politics out of tariffs, and in the end the politicians had carried the
day, exposing him as a weak and inexperienced legislative manager
with no real control over his party. His claim of victory on the flexible
tariff provision was mere face saving: the slightly improved process
would prove just as cumbersome and seldom used as the old.

Ugly as it was, the end of the tariff fight was liberating for Hoover
on several fronts. It brought an end to an embarrassing political spectacle. It signaled the finish of the Second Session of the Seventy-First
Congress and the beginning of a five-month break in legislative activity on the Hill. It also removed a cloud of uncertainty from the economic horizon.[35]

There had undoubtedly been a slump in the first quarter of 1930.
Automobile production, steel production, and petroleum production
were all down, as were department store sales and wholesale prices.
The depth of the decline, however, was difficult to ascertain. Hoover
read economics texts by the dozen and continued to look backward
at recoveries from previous downturns, studying month-by-month
data to estimate where the nation might be in the business cycle. He
recognized that this was an imprecise exercise and grew frustrated by
the dearth of reliable economic data. As always, he turned to experts
to fill the gaps, appointing, for instance, a committee of statisticians
to advise the government on methods of determining true rates of
unemployment, which were elusive at the time. As he waited for its
work, he had no choice but to guess and, true to a defensive nature,
he tended to choose the most optimistic slices of whatever data was

available. In fairness to him, even the more pessimistic reckonings of unemployment in early 1930 indicated that unemployment was nowhere near the peaks of 10 percent or 12 percent reached during the depression of 1921. Nor did the GDP appear to be headed for anything like the 23 percent decline of that previous calamity.[36]

By June, with the weather warming and the White House gardens in full bloom, Hoover was increasingly optimistic about the overall state of the economy. Among other positive signs, business and political leaders appeared to be following his advice to increase capital spending. The $4 billion worth of projects that had been inaugurated by the end of January was augmented in ensuing weeks. By March, thirty-six states were reporting either no unusual unemployment or only moderate and declining unemployment. Joblessness amounting to distress was centered in just twelve states, and in all but one of them governors reported that conditions were improving. The stock market was up 16 percent over the first half of 1930, recovering the level it had held the previous spring. Commodity future prices were above actual prices. Foreign lending was back to the pace of 1929 and industrial production was accelerating. With the Federal Reserve discount rate at 3 percent and falling, credit seemed cheap, and there had been no major banking or industrial failures. Employers had more or less kept their commitment to hold wages, and labor was at peace. Weaknesses remained, notably in steadily declining price levels, but a corner appeared to have been turned.[37]

Hoover went out on a short limb and assured Americans that "we have now passed the worst." He told the Chamber of Commerce at its annual dinner in the Washington Auditorium:

> We are not yet entirely through the difficulties of our situation. We have need to maintain every agency and every force that we have placed in motion until we are far along on the road to stable prosperity. He would be a rash man who would state that we can produce the economic millennium, but there is great assurance that America is finding herself upon the road to secure social satisfaction, with the preservation of private industry, initiative, and a full opportunity for the development of the individual.[38]

In thanking the business leaders in his audience for their part in the fight against economic ruin, Hoover made a bid for the historic nature of their mutual campaign:

> On the occasion of this great storm we have for the first time attempted a great economic experiment, possibly one of the greatest of our history. By cooperation between Government officials and the entire community, business, railways, public utilities, agriculture, labor, the press, our financial institutions and public authorities, we have undertaken to stabilize economic forces; to mitigate the effects of the crash and to shorten its destructive period. I believe I can say with assurance that our joint undertaking has succeeded to a remarkable degree.[39]

Hoover was not alone in his optimism. Salvation Army workers in the Bowery reported that breadlines, swollen by as much as 50 percent over the winter, were now closing. Summer bookings for European travel were at a record high. Financial forecasters, including Moody's, predicted rapid economic improvement, and the Harvard Economic Society, which had in November declared that a serious depression was "outside the range of probability," which had in January declared that "the severest phase of the recession" was over, which had in March declared that America was "definitely on the road to recovery," now declared that a "vigorous" upturn was due in the third quarter. One of the better minds in the Democratic Party, Bernard Baruch, lamented to a friend that Hoover would "have a rising tide" before the 1932 election, "and then he will be pictured as the great master mind who led the country out of its economic misery." That the predicted uptick in economic activity did not transpire in the summer of 1930 had little effect on the optimistic consensus. "Untoward elements have operated to delay recovery," said the Harvard experts, "but evidence nonetheless points to substantial improvement."[40]

Hoover spent the summer resisting further countercyclical measures on the understanding that recovery was on the way and that further effort would gild the lily. He instead directed his energies toward a drought that scorched large parts of the Midwest and the South in July and August, threatening the crops and livestock of a million farm families. At the drought's epicenter in Arkansas, temperatures reached one hundred degrees every day but one in a forty-three-day period. Farmers spoke of apples cooking on the tree and corn popping on the stalk. Feed stock was destroyed in the hardest-hit states, and some two thousand farm families in Arkansas lost their food crops as well.[41]

It was the kind of emergency Hoover had addressed so many times before, and he approached it, said his friend Mark Sullivan, almost with a sense of relief: like the prison crisis of the previous summer, the drought was a tangible problem, something he could get his hands on, unlike financial panics or slippery tariff boosters. A presidential holiday to the Rockies was canceled. Governors of the affected states were invited to Washington to make "definite plans for organization of relief." The Red Cross, among other charitable institutions, pledged $5 million in aid to afflicted families. Drought committees were set up in every state under the auspices of prominent citizens. Railways would haul feed to afflicted areas at half rates. Road-building projects were organized to create temporary work for busted farmers.[42]

In early September, a sudden deluge brought relief to the parched acres, and the drought receded from the nation's front pages, although not before ensuring another harsh year for farmers in the months leading to the midterm congressional elections.


Hoover was concerned for his party's fate in the midterms. He did not much care what happened in the Senate, doubting that the chamber could do worse. The House was another matter: he was desperate to hold his advantage, feeling that anything less would reflect poorly on his performance and make it difficult for him to govern effectively. He understood that the usual dynamic was for incumbent parties to lose seats in the congressional election, but it was not historic norms, or the state of the economy, or the tariff outcome that seemed to him the greatest threat going into the election season. His deepest concern was over something new and, for Hoover, ominous in American political life.

James MacLafferty, a bouncy former California congressman

who served as the administration's liaison with the House, had a habit of stopping by the White House around 8 a.m. to catch the president before he started his day. He happened to be in Hoover's office one August morning in time to hear an anxious rant about John J. Raskob's Democratic National Committee and its determined efforts to "malign me and to undermine my influence."

It had been customary for the national committees of the two great parties to remain silent and even shut down between presidential campaigns. Throughout the 1920s, the single permanent employee of the DNC had been an obscure and shiftless wreck of an ex-newspaperman who needed the paltry salary. After the 1928 election, however, the Democrats had retooled in a magnificent way. Raskob, as party chairman and chief financier, had committed $250,000 to what *Scribner's* called "a first-class, high-grade, sixteen-cylinder publicity machine." It would spend the entire interval between national elections attempting to reduce Herbert Hoover to human scale. Raskob rented a whole floor in the National Press building, filled it with clerks, secretaries, stenographers, and enough equipment to run a state-of-the-art media company. Installed at the center of this emporium was Charley Michelson, a fair-haired man with a patrician air that belied his frontier origins. A fine writer and a world-class controversialist trained in the Hearst stable, Michelson had abandoned the Washington bureau of the *New York World* to attack Republicans full-time. He was a thick cut above the hacks typically employed in political offices, and he had a $25,000 salary to prove it.[43]

Since Inauguration Day, 1929, Michelson had been bedeviling Hoover in an extraordinary and unprecedented manner. He had written many thousands of words magnifying Hoover's mistakes and belittling his achievements. On learning that a colony of unemployed men in Chicago had dubbed their shanty town "Hooverville," Michelson adopted the phrase and made it a national joke. He found more defects and weaknesses in Hoover than one man could possibly possess, and succeeded in imprinting in at least part of the public mind an image of an inept and indecisive leader bewildered by events and the responsibilities of office. The burden of practically every line Michelson wrote was to ask how a supposed economic genius had landed the country in a depression.[44]

What added immeasurably to Michelson's potency was his novel method of distribution. Publicity offices of the major parties had traditionally produced reams of canned editorials and statements that only partisan newspapers would find publishable. Michelson, with no pride of authorship, put his words in the mouths of Democratic members of the Senate and House, who delivered speeches and granted interviews that landed Michelson's barbs and insights on the front pages of even the quality papers. The Democratic base perked up. Wayward Democrats found their way back to the fold. More tension developed between Hoover, his partisans in the House and Senate, and the American people. Michelson was almost single-handedly bringing the party of Al Smith back from the dead at a time of unaccustomed vulnerability for Republicans.

Hoover had no answer for Michelson. The Republican National Committee had closed its national publicity office after Hoover's victory. The committee was so weak in leadership that the president felt obliged to manage the congressional elections out of his own office. He and MacLafferty produced speaking notes blaming Democrats for the delay in passing the tariff and for the weakness of the economic recovery. MacLafferty repeatedly asked permission to unleash the Ku Klux Klan on Raskob, a noted Catholic. Hoover's "natural sensitiveness was wounded" at this suggestion, said MacLafferty, who thought him weak. As a team, the president and his men were hopelessly outclassed by Michelson.[45]

At Hoover's insistence, his office camouflaged its part in the congressional races, modest as it was. He did not want the accountability, and he did not want the bother. To campaign personally would have been to expose himself to the endless annoyances of receptions and parades, of glad-handing, posturing, and speechmaking on someone else's behalf. He might have had to travel, and he might have to answer questions to which he had no answers: the future of Prohibition, for instance. He preferred to work at his desk on what he considered the real problems vexing the nation.

Congressional Republicans did not miss him in the campaign. Hoover's leadership of the party was increasingly nominal. He had made little effort to know his caucuses and as a result he was unknown to them. He operated as though he did not need them and owed them nothing, and they learned to reciprocate. They did not fear him or crave his regard or affection. They were increasingly indifferent to him. Stubborn and inexperienced, he remained baffled that they could not face an issue as he faced an issue and see what he saw.

The truth was that Hoover and his congressmen were looking past one another, playing different games. The latter, as a body, had an experience of politics that was more personal and tribal than anything the president knew. In Washington, they were each one of 531 elected members of Congress. The press did not camp on their doorsteps, they needed to shout to be heard, they accumulated influence on the Hill by force of personality, by strategic alliance, and by seniority. They maintained their relevance back home by pushing local priorities, by riding single issues, and by grabbing headlines. The game was not of their making. It was a consequence of the constitutionally mandated congressional system.

Hoover was so sincere and determined in his efforts to rise above partisan politics that it probably never occurred to him how injurious his antipolitical lectures were to fellow Republicans. He was forever contrasting the high-minded, knowledgeable, and dispassionate public servant with the noisy, vote-grubbing, lobby-haunting politician, the man "prolific with drama and the headlines," the man of "reckless ambition" and "demagogic folly," of "vainglory," of "the hustings." He seems not to have been entirely conscious of the fact that his answer to almost every problem, whether Prohibition, the tariff, or the economy, was to take the politics out of it and hand it over to the experts or commissions of impartial thinkers he considered to be free of political toxins. His conferences, of which there were as many as two dozen running at a time in Washington, were a deliberate effort to bypass Congress and treat problems of government in the efficient and evidence-based manner he believed necessary in an increasingly complex and fast-changing world.[46]

Hoover was neither the first nor the last political leader to recognize that his job would be easier without politics. Congress has always been a circus, and compromise with it has always been to some extent self-defeating, and the increasing complexity of government has long required the best intelligence the nation has on offer. Hoover had his points, yet they were all beside the point. He was again misreading the requirements of his position: he needed to lead his party, Congress,

and the people, as well as to solve problems. His efforts to bypass necessary political institutions were doomed to failure. Taking the noise,
the conflict, the special pleading out of the system was taking the air
from the legislators' lungs and denying electors their representatives.
His choice was between political engagement and political defeat.

Election day, November 4, was dull and rainy across the Eastern
Seaboard. The cabinet met and engaged in a morose discussion of
Republican prospects. The secretaries blamed Prohibition as much
as the economy for what they expected would be a poor showing.
Stimson's diary record of the conversation proves the extent to which
Hoover had built his cabinet in his own image:

> The sentiment of the meeting was that the prohibition ques-
> tion must be put up in some way to the electorate in the form
> of a new amendment put forward but not endorsed by the
> Administration or the Republican party, so as to give the peo-
> ple of the nation a chance to vote on the question again and
> settle it, and, if possible, take the embarrassing question out
> of politics.[47]

The Republicans lost fifty-two seats in the House but still held a
one-seat majority when the polls closed. They lost eight seats in the
Senate, leaving them tied with the Democrats. The vice president's
tie-breaking vote gave the GOP nominal control of the Senate, but
the insurgents returned a sizable caucus, leaving real control as elusive
as ever. More impressively, Republicans maintained a nine-point lead
over the Democrats in the popular vote. Their losses were concentrated in farm states and in the South, where Democratic voters, no
longer alienated by Al Smith, resumed their traditional allegiances.
The elections, in sum, were a setback, not at all a repudiation.[48]

Hoover nevertheless took the outcome hard, reading it as a vote
of nonconfidence in himself. MacLafferty rolled into the president's
office the morning after, bearing results that had missed the deadlines
of the morning papers. "Well?" asked Hoover, his face pale and serious, his eyes red and tired "as if he had been concentrating on close
work." MacLafferty informed him that the Republican margin in the

House was unlikely to hold and then took him state by state through the Senate races. "It looks bad," said Hoover with discouragement in his voice. He got up from his chair and paced the floor.[49]

MacLafferty blamed the results on Michelson's "dirty work," and got no argument from his leader. They discussed the need for a new RNC organization and tried, with no success, to think who could chair it. "That's the trouble," said Hoover as he stopped pacing. "I canvassed lists for weeks to find the right man. Lists of lawyers, businessmen, and others. I simply could not find the man, it seemed impossible." They also discussed Prohibition, with MacLafferty arguing that the Republicans needed to consider a repeal of the Eighteenth Amendment. He believed it had caused them more trouble than the economy in the midterms and that it would cause them more trouble still in 1932 when the Democrats were likely to run on a wet platform. Hoover countered that aping the Democrats would do nothing to sustain the authority of Republicanism.

Both the chairmanship of the RNC and the party's Prohibition stance were left unresolved at the end of their conversation. MacLafferty left the White House shaking his head at Hoover's lack of political guile and regretting that the president could not be excused from political duties. "What a pity," he said, "that Herbert Hoover is not permitted to give all his thoughts and time to serving the people of our country instead of being plagued and tortured by those infinitely beneath him in character, ability and decency."[50]

# CHAPTER 21

# Just When We Thought It Was Over

*When one walks around New York now, away from its more cosmopolitan paths, in streets where flow the business and industry of the city, one finds the unemployed on every corner, in almost every doorway where there is no activity. They saunter by silently, and strangely enough they seldom beg. . . . These men want work, and they want it badly, so badly they don't like to speak of their need.*

That paragraph, written in the last weeks of 1930 by the legendary New York newsman Russell Owen, described a recent phenomenon on the city's streets: the new unemployed, men who had little in common with the perpetually unemployed, the "floaters" and casual laborers who haunted the city's breadlines and soup kitchens even in good times. These were "white collar" workers, former managers and supervisors, people accustomed to providing for families, and it was their presence on the street that "stamps this unemployment situation as somewhat different from that which existed in previous years."

Although many of these men had sold their overcoats, wrote Owen, they were generally neat and well dressed. Some carried bundles under their arms with spare shirts, a clean collar, a bar of soap, and a canvas sheet under which to flop at night. They slept on benches or rode the streetcars until dawn and visited employment offices in daylight, or sold apples on street corners. They slid timorously into the doorways of Salvation Army shelters for their meals, lining up for bowls of soup, hats low over their eyes, staring straight ahead, silent, "bent on some inner misery of spirit."[1]

· · ·

Owen's was among the very first in an emerging genre of stories describing a profusion of human damage that marked this depression as out of the ordinary. Now heading into its second winter, the slump was frighteningly deep and tenacious, compounding the suffering of the indigent and sharing their pain with classes of people generally buffered against severe loss and privation. The last weeks of 1930 mocked earlier assumptions of a quick economic rebound. In addition to the social trauma described by Owen, they brought an abrupt end to what had been the most reassuring trend of the decline. Hoover had been one of many to take solace in the absence of bank failures since the crash. A mid-November crisis in Nashville robbed him of that crutch.[2]

Caldwell and Company was the largest banking chain in the South, with $200 million in assets. It was also overextended and vulnerable to the drought and collapsing farm incomes. It closed its doors in mid-November and was followed in short order by more than a hundred associated institutions in Kentucky, Arkansas, North Carolina, and elsewhere in Tennessee. The closures shook the faith of depositors, who began pulling funds from even healthy banks throughout the region. Only the quick action of the Federal Reserve Bank of Atlanta, which pumped liquidity into the regional banking system, checked the spread of the panic.[3]

Before the dust had settled in Nashville, the sloppily managed Bank of United States, fourth largest in New York, began crumbling under the weight of a huge portfolio of unsalable real estate. Mounted police were called to keep stampeding customers from its doors. State banking officials sought a merger partner or a buyer of the institution's assets, but as none was forthcoming they gave it up as insolvent. The Bank of United States became the largest commercial bank failure in U.S. history to that time. The Federal Reserve Bank of New York followed the lead of its southern cousin, making cash and liquid assets available to banks in its jurisdiction, and again a broader panic was avoided.[4]

The twin collapses at the end of 1930 confirmed in Hoover's mind that the banking sector was a weak link—perhaps the weakest—in the American economy. There were some twenty-five thousand banks in

America, most of them single, independent units, some with as little capitalization as a corner store. They were overseen by fifty-two separate regulators of varying quality, and even in good times they failed at a rate of five hundred a year. Hoover had asked Congress to study the banks in the wake of the crash of 1929. Specifically, he had wanted to understand if the growth of chain banking would increase the stability of the system, and if something might be done to prevent the flight of bankers from national charters to less restrictive state regulations, another development that diminished oversight. His request of Congress had gone unheeded, perhaps in part because Hoover was at the same time reassuring the country that the financial system was fundamentally secure.[5]

Unnerving as the problems in New York and Tennessee were, the fact was that they did not spread, indeed, they seemed to pass almost as quickly as they arrived, an immense relief to the president. It was not long before he could take the resolution of yet another potentially devastating situation as a sign of encouragement. It might seem strange to find positive signs in a round of bank failures, however brief, but by a compelling twist of logic the persistence of the depression, together with the fact that the recovery of the previous spring had proved a false dawn, made an imminent rebound seem all the more likely. Surely by the time a slump had produced new classes of vagrants and delivered seismic jolts to the financial sector, the worst had passed. Hoover was not at all alone with this line of thinking. "The depression," wrote the *Commercial & Financial Chronicle*, "has continued so long and has proceeded so far that it seems hardly tenable to believe that the end is still far off." The latest prediction of the *Harvard Economic Review* was for "the end of the decline in business during the early part of 1931" and steady revival for the remainder of the year. Few experts dissented from that outlook. Businessmen, too, were voicing a new confidence.[6]

Expecting that the anticipated recovery might take weeks or months to gain traction, Hoover, before Christmas, still took the precaution of asking Congress for an emergency appropriation for further public works to bolster what was already "the greatest program of waterway, harbor, flood control, public building, highway, and airway improvement in all our history." He also recommended loans to drought-stricken farmers to purchase seed. He hoped these initiatives

would boost employment, stimulate agriculture, and forestall more
ambitious relief plans in Congress. New spending proposals worth
a total of $4.5 billion were floating around the Hill. Hoover thought
any substantial increase in federal spending reckless in light of the
probable upswing.[7]

He took a confident tone to the Gridiron Club at the end of 1930.
After opening his speech with bitter teasing of the gallery for priori-
tizing news of political combat and personal grievance over the activities of "the honest, plodding public official, intent upon building up
safety and welfare of the people," he offered assurances that America's
prevailing troubles were momentary, and that no one would go cold
and hungry over the winter. He professed astonishment at the pressure brought against him to reconsider the fundamentals of American
government in relief of a passing economic storm. "Not an hour has
gone by," he said, without "some demand, backed by some important influence, that we should take over more and more responsibilities and more and more functions from the citizens, the States, and
municipalities." It was time "to abolish the illusion," he said, that the
national government was a remedy for every ill. No federal dole, he
chided, could provide wage earners with the broadly distributed benefits of his program of wage maintenance and public works investment:

> No proposal of charity by the Government can equal a small
> part of the sums attained by the thousand earnest local com-
> mittees now engaged in relief of distress in our counties and
> towns. I do not believe they will fail and I believe that we shall
> again demonstrate the strength and devotion of our people to
> the fundamentals of our democracy.[8]

It was in this spirit that Hoover wielded his veto like a righteous
sword over the final months of the Seventy-First Congress. The
Senate passed a bill in the first weeks of 1931 providing for federal
operation of a wartime dam and nitrate plant at Muscle Shoals on
the Tennessee River. This was a pet project of Nebraska's Senator
Norris and his fellow insurgents, who wanted the government to use
the facilities to make fertilizer and generate power, as well as to build
transmission lines, all in competition with private industry. When it

made its way to his office, the president smote it on grounds that close examination of "the capital invested, the available commercial power, the operating costs, the revenue to be expected, and the profit and loss involved from this set up, were discouraging, even before asking whether the Federal Government should or can manage a power and fertilizer manufacturing business."[9]

Hoover proceeded to ask whether Washington should or could operate the Muscle Shoals plant. Here was the first hint of a new Hoover approach to legislative matters, an adjustment urged by the embarrassments of the first two years of his mandate. Rather than hold the battle on the field of economic feasibility, he frankly acknowledged that the question of government involvement in the power business was a political one, and that the Norris Bill had become a potent symbol for those favoring a more direct role for federal administrators in the economy. Regardless of the fact that the Muscle Shoals project had much in common with the Boulder Canyon project he had championed, he denounced the legislation on political grounds.[10]

There might be national emergencies, he said in his veto message, that require the government to "temporarily" enter a field of business, and there might be localities in which Washington would be justified in constructing dams and reservoirs to aid navigation and to control floods, and power production might be a "byproduct" of these efforts. But for the federal government to deliberately "build up and expand . . . a power and manufacturing business is to break down the initiative and enterprise of the American people; it is destruction of equality of opportunity amongst our people; it is the negation of the ideals upon which our civilization has been based." He closed his message:

> I hesitate to contemplate the future of our institutions, of our Government, and of our country if the preoccupation of its officials is to be no longer the promotion of justice and equal opportunity but is to be devoted to barter in the markets. That is not liberalism, it is degeneration.[11]

A second fight with Congress was over a bill from the House of Representatives proposing to let veterans borrow against compensation due them in 1945 for service in the Great War. The administrator of veterans' affairs told Hoover that if the House had its way and soldiers were permitted to borrow up to 50 percent of the value of the promised payments, the drain on the public purse could reach one billion unbudgeted dollars. The president and his cabinet were united in opposition to the so-called bonus scheme, seeing it as a misguided product of effective lobbying. Most of the country's 387,000 veterans were employed, and the government, having spent $5 billion on various pensions and disability allowances since the Great War, could not be accused of shirking its obligation to them or their dependents. Even if the administration, already running a significant deficit, wanted to spend more on relief, there were far better ways to spur employment and industrial activity than to write checks to hundreds of thousands of men able to care for themselves.

Hoover claimed that the bonus bill would do the veterans more harm than good in the long run: "The future of our World War veterans is inseparably bound up with the future of the whole people." Improvident use of federal funds would inflict "injury to the country as a whole" and leave all Americans, including veterans, in worse shape. In a demonstration of veterans' enormous influence, Congress immediately summoned the votes to pass the Bonus Bill over Hoover's objections.[12]

His third veto gored the handiwork of Democratic senator Robert Wagner, who introduced a bill for a system of federal employment agencies. This was a delicate situation for Hoover. Wagner was a man close to his own heart, a champion of scientific measurement of social phenomena and a supporter of countercyclical public works spending. He liked to quote Hoover's speeches from the 1921 President's Conference on Unemployment and he cited as precedents for his proposed emergency relief to drought sufferers Hoover's humanitarian efforts in Belgium and Russia. Hoover, moreover, was on record as wanting to improve federal employment services.

His objections to Wagner's bill were, again, political. The senator and like-minded Democrats were working in lockstep with the insurgents, and Hoover was loath to allow them any semblance of momentum in the waning days of the lame-duck session and on the eve of an anticipated recovery. He blocked the bill on grounds that it would abolish existing federal employment offices and take months if not years to replace them with new services.[13]

The vetoes came at a cost. Borah, favoring a more aggressive use of government resources to combat the depression, denounced each in turn and also attacked Hoover for indifference to the suffering of southern drought victims in another of his floor-shaking speeches in the Senate. Borah quoted a letter from a Red Cross worker in the South who visited the home of a widow with four emaciated children with nothing to eat but rancid food. Here, shouted Borah, was a family being fed "in a way that no one would feed his dog." Why was Hoover, who had famously relieved drought sufferers along the Volga, refusing to do more for the hungry and needy of America? Borah demanded a gift of $25 million to the Red Cross for drought sufferers and another special session of Congress to deal with drought relief. A majority of his colleagues rose to their feet in a roar of approval. Republican members sat in silence and offered no reply.[14]

Hoover stated the obvious in conversation with Stimson. Borah, he said, was "very bitter" toward him. He also told Stimson that he had it on "very good information" that the Idaho grandstander was maneuvering to organize a third party comprised of progressive Democrats and Republican insurgents. Stimson thought him paranoid and crazy. In fact, Hoover's intelligence was accurate. Senators Borah and Norris, and a coterie of progressives from both the Democratic and Republican parties, met the second week in March to devise a policy platform intended as the foundation of a new party with an eye to the 1932 presidential race. What Hoover overestimated was the ability of this pack of mavericks to work constructively in harness. The progressive conference went nowhere.[15]

The White House had little in the way of an immediate answer to Borah's attack. It released a calm statement reiterating Hoover's faith in private drought aid, and he promised to lay the matter before Congress in the event that local efforts proved insufficient. He waited a week, and then a few days more, to offer a fulsome, if indirect, riposte to Borah.[16]

Hoover had developed a habit of using public holidays and historical anniversaries as opportunities to explain to the public the philosophical underpinnings of his policy. Perhaps no date in the calendar held more significance for him than February 12, the birthday of the founder of the Republican Party, and an occasion Hoover, alone among Republican presidents, always honored with a public speech. On this evening in 1931 he addressed national audiences over the NBC and CBS networks directly from the Lincoln Study. He spoke with reverence of sitting in the very room in which the great man had toiled by day and night that the Union might survive its most desperate trial. He said he could feel Lincoln's spectral presence in the furniture and in his portrait over his mantelpiece. The speech reminded the American people that they had endured greater disasters than this depression, and identified one issue from Lincoln's time as distinctly relevant to their own:

> In Lincoln's day the dominant problem in our form of government turned upon the issue of States' rights. Though less pregnant with disaster, the dominant problem today in our form of government turns in large degree upon the issue of the relationship of Federal, State, and local government responsibilities.[17]

Recognizing that the federal government had assumed greater responsibilities than in Lincoln's time, and that it might do more in the years ahead, Hoover nonetheless insisted that federal action, particularly in social and economic matters, be limited to supplementing rather than superseding lower levels of government. To do otherwise would threaten the principle of local government, which was the basis of self-government: "Where people divest themselves of local government responsibilities they at once lay the foundation for the destruction of their liberties."[18]

Hoover set these ideas in the larger context of his conception of government as outlined in *American Individualism*. The purpose of a national government, he said, is to provide ordered liberty and equality of opportunity so that every individual might rise to the level of attainment of which he or she is capable. It is on this fair playing field that the character of individuals is formed, and they make their character by shouldering responsibilities, not by escaping them. National governments destroy character when they direct lives, undermine initiative, and reduce citizens to servants of the state. This, said Hoover, was Lincoln's understanding of government, and the critical test facing Americans in a depression was to respond in the spirit of that understanding, to preserve the principles of American life laid out by the Founders just as Lincoln had preserved them in his time. Half the world, Hoover observed in conclusion, was enmeshed in social and political revolution, fighting for or against new governments and ideologies. Amid this turmoil, America was a beacon of progress and stability. He counseled against despair. He told the people they need only have faith in one another and in the leadership of his government:

> Never before in a great depression has there been so systematic a protection against distress. Never before has there been so little social disorder. Never before has there been such an outpouring of the spirit of self-sacrifice and of service. . . . The resourcefulness of America when challenged has never failed. . . .
>
> Victory over this depression and over our other difficulties will be won by the resolution of our people to fight their own battles in their own communities, by stimulating their ingenuity to solve their own problems, by taking new courage to be masters of their own destiny in the struggle of life. This is not the easy way, but it is the American way. And it was Lincoln's way.[19]

While economic news and the president's vetoes made their share of headlines in the early months of 1931, the dominant story and the preoccupation of the administration was, in fact, Prohibition. George Wickersham's National Commission on Law Observance and Enforcement delivered its report on Prohibition enforcement to the White House on January 7. Having heard that the commission would not take the clear dry position he wanted from it, Hoover dreaded receipt of the document. An ambiguous outcome would only exacerbate the debate and "split the Republican Party from top to bottom." Hoover sat down and read all ninety thousand words of the report in a day, and his heart sank.[20]

Two members of the eleven-member panel wanted to repeal the Eighteenth Amendment, five were for its revision, and four advised further trial. One of the few points of unanimity was that "there is yet no adequate observance or enforcement" of Prohibition, hardly the endorsement Hoover wanted for his compliance campaign. Matters were further confused by the personal comments of several panelists appended to the general report suggesting that the commission had agreed upon immediate revision. It was, as one newspaper aptly noted, "a Wickershambles."[21]

On an afternoon shortly after Hoover's receipt of the report, Stimson walked in on a discussion of its merits between the president and Mark Sullivan. To the secretary's suggestion that it was a fine piece of work, Hoover leaned back in his chair and said, "Well, we were just coming to the conclusion that it is a rotten report."[22]

Stimson pressed his case. "You can't afford a split on your own baby," he said. It would look better for the administration to embrace the document for what it was. Most people, said Stimson, believed that the outcome was fixed, that Wickersham would deliver a dry report whatever the evidence. "It's up to you to show that it isn't a joke," he told the president, but instead "a really thoughtful, analytical report and the best thing that has yet been put out on the subject."[23]

Stimson was ingenuous: no amount of lipstick was going to save the Wickersham Report, and the president was in trouble. Like the eleven-member panel, Americans were hopelessly divided on the Eighteenth Amendment. Michigan was handing out life sentences for a fourth conviction of trading in liquor, and Kansas was threatening the death penalty for bootlegging gangsters, while the New York police commissioner reported thirty-two thousand speakeasies operating in his jurisdiction, and Maryland had quit enforcing the Volstead Act entirely. Wickersham found that "taking the country as a whole, people of wealth, businessmen and professional men, and their families, and, perhaps, the higher paid working men and their families, are drinking in large numbers in quite frank disregard of the declared policy" of Prohibition. The volume of alcohol consumption appeared to be growing, and social attitudes toward liquor, especially among women and the young, were notably looser than they had been a decade or two earlier. Hoover's sincere efforts to improve enforcement had achieved nothing, as had his attempt to broaden the debate beyond wet versus dry.[24]

An honest reading of the report argued for Hoover to retreat from his firm dry position. Many in his circle, including MacLafferty,

Edgar Rickard, and Jerry Milbank, head of the Republican National Committee, were nudging Hoover toward a compromise, whether it be legalizing low-alcohol beer or giving states more latitude in enforcement. Milbank worried that a staunchly dry position would make fund-raising a chore for the party. Hoover would not budge. He did not want to go down in history as the leader who had frustrated the cause his mother and her forebears had so long upheld, and politics also argued against a retreat. Support for Prohibition had won him Borah's endorsement and had helped him get elected. The dry ranks, while undoubtedly thinning, remained considerable, and they could be counted on to vote Republican in 1932. Hoover was also tormented by the thought that Borah would use any moderation on his part as an excuse to raise a third party of dry Democrats and insurgents. When he could get his mind off Borah, he was convinced that Gifford Pinchot, recently sworn in as governor of Pennsylvania and reckoned as a Republican presidential aspirant, would exploit any softening of his position to pry away his dry support and steal his leadership. Neither scenario was likely. The fact that Hoover was so easily spooked was further evidence of his unfamiliarity with political strategy and the workings of his party.[25]

Feeling trapped, seeing no clear and politically advantageous way forward, Hoover tried a dodge. He forwarded the Wickersham Report to Congress with a message declaring it to be unambiguously dry and supportive of still more enforcement:

> I am in unity with the spirit of the report in seeking constructive steps to advance the national ideal of eradication of the social and economic and political evils of this traffic, to preserve the gains which have been made, and to eliminate the abuses which exist, at the same time facing with an open mind the difficulties which have arisen under this experiment.[26]

Hoover made it clear that he opposed any manner of revision. His message only added to the confusion and disappointment surrounding the report and intensified the debate among wets and drys over whether to keep, dump, or rewrite Prohibition.

·   ·   ·

The president's faith in the underlying strength of the American economy seemed to be rewarded in the first months of 1931. For the second time since the crash, there was evidence of recovery, as anticipated by Hoover, Harvard, and the *Commercial & Financial Chronicle*, among many others. Industrial production and business activity were picking up by most measures. Payrolls were gaining. Bank failures were fewer.[27]

There was more good news in that reports to the cabinet suggested Americans were receiving sufficient aid to make it through the winter. Predictions of starvation in New York had come to naught, and Arkansas, the epicenter of the drought and the most severely afflicted state in the Union, was from the perspective of its governor, Harvey Parnell, answering the call of the destitute with local charities and the Red Cross. Parnell saw no need for federal assistance. Having learned from the mirage of the previous spring to be cautious in his public declarations on the economy, Hoover said little at this point. He was keenly aware that the depression was not well understood. It seemed to have a mind of its own, bent on defying prediction.[28]

Just how strange and perplexing a phenomenon the depression had become was apparent at a series of meetings hosted by the League of Nations in Geneva in March. The economic councils and research institutes of fifteen nations had sent their best minds, including future Nobel Prize winners Friedrich Hayek of Austria and Bertil Ohlin of Sweden, to investigate the causes of the downturn.

Edward Eyre Hunt, a veteran of the Belgian relief and a favorite Hoover policy adviser, represented the United States, the only non-European country at the meeting. Summarizing the administration's experience of the depression to date, Hunt emphasized how economic forecasts had driven policy:

> The business leaders whom the President summoned to the White House conferences in November 1929, the economists who met in Washington in December of the same year, agreed that the depression would be like [the light recession of] 1923 rather than like [the deep recession of] 1921. Private as well as public policy under aggressive Government leadership was based upon the belief that the depression would be short. We had a false dawn in the spring of 1930. This, most

of us believed, marked the beginning of the end. Instead it
marked the beginning of still deeper depression.[29]

Hunt went on to say that there was general agreement in America that the economy was improving in the early months of 1931,
although some worried that this might be another mirage. The government estimated that between 4.5 and 5 million Americans were
unemployed, with many more working part-time. It was not confident of the accuracy of its numbers.

In a private memo to Hoover, Hunt wrote that the economists at
the gathering were a surprisingly youthful group, with only a single
bald head among them. They spoke English, and many had studied
in the United States. Despite these commonalities, they could agree
on little more than that the depression had started outside of the
United States and that it was harsh. The list of possible causes of the
depression ran to several pages. Poland, Finland, and Germany dated
it from 1928, other countries from 1929, and Denmark from 1930.
Some viewed it as a domestic problem, others as an international one.
Some considered it the downside of a routine business cycle; others
thought it represented structural economic change and a flaw in capitalism requiring a new economic system; some thought both. No one
could adequately explain why prices were falling so sharply. There
was no certainty around the role of capital movements, or the effect
of the crash of 1929, the impact of tariff reforms, or the influence
of political events and psychological factors. There was no unity on
whether it was best to have workers fully employed and making goods
at lower prices or to tolerate a 10 percent increase in unemployment
and see goods sold at higher prices. There was no agreement on the
afternoon of the second day on how long to adjourn for lunch, the
Nordics wanting to get back to work, the Latins holding out for a
three-hour break.*

Of course, Hoover's understanding of what was happening in
the economy was also flawed. Like every other responsible actor on
the world stage, he took a gold-based monetary regime as something

---

* There was relatively little discussion throughout the conference about monetary policy
and the gold standard, which we now know to have been critical factors in the Great
Depression.

approaching divine law. He also harbored his share of bizarre ideas, including the conviction that his enemies had organized "concerted bear raids for political purpose" on New York stock markets and Chicago commodity markets. These raids, he believed, were designed to drive down prices, making money for the perpetrators and spreading distress to undermine his administration. At his request, the attorney general's department investigated his suspicions, finding plenty of short selling but no illegal activity, and no plot to torment the president.[30]

These lapses notwithstanding, few men alive could match for depth and breadth Hoover's perspective on the global economy. He attributed the depression to a combination of factors. Domestically, easy money, speculation, and an imbalance of production and consumption had led to the crash of 1929 and a rather predictable downturn in the business cycle during the first half of his term. Behind all this, and moving center stage in the second half of his term, were a multitude of global forces, most of them traceable to the Great War, its destruction of life, property, and productive capacity, and its legacy of economic instability and political hostility.

Germany and Austria, two countries groaning under the weight of reparations due the Allies, notwithstanding two rounds of renegotiations that had lightened their obligations, were in Hoover's estimation ground zero in the global depression. Their troubles had been aggravated in 1928 by the Federal Reserve's decision to raise its rates, a move that pulled funds home to America and deprived Central Europe of much-needed capital. In response, German chancellor Heinrich Brüning raised interest rates to defend his own currency, a move that inflicted more economic pain on his people, and still recovery eluded him. The unpopularity of his policies fueled his political opposition, most alarmingly Adolf Hitler's National Socialist Party. To sustain his popularity, Brüning competed with the Nazis in expressing bitterness over the terms of Versailles. He expanded his navy in contravention of the treaty and talked of a customs union with Austria, which the French saw as a first step toward annexation, also forbidden by the treaty. Brüning further threatened to suspend payments on reparations, a move that seemed calculated to drive France mad.[31]

Hoover had been studying the German and Austrian problems along with other elements of what he called "the malign inheritances" of the Great War. He viewed its economic, political, and military legacies as inextricably linked. He had his Commerce Department furnish him with memoranda on the war debts of the combatant states, as well as their intergovernmental debts, volumes of trade, and past and present levels of military spending. He was aghast to find that the world was spending $5 billion annually on arms, 70 percent more than prewar levels. France had doubled its arms spending from pre-crash levels in reaction to what it considered the deliberate anti-Versailles provocations of Brüning and the rise of German extremism. Millions of European soldiers had yet to be demobilized despite the Armistice and the signing of the Kellogg-Briand Pact. This was "a gigantic waste," said Hoover. The potential savings from rigorous demilitarization would buy a great deal of economic recuperation.[32]

He had already made headway in his campaign for disarmament. The London Naval Conference, a child of his meetings with Prime Minister MacDonald in the autumn of 1929, had seen the United States, Britain, Japan, Italy, and France agree to restrictions on submarines, destroyers, battleships, and other classes of vessels. Hoover hailed the agreement as a net savings of more than $2 billion and a diplomatic landmark representing "the final abolition of competition in naval arms between the greatest naval powers, and the burial of the fears and suspicions which have been the constant product of rival warship construction."[33]

He proposed to the International Chamber of Commerce that the naval agreement be followed by sharp reductions in total arms spending to allow governments to lower taxes, balance their budgets, invest in productive industries, and reduce tensions around the world. He also wondered if some sort of moratorium on reparations and international war debts, including the enormous sums owed to the United States, would further alleviate the pressures on European economies. It seemed a necessary measure, albeit one fraught with political danger, at home as well as abroad.[34]

America had yet to own up to the relationship between war debts and reparations, although the connection was obvious to the rest of the world. Throughout the 1920s, heavy lending by Americans assisted

Germany in making its reparations payments to the Allies. France and Britain, in turn, relied upon German payments to service their war debts to the United States. And so the money passed from capital to capital in a circle of enablement and dependency that Americans, led by their politicians, most notably Coolidge, stubbornly refused to acknowledge. Even when the withdrawal of Wall Street credit disrupted the circle in 1928, leaving Germany exposed, Washington still wanted to collect the $10 billion owed it by the Allies. Why, asked Main Street, should taxpayers be left holding the bag for Europe's war? Why should they contribute another cent to the sustenance of ancient, irredeemably corrupt, war-mad peoples on the other side of the Atlantic when their own economic futures seemed so uncertain?

Wall Street viewed the issue differently. The reduction or nullification of intergovernmental debts would lend a measure of security to its outstanding private loans to Germany. Financiers were all for cancellation, an attitude that did nothing to endear them to the people, or to the president. "Sitting in New York, as you do," Hoover told Thomas Lamont of J. P. Morgan, "you have no idea what the sentiment of the country at large is on these inter-governmental debts."[35]

Although conscious of the plight of Central Europe, Hoover did not move until a crisis approached. On May 5, his ambassador to Germany, Frederic Sackett, returned to Washington warning of a perilous state of affairs at his post. "The political disturbances are so extreme," he said, "the misery of the people is so great," and the pressures of reparations so high, that Germany was facing ruin or revolution without immediate assistance. Sackett's bleak view was validated just six days later when Creditanstalt, known to Hoover as the most important banking institution in the old Austrian Empire, suddenly collapsed. Riots broke out in the streets of Vienna, and the country's entire banking structure seemed ready to topple. The panic spread to Germany, causing more social unrest and threatening its much larger banking system. Money and gold fled both countries despite high central bank rates. Much of the specie landed in the United States, where, of all places on earth, it was least needed. New York markets watched the havoc and went weak in the knees. The Dow Jones Industrial Average, which had rallied in the first quarter of 1931, the second false dawn, now sank to a new low of 122 points, one-third of its pre-crash high.[36]

"Just as we had begun to entertain well founded hopes that we were on our way out of the depression," wrote Hoover in the immediate wake of these events, "our latent fears of Europe were realized in a gigantic explosion which shook the foundations of the world's economic, political, and social structure."[37]

Only months into his new job, Hoover's new press secretary, Theodore Joslin, was still grappling with the vagaries of his master's moods and habits. He noted in his diary that while lesser matters prompted the president to shout " 'damn' with the best of them," the great pressures now descending on him seemed somehow to compose him. He went about his business without any outward evidence of disturbance except, in the most trying of moments, a slight twitch in his facial muscles. He complained only once, when Joslin one day walked into his office, found him pacing the floor, and asked what was the matter. "This is a cruel world," said the president before quietly returning to his work.[38]

Henry Stimson returned to his office late on the unbearably warm afternoon of June 5 to find a telephone message from the president summoning him to the White House. Hoover was alone when he arrived. Secretary Mellon and his undersecretary, Ogden Mills, were called in from another room down the hall. Hoover launched directly into a description of the rapidly degenerating European situation. The failure of Creditanstalt, he said, had brought Austria and Germany to the brink of financial collapse, and an overthrow of the German government was a distinct possibility. The movement of gold to the United States was "paralyzing central banking institutions the world over." He recorded what followed in his own aide-mémoire:

> I had a definite proposal to lay before them. That was that we should postpone all collections on Allied debts for one year in consideration of all the Allies making similar postponements of reparations and all claims during the same period. I further explained that the world needed some strong action which would change the mental point of view, and that I felt perhaps such an action might serve this purpose of general reestablishment of courage and confidence.[39]

Hoover went around the table and asked his secretaries for their thoughts. Stimson was favorable. He predicted that the proposed moratorium would buoy public opinion on both sides of the Atlantic. Mellon opposed the whole scheme. Mills agreed with Mellon and pointed out that Hoover had no executive authority to effect such a bargain, and that it would be impossible to secure approval without a special session of Congress. Stimson lingered in Hoover's office after the meeting and found the president determined to forge ahead whatever the obstacles. The Great War, he said, had been prolonged by a lack of initiative from all concerned parties. He wanted to meet the European situation head-on rather than let it come.[40]

Later that evening Hoover presented Joslin with several pages of notes summarizing his position. "This," he said, "is the most daring statement I have ever contemplated issuing." He wanted it known, however, that he had not yet decided to release it.[41]

The next week brought flurries of cables and transatlantic telephone calls among administration officials and European governments and bankers, as well as tense and private communications with Eugene Meyer of the Federal Reserve and Wall Street power brokers Owen Young and Bernard Baruch, among others. Hoover received daily briefings on the volumes of gold exiting Central Europe and on how Brüning was faring in the Reichstag.

In spare moments, the president and Stimson argued heatedly over whether to act alone and unconditionally or in concert with other nations, whether to hold reparations and international war debts separate or admit that they were related, whether to bind the moratorium to arms reductions or to keep those issues separate, whether to impose a one-year or a two-year moratorium. They challenged each other, they wrote and rewrote statements, they waffled, they switched sides, and they apologized for intemperate language. Their options and their outlooks changed daily, and sometimes hourly. In one moment they would be concerned about getting France, "the fussy nation," to agree to a multiparty deal, and in the next they would fear France and England might forge their own bilateral agreement and dump an objectionable solution in America's lap. Few things scared

both men more than the prospect of the United States being transformed into a direct claimant against Germany for her reparations
payments. Through it all, the situation continued to deteriorate. Germany announced that it could no longer afford to pay reparations,
leading to a swirl of rumors that it would soon disallow foreign withdrawals of gold and capital.[42]

Stimson, like Joslin, spent a good part of his time in the executive presence trying to crack Hoover's code. Being the better observer
and having the advantage of sitting in the cabinet, he registered a
greater range of emotional activity in the president than did Joslin.
He watched Hoover agonize over every error, perceived error, and
narrowly avoided error. He logged in his diary "discouraging, pessimistic blasts" and black moods during which the president would
take the grimmest view of every problem, drawing down the administration's "stock of optimism" and adding to the almost insuperable
burdens of the cabinet and staff. That he was so sensitive to rumor,
criticism, and opposition, losing whole nights of sleep when under
attack, left Stimson pained and baffled. "If he would walk out his own
way," said the secretary, "it would make matters so much easier."[43]

While Stimson would never entirely acclimate to Hoover's dark
moods, he did come to appreciate that they represented a psychological process more than the true state of his morale and his willingness
to fight. He marveled at how the president's public comments, the
deliberately drafted products of careful reflection, continued to be
upbeat and inspirational in the most trying of situations. Said Stimson:

> In every important crisis which I have had with him and
> which we have faced together, he has always gone through
> a period in which he sees every possible difficulty and gets
> terribly discouraged over it, and seemed for a long time to be
> going backwards. When he finally does make up his mind and
> does act, he turns to it with great courage.[44]

It was not until Stimson's spirit had been almost crushed that
Hoover finally decided on a course of action for Central Europe.
Over a weekend at Rapidan, he determined to push for a one-year

moratorium on reparations and war debts. He gave up his Sunday, June 14, the last day of trout-fishing season in Virginia, to polish three speeches for delivery on a three-day swing through the Midwest in the coming week. On his return, he would seek bipartisan congressional support for the moratorium and then announce it to the world.

# CHAPTER 22

# "It Seemed Like the End of the World"

Political reporters were eagerly anticipating Hoover's western junket, which they viewed as the informal kickoff to the 1932 election cycle. A score of newspapermen boarded Hoover's special train bound for Indiana and watched what looked to them very much like a campaign trip. The president appeared on the train's rear platform and met state party chiefs, women's committees, and other delegations at every major stop on the route to Indiana. He arrived in Indianapolis on Monday evening, June 15, for an address to the Indiana Republican Editorial Association and was greeted at the two-acre Manufacturers Hall on the state fairgrounds by a standing ovation. He was served a plate of fried chicken heaped so high and served by a waitress so fetching that he momentarily stopped scribbling notes on his speech, looked up, and beamed. He received another lengthy ovation when he stood to speak, and still more cheering when he invited the men in the crowd to take off their coats in consideration of the oppressive heat. He finally addressed his audience with more vigor than he had shown at any time since assuming office, and he gave them perhaps the best speech of his presidency.[1]

Hoover repeated his thesis that the depression was rooted in the Great War and told the editors that its spread around the world could not be explained simply in terms of shrinking global trade and lower commodity prices. The U.S. economy was sufficiently self-contained to withstand those blows. More virulent and damaging was the cli-

mate of fear Hoover had been striving to allay since the first days of
the Great Crash.

> Fear and apprehension, whether their origins are domestic
> or foreign, are very real, tangible, economic forces. Fear of
> loss of a job or uncertainty as to the future has caused mil-
> lions of our people unnecessarily to reduce their purchases of
> goods, thereby decreasing our production and employment.
> These uncertainties lead our bankers and businessmen to
> extreme caution, and in consequence a mania for liquidation
> has reduced our stocks of goods and our credits far below any
> necessity. All these apprehensions and actions check enter-
> prise and lessen our national activities. We are suffering today
> more from frozen confidence than we are from frozen securi-
> ties.[2]

The president urged people to stop staring at "the empty hole
in the middle of the doughnut," an apt metaphor for his own private habit of mind. He asked them to remember America's bounty of
resources "in land, mines, mills, manpower, brainpower, and courage." These resources combined with "patient, constructive action in
a multitude of directions" would ultimately lead America to victory in
"this battle upon a thousand fronts."[3]

Government, he continued, had a role to play in aiding and guiding a recovery, and he recited the many activities of his own administration, but America was not going to legislate its way out of a global
depression rooted in a world war. He attacked what had become a
vogue that summer, in such publications as the *New Republic*, *Harper's*,
and *Forum*, for the replacement of capitalism with Stalinesque multi-
year economic plans. These plans, said Hoover, "through which Russia is struggling to redeem herself from ten years of starvation and
misery," were dead ends:

> I am able to propose an American plan to you. We plan to
> take care of a 20 million increase in population in the next 20
> years. We plan to build for them four million new and better
> homes, thousands of new and still more beautiful city build-
> ings, thousands of factories; to increase the capacity of our

railways; to add thousands of miles of highways and waterways; to install 25 million electrical horsepower; to grow 20
percent more farm products. We plan to provide new parks,
schools, colleges, and churches for this 20 million people. We
plan more leisure for men and women and better opportunities for its enjoyment. We not only plan to provide for all
the new generation, but we shall, by scientific research and
invention, lift the standard of living and security of life to the
whole people. We plan to secure a greater diffusion of wealth,
a decrease in poverty, and a great reduction in crime. And this
plan will be carried out if we just keep on giving the American
people a chance. Its impulsive force is in the character and
spirit of our people. They have already done a better job for
120 million people than any other nation in all history.[4]

Some groups believe this plan can only be carried out
by a fundamental, a revolutionary change of method. Other
groups believe that any system must be the outgrowth of the
character of our race, a natural outgrowth of our traditions;
that we have established certain ideals over 150 years upon
which we must build rather than destroy. . . .

Shall we abandon the philosophy and creed of our people
for 150 years by turning to a creed foreign to our people?
Shall we establish a dole from the Federal Treasury? Shall we
undertake Federal ownership and operation of public utilities
instead of the rigorous regulation of them to prevent imposition? . . . Shall the Government, except in temporary national
emergencies, enter upon business processes in competition
with its citizens? Shall we regiment our people by an extension of the arm of bureaucracy into a multitude of affairs?

The future welfare of our country, so dear to you and to
me for ourselves and our children, depends upon the answer
given.[5]

The speech hit unexpected notes for newsmen anticipating a partisan preelection speech. Hoover did not mention the Democrats, or
the insurgents. Nor did he rail against his critics, or against Congress.
Rather, he went out of his way to praise legislators who had collabo-
rated in the fight against the depression. He was generous, buoyant,

and undaunted. He stood on the higher ground on which he had
always intended to lead, and in that troubled moment it struck editorialists as inspired. "If Americans like a public man who is not afraid,"
wrote the *New York Times*, "they also like one who is not discouraged
or despondent." The president had every right to be "haggard with
anxiety" over the state of the nation, yet he "so plainly inclines to
hope rather than fear that it will tend to quicken the hopes and banish
the fears of great numbers of his fellow-countrymen."[6]

The next day was in many ways an even more surprising occasion. Hoover visited the lonely tomb of Warren Harding in Marion,
Ohio, and performed the dedication that had been wanting through
the Coolidge years. In a dark suit, with somber face, he laid a wreath
and delivered a brave and touching encomium that did not shirk from
damning the Harding scandals, or from acknowledging his friendship
with Harding, or from defending Harding's character. He presented
the late president as a man betrayed by those closest to him:

> There are disloyalties and there are crimes which shock our
> sensibilities, which may bring suffering upon those who are
> touched by their immediate results. But there is no disloy-
> alty and no crime in all the category of human weaknesses
> which compares with the failure of probity in the conduct of
> public trust. . . . The breaking down of the faith of a people
> in the honesty of their Government and in the integrity of
> their institutions, the lowering of respect for the standards
> of honor which prevail in high places, are crimes for which
> punishment can never atone.
>
> But these acts never touched the character of Warren
> Harding. He gave his life in worthy accomplishment for his
> country. He was a man of delicate sense of honor, of sympa-
> thetic heart, of transcendent gentleness of soul—who reached
> out for friendship, who gave of it loyally and generously in his
> every thought and deed.[7]

Hoover rounded off his tour with a nod to "our greatest American," rededicating the magisterial granite memorial to Abraham
Lincoln in Springfield, Illinois, on a blistering afternoon. The Lincoln Liberty Chorus, an all-black group from Chicago, opened with

"Swing Low, Sweet Chariot" before Hoover reiterated his views on the necessity of obedience to and enforcement of the law. By happy coincidence, the morning headlines had announced that the gangster Al Capone had pled guilty to federal charges of tax evasion and conspiracy the previous day, a rare victory for Prohibition enforcement.[8]

The return train to Washington set what some reporters considered a land speed record from Springfield, no doubt at the president's request. He was in a positive frame of mind. He had been encouraged by reports from midwestern business and political leaders that unemployment was dropping and that the crop season was promising. On the night of his speech in Marion, the statistician and investment guru Roger Babson, one of few men with a legitimate claim to calling the Great Crash, and Dr. Lewis H. Haney, director of the Bureau of Business Research at New York University, had both stood up at New York's Hotel Astor to assure the Advertising Federation of America that the business cycle had bottomed out and prosperity was on its way. Hoover was eager to wrestle agreement on his moratorium from congressional Democrats and add a measure of international stability to these fresh signs of momentum.[9]

Over three days, Hoover in person and on the telephone canvassed support for the moratorium deep into the senior ranks of the House and Senate Democrats, as well as within his own party. Once again standing in the front line of a legislative charge, he made personal appeals for the necessary votes. He urged the moratorium as crucial to stabilizing Germany and Europe, financially and politically, and to protecting American banks with exposure to those markets. He asked members for their approval on the understanding that a formal vote would await the meeting of Congress in December. The response was better than the administration had anticipated. Republicans and Democrats both were overwhelmingly supportive.[*][10]

* The only Republican to give Hoover trouble was New Hampshire senator Henry Keyes, who, if Joslin is to be believed, refused to cooperate because the president had not permitted his wife, the novelist Frances Parkinson Keyes, to quote him in an article for *Good Housekeeping*. (Joslin Diaries, June 19, 1931, Herbert Hoover Presidential Library and Museum.)

The White House was in a state of high excitement on the afternoon of June 20 as Hoover, confident of a majority in both chambers
and fearing a leak to the press, invited reporters on short notice to
a briefing at 4:30 p.m. With the "sense that it was a very historic
occasion," Stimson watched the president, purposeful, confident, "a
man transformed," read a statement proposing a one-year postponement of payments on intergovernmental debts and reparations. He
placed the names of supportive congressmen and willing nations on
the record. He assured the American people that he was not proposing cancellation of debts, merely postponement as "wise creditors"
interested in peace and economic stability. As the reporters hustled
off to meet their deadlines for Sunday-morning editions, Hoover
called Joslin into his office: "Well, Ted, we've had a hard siege. Get
your wife and the boys and we'll go down to the camp for over Sunday." And they did, although both of them would spend almost the
whole of Sunday on the telephone speaking to Senators, advisers, and
diplomats about the bombshell they had dropped.[11]

Given the vehement isolationism that had gripped the nation
since Wilson's return from Versailles, the reaction of Americans to
the moratorium was amazingly positive. An impartial survey of two
dozen major newspapers found them unanimously favorable to the
president's initiative. Congress, led by the mercurial Borah and other
members of the Senate Foreign Relations Committee, was firm in its
support. Wall Street, as expected, was full of praise for the president's
initiative. Another chorus of approval came from capitals around the
globe, echoed in the international press, with the *Times* of London
describing Hoover's move as the most important act of statesmanship since the Armistice. The effect of what became known as the
"Hoover Holiday" on the world's bourses was almost magical. Paris,
Berlin, and London jumped as a wave of buying hit bonds and securities. The Dow Jones Industrial Average gained more than 11 percent
in two days of heavy trading, the swiftest two-session advance in a
generation (leaving aside one violent fluctuation during the week of
the Great Crash). The inculpation of debts and reparations in the
global depression, if still not entirely understood, was now indisputable. After nineteen months of struggle and two false dawns, this was
a welcome break.[12]

Joslin collected the piles of telegrams and cables flowing into the

White House, every last one favorable, and arrived, his face beaming excitement, before the desk of the president. He began reading excerpts aloud. Hoover brought him up short. "Don't forget for a moment," he said, "that some people, a lot of people, will see another side to this picture. Everything is pleasing now, but there may well be a ground swell against my proposal." It was, said Joslin, "like a dash of cold water." The admonishment, however, was warranted. This would be Hoover's third false dawn.[13]

For the moratorium to be effective, it needed to do more than jolt the global economy. It needed to convince businesses and financiers and governments that the run on Germany would stop in its tracks, that her financial system could henceforth heal itself from within, that the advances of the communists and Nazis in Central Europe were checked, that the economic drag of debts and reparations that had held the Continent back since the Great War was lifted, that sixteen governments, several of whom were paying more than 20 percent of GDP to service their war debts, would receive a sudden gush of cash, a gigantic stimulus to productivity and recovery, and that they would put it to good use, abandoning their mutual mistrusts and working toward common goals of peace and prosperity. It was a tall order.

As it happened, the University of Chicago was at the moment of Hoover's announcement entertaining an eminent English economist with a heavy brow, piercing dark eyes, and a bristling mustache. "A fine piece of policy," was Keynes's verdict on the moratorium. It would give affected countries breathing space and restart investment, "provided that it is accepted by other interested parties." By other interested parties, Keynes meant France, the fussy nation.[14]

And there was the rub. Hoover needed instant acceptance of his proposal from all affected countries for it to have a chance at lasting impact. Public opinion in France would not accept further economic aid to Germany without political concessions. Even before Hoover had released his plan, the French were moving behind the scenes to, as Stimson said, "blackmail" Austria by linking approval of reparations relief to disavowal of a customs union with Germany. Once the initiative was public, Paris pretended to be surprised and denounced "America's shock tactics." Its real complaint was that Hoover's scheme was being foisted on Europe, whereas previous renovations of the Versailles framework had been arranged through negotiation. There

followed a long list of French reservations. Italy felt much the same
way. Stimson felt as though the French dissenters were picking the
pockets of the drowning man he was trying to pull from the water.[15]

The French, concerned for their security if Germany were
unbound, stalled, haggled, and pushed their misgivings hard enough
over the next several weeks to break the spell of progress. It became
clear that the moratorium, when finally ratified, would be but a brief
one-year recess and not an end to France's demands to collect German
reparations. Brüning did damage of his own by downplaying his ability to subsist without further international loans, contrary to Hoover's
assurances that the moratorium would deliver Germany from threat
of default. These complications and the evident inability of the leading European nations to escape their "malign inheritances" quickly
rekindled questions of Germany's financial and political stability and
the ability of its neighbors to manage their indebtedness and rally out
of the depression.[16]

The rest of the summer brought bank collapses and forced banking holidays in Central Europe. Trouble spread across the Continent
and even to Britain, which held a large share of Germany's long-term
debt. A run on the pound was soon under way.

The president's answer to the discouraging outcome of the moratorium was to put in more hours at his desk, driving himself still harder
in his "battle on a thousand fronts," and what the rest of the world
was coming to appreciate as the Great Depression. He read analyses of the causes and duration of every economic downturn dating
back to the Napoleonic Wars. Late in the evenings, he snuck advisers,
business executives, and congressmen past the press sentries at the
entrance to the White House for private consultations. The workload
left him more pasty and slumped than usual. "I am so tired that every
bone in my body aches," he confessed to staff. The benefits of his
weekend respites at Rapidan now seemed to disappear within hours
of his return to the office. "Worn, worried, and harassed," was how
Joslin described him.[17]

Hoover's negativity was now accompanied by a higher magnitude
of defensiveness and paranoia. In addition to brooding over the activities of the short sellers and the insurgents, he obsessed over his press

coverage. He divined opposition to his economic policies and Prohibition stance even among Republican writers. He could not accept, as Joslin told him, that most of the reporters were honest men reporting on the administration as they understood it. Nor would he accept that his office's constant requests for corrections and retractions of stories contributed to ill feelings.[18]

He saw larger conspiracies, believing that Owen Young, chairman of General Electric and a leading Democrat, had locked arms with the Hearst press, the Scripps-Howard newspaper chain, and the *New York Times* to foist upon the nation what Hoover believed to be "an impossible and wholly uneconomic plan" involving the replacement of free markets with a collectivist scheme amalgamating Mussolini and Lenin.[19]

The stresses on the administration began to produce fissures in the cabinet. In sullen moods, Hoover groused about the inadequacies of certain appointments, particularly Mellon. He had heard enough of the Treasurer's impassive counsels of nonintervention, or what Stimson called his "long childlike narrations" on the economic situation.[20]

In his midseventies, richer than ever, Mellon took a long vacation on the French Riviera during the critical summer of the moratorium and devoted himself to wheedling Titians, Rembrandts, and van Dycks from the Hermitage Collection of Petrograd. Mills, his vigorous undersecretary, was doing all of the important work at Treasury. He and Governor George Harrison of the Federal Reserve Bank of New York had the president's ear. Mellon still mattered to Republican businessmen, and to himself. It annoyed him that he was not permitted to speak without the White House preapproving his remarks, and that Hoover no longer consulted him on making appointments.[21]

Hoover's relationship with Stimson, although far more productive and respectful, also showed strains. The secretary of state had an insouciant, optimistic manner alien to his boss. He also had a mind of his own, which at times tested Hoover's patience. Dispatched overseas to finalize the details of the moratorium, Stimson was as assiduous in begging the president to modify his demands as he was in negotiating with the Europeans. "Goddamn it," exploded Hoover, "I wish I had an ambassador over there who would do as I direct him, rather than a hard-headed Secretary who thinks he can do as he pleases."[22]

"I don't think he realizes how hard it is to work for him," wrote

Stimson in the same diary in which he complained of the president's grim and grinding ways, of dull cabinet meetings that went on week after week, year after year, without a single joke.[23]

Despite these tensions, Hoover and Stimson generally found their way to common ground, something the president and Mellon seldom managed. Each showed an unusual solicitude for the other's well-being in the face of their mutual challenges. Stimson had a weak constitution, finding it difficult to work hard for more than a few hours at a time. As the depression deepened, he confessed to feeling "dreadfully dull and stale." He worried that he was "a loafer" compared to other members of the cabinet. Hoover, aware of Stimson's infirmities, was careful not to push him too hard. "I must consider his physical disability," he would say.[24]

Stimson, for his part, bled for Hoover and the load he was carrying. "How I wish that I could cheer up the poor old President," he wrote in his diary, "and make him feel the importance of a little brightness and recreation in his own work. But after all I suppose he would reply and say that he gets his recreation in his own way, and that my way would not suit him at all."[25]

Stimson joined Hoover at Rapidan the weekend of September 12, 1931, delighted to escape the still and steamy city for a couple of days. It was warm at camp, too, but comfortable enough to play deck tennis in the afternoons and to dine outdoors, under the trees, in the evenings. Stimson accompanied the president on long walks down sun-dappled trails where they filled their lungs with clean mountain air and added their voices to the birdsong and rustling leaves. Hoover guided the secretary by the arm and described the many ways he had been disgusted at France's behavior in the moratorium negotiations. As the sun lowered, the men of the Rapidan party sat around the Town Hall, as the main camp room was called, telling stories and reminiscing.

Stimson returned home refreshed and wiser to the camp's salubrious benefits to himself and his leader. "The President strikes me as being in very much better condition," he wrote. "His poise is better and he is more cheerful, and although he is oppressed by the terrible state of the country, he does not strike me as fretting as much."[26]

. . .

The state of the country was, indeed, terrible. The slight optimism of spring, the third false dawn, was scorched through summer. Unemployment, still impossible to pinpoint, was undoubtedly worse. The most recent census report had put the number at 6 million, representing 30 million Americans if one counted their families. Hoover hated that sort of math, arguing that some families had more than one breadwinner, that some of the unemployment was seasonal, and that some of the jobless were perpetually unemployable:

> Certainly we will have a serious problem but the envisaging of the problem in the light of large numbers is very seriously disturbing to public minds . . . and one result of that is the tightening of people's belts who have resources and decreasing the purchasing in the country, and thereby increasing unemployment again.[27]

Among other indicators, the gross national product had slid from $105 billion in mid-1929 to $75 billion in late spring of 1931. Business activity had slowed to a crawl, whether measured by factory payrolls, construction contracts, or industrial production. The Dow Jones Industrial Average had drooped below 100 in the warmer weather and was now down 50 percent from April, and three-quarters from its 1929 high. Commodities found new lows: the price of wheat had fallen from 74 cents a bushel to 55 cents since April. The Farm Board, able to support prices early in the depression, had exhausted its funds and could do no more. Cotton was so weak that Hoover worried it could wipe out most of the banks in the South.[28]

The banks remained a major concern in every region of the country. A new wave of suspensions had hit the Chicago suburbs and parts of Pennsylvania. Hoover spoke privately in early September of "a suppressed panic" in the American financial system. He had data showing that skittish depositors, disturbed by the shakiness of banking globally, had pulled enormous sums from U.S. institutions. He believed a major run of failures was only a matter of time.[29]

The drought was now in its second year and aggravated by grasshopper infestations. Farmers in the central and northwestern states, from Iowa to Montana, were hardest hit. "Suffering within the areas affected is acute," Hoover admitted. His official position was that the

Red Cross and local community relief areas were managing the problem, and he continued to promise that every agency of local, state, and federal government would work to ensure that no one would starve or go hungry or cold in America. Privately, he was worried. He was painfully aware that he did not have much to show for his depression-fighting efforts to date. A third lean winter was in prospect. Congress would return in December, with cohorts in both chambers eager to blame him for the economy and to float their own ideas for how to fix it and relieve its victims. Some of his own appointees were asking him to provide direct aid to the unemployed. Not least of these was Arthur Woods, a former New York City police chief who had been coordinating national charitable relief on behalf of the administration.[30]

In the late summer of 1931, Hoover took the unusual step of asking his surgeon general to report on the state of public health in the depression. Hugh S. Cumming, a distinguished soldier and Virginia physician, was the nation's fifth surgeon general and among the most credible voices in the American medical community. He had been guarding the health of the American people for eleven years, with special attention to its veterans, immigrants, prisoners, addicts, and lepers. He promptly answered the president's query with a survey of populations in thirteen states representing 43 million people. He compared their health over the recent winter of 1930–31 against the full-employment winter of 1928–29. He found mortality rates had improved from 13.7 per thousand to 12 per thousand. Incidences of infant mortality and death by tuberculosis, diphtheria, typhoid, and smallpox were similarly reduced. "In view of the agitation in general with respect of the effect of economic conditions on health," wrote Cumming, "public health workers have been surprised at the excellent health conditions that are found upon studying the available facts."[31]

Hoover, relieved by these findings, could not resist the opportunity to polish them. "The public health," he stated, "has apparently never been better than it has been over the past six months." Of course, that he was reduced to investigating whether or not the economy was killing people was not in itself reassuring. "It would be hard to persuade the American people that destitution and anxiety are not detrimental to health," said Lippmann.[32]

·  ·  ·

There were more defensive announcements. The White House released a statement from the Association of Community Chests and Councils advising the president that its organizations in 227 cities had "complete confidence that they, in cooperation with municipalities and other local agencies, will be able wholly to undertake the unemployment relief situation during the forthcoming winter." Hoover reminded the nation that his government was spending heroically in aid to employment, pouring more than $700 million into construction and maintenance, an amount triple to precrash levels. These projects gave work to 760,000 Americans compared to 180,000 in normal years.[33]

Popular opinion on the need for federal relief was difficult to gauge. Hoover tried to convince Republican governors to stand up and say that federal aid was unnecessary. Only three of the "spineless" lot would oblige him. This might indicate that the governors believed more relief necessary, or it may have been a reflection on the state of their relations with the White House.[34]

The Community Chests, closer to the problem than the governors, believed they could manage the distress. A *New York Times* survey of the mayors of twenty-four major American cities found them almost unanimous in their determination to get through the winter without federal assistance. The two exceptions were Detroit, where auto production had screeched to a halt, and Minneapolis, struggling under a mountain of debt.[35]

The vast majority of mayors agreed with Hoover that economic relief was a municipal and state function. Most were offended by the notion that they did not have the situation in hand and needed to be rescued by Washington. "I will positively say," harrumphed Philadelphia mayor Harry Mackey, "that no matter what the situation may be next winter, Philadelphia will take care of her own." Replies such as these, wrote the *Times*, "reveal in an impressive way how deep-seated is the American sentiment in favor of self-help and local action." The president's ideas about American character and the role of the federal government appear to have been well within the mainstream of national opinion.[36]

Nevertheless, Hoover continued to fret, fixating on what he called, in the infelicitous language of an engineer, "the probable volume of the load of distress which will need to be provided for."

Small businesses were laying off workers. Local and state governments, strapped for cash, were cutting payrolls and curtailing building programs, offsetting the impact of much of their relief work and
Washington's spending and hiring. Anxious to seize the initiative with
Congress due back in December, and genuinely concerned with the
mounting numbers of jobless Americans, Hoover launched a new
program of his own.[37]

The President's Organization for Unemployment Relief, headed
by AT&T president Walter S. Gifford, was a voluntary nationwide
campaign to raise funds to assist the unemployed. It coordinated
charitable activities, stimulated local employment projects, placed
workers in jobs, and provided relief to those unable to find work.
Its advertisements appeared in publications and on billboards emblazoned with the slogan "Of Course We Can Do It." Hundreds of benefit air shows and sporting contests were organized with a goal of
doubling the relief funds available the previous winter.[38]

Within weeks of the announcement of Hoover's program, New
York governor Franklin Roosevelt, a leading candidate for the Democratic nomination in 1932, launched what he christened the Temporary Emergency Relief Administration (TERA). It provided $20
million in relief to the unemployed directly from the New York State
Treasury. Roosevelt and his Democratic followers, then and ever
after, positioned TERA as a bold and compassionate alternative to the
thin gruel of Hoover's plan. This was consistent with the Democratic
National Committee's emerging portrayal of Hoover as indifferent to
human suffering and dogmatic in his insistence on a limited national
government.[39]

In fact, there was little to choose between the positions of the
two leaders. Hoover entirely supported direct relief at the state level.
Roosevelt was vague on what he wanted Hoover to do at the federal
level, and Democrats in Congress were by no means aligned with the
New York governor on the need for Washington to do more. Both
men were opposed to anything resembling a dole, or direct federal
payments to the unemployed, hence the emphasis on "temporary"
and "emergency" in the title of Roosevelt's agency. As for the effi-
cacy of their approaches, Roosevelt put $20 million into his fund for
the entirety of New York State. Gifford's Committee helped increase
annual municipal relief spending in New York City from $9 million

in 1930 to $58 million by 1932, and to quadruple private donations to a total of $21 million over the same period. Together the programs could barely keep up with the swelling ranks of newly unemployed New Yorkers.[40]

Hoover, while convinced of the rightness of his policy, was indignant at the suggestion that callousness or incompetence prevented him from doing more. He struck back at his critics, lumping Roosevelt in with a free-spending congressional minority eager to demonstrate its generosity at the expense of the public purse, and willing to "play politics at the expense of human misery." These sallies boosted his morale. Still, he brooded, as did many Republicans, over the damage the depression and Democratic attacks had done to his chances for reelection in 1932, especially with the conventions ten months away.[41]

After three years in office, Hoover continued to pretend disinterest in his political fortunes. Joslin would try, from time to time, to turn the president's attention to the coming election, only to incur his wrath:

> I don't give a damn, Ted, whether I am re-nominated or not. I shall not turn a hand to get another term. The convention can nominate me if it wants to or it can nominate some one else. It can do as it damn well pleases. Let's not bring up the subject again.[42]

Joslin knew well that the president desperately wanted a second term. His inaugural had outlined two terms' worth of initiatives, most of them sidelined by the long tariff fight and the depression. Items dear to his heart, such as child welfare, social reform, and a reorganization of the federal administration, would at this late stage almost certainly require a second term. He also yearned for a chance to demonstrate his ability under something approaching normal economic conditions.

Hoover's true feelings about 1932 were better reflected in his actions than his words. In midsummer, he gave his blessing to the efforts of his aide, James MacLafferty, to assess the readiness of the Republican Party to fight a national election. MacLafferty gave up his Washington rental accommodations, put his household goods in storage, and drove his majestic Cadillac 314 coupe almost fifteen thousand miles in big loops across the map, fancying himself "a sort of political Lindbergh." He attended more than 120 meetings of county Republican organizations and friendly service clubs. He preached the word of the administration and listened carefully to local assessments of the national political situation, Hoover's performance, and Republican prospects.[43]

MacLafferty's regular reports back to Robert Lucas, executive director of the Republican National Committee, carried discouraging news on both the state of the party and the president's profile. As MacLafferty had expected, Republicans were deeply divided over Prohibition and reeling from the depression, which by now had made its way to almost every doorstep. What surprised him was the distribution of blame. While most Republicans were inclined to sympathize with Hoover over the hand he had been dealt, or to direct their anger toward Congress, and the Senate specifically, for frustrating administration policy, an unmistakable and vocal minority pointed fingers at the president. They had no coherent case against him: they blamed him for the drought, the grasshoppers, the price of corn, the lack of jobs, the failure of the Eighteenth Amendment, their own personal misfortunes, and the defeatist state of mind in the party. In some pockets of the country the animosity against Hoover amounted to "a pure and holy hatred," and MacLafferty could say nothing to change minds.[44]

Equally inimical to the party's hopes were the signs of disorganization and schism MacLafferty found everywhere he traveled:

> Republicans seem not to be trained to meet political adversity. They have been used to success nationally and have gotten away with the "Republican Prosperity" talk. Now that they find adversity has come during a Republican administration they do not know how to act.[45]

MacLafferty's reports suggested a significant decline in Republican fortunes since the midterm elections less than a year past. The president's neglect of the party was draining its enthusiasm to stand with him, let alone fight for him. There was still time to bring most

Republicans around, thought MacLafferty, who was far from ready to concede the 1932 election. He nevertheless warned Lucas that a great deal of work would be required to right the ship.

The "political Lindbergh" did not level with Hoover about the mood of their party. Aware of the president's sensitivity to criticism, he picked out discreet ideas or messages he felt would be helpful and encouraging to him. For instance, he suggested the president be more aggressive in holding the Senate to account. Hoover listened carefully, and offered his own complaints about the state of the leadership of the Republican National Committee, its inability to pay for good staffers, and the difficulties of fund-raising. The two men agreed that the state of their national committee was disastrous compared to the super-charged machine Raskob and Michelson were operating. Even so, Hoover was reluctant to act on the matter. MacLafferty had to goad him into intervening to prevent an anticipated round of salary cuts at Republican headquarters.

Even as MacLafferty was making his way home to Washington, international events were conspiring to worsen the odds on Republican reelection, and to render Hoover's estimates of the probable volume of the load of distress obsolete. Central Europe's troubles had crossed the English Channel over the summer and Great Britain's gold reserves were dangerously close to the legal minimum. Austerity measures designed to renew confidence in the pound had instead led to widespread protest and strike actions, including, remarkably, a pay-cut mutiny by the Royal Navy. With banks frozen and unemployment above 20 percent, British policy makers could see no way forward. Winston Churchill, now in opposition, warned in Parliament that the "hoarding" of gold by the United States and France at the expense of the rest of the world was dooming civilization to a "bleak, ferocious barbarism."[46]

Hoover admitted to reporters in Washington in early September that as much as half the planet's stock of gold was within U.S. borders. This he attributed to "the flight of capital from practically the whole world to the United States in refuge." While agreeing with Churchill that the situation was abnormal and unprecedented, he rejected the charge of hoarding: "It is fundamentally due to the lack of confidence of people in their own governments and their own circumstances in their home countries."[47]

On the evening of September 20, the British government staggered the financial world by announcing the indefinite suspension of its efforts to hold the pound at its traditional rate of convertibility. In short, it was off the gold standard. The pound lost a fifth of its value overnight. Overwhelmed by a new wave of fear and uncertainty, security and commodity markets closed from Amsterdam to Vienna. Only Paris remained open, and even there, trading seized. "It seemed," said Hoover's friend, the New York banker Jackson Reynolds, "like the end of the world, to financial thinking." If Great Britain, still the leading nation in international finance, could be forced to capitulate, there was no safe haven for capital anywhere.[48]

Speculation followed as to whether America, with its large holdings of British and German paper, might be the next domino to fall. Central bankers, investors, and speculators, battered and risk averse, rushed for the exits without waiting for an answer. Thus began what the Federal Reserve Bank of New York called "the most rapid outflow of gold experienced by this country, and probably by any country." No amount of reassurance from the leadership of the Federal Reserve System could stop the run. The Bank of England, after all, had been full of encouragement until hours before its surrender. A hike in discount rates from 1.5 percent to 3.5 percent provided a measure of protection for the dollar but not enough to change sentiment. Meanwhile, the higher rates produced further deflationary momentum in an already flaccid economy. Prices and industrial production sank again. Consumers and businesses were more reluctant than ever to borrow or spend. On the evening of September 22, the United States Steel Corporation announced 10 percent pay cuts to employees, a move immediately emulated by other major companies, breaking the agreement on employment that Hoover had enforced with corporate America for almost two years, and stirring more fear among the nation's workers.[49]

The administration's official response to Great Britain's move was to proclaim business as usual. London, said Hoover, had not abandoned the gold standard, it had merely suspended its usual rate of convertibility in favor of a variable standard, a decision that might be reversed at any time in the future. Hoover reminded the press that Britain had found its way back to its usual mark after a similar situation during the war. In the meantime, business transactions would continue to be conducted in gold, and the president did not anticipate "any great effect in the United States."[50]

In truth, Hoover considered Britain's departure from gold a disaster, a massive breakdown in the machinery of international finance, with dreadful implications for his own banking system. He leveled with the press gallery in an off-the-record briefing, admitting that the crisis in London had rent the economic fabric of the world and that everything now depended on the United States, which he described as "the Verdun" of global stability. He asked the newspapermen to help him keep the country "steady in the boat" by avoiding alarmist reports. For the moment, they obliged.[51]

Despite his efforts at containment, the suppressed panic Hoover had identified weeks before London's move now broke all restraints. U.S. financial institutions were hit with both barrels. There was an external shock as international investors and central bankers pulled gold and capital out of America, and as the value of German and English assets held by U.S. banks plummeted. There was a domestic hit as American depositors pulled their funds from risky banks and hid them in teapots and under mattresses. The net effect was a liquidity crisis of catastrophic proportions.[52]

Hoover never seriously considered following Britain's lead and suspending the gold standard in the United States. Virtually all economic theory and every reputable economist agreed that its maintenance was a necessity. There was no recognized alternative to assessing the relative values of currencies, no other basis on which to conduct international trade. Untethered prices were considered arbitrary, unreliable prices. Without gold, as Hoover said, a merchant could not know on making a sale "what he might receive in payment by the time his goods were delivered."* However desperate matters

---

* John Maynard Keynes was in 1931 developing a theory of monetary management independent of the gold standard. His ideas were not as yet fully developed or widely known, let alone accepted as workable by policy makers.

were at the moment of Britain's breach, it was easy to imagine worse if the United States were to follow suit.[53]

Through the rest of September and into October, bank suspensions swept the nation at a rate of 125 a week, ten times the average during 1929. Depositors pulled their funds from weak and strong banks alike, forcing those institutions still open to call loans and to restrict short-term credit, measures detrimental to industry and commerce. Hoover understood that the banking system was desperate for liquidity. More credit would relieve the pressure from the banks, allowing them to resume lending for business purposes, encouraging businessmen to invest and consumers to spend money. He also knew that the necessary measures would not come from the Federal Reserve System, which did not see the restoration of confidence as its problem. In any event, many faltering banks were not members of the Federal Reserve or did not have eligible commercial paper to pledge as collateral to borrow from the system. The administration would need to step in. The question was how.[54]

Hoover wanted New York's leading bankers to voluntarily fund a bailout of weaker banks, forestalling further suspensions. This was how a crisis had been averted during the Panic of 1907, when the legendary financier J. P. Morgan and his colleagues had pledged their own wealth to stabilize the financial system. Hoover engaged Federal Reserve chairman Eugene Meyer to help organize such a pool, although Meyer was never convinced that the bankers would respond favorably. He had an alternative in mind. He wanted the federal government to create its own fund for failing banks on the model of the War Finance Corporation, which had loaned to industry and bankers in aid of the war effort.

Hoover was not entirely averse to Meyer's idea. He was uneasy, however, about setting a precedent of peacetime support for the banking industry, and he did not want to recall Congress in extra session to that purpose. Moreover, he believed the bankers would prefer to stand up, rescue their own industry, and do their part in promoting recovery, rather than fall back ignominiously on public assistance.

When the cabinet discussed the question of private versus public relief for the banking sector, the president pushed his views with unusual heat. He was inwardly furious at his Treasury secretary for

having failed to assist institutions in his own backyard earlier in the
summer. The Bank of Pittsburgh had suspended operations. It was
the largest non-Mellon bank in the Steel City, and one that the Treasury secretary had long coveted. Leading Pennsylvania financiers had
attempted to raise a subscription to save the bank, but Mellon refused
to participate unless given complete control and the Bank of Pittsburgh went under, triggering a spate of failures in Pennsylvania. So
far as Hoover was concerned, Mellon had put his personal interests
ahead of the national interest and had made of himself an unhelpful
and conspicuous example when banks across the country were struggling to maintain the confidence of their depositors. The people of
Pittsburgh took the president's side. The Mellon name would never
entirely recover in the city.[55]

Hoover ultimately insisted on the administration adopting his
privately funded bailout scheme. He arranged to meet with nineteen
leading bankers, most of them from New York, on Sunday, October 4.
Although his habit of sneaking businessmen and external advisers into
the White House for evening meetings had served him well through
the summer, he now changed venues. His chances of slipping Thomas
Lamont of J. P. Morgan and William Potter of Guaranty Trust past
the newspaper sentries at the White House were slim. They gathered
instead amid the Gainsboroughs and Turners in Mellon's opulent
fifth-floor penthouse in the McCormick Building. It undoubtedly
pleased the president that the Treasury secretary was thoroughly
implicated in his project.

The bankers gathered just after dark, made quick introductions
on Mellon's priceless oriental carpets, and settled without further preliminaries into his eighteenth-century French furniture for a presentation by the president. "You know the picture better than I do," he
told them, before painting it for them anyway:

> Owing to the prolonged business depression, the succession
> of events abroad, the failure of banks in constantly increasing
> numbers, and the destruction of confidence and increasing
> fear throughout the country, a situation exists which calls for
> concerted action on the part of our leading bankers and strong
> banks to avert a possible threat to our entire credit structure.[56]

Hoover counted 1,215 bank suspensions since the beginning of the year. These had tied up billions of dollars in savings and investments. Close to a billion more had been withdrawn from banks by skittish depositors. He discussed the problems of membership and eligibility that prevented the Federal Reserve from coming to the rescue of sick banks. He reminded the bankers that their industry had in the past met crises of confidence and liquidity themselves.[57]

What was needed, he said, was for the strong banks to recognize their obligation to weaker banks around the country and pledge 2 percent of their assets to a $500 million support fund that would lend to troubled institutions on less rigid terms than the Fed required. "I consider some such program essential in the public interest," he said, adding that "if present tendencies are allowed to continue unchecked, there is no telling where the movement will stop."[58]

Many of the bankers, having been tipped by Governor Meyer as to what the president wanted, had come to the meeting reluctantly. They were unenthused by Hoover's proposal. They believed that 1907 was ancient history, and that the creation of the Federal Reserve System in 1913 had relieved them of collective responsibility for the financial sector in such crises. They asked why they should risk their own balance sheets in service of banks they viewed as not simply illiquid but insolvent. They saw Hoover's plan as throwing good money after bad and suggested the government furnish the bailout pool.

This was a major miscalculation by Hoover. He had thought the bankers, a conservative lot, would be hostile to a direct and unprecedented federal intrusion into their sector. He had wielded the publicly funded option as a threat, and he was dumbfounded when the bankers welcomed it. He returned to the White House annoyed at the timidity and condescension of the Wall Street heavyweights, who had seen fit to lecture him on the basics of banking and finance. Meyer stayed behind at Mellon's residence and convinced those gathered to subscribe to a pool as requested by Hoover. They agreed, huffily, on condition that a public solution would follow in the event of failure. The very existence of this backstop, obviously, did not bode well for their commitment to making the private fund work.[59]

·   ·   ·

The next day Hoover traveled to Shibe Park in Philadelphia for the third game of the World Series between the Athletics and the St. Louis Cardinals. He was enough of a baseball fan to have marked the occasion on his calendar the previous February, ensuring the day would be free. He considered canceling at the last minute under pressure of events but attended anyway on the theory that his presence would be reassuring to the public under the circumstances.[60]

Sitting with Lou in an open box, he threw out the first pitch without loosening his tie or removing the jacket of his three-piece suit. The ball sailed far over the head of catcher Mickey Cochrane. The crowd of thirty-four thousand greeted him warmly regardless of his aim, and he received more applause later on that Indian summer afternoon when he stood for the seventh-inning stretch. Several reporters heard isolated booing directed at the president, but he does not appear to have noticed (although he left the stadium with the chant of "We Want Beer" ringing in his ears). Sadly for the Athletics, who had come to view Hoover as a good-luck charm—they had not lost in his two previous visits to Shibe—the Cardinals managed a 5–2 victory.[61]

The following evening the president made another sortie in his battle to save the banks, hosting a meeting of thirty-two leading senators and representatives at 9 p.m. at the White House. There was no hiding from the press this time. Invitees had been contacted on short notice and told only that the agenda was of urgent national importance. An army aircraft was made available to anyone requiring travel assistance. John Nance Garner, in Uvalde, Texas, took up the offer and flew two thousand miles in fourteen hours to make the meeting. He arrived at the White House just before 9 p.m. and, like every other guest stepping out of a taxi or limousine, was greeted by an explosion of flashbulbs and a cordon of a hundred correspondents wanting to know more about the purpose of the gathering.[62]

The guests were ushered to the Lincoln Study, where Hoover did most of the talking. Once again, and with more drama than ever, he rooted the crisis in the malign inheritances of the Great War:

> The nations of Europe have not found peace. Hates and fears dominate their relations. War injuries have permitted no abatement. The multitude of small democracies created by

the Treaty of Versailles have developed excessive nationalism. They have created a maze of trade barriers between each other. Underneath all is the social turmoil of communism and fascism gnawing at the vitals of young democracies. The armies of Europe have doubled since the demobilization. They have wasted the substance which should have gone into productive work upon these huge armies and massive fortifications. They have lived in a maze of changing military alliances and they have vibrated with enmities and fears. They have borrowed from any foreign country willing to lend, and at any rates of interest, in order to carry unbalanced budgets. . . . Nineteen countries in the world, in two years, have gone through revolutions or violent social disturbances. Whether or not Germany and Central Europe will avoid Russian infiltrated communism or some other "ism," is still in the balance, and that does not contribute to a revival of world confidence.[63]

Hoover talked his way through the British debacle to the pressure on American banks, the "Damoclean sword over our credit structure." There was utter silence in the room. "We are now faced with the problem," he said, "not of saving Germany or Britain, but of saving ourselves." His guests, he wrote later, seemed stunned.[64]

With help from Meyer and Ogden Mills, the president outlined his plans for a private fund in support of troubled banks, backed by a new federal agency if necessary. He unveiled plans to inject more capital into the Federal Farm Loan system to provide additional low-interest credit to farmers. He disclosed that he had asked the Federal Reserve banks to work with bankers in their districts to free some of the assets frozen by bank suspensions, putting money back in the hands of depositors. All of this was intended to liquefy the financial system, mobilize the banking resources of the country, and get the economy moving again.

Hoover asked approval in principle for his plans. Garner, who may have had a drink or two in the course of his long journey, spoke first. He abruptly declared his refusal to be bound in any manner by the administration's plans. The room fell quiet. Apart from the cigar smoke swirling around Mellon's chandeliers, nothing moved. The prospects for a rescue looked bleak.

After what seemed like an eternal pause, deliverance came from an unexpected quarter. Mississippi senator Pat Harrison was a Democrat and a respected member of the Senate Finance Committee. He spoke of the fragility of the economy and gave his blessing to Hoover's plan. Joe Robinson, Senate Minority Leader, and his colleague Carter Glass, the leading financial mind in the Democratic caucus, added their approval. The moment was saved. Hoover produced a public announcement that he wished to release to the press. It denounced the "foolish alarm" behind the mass withdrawals from American banks, asserted that fear for the financial system was "wholly unjustifiable," and outlined the president's program. All in attendance except Garner and Senator Borah gave their assent. Around midnight, the guests trickling out of the White House divulged to reporters the purpose of the meeting and announced their support in principle for Hoover's proposals.[65]

# CHAPTER 23

# The President in His Fighting Clothes

Even with bipartisan support, there was every chance that the president's program to save the banking system would fail. Two years into what was supposed to be a brief setback, with industry still retrenching, with wages dropping and thousands upon thousands of jobs disappearing every week, with apprehension crushing optimism in the weary hearts and minds of the public, confidence was not easily conjured. People knew that much had been tried, far more than had ever been tried in answer to any previous downturn, and that after several false dawns, much had failed. Why trust this latest trick, six months after the disappointing moratorium trick? Even to Hoover, it seemed as though the harder he rubbed his lamp, the smaller the genie. And yet between the wee hours of October 7, when White House reporters had returned to their desks to file their stories, and the middle of the next day, when their news had made its way around the country, America brightened.

The stock market was first to respond, with the NYSE recording its strongest day of advances since the Great Crash. Bankers were lavish in their praise of the president's plan, whatever their private doubts. They characterized it as "a powerful turn of the flywheel" to set America's economic machinery humming again. Congressional leaders stuck to the script, marking the second time in six months that Hoover had forged a bipartisan consensus on a groundbreaking measure. The press not only avoided doom-saying reports, as requested, but went out of its way to signal approval for the president's actions.

A national survey of twenty-four papers of all stripes found unanimous praise for the new program. The Hearst papers said Hoover had delivered a death blow to "the utter folly and recklessness" of "outmoded laissez-faire doctrine in economics." Added Hearst's competitor, the *New York Herald-Tribune*:

> Once again President Hoover has cut swiftly and decisively through a tangle of mingled fact and fear. By careful preparation and skillful leadership he has been able to marshal the best financial minds of the nation and its entire financial strength behind a simple and understandable plan. Practically overnight the country's credit resources have gained the benefits of a unified command.[1]

As chance would have it, another eminent European economist was visiting America during this episode, as Keynes had been for the moratorium announcement. Melchior Palyi was an adviser to Deutsche Bank und Disconto-Gesellschaft, and a former professor at the Handelschochschule in Berlin and Oxford University. He was soon to become a leading light in the University of Chicago economics department. He applauded Hoover's National Credit Corporation, as the privately financed $500 million fund was labeled. The support of failing banks was crucial, said Palyi, even though some by their own mismanagement deserved to fall: "Wait until the panic is over before punishing bankers, and by the extension of liberal credits permit all banks to stay open and thus spread prestige and confidence in financial institutions, and the panic is over."[2]

The panic was indeed over, at least for the time being. At a cabinet meeting on October 20, it was agreed that the president's banking plan was bearing fruit. Domestic runs on banks slowed each successive week during the month, as did the exodus of gold and the domestic hoarding of currency. The markets gained steam once again. Hoover used the breathing space to stand up another pillar of his recovery strategy.[3]

For the first two years of the depression, Hoover had been pleased to loosen the federal purse strings with the intention of creating jobs and supporting employment. He had run deficits to take the edge off the downturn, trusting that there would be time to balance the books when the economy improved. He had cut taxes in the expectation that government revenues would rise as they had after three Mellon tax reductions in the twenties. Hoover aimed his cuts at people with large incomes who, given lower rates, could be expected to take money out of tax-free municipal bonds or savings accounts and invest it in new production. These attempts to put the national government to work in service of recovery amounted to a radical new approach to economic management. The net stimulative effect of Hoover's policy in 1931 would be larger than in any other year in the twenties or thirties. Hoover was so confident in this direction that he had overridden the collective wisdom of Mellon, Mills, and the Federal Reserve's Meyer, who had each advised letting nature take its course. Now, in the wake of Britain's departure from gold, Hoover performed a dramatic reversal, raising taxes, cutting spending, and pursuing a balanced budget with the ferocity of a latter-day Coolidge.[4]

It was an unexpected, mind-bending turnabout, made sensible by the new circumstances in which Hoover suddenly found himself. In the wake of Britain's decision, gold was no longer flowing into America; it was flowing out. Interest rates were not low but high, and asset values were deflating rapidly. The country was in the midst of a credit squeeze. To continue to finance deficits in such an environment would have put government in competition for credit with industry and the nation's wobbly banking sector. More government borrowing would have put more upward pressure on interest rates and further depressed security prices and the value of bank assets, leading to more bank failures. An unbalanced budget, moreover, might in the wake of Britain's experience make the government look weak and increase the outflow of gold.[*][5]

Hoover's best option, under the gold standard regime which, again, was viewed as inviolable, was to prove that his government, unlike Britain's, had its budget under control. He laid out a plan to increase tax revenue by 30 percent, or $900 million, in the next fiscal year. "Our first step toward recovery," he explained, "is to reestablish

---

[*] An alternative to borrowing would have been for the Federal Reserve to create more money to support a deficit. Its leadership was not prepared to do so. Nor would it exert itself to prevent bank failures. It was preoccupied with the specific task of defending the convertibility of the dollar to gold.

confidence and thus restore the flow of credit which is the very basis of our economic life. . . . The first requirement of confidence and of economic recovery is the financial stability of the United States government."[6]

Higher taxes and spending cuts were harsh medicine in the midst of an epochal depression. Hoover understood that the measures would tend to slow recovery but he considered it a necessary price to pay to secure the stability of the entire financial system. His plan faced no serious opposition in Congress or anywhere else.[7]

If Hoover had any fantasies in these months about carving out time to return to his original constructive agenda for his presidency, an explosion on a section of track along the Japanese South Manchurian Railway in September 1931 blew them up. One Japanese guard was dead. The Japanese army, with a strong presence in the region, blamed Chinese nationalists for the blast and began seizing towns and cities along the route. These actions were well timed to take advantage of civil strife in China, which was largely powerless to respond. China appealed to the League of Nations. Japan, after all, had signed its covenant. The League, with no enforcement mechanisms of its own, turned to the United States. The United States protested to the Japanese government, which, despite its imperial ambitions, had not approved its army's actions. Meanwhile, the Japanese army, claiming a need to put down bandits, continued to occupy strategic sites in resource-rich Manchuria.[8]

Hoover and Stimson were initially confused by the situation, in part because Japan and China were offering contradictory reports on events, and also because the Japanese government and the Japanese army appeared to be operating independently. There was no question that Japan was formally afoul of the League of Nations covenant, the Kellogg-Briand Pact, and several other international agreements. However, with so many economic problems to deal with, the administration's first concern, said Stimson privately, was "not to allow under any circumstances anybody to deposit the [Manchurian] baby on our lap." Its second concern was to avoid backing itself into "a humiliating position." These goals overrode Hoover's desire to prove that the international world could be governed by pact and treaty. Stimson, for his part, believed that European peace treaties no more fit the peoples of Russia, Japan, and China than "a stovepipe hat would fit an African savage."[9]

The United States minced around the Manchurian situation for months, wanting to help China but anxious about a confrontation with Japan. Stimson tried to engineer a peace brokered by the League of Nations, but his initiative went nowhere. The Japanese government, its control of the situation still uncertain, sent conciliatory notes to the administration while its army expanded its reach to the whole of Manchuria. Stimson and Hoover rightly worried that the situation was making "rather a mockery" of the president's bid to lead the world to a sweeping new disarmament agreement.[10]

They continued to discuss their options. Military action was out of the question. "Neither our obligation to China, nor our own interest, nor our dignity requires us to go to war," Hoover would later write. He dismissed an economic blockade as likely to lead to war and also opposed the withdrawal of the U.S. ambassador from Japan as a provocation. Faced with the likelihood that Japan would set up a puppet government in Manchuria and disavow taking an inch of territory, he told the cabinet that such a result would not represent a diplomatic defeat for the United States. China in the long run would throw off Japan's effort to dominate it as it had done with every other outsider. He continued to stand on moral suasion and international agreement. "The poor old President," said Stimson, who favored more aggressive action, had "outstripped the progress of the world by taking too high a position."[11]

On November 9, Hoover suggested to Stimson that their best move would be to announce a refusal to recognize any territorial changes or treaty between Japan and China executed by force. The policy, consistent with the spirit of the Kellogg-Briand Pact, would be officially announced in the New Year. It would be known, to Hoover's annoyance, as the Stimson Doctrine. It would have no positive effect on the conflict whatsoever. The Japanese resented the U.S. intrusion and marched on Shanghai in a matter of months. Manchuria would continue to occupy a share of the president's attention for the rest of his term.[12]

.  .  .

Another set of issues occupying Hoover's mind in the fall of 1931 was as petty as the Manchurian crisis was profound. *Mirrors of 1932*, by Anonymous, was an early entry in a spate of malicious books examining Hoover, his life, and his presidency. It portrayed him as an "unloved and unpopular" opportunist whose party would cast him aside given a convenient opening.[13]

Close on the heels of *Mirrors*, and more vexing to Hoover and his friends, was John Hamill's *The Strange Career of Mr. Hoover Under Two Flags*. The Firm had known of Hamill's investigations for more than a year: the author, pleading penury, had tried to sell his researches to Hoover through the agency of Edgar Rickard. When no deal was struck, he published. Hamill's book resurrected and embroidered on every scandal ever to have touched the president, cleverly mixing fact and fiction, placing official paperwork alongside hysterical claims that Hoover had murdered mine workers in his lust for gold, that his mining syndicates were a species of organized crime, and that he had renounced his American citizenship while living in London. Written in a hyperbolic tone, Hamill's book was published by the thrice-convicted pornographer Samuel Roth, purveyor of *Venus in Furs* and *Celestine—Diary of a Chambermaid*.[14]

A third book, by the radical left-wing reporter Walter Liggett, used some of Hamill's documentation and added more of its own to make salient points about the embarrassing speculations of the Bewick, Moreing crowd and the involvement of Hoover colleagues in grain speculation while he served as food czar. Although Liggett sometimes shared Hamill's inability to distinguish suggestion from fact, he was more careful in his research and relatively restrained in his conclusions, perhaps explaining his slighter sales.[15]

These and several other volumes, including *The Great Mistake*, by John Knox, and *Hoover's Millions and How He Made Them*, by James J. O'Brien, came to be known collectively as "the smear books." In aggregate, they showed the president as an irresponsible, timid, petty, callous, arrogant, unscrupulous, malicious, devious, greedy, violent, ignorant, and reactionary fraud. The mainstream press largely ignored them.[16]

Hoover would have been wise to do the same. Indeed, he was advised by friends to do the same. He was reminded that every president since Washington had been subjected to scurrilous attacks. He chose instead to be tormented. Wrongly convinced that the hand of Raskob was behind the books, he tried desperately to trace them to the DNC. He had his aides engage naval intelligence and the FBI in fruitless efforts to discredit the authors and their work. He plotted campaigns of magazine articles responding to his critics and celebrating his record. He considered asking the publisher Russell Doubleday to produce a retort to the smears and an exposé of Raskob and Michelson, his enemies in Congress, and the press. Hoover's inner circle met almost daily through the fall to worry over the attacks and succeeded in manufacturing a small shelf's worth of fawning magazine articles and biographies, all of which passed as unheeded as the smear books. The sum of all this handwringing and drama was merely to add an enormous weight of personal anxiety to the dreadful load Hoover was already carrying.[17]

The one encouraging aspect of the smear episode, so far as the Firm was concerned, was that Hoover had at least managed to contain his feelings behind closed doors. He presented himself to the outside world as unruffled. The abuse, said reporters, has "failed to embitter him, and he has learned to relax and smile" in the face of it. He was "almost Oriental" in his calm. McCormick noticed in the president "a limbering up of manner and attitude, a new, less personal view of events." He was genial, at ease, fidgeting less, doodling less, looking his visitors in the eyes, laughing off the insults. There was personal growth here. As his reputation tumbled from absurd heights to unaccustomed lows, he at least managed to appear to be philosophical about it.[18]

The strains, piled on top of his backbreaking work habits and the usual pressures of the presidency, nevertheless showed. He was aging on the job, already by the end of 1931 several shades grayer than the man elected in 1928. His skin had lost some of its elasticity, deepening the creases on his face and loosening his jowls. The corners of his eyes drooped. He was leaner and slightly more stooped than he had started, although fitter due to his dedication to Hooverball.

Hoover gave more effort to his 1931 State of the Union than to any speech since his inauguration. He wrote the first draft at the beginning of November, five weeks before it was due. At that time, there were signs that the bankers' pool was having its intended effect, but the signs did not last, making the autumn of 1931 Hoover's fourth false dawn. The bankers, never enthusiastic about the idea, used the uptick to question the necessity of the fund and delay their participation in it. Almost no money was loaned, and before November was out another spasm of pain shot through the financial system. Bank suspensions ramped up again, markets tumbled further, and the lay-offs kept coming. The federal government, with its tax receipts plummeting and its expenditures on public works at record highs, was for the fiscal year ending June 30, 1932, facing a deficit approaching $2 billion on spending of just over $4 billion notwithstanding Hoover's austerity plan. The new President's Organization for Unemployment Relief was looking increasingly inadequate to the escalating problem of joblessness. "Everything is down again," wrote Stimson in his diary. "Everything is blue." Hoover asked Governor Meyer to begin drafting legislation for an updated version of the War Finance Corporation that would do what the bankers would not.[19]

These shifting circumstances forced continuous alterations to Hoover's address. So did his estimations of what it would take to win reelection. He viewed the winter congressional session as his last chance to derail the economic crisis that had played havoc with his term and to demonstrate the soundness of his judgment and leadership. He knew that the patience of the American people was wearing thin. It took him twenty-two drafts to get the speech where he wanted it, and even then, after finally handing it to Joslin at 9:30 a.m. on the morning of Sunday, December 6, he promptly asked for it back to make further alterations. An exasperated Joslin told him it was already in the hands of the printer. "Well, that ends it," said Hoover with an awkward chuckle.[20]

The two chambers of the Seventy-Second Congress were read Hoover's speech independently. The Senate was more or less unchanged from the Seventy-First, with a slightly narrower and still unworkable Republican majority. In the House, a high rate of mortality among Republican members in recent months had allowed an eight-seat swing in favor of the Democrats, giving them a viable majority. At the opening of the House session, Representative Jack Garner of Texas was elected Speaker to wild cheering from a joyous Democratic caucus as Republicans looked on sullenly.

Hoover was ambivalent about the shift in leadership. The Democratic ascendency, having come at the expense of his party, was unquestionably a defeat, but he had never enjoyed the support he believed he deserved from Republican representatives. Not more than ten of them could be counted on to stand up and defend him. He expected the Democratic leaders would be inclined to work with him in order to take credit for his successes. He also hoped that their rash spending plans might be checked by the burden of responsibility for the House.[21]

The address opened with the president's usual appeal for Americans to look on the bright side, to appreciate that for the first time in their history a major downturn had brought no labor strife or public disorder, that their charity and generosity had through two hard winters helped millions to keep body and soul together. It is unlikely that by this point in the depression, Americans were comforted by any of this, or by another recitation of the litany of measures the government had employed in its failed bid to fix the economy.

What was new in the speech was a package of initiatives that dramatically escalated the administration's attack on "credit paralysis." Only by putting "some steel beams in the foundations of our credit structure," said Hoover, could government improve public confidence, and the economy and the banking system stabilize. The first requirement was a balanced budget: he would raise taxes and cut spending. He asked Congress to permit a reorganization of federal departments to eliminate overlap and allow more savings. A portion of the deficit would have to be financed through borrowing.[22]

Building on this base of fiscal stability, Hoover laid out plans for Federal Land Banks to make capital available to farmers at low rates, and for home-loan discount banks to support residential housing. He asked that Congress and the Federal Reserve work to return to depositors some portion of funds stuck in closed banks, and he appealed for a full range of banking reforms, including deposit insurance and a separation of investment banking from commercial banking. The centerpiece of the speech was his proposal for creation of the Reconstruction Finance Corporation, successor to the War Finance Corporation. Hoover recommended the RFC as a multipurpose agency that would expand the capital stock of the financial system and lend to a broad range of financial institutions. The first $500 million of the

RFC's funds would come from the Treasury, with another $1.5 billion raised through debentures.

In conclusion, Hoover insisted that local communities, lower levels of government, and individual Americans retain primary responsibility for relief of unemployment. The speech said nothing about Prohibition or foreign affairs—nothing of note about anything other than the economy. Hoover was betting his presidency on kick-starting recovery.

Minutes after the reading of the State of the Union, identical bills to create the Reconstruction Finance Corporation were delivered to the Senate and House Banking and Currency Committees. The administration and its congressional allies fanned out to press for immediate action. The president made it known he wanted the legislation approved before the Christmas recess. While that was an optimistic deadline, Democratic leaders, as Hoover had expected, were cautious in their criticisms of his proposals, and both chambers sprang into action. There was informal bipartisan agreement that the RFC should come to life by February 1.[23]

It was a momentous decision to use public funds to bail out the financial sector in peacetime. Nothing like it had been done before. Some found it mind-boggling, not least because it came from Hoover. Said Senator Norris, among the most radical of the insurgents: "I have been called a socialist, a Bolshevik, a communist, and a lot of other terms of a similar nature, but in my wildest flights of imagination I never thought of such a thing as putting the Government into business as far as this bill would put it in."[24]

Rex Tugwell, the Columbia University economist and future New Dealer, said that Hoover, overcoming his "expressed horror of governmental interference," had intruded so far into the banking sector that "one may imagine what pictures of government in business one pleases."[25]

The incredulity of Norris and Tugwell at the president's radical initiatives relied upon a caricature of the man as an obstinate champion of laissez-faire. This picture, drawn primarily by Democrats in the middle years of the president's term, ignores Hoover's early advocacy of countercyclical government spending and expensive economic development projects. It forgets that he had applied $500 million in government funds to stabilize agricultural prices through the Federal Farm Board. There were places Hoover would not take the government—Muscle Shoals being the shining example—but he had never been shy about federal interference in the economy. Hoover was especially comfortable with intrusive government in exceptional circumstances, and he did not view the nation's predicament as the usual course of business. He often compared fighting the depression to fighting a war, and he considered the depression a legacy of war. It followed, in his mind, that the country should mobilize all of its resources against the emergency, as it would in wartime. He saw it as both a moral imperative and the first requirement of leadership for the administration to step into the breach. "Governments," he told the Methodist Ecumenical Congress in a radio address six weeks before the State of the Union, "are tested at last by their attitudes to the welfare of men and women."[26]

Notwithstanding the unprecedented nature of the RFC and the dollars involved, equal to half of the federal budget, there was scarcely any opposition to its specifics, and to the entire State of the Union, from economists, editorialists, or politicians. There was general agreement that a balanced budget, easier credit, and a stable financial system would cure what ailed America. What little opposition developed to Hoover's plans emphasized what he had left out rather than what he had proposed. A growing body of opinion thought it insufficient for the government to fight the disease of depression. It wanted action on the symptoms, and the president had offered no direct succor to the millions of unemployed and their families.

Just after the Christmas break, a subcommittee of the Senate Committee on Manufactures began hearings on two bills authorizing hundreds of millions of dollars in direct federal spending for unemployment relief. The bills' sponsors were Senators Edward Costigan, Democrat of Colorado, and Robert La Follette Jr., an insurgent Republican from Wisconsin and chair of the Committee on Manufactures. In two weeks of testimony in Room 412 of the Senate Office Building, a parade of social workers, charity leaders, labor chieftains, civic employees, and local politicians gave graphic and moving testimony to the strain on community relief resources and the human devastation wrought by the depression.[27]

A director of Jewish charities in Chicago told the committee that more than 600,000 were unemployed in his city alone, and that privation was so widespread that even after ensuring relief applicants had drained their bank accounts and borrowed against insurance policies or home equity, local agencies were struggling to provide a bare minimum of food and shelter for the needy. The Cook County Bureau of Public Welfare had been unable to pay its milk bill for almost two years. Requests for beds had been answered with chairs, until the supply of chairs ran out. More than two hundred women were sleeping in Grant and Lincoln Parks every night.

The American Association of Public Welfare Officials reported that the southwestern states were no longer able to cope with hordes of jobless, penniless, transient young men. Los Angeles alone counted seventy thousand of them, with 1,500 more arriving daily on freight trains.

Sidney Goldstein, chairman of a national umbrella group of unemployment relief agencies, spoke of overcrowding in orphan asylums and mental institutions, and rising rates of suicide over the previous two years. He had sat across the table from a man on the cusp of a breakdown who, hands trembling and face twitching, had said, "I can not go home to my wife and children and hear them cry for a little bread. The whole thing is driving me mad."[28]

Aid workers in the coalfields of West Virginia and Kentucky counted at least twenty-five thousand children wanting food and warm clothing. In some schools up to 90 percent of the pupils were underweight and exhibiting "drowsiness, lethargy, sleepiness." Thousands were too weak to even attend class. Evicted families were living in tents through the winter. Toddlers were seen barefoot in the snow.[29]

The testimony ran on for several hundred pages, managing to underscore both the heroic work of the thousands of private and public agencies answering the seemingly endless calls of distress, and the heart-wrenching tragedy of an economic disaster that had blighted cities, gutted industry, broken families, and shattered lives.

The witnesses were largely in favor of direct federal relief as a temporary expedient. This, of course, put them at odds with the administration, represented toward the end of the hearings by Chairman Gifford of the President's Organization on Unemployment Relief. He attested that his committee had raised in excess of $100 million in three months, and that his nationwide coalition of local and state agencies would see America through its third winter of want.

The president was not a factor in the hearings, apart from some quarreling with his assessments of the state of public health, isolated cutting remarks about "Hoover prosperity," and one question, the best asked in all the days of testimony, that could only be answered by him. "Of those who believe that it is not quite timely as yet to give relief," said Sidney Hillman, president of the Amalgamated Clothing Workers of America, "I would ask by what standard are we to gauge the time? Must we have hundreds of thousands of people actually dead and dying from starvation? Must we have bread riots? What is necessary to convince them there is need for Federal and speedy relief?"[30]

As Costigan and La Follette pressed on, the larger Congress found itself debating Hoover's legislative proposals, a batch of once-unthinkable solutions to unprecedented economic problems. There was an eerie sense of déjà vu about the deliberations on the Hill. Each stage of the battle on a thousand fronts had pushed the national government further out into policy frontiers few had ever expected to visit. Each administration initiative to date, from Hoover's first confidence-building meetings in Washington, through his counter-cyclical spending, the drought aid, the moratorium, the unemployment agencies, the bankers' pool, had seemed, in its day, novel, momentous, and daring. Now the RFC alone was proposing to commit a sum equivalent to two-thirds the entire pre-crash federal budget to resuscitate the financial industry, and it seemed to Congress as though it had no choice but to assent.[31]

No one could say for certain that any of Hoover's radical initiatives would pull America from the ditch. Nor could anyone articulate a Plan B. If Hoover failed, would he, or his successors, go further or turn back? It was, and still is, notoriously difficult to distinguish, at the inception of a new policy, between a temporary expedient and a new paradigm of governance, and it is not always up to the person who introduces the policy to decide which it might be.

A measure of novelty was supplied to the RFC debate by unusually cooperative relations between the White House and Congress. When it had come time to vote, earlier in the session, on the previous summer's international debt moratorium, a handful of Democrats made predictable speeches asking why Hoover was giving breaks to foreign debtors while American families were suffering. They were promptly upbraided by one of their own, Democratic representative Fiorello La Guardia, for failing to appreciate the emergency before them. The necessary legislation passed and was signed by the president on December 23. Learning something from his moratorium success, Hoover was now exerting himself as never before with congressional figures, meeting frequently, mostly in small groups, to hash out the details of the RFC and his proposed banking reforms. His office, as well as the White House breakfast, lunch, and dinner tables, opened in these months to an endless stream of senators and representatives.[32]

Thanks to the urgency of the situation and this new spirit of collaboration, the Reconstruction Finance Corporation, with Eugene Meyer as its chairman and General Charles Dawes as president, was made official as soon as January 22. Hoover made a statement thanking the congressional leaders who had aided passage of the legislative package for their patriotism. Charitable as that sounds, he left three leading Democratic patriots standing unawares in his office late that same afternoon as he signed the historic legislation alone before newsreel cameras.[33]

Five days later, the president got back some of his own on signing a bill releasing $150 million to the Federal Land Bank System. Democratic representative Henry B. Steagall hailed the legislation as important, groundbreaking, and entirely to his own credit. If the administration had listened to him earlier, he said, thousands of farmers would not have been thrown out of their homes and reduced to living with their families in highway ditches. But the collaboration continued.[34]

Hoover, through gritted teeth, gave Steagall, chair of the House Banking and Currency Committee, the honors in preparing the emergency bank legislation wanted by the administration. Steagall and Senator Glass, who chaired the corresponding committee in the Senate, produced the Glass-Steagall Act, which expanded the definition of acceptable collateral for Federal Reserve lending and so enabled an expansion of credit to member banks. It also permitted the inflationary tactic of supplementing the system's gold reserves with government bonds. Hoover called the moratorium, the RFC, the recapitalization of the Federal Land Banks, and the Glass-Steagall Act his "thoroughly nonpartisan patriotic program of reconstruction." It represented as fine a run as any president had managed with Congress dating back to Wilson's first term.[35]

On March 23, Hoover also signed the Norris-LaGuardia Act, a progressive piece of labor legislation that prohibited judges from using injunctions to stop nonviolent strikes, and outlawed "yellow dog" contracts that prevented employees, as a condition of employment, from joining unions.

What was avoided was as important to Hoover as what was passed. In February, he had dodged the attempt by Costigan and La Follette to pass a bill providing direct federal relief for the unemployed. The Senate defeated what was popularly known as the "dole bill" by a vote of 48–35. Not only did a solid majority of senators oppose the bill, they did so for Hoover's reasons. The question, said Democratic senator Hugo Black of Alabama, was whether federal bureaucrats should intervene in the affairs of the states and tell them whether or not they should aid the unemployed and how they should do it. Hoover's insistence on local sovereignty over relief remained consistent with the American consensus.[36]

The administration's winning streak was all the more remarkable for the fact that both chambers were effectively in opposition hands. It helped that the Democratic House was more concerned with avoiding mistakes on the road to the 1932 elections than with pushing a program of its own. Just the same, credit rests with Hoover. He was hard to beat in a crisis: first with a plan of action and relentless in its pursuit. He had overcome his personal reluctance to crawl into the legislative trenches, much as he hated them. He would sometimes emerge from meetings with congressmen red-eyed and furious, cursing in profanity his aides traced to his mining days. He refused to backslap the lawmakers or share intimacies or forge any kind of personal communion with them. But he was playing their game, playing it effectively, and he had toughened up. He had a brown double-breasted suit that he wore when it was his turn to go on the offensive. The press knew the ensemble as "his fighting clothes."[37]

He was evolving in other ways as well. Hoover had long demonstrated an inclination to take the heaviest loads on his own back, leaving lighter chores to staff and the cabinet. This tendency was so pronounced that Irwin "Ike" Hoover (unrelated), in his fifth decade as an usher, and now chief usher, at the White House, thought it advisable to pass along management tips to the chief executive through press secretary Joslin. "He is the ablest, hardest working President of the lot," said Ike. Nevertheless, "he should delegate all but the most essential work." Unwilling to go as far as his usher advised, Hoover did in fact show unusual trust in two individuals in the last year of his term.[38]

The first of these was the hard-drinking, blue-blooded, Harvard-educated lawyer Ogden Mills. As undersecretary of the Treasury, Mills had proven himself responsive, energetic, and useful, in sharp contrast to Mellon, who was primarily an ornament in Hoover's cabinet. Early in 1932, Mills, the third-richest man in Washington, moved to the foreground in Treasury as Mellon, the richest, was swept aside, in part because the ornament had become an eyesore.

The House Judiciary Committee was investigating reasonably credible charges that Mellon had continued to operate his family business while overseeing Treasury. Hoover asked for and after some prevarication received Mellon's resignation from the cabinet and in return permitted him an elegant retirement as ambassador to the Court of St. James's. Mills was promoted to the cabinet post he had long deserved. Hoover trusted him implicitly, even with such crucial challenges as whipping the Glass-Steagall legislation into acceptable form. "I haven't the time to attend to every detail," Hoover told him. "You are the only one who can do it."[39]

The second trusted lieutenant was General Charles G. Dawes, the former vice president, former comptroller of the currency, and onetime Hoover rival for leadership of the Republican Party. Dawes had been Mellon's predecessor in the United Kingdom until Hoover begged him to return to the United States to head the Reconstruction Finance Corporation. Once Dawes was back in Washington, Hoover applied his abilities to a range of financial issues. He liked especially to set him loose on recalcitrant Democratic congressmen. A red-blooded, narrow-eyed force of nature, Dawes lived for political drama. He was a shouter, bellowing hard and fast around conference tables to make himself heard over the machine-gun pounding of his own fist. In full fury, he would spew fact and hyperbole in such torrents that conferees could scarcely catch his meaning. His stamina won as many points as his reason. "Thank Goodness," said the president, "I have the General here with me. He surely put the fear of God in the hearts of those Democrats. I would never have gotten away with it alone."[40]

Hoover needed the help as the pace of activity in the White House, unparalleled at the start of his term and cranked up as the depression deepened, now found another gear entirely. Joslin scrambled for the right analogy. It was "a mad house," he said. Or it was like the emergency ward at St. Elizabeth's Hospital, "the only difference being . . . that we go home nights." Hoover had his own description. "This job," he exclaimed, "is nothing but a damned twenty-ring circus, with hell breaking loose everywhere." MacLafferty would wander around the White House offices early in the morning and find conference rooms littered with wadded paper and crowded ashtrays, the debris of meetings that had run well past midnight. He would inspect the floor to find the small pile of discarded gold bands bearing the inscription "Ramon Allones No. 2 Habanas" and know where the president had been sitting.[41]

Hoover continued to rise at six and arrive at his desk just after eight no matter how late he had worked. "The terrible grind of responsibility," said MacLafferty, showed in his face. He looked tired and haggard, like "a poor, worried human being."[42]

He took measures at the start of 1932 to lighten his schedule. "Missionary work," Hoover's term for meetings with delegates to the White House, was curtailed. The 160 organizations with plans to meet the president in the first half of 1932 were informed that they were welcome to visit the White House without shaking the chief executive's hand. He needed his time for "proper consideration of matters of the greatest moment to the Nation." These adjustments,

meant to buy him personal time, only made way for more meetings, and he still managed to greet some twenty thousand individuals in the first five weeks of the year, including Rudy Vallee, the pop
crooner who dropped by to show off the second of his four wives,
actress Fay Webb. Joslin allowed Senator Smoot to come around on
a hectic afternoon with the president of the Mormon Church, after
which Hoover vented to his staff, "I don't care if you announce God
Almighty I won't see him."[43]

There were few escapes from the pressures of the presidency in
the winter of 1932. Rapidan was closed for the season. There was no
time for vacation. Sundays were working days. The Hoovers were
required to attend or host social functions several nights a week. Iron-
ically, one of the precious few moments of pleasure afforded Hoover
in these months was among journalists. After repeatedly saying that
he would not attend the official opening of the new offices of the
National Press Club, Hoover relented at the last moment and agreed
to show his face for ten or fifteen minutes. It was the right thing to
do in an election year. Refreshed by a late afternoon nap, he arrived
shortly before 10 p.m., received a good hand, and witnessed the opening ceremony. His fifteen minutes up, Joslin leaned over and asked if
he was ready to leave. "No," he said. "This is good. Let's stay a while."
He stayed for the whole program of songs and speeches and would
have stayed longer had the floor not been cleared for the ball that was
to follow. He remained in good form in the car on the way home,
chuckling over what a "flat tire" Senator Robert Bulkley of Ohio had
been.[44]

Knowing that his productive run with Congress would not last,
Hoover's intention was to keep both chambers off balance long
enough to get his full program approved. "The Democrats," he told
an aide, "have taken my program because the country compelled them
to and because they have no ideas of their own. They would murder
our plans in a moment if they dared."[45]

They began to dare as February bled into March. Representative
La Guardia grew tired of hearing the president thank the Democrats
for their cooperation. He reverted to partisanship. "This isn't a session of Congress," he complained. "This is a kissing bee."[46]

The months between this congressional reversion to the mean and the party conventions in June were given over to furious debates over the balancing of the federal budget, the last major item of Hoover's program. There was no serious disagreement with the president's insistence that "rigid economy is the real road to relief." It was accepted that the government's ability to borrow and to command public confidence depended on its fiscal stewardship, and the situation was made more ominous by the fact that lower levels of government also appeared to be tapped out. The pertinent questions were how much to cut, and where, and whether or not to raise taxes.[47]

The budget gap was huge: the deficit for fiscal 1932 would come in at 43.3 percent on spending of $4.7 billion. Hoover wanted a massive overhaul of the executive branch to eliminate waste and duplication, and he also believed tax increases were necessary as there was not much room to cut expenditures. Congress, reluctant to delegate him the powers to reorganize, had ideas of its own. Speaker Garner staked his bid for the Democratic nomination on a scheme to balance the budget by introducing a sales tax and failed to push it through. Countless other proposals, counterproposals, and amendments were floated and shot down. Meanwhile, to Hoover's horror, new initiatives for deficit-swelling relief spending were warmly received on the Hill, including the suggestion that world war veterans be allowed to immediately cash out another $2 billion in bonuses.[48]

Assailed by congressional Democrats for the size of his deficit (notwithstanding their own spending plans), Hoover again accused Congress of playing politics in the face of disaster. He caused a sensation by showing up at the Senate in person one afternoon in May on two and a half hours' sleep and, as the first president to address either house since Harding, blamed its members for undermining "the unquestioned beneficial effect" of his recovery program and for disturbing the public mind. He demanded immediate legislative action with a force some congressmen decried as bullying and dictatorial. He was as hard on his own party as he was the Democrats. Republican members of the Senate Appropriations Committee, he said to a staffer, "are a dusty-brained, foozle-witted lot. You can't imagine the difficulty I had last night in making them appreciate the necessities of their situation."[49]

The bill that finally emerged from the fracas increased personal tax rates for most people from a low single digit to a high single digit. Corporate taxes and other wealth taxes were introduced, including surtaxes on top incomes at rates of up to 63 percent. Although Hoover would have preferred a lower high-income surtax and higher estate taxes, which he considered a more effective means of redistributing wealth, he nevertheless signed the Revenue Act of 1932, which would stand as the most progressive tax legislation of the thirties.[50]

There had been signals in the last days of the kissing bee that Hoover's "thoroughly nonpartisan patriotic program of reconstruction" was finally going to break the back of what was by now universally recognized as the worst economic calamity America had ever known. The epidemic of bank failures ended in the first five months of 1932. The Dow Jones Industrial Average, although under 100 points, less than a quarter of its pre-crash high, once more scratched its way into positive territory and it held its gains into spring. The administration was cautious about suggesting the economy had turned a corner, a tentativeness shared with most other forecasters. In fact, the tall foreheads of the Harvard Economic Society, humiliated by their long run of spectacularly misguided projections, had quietly disbanded. The uptick nevertheless registered in certain circles, including among the Democratic organizers readying for their nominating convention. "There is a distinctly better feeling," said the Democratic financier Bernard Baruch, citing a steadily improving bond market as evidence. "I have been looking into it carefully and I am sure of it." Baruch added that many Americans, at least of the class he knew, thought the president appeared "courageous and surefooted" in his handling of the crisis, even "gallant" in his unwavering commitment to finding solutions.[51]

The distinctly better feeling identified by Baruch was yet another mirage, much like the one that had followed the British gold suspension the previous autumn, and the three before that. It would not last the spring, and it would not convince Americans of Hoover's gallantry—indeed, his popularity was at an all-time low. Democratic efforts to saddle him with responsibility for the depression were find-

ing eager ears, and he was loathed in many parts of the country. "The
only mistake starving unemployed of this country have made," wrote
Heywood Broun, "is that they did not march on Washington [dis-
playing] banners reading 'We are Belgians.'" Hoover did not help his
own cause by resisting efforts to polish his image. Once, on his way
back to the White House, Hoover stopped to cheer a group of boys
on a baseball diamond. His staff learned of the incident and asked
him to do it again the next day with reporters present to capture the
moment. He refused, consistent with his natural diffidence, and perhaps more so because he was reluctant to use children as props.*52

Damaged though he was, Hoover was far from finished. The Democrats had yet to identify a capable leader, and the Republican brand
was still powerful in America. The *Pathfinder* magazine poll released
at the end of March showed Hoover favored for reelection among its
readers. The *New York Evening Post* in mid-April cited bettors in New
York giving six-to-five odds that he would gain a second term. They
were posting money at two to one that the next president would be
a Democrat. Replies to a survey of college editors in late April asking "Whom do you think will be elected" ran fifty-seven for Hoover
against thirty-one for Governor Roosevelt or "any Democrat."53

By June, a supposedly scientific nationwide survey of opinion by
the Babson statistical organization of Wellesley, Massachusetts, had
the Democrats leading with about 60 percent of popular support. Its
authors, however, contradicted their own findings in a press release
accompanying the data, claiming much had changed since they were
in the field. They ventured that the "demoralizing tactics of the
Democratic Congress," a "recent assertion of vigorous leadership
by President Hoover," the lack of a strong Democratic leader, and
the possible improvement in farming and business all pointed to a
Republican victory.54

The *Philadelphia Public Ledger* jumped in with a fair-minded piece
of commentary:

* Similarly, Lou Hoover destroyed letters relating to her personal efforts to aid individual Americans who wrote the White House seeking relief from the depression. These
records reflected well on Lou and her family, but she believed the correspondents were
proud people who did not wish to be remembered to history as needy. (*New York Times*,
June 14, 1952.)

The task was one for a superman. Mr. Hoover's admirers will tell you he has succeeded. His enemies will insist he has been a dismal failure. An unbiased observer, if there is any these days, would probably say he has done all that was humanly possible for a President to do. Nevertheless, the habit of the American people is to hold the party in power responsible for economic conditions, good or bad, and Mr. Hoover must enter the presidential contest this year with a section of the voting population disappointed because he has performed no miracles. The closest election since 1916 is in prospect.[55]

# CHAPTER 24

# "A Human Creature
# Desperately Hurt and Pained"

The convention will be very dull, everyone says," Lou Hoover wrote Allan in anticipation of the June 1932 Republican Party gathering at which her husband was to be nominated for a second term. That Lou was correct, and that the national convention would be very dull in part because the president's renomination was a foregone conclusion, does not make her comment any less odd. Her husband was charged with rousing the Republican Party for its quadrennial battle against the rejuvenated Democrats. "Very dull" did not bode well for his chances.[1]

Lou was also under the impression that the president was concentrating on the state of the economy to the exclusion of partisan affairs, which was not entirely the case. Anxious about his prospects, he was discussing with insiders the possibility of replacing Vice President Curtis with General Charles Dawes to recharge the ticket, a plan that fell apart when the latter bolted to Chicago to save his family bank. Hoover was also meeting regularly, and in secret, so as to maintain his disinterested pose, with party officials drafting the Republican platform. He was obsessed with the Prohibition plank.[2]

In the days before the delegates gathered at Chicago Stadium, home of the National Hockey League's new Blackhawks franchise, Hoover tried to engineer a straddle on the Eighteenth Amendment. He could feel the wet tide rising across the country, and he expected the Democrats to run on repeal of Prohibition. He still leaned dry himself. To his many friends and advisers asking him to soften his stance, he offered bits of cherry-picked evidence suggesting that Americans were preponderantly with him. He sent Secretaries Mills and Stimson to Chicago to wring a straddle out of the Republican platform committee, but they ran into a wall of opposition within the committee. "That convention is dripping wet," Hoover fumed to Joslin. "We can't do anything with them. But they have got to adopt the right kind of plank. It cannot be too wet."[3]

Support for outright repeal was so strong among conventioneers that the president, in a histrionic fit, drafted a letter withdrawing his candidacy. "If the convention goes for repeal," he told Joslin with eyes flashing, "I shall refuse to accept the nomination."

"You can't do that, Mr. President."

"Yes I can. I shall have to."

Joslin advised him to accept the platform as drafted and repudiate the Prohibition plank during the campaign, as Smith did in 1928.

"I won't stand for repeal. My conscience would not permit me to do it."[4]

The withdrawal letter was almost certainly a bargaining tactic; nothing was going to keep him from his chance at reelection. In any event, Hoover eventually got his way. The plank stated that a Republican administration would redraft the Eighteenth Amendment to allow states to deal with Prohibition as their citizens saw fit, a compromise that satisfied few besides Hoover. Polite Republican papers called it "weak and ambiguous." The Chicago Tribune saw a product of "political cowardice and hypocrisy," as "futile as it is fraudulent."[5]

The rest of the Republican platform was given over to a defense of the president's record and critiques of a Democratic agenda that had yet to be announced. That left, as its headline, the Prohibition half-measure, an outcome that put more pressure on Hoover and his leadership to carry the party through the election.

At noon on June 16, the president sat in the Lincoln Study in the White House listening to the Republican nominating speeches with Lou and a handful of staffers. "His eyes twinkled and he laughed and joked as the orators cut loose," said Joslin, although he turned serious when the balloting began. He received 98 percent of the votes, slightly higher than the 96 percent Coolidge had taken in 1924, and not quite the 100 percent Theodore Roosevelt had managed in 1904. It was a remarkable showing given the challenges of the times and the persistence of the Republican insurgency. "Well, it wasn't exactly unexpected," Hoover said when the totals were announced. "I guess I will go back to the office now." There were no congratulations, not so much as a smile, as he walked out of the room to work on his convention speech.[6]

The delegates in Chicago renominated Curtis as vice president, putting to rest a minor and nonsensical panic among the Hooverites that Coolidge might be drafted to the bottom of the ticket. That was the final substantive note of the convention. An admirer of Hoover, William Allen White, was disappointed that the whole affair had indeed been very dull. "If ever there was a time in American history which called for challenge, for combat, and for criticism, constructive or otherwise, it would seem to be now."[7]

If Hoover could have handpicked his opponent from among the Democratic contenders in 1932, he would have selected New York governor Franklin Delano Roosevelt, the Groton- and Harvard-educated scion of a wealthy and socially prominent family from Dutchess County, New York, and the fifth cousin of the former president.[8]

Hoover had been rooting for Roosevelt at least since January, partly because they had been friendly in the years after Hoover's return from Europe, and partly for reasons best articulated by the journalist and administration insider Mark Sullivan after watching FDR deliver a speech over the winter:

> He does not possess the imagination of leadership. He does not fit the picture. He is not what the hour demands. He will not pass muster. There is nothing to Franklin Roosevelt.[9]

The Hoover camp feared Al Smith, believing that the Prohibition issue was less damaging to him in 1932 than it had been in 1928, and that he would put up a better fight a second time around. Joslin guessed that the Democrats would turn to Smith when it dawned on them that the paralytic Roosevelt, an adult victim of poliomyelitis, did not have the strength to handle the presidency. Hoover agreed that health was an issue. FDR, he said, was a sick man who would not last a year in the White House. Lou, while also sizing up Roosevelt as a lightweight and an invalid, feared that many people admired him for his grit in overcoming his affliction: "And heaps of people would vote for him just because he has put up such a game fight."[10]

At the opening of the Democratic National Convention in Chicago at the end of June, Hoover was still lamenting that things looked "bad for Franklin." He improvised bold speeches that FDR or his supporters could make to improve his chances. "Our salvation," said Hoover, "lies in his nomination."[11]

Roosevelt triumphed on the fourth ballot, setting up what one news service called the first contest in U.S. history between two millionaires for free rent at the White House. An usher carried the message to the president at dinner. He smiled more broadly than he had in months. House Speaker John Nance Garner rounded out the Democratic ticket and, as expected, the party embraced repeal of the Eighteenth Amendment.[12]

Hoover's low estimation of Roosevelt was conventional wisdom in the summer of 1932. He was "Feather Duster Roosevelt," the foppish postwar generation's answer to Warren Harding, with benefit of royal blood. Lippmann considered him a parody of a politician, allergic to hard stands, brimming with "two-faced platitudes," attempting the ridiculous feat of straddling the whole country. Two independent surveys of newspaper opinion in the wake of his nomination found few editors willing to credit Roosevelt with much more than ambition, geniality, and a magical name. The *Pittsburgh Post-Gazette* believed Hoover's odds of reelection were improved by FDR's triumph.[13]

One of the reasons Roosevelt was held in such middling esteem was that his speeches during the nomination race were indeed inconsistent and half-baked. He pronounced the American system sound, and promised to fundamentally change it. He adopted Hoover's call for renewed public confidence, yet was frankly pessimistic about the nation's future. America, said Roosevelt in an astounding address at Oglethorpe University, had crossed a threshold, leaving its best days of economic growth in the past: "It seems to me probable that our physical economic plant will not expand in the future at the same rate at which it has expanded in the past." Americans needed to turn their attention from making their way in the world to remaking society to permit a "wiser, more equitable distribution" of wealth. This was a reality, he said, that the benighted Hoover administration lacked the courage to face.[14]

Given his evident weaknesses, it was easy to miss the fact that Roosevelt had a firm two-handed grip on one of the central issues in the election. He had an encyclopedic knowledge of the failures of the Republican administration and the vulnerabilities of its leader. He threw the book at Hoover, in grand prosecutorial style, and left it for the court of public opinion to decide what would stick. He sometimes attacked from the right, excoriating Hoover for his deficits and demanding cuts "of not less than 25% in the cost of the Federal Government." He sometimes attacked from the left, promising long-term economic planning and a more generous, interventionist government. He ridiculed the president's judgment and leadership, lambasting him as a general out of touch with his troops, bailing out bankers and financiers while doing nothing to restore the purchasing power of farmers and working-class Americans. He faulted the Republican tariff for protecting the profits of businessmen while raising prices for consumers.[15]

In the manner of Michelson and Raskob, Roosevelt laid entire blame for the crash of 1929 and the Great Depression at Hoover's feet, to the extent of refusing to acknowledge its international dimensions. He portrayed the president as a slow and tentative executive, all but inert in the face of crisis. To dramatize his own contrasting dynamism, he traveled almost ten hours from Albany to Chicago in a Ford tri-motor airplane to accept his nomination in person, a brilliant stroke.[16]

Roosevelt's acceptance speech, together with another address weeks later in Columbus, Ohio, doubled down on his attacks on the president. Hoover now emerged as a witless, heartless sluggard clinging to self-evidently absurd policies as the nation's mothers scrounged for food. Roosevelt gleefully recited every prediction of prosperity and recovery that Hoover had ever uttered. He mocked the president's stance as a champion of individualism: it was a fraud, he said, a "ghastly sham." Hoover was in fact a dangerous and dishonest man exploiting the American people on behalf of the "not more than five human individuals" who controlled America's wealth. He was abetting the "crooks" in high finance as they robbed hardworking citizens of their savings.[17]

Over the previous three years, Michelson and Raskob had succeeded in "whittling Hoover down to our size," as Jack Garner said. Roosevelt had now upped the ante, viciously and ingeniously casting Hoover as the villain. It was smoothly executed. Roosevelt was always careful to regret the necessity of his blows. He took pains to separate Hoover from the Republican herd, blaming leaders, not followers. He developed a confidential, intimate rapport with voters, exhibiting a highly developed political talent that could make the smarmiest of phrases radiate with sincerity: "You and I as common-sense citizens know . . ." Perhaps most importantly, Roosevelt acknowledged the genuine hardships endured by millions of Americans in the depression, a welcome message that Hoover, bearing more responsibility for the situation, choked on.[18]

As with Harding, another compromise candidate, pundits were reluctant to credit Roosevelt's political gift. Lippmann sneered that FDR's evasions and equivocations were "probably shrewd politics." Thoughtful critics of the democratic system, including Hoover, have always struggled with the reality that a man of second-rate intellect and questionable character could by a keen appreciation of the real business of politics—the assembling of voting constituencies in pursuit of power—outperform more accomplished or admirable individuals.[19]

Roosevelt shared Harding's talents for projecting confidence, for radiating comfort and cheer, and for assuming whatever shape voters required of him. He had a deeper self-assurance than Harding, and he was far more ruthless, prepared not merely to elevate himself but to tear others down by any available means, not least a class war.

The tone of the Democratic campaign rhetoric soon had Hoover reconsidering his preference for Roosevelt as a candidate. He was slow to fight back: if it had been beneath Hoover's dignity to mount a vigorous campaign for the presidency as a nominee in 1928, it was more so for an incumbent in 1932. He was under the impression that no president seeking reelection had ever campaigned (he had been out of the country when Taft and Wilson had stumped for second terms), and he refused to tour the country. He planned to make, at most, three speeches before voting day. Wanting to impress upon the people that he was still working hard on their behalf, he rarely left his office in the two months following his renomination. This was not entirely out of step with the campaign rhythms of the day. Roosevelt had left the Democratic convention for a sailing expedition.[20]

There was also a measure of necessity to Hoover's attachment to his desk. In the last days before the adjournment of the Seventy-Second Congress, two powerful Democrats, House Speaker Garner and New York senator Robert Wagner, were determined to enact one more piece of legislation to relieve human suffering in the depression. Hoover supported their intent, with strong reservations on some of their specifics. Garner's plan for public works entailed new post offices in key Democratic congressional districts, which the president opposed as pork-barreling. There was a similar intent in Wagner's proposal to allocate money to states on the basis of population as opposed to their share of the unemployed. After weeks of lively negotiation and one presidential veto, Congress approved a compromise version of what came to be called the Emergency Relief and Construction Act in July. It directed another $1.5 billion into the RFC, made $300 million available to the states, and answered all of Hoover's important stipulations save one.[21]

Garner had refused to let go of a clause that publicized the names of banks seeking RFC funds. This was in part due to the fact that the Dawes family bank in Chicago had recently received a huge loan, a legitimate yet politically unseemly use of public money, given Dawes's connections to the administration and the RFC. Garner's insistence on exposing borrowers ensured that troubled institutions would lose public confidence by applying to the RFC, aggravating rather than alleviating their problems. By now second on the Democratic ticket, Garner did not care: he was frankly pleased to force the president to defend secret loans to his friends in high finance. Hoover signed the bill on July 21.[22]

The Emergency Relief and Construction Act delivered on Hoover's long-standing promise to use all the resources of the national government to backstop depression relief, even to the extent of direct aid to states if conditions warranted. The RFC, universally recognized as the president's creation, was with this new injection of capital a massive $4 billion depression-fighting behemoth. The *New*

*York Times* credited Hoover with the only "positive achievements to come out of the session." The Democrat-controlled Congress was widely seen to have embarrassed itself at the trough.[23]

Another issue keeping Hoover at his desk, quite literally, was the so-called Bonus Army. Unemployed veterans of the Great War, some accompanied by their families, had been gathering in Washington from all points of the compass through the summer to once more press their case for an early payout of the war service funds due them in 1945. By July, they numbered more than ten thousand, camping throughout the capital in tents and makeshift shacks, or squatting in abandoned buildings. The presence of so many unoccupied men, many of them begging on street corners, and the suspicion that political radicals and communists had infiltrated the movement, cast an ominous spell over the city, notwithstanding a remarkable lack of civil unrest in America during the first three years of the depression. There were rumors of impending violence and rioting. In yet another way, the Great War was haunting the Hoover presidency.[24]

Unsettled by the veterans, Hoover and his staff canceled at least one public appearance. There were "too many fellows in town who are willing to throw bricks," he said privately. At the same time, he quietly distributed food, clothing, blankets, and camp kitchens to their encampments, and the Sixth Marine Barracks provided medical care to hundreds of veterans a day. This assistance was provided without publicity so as not to invite more veterans to the city, and also to forestall criticism from the likes of the *Washington Post*, which warned that it would be "a stupid and deadly mistake to coddle the communists."[25]

On July 7, the Senate soundly defeated a bill that would have distributed $2.5 billion to the veterans. Its members agreed with Hoover that the veterans represented a small segment of the depression's victims, and that paying out the bonus would preclude other plans for relief. Most of the Bonus Army called it a summer and returned home. Hoover authorized $100,000 in transport subsidies to ease their way. A militant minority, however, refused to leave, and in the weeks that followed, tensions heightened, rumors spread that veterans planned to storm the White House and were arming themselves with machine guns and grenades. Security at the executive mansion was stepped up, the gates closed, the curtains drawn, and more agents put on patrol.

District of Columbia police tried to evict veterans squatting in several buildings along Pennsylvania Avenue on the morning of July 28. A riot ensued. Two marchers were shot dead and six policemen were hospitalized. District of Columbia authorities asked for the help of federal troops in clearing the buildings, and Hoover obliged, with strict instructions that the veterans were to be gently herded back to their main camp across the Anacostia River.

Army chief of staff General Douglas MacArthur, sniffing "incipient revolution in the air," organized a detachment of mounted cavalry, six tanks, and a column of infantry and met a ragged band of veterans at the foot of Capitol Hill. Tear gas and bayonet points were used to push the protesters over the Eleventh Street Bridge. Ignoring his orders from the president, MacArthur followed them across the river, drove the men and their families from their tents and shacks, and torched the entire encampment of Anacostia Flats. He then held a press conference congratulating Hoover on his firm hand: "Had the President not acted within twenty-four hours, he would have been faced with a very grave situation." Secretary of War Hurley backed MacArthur and insisted that a large proportion of the "mob" were criminals and communists who had never served their country.[26]

Decades after these events, Roosevelt partisans Rexford Tugwell and Felix Frankfurter would separately claim to have been in the presence of the Democratic nominee as he absorbed news of the armed rout of defenseless veterans. He is said to have immediately concluded that reports of a callous president loosing the dogs of war on victims of his own economic incompetence would turn the country against the Republicans. Tugwell, who visited the candidate as he read his morning papers on July 29 in his Albany bedroom, wrote: "If Roosevelt had had any doubt about the outcome of the election, I am certain he had none after reading the *Times* that day." Frankfurter recorded that FDR turned to him on the porch of his Hyde Park home and said, "Well, Felix, this will elect me." These accounts have heavily influenced the historiography of the 1932 campaign.[27]

The stories of Tugwell and Frankfurter ring false. The editorial attitude of the *New York Times* in the wake of the clearance was vehemently pro-Hoover. The Bonus Army, it said, had been acting in "violent defiance of the law and the public authorities." The protest had become "a national reproach and even [a] danger." The *Washington Post* and the *Washington Herald* were similarly complimentary to Hoover. The Associated Press surveyed editorial comment among America's leading dailies on July 29 and found them "practically unanimous in expressing the opinion that President Hoover was justified in his course." A *Literary Digest* roundup of newspaper opinion on August 6, 1932, reached the same conclusion. The principal exceptions to this line of comment were the Hearst papers, and their dissent from the administration's management of the incident was slow to emerge.[28]

More tellingly, Roosevelt, never one to miss an opportunity to bash the incumbent, was silent about the Bonus Army during the campaign. He was savvy enough to see that the first duty of a chief executive is to uphold the law, and that the American people would applaud decisive action against drifters and agitators menacing the peace. Weeks later, after it emerged that the proportion of communists and criminals within the ranks of the Bonus Army had been much smaller than MacArthur and Hurley and, on their advice, Hoover had led the public to believe, Roosevelt still held his tongue. Indeed, before election day, he sided with the Senate against early payment of the veterans' funds. The *New York Times* synopsis of the major issues in the campaign would omit any mention of the Bonus Army clearance. There is no compelling evidence that it was a decisive or important factor in the campaign of 1932.[29]

Roosevelt, rather, continued to chronicle the "failure," the "folly," and the "futility" of Hoover's economic record, and here he had a wealth of material. Coming out of the conventions, gross national product was at $60 billion, down from $75 billion a year before, and a peak of $105 billion in 1929. Unemployment was higher than ever. Later estimates would put it over 20 percent in the summer of 1932. The Dow Jones Industrial Average that month bottomed at 41.2 points, a sickening slide from its peak of 381.2.[30]

The numbers, however grim, tell only part of the story. Among those who retained their jobs were millions who had seen their hours or their wages drastically cut. They were struggling to pay the rent and to feed their families, living daily in dread of joining the less fortunate who squatted in Central Park, or who camped in vacant lots in Philadelphia, on public roadsides in Los Angeles, or in caves in Arkansas. They knew they were one bad day from joining the needy scavenging for edibles in the St. Louis dump or waiting for table scraps in the alleys behind Chicago restaurants. Private charity was by now exhausted in many cities and states. New York was offering a measly two dollars a week to people in distress. Dallas and Houston were refusing aid to blacks and Mexicans.

The public still had no exact understanding of what was happening to the economy, nor did the experts. The Institute of Public Affairs at the University of Virginia hosted a 560-member roundtable discussion that summer on the topic of the Hoover administration's performance during the financial crisis. Right-wing critics condemned the president for retarding recovery by "driving the government deeper and deeper into the business structure." The left assailed him for refusing to admit the collapse of capitalism: "The time has come," said Dr. William Jett Lauck of the Bureau of Applied Economics, "when the Federal Government must take control of private industry, start it into operation and put the unemployed of the country back to work." After six days of discussion, the attendees reached no agreement on what Hoover should have done differently. They announced an insipid sixteen-point program of relief, calling for more unemployment offices and more subsistence farming. They were nevertheless unanimous in their verdict that Washington had failed.[31]

Here was Hoover's major problem: Given the manifest state of the economy, who could say he had succeeded? Who would accept his assertion that things could have been much worse without him? Roosevelt recognized the president's predicament and allowed him no quarter. Hoover was out of touch, incompetent, a fraud, a tool of the plutocrats, and an enemy of the common man. Increasing numbers of Americans found Roosevelt's message compelling and grew more inclined to interpret the president's notes of optimism and resilience as cluelessness.

That Roosevelt's messages were hitting home with voters was confirmed by Lou Hoover, always a reliable barometer of both public receptivity to attacks on the administration, as well as the state of her own household's morale. She had been trying to stay calm in these months, reading the Stoic philosopher Marcus Aurelius. He does not seem to have taken. Of all the misrepresentations, insinuations, and falsehoods she heard, nothing stung quite like Roosevelt's distinction between himself as a man of generosity and humanity and her husband as an elitist Scrooge. She was sufficiently moved to write another long letter to her boys.

Her missive is in part a recitation of Hoover family mythology, in which "Daddy" is a saintly figure whose animating purpose, since his earliest jobs swinging pick and shovel underground, has always been the welfare of "people less fortunately situated than himself." The safety and comfort of his miners had been his first concern. He had never suffered a labor disruption as a mine manager. He had never sought public office. His climb to the presidency had been one long and barely endurable sacrifice for the good of humanity.[32]

Obvious embellishments and elisions aside, Lou made a strong case for the unfairness of Roosevelt's characterization of her husband. He had fought the "big men" on behalf of starving millions in Belgium and Northern France. His philosophy of government was built around the provision of equality of opportunity for all, and he had long been a tireless champion of the rights and needs of "the most-needy members of the population," be they laborers, children, prisoners, flooded-out sharecroppers, struggling farmers, or Native Americans. He was also an enemy of great fortunes, working with titans of capital to right the economy out of necessity rather than by choice. "Look back through the past three years," demanded Lou, "and recognize that . . . it is the 'small man' that the President has been ceaselessly working for."

In her anguish, Lou was coming to hate Roosevelt. In a separate letter, she called his caustic Columbus speech "downright untruthful." She was outraged that a man who would not publicly admit that he could not stand or walk without support would call her husband a fraud:

This posing before the world as a normal, sturdy man, and going to any amount of trouble and subterfuge to hold the truth of it from the public, shows up painfully a flaw in the man's own truthfulness and forthrightness. Incidentally, doctors say that almost invariably that disease does affect the brain and nervous system structure, the first symptoms of which are to develop an overpowering ego in the patient. And this probably accounts for the desire to appear so much stronger physically than he is.[33]

While Hoover had his own misgivings about Roosevelt's health, he insisted his campaign make no mention of the challenger's physical handicap and refrain from personal abuse. He disliked ad hominem politicking, and he was not keen to make a martyr of Roosevelt.

Meanwhile, it was Republicans who were at the brink of physical collapse. Mrs. Eugene Meyer pleaded in vain with Hoover to release her frazzled husband from the double load of chair of the Federal Reserve Board and head of the Reconstruction Finance Corporation. Stimson, "frightfully stale," unable to sleep, worried that he had reached "the end of my tether." Secretary Hyde was on the verge of a nervous collapse until the president ordered him to take a fishing trip. "I guess there are no other casualties for the moment," Hoover said to Joslin, "but it's a wonder there are not more."[34]

His closest associates worried about the state of the president's health. Secretaries Stimson and Hurley grabbed Dr. Boone after a cabinet meeting and demanded he examine Hoover's "mental condition." They considered him to be exhausted and suffering from some variety of nervous conditions. Boone agreed to keep a close watch.[35]

On August 11, hours after Hoover had delivered his speech officially accepting the Republican nomination, Stimson visited Hoover in his office and found him at his desk, wrapped in thought. "I feel more depressed and troubled," said the president, "than I ever have been in my life." He was especially upset about the Republican straddle on Prohibition, which he had dictated and, moments before, publicly endorsed for the first time. He was conscience-stricken at having broken a promise on which he had been elected in 1928, and at having broken faith with the dry tribe. "All my life," he said, "I have been connected with the God-fearing people of this country. I believe that they represent all that is best in this country, and I feel now that I have made a decision which will affront them and make them feel that I have betrayed them." The secretary was struck by the president's earnestness. He had for four years "worked to the limit" on behalf of the American people. Stimson compared him to "the untried, rather flippant" Roosevelt, so disjointed and opportunistic in his policies, and grew depressed himself.[36]

It was clear by the time the president finally launched his fight for reelection that he was spent. Joslin had invited twenty-six newsmen out to Rapidan in August for what was supposed to be an intimate gathering and photo opportunity. Hoover was coaxed onto horseback and, additionally, made to sit, supposedly relaxing, in an easy chair next to Lou. He was glum all day long, however, and he would not answer questions from the reporters. His staff was crushed, knowing that an opportunity had been wasted.[37]

When he finally took to the stump after Labor Day, Hoover was virtually alone in his campaign. MacLafferty's warnings about the unpreparedness of Republicans to meet adversity had been apposite. The dullness of the June convention had leaked to the hustings and there was little in the way of organization or fund-raising behind the candidate. Whereas in 1928, Republican luminaries such as Borah and Charles Hughes had campaigned exuberantly for Hoover, none but his cabinet members would do so now, and chosen for their administrative competence rather than their political acumen, they had their limits. Stimson was appalled to be asked to criticize Roosevelt's record as governor of New York. He at first claimed that it was beneath the dignity of the secretary of state to engage in such activities. He next protested that it was unwise to hold to account "a presidential candidate who is a cripple." He ultimately decided that in a campaign of personalities, the president had to speak for himself.[38]

Regardless of the state of his party, Hoover believed he could win the election. He had thought so in the wake of the conventions, and nothing since had changed his mind. Indeed, the spasmodic economy, by September, again seemed to be turning up, and in more convincing fashion than ever. The passage of Hoover's reform packages and the settling of the federal budget before the conventions had put virtually every important economic indicator on a positive track. The outflow of gold from the United States was dramatically reversed. Industrial production had arrested its three-year slide and improved by 15 percent in the third quarter. Three-year slumps in production of consumer goods, production of durable goods, and production of machinery, of capital expenditures for plant and equipment, of the general price index, of the wholesale price index, and of employment, had all been broken and turned around. The Dow Jones Industrial Average had shot from its June low of 42.8 points to 71.6 in August, an astounding 67 percent gain. Real gross national product, which had declined an average of 9.3 percent a year in 1929, 1930, and 1931, fell a mere 1.3 percent in 1932 and was likely flat in the second half of the year given everything else going on in the economy. The more finely calculated metric in the thirties was industrial production, and it would never again reach the lows of July 1932; nor would the Dow repeat its bottom of June 1932. After three years of backbreaking work, Hoover had in fact stopped the depression in its tracks and by most relevant measures forced its retreat.[39]

It remained to be seen if the improvements would last. Perhaps the best measure of the febrile temper, the maddening volatility of the times comes from the 130-year-old Dow Jones Industrial Average. Fourteen of its top twenty single-day percentage increases occurred on Hoover's watch, as did six of its top twenty record losses. There was no predicting anything in such an environment.

It also remained to be seen if economic gains would repair Hoover's political standing. The immediate signs were mixed. He was shaken in mid-September by the strength of the Democrats in Maine, which held a separate state election. They had upset the established Republican order by taking the governorship and two of Maine's three congressional seats. A week later, Hoover was buoyed by the first edition of the influential *Literary Digest* national poll, which on September 24 gave him 28,193 straw votes to Roosevelt's 27,654. "It is not the crushing blow that I had feared," he told Joslin. An internal poll commissioned by the Republican National Committee showed the Democrats ahead in voter intention. The massive Hearst presidential poll indicated Hoover had a slight lead in electoral college votes. There was cause for concern. There was no objective cause for despair.[40]

Convincing the Republican Party that it was still in the fight nevertheless proved difficult. Iowa organizers tried to talk Hoover out of making an October 4 speech in Des Moines, less than a two-

hour drive from his hometown. They were "panic-stricken," said Joslin, that angry farmers, armed with eggs, or worse, would do "bodily
harm" to the president. When Hoover would not be deterred from
the appearance, they tried to convince him to cut his proposed eleven-
thousand-word, two-hour speech to give him a chance of holding his
radio audience. This was useful advice. Again he refused, and boarded
a train to Iowa with the long draft in his pocket.[41]

Hoover's entourage, including the Secret Service, was jumpy
on the train. Lou chattered nervously at dinner about the McKinley assassination. The president, unperturbed, continued to work on
his speech. It was his most interesting effort of the campaign, more
a stubborn apologia than a conventional campaign address. It had
two principal objectives. First, Hoover wanted acknowledgment that
his depression-fighting efforts had been fruitful. The relief program
installed during the first half of 1932, he insisted, had restored confidence in the American dollar:

> Since June, $275 million of gold has flowed back to us from
> abroad. Hoarders in our own country, finding our institutions
> safeguarded and safe, have returned $250 million to the use-
> ful channels of business. . . . The rills of credit are expanding.
> The pressure on the debtor to sacrifice his all in order to pay
> his debts is steadily relaxing. Men are daily being reemployed.
> If we calculate the values of this year's agricultural products
> compared with the low points, the farmers as a whole, despite
> the heartbreaking distress which still exists, are a billion dol-
> lars better off. Prices have a long way to go before the farmer
> has an adequate return, but at least the turn is toward recov-
> ery.[42]

Second, and more important to him than the "dreary" and complex matters of currencies and budgets, he wanted Americans to know
that Roosevelt had no monopoly on concern for their welfare. "We
have fought to preserve the safety, the principles, and the ideals of
American life," he wrote. The overriding objective of his policies had
been to protect "the interest of the people in the homes and at the
firesides of our country . . . the millions of homes of the type which I
knew as a boy in this State."[43]

We are not a nation of 120 million solitary individuals, we are a nation of 25 million families dwelling in 25 million homes, each warmed by the fires of affection and cherishing within it a mutual solicitude for kinfolk and children. Their safety is what we are striving for. Their happiness is our real concern.[44]

There was much more to the speech, on the causes and the course of the depression, on how he had avoided the "class bitterness" that Roosevelt was fomenting, on the virtues of the tariff policies Roosevelt had attacked. On it went for ten thousand words, an earnest, fascinating attempt to justify the ways of the Hoover administration to Americans. He was also trying to justify himself to Roosevelt, on whose terms Hoover was now conducting his campaign: he was writing a two-hour speech denying that he was a heartless fraud, looking backward at the ruins of his term, and defending actions and policies that, however bold, however well intentioned, and however promising, had patently failed to avoid calamity.[45]

As it turned out, Hoover had no cause to be concerned for his safety in Des Moines. He arrived, he delivered his long speech, it was carried by radio to over one hundred cities, and he left the next day without a single egg thrown in anger. There had been a minor protest with farmers bearing signs reading IN HOOVER WE TRUSTED— NOW WE'RE BUSTED. Police were called, not to quell the protest but to protect the farmers from angry Hoover sympathizers. Septuagenarian senator James A. Reed, Hoover's bête noire from his days as America's food czar, came out of retirement to follow the president to Des Moines and remind Americans that as the son of a blacksmith he knew nothing of farming, and that as a man who had spent most of his adult life abroad, he knew nothing of America.[46]

All in all, Joslin was elated:

We are on the way back East from Des Moines, after the most successful day imaginable. . . . At Des Moines we headed a parade that was witnessed by 125,000 people. The Coliseum was packed and what a response the President got. He deserved it for his speech was the best he ever made, not only in substance, with a lot of fight in it, but in delivery. He threw himself into it, revealing himself as he never has before in public. The crowd responded instantly to him. I believe he has helped himself a great deal.[47]

Hoover made at least sixteen stops on the way home from Des Moines, speaking to crowds ranging from one thousand to fifteen thousand. Joslin saw them as uniformly warm and enthusiastic, and a tonic for the president. The newspaper response was similarly uplifting. The *New York Times*:[48]

It will be said that it was a new Hoover who disclosed himself yesterday in Iowa. It was at least a Hoover standing up with a new vigor of language in his own defense, and making an appeal to his countrymen which was touched with an emotion not hitherto supposed to be characteristic of him. Whatever the effect of the speech upon the presidential campaign, he may rest in the belief that in it he has put forth the best that is in him.[49]

The president returned to the White House groggy, exhausted, eyes bloodshot. A reporter who saw him up close in this stretch of the campaign said he looked like "a human creature desperately hurt and pained," a man "tortured intolerably and interminably." Hosting a judicial reception on October 13, he shook hands with at least two thousand people and, seeing as many yet to come, said, "I can't go on. I don't want to faint here." The receiving line was broken up and the president shepherded to his study.[50]

Within thirty-six hours, he was back on the campaign trail, bound for Cleveland. The crowds were less friendly on this trip. Boone recorded that somewhere around Pittsburgh they became "dangerously hostile." There was heckling, and an egg splattered against the window of the train as it rolled by the steel mills. Regardless, Hoover insisted on walking among the people at most stops, a practice that terrified the war hero Boone. In the doctor's estimation, the citizenry was in a "very highly agitated, inflammatory, abusive state of mind." He worried that someone in despair might take a shot at Hoover, even as he stood on the platform.[51]

With two weeks left in the campaign, Hoover learned that his party, accustomed to vastly outspending its opponents, had run out of money. His Chicago organizers told him that paid staffers had to be dismissed, and that his upcoming speech in Detroit could not be broadcast for want of funds. The president gave $20,000 of his own money to book the hall and pay for the radio. Ogden Mills and Stimson each chipped in $5,000, and Mills was instructed to demand $150,000 of Andrew Mellon. Hoover, still convinced that he could win if he could refill his war chest, returned to his office to personally dial up more donations. "My God," said Joslin, "what a job."[52]

After having insisted for months that he would not make the great pilgrimage across the country his staff had urged on him, Hoover relented at the eleventh hour and announced that his one-man show would travel by rail to Palo Alto in the last week of the race, meeting a heavy schedule of speeches and platform appearances along the route. That the Literary Digest survey as well as internal Republican polling now had Roosevelt with a substantial lead undoubtedly helped to change the president's mind. He was to leave Washington on November 3. On that day, Lou piled into their limousine under the north porte cochere at the White House and waited for him to join her for the short ride to Union Station. He had been working frantically all morning to clear his desk. She waited an unusually long time, and when he finally appeared, he slumped in his seat, drained and pale. "I am so exhausted," he whispered, "I do not believe I will survive the trip." When they arrived at the station, Lou instructed the physician Boone to remain at his side every step of the journey.[53]

The mounting evidence of Roosevelt's momentum undermined Hoover's commitment to wholesome campaigning in the last days of the race. Before leaving for Palo Alto, he had pounded his opponent for irresponsible appeals to class and sectional differences, enumerating Roosevelt's inconsistencies and damning him as "a chameleon on the scotch plaid." He had warned that the elimination of protective tariffs would cause "grass to grow in streets of a hundred cities, a thousand towns," a piece of hyperbole in league with the Democrats' claim that Smoot-Hawley had caused the Great Depression. He now continued in this vein through the heartland, deriding Roosevelt, accurately and forgettably, as "nebular and inconsistent" to an audience in St. Louis.[54]

Stung by Democratic emphasis on his faulty economic predictions, Hoover tried to turn the table, reaching back to the last time the Democrats had held the White House and quoting President Wilson and Treasury Secretary William McAdoo as stating that the creation of the Federal Reserve System would prevent all future panics. This made the president feel better. As a political message, however, it was old news that served only to remind voters that he had been wrong in his own forecasts.[55]

Edgar Rickard listened to a broadcast of Hoover's speech in St. Paul and was "stunned" by the weakness of his friend's delivery. He feared he might collapse before the end of the campaign. Joslin, who saw the performance in person, said that Hoover's voice "was worn out and so were his eyes for he spoke haltingly and frequently lost his place."[56]

Boone, as per Lou's instructions, had the most intimate view at St. Paul. Seeing the president lose his way in the middle of the speech, he stepped quickly to his side and put his finger at the right section. Hoover stood there without saying a word, looking like he was going to faint. Boone used his foot to push a chair behind the president in case he toppled backwards. Instead, Hoover took a deep breath and continued on his way. The doctor afterward tried to excuse the mishap, noting that the light over the podium had been weak. "There was nothing wrong with the light," said Hoover. "I reached a point where I couldn't see the damn print."[57]

The most memorable moment on the home stretch happened at a dusty railroad siding in the one-street town of Elko, Nevada, on the last day of campaigning, November 7. The train stopped at twilight, and Hoover spoke to the nation from a radio hookup in the dining car, with Lou, his retinue, and his escort of journalists all crowded around. It was an unremarkable little speech made remarkable by the circumstances. It seemed a wonder to everyone on the train that they could pull up in the middle of nowhere, in a town whose name in the original Shoshoni means rocks piled on one another, and with the flip of a switch allow the president to address the whole of the American people.[58]

It also seemed a fitting finale for a man who throughout his time in Washington had ushered in one technological wonder after another. There was dead silence in the car as he spoke:

> Four years ago I stated that I conceived the Presidency as more than an administrative office: it is a power for leadership bringing coordination of the forces of business and cultural life in every town, city, and countryside. The Presidency is more than executive responsibility. It is the symbol of America's high purpose. The President must represent the Nation's ideals, and he must also represent them to the nations of the world. After four years of experience I still regard this as a supreme obligation.

Hoover by now knew he was finished, yet he betrayed nothing of what he was feeling about the election until the very end of his address, when he stopped, looked straight ahead, and, with a slight quaver in his voice, said, "Good night, my friends, good night."[59]


It is unsurprising that Hoover, who could never gather enough data, commissioned the research that best explains his defeat. The New York firm Houser Associates undertook what appears to have been the first scientific national election poll for either party. Face-to-face interviews with a random-sample of five thousand American voters were conducted in and around fourteen metropolitan areas. The survey report was delivered to Lewis Strauss, Hoover's friend and the vice treasurer of the Republican National Committee, with three weeks left in the campaign. It is an invaluable document, perhaps the only empirical tool capable of penetrating the heaps of supposition and conjecture under which the 1932 campaign was fated to be buried.[60]

The Houser survey indicates that the Democrats had a sizable lead among decided voters, 1,692 to 1,431. It found that Prohibition, more than any other issue, was driving Republicans into Roosevelt's arms. Among those defecting, 83.6 percent believed that repeal would be good for the country (a position shared by the vast majority of traditional Democrats). Majorities of both defectors and Democrats

believed that opening the taps would create jobs and fire the economy. The Republican base was split on the benefits of repeal, suggesting that the president's agony over the issue was warranted. That so
many voters saw a connection between the Eighteenth Amendment
and economic recovery shows that the issues were connected, and
makes it tricky to weigh the relative impacts of Prohibition and the
depression on the final outcome.[61]

The depression undoubtedly did its own damage, although in different ways and perhaps to a lesser extent than is generally supposed.
Fifty-eight percent of defectors held Hoover "at least somewhat
responsible" for the downturn. At the same time, 68 percent believed
that his government had done something to make the depression
less severe, with the Reconstruction Finance Corporation receiving
much of the credit. The majority of respondents, and 64 percent of
decamping Republicans, said financiers and businessmen were "most
to blame" for the ruined economy. Wall Street, vilified alongside
Hoover by Roosevelt, was the greater bogey.[62]

The poll's most interesting revelation on the depression is that the
vast majority of Americans believed it was over. Almost two-thirds of
respondents agreed that "business in general is picking up," as Hoover
had insisted during the four months of the campaign. His final upturn
had been no mirage. It held until Election Day. Eighty-two percent
of Republican defectors looked forward to declining unemployment
in the year ahead. Republican regulars were slightly more confident.
The expectations of regular Democrats are not provided, but it is reasonable to assume they would have aligned with the defectors, as they
did on almost every other question.[63]

For all the discussion in Congress about unemployment relief,
a mere 5.4 percent of Republicans and 16.5 percent of Democrats
thought "the government should give money directly to the unemployed." This suggests that Hoover was not much damaged by the
particular issue of his opposition to the dole.[64]

There are other insights to be gleaned from the Houser survey.
Hoover was injured by his tariff stance: 70 percent of Republican
deserters objected to existing rates, no doubt inspired by the Michel-
son/Roosevelt demolition of Smoot-Hawley. The defecting Republicans evinced some of the same contradictions as Roosevelt. They
tended to believe more strongly in a generous, activist national gov-

ernment and, at the same time, were more inclined than the Republican base to want the national budget balanced through spending reductions. They also shared Roosevelt's professed isolationism, doubting a European role in the depression, and feeling less of an obligation toward aiding European recovery.[65]

In a pyrrhic victory for Hoover, a slight majority of Americans now accepted his long argued point that business could be "planned and arranged" so as to offset depressions. It was Roosevelt, however, who had made an issue of economic planning in 1932.[66]

Valuable as it is, the Houser survey has severe limits. Most significantly, it asks no questions about leadership and is therefore mute on the impact of Roosevelt's manifest political skills and Hoover's shortcomings. The president was undoubtedly injured by his inability to project empathy for the victims of the depression, and he failed to place the same blame on Congress that Roosevelt had laid upon him. His credibility was reduced by his three years up and down the depression roller coaster. It would be unwise to underestimate the role of leadership in the campaign.


At home in Palo Alto on election night, November 8, the Hoovers presided over a throng of friends and neighbors in their oversized living room. One guest said the couple looked tired and thin, "as though they had been pulled through a knothole." Around 9 p.m., as Stanford students gathered outside on the street to serenade the president, he slipped off to his study to compose his letter of congratulations to Roosevelt.[67]

There was no ambiguity about the result. The man who had won election by an emphatic margin of victory four years earlier lost by an even greater margin. Roosevelt took 472 electoral college votes and 57.4 percent of the popular vote to Hoover's 59 and 39.6 percent. The Democrat carried forty-two states to the Republican's six, all of which were clustered in the northeast. Hoover suffered the humiliation of seeing his home state of California and his native states of Oregon and Iowa each give 58 percent of their vote to the challenger. At 9:30 p.m., the crowd in the living room hushed as the concession telegram was read aloud. A few minutes later, Hoover, with Lou by his side, appeared on the front balcony of the house to address the students.

They gave him a solid four minutes of applause and lit fireworks until the sky was bright as day and the president was enveloped in smoke. He stood smiling and waving. After a series of boom-rah cheers, the students were hushed by a cheerleader.[68]

"I thank you for your fine loyalty," said Hoover with emotion, "and I deeply appreciate this very hearty greeting. Thank you." He turned away and walked back into the house.[69]

"Democracy," he later wrote, "is a harsh employer."[70]

Hoover was not long in Palo Alto. Defeated or not, he had four months left in his term. There was scant opportunity to regain his bearings and salve his wounds. The pace of events seemed only to increase after the election.[*]

The one-year moratorium on war debts and reparations Hoover had negotiated in 1931 was to run out at the end of 1932. International sentiment was largely in favor of outright cancellation of the debts, an outcome still objectionable to the American people. Not wanting to write off the $10 billion owed the U.S. Treasury without receiving anything in return, Hoover advanced an imaginative scheme to establish a commission that would link further concessions on indebtedness to limits on military spending. He believed the proposal, if accepted, would help to stabilize Europe's politics and finances, and forestall revolution in Germany.

The major roadblock to his plan was that Congress had placed strict limits on the executive's ability to renegotiate the debt payments, and congressional leaders were now looking to Roosevelt rather than him for guidance. Hoover thus made an unprecedented approach to the president-elect, asking his cooperation in advancing the international debt plan, even offering to create a bipartisan working group to see the measure through. Editorial opinion was firmly in the president's court: Democratic papers wrote that "no one but a churlish partisan could have failed to feel a glow of satisfaction" on reading Hoover's offer, inspired as it was by "unselfish and non-

---

[*] Hoover's was the last of the long interregnums. The Twentieth Amendment to the Constitution, ratified in February 1933, would move up the start of the presidential term from March 4 to January 20. The new dates would take effect in 1937.

partisan and public-spirited motives." This was largely, although not entirely, the case. Hoover would have been happy to have Roosevelt accept his scheme and implicate himself in an international solution to a depression that he had insisted was a domestic phenomenon.[71]

While publicly crediting Hoover with excellent intentions, Roosevelt was unenthusiastic about the debt plan, which his adviser Raymond Moley compared to an "explosive" package left at the president-elect's door. Roosevelt appears to have sincerely believed that a domestic solution to the depression was possible, and many of his supporters were against debt concessions of any kind. He also had no interest in helping Hoover solve the depression, and he did not want responsibility for the outcome of any negotiations that Hoover would conduct with the Europeans. Resolving not to cooperate with the president, he agreed only to an informal courtesy call at the White House.[72]

The meeting was held in the Red Room of the White House on November 22. The mood was tense. There was, by this time, palpable animosity between the two old friends, now president and president-elect. Eleanor Roosevelt, in a memoir written almost two decades after these events, suggests that it dated to the Governors' Conference of the previous spring when Hoover had left Roosevelt, whose weight was supported by crippled legs encased in heavy steel braces, waiting in a predinner receiving line for an agonizing half hour. This appears to be overstated.* More likely, the ill feelings were mostly on Hoover's side and attributable to the jabs he had caught on the campaign trail. He was as unable to forgive Roosevelt's rhetoric as Roosevelt was unwilling to believe that a politician could hold a grudge

---

* Mrs. Roosevelt admitted that staffers had twice offered her husband a chair at the Governors' Conference, and that the cause of his wait was late-arriving guests. She also allowed that accusing Hoover of deliberately torturing FDR seemed preposterous but added that "in political life you grow suspicious." Alonzo Fields of the White House domestic staff casts doubt on her story. He recalled in detail (also much later) his encounter with Franklin Roosevelt at the Governors' Conference, saying that he was given instructions and training on how to assist the governor, who arrived early, was promptly placed in an elevator, and conveyed to the upstairs dining room where he was immediately seated. This is consistent with Hoover's decision to break protocol in the Senate chamber during Roosevelt's inauguration so that FDR would not need to stand waiting for him. Alonzo Fields Oral History, 1970, HHPL; Eleanor Roosevelt, *This I Remember* (Garden City, NY: Dolphin Books, 1961), p. 69.

over words uttered for partisan advantage. They would remain mutually suspicious, questioning each other's motives and missing each other's points, for the rest of their lives.

Roosevelt used the White House elevator and entered the Red Room with his usual bonhomie. His adviser Raymond Moley found the president "grave, dignified, and somewhat uneasy." Hoover, sitting alone on a divan, dominated the conversation, rarely looking at Roosevelt, choosing instead to watch the afternoon light retreat from the seal of the United States on the deep red carpet. Moley admired Hoover's "mastery of detail and clarity of arrangement," and doubted that anyone understood the issues better. Roosevelt asked a few brief questions and left it for Moley to explain on his behalf that the incoming administration disagreed with Hoover's assessment of the debt problem and his proposed solutions.[73]

The meeting was a bust, with Hoover later telling Stimson that he had spent much of his time "educating a very ignorant . . . well-meaning young man." Roosevelt publicly suggested that Hoover do what he liked with the remainder of his term. Asked by reporters about the debt issue, the president-elect answered that he would "leave that baby on Mr. Hoover's lap," and noted that there was no constitutional provision for the involvement of an incoming chief executive in his predecessor's work.[74]

Hoover, in fact, could not do as he liked, given the limits Congress had placed on his ability to renegotiate the debt payments. He had already met with congressional leaders and learned, as he had suspected, that they would not change their stance without Roosevelt's support. Seized with the urgency of the moment, he continued to bombard his opponents with proposals for cooperation toward solutions, going so far as to suggest that Democratic nominees, not Republicans, be sent to Europe to engage in negotiations, all to no avail. Notwithstanding what editorialists called his "personal and moral responsibility" to engage with the outgoing administration, Roosevelt had instructed Democratic leaders in Congress to not let Hoover "tinker" with the debts. He had also let it be known that any solution to the problem would occur on his watch—"Roosevelt holds he and not Hoover will fix debt policy," read the headlines. Thus ended what the *New York Times* called Hoover's magnanimous proposal for "unity and constructive action," not to mention his twelve-year effort to convince America of its obligation and self-interest in fostering European political and financial stability. League of Nations spokesmen in Geneva expressed dismay and wondered what hope there was for international cooperation when outgoing and incoming American administrations could not work together.[75]

As it happened, England made its next payment on time, France defaulted, and Germany, sensing that the United States was turning inward, announced that it was seeking to cancel all of its reparations.


During the debt discussions, and to some extent as a result of them, the economy turned south again. Several other factors contributed. Investors were exchanging U.S. dollars for gold as doubt spread about Roosevelt's intentions to remain on the gold standard. Gold stocks in the Federal Reserve thus declined, threatening the stability of the banking sector. Confidence in the banks was further undermined by an ill-timed, widely publicized Senate investigation into skullduggery on Wall Street. The chamber would have been wiser to heed Melchior Palyi's advice to wait until the dust had settled to "punish the bankers." What's more, the effectiveness of the RFC, which had succeeded in stabilizing the banking system, was severely compromised by Congress's insistence on publicizing its loans, as the administration had warned. For these reasons, Hoover would forever blame Roosevelt and the Democratic Congress for spoiling his hard-earned recovery, an argument that has only recently gained currency among economists.[*76]

Alarmed at these threats to recovery, Hoover pushed Democratic congressional leaders and the incoming administration for action. He wanted to cut federal spending, reorganize the executive branch to save money, reestablish the confidentiality of RFC loans, introduce

* Eichengreen in *Hall of Mirrors* explains how Roosevelt's apparent inclination to tamper with the monetary standard drained gold from the Federal Reserve and the country, undermining the banking sector. Butkiewicz illustrates how the Reconstruction Finance Corporation was working effectively until Congress began publicizing the identity of borrowers, reducing its volume of loans in September and leading to a decline in industrial production in October. Barry Eichengreen, *Hall of Mirrors* (Oxford: Oxford University Press, 2015), p. 164; James Butkiewicz, "The Impact of a Lender of Last Resort During the Great Depression," *Explorations in Economic History* 32 (2005), pp. 197–216.

bankruptcy legislation to prevent foreclosures, grant new powers
to the Federal Reserve, and pass new banking regulation, including
measures to protect depositors. He also wanted to extend federal
regulations to banks operating on an interstate basis, and to separate
investment banking from commercial banking. He was frustrated at
every turn by Democratic leaders taking cues from the president-elect.
While pretending to stay out of Hoover's way, Roosevelt, reported
the *New York Times* on January 1, was calling the shots, "more and
more assuming, in a political sense, the domestic section of the burden which will be officially his on March 4." As Garner, Democratic
Speaker of the House and incoming vice president said, "it is a waste
of time to try any legislation to which [Roosevelt] will not agree."[77]

On February 5, Congress took the obstructionism a degree further by closing shop with twenty-three days left in its session. Virtually all work was put off until the incoming administration was in
position to introduce its own sweeping reconstruction program. It
was common knowledge in Washington that Roosevelt had asked
the next Congress to give him a free hand to implement his as-yet-
unannounced plans.[78]

Hoover was meanwhile pilloried by the same Democratic congressmen who refused him cooperation over the size of his deficit and
his unwillingness to reduce it. Not going down without a fight, he
surprised Congress on February 20 with a special message repeating
many of his requests, only to be told by Democratic leaders that he
was too late. He tried once more to have the publication of RFC loans
discontinued and briefly gained the crucial support of Senate minority leader Joseph Robinson until he, too, decided to stand down and
await the advent of Roosevelt.[79]

The president, by this time, would have been content to admit defeat
and quietly play out the string on his term. He was in a wretched
mood. His Research Committee on Social Trends had just delivered
its awe-inspiring two-volume report on the state of America. It was
easily the most comprehensive study of its kind ever attempted, examining demographic patterns, education, moral attitudes, childhood,
family life, urban life, the status of women, consumerism, labor issues,
the arts, health and medical practice, religion, and public administra-

tion, among many other issues. It had been intended to provide a factual basis for the promotion of actively managed change in all of these areas, to help the country "see where social stresses are occurring and where major efforts should be undertaken to deal with them constructively." This had been the work Hoover had most wanted to undertake during his presidency. Distracted by the depression and deprived of a second term, all he could do was append his signature to the report's 1,600 pages and leave it to the fates.[80]

He would not have contacted Roosevelt again until the inauguration had not conditions deteriorated further. A full-blown banking crisis in February forced president and president-elect into another unwanted embrace.

The scene of the crisis this time was Detroit, where the mammoth Guardian Group, headed by Edsel Ford, the arrogant and irresponsible only son of Henry, was in desperate need of capital. The firm had blown a great deal of money on a towering Art Deco, Mayan Revival headquarters on Griswold Street in Detroit, funded the stock speculations of its officers, and overextended itself in home mortgage loans, among other objectionable practices. Ford applied for RFC funds and after a series of meetings with administration officials, he was told that he would need to make several concessions and to inject some of his own money as security for RFC assistance. Ford balked. No such demands had been made upon the Dawes family bank when it hit the rocks the previous summer, he complained. He had a point, but Congress had been less alert then. Believing that Washington would never risk systemic chaos by allowing his bank to fail, Ford refused to cooperate. The RFC, over Hoover's strong objections, bowed to congressional pressure and refused Guardian Group the loan, and down it went.[81]

Its failure triggered runs on other banks, in Michigan and throughout the country. Individual depositors hustled to their local tellers and filled their pockets and purses with what was left of their savings, compounding the stress on the system. Among them were two Hoovers: Lou withdrew $2,000 in cash because it was very possible, she told Allan, "that any or all banks in the country might unexpectedly stop cash payments one of these days"; her husband had meanwhile filled a safe deposit box with cash drawn on February 13, a day before Michigan declared an eight-day bank holiday.[82]

All of the positive indicators that Hoover had been so relieved to see in the second half of 1932 were by now dismal again. In the last half of February, the Federal Reserve Bank of New York saw almost a quarter of its gold evaporate. Wholesale prices declined. Industrial production sank. Unemployment increased. State after state followed Michigan's example of implementing a bank holiday. Robbed of his long-awaited recovery, Hoover blamed Democrats for the new slump and Congress more generally for dismissing his three years of calls for bank reform. He prepared a legislative package to meet the bank runs and gold withdrawals. Of course, it, too, would require congressional assent, and Congress would not yield without the president-elect's approval; so, once more, he picked up his pen.[83]

At 4 p.m. on the afternoon of February 18, 1933, Secret Service operative John S. West was called to the White House, where Lawrence Richey handed him a sealed envelope and instructed him to place it in the hands of President-elect Roosevelt that evening. West boarded the five o'clock train, arrived in New York at 10 p.m., tracked the president-elect to a banquet at the Astor Hotel, and placed the package in his hands.[84]

Roosevelt took one look at the envelope and noticed that Hoover had dropped the first *e* from the spelling of his name. He took this as a personal slight, unaware that Hoover was capable of misspelling his son's name. Inside the envelope he found the president's handwritten letter announcing that "a most critical situation has arisen in the country of which I feel it is my duty to advise you confidentially." Fear and apprehension, wrote Hoover, were once more rampant in the country. "I am convinced that a very early statement by you upon two or three policies of your administration would serve greatly to restore confidence and cause a resumption of the march of recovery."[85]

In particular, Hoover wanted Roosevelt to commit to balancing the budget, and to promise that there would be "no tampering or inflation of the currency." It would also help, said Hoover, if congressional leaders were to cease publication of RFC business. With the exception of the last point, Hoover asked nothing that had not been promised by Roosevelt during the campaign, and by the Democratic

platform. Indeed, Roosevelt had lambasted Hoover for his deficits
and for employing inflationary tactics that had weakened "public confidence in our Government credit both at home and abroad." Hoover
did not directly accuse Roosevelt of reneging on his promises. He
blamed the public fright on loose talk in congressional circles raising
concerns that the platform might be abandoned, and insinuated that
the president-elect and his circle had contributed through words or
actions to the general hysteria. On the whole, the letter was conde-
scending in tone and unnecessarily provocative in laying responsibility for the immediate crisis at the feet of the Democrats.[86]

Moley was quick to note in the letter Hoover's desires to legitimate his own management of the financial crisis and to handcuff the
incoming administration. It would later come out in private correspondence that Hoover hoped to scare Roosevelt into endorsing Republican views on the depression and renouncing New Deal
promises of change and experimentation. He would be disappointed.
Roosevelt, said Moley, either "did not realize how serious the situation was" or "preferred to have conditions deteriorate and gain
for himself the entire credit for the rescue operation." The latter is
the more likely explanation. Bernard Baruch and Carter Glass, two
of the Democratic Party's most respected voices, together with the
Federal Reserve Advisory Board, echoed Hoover's requests of the
president-elect, with the same sense of urgency. Glass had refused
to sit as FDR's Treasury secretary over the same policy uncertainty
identified by Hoover. The seriousness of the situation was abundantly
clear. Roosevelt responded as he did out of his frequently articulated
belief that "the goad of fear and suffering" facilitated his "progressive
purpose." A totally devastated U.S. economy, along with any credit
he might receive for an upturn, would bring Roosevelt the political
capital he needed for the legislative onslaught he had in mind for his
first hundred days. He deliberately left Hoover's letter unanswered
for eleven days, by which time more than thirty states had closed their
banks.[87]

Moley was impressed at Roosevelt's sangfroid. He showed no
more concern for the imminent collapse of the nation's banking system than he had for the assassin's bullet that had missed him by a
few inches in Miami on February 15, killing Chicago mayor Anton J.
Cermak instead. Moley kept waiting for Roosevelt to break out in a

sweat, or for him to at least produce a hint of "false gaiety." It did not seem an unreasonable expectation. "Terror," said Moley, "now held the country in grip." Yet he saw nothing from Roosevelt except poise and unshakable confidence.[88]

The day before the inauguration, Hoover hosted Roosevelt for a traditional pre-inaugural tea at the White House. The New Dealers, under the mistaken impression that custom dictated a dinner, took the tea as a slight. Hoover used the occasion to again beg Roosevelt's assistance. He proposed they resort to a relic of the Great War, the Trading with the Enemy Act, to restrict gold shipments and bank withdrawals. The attorney general had advised Hoover that he required approval in advance from Congress to invoke the act. Congress would still not move without a signal from the president-elect, and Roosevelt again answered Hoover with polite evasions.

Later in the evening, the president made a telephone call to Roosevelt. Hoover had come under pressure from the Federal Reserve to declare a nationwide bank holiday to relieve the pressure on the system. Hoover thought the idea unnecessarily drastic, punitive to unaffected regions of the country, and unfair to his successor in that it limited his options in managing the crisis. Perhaps most of all, Hoover was not keen to leave office with the heart of the national economy stopped. Believing that the states should be left to decide whether or not to close their banks, he spoke to Roosevelt, who claimed to agree that a national holiday was unwise.

The Hoovers said good-bye to the White House and its staff on the morning of Roosevelt's inauguration. Lou had packed up their things, placing boxes in storage, where they would lie forgotten for many years. She gave away hundreds of books on economics her husband had collected and studied during his great trial. Hoover and Roosevelt drove together the next morning down Pennsylvania Avenue to the Capitol. Magazine covers would portray a chill between them, which was undoubtedly present, although several photographs show Hoover greeting the president-elect warmly. Hoover, on the whole, behaved much as he had when riding with Coolidge in 1928.

Sitting stone-faced through the inaugural, he had to have noticed Roosevelt's clear, mellifluous voice and charismatic delivery. He had to have been wounded by Roosevelt's indictment of "the rulers of the exchange of mankind's goods" who had failed "through their own stubbornness and their own incompetence," and who had been "rejected by the hearts and minds of men." He had to have been annoyed at Roosevelt's declaration that Americans had "nothing to fear but fear itself." The line, which did not cause a ripple in the crowd, or receive prominence in newspaper summaries the next day, would have stuck out for Hoover simply because he had expressed the same sentiment ad nauseam throughout his term only to be mocked as a Pollyanna by Roosevelt during the campaign. When Roosevelt told the American people that they could now expect to hear truth from their president, Hoover, according to Boone, "looked as though somebody had cracked him across the face with a riding crop."[89]

Hoover left the Capitol directly for Union Station. Because of the recent Bonus Army fiasco and the attempt on Roosevelt's life, there had been heavy security at the inaugural, including machine-gun nests up and down Pennsylvania Avenue. Having at least as much reason to feel vulnerable as Roosevelt (the man who took a shot at the president-elect had been originally targeting Hoover), he had asked the incoming administration for a Secret Service detail to accompany him on the train home. He was angered to learn that he would be covered to Union Station and no farther.

In this spirit of mutual antagonism, with each man nursing slights real and imagined, with the country frightened and demoralized as never before in peacetime, Roosevelt and Hoover parted, never to meet again.

# ★ BOOK V ★

★ BOOK V ★

# CHAPTER 25

# Through the Abyss in a Buick

The White House had been one of the firmer bases of operations in the Hoovers' thirty-four-year marriage. They had lived under its roof almost constantly through his term, rarely traveling farther than Rapidan for work or pleasure. It was their intention on leaving Washington to finally make a home of the Stanford mansion Lou had built a decade earlier. She had doubts about how long the arrangement would last, knowing her husband's attraction to the East Coast, but she was convinced that California would serve his recovery. He was "utterly brain tired," she wrote Allan, having endured "a long, dull, deadly grind, and it will be a slow process getting back to normal . . . like recovering from an illness."[1]

Although the Palo Alto house, he confessed to friends, was not to his taste, Hoover tried to make it work. He truly occupied his study for the first time, using it to deal with his voluminous correspondence, as many as 1,500 letters a day. He also became a regular visitor to the nearby Hoover War Library, an institution he had founded and filled with books, posters, and documents from the Great War, the Versailles conference, his relief administrations, and earlier conflicts and famines that interested him. He followed the news and kept a close eye on the "anti-Hoover literature" that was accumulating at a depressing rate in the library. Doing his best to appear relaxed and busy, he spoke of "a complete exultation and release at no longer having to make ten vital decisions a day. I now could get into my automobile and drive anywhere I liked."[2]

The trouble was that he had nowhere to go. Ray Lyman Wilbur visited Hoover in April, a month after his arrival at Stanford, and found him "lonely beyond measure" and "terribly isolated." Edgar Rickard wrote of Hoover's epic letdown after twenty-two years of intimacy with "national and international affairs and men of importance and position." Another acquaintance used the term "broken-hearted" to describe him: "When I went to see him I would find him playing solitaire by himself. It made one feel like crying to see his low state of mind."[3]

Having been delivered from West Branch as a boy due to circumstances beyond his control or understanding, Hoover had managed through will, resourcefulness, and strong native intelligence to establish an identity, build a life for himself, regain his sense of self-worth, and find a series of communities to which he belonged and in which he was appreciated. With drive and astounding self-discipline, he had put himself in a position to successively care for himself, his family and friends, for tourists stranded by war, for starving populations in Europe and Russia, and ultimately the whole of the American people. He had sought power and control as antidotes to his own sense of vulnerability and out of a solemn sense of duty to improve the lives of others, to give them the sense of connection and community that he had come through painful experience to understand as fundamental to life. When the markets blew out in 1929, he had genuinely believed that his mastery and hard work could keep the economy on its hinges. He had wanted nothing more than to triumph over the Depression or, at least, to help the American people, at their self-reliant and community-minded best, to recognize it as a temporary setback, one they would overcome before marching further down the path of advance and achievement they had trod for 150 years. In the end he had been adjudged a failure, beaten again by circumstances beyond his control or understanding, rejected in the hearts and minds of voters, drummed out of office, and made both a punching bag and punch line by the people he had sought to serve. The tender psyche that so desperately wanted an honored place in the American story was devastated.

Hoover now resembled, in all but corporeal ruin, his old friend Franklin Lane who at the start of Hoover's political career had written from his deathbed wondering if all the anxiety, insult, and humiliation of public life had been worthwhile when, at the end of the day, his high hopes and ambitions had led him into a world "awry, distorted, and altogether perverse," where he could only stare in wonder at the gap between intent and effect.[4]

California was the wrong place for a man who rarely ate a meal alone, who needed to belong, who dreaded rejection and isolation. He knew few people in Palo Alto, and he had nothing much to do beyond suffer the full weight and pain of his repudiation, and make lists of people he felt had been disloyal to him.

It would have been a difficult adjustment even without the defeat. The American presidency is a pinnacle like no other. What follows is necessarily a descent or, at best, an eclipse. Certainly none of Hoover's recent predecessors offered much to emulate in the way of a post-presidential career. Not Harding (died in office), Wilson (all but died in office), or McKinley (assassinated). Cleveland and Coolidge (the latter had died during the Hoover-Roosevelt interregnum) had each retired to the quiet obscurity of a country home in declining health, again nothing Hoover would want. He was fifty-eight, not yet old, in the prime of life as leadership goes. He would reclaim his physical vitality with a week or two of decent sleep. He wanted a future of purposeful toil commensurate with his abilities. He might have envied Taft, who made a successful transition to the Supreme Court, an avenue closed to Hoover, who had not studied the law.

The only remaining example from recent presidential history was Theodore Roosevelt, who on leaving office had traveled, hunted like a madman, and haunted his party until he broke it. Hoover had begun his term with the example of the great Bull Moose in mind. He would now follow loosely in his postpresidential footsteps, nursing the same sense of unfinished business. He would fish, travel like a madman, and haunt the successor who had broken him.

He considered, at least momentarily, taking a job. His finances were in poor shape; four years in office had been a major expense, and he had given a fifth of his salary back to the government in 1932 (the amount allowed by law) and donated the rest to charity in an unprecedented yet futile gesture of solidarity with the American people. He had continued to be generous with friends, family, and associates, supplementing incomes and lending cash that would probably never be repaid, and the Depression had devastated his investments. His nest egg, by one estimate, had been reduced from several million to $700,000.* Given the state of the economy, it would no longer provide the level of income to which the family had grown accustomed.

Henry Ford offered to secretly underwrite a ten-minute weekly radio broadcast by Hoover to the tune of $3,000 a week. Always conscious of his dignity, and uneasy about appearing before a public that had discarded him, Hoover dismissed the opportunity. He also rejected the alternatives of salaried positions with financial institutions or mining firms: putting himself on the payroll of corporate America would tend to confirm his alignment with Roosevelt's crooks and enemies of the people, and he was as yet unwilling to admit that his political career was over. He decided instead to trust his own business savvy to rebuild his fortune and took a more active part in his investments.[5]

Lou, stout as ever, took the loss of the presidency and their reduced circumstances in stride. "For the coming year or years I am going to have very little money to run our family on," she wrote Allan. "We have spent in the past, instead of being thrifty." She mused whimsically about using the sums of cash she had squirreled away to purchase a cheap plot of land where they could all live simply with chickens and a cow. "It will be rather fun," she said, "and not any hardship really." In the same breath she asked Allan to inquire about the cost of a grand piano. All things considered, the Hoovers remained well-to-do.[6]

The boys were more or less self-supporting. Herbert Jr., turning thirty, had followed his degrees at Stanford and the Harvard Business School with a Guggenheim fellowship to study aviation economics. A key figure in the growth of commercial aviation, he had made the cover of *Time* magazine in 1930 as the first president of Aeronauti-

---

* Theodore Joslin records in his diary on July 30, 1932, that he showed Hoover an advance proof of an article in *Fortune* magazine claiming his fortune had dwindled to $700,000 from $4,000,000. "[Hoover] read it through carefully, looked up with a smile and said, 'Well, Ted, for your information there is not an accurate sentence in that entire article.'"

cal Radio Inc. He resigned that position months later, after the 1930 elections, when it was alleged that he owed his success and his firm's contracts to his father's influence. After a long convalescence from a bout of tuberculosis, he worked at Transcontinental Air Express and taught economics to engineering students at the California Institute of Technology.* Allan Hoover had followed his brother through Stanford and Harvard Business School. After a spell in the Los Angeles financial industry, he took over management of the family's farming operations in California's Imperial Valley.[7]

Had there been some crisis in his finances or in his family, something urgently requiring his attention and energy, Hoover's transition out of the battle on a thousand fronts might have been easier. As it was, his days were relatively empty. He craved news, despite reading dozens of newspapers a day. He was constantly in touch with Washington through the mails and by telephone. His friends transmitted gossip about Roosevelt: how he stayed in bed until 10:30 in the morning; how he addressed newspapermen by their first names; how his adviser Louis Howe, living in the White House, came down to breakfast without shaving and gave orders to domestic staff as though he owned the place. They kept Hoover abreast of the progress of the New Deal, which would have done little to alleviate Hoover's suffering, both because it was popular and because he was skeptical of Roosevelt's policies.[8]

Hoover meanwhile retained full ownership of the Depression. Every job lost, every mortgage foreclosed upon, was noted on his side of the ledger. Every ray of hope and all credit for effort fell to the new president. Economists and political scientists developed the habit of charting the economy's gains from Roosevelt's inauguration rather than from his election, not an unreasonable practice given that March 3 was FDR's official start date, but one that exaggerated Hoover's culpability and absolved the Democrats of any responsibility for decisions during the interregnum.

---

* Herbert Jr. would later make a significant contribution to California's emergence as a technology leader by founding Consolidated Engineering Corporation (CEC) and winning a patent for a mass spectrometer. "A marker in a Tommy's Burger parking lot in Pasadena, California, commemorates his company and his patent," says Thomas Schwartz, director of the Herbert Hoover Presidential Library (letter to the author, January 30, 2017). CEC was acquired by Bell and Howell Corp. in 1960.

Hoover spent an immense amount of time behind the wheel of his car, not in complete exultation, as he claimed, but in a desperate, primal response to hostile circumstances. Travel had been his resort when legal troubles had smashed his nerves during his business career, and it was his resort now. He sped through Grass Valley, the High Sierras and Yosemite, and down along the Pacific Coast, putting eight thousand miles on his odometer in the spring of 1933 in a vain effort to outrun his failure and his feelings, and for the sheer need of something to do.

He seems mainly to have been drawn to the Sierra Nevada, the same 40-million-year-old granite peaks he had visited as a geology student in the company of Professor Lindgren. It was there he had gotten his first "whole jug full" of learning and experience, where he had become intoxicated by the majesty of the scenery, and where he had forged his romantic sense of identity and destiny as an indomitable man of science. It was there he had nurtured his ambition, the intent that he had fulfilled to such awful effect. Just what he wanted in his return is impossible to say: answers, inspiration, nostalgia? It is unlikely that Hoover, largely a mystery to himself, had a clear idea. He was aware of little more than his hurt.[9]

He returned to Bohemian Grove along the Russian River in the summer of 1933 for the first time since Coolidge had announced that he would not seek reelection. Anxious about how a man who had lost the country would be received by this pack of power brokers, Hoover would not stray from his cabin and the loneliest of the Grove's redwood trails during his first week in attendance. It was only when he was introduced to a standing ovation at a Saturday-night gathering of a thousand campers that he finally let his guard down. At Bohemian Grove, at least, he still belonged.[10]

Strangers he continued to avoid. One of the appeals of the many short fishing trips Hoover took in this period was that he could hide from the world. In October, he was in Oregon with the Iowa cartoonist J. N. "Ding" Darling and others. Their long black limousine pulled up in front of a village grocery near the Oregon border so the driver could pick up supplies. Hoover slouched in the back seat, fearing the lash of judgment in the eyes of the locals. To his dismay, the arrival of so unusual a vehicle in rural Oregon drew the townspeople from their lairs. The local newspaper editor came out, under his green eyeshade, with a box of pink pears. A group of students descended on the car with pencils and paper, asking for autographs.

"Now look what you've done," Hoover snapped at Darling.[11]

The townsfolk kept coming, among them a kindly elderly lady in a lace cap and shawl who elbowed her way to the front of the crowd and stuck her hand in the car.

"Is that really you, President Hoover?" she said. "We all love you and I just want to go home and tell my family that I have seen you and shaken your hand."

Hoover would not look up. He briefly clasped the woman's hand as the limo pulled away.

"Did you see that sweet little old lady, who only wanted to shake your hand?" asked Darling.

"Yes," Hoover answered.

"Well you didn't act like it."[12]

The rest of the drive passed in silence.

Several days after that unhappy episode, with the fishing party camped on the Klamath River, a local schoolteacher approached one of its members and asked if the former president would honor her students with a visit to her one-room schoolhouse. Informed of the request at dinner that evening, Hoover was vehement: "I won't do it." Unintimidated, his fellow fishermen told him he had a duty to the children. Hoover became peevish and silent.[13]

The next morning he toured the school. He noticed that the children seemed underfed. The teacher confessed that she used part of her salary to keep a soup kettle on the woodstove so that her charges would be guaranteed at least one hot meal a day. Hoover returned to camp and asked his friends to help him donate $100 to the school, sufficient to buy the children lunches for a year, and they did.

As Lou expected, time would heal much of Hoover's pain, although it is doubtful that she anticipated how long it would take, or that parts of him would never entirely recover. It certainly did not help that in the first years of his postpresidential life, Hoover had reason to consider himself a hunted man.

The Roosevelt crew and the Democratic Congress did their best to scandalize his administration, one of the cleanest on record. The tax bureau was loosed on Andrew Mellon in a determined although ultimately unsuccessful effort to prosecute him for tax evasion. The distribution of airmail contracts under Hoover's postmaster general, Walter Brown, was probed. The investments and tax returns of all four Hoovers were closely inspected. Nothing was found, much to the relief of Edgar Rickard, who had done Hoover's taxes since the Great War.[14]

The main effect of this unusual attention was to heighten paranoia in the family and the Firm. They were convinced that they were being watched, that Rickard's letters to Hoover were being opened prior to delivery, and that their offices would be raided. They often communicated in cypher, under assumed names. Rickard, most loyal of the Hooverites, looked forward to separating his own financial relations from those of his best friend in part to avoid further scrutiny. Herbert Jr. said that his father's presidency had been the "worst thing that ever happened to the family." They would all have been better off if he had "rested on his oars with his European engagements."[15]

Inevitably, Hoover's hatred of his successor grew. Roosevelt was constantly in his thoughts as he wore out his odometer, racking up forty-five thousand miles and visiting twenty-eight states in his first two years of retirement. He noted and abhorred each of FDR's broken promises, each revision of or departure from the Democrat's New Deal platform, and every contradiction of word or deed committed by Roosevelt and his "starry-eyed young men," the "collegiate oligarchy" that would come to be known to history as the "brains trust."[16]

The New Deal, as manifest in Roosevelt's famous Hundred Days of legislative activity, was an odd amalgam of policies, some initiated by Roosevelt, others urged upon him by advisers or circumstance. Its constituent parts were intended to either promote economic recovery, relieve victims of the Depression, or reform government, or to achieve some combination of the three. It never amounted to a coherent program, not least because his recovery, relief, and reform measures often conflicted with one another, especially when it came to budget matters. Nevertheless, there were important consistencies to it.[17]

Roosevelt delivered on his promise of bold, persistent experimentation. He also clung to his view of the Depression as an essentially American phenomenon requiring domestic solutions. Convinced that the U.S. economy was past its prime, he paid more attention, as promised during the campaign, to the alleviation of distress and the distribution of national wealth than to spurring growth. And running through the whole of the New Deal as perhaps its most consistent feature was a bright thread of partisanship. Roosevelt was determined to use policy to weld together a formidable, durable Democratic advantage in America. The political calculus of the program often introduced contradictions and incoherencies that to this day flummox both its critics and supporters. Roosevelt nevertheless succeeded in his objective. His party would dominate national politics through the middle decades of the twentieth century. His partisanship was disgusting to Hoover, whose noble and self-defeating view was that legislation should never be written in service of political agendas.[18]

Roosevelt's most important moves in the days after his inauguration concerned the banking crisis. He immediately declared a national banking holiday, closing all of the banks in the United States while their books were inspected. Although the examinations were cursory, the four-day holiday served to break the spell of panic. The vast majority of banks reopened a week later in an environment of renewed confidence. Roosevelt also called a special session of Congress, which passed the Emergency Banking Act, an amendment to the Trading with the Enemy Act, granting Roosevelt increased power over the economy including the ability to curb gold and capital outflows from the United States. The Reconstruction Finance Corporation was permitted to inject new capital into banks by taking equity positions in them. Congress, in a stunning volte-face, voted to make RFC loans confidential. These were all components of Hoover's plans, with the exception of the bank holiday, which proved a strong tonic and which he had refused to enact with Roosevelt's apparent agreement. Hoover's Treasury secretary, Ogden Mills, stayed on to steer the new administration through the crisis while Arthur Ballantine, Hoover's undersecretary of the Treasury, helped to write Roosevelt's first fireside chat in which he explained the program.[19]

This initial blast of activity was a great success. When the New York Stock Exchange opened along with the banks on March 15, the Dow Jones Industrial Average shot up 15 percent, its largest single-day increase in history. Gold and bank deposits returned to the financial system.* The banking sector would remain stable for the duration of the Depression, and the new administration received credit for solving the crisis. Hoover would always believe that Roosevelt had pushed the economy off the dock so that he could play the life saver after his inauguration.[20]

In any event, a pattern was established that would play out time and again over the next four years, with New Dealers taking applause for initiatives that had been fathered by Hoover. "When we all burst into Washington," wrote Raymond Moley, "we found every essential idea" of the New Deal anticipated, in whole or in part, by the previous administration. Especially at the start, Roosevelt had hewed closely to Hoover's program of bank relief, agricultural aid, labor reform, industrial cooperation, federal aid to local government, and cuts to conventional spending. He was at least as keen as Hoover to produce balanced budgets. FDR also invoked the spirit of wartime collaboration to encourage adoption of his initiatives, some of which were in whole or in part voluntary, and most of which were considered emergency measures, and therefore temporary. "We must not take the position," he said, "that we are going to have permanent Depression in this country."[21]

The New Deal's justly celebrated Glass-Steagall banking reforms, which divorced commercial from investment banking and introduced a federal deposit insurance program, were another example of Roosevelt presenting Hoover's initiatives as his own. Such new agencies as the Civil Works Administration and the Civilian Conservation Corps followed Hoover's example of using public works to create new employment. Hoover's Reconstruction Finance Corporation, dubbed by one of Roosevelt's advisers "the greatest recovery agency" of the Depression, would become indispensable to the New Deal. Another administration insider, Rexford Tugwell, later traced a long list of New Deal ventures to Hoover's years as secretary of commerce and

---

* Hoover believed this turnaround happened because investors wrongly interpreted Roosevelt's moves as a commitment to sound currency. Economist Barry Eichengreen argues that gold and deposits returned because the banking sector had been suffering from a run-of-the-mill panic rather than fear of the New Deal, as Hoover wanted to believe.

as president and concluded that "the New Deal owed much to what he had begun."[22] This is to say nothing of the invaluable lessons from Hoover's three years of effort, successful or not.

Moley and Tugwell still overstate the case. Roosevelt did proclaim the banking holiday, going further than Hoover thought advisable. He legalized beer in his Hundred Days, after the lame-duck Congress had already passed a bill repealing Prohibition. Roosevelt also created the Tennessee Valley Authority, a public corporation designed to create and distribute hydro power at Muscle Shoals and the centerpiece of an ambitious plan to develop the Tennessee Valley. Hoover had opposed all of this. In other policy realms, Hoover had merely dabbled where his successor shot the moon. Roosevelt's Civil Works Administration put five times more people to work in one winter than Hoover had employed at the peak of his efforts. Whereas Hoover had asked business to maintain wages and encouraged voluntary planning to reap efficiencies in industry, Roosevelt signed the National Industrial Recovery Act permitting the imposition of hours-of-work standards and minimum wages, and empowering a bureaucracy to regulate industrial competition. Hoover's efforts at farm price manipulation, daring at the time, were eclipsed by the New Deal's Agricultural Adjustment Administration, which paid farmers to kill 6 million piglets and destroy 10 million acres of cotton in a bid to increase prices through forced scarcity.[23]

Some New Deal measures, most notably the bank holiday and the ending of Prohibition, were successful. Others, like the Tennessee Valley Authority and the Agricultural Adjustment Act, had mixed results. Some, like the National Industrial Recovery Act, were abject failures. Hoover despised them all. He was further outraged by FDR's funneling of relief funds to strategic Democratic districts, a vote-buying scheme that smacked of Tammany Hall. (Al Smith would join Hoover in denouncing Roosevelt for playing Santa Claus with public money.) The rhetoric used by the administration to justify the New Deal also infuriated Hoover. It was socially divisive and unapologetically antibusiness. Republicans and the captains of industry were rechristened "social Neanderthals" and "corporals of disaster." Their "murderous doctrine of savage and wolfish competition" was cited as the cause of the Depression.[24]

On top of all this stood the single issue that drove the sharpest divide between the two administrations and confirmed Hoover's opinion of Roosevelt as a dangerous radical: the gold standard. Hoover was not obstinate about gold. He understood that much of the Depression's pain was caused by a monstrous global deflation transmitted from nation to nation by means of the gold standard. Elements of the Reconstruction Finance Corporation, together with his tinkering with the Federal Reserve System, were intended to loosen gold's shackles and expand the U.S. monetary base. He had talked with Stimson and French prime minister Pierre Laval about the possibilities of bimetallism, using silver to supplement gold in order to relieve debts, raise prices, and restore economic confidence. His consideration of the Trading with the Enemy Act also envisaged a disruption of the usual workings of the gold standard. He nonetheless believed that there was no workable long-term alternative to gold as a basis for international exchange.[25]

Roosevelt, during the campaign, and again after his inauguration, had claimed to be "absolutely" committed to gold. Hoover, unconvinced of FDR's sincerity, felt vindicated when the new president crowned the Hundred Days by announcing that the United States would adopt a managed currency, its value untethered to gold or any fixed international rate of exchange.[26]

Roosevelt, on this tack, was operating on political instinct more than on sound monetary knowledge or theory. At the time, elite world opinion was solidly behind coordinated action to stabilize the global monetary environment, avoid inflation, and return to the gold standard. Some of Roosevelt's own advisers considered his departures from consensus economics as "harebrained and irresponsible." Regardless, the new president, eager to win the political loyalty of the heavily indebted farm belt, bet that suspending gold and inflating the currency would ease the farmer's debt burdens, raise commodity prices, and help put the country back on track. The bet paid. The move to a managed and, ultimately, a significantly devalued currency eased debt burdens and allowed an expansion of the monetary base, a crucial step toward recovery.[*27]

---

* After months of personally managing monetary policy and dictating the price of gold, Roosevelt in early 1934 repegged the currency at $35 per ounce of gold, representing a devaluation of 40 percent from the previous level of just under $20.67.

Hoover had two principal objections to inflation. First, it benefited speculators, bankers, foreigners, landholders, and stockholders, while degrading the incomes of workers on fixed wages and salaries, as well as the investments of prudent Americans who had carefully saved and purchased insurance policies and avoided debt. Second, and more importantly, Hoover believed that America's place in the world demanded its participation in efforts to reestablish global exchange rates and achieve a coordinated international reflation. "Ever since the storm began in Europe," he said, "the United States has held staunchly to the gold standard. . . . We have thereby maintained one Gibraltar of stability in the world and contributed to check the movement of chaos." Unilateral U.S. inflation would render these objectives, and American leadership, impossible.[28]

This was an important point. Roosevelt's refusal to collaborate with Hoover on the debt issue, along with his pursuit of a nationalist economic policy, had led Nazis, fascists, and other militarists to infer that they had nothing to gain or fear from America. Japan promptly dropped out of the League of Nations and continued its assault on China. After the torching of the German Reichstag, Adolf Hitler assumed absolute powers in Berlin and began his attacks on academics, clerics, labor unions, and Jews. Roosevelt's declaration of July 3, 1933, that the United States would not return to gold in the foreseeable future, nor participate in any joint effort to stabilize exchange rates, further confirmed that the nation had turned its back on the world. It may be that there was no deal to be had on international cooperation by the time Roosevelt made his fatal decision. Hoover held that one was possible, and he had been a party to several going back to the Dawes plan. He certainly believed that the United States owed it to the world to try again.[29]

One of the ironies of Roosevelt's decision to devalue the dollar is that it compounded the negative impact of the high tariffs he had so effectively denounced during the campaign. Devaluation, more than Smoot-Hawley, made European goods less competitive, exports to the United States less attractive, and loans from the United States more burdensome. For Germany, heavily indebted to Wall Street, the pain was acute. Nevertheless, the new president maintained high tariffs through his first term, making no serious effort to reduce them until the opening of the 1936 campaign.

. . .

Thoughts on Roosevelt's performance and the state of the world rattled in Hoover's head as he steered a long, tall Buick down thousands
of miles of new California highway built during his time in Washington. He tried to make sense of the New Deal. There were parts of it
for which he wanted credit, and parts he abhorred. At times the whole
program seemed preposterous: the New Deal was an empty phrase
sanctifying "a muddle of uncoordinated and reckless adventures in
government." He would never be entirely sure that it deserved to
be taken seriously. But as his thoughts distilled with each tank of gas
burned, ominous elements of the program absorbed his attention,
and he eventually arrived at a new and life-altering perspective on
Roosevelt's advance.[30]

David Lawrence's original assessment that Hoover would be "as
radical as the times demand" had held true at least until the last year of
his presidency. He had adhered to an expansive vision of what government could do. While he had not moved as fast as other progressives
wanted, he had moved steadily. Roosevelt brought him face-to-face
with the limits of his radicalism.[31]

In Hoover's judgment, the New Deal's scale, reach, and coercive
nature were so far beyond anything America had known as to represent a new and dangerous doctrine in national political life. Roosevelt
was clearly bent on a massive expansion of the federal bureaucracy,
having launched forty new agencies in his first year. There was a pattern in his initiatives of requiring Congress to delegate authority to
the executive branch, resulting in a vast expansion of presidential
powers that Roosevelt was not shy about wielding with partisan purpose. Government, in this new world, was no longer an umpire in
the marketplace: it was directing and dictating wages and prices, and
competing against private enterprise. This, thought Hoover, was not
"change that comes from the normal development of national life."
This was an attempt to "alter the whole foundation of our national
life." It was "a radical departure from the foundations of 150 years
which have made this the greatest nation in the world."[32]

His hatred of the new president and his sensitivity to the administration's withdrawal from the world convinced Hoover that Roosevelt was launching a mass nationalistic movement "dipped from the

cauldrons" of Russian Communism, German National Socialism, and Italian fascism. As he later wrote:

> All those movements sprang from the soil of postwar misery, the strivings for power, greed for the possessions of others, boredom with the routines of life, yearnings for adventure, or just frustration. These mass movements had many common characteristics. They exaggerated the miseries of the times. They condemned the existing economic and social systems as bankrupt. They cried, "Emergency! Emergency!" They promised Utopia. They envisaged a national devil. They stifled criticism with smearing and misrepresentation through the powerful agencies of government propaganda. They subjugated the legislative and judicial arms and purged their own party oppositions. They spent public moneys in subsidies to pressure groups. They distributed patronage to their adherents. They sought ceaselessly for more power.[33]

Hoover saw Roosevelt's popularity as proof that he was corrupting the American people. They had been hypnotized into believing a new millennium had dawned. They were being made dependent on government by Roosevelt's "habit of carefree scattering of public money." While many Americans would have quarreled with Hoover's suggestion that their economic miseries were being exaggerated, he continued to describe the Depression as a temporary setback and argued that the U.S. economy remained the strongest in the world. The rate of home ownership had never been higher, and there were 23 million cars on the road. He was correct, if somewhat beside the point.[34]

Here was Hoover's Rubicon. Exactly where he crossed it is unknown, whether in the morning coastal fogs of Pescadero or under the unforgiving sun of Modesto. Somewhere along the road, his experiences, the nation's postwar gyrations, the Depression, and Roosevelt's radical New Deal had brought him to believe that the United States now had more to fear than to gain from further expansion of the federal government.

. . .

He had been planning, since his election loss, to renew his literary production. His former researcher, French Strother, a journalist by training, had agreed to help him mount a multivolume defense of his administration, only to die of pneumonia ten days after the inauguration. Hoover now proceeded on his own.

Published in 1934, *The Challenge to Liberty* is an abstract critique of the New Deal that never mentions its programs or its leader. The book discusses American freedom in historical and international perspective. It describes the individual rights guaranteed Americans by the Constitution and reminds readers that the nation had been built upon a strong distrust of concentrated authority. The Founding Fathers had believed that the best guarantee of liberty and justice was in the constraint of power. They had put severe limits on the national government's capacity to intrude in everyday life and in the organization of the economy. Their foresight had left Americans with a legitimate claim to being the freest society on earth.[35]

*The Challenge to Liberty* sees threats to individual rights in heavy regulation and bureaucratic expansion. It perceives a forced regimentation in government efforts to plan industry and agriculture, to set wages and prices, to manipulate the currency, and to compete with private business. It charts a deterioration of public morals in the repudiation of debt through inflation, the creation of class division, and the exploitation of a temporary crisis to break with fundamental American values. Reviewing the checks and balances of power devised by the nation's founders, it abhors the denigration of Congress in favor of one-man rule.

In its conclusion, it steers America back to the foundation of the individual, responsible to himself and serving his neighbors, building local institutions and governments—what we would now describe as social capital—and turning to the national government only when all else fails. The book does not deal with Prohibition, an enormous federal intrusion that Hoover had supported, and it betrays a suspicion of "temporary" expansions of federal authority to fight emergencies that had been lacking during his own administration. It is nonetheless one of the more trenchant critiques of New Deal liberalism to emerge in Roosevelt's first term.

Hoover's closest friends wished that he would not publish the book, knowing that it would be received as the bitter musings of a defeated man rather than as a thoughtful treatise on big government. Rickard also sensed, accurately, an unspoken, "unrelenting animus" toward Roosevelt in its pages. Hoover would not be dissuaded. The book sold over 100,000 copies thanks to a friendly deal with the Book of the Month Club.[36]

"The gospel according to Palo Alto," as Hoover nicknamed *The Challenge to Liberty*, did little, if anything, to improve his public persona. Republicans were unresponsive. The *Washington Post* supposed the work might have enjoyed a better reception if written by a different author. The left was contemptuous. *The Challenge to Liberty*, wrote Harold Laski, the British Marxist, epitomized "the terrified anger of a high priest of the Ptolemaic astronomy watching the growth of the Copernican hypothesis."[37]


The author's hope that the book might influence the midterms of 1934 was dashed when Roosevelt and the Democrats increased their dominance over Congress. Hoover was dumbfounded: "Daily the world goes back toward the regimentation of the Middle Ages, whether it be Bolshevism, Hitlerism, Fascism, or the New Deal." He stepped up his opposition, visiting newspapermen and making speeches across the country, defending his record as president and intensifying his attacks on the New Deal. He had plenty of ammunition. Indeed, it accumulated as he traveled, for, as a practical matter, the Depression survived Roosevelt's remedies. In the summer of 1935, industrial production, wholesale prices, and the Dow Jones Industrial Average, while improved over Hoover's worst year, remained exceptionally weak by postwar standards. Unemployment ranged from 17 percent to 22 percent in the two years after the Hundred Days, hardly a recovery.[38]

Nevertheless, Roosevelt was spectacularly popular. He unleashed another barrage of legislation in 1935, known as the Second New Deal. The Social Security Act brought the United States up to date with other industrial countries through the introduction of old-age pensions and unemployment insurance. The Wagner Act guaranteed employees the right to collective bargaining through unions of their own choice. The Works Progress Administration put millions to work in low-wage jobs building public infrastructure including, famously, LaGuardia Airport in New York, the River Walk in San

Antonio, and Griffith Observatory in Los Angeles. Roosevelt's optimism and constructive works kept the spirits of the country high and foiled all opposition.

The nation's idolization of Roosevelt left Hoover aghast. He could not understand how people were missing what he saw, and he would not hear a word in favor of the president. When his old friend Mark Sullivan advised not speaking against the New Deal until FDR's popularity had abated, Hoover suspected Sullivan of sordid motives. He told Edgar Rickard that the journalist was being easy on the new administration to gain access to the New Dealers, maintain the relevance of his syndicated newspaper column, and protect his income.[39]

Sullivan, in fact, was trying to protect his friend. With his wide acquaintance in Republican circles, he understood that the party was eager to turn the page and forget about its Depression president. It wished Hoover would pipe down. Three credible journalists—Frank Kent, David Lawrence, and W. M. Kiplinger—transmitted similar messages to the Firm: Hoover, never a true member of the Republican guild, now represented its greatest disaster, and it was time he step aside for new leadership. Another argument against Hoover was that many congressional Republicans believed the party needed to adopt elements of Roosevelt's plan rather than to fight it. They thwarted his efforts to rally the party around a general statement of anti–New Deal principles.[40]

Hoover, aware of the hostility toward him, was "very much hurt," said Rickard. It troubled him that his fellow Republicans sat mute as Democrats belittled the accomplishments of his administration: "He cannot see why it is not generally publicized that he broke the Depression in June and July of 1932."[41]

With a courage bordering on delusional, Hoover ignored his advisers and set his sights on the Republican nomination in 1936. As usual, he would not overtly campaign for it. He told his friends that if they felt "sufficiently keen and confident, they should get out and 'spread the gospel,' and create a background in his favor, and only with a strongly manifest support could he be induced to accept any overtures." He meanwhile advertised his availability through innumerable speeches, copies of which were circulated to vast mailing lists. Grossly overestimating both the receptivity of his party to his message, and FDR's vulnerability, he thought he had a chance to win.[42]

In late February of the election year, Hoover, Larry Richey, Edgar Rickard, and others were guests of Lewis Strauss at the offices of Kuhn, Loeb and Company in New York. They shared their bad news: Hoover did not have a chance at the nomination. A poll of 1,600 Republicans in the bellwether state of Ohio showed a pathetic 4 percent support for him as leader. Moreover, money was scarce, and the practice of printing and distributing his speeches would have to stop. The consensus of the meeting was that Hoover should abandon his shadow campaign. Unconvinced, he fought on, dedicating every waking hour to his candidacy and running up "a terrific telephone bill," said Rickard, through the primaries season. He failed to gain traction.[43]

William Allen White joined the circle of friendly journalists wishing that Hoover would keep his head down. The man was hated, wrote White, who was personally upset by this "mob rage at an honest, earnest, courageous man. Yet it is here. It still hangs on. And everything he says, as well as everything his friends say, is discounted. It is unbelievable."[44]

Hoover finally folded his hand in the last days before the Republican convention. "It should be evident by this time that I am not a candidate," he said. "I have stated many times that I have no interest but to get these critical issues before the country." He was devastated. "Edgar," said Hoover to his friend Rickard, "I am out of public life."[45]

Of course, he was not really out. Hoover elbowed his way to a prime-time address before the convention in Cleveland on June 10, hoping for a last-minute miracle. Eight thousand people greeted him at the train station that afternoon, summoned by a truck circling the city with a megaphone. He arrived in his old blue serge uniform, looking cheerful and healthy, notwithstanding the pounds he had gained in the absence of Hooverball.

At 9 p.m., he walked through the throngs in the jam-packed auditorium and mounted a rostrum that rose like a pulpit in the middle of the convention floor. It was rigged with an unobtrusive metal stand on which he could place his speech and read its pages at eye level. This was one clue that Republicans were about to see a different Hoover.

Before he could utter a word, delegates from California broke into a wild demonstration, unfurling an enormous blue silk banner and parading it through the aisles. They pulled in delegations from seventeen other states behind them. Republicans stood on their chairs, waved their hats, and howled their approval. Hoover kept his poise. His eyes looked out over the throng, not down at his feet. He smiled and occasionally motioned for calm as the procession marched on. It was fifteen minutes before he could speak.[46]

When, finally, the delegates were quelled, he launched into the most bracing attack on Roosevelt's policy yet heard from a senior Republican. He first described what he called his "charitable" view of the New Deal: "that it has no philosophy, that it is sheer opportunism, that it is a muddle of a spoils system, of emotional economics, of reckless adventure, of unctuous claims to a monopoly of human sympathy, of greed for power, of a desire for popular acclaim and an aspiration to make the front pages of the newspapers." If the New Deal was indeed quackery, he said, it would lead to chaos. What worried him, however, was that it had a true purpose, that it represented "a cold-blooded attempt to Europeanize the country."[47]

Hoover did not have to explain, with Mussolini and Hitler triumphant in Italy and Germany, and with fascists warring against republicans in Spain, that "Europeanizing" America meant the extermination of liberal democracy. He identified class hatred, centralization, utopian planning, collectivism, regimentation, unsound money, spoilsmanship, and a monarchical presidency as harbingers of despotism, and he traced their presence in New Deal thought and action. He railed at Roosevelt for spending $15 billion more than his own administration had spent, and he condemned Congress for abandoning its responsibility to control the public purse. He protested a reckless orgy of experimentation that had put "a few hundred thousand earnest party workers" on the federal payroll but returned unemployment to the same level it had notched on election day in 1932.[48]

His delivery, by Hoover standards, was superb. The stand for his notes kept his chin from his chest. It gave him the impression of being aware of his audience, although he was obviously reading his text. His tone, formal and crisp, was mildly modulated. He was repeatedly interrupted by vigorous applause. The *New York Times*, perhaps reflecting its low expectations, said he performed with "the aplomb of a man who is not naturally an actor but who, with the determination of Demosthenes, has mastered the platform technique."[49]

In closing, Hoover demanded that the party fight the "poisoning of Americanism" and stop cowering in the face of the New Deal:

> Republicans and fellow Americans! This is your call. Stop the retreat. In the chaos of doubt, confusion, and fear, yours is the task to command. Stop the retreat, and turning the eyes of your fellow Americans to the sunlight of freedom, lead the attack to retake, recapture, and re-man the citadels of liberty. Thus can America be preserved. Thus can the peace, plenty and security be re-established and expanded. Thus can the opportunity, the inheritance, and the spiritual future of your children be guaranteed. And thus you will win the gratitude of posterity, and the blessing of Almighty God.[50]

The Republican throng exploded again, chanting "We want Hoover!" State delegations jumped up to resume their marches. The band played "The Battle Hymn of the Republic." The auditorium was a circus of color and motion. Everyone seemed to be singing or yelling. Women were seen weeping. The shrieking and cheering continued for a half hour after the convention chair announced that Hoover had left the building to catch his train.[51]

After his speech, there was the briefest discussion among California delegates that their man might have a chance at renomination. Cooler heads prevailed. The ecstatic reception had been more a tribute to the ex-president than a wish to see him returned to office. Alfred M. Landon of Kansas, one of only two Republican governors to be reelected in 1934, took the convention. Roosevelt, who had money on Hoover, thought the Republicans had made a mistake.[52]

Hoover, according to Rickard, returned to New York in "great good humor," buoyed by his reception and eager to take to the hustings and resume on Landon's behalf his attacks on Roosevelt. His high did not last, as Landon, who found much to admire in the New Deal, refused the proffered assistance. Hoover was permitted to make just two speeches in the campaign.[53]

Roosevelt's reelection was never at serious risk. The economy had improved steadily in the second half of his term, due largely to an expansion of the monetary base fueled by the flight of gold to the United States from an increasingly dangerous Europe. The New Deal, so far as most Americans were concerned, had stabilized the economy and the financial system, brought a new sense of fairness to the workplace, made home ownership more achievable, and made old age and unemployment less unsettling. Millions of families had received employment or checks from Washington. The rapacious denizens of Wall Street had been put in their place.

Republicans could grumble all they wanted about how voters had been bought with their own money, how Roosevelt was paying the young, the elderly, and the farmer not to work and paying healthy young men to do make-work, and still producing double-digit unemployment figures—it did not matter. FDR was wildly popular. To the extent that he had opposition, it had been from the likes of Louisiana governor Huey Long and California gubernatorial candidate Upton Sinclair, who believed the New Deal not radical enough. Landon won only 8 of 531 electoral college votes, a worse showing than Hoover in 1932. Only Maine and Vermont stood between Roosevelt and unanimity.[54]

Hoover might at this point have kept his vow to Edgar Rickard to retire after the election. He had other work to do, having signed on as a director of New York Life Insurance Company and expanded his farms in the Imperial Valley. He was bombarding Rickard with investment instructions. He became honorary national chair of the Boys Clubs of America Inc., a cause dear to his heart due to his own struggles as a youth, and also because he believed boys required outlets for their energies denied them by the rampant urbanization of American life. He set a lofty fund-raising goal of $15 million, sufficient to build a hundred new clubs in fifty cities in three years, and easily surpassed it. He also remained active at Stanford and his War Library. All of this would have sufficed for many an American male of sixty-two years. Not Hoover, and definitely not Hoover after he had been so warmly received by his own party in Cleveland and after Landon had run such an abysmal campaign. It was plain to him that no other Republican had the stature, intellect, and vigor to lead a crusade against the New Deal. He was correct insofar as no one else was clamoring for the job. Rickard soon found him determined to regain leadership of the GOP, wiping the slate clean of "pinhead politicians" of the Landon ilk.[55]

# CHAPTER 26

# Father of the New Conservatism

If Hoover had needed any additional spur to resume his public life, Roosevelt provided it with his bold attempt to pack the Supreme Court in the first weeks of 1937. The court and the executive branch had been at loggerheads throughout Roosevelt's first term. Almost every major component of the New Deal had been threatened with judicial nullification. Important parts of the National Industrial Recovery Act and the Agricultural Adjustment Act had been eviscerated by the justices, while Social Security and other acts awaited their day in court, their prospects dim.[1]

Primary among the Supreme Court's concerns with Roosevelt's legislation were what it considered unwarranted intrusions of the federal government into state affairs, and an unlawful delegation of congressional powers to New Deal agencies under the administration's control. Roosevelt, enraged by unelected judges frustrating the will of the legislature, advanced a proposal that would have empowered him to appoint additional justices to the Supreme Court, to a maximum of six, for every member of the court over the age of seventy. At that moment, six of nine members were overripe by the proposed standard. Roosevelt's public rationale for the Judicial Procedures Reform Bill was that workloads were heavier than "aged or infirm" members of the court could manage. Over time, he came to rely on the more forthright argument that the court had mistaken itself for a legislature and that he was attempting to "restore" it to "its rightful and historic place in our system of Constitutional government."[2]

Hoover, on balance, took a conservative view of the court, as had been evident in his appointment of Charles Evans Hughes to serve as chief justice in 1930.* He had also anticipated Roosevelt's move against the judiciary, warning in his convention speech the previous summer that FDR, already possessed of enhanced executive powers and overwhelming majorities in both houses of Congress, might subvert the last major barrier to absolute control of the national government. In Hoover's opinion, the justices of the Supreme Court, ancient or not, were learned, duly appointed, and as constitutionally legitimate as the president himself. The proposed bill was an outrage. "The sword of the people," he thundered, was being reduced to "a tool of the executive."[3]

Disgusted once more at the feeble response of his fellow Republicans to Roosevelt's chicanery, Hoover assigned himself the role of Jeremiah. He crossed the country again making fiery speeches that were reprinted in hundreds of dailies: "If Mr. Roosevelt can change the Constitution to suit his purposes by adding to the members of the Court, any succeeding President can do it to suit his purposes. If a troop of 'President's judges' can be sent into the halls of justice to capture political power, then his successor with the same device can also send a troop of new 'President's judges' to capture some other power. That is not judicial process. That is force."[4]

Hoover was finally on to a popular issue. The mails to Congress ran eight to one against the court bill. Roosevelt, said Walter Lippmann, was "drunk with power." By May, the White House was trying to salvage its initiative with a compromise. It did not fly, leading to a bitter political defeat for the administration. Hoover claimed credit, although the justices themselves, and the Democrats in Congress who stood up to the president after four years of rubber-stamping his agenda, were the critical players.[5]

The repercussions of the court-packing escapade were several and profound. The political momentum Roosevelt had gained in the recent elections was wasted, and he slipped significantly in public

---

* Hoover, during his term, placed two other justices on the Supreme Court. Owen Roberts was appointed in 1930 after Hoover's initial nominee, John J. Parker, was rejected by a single vote in the Senate after protests from the NAACP and organized labor. The appointment of the liberal Benjamin Cordozo in 1932 was universally commended.

esteem. Progressive Republicans and conservative Democrats abandoned the New Deal coalition, hobbling progress on the president's domestic agenda. On the other hand, Roosevelt had housebroken the Supreme Court: it almost immediately reversed its opposition to New Deal labor legislation and never again posed a serious threat to the president's will.

The administration might have rebounded from the court setback had its burdens not been aggravated later in the year by yet another economic slump, known to posterity as the Roosevelt Recession. In a twelve-month period beginning in September 1937, industrial production and payrolls dropped by a third, national income by 13 percent, and profits by 78 percent. The Dow Jones Industrial Average gave up most of the gains it had made since the bank holiday of 1933. Despite Roosevelt's having put an additional 3.5 million people on the federal payroll, unemployment, never to decline beneath 11 percent on his watch, soared back up to 20 percent.[6]

Chief among the several causes of the Roosevelt Recession was the decision by Treasury Secretary Henry Morgenthau, who worried about inflation with foreign gold still pouring into America, to take a volume of gold out of circulation, tightening the money supply and discouraging bank lending. The rising costs of labor, a consequence of administration policy, and FDR's hostility to the financial sector also hurt the economy. Nor did it help that Roosevelt, believing a balanced budget essential to a healthy economy and worried that his temporary relief programs, if extended, would have the "narcotic" effect of a permanent dole, rushed to cut spending. Hoover had also moved to eliminate his deficits, although he had been fighting a run on gold while Roosevelt enjoyed an abundance of it.[7]

America was perplexed to find itself back on the breadlines after Roosevelt's volleys of legislation and new spending. The New Deal was exposed as having prioritized the president's political agenda over the nation's economic recovery. "Incredible as it sounds," wrote Walter Lippmann, "the New Deal does not have any program, good, bad, or indifferent, which even pretends to have any relation to the economic crisis." Hoover's new line was that the planned economy had resulted in "two families in every garage."[8]

Americans were also disturbed by a new wave of labor unrest. Workers introduced the novel tactic of the sit-down strike at a General Motors factory in Flint, Michigan, in February 1937. They occupied the premises and barred the doors, demanding higher wages and shorter work weeks, and crashed GM's production from a rate of 12,500 cars a week to as few as twenty-five. Management and the State of Michigan had no answers. After forty-four days, the strikers won recognition for the United Auto Workers as representative of employees in GM factories, a great victory for industrial unionism in America.[9]

The sit-down strike and the new labor militancy quickly spread to factories and steelyards across the country, sometimes with savage results. On Memorial Day, a crowd of UAW pickets and their sympathizers squared off against a police cordon along a hundred-yard line at the gates of Republic Steel Corporation's South Chicago Mill. The melee left ten dead, and thirty others seriously wounded. Similar tensions led to the imposition of martial law in Pennsylvania and Ohio.[10]

Roosevelt, having traded toleration of sit-down strikes for organized labor's support, did his best to stay above the fray. To many who recalled his anti-business rhetoric, he appeared indulgent of the new militancy. The public increasingly took the side of order, and the gulf between Roosevelt and conservative members of Congress widened.[11]

The president's troubles were good for Hoover's bookings. The public appetite for screeds against the New Deal was sharpening, especially in the business community, long intimidated by Roosevelt's popularity and apparent moral authority, and slow to raise its voice against him. It was angry and loud by December 16, 1937, when Hoover appeared before the elite of midwestern commerce at the Economic Club of Chicago.

His speech was written as they all were now: lead pencil on paper, sitting at a desk with his feet clenched around his chair, his free hand twirling his forelock. It gave his audience what it wanted in the way of condemnations of government meddling, wasteful spending, inflation, regimentation, democratic decay, and other New Deal scourges. He was just short of gleeful in his descriptions of the court-packing debacle, the depths of the Roosevelt Recession, and the failure of the

New Deal to build a New Jerusalem. It was nevertheless a different style of address than Hoover had become accustomed to deliver.[12]

Over the previous three months, he had been attempting to move beyond abstract essays on liberty and takedowns of New Deal initiatives toward a positive statement of an alternative approach to governance. The Chicago crowd was treated to the fruits of this labor. His speech, prosaically entitled "Economic Security and the Present Situation," asserted that the primary objective of any economic system should be "to eliminate poverty and the fear of it." Government must also address business abuses, remedy social ills, look after the homeless and the aged. It should strive for an equitable distribution of wealth and require "the economically successful [to] carry the burdens of social improvement for the less fortunate by taxes or otherwise." These objectives were not markedly different from those articulated by Hoover while in Commerce and the White House. Nor were they incompatible with the New Deal. Hoover and Roosevelt were both attempting to enhance the economic security of the American people. It was the means to this end that fundamentally distinguished Hoover's option.[13]

Hoover doubted that "transient political officials" could plan and secure the economic prosperity of a nation of 120 million. The only real security available to Americans, he said, was through job creation, wage growth, and rising standards of living, and those were generated not by government but by individual initiative and private enterprise:

> We cannot increase standards of living by restricting production. We cannot spend ourselves into prosperity. We cannot hate ourselves into it either. We cannot constantly increase costs of production without increasing prices and therefore decreasing consumption and employment. We cannot place punitive taxes on industry without stifling new enterprise and jobs.[14]

Despite eight years of depression, Hoover had not given up on the ability of his countrymen to govern themselves. Whereas Roosevelt believed that the nation's entrepreneurial fires were dying and that the age of American growth was over, Hoover held that free men could repair their losses, repay their debts, bury their mistakes, and resume the march of progress. The "competence, the self-discipline, and the moral stamina" of the American people, he insisted, were undamaged:

> What they want of government is to keep the channels of opportunity open and equal, not to block them and then send them a tax bill for doing it. They want rewards to the winners in the race. . . . To red-blooded men and women there is a joy of work and there is joy in the battle of competition. There is the daily joy of doing something worth while, of proving one's own worth, of telling every evil person where he can go. There is the joy of championing justice to the weak and downtrodden. These are the battles which create the national fiber of self-reliance and self-respect. That is what made America.[15]

Hoover disliked political labels. Terms like *liberal, conservative, radical, Tory,* and *reactionary,* he said, were mostly used by one group to disparage another.* In the past, when pressed, he had described himself as a liberal, in the classical sense of someone who "seeks all legitimate freedom first, in the confident belief that without such freedom the pursuit of other blessings is in vain." Over time, however, *liberal* had been distorted in common parlance to describe people favoring the use of government to achieve social and economic outcomes. The New Dealers were liberals; he needed something else. "If the connotation of 'liberalism' is to continue to be coercion," he decided, "then that alternative party may be dubbed 'conservative' without disturbing my sleep."[16]

So it came to be that the man who had arrived in Washington two decades earlier as a darling of the progressives was now, after an ardu-

---

* He did not like to use labels, but he understood them: "Taking a compound of definitions coming out of Washington, the impression would be that the Tories do the money changing. The Reactionaries are members of well-warmed and well-stocked clubs. The Conservatives are greedily trying to keep their jobs and their savings. The Liberals have the exclusive right to define the opinions of others. The Radicals do not know what to do but do it in every direction."

ous slog to power, a turbulent presidency, and five years of the New Deal, self-identifying as a conservative. On this icy winter evening in Chicago he laid down the core values of his new creed. Economic security on Roosevelt's terms, he said, was not worth having. Security was worthless unless joined to the higher good of American liberty, "the greatest possession any nation has ever had." He was again echoing Lincoln on the essential democratic character of the Union, on the principle that all men are created equal, and that the nation advanced by unleashing the talents and genius of free individuals:

> The main anchor of our civilization must be intellectual and spiritual liberty. Ideals, invention, initiative, enterprise, and leadership spring best from free men and women. The only economic system which will not limit or destroy these forces of progress is private enterprise.[17]

Rickard, listening on the radio, thought Hoover's delivery poor and believed that he must have lost his place at certain points. Press reports were kinder, saying only that he was frequently applauded and that he had received loud cheers.[18]

As it happened, the very day that Hoover made his address, a bipartisan group of conservative senators, including Hoover's associate Arthur Vandenberg of Michigan and North Carolina Democrat Josiah Bailey, a dissenter from the New Deal, published their own manifesto in the *New York Times*. Citing the need for quick action to reverse the Roosevelt Recession, the senators presented a ten-point program entirely consistent with Hoover's new creed. It sought, among other measures, to encourage private investment, lower capital gains taxes, reduce friction between capital and labor, maintain states' rights, end government competition in the economy, and above all to preserve and rely upon "the American system of private enterprise and initiative." These, said the senators, were the constituent elements of the "American form of government," which was "far superior to and infinitely to be preferred to any other so far devised. They carry the priceless content of liberty and the dignity of man."[19]

The emergence of the manifesto on the day of Hoover's speech may have been a coincidence, but their similarities were not. Hoover had been a leading critic of the New Deal since 1934, and much of the substance of his creed had already been published piecemeal in magazines and newspapers over the autumn. Senator Vandenberg, moreover, had been one of Hoover's partners in a high-profile and ultimately abortive campaign to unite Republicans around a general statement of anti–New Deal principles. The ex-president's influence on the manifesto is obvious, right down to the assertion that "the heart of the American people is sound."[20]

Conservatism was by no means new to America in 1937. It had a long and manifold history dating at least to Alexander Hamilton and the Federalists. Its character had been mostly oppositional: conservative Whigs had fought to protect a burgeoning industrial economy from the agrarian-populist ravages of Jacksonian democracy; conservative Democrats had beaten back radical Republicans seeking to punish Confederates and protect freedmen during Reconstruction. In Hoover's lifetime, the likes of Grover Cleveland, William McKinley, William Howard Taft, Harding, and Coolidge, although differing markedly on such issues as industrial trusts and the tariff, had consistently upheld an orthodoxy of small government, low taxes, and the rule of law, the essence of conservatism through most of Hoover's lifetime.

Modern American conservatism, conceived as an antidote to the New Deal, was born on December 16, 1937, with Hoover as its prophet and philosopher, and the signatories to the Senate manifesto, whose spirit would dominate Congress until the Kennedy era, as its first generals.

Leaving his divided party to mull his words and its future direction, Hoover and a small entourage boarded the ocean liner *Washington* on February 9, 1938, for his first visit to Europe in nineteen years. He had been planning a return to Belgium, and the sites of his relief and reconstruction triumphs, since 1935. He was curious about the state of the Continent and eager to remind Americans of the prestige he had once held on the international stage. Various roadblocks, including a reported reluctance by Brussels to grant a hero's welcome to one of Roosevelt's chief critics, had delayed what he called his "sentimental journey."[21]

The Belgians were not wrong to be cautious about their invitation.

Another motive behind Hoover's trip was a desire to open a foreign-policy front in his ongoing war against Roosevelt. When he arrived in Le Havre, Belgium embraced him regardless. He was paraded from town to town, meeting old colleagues and soaking up the gratitude of the beneficiaries of his humanitarianism through dozens of receptions, speeches, toasts, and dinners. He visited the universities that had been revitalized by the $25 million surplus of the Committee for the Relief of Belgium. He left flowers on the tombs of his old friends, King Albert and Queen Astrid.[22]

After eight days of round-the-clock adulation, loaded down with scrolls and medals, Hoover moved on to France, Switzerland, Austria, and ten other stops in what became a fourteen-nation grand tour. All along the way he received the friendly press coverage he had anticipated, including a multipage spread in *Life* magazine that showed him standing awkwardly and somewhat endearingly in a tall ceremonial hat as he received a PhD in Helsinki.[23]

The more substantial benefit of the journey was the access he gained to heads of state, senior officials, and eminent personages in and out of the governments of every country he visited, including Nazi Germany. He traveled to Berlin by automobile purposely to experience at first hand the Third Reich's celebrated housing projects and autobahns. He was astounded, as were so many others, by how quickly Germany had rebounded from the depths of depression in 1933 when, said Hoover, it was as near "to a complete state of chaos as any modern nation has ever reached."[24]

Before noon on his first morning in the capital, Hoover presented himself, along with Hugh Wilson, American ambassador to Germany, at the Reich Chancellery. He was escorted through a large door, over which the initials AH were carved on the marble transom. He came face to unmistakable face with the Führer and Reich Chancellor of the German people. Hoover took a seat in the middle of a large sofa behind a tall round coffee table, Hitler to his left in a matching upholstered chair. The Führer wore black slacks, a quasi-military doubled-breasted tan jacket, and a swastika band on his left arm. Their conversation, conducted through interpreters, centered on the German economy and agriculture. Hitler did most of the talking, punctuating his discourse with red-faced tirades about Jews and

Communists. Revolted by these displays of temper, Hoover never-theless admired the Führer's intelligence and his "ability for logical arrangement of facts." He decided that pundits who dismissed him as the puppet of a Nazi Party hierarchy had underestimated him.[25]

Their interview lasted just over an hour, after which Hoover trav-eled by motorcade thirty-five miles out of Berlin to Carinhall, the massive lakeside hunting lodge of Germany's number two, Minister President General Field Marshal Hermann Göring. Greetings were conferred at the entrance to the estate by sixteen huntsmen in medi-eval costume blowing the hunting song from Wagner's *Siegfried* on French horns. Göring shared none of the asceticism that Hoover had sniffed on Hitler. The Americans estimated Carinhall must have cost several million dollars to build. Its great room, two hundred feet long, was packed with a museum's worth of Old Masters, rare tapestries, and statuary, and on the table at which they lunched was a full-sized solid-gold bust of Göring's first wife on a revolving stand.[26]

Through such entertainments, as well as individual meetings with Germans of varying degrees of loyalty to the Reich, Hoover sharp-ened his views on the meaning and implications of Nazi rule. There was no question that Hitler had in a short time restored economic virility and political order to the nation, and dignity to its people. "I don't wonder," he said, "they idolize the man who brought it about." Yet this transformation had come at an awful price. Individualism and community were suppressed in the name of a "new Sparta." The uni-versities and the intellectual life of Germany had been crushed, along with any and all political dissent. Discipline and devotion to the state were enforced through intimidation and concentration camps, and there was a serious menace in the Reich's racial intolerance and fever-ish rearmament.[27]

As for Hitler's ideology, Hoover deemed it built on the rudi-ments of Italian fascism, fortified by German skill and thoroughness, and enveloped in an "atmosphere of mysticism," an ecstatic vision of Germany's collective destiny that spoke to "the tribal instincts" of its people. Hitler was "an extraordinarily emotional character" whose mind "gets to mysticism at a jump." His speeches were unremarkable to read, yet they had "a very persuasive effect on a crowd." Hoover listened to one on the radio and could feel its power, "even though I understood only about twenty per cent of what he said. And then the Germans are the only people in the world who can stand a three or four-hour speech and like it."[28]

Nazism, decided Hoover, was a phenomenon "of the most terrible order for the rest of the world." It represented, in economic and military terms, something "more focused and potent" than anything before it. Hitler would inevitably bust out of his Versailles cage and unite the German people in Austria, Czechoslovakia, Poland, and wherever else they might be. Hoover considered it a blessing that this appeared to be the extent of his territorial ambitions. He was convinced the Nazis were not a mortal threat to England, Belgium, or France. If the Nazis were to expand, they would seek agricultural land in the east, bringing them ultimately into the path of the Soviet Union. Hitler despised the Soviets and was obsessive about the threat of Communism. He had consolidated conservative power in Germany through an anti-Communist stance. It was far likelier that he would challenge the Soviets than the West, said Hoover, who, sharing the Führer's hatred of Communism, was sanguine about that prospect.[29]

Surprising as it may seem in retrospect, Hoover was correct, at this point in time, about the Führer's strategic direction, notwithstanding Germany's remilitarization of the Rhineland along its borders with France and Belgium, and its heavy contributions to the war in Spain. Hitler's attention was riveted on Czechoslovakia and the east, he had not articulated any designs on Western Europe, and neither he nor his generals had confidence, given their state of preparedness, that they could fight in both directions at once.[30]

After seven weeks of travel and a final stop in England, Hoover returned to America eager to inform his countrymen of Europe's "terrible and disheartening" condition, to warn them of what lay ahead, and to fire the first salvo in his new battle with Roosevelt.[31]

Nineteen years after Wilson's crusade to make the world safe for democracy, said Hoover, liberal institutions were in retreat across the Continent. The League of Nations was in a "coma," and the notion that peace could be imposed by collective action was, for the moment, "dead." More than a dozen European nations were in the iron grip of authoritarian dictatorships, some of them nationalist, some imperialist, some militarist, and all of them with a brutal disregard for life and justice. Political trials, concentration camps, the aerial bombing of civilian populations in Guernica, and the "heartbreaking persecution of helpless Jews," said Hoover, "are but the physical expressions of an underlying failure of morals terrible to contemplate." Civilization was once again on the brink of disaster. He did not believe another general war was "an immediate prospect"—military preparations were as yet incomplete—but it would not be long given the terrifying pace of rearmament.[32]

As disturbing to Hoover as the probable fate of the Continent was the casual assumption of so many Europeans he had met that the United States would be drawn into the coming conflict as a defender of democratic ideals. Roosevelt, they believed, had assured them of this eventuality.

Foreign policy had not been central to Roosevelt's first term. He had followed Hoover's Good Neighbor Policy in the Western Hemisphere and was thwarted in his efforts to bring the United States into the World Court (Hoover, with the Senate against him, had not tried). Roosevelt's boldest move had been to recognize the Soviet Union, largely to enhance American commercial prospects, and also in a bid to limit Japanese expansionism in Asia. Hoover had objected to this decision. America's policy of nonrecognition, he said, had been inaugurated by Wilson after the Soviet Union had refused to honor czarist Russia's debts to the United States and seized American property without compensation. What's more, a nation that had snuffed liberalism within its borders and ruled by terror did not belong among "respectable members of the family of nations."[33]

The Roosevelt administration had been at least as isolationist as the 1920s Republican regimes of which Hoover had been a part, until late in 1937 when the president had announced that it was time to "give thought to the rest of the world." He did not thoroughly explain his change of heart. He cited a deplorable "reign of terror and international lawlessness" that, while certainly exacerbated in 1935 by Mussolini's invasion of Ethiopia and by the outbreak of the Spanish Civil War in 1936, had been evident since his first inaugural. Unlike Hoover, who did not believe totalitarian governments posed a major security threat to the United States, Roosevelt was now seized with the menace of Germany, Japan, and the march of despotism:

Let no one imagine that America will escape, that America may expect mercy, that this Western Hemisphere will not be attacked and that it will continue tranquilly and peacefully to carry on the ethics and the arts of civilization. . . .

The storm will rage till every flower of culture is trampled and all human beings are leveled in a vast chaos.[34]

Roosevelt's answer to the new challenge was a proposal for peace-loving nations to "quarantine" the forces of international anarchy and barbarism. This required an ill-defined form of active engagement between the United States and European democracies for the purposes of upholding international "morality" and protecting the right of nations "to be free and live in peace." It was this indistinct project that had convinced so many Europeans that Roosevelt would come to the rescue of Continental democracies if they were threatened by fascism. They were less cognizant of FDR's promise to domestic voters that he would take every "practicable measure" to avoid a resort to arms.[35]

Unable to credit the president with a principled stand on the issues, Hoover decided that Roosevelt was duping the American people. He believed the president wanted a piece of Europe's action either to distract from his stalled domestic agenda or to generate the state of crisis that would perpetuate his administration and facilitate his state-building ambitions, or both. Terms such as "actively engage" and "quarantine," said Hoover, could only be read as promises of military or economic support to England and France, and this was the last message the United States should be sending. It implicated the United States in the security of Great Britain and its global empire. It committed America's might not only to France but to its ally, the Soviet Union. What good was a war for democracy, he asked, when "we would be supporting Stalin?"[36]

Worse, in Hoover's reading of the situation, was that Roosevelt's statements sent a provocative message to Europe that America would join Great Britain and France in league against Hitler. This was making Great Britain and France incautious, while drawing the Führer's attention from the east, raising, rather than reducing, the chances of continent-wide conflict.

Neither an isolationist or a pacifist, Hoover, having grappled for two decades with the horrid legacies of the last war, simply wanted no direct role in another. He knew it would be more encompassing, more expensive, and more technologically advanced; that it would spill more blood and destroy more homes, towns, cities, and nations; that it would be, in all likelihood, "the most barbarous war that we have ever known." The victors would suffer "almost equally" with the vanquished, the world would be changed beyond recognition, and the United States, if it participated, would change along with it. Another massive mobilization would leave America heavily indebted and with a permanently centralized, swollen, and increasingly authoritarian national government. "Those who would have us go to war to save liberty might give a little thought to the preponderant chance that we should come out of such a struggle with personal liberty restricted for generations," he said. "We should have none of it."[37]

Hoover believed the sane thing was to "harden our resolves [to] keep out of other people's wars" and resist the temptation to pose as a global guardian of liberal democracy. Wilson had tried and reaped a continent seething with dictatorship. "We cannot herd the world into the paths of righteousness with the dogs of war," said Hoover. "We cannot become the world's policeman unless we are prepared to sacrifice millions of American lives—and probably some day see all the world against us. In time they would envisage us as the world's greatest bully, not as the world's greatest idealist."[38]

If Hitler was determined to expand, Hoover continued, let him head east, not west. Let America protect the home front, which, contrary to Roosevelt, he believed was safe from serious military attack by Germany. Better for the United States to "keep the lamp of liberty alight" until such day as Europe realized its error, as he was sure it would: "The spirits of Luther, of Goethe, of Schiller, of Mazzini and Garibaldi, are not dead."[39]


Events marched on. Germany had annexed Austria by the time Hoover returned to America. Hitler next menaced Czechoslovakia until, in October 1939, British prime minister Neville Chamberlain and French prime minister Edouard Daladier permitted his occupation of the country's ethnic German Sudeten region in exchange for his pledge to cease his territorial demands. Five months later, Hitler helped himself to most of the rest of Czechoslovakia, snuffing out the last bastion of democracy in the neighborhood to his east. Fearing that Poland was next, Britain and France made a hasty guarantee of Polish independence. On the pretext that Britain, France, and Poland were trying to encircle Germany, Hitler renounced his nonaggression pact with the Poles in favor of a nonaggression pact with the Soviet Union. He and Stalin secretly divided Poland and other nations between them. German bombers flew over Warsaw on September 1, 1939, and the Second World War was under way.

Hoover and the American people watched with mounting horror this grim spectacle, which, unlike the abrupt start to the earlier war, seemed to move in slow motion. Even after Poland, there was no popular appetite in the United States for intervention. "If the world is to become a wilderness of waste, hatred, and bitterness," said Pennsylvania governor George Earle, a liberal Democrat, sounding a lot like Hoover, "let us all the more earnestly protect and preserve our own oasis of liberty."[40]

Between 1935 and 1939, Congress passed five pieces of neutrality legislation designed to insulate the nation from the storms in Europe. The acts forbade Roosevelt to sell arms and war materials to belligerent nations or to lend them money. U.S. ships were prohibited from carrying goods or passengers to warring nations. Peace marches and pacifist oratory were commonplace in Washington and around the country. Fear of contamination by the bacillus of war was so extreme that a mere 5 percent of Americans supported the relaxation of immigration quotas to accept European refugees.[41]

It stood to reason in 1939 that the popularity of peace would be of some political benefit to an arch-peacemaker like Hoover, or so he believed. He also noticed that neither of the leading candidates for the Republican nomination in 1940, Senator Robert Taft of Ohio and Senator Arthur Vandenberg of Michigan, had anything like his experience and knowledge of global affairs. Still more enticing, the Democrats seemed to be at the end of their rope. Roosevelt was likely to retire, as per tradition, after his second term, and he would leave a party divided by his meddling in Europe, by the court-packing episode, and by the New Deal. Although Democrats clung to both houses, Republicans had made gains in the 1938 election. The result, wrote Joseph Alsop, was a "repudiation of precisely the intellectual liberalism for which the New Dealers stand." The economy, while improving, remained weak by historical standards. This illusion of opportunity was encouraged by the fact that Hoover had been feted in Europe and heard on his return. Journalists were speaking of the "renaissance," the "comeback" of America's only living ex-president.[42]

Another hint that he had escaped the political desert came in the form of overtures from the White House. Through Norman Davis, chair of the American Red Cross, Roosevelt inquired as to Hoover's availability to coordinate relief for the millions of Europeans who had been displaced by the outbreak of war. Hoover was suspicious of this proposal. He had been hounded from office and pilloried by FDR. "Few administrations in American history," wrote *Newsweek*, "ever went to greater lengths to smear a predecessor than the present one, and the former president had every right to question the sincerity of a sudden peace gesture." He declined to pursue the opportunity.[43]

FDR next had his wife, Eleanor, call publicly for Hoover to head an agency that would manage relief work. He refused again, convinced that the Democrats were attempting to derail his unannounced campaign for the Republican nomination or to buy his silence on domestic and foreign policy. In fact, Roosevelt, to the extent that he was interested in Hoover, saw him as a pawn in a larger scheme to build an aura of bipartisan legitimacy around his administration in wartime.

Candidate Hoover continued with his noncampaign, working maniacally to keep himself visible while refusing to admit his intentions. He revived his arguments against the New Deal and wrapped himself in the mantle of traditional American foreign policy, defined as the avoidance of foreign entanglements, an emphasis on self-defense of the territorial United States, and the promotion of peace, liberty, and economic prosperity. He dared Roosevelt to come out with a "vigorous, definite statement" that the United States would not go to war with "anybody in Europe unless they attack the Western Hemisphere." He assailed the president's coalition cabinet, which placed Hoover's former secretary of state, Henry Stimson, in the War Department, as another attempt to stifle political opposition and establish one-man rule.[44]

The nomination proved as elusive to Hoover in 1940 as it had four years earlier. He was damaged beyond political repair by the failure of his presidency and the anti-Hoover mythology artfully perpetuated by Roosevelt. The best part of every FDR campaign speech in the thirties was his description of the state of America when he first took office, bequeathed a country "afflicted with hear-nothing, see-nothing, do-nothing government":

> The nation looked to government but the government looked away. Nine mocking years with the golden calf and three long years of the scourge! Nine crazy years at the ticker and three long years in the breadlines! Nine mad years of mirage and three long years of despair! And, my friends, powerful influences strive today to restore that kind of government with its doctrine that that government is best which is most indifferent to mankind.[45]

Roosevelt did not need to mention Hoover's name in these speeches. His listeners knew where the finger was pointed. This was one of FDR's more sublime political achievements: he had by now overseen six years of the Great Depression to Hoover's three. While the nadir of the downturn was in 1932–33, much of its trauma was inflicted by its duration, by the endless anxiety, the fruitless searches for work, the persistent hunger, the long erosion of confidence, and the gradual turn to disillusion, bitterness, and radical solutions. All of this made of the Great Depression a national trauma, opening the door to sweeping political reforms and searing its imagery into the American psyche.

The Depression had begun to take shape as a cultural phenomenon in the last months of Hoover's administration, with a *Fortune* magazine article lambasting his employment record and Bing Crosby's version of the jobless anthem "Brother, Can You Spare a Dime?" both landing in the midst of the 1932 campaign. Otherwise, the rich trove of critical and artistic expression inspired by the Depression accumulated in the Roosevelt years. Charlie Chaplin's *Modern Times* and Gregory La Cava's *My Man Godfrey* both date from 1936. The most searching books, *You Have Seen Their Faces*, by Erskine Caldwell and the photographer Margaret Bourke-White, and *Let Us Now Praise Famous Men*, a collaboration between James Agee and photographer

Walker Evans, were released in 1937 and 1941 respectively. Dorothea Lange's iconic *Migrant Mother*, a family portrait of Dust Bowl victims, was taken in 1936. Indeed, the black clouds of the Dust Bowl, fueled by drought and wind erosion, and used to magnificent metaphorical effect in Steinbeck's *The Grapes of Wrath* (1939), provide the most poignant imagery of the Depression. The Dust Bowl (a phenomenon distinct from the droughts of 1930–31) came in three waves between 1934 and 1940.[46]

Roosevelt not only shepherded the economy through six desperate years while attracting little of the blame, but his administration sponsored an enormous volume of artistic endeavor during the Depression, confident that it would hold to the narrative of Republican failure and sustain rather than undermine Roosevelt's authority. As his advisers anticipated, every new tent city that sprang up in the Roosevelt Recession of 1937–38 was called a Hooverville.[47]

William Allen White, who had bled for Hoover in 1936, bled for him once more in 1940. He esteemed the former president as an "honest, intelligent, and courageous" leader and believed that the nation could not afford to ignore the advice of so valuable a man, yet there was no doubt "Hoover is poison . . . he is a sort of political typhoid carrier."[48]

The Republican Party chose a dark horse as its nominee: Wendell Willkie was an inebriate, apostate Democrat and anti–New Dealer seeking to leap directly from the utilities industry to the White House. His timing was excellent. The Nazi boot crushed France on the second day of the Republican convention in Philadelphia. The eyes of the world immediately shifted across the channel for the much-anticipated Battle of Britain, which would run concurrently with the national campaign. Willkie was the leading Republican proponent of giving Churchill every support short of a military action, an increasingly popular position now that Great Britain, America's friend and erstwhile ally, had its back to the wall.

To the delight of Democratic organizers who could feel their prospects brighten every time the Republican Party acknowledged its last president, Hoover was permitted to speak to the convention in a prime-time spot in Philadelphia. The moment was broadcast nationally on radio as well as television for the first time.

It is sometimes said that a great leader can ask more of people, admit the hard truth of a situation and call on his followers to make the necessary sacrifices rather than settle for promises of easy solutions. Hoover tried a great leader speech in Philadelphia:

> The New Deal has contributed to sapping of our stamina and making us soft. . . . The road to regeneration is burdensome and hard. It is straight and simple. It is a road paved with work and with sacrifice and consecration to the indefinable spirit that is America.[49]

This message was consistent with Hoover's vision of America, and it contained some home truths. It was nothing, however, that Americans were prepared to take from a man they saw as the cause of their economic miseries. On the first ballot, a thousand votes were cast for ten candidates, with Hoover receiving seventeen and finishing ninth. Willkie was nominated on the sixth ballot, and he had no more use for Hoover than had Landon in 1936. The ex-president was permitted to make two speeches on behalf of the campaign, which would not pay to have them broadcast.

Roosevelt, at the last minute, decided that America needed his skills and experience for a third term and to meet the Nazi threat. He dumped his running mate, John Nance Garner, in favor of his agriculture secretary, Henry Wallace, and swept the country with 449 electoral college votes, leaving the Republicans and Willkie with 82, in double figures (or less) for the third consecutive election.[50]

The New Deal never did deliver full recovery, or resolve the interminable farm crisis, or produce a coherent social or economic philosophy to replace what had stood before it. At the same time, neither did it massively redistribute national income, or compete with business in a major way, or bring America to the doorstep of totalitarianism. Roosevelt, whatever his methods, did manage to shepherd the country through the greatest domestic crisis since the Civil War with its institutions intact, with domestic extremists at bay, without widespread social unrest, and with his own popularity largely undisturbed.

Hoover, for obvious reasons, would only see the New Deal's faults and never admit its accomplishments.[51]

His third mandate assured, Roosevelt adeptly led or, as Hoover would have said, backed the American people into war. He had already been operating secretly to assist China in fending off the Japanese, and he had begun a quiet correspondence with Churchill to discuss means of supporting Great Britain. He steadily pushed against neutrality laws and the U.S. arms embargo and overcame congressional reluctance to extend credit and deliver weapons to belligerents through his cash-and-carry policy. He convinced his countrymen that the United States should serve as "the arsenal of democracy." In practical terms, this meant adoption of the Lend-Lease program under which America sent food, oil, and weapons, including planes and warships, to Britain, France, and China in exchange for leases to strategic military bases around the globe. He denied, through it all, any intention of sending American soldiers to fight.[52]

Hoover continued to dog Roosevelt's every step through 1941, making principled arguments and thoughtful policy suggestions, and above all warning Americans that the president's maneuvering would trap them into war. The United States, he insisted, had nothing to fear from Hitler. If Germany had failed to negotiate the English Channel and invade the United Kingdom, there was no threat of it crossing the Atlantic.

Hoover was enraged when Roosevelt extended the Lend-Lease program to the Soviet Union—"one of the bloodiest tyrannies and terrors ever erected in history," "an enemy of human rights and human liberty," a "militant destroyer of the worship of God"—after it was invaded by Germany in June 1941. It left America in the position of underwriting the Red Army's charge westward into Europe on a front extending from Finland to Romania. The proper course of action for Roosevelt would have been to stand back and let "those two bastards [Hitler and Stalin] annihilate themselves." Western civilization, said Hoover, had instead "consecrated itself to making the world safe for Stalin."[53]

Close behind Soviet appeasement on Hoover's list of Roosevelt's diplomatic blunders was his inflammatory rhetoric and economic sanctions against Japan. He compared the administration's policy to poking a rattlesnake with a pin. "I am afraid," he wrote an associate on November 16, 1941, "that [FDR's officials] are so anxious to get into the war somewhere that they will project it. They know there will be less public resistance to this than to expeditionary forces to Europe." He was already on record expressing "a foreboding that we have taken on a situation [in the Pacific] from which sooner or later we will see outrages upon American citizens and other incidents which will inflame the country and draw us into war in the east."[54]

He had the good sense to hold his tongue when Japan bombed Pearl Harbor on December 7, and Germany and Italy, allied with Tokyo, declared war on the United States. He immediately pledged his support to Roosevelt and recommended America "fight with everything we have."[55]


It was a long, dreary war for Hoover. His position that totalitarian governments did not threaten the security of the United States was untenable after Pearl Harbor. For his counsels of restraint, he was flayed by Democrats and even some Republicans as an isolationist and an appeaser. Especially in retrospect, it would appear that he had failed to recognize potentially devastating threats upon looking them in the eye. Roosevelt, whose motives, while mixed, were nobler than Hoover would admit, received credit for anticipating and preparing America for the inevitable conflagration. None of that is quite as simple as it appears.

Hoover did recognize Hitler as a madman and a menace to the peace. His hope, again, was that the West would avoid a direct conflict. Whether or not Hitler could have been placated (or depleted) by eastern expansion is one of history's unknowables. It seems unlikely that continental war could have been prevented given the legacies of the Great War, Hitler's mad ambitions, and the pace of rearmament among Europe's powers, but the fact is that Germany only reluctantly turned its attention to the west when it was clear that Great Britain and France, with presumed material support from the United States, were obstacles to its designs on Czechoslovakia and other eastern points. This occurred well after Hoover and Roosevelt had staked their positions, while the situation in Europe was still fluid. War was not preordained. Nor was direct American military involvement.[*] As always, war was a consequence of a series of choices made by leaders in evolving situations. More than one principled stand was available and alternative outcomes, of more or less desirability, were possible. None of which changes the position of Hoover in 1941: "We are the lepers," he told a friend as America mobilized. "At least our consciences are clear."[56]

He did his best to rekindle some of the humanitarian magic he had possessed in the previous conflict, but without a mandate from Roosevelt and with the belligerents reaching new heights of savagery he could not find a footing to deliver substantial food or aid to any part of Europe. He continued to speak and write with what one journalist called "his habitual air of grumpy wisdom." His anti-interventionist book entitled *America's First Crusade*, treating the failed aims of Wilson's war, had the misfortune to be released on the eve of Pearl Harbor. Its own publisher, Scribner's, did its best to ensure no one bought it.[57]

A 1942 volume, coauthored with Ambassador Hugh Gibson and entitled *The Problems of Lasting Peace*, examined the failures of peacemaking in 1919 and argued against putting the vanquished on a "treadmill of punishment." It outlined a constructive, staged approach to restoring order and resolving such issues as borders, debts, and reconstruction. The staging was crucial to wringing emotion from the process. The book would help to move Republicans to accept the necessity of a new League of Nations in the postwar world.[58]

In his expanding spare time, Hoover fished, smoked cigars by the drawerful, and invested in mining opportunities in Nevada and Utah. He traced in the press ideas he had floated in speeches that had been adopted by others without attribution. He grimly chronicled every perceived error in strategy and judgment made by the Roosevelt administration in the management of both the war and the American

---

[*] Winston Churchill believed war avoidable through a strategy diametrically opposed to Hoover's. "No event," Churchill would write, "could have been more likely to stave off, or even prevent, war than the arrival of the United States in the circle of European hates and fears." Winston S. Churchill, *The Second World War* (London: Bloomsbury Revelations, 2013), p. 110.

home front. "HH continues to be most despondent," wrote Rickard, who was trying to break his friend of his feeling "that all the world is working against him." Hoover also suffered "periods of acute depression over the affairs of government."[59]

He ruled himself out of contention well in advance of the 1944 election and made no attempt to organize, covertly or otherwise. The Republican nominee was New York governor Thomas Dewey, former star of the University of Michigan glee club, with slick dark hair and a push-broom mustache. Dewey had shot to prominence by hanging a thirty-year jail sentence on Mafia kingpin Charles "Lucky" Luciano. He would have the honor of becoming the fourth consecutive Republican to fail to win one hundred electoral college votes against FDR. Hoover did not participate in the race, submitting rather meekly to Dewey's request that he publicly disassociate himself from the Republican side.

"It having been plainly indicated that I was a liability," Hoover wrote his old friend Ruth Hanna McCormick Simms, "I naturally took to the mountains. I . . . have given great attention to the fish. Of course, every new candidate has to make his own campaign and the problems, of course, are new and the experience of other campaigns never seems very real." In other moments, he was less sanguine. "A man couldn't wear a mustache like that," he said of Dewey, "without having it affect his mind."[60]

He met his seventieth birthday in 1944 defeated in his efforts to rehabilitate himself, marginalized as a humanitarian, a politician, and a public servant. He met it as a man in exile, both from Washington, where 2300 S Street had been put up for sale, and from California, which he had officially abandoned for the Waldorf after the state's Republicans had failed to support his unofficial candidacy in 1940. He also met it alone.


The postpresidential years had been easier for Lou Hoover than for her husband. She continued her work with the Girl Scouts and indulged her love of music, organizing and underwriting classical concerts in Palo Alto. She founded an organization called the Friends of Music at Stanford in 1937, dedicated to the encouragement of performance and education. She supported Republican women's organizations and her husband's attempts at stewardship of the party without entirely appreciating how badly he wanted another shot at the White House.[61]

Her health, always robust, weakened in 1943. Limiting her activities on medical advice, she also spoke with her lawyer about preparing a will. She wrote her sons to tell them "you have been lucky boys to have had such a father, and I a lucky woman to have my life's trails alongside the paths of three such men and boys." She spent a last summer at her home at 623 Mirada in Palo Alto and picnicked at her favorite spot in Mount Tamalpais in Marin County. That autumn the Hoovers rented 623 Mirada to the university and for the first time since the earliest years of their marriage occupied just one residence, suite 31-A at the Waldorf in New York.[62]

At half past six on the evening of Friday, January 7, 1944, Lou attended an afternoon concert given by the harpist Mildred Dilling in New York. She returned to the apartment. Edgar Rickard and Hugh Gibson were there, waiting to take her husband to dinner. He was tuned in to Lowell Thomas's nightly broadcast on NBC. When he was finally ready to go, he went to say good night to Lou and found her unresponsive on her dressing room floor. Rickard called for the Waldorf doctor, who arrived at 7:05 p.m. A few minutes later, Hoover emerged from the bedroom to report to his friends that his wife of forty-four years "was gone," dead of a heart attack at age sixty-nine.[63]

An undertaker was contacted, and Lou's body was moved that evening across the street to St. Bartholomew's Episcopal Church. Flight arrangements were made for Herbert Jr. and Allan. Hoover, said Rickard, went to bed at 11 p.m., having kept his head all evening.

Fifteen hundred mourners, including two hundred Girl Scouts, attended a service at St. Bartholomew. Afterward, the three remaining Hoovers flew with the casket to Palo Alto, where Lou was buried. Her obituaries emphasized her role as a political wife and said relatively little of her independent interests and accomplishments.

Among Hoover's neighbors at the Waldorf was the Duke of Windsor, who had given up his throne in the United Kingdom to marry the American Wallis Simpson in 1936. After Lou's funeral, he invited Hoover to join him for a few days of recuperation in the Bahamas, where the duke served as governor. The two men were photographed together at Government House in Nassau, standing stiffly side by side under a hot sun in double-breasted suits.

In typical fashion, Hoover said almost nothing to anyone about his loss. Lou's papers, including two wills, were scattered across the country and required considerable effort to arrange. On February 7, Rickard and Hoover dissolved the Seeing Cairo Fund they had assembled from their windfalls thirty-five years earlier and sent $250 to the Hoover War Library as a memorial in Lou's name.[64]

# CHAPTER 27

# Reborn in a Darker World

The war had taken a physical toll on Franklin Roosevelt, so much so that in the early months of 1945 close observers were beginning to doubt his competence. Anthony Eden had found him "vague and loose and ineffective" with Churchill and Stalin at the Yalta conference in February where they discussed the governance of postwar Europe. Eden did not know that FDR had been diagnosed with heart disease almost a year earlier. No one did. At the end of March, with the fall of Nazi Germany in sight, the president traveled, ashen and weak, to what had become known as the Little White House in Warm Springs, Georgia, for a vacation. Just after noon on April 12, while signing letters and having his portrait painted in the living room of his cottage, he felt a sharp pain, grabbed his head, and lost consciousness. Within three hours, he was dead.

Herbert Hoover had just finished saying to the journalist Felix Morley that he hoped Roosevelt would "live long enough to reap where he had sown" when the announcement of his death came over the radio.[1]

"The nation sorrows at the passing of its President," wrote Hoover for public release. "Whatever differences there may have been, they end in regrets of death. It is fortunate that in this great crisis of war our Armies and Navies are under such magnificent leadership that we shall not hesitate. . . . While we mourn Mr. Roosevelt's death, we shall march forward."[2]

Having served for twelve years as the president's all-purpose scapegoat, Hoover was not long in mourning. Rather, he seized on the opportunity of a changing guard. Former Missouri senator Harry S. Truman, the third vice president of the Roosevelt era, had taken the presidential oath of office in the White House Cabinet Room four hours after FDR's demise.

Hoover thought he might hear from Truman immediately, for two reasons. Although he had no relationship with the new president, the Dumbarton Oaks Conference of the previous autumn had established a framework for the creation of the United Nations, and a follow-up meeting with delegates from fifty allied countries was set to convene in San Francisco late in April. Hoover had lately been free and public with his advice on international institutions. It seemed reasonable to expect an invitation to San Francisco.

There were also rumors in Washington, false as it turned out, that Truman would remake FDR's cabinet. Hoover told Edgar Rickard that he would like to serve as secretary of war, a post that would give him command of shipping and permit him to relieve Europe when the shooting stopped and the continent confronted its ruin. "Now that there has been a change in Washington," he wrote his sister, "I may be on the move often."[3]

As it happened, Edward Stettinius Jr., secretary of state, sent Hoover an invitation to the opening of the meeting at the San Francisco Opera House on April 25, and Hoover blew it off. He had assumed his invitation would come directly from the White House. Bruised and paranoid from the drubbing he had suffered throughout the Roosevelt era, he took Stettinius's invitation as either a bureaucratic mistake or some sort of setup. Another approach came at the end of the month from his old colleague Henry Stimson, now secretary of war. He asked Hoover to visit him at home in Long Island, and Hoover again declined, supposing that the secretary was operating without presidential approval. Stimson, undeterred, waited a few days and suggested Hoover join him in Washington to discuss postwar Europe. He made it known that Truman had approved his overture.

This, thought Hoover, was better. He was now confident that he had the administration's attention. An old hand at leveraging attention into opportunity, he promptly refused Stimson again, standing on ceremony: as an ex-president, he could not travel to Washington for anything less than a meeting with the president, at the express invitation of the president. He did not want to appear "a seeker of interviews."[4]

Banking on the familiarity of their years together, and unaware that Hoover wanted his job, Stimson begged his former boss to show some flexibility. Hoover, prepared for this line of reasoning, reminded Stimson of the abuses he had endured at the hands of the New Dealers, how Roosevelt's press secretary, Steve Early, had said that if Hoover wanted anything "he would have to come down on his knees to get it." Early was now in Truman's press office, proof to Hoover that "the old vindictiveness" was still alive in the Democratic Party. If he was being inflexible, he told Stimson, it was for his own protection. If Truman "did not think it worth while to pay this small courtesy to me for the benefit of my advice," he said, he had "better not continue to attempt to get it." Stimson and others tried to change Hoover's mind, to no avail.[5]

As this drama played out, curtains were falling on the European war. With the Allies in possession of Rome and headed north, Benito Mussolini bolted for the Swiss border only to be intercepted by communist partisans. They executed him with a submachine gun on April 28 and dumped his corpse in Milan's Piazzale Loreto, where it was defiled by a mob and left swinging upside down from the canopy of an Esso station. Two days later, with Soviet troops fighting street by street to the center of Berlin, Hitler blew his brains out in his bunker fifty-five feet below street level. Germany surrendered unconditionally on May 8.

The next day, Hoover appeared at Carnegie Hall at the behest of the Save the Children Federation to kick off a series of speeches warning that none of the nations of Western Europe had enough food to hold them until harvest. It was "11:59 on the starvation clock" and Americans needed to move quickly to save the destitute. "This is a problem of the next ninety days," said Hoover, turning up the heat on Washington to take action. "It is urgent. It is urgent as a matter of humanity. It is urgent as a matter of preserving order. It is urgent in protection of our boys in Europe. It is a job so long delayed that only the American Army can solve it."[6]

Meeting in Long Island, Stimson again pleaded with Hoover to call Truman. He promised that the president agreed with him on the destitution of Europe, on the inability of the United Nations Relief and Rehabilitation Agency to manage food relief, and the need to involve the army, not least of all because the United States was still at war in the Pacific. Stimson spoke so persuasively of Truman's sincerity and positive qualities that Hoover came away believing he might be preferable to Dewey as president. Nevertheless, he dug in his heels and refused to call the White House.

Increasingly anxious to either bring Hoover on board or put a cork in him, Stimson next sent a high-ranking delegation from the War Department to New York on May 23. The delegation seemed intent on convincing Hoover that the army was powerless to act with UNRRA already in the field. Hoover lectured his visitors on the need for an army-staffed relief effort under a single mind given dictatorial powers over economies of the liberated countries throughout Europe. Failure to adopt his plan would mean "the liberated countries are likely to go communist." While his conclusions were arguable, no one alive had more credibility on the subject of mass food relief than Hoover, and he showed no signs of holding his tongue.[7]

Two days later, Truman surrendered. "If you should be in Washington," he wrote to Hoover, "I would be most happy to talk over the European food situation with you. Also, it would be a pleasure to me to become acquainted with you."[8]

Hoover, his long ostracism at an end, was jubilant. He gladly accepted the invitation and made his preparations to rejoin the official life of the country. FDR partisans in Washington were stung. Hoover, complained Steve Early, did not deserve the attention. In twelve years, he had never come to the White House "to pay his respects."[9]


Harry S. Truman was a pleasant, clean-shaven, weak-eyed man from Independence, Missouri. He had abandoned two attempts to expand his education beyond high school. He had performed better in the Great War, seeing action in France and establishing himself as a capable leader of men. Struggling to launch himself in a career after his discharge as a major in 1919, he tried haberdashery and was crushed by the depression of 1921. Turning to politics, he made a modest living as a local cog in the notorious Democratic machine run by Boss Tom Pendergast out of Kansas City. After more attractive candidates turned him down, Pendergast supported Truman for the U.S. Senate in 1934. On winning, Truman served ten unremarkable years before President Roosevelt tapped him in 1944 as replacement on the Democratic ticket for Henry Wallace, who had been deemed too liberal and labor friendly by the party brass. Truman had been vice president for eighty-two days when FDR died.[10]

He and Hoover both left records of their meeting. Hoover's was businesslike: he had arrived at 10:30 on May 28, 1945, and left fifty-five minutes later having discussed with the president elements of European food relief, some ideas on how to end the war in the Pacific, and how to deal with the Russians. Hoover advised treating the latter as "Asiatics," by which he meant dishonorable people unlikely to abide by their treaties or agreements. There was no sense in going to war with them. It could lead only to "the extinction of Western Civilization, or what was left of it." Privately, Hoover told friends that he had deliberately used words of a single syllable in speaking to the new president.[11]

Truman noted in his diary that he and Hoover had "a pleasant and constructive conversation on food and the general troubles of U.S. Presidents—two in particular." They discussed the "prima donnas" on their White House staffs "and wondered what makes 'em." Years later, Truman would recall that Hoover, eyes welling with tears, struggled to compose himself as they took their seats on his return to the Oval Office.[12]

It was left unsaid in both accounts that Hoover hinted he was available for assignment, and that Truman had long before agreed with Stimson that the visitor was only wanted for occasional advice. Both participants received something of what they wanted from the meeting. Truman was lauded in the press for a "fine nonpartisan gesture." Hoover told reporters that the president was doing an admirable job and taking "very wise steps." Rickard found his old friend upbeat on his return to New York. He soon received a letter from the White House: "I appreciate it very much your coming to see me," wrote Truman. "It gave me a lift."[13]

Hoover was disappointed, however, that the president had no intention of making use of him. He kept up his criticisms of the administration's relief management, among other elements of its foreign policy. He was vocal, for instance, after Truman dropped nuclear weapons on Hiroshima and Nagasaki in August 1945, instantly killing about 150,000 people and bringing the Pacific War to an end. Hoover had advised Truman to negotiate a Japanese withdrawal from China in return for Korea and Formosa (Taiwan), which he estimated would save a half million lives. He was unaware of the existence of the atomic bomb until it was deployed. Its use, "with its indiscriminate killing of women and children, revolts my soul," he said.[14]

> This is the most terrible and barbaric weapon that has ever come to the hand of man. Despite any sophistries, its major use is not to kill fighting men, but to kill women, children, and civilian men of whole cities as a pressure on governments. If it comes into general use, we may see all civilization destroyed.[15]

He made public pleas for the United States to keep the secrets of atomic weaponry to itself until proper methods could be devised for their control. He wanted the bomb eliminated from all arsenals, along with chemical and biological weapons, and he sought assurances that the United States would not use it as a threat in its diplomacy. He was incredulous at proposals in Washington to share the technology with the Soviets: "And now we propose to give her [Russia] military power over us? Why not give her half our fleet?" (He later softened his stance on use of the atomic bomb with the Soviets in mind: "We should be willing to agree that it will never be used except in defense of free men.")[16]

In the months that followed, Hoover also made an interesting set of observations on the corruption of language in the emerging postwar world, or what, in bitter moments, he called the world left by Franklin Roosevelt. He seized on the word *appeasement*, not least because it had been hurled at him as a rebuke after Pearl Harbor. "It is a term of vile reproach never to be used any more now that Hitler is buried," he said. Yet since then Roosevelt and Churchill had given Stalin "a 'sphere of influence' over 150,000,000 people in a dozen independent nations, all of which cynics might say was appeasement," not to mention a violation of the freedoms for which the United States supposedly went to war.[17]

It was a strange world, he continued, where Soviet expansionism could be called, in the Yalta definition, "establishing a broad democratic basis," and where a single-party government that used secret police to educate its citizenry qualified as a democracy. It was stranger still when a leader could be called a dictator—the fascist Perón of Argentina was one, the fascist Vargas of Brazil was not—depending on his usefulness to U.S. foreign policy.[18]

These complaints were appended to Hoover's larger catalog of the new liberalism's sins: empty sloganeering, duplicitous policies, arrogant economic planning, sprawling bureaucracies, the buying of people with their own money, the creation of dependencies on the state, intolerance of opposition, the rewriting of history, the use of whipping boys to evade accountability, the turning of citizens against one another by promotion of class division, and an overarching belief, evident in the court-packing episode, that "the objective," to use a favorite New Deal term, justified the means.[19]

These all became proofs in Hoover's larger argument about the increasingly manipulative, overbearing nature of government, and the resulting degradation of public morals and true liberty:

> There is no double standard of morals, one in public and one in private life. Self-government in people decays when moral standards in the people fail. Moral standards in the people are sullied when moral leadership in government fails. It is alone the spirit of morals that can reconcile order and freedom. A people corrupted by their government cannot remain a free people.[20]

He did not blame everything on Roosevelt. The cataloged evils had been exacerbated by war. The first result of total war, he wrote, "is the mass slaughter of truth." Propaganda is perfected to boost morale and cover blunders and failures. Vocabularies become confused, and familiar phrases are stuffed "with perversions of truth."

For instance, the West was claiming victory in a European war that had left "hundreds of millions of human beings [breathing] less independence, less liberty, less freedom from fear than before we started on this crusade." America was also celebrating victory in a Pacific war ended by the mass slaughter of women and children at Hiroshima and Nagasaki. "Even if we grant that it was necessary," he said, "it is not a matter to exult over."[21]

It had been fear of this sort of debauchery that had led Hoover, from 1939 to 1941, to warn Americans that their country might not emerge from another great war with its traditional values intact, that such a war might actually decrease the amount of freedom known to individuals and leave the United States on a permanent war footing. Mixed as his arguments were with his well-established animosity toward Roosevelt and the Democrats, Hoover was seldom taken seriously. To a country largely content with Roosevelt's leadership and the outcome of the war, he sounded shrill and resentful. He was nevertheless making important points, and he was not alone. Walter Lippmann kept his own inventory of Roosevelt's "concealed purposes," "lack of good faith," and "lawless legality." The *New York Times* bemoaned the late president's "political sharp practice" and "indirectness." Other Democrats had regretted his "lack of frankness," "intent to deceive," deviousness, camouflage, and hypocrisy.[22]

While these criticisms of Roosevelt were often just, the phenomena Hoover had identified were larger than the New Deal and, indeed, larger than America. His complaints were staples of postwar literature on both sides of the Atlantic, coloring the works of a wide variety of authors, including Norman Mailer, Joseph Heller, Ayn Rand, J. D. Salinger, Evelyn Waugh, William Golding, and Anthony Powell. Easily the best articulation of Hoover's core thesis came in George Orwell's 1949 dystopian masterpiece, *Nineteen Eighty-Four*, set in a militaristic totalitarian superstate that persecutes its own citizens for acts of individualism and tortures the language for reprehensible purposes. Orwell and Hoover had very different minds, yet they shared a capacity to look unforgivingly at the creep of illiberal and tyrannical practices into Western societies. Orwell described his novel as:

> a show-up of the perversions to which a centralized economy
> is liable and which have already been partly realized in Com-

munism and Fascism. I do not believe that the kind of society I describe necessarily will arrive, but I believe . . . that something resembling it could arrive. . . . The scene of the book is laid in Britain in order to emphasize that the English-speaking races are not innately better than anyone else and that totalitarianism, if not fought against, could triumph anywhere.[23]

Hoover could not have said it better; nor could he say it well enough for it to resonate with his countrymen. The world wars profoundly shifted the relationship of individuals to the state. Even if one accepts that a rebalancing was advisable, or necessary, there is no question that it came at the expense of individual liberties and other humane values, and that the permanent war footing has for many nations become a reality. In the United States, there was no drive for normalcy after the Second World War. It led directly to the Cold War. The nation would keep well over a million men in uniform and establish what Dwight Eisenhower would later call the military-industrial complex, as well as a permanent national security apparatus, while also massively expanding the scope and the budget of the Federal Bureau of Investigation. The American people would learn to live in an ominous new world, fearful of communist aggression, real and imagined, and under perpetual threat of nuclear annihilation. The old America, as Hoover had foreseen, was gone.

Another prediction that was borne out: the food situation in Europe deteriorated as Hoover had predicted, prompting Truman in March 1946 to invite his predecessor's predecessor back to the White House. Hoover this time came away thinking the president "really dumb" and incapable of grasping "the vital points of any issue." He did not believe the country had ever been governed "by such a mediocre type of man." He nevertheless accepted on the spot an appointment by Truman as honorary chair of the President's Famine Emergency Committee.[24]

On a gray, chilly Sunday morning, March 17, a white-haired, seventy-one-year-old Hoover arrived at LaGuardia Airport in his customary double-breasted blue suit and, a concession to the times, a conventional point collar on his white shirt. He climbed briskly into an Air Transport Command C-54, accompanied by a small entourage and a camera crew, and disappeared into the heavy clouds. Most of the reporters gathered to watch him leave had not known him as a president, let alone as the international humanitarian of the Great War. They were shocked to see this failed politician transformed into "a dramatic symbol of sympathy and hope."[25]

"I've been called back again like an old family doctor," Hoover, smiling, told the press on landing in Paris. He talked up his mission as "the most prodigious call [the American people] have ever received in history," and assured Europe that it would be answered "magnificently." That said, he would not reprise his role as food dictator and all-around economic manager from the First World War. He operated as an adviser and a figurehead this time. Regardless, it was a bravura performance.[26]

He traveled thirty-five thousand miles in five weeks, instructing the Poles and Finns on how to negotiate with the Russians for food, urging the Swedes to make 100,000 tons of fish available to the Germans, encouraging the British to reduce their cereal consumption from 400 to 300 grams a day, counseling the Egyptians to send 30,000 tons of wheat and millet to Greece and Italy, the Iraqis to export their 140,000 tons of surplus dates, and on and on through India, Siam, China, and Japan.[27]

Hoover displayed his usual command of the logistics of agricultural production and international distribution. He was, once more, his own publicity machine, proclaiming that he faced "the grimmest specter of famine in all the history of the world," with hunger hanging over the homes of "over one third of the people on the earth." He demanded assistance and sacrifices from the people of each of the twenty-five countries he visited. As always, he paid close attention to the needs of children, who, unless they were better fed, would develop tuberculosis, rickets, and anemia, among other diseases, and grow up into a generation of political "malevolents."[28]

Along the way, he jingled coins in his pockets, toured fish markets and refugee camps, and signed autographs for strangers in the streets. He was photographed with Pius XII in Vatican City and Gandhi in New Delhi. He recited nursery rhymes with poker-faced Finnish leaders to lighten the postwar gloom. After rummaging through the ruins of Hitler's offices in Berlin and the bunker where the Führer had met his end, he drove around the shell-pocked city of Vienna in Hitler's Mercedes, which had been confiscated by the American military in Berchtesgaden.

He returned home and on May 13 reported his findings to Truman, who thanked him profusely and sent him on the road again to South America. Hoover's efforts alleviated the suffering of many millions in a shattered and dysfunctional postwar world. "No one seems to question for a moment," wrote Edgar Rickard, "that his trip around the world saved the world from a terrible disaster." Nor was there any doubt that the assignment was a tonic for Hoover: "overnight he shook off his depression and entered into his job with the same keen enthusiasm and wise planning which made him successful."[29]

The following year Hoover would be dispatched again, back to Germany on an unpressurized DC-4 that left him with permanent hearing damage. He slept for two weeks in unheated hotel rooms in decrepit, bombed-out cities, assessing the economic conditions of Central Europe. The rebuilding of German industry, he informed Truman, should be the first priority of any program for European reconstruction. The economies of the Continent were inextricably linked, he said, and all roads pointed to Germany. What's more, a thriving European economy was the best bulwark against the spread of communism. It would also bring relief to American taxpayers, who at the time were spending billions annually in aid to defeated nations.

While Hoover's report encouraged an emerging consensus in Washington on America's interest in European recovery, he was not seriously consulted on the Marshall Plan, which put $13 billion toward Western European reconstruction, nor on the establishment of the United Nations or any other international institution. He was, in these years and hereafter, a secondary figure in the conduct of American foreign policy.

To everyone's surprise, including his own, it was in the realm of domestic policy that Hoover reestablished himself as a significant force in Washington. The midterm elections of 1946 had produced the first functional Republican Congress in a generation. It passed legislation establishing a committee to investigate the reorganization of the executive branch of the federal government. This was one of

Hoover's oldest and fondest projects, although he had opposed reorganization efforts on Roosevelt's watch for fear that they would be "an attempt by indirection to increase the Presidential authority over legislative and judicial functions and bring about an extension of the spoils system." He was appointed to the new committee by Joseph Martin, Speaker of the House, and chosen as its chair by his fellow commissioners.[30]

The Hoover Commission, as it became known, was delayed by a painful attack of shingles that laid low its chairman in the late summer of 1947. For one of the few times in his life, he was hardly able to work. It was not until September 29 that he was fit to announce "the most formidable attempt made yet for independent review and advice on the business methods of the Executive Branch." The goal of the commission, and the twenty-four expert task forces Hoover established under it, was to enhance the efficiency and economy of a national government swollen over twenty years from 580,000 employees to 2.5 million, more than America's state and municipal governments combined. It had grown haphazardly, without clear lines of command and accountability, and with scores of insufficiently supervised agencies and departments overlapping in purpose and function. The government was running paint factories, meat-cutting plants, auto repair shops, ice cream manufacturers, a Virgin Island distillery, a Panamanian railroad, and a fertilizing plant in the Tennessee Valley. It could account for few of the million motor vehicles and very little of the $27 billion in property that it owned.[31]

Hoover's expectation was that his commission would report after the 1948 election, by which time a Republican government might be in power and his personal objectives of unwinding some of the New Deal's administrative structures and laying off whole corps of federal employees might be welcome. He took an active interest in the campaign that year and was pleased to find that candidates for the Republican nomination wanted meetings with him and even said so in public. He made a speech at the convention, which had returned to Philadelphia, regretting again that two wars conducted in the name of liberty had left America "the only obstacle to the annihilation of freedom," the sole power "able to resist the hordes from the Eurasian steppes who would ruin Western Civilization."[32]

It no longer mattered, he said, "whether some of us who foresaw that danger and warned of it were right or wrong, and whatever the terrible efforts of American statesmanship that helped bring it about, we are today faced with a world situation in which there is little time for regrets." He warned of "creeping totalitarianism" that was slowly reaching "its tentacles into our labor unions, our universities, our intelligentsia, and our Government."[33]

His support for the Republicans was not based on ill will toward Truman. Quite the contrary. The president's attentions and assignments had warmed Hoover to him, slow-witted or not, as had news that the administration was reconsidering the name of the Boulder Dam. It had initially been called the Hoover Dam. Roosevelt's spiteful secretary of the interior, Harold Ickes, had with his president's approval changed it to Boulder Dam. Congress, with Truman's support, changed it back in 1947, in part because it was deserved, and also as a reward to Hoover for his service.

It was a shock, then, when Truman, in the final days of 1948's tight race against Thomas Dewey, second-time Republican candidate, resumed Roosevelt's tradition of running against the Hoover presidency as much as the official GOP nominee. Truman told an audience in Boston that Hoover had stolen the presidency from Al Smith in 1928 through "a vile whispering campaign spearheaded by the Ku Klux Klan." On being sworn in, Hoover, "the great engineer," had backed the American train into the station, "all the way into the waiting room and brought us panic, depression and despair" until "the courageous leader and great humanitarian, Franklin D. Roosevelt," put the nation back on track.[34]

Hoover had assumed that his own habit of lambasting the Democratic Party in general and sparing Truman in particular would insulate him from such criticism and recrimination. Loyalty mattered to him—he still had his long lists of names of people he had known, divided into those who had stuck with him and those who had "repudiated the faith"—and he believed it was due him from the president. After Truman defeated Dewey in one of the great upsets of American electoral history, Hoover returned to the White House to discuss the progress of his commission. "Mr. President," he said, "I would be less than frank if I didn't tell you that your Boston speech was both personally offensive to me and, I believe, uncalled for."[35]

Truman immediately apologized. "I feel the same way about it," he said. "It was one of those damned speeches that someone had writ-ten for me and when I got into the part when I attacked you, I wasn't smart enough to know how to improvise at the moment, and then I remembered the speech had been released to the press and I had to go through with it."[36]

It was a weak explanation, the whole Boston speech having been constructed around an indictment of the Hoover administration. It was hardly the sort of attack that occurs without consultation and deliberation, especially when its target is running a high-profile federal commission. In any event, Truman's story was sufficient for Hoover to rationalize forgiveness and continue in his office with his dignity unimpaired.


Hoover watched over his commission's task forces like a hen with twenty-four chicks, using his personal authority and unparalleled command of the facts to overcome internal disagreements and divi-sions, and to ensure that each delivered substantive recommendations. It was a monumental undertaking: in a two-month period starting in February 1949, the Hoover Commission sent to Congress nineteen reports, each released separately for maximum publicity. The reports contained 273 recommendations for changes to the government's administrative structure. No corner of the executive branch escaped the reformer's broom. The reports called for clearer lines of authority, the elimination of two-thirds of the sixty-five government agencies reporting to the president, a reorganization of services and agen-cies by purpose and function, a civil service commission to enforce employment standards, a consolidation of public works in the Interior Department, the clustering of lending agencies in Treasury, and the creation of what became the General Services Administration, which oversees procurement, communications, transportation, office space, records management, and other needs of the federal government.

Unfortunately for Hoover's plans, the election that had returned Truman to office had also put both houses of Congress back in Dem-ocratic hands. This did not bode well for his hopes of shrinking the national government and rolling back Roosevelt's handiwork. Rumors circulated in Washington that Hoover might resign, as they always did when he wanted attention from the White House. On receiving signals from Truman that he wanted the commission to proceed uninterrupted, Hoover showed his flexibility, jettisoned his dreams of eliminating New Deal agencies, and lined up with the administration. "Our job is to make every Government activity that now exists work efficiently. . . . It is not our function to say whether it should exist or not."[37]

To increase the odds of his proposals gaining a fair hearing, he founded the Citizens Committee for the Hoover Report. It recruited members, lobbied congressmen to implement the commission's proposals, and repeatedly testified before congressional committees studying the recommendations. Hoover, its chief fund-raiser, saw the Citizens Committee as a necessary instrument when virtually every agency and department in government was badgering the Capitol to maintain its standing and budget. They all agreed on the need for change, said Hoover, "in every branch except their own."[38]

A two-year stream of executive orders and legislation implemented at least one hundred of the commission's recommendations, resulting in the State Department Reorganization Act, the Military Unification Act, and the birth of the General Services Administration, among other achievements. While disappointing to Hoover and some Republicans in its failure to reduce the size, cost, and reach of the federal government, the commission left the executive branch with a more rational and effective structure, and the presidency with the enhanced managerial capabilities necessary to a modern expansive government. Hoover could at least take pride in having helped to clean up what he believed to be Roosevelt's mess.


By the time the Hoover Commission and the Citizens Committee had done their work, Hoover had passed the milestone of seventy-five years. There were heavy-framed eyeglasses on the tip of his nose, and a detested hearing aid in his ear. His voice was huskier and his cheeks sagged, making of his mouth a permanent frown only slightly alleviated when he smiled what *Time* called "his slightly pained and embarrassed smile." His jawline was as impressive as ever. The receding white hair and ruddy cheeks gave his face a tenderness it had not conveyed since boyhood.[39]

He spent increasing amounts of time high above Park Avenue at the Waldorf. The building, with its A-list clientele, 155 telephone operators, two hundred cooks, corps of interpreters, security officers, and service staff, met all of his needs. He called his four-room suite, 31-A, a "comfortable monastery," although it saw enough traffic to pass as a king's court. A living-room portrait of Lou watched over her husband's pipes and a cabinet displaying eighteen of her beautiful blue and white porcelains.[40]

He worked at a large desk, keeping three secretaries, and at peak times four with an additional researcher, busy for twelve hours a day on his correspondence, speeches, and multiplying literary endeavors. The life of an ex-president, as Hoover arranged it, was a grind, and as he was the only living example, no one could argue with him. He hated the idea of retirement. "There is no joy to be had from retirement," he said, "except some kind of productive work. Otherwise you degenerate into talking to everybody about your pains and pills. . . . The point is not to retire from work or you will shrivel up into a nuisance to all mankind."[41]

A young woman visited him at the Waldorf, and in response to his query told him she was content with her life. He looked at her with what she described as "total horror," and said, "How can you say a thing like that, because I want more. I want to write a better book. I want to have more friends—I just want more—and I think you should never sit back and say, 'I want the status quo.' "[42]

Into his late seventies, he received well over a hundred speaking invitations a month, accepting only two or three of them. He claimed to have written 55,592 letters in a single year, "not counting acknowledgements." He released three volumes of memoirs in 1951–52, published by Macmillan with a $70,000 subsidy from the author. They were a prolonged, turgid, intermittently reliable, and occasionally illuminating exercise in validating and vindicating his public service. While an important historical resource, they have seldom been read for pleasure. He published eight volumes of his speeches under the title "Addresses Upon the American Road" between 1938 and 1961.[43]

The secretaries, omnipresent in 31-A, satisfied his need for constant human companionship. Although they were dear to him, he rarely spoke with them. He passed his requests in the briefest of penciled notes, and they would answer in kind. His only breaks during the day were five or ten minutes for a bolted lunch and visits with the friends and callers who dropped in from around the city, from Congress and embassies in Washington, from Stanford and elsewhere in California, and, indeed, from around the world. All of them found an eager ear and a prodigious source of gossip and intelligence.

His evenings began with the television news, followed by two martinis mixed in a glass teapot. He revered the cocktail hour "as the pause between the errors and trials of the day and the hopes of the night." Dinner was usually served from the Waldorf kitchens, although on occasion, for a treat, he would order beans and cornbread from the Horn and Hardart automat. A regular group of friends and neighbors stopped by regularly for gin rummy or canasta.[44]

He traveled to speak and to fish and, in summers, for the annual pilgrimage to Bohemian Grove. His recreation was otherwise limited to long walks around Manhattan. In spare moments he liked to take apart clocks and telephones, studying their works, and reassembling them.

The Firm had disbanded with the close of Hoover's political career. Larry Richey had been generously pensioned off. Old friends began to die in droves. Will Irwin and Ray Lyman Wilbur, his closest Stanford chums, were gone, as were Mark Sullivan and Edgar Rickard. The loss of Rickard was exceptionally painful. Although he had several years earlier given up oversight of the Hoover mail, the Hoover investments, and the Hoover liquor purchases, the men remained close. Rickard was in these last years more friend and less an aide-de-camp to Hoover; their relationship grew more balanced than it had been in the past. Both widowed, they would dine together every night for months on end. When Rickard spent ten weeks in a hospital well outside the city, Hoover visited him every other day.[45]

Hoover outlived his family, as well. He had been irregularly in touch with his sister, May, although he continued to support her financially until her death in 1953. He was rarely in touch with Theodore, who had drifted off when Bert's public life took flight, not wanting, as he said, to be a tail to his brother's kite. Bert failed to mark Theodore's eightieth birthday, belatedly writing him, "I am glad you continue to live and work." Theodore passed in 1955. His brother did not attend his funeral, pleading pressing commitments.[46]

Hoover believed that his reputation was recovering as the years passed, and it was. His work for Truman had earned him a relatively admiring press. A flattering biography by Eugene Lyons had been published in 1947 and distributed with Hoover's generous assistance. Better still, a smattering of scholars, some granted access to Hoover's voluminous files, were chipping away at the edges of Roosevelt's still considerable prestige. Reporters were noting that Hoover had adopted a dash of self-deprecating humor: "I am the only person of distinction who's ever had a depression named after him," he would say. Wrote *Collier's*, "A lesser man of lesser faith might well have grown bitter. He might have retired to a life of prosperous idleness which Mr. Hoover could always have had and which he always scorned."[47]

Despite his age, and because of his improved stature, job offers continued to roll in for Hoover. New York's governor Dewey, once reluctant to be associated with him, offered Hoover the seat of retiring New York senator Robert Wagner in 1949. He declined, suggesting the party turn to a younger man: "I will not be physically able to undertake the necessary strain of the nomination and election campaign four months hence. . . . The Republican Party needs young blood on its fighting fronts."[48]

Another reason for his refusal was that Hoover had recently committed to lead a major fund-raising campaign at Stanford, one of his many charitable interests alongside the Carnegie Institute, the Huntington Library, and the Boys Clubs of America. The War Library was expanding to include research activities, a process that would see it develop into a world-class think tank and repository known as the Hoover Institution on War, Revolution, and Peace.

Truman, too, offered another assignment. The president was growing in office, and he was growing on Hoover. They shared simple midwestern backgrounds, heartfelt patriotism, and an appreciation for Hoover's capacities.

The advent of the Cold War, with its high political and military tensions between Soviet bloc countries and Western powers, had brought a new alertness in America to communist efforts to subvert the national government. The House Un-American Activities Committee and its cleverest member, Congressman Richard Nixon, had riveted the nation in 1948 with their prosecution of State Department official Alger Hiss on charges of spying for the Soviet Union. Truman wanted to get to the bottom of the alleged Soviet penetration of Washington. He turned to Hoover, for whom few subjects were more animating than the Soviet Union. He continued to believe that Roosevelt had been wrong to recognize Communist Russia in 1933, and that the president and Churchill had been duped by Stalin's supposed acceptance of the Atlantic Charter, a 1941 agreement that pledged its signatories to foreswear territorial aggrandizement and respect the self-determination of peoples, and by every other promise the Soviet leader had made, up to and including Yalta, after which Moscow installed a Communist government in Poland instead of permitting free elections as promised.

Hoover considered the Soviets at least as evil as the Nazis, and the greatest remaining global threat to peace, liberty, and free commerce. He was sickened by the Roosevelt-Truman pattern of "military alliance and political collaboration and appeasement with the Kremlin." It had resulted, he wrote, in a "long line of tombstones over 21 free peoples and 900,000,000 human beings."[49]

While generally supportive of Nixon's efforts to expose communists and fellow travelers in the United States, Hoover did not think the problem widespread enough to warrant Truman's proposed committee of investigation. The real problem, he told the president, was not Communists but the "men in government whose attitudes are such that they have disastrously advised on policies in relation to Communist Russia" throughout the Roosevelt era, and yet remained in office. He would later change his mind on the threat of Communist activities in the United States, but never on Roosevelt's advisers.[50]

Although finally free of ambitions for office, Hoover still followed partisan politics, and continued to dispense advice to the Republican Party. He urged it to "point out that the Democratic party gained power and held it for 20 years by lying about the Hoover Administration." He hoped that the GOP could gain power and hold it as long "by telling the truth about the Roosevelt and Truman administrations." He had come to embrace the label of "conservative," and he wanted Republicans to do the same. Being a conservative, he said, "is not a sin":

> It means today the conservation of representative govern-
> ment, of intellectual freedom and of economic freedom
> within the limits of what does not harm fellow men. It means
> the conservation of natural resources, of national health, edu-
> cation and employment. A conservative is not allergic to new
> ideas. He wants to try them slowly without destroying what
> is already good.[51]

He retained a weakness for the term *liberalism*, in the classical sense, but advised Republicans to give it up. Socialists and Commu-nists, he said, "have nested in this word until it stinks. Let them have [it]." He would soon find his way into the orbit of William F. Buckley Jr., where he played uncle to an emerging generation of intellectual conservatives.[52]

His wariness about the projection of American military power had heightened. He publicly supported Truman's deployment of U.S. troops to defend the Republic of Korea from Soviet-backed invad-ers from the north in 1950, but lamented that the United Nations and Western Europe showed no interest in helping to counter Com-munist aggression. He thought that Washington should threaten to withdraw from Europe in order to galvanize Western European nations against the Soviet threat. While he did not oppose the cre-ation of the North Atlantic Treaty Organization, he worried that it would function as a blank check for a continent unwilling to rearm and defend itself.

He further believed that the United Nations had erred by allow-ing Communist states into its councils. The institution seemed to Hoover more effective in legitimizing than in resisting "Red imperial-ism." He wanted either a Communist-free UN or a new organization of free states capable of resisting Communist expansionism. If none of these measures were feasible, said Hoover, the United States should "retreat into the Western Hemisphere to save our own civilization from exhaustion." It could not go on indefinitely defending the per-sonal freedoms of people who would not defend themselves. It could not "change ideas in the minds of men and races with machine guns or battleships." It could develop its air and sea power sufficiently to make of the Western Hemisphere an impregnable Gibraltar of liberty.[53]

Hoover's speeches on foreign policy once again brought him accusations of isolationism or, at least, "retreatism." He was not swayed. Indeed, his position hardened with time. Americans, he said, needed to accept the fact that the world was full of peoples with "aims, ideals, objectives, traditions, fears, hates, and national interests" different from their own. He described as "silly" the view that "if we start drawing in our horns and minding our own business that Russia will advance every foot we retreat until we will eventually find North America standing alone in a communist world." There remained many people on earth unwilling to live under Stalin's yoke, he averred.[54]

At the 1952 Republican convention, Hoover's worldview, represented by his friend and colleague Robert A. Taft, went down to defeat at the hands of Dwight D. Eisenhower, five-star general, hero of the Second World War, supreme commander of NATO, and standard-bearer of the internationalist, liberal wing of the Republican Party. Inclined to dismiss Eisenhower as a free spender and a naive internationalist who would "jabber about leading the world," Hoover was brought around by an application of Eisenhower's diplomatic finesse. The latter paid homage to the last Republican president, asking his advice, and bringing him just close enough to the campaign to win him over.[55]

By election day, November 6, Hoover was watching the returns on his television at the Waldorf in a state of high excitement. His friend, the author and conservative activist Clare Boothe Luce, stopped by on her way to join Eisenhower's crowd at the Commodore and found Hoover "as close to happy" as she had ever known him. To their mutual satisfaction, the Republicans snapped the twenty-year string of Democratic rule that evening. Hoover took it as a personal vindication of his principles and his tenacious opposition to the conduct of policy in the Roosevelt-Truman era.[56]

At the end of the evening, Eisenhower, exhausted by a long campaign, was impatient to get to bed. Mrs. Luce begged him to do one last thing before he turned in. She dialed Hoover's number at the Waldorf and put the president-elect on the line. Eisenhower said that he would try to instill as much integrity into the White House as Hoover had done, and that he would welcome his advice. Actually, Eisenhower never asked for much advice, although he did invite Hoover to his inauguration. He also took him fishing, and assigned him to his last major piece of public service.[57]

In one of its first moves, the narrowly Republican Congress elected along with Eisenhower launched the new Commission on the Organization of the Executive Branch of the Government. It was more directly targeted than the first commission at rolling back expenditures and nonessential services and agencies that competed with private enterprise. Critics viewed it as a full-bore attack on the New Deal.

On July 13, 1953, Eisenhower asked Hoover, a year short of his eightieth birthday, to head what would become known as the Second Hoover Commission. "Unending public chores seem to have become my privilege in life," said the new chairman.[58]

The Second Hoover Commission ran with all accustomed discipline and oversight. Hoover this time was able to appoint many of the members of his task forces and define their areas of inquiry. He pushed them, and himself, hard, said Herbert Brownell, who served on the commission:

> Joe Kennedy and I sat together and we really admired Mr. Hoover. He worked like a Trojan. That's my recollection of him during that time—how hard continuously he worked. He just begrudged every minute we took out for a sandwich and coffee in the middle of our all day meetings, you know, because he wasn't getting anything done. We used to joke with him a little about it, and he would laugh about it but he'd go right on with business during lunch.[59]

Hoover hoped to meet the objectives of his congressional sponsors and not simply repair but reduce the many offices and agencies reporting to the executive branch. He fanned his own flames by making it known that twelve separate government agencies were giving competing weather reports, and the revelation that the navy had stored enough canned hamburger to last sixty years when the product had a shelf life of two years. He took special aim at Roosevelt's Tennessee Valley Authority, which continued to operate in competition with private power producers. He also wanted to purge the thousands of policy-making and policy-advising officials baked into the Civil Service whose chief task, he said, was to perpetuate the growth and reach of government.[60]

The Second Commission, like the first, would fail to substantially reduce the size and scope of the executive branch. That the panel had a Republican majority, unlike the bipartisan original, made it less credible in the eyes of congressional moderates, who inevitably came under pressure from bureaucrats and special interests to oppose proposed cuts. The Eisenhower administration was not prepared to take bold action. Hoover found some of the Republican appointees to the commission difficult to manage: "My relations with the New Dealers four years ago were more pleasant," Hoover told Hugh Gibson. He wished he had "dictatorial powers, and the right to have about one man hung every month without trial."[61]

He had no luck in shutting down the TVA or turning back the clock on the growth of the public power sector, although he did excise some six hundred other government activities seen to be competing with private enterprise. More successful were the commission's efforts to streamline government processes and eliminate red tape and duplication. Federal budget expenditures were put on an annual basis, eliminating millions in holdover appropriations. The new Department of Defense was granted effective control of the three armed services under its purview. A foundation was laid for the creation of the Department of Health, Education and Welfare, and the managerial capacities of the White House were further enhanced in a manner that would guide successive administrations through the balance of the century.[62]

Notwithstanding its frustrations, the *New York Times* called the Second Hoover Commission "a milestone in the history of American government." Of its 314 recommendations, more than half were enacted in whole or in part. They not only effected a crucial rationalization of the executive presence in national government but spawned imitative bodies at the state level, including California's "Little Hoover Commission," which remains devoted to the promotion of "efficiency, economy, and improved service" in government to this day. Said the *New Republic* of its chairman at the end of the Second Commission's mandate:

His Party is again in power, and it has granted him the opportunity of making a final testament to the country of his years
in public life. Ninety-five percent of the press has hailed his
efforts. He was applauded as he left the conference room last
week. The dark memories of the New Deal are past. In his
own eyes, Hoover has been finally redeemed. And now he
can retire.[63]

Hoover never did form much of a relationship with Eisenhower. It
was Truman, rather, whom he accepted as an intimate in his later
years. Their relationship had nearly died again in the 1952 campaign
when the retiring president and the new Democratic nominee, Adlai
Stevenson, took turns campaigning against Hoover Republicans.
Injured anew, Hoover skipped Truman's seventieth birthday celebrations in 1954. A year later, Truman visited the Waldorf and managed
to smooth things over. The thirty-first president eventually wrote one
of the warmest letters of his life to the thirty-third, expressing gratitude for his rescue from ostracism:

> Yours has been a friendship which has reached deeper into
> my life than you know.
>
> I gave up a successful profession in 1914 to enter public
> service. I served through the first World War and after, for a
> total of about 18 years.
>
> When the attack on Pearl Harbor came, I at once
> supported the President and offered to serve in any useful
> capacity. Because of my varied experiences during the
> first World War, I thought my services might again be
> useful, however there was no response. My activities in the
> second World War were limited to frequent requests from
> Congressional Committees.
>
> When you came to the White House, within a month
> you opened the door to me to the only profession I knew,
> public service, and you undid some disgraceful action that
> had been taken in the prior years.
>
> For all this and your friendship I am deeply grateful.[64]

Hoover returned to West Branch, population 769, for his eightieth birthday, the biggest occasion in town since his presidency. *Time* sent a reporter:

> The Lions International club pushed a campaign to get the town's homes gleaming with new paint, and front yards trimmed to the quick. Work was rushed on the new elementary school so that the famous guest could dedicate it. The night before the big day, the women's society of Christian Service of the Methodist Church stored gallons of pickled beets and great bowls of applesauce in the demonstration refrigerators of Rummel's appliance store on Main Street. At midmorning the ladies began carrying the food to a special luncheon tent along with 60 fried chickens, cords of fresh sweet corn, and the 100-egg birthday cake baked by Mrs. Harold Heick.[65]

The famous guest visited the graves of his parents and planted a tree at the school named in his honor. The next year he celebrated his birthday in Newberg, Oregon, touring his uncle's home, which had been opened to the public. He wandered through the rooms and stood silently, eyes glistening, in his old bedroom. He made a nostalgic speech about the American way of life and fondly recalled his happy days in the streams and lakes of Oregon, all memories of a "pretty stiff time" extinguished. The year after, he marked the occasion at a party aboard an American President Lines ocean-liner christened *The President Hoover*.

In addition to farewell visits to West Branch, Newberg, and Stanford, there were farewell conventions: four, to be precise. Each of the 1948 and 1952 Republican affairs had been a valediction, the latter with a genuine air of finality to it. Hoover had no intention of attending in 1956 until Eisenhower personally asked him to "arrange your plans so that you can attend. . . . You exemplify in more ways than I am sure you realize the dignity and the spirit of the Republican Party and I know that every delegate to the Convention would be keenly disappointed, as would I, if you were not there to lend your counsel and advice." Hoover appeared for an affectionate send-off from a packed house at the Cow Palace in San Francisco.[66]

The organizers of the 1960 convention in Chicago that would nominate Richard Nixon invited Hoover back once again. Now eighty-five, he begged off. When they persisted, he agreed to make a closed-circuit television appearance from the Waldorf. As the date approached, he decided he might as well attend. Introduced as our "beloved chief" and the "grand old man of the Republican Party," he stood before the assembly on opening night, looking trim, fit, and erect, the floodlights beaming off his forehead. He was the delegates' first opportunity to loose their convention spirit, and they made the most of it. The Texans shouted, "Viva! Viva!" The Utahns paraded under a giant bee, their state symbol. Everyone howled and cheered for a full five minutes.

"It would be a tired Republican heart," said a television announcer, "that would not be stirred by the sight of Herbert Hoover, wouldn't it?"[67]

"I had not expected to speak at this convention," Hoover began when the noise finally subsided. "At each of the last three I enjoyed affectionate goodbyes. My goodbyes, however, did not take, and I have been bombarded with requests to do it again for the fourth time. Now unless some miracle comes to me from the Good Lord, this is finally it." Cries of "no! no!" filled the hall.[68]

His speech, delivered in a discernibly weaker voice, bemoaned America's "moral slump," as indicated by rising crime rates and headlines about government corruption. He blamed this in part on an "infection from Communist Russia," and in part on the "beatniks and eggheads" who, ashamed of their civilization and bereft of religious faith, were destroying America's national pride. He sounded very much an eighty-five-year-old man, but he rallied at the end to express confidence in the capacity of the American people to rejuvenate themselves.[69]

The last presidential election he was to witness, in 1960, was of great personal interest to Hoover. He knew Richard Nixon, having encouraged him years earlier to quit his law practice and run for public office. A fellow birthright Quaker, Nixon considered their "breakfasts and other meetings in your apartment in the Waldorf . . . among the most cherished memories of my fourteen years of government service."

Hoover advised the Republican candidate during the campaign to forgo a fifth televised debate with Kennedy for his own good. Nixon received a lot of advice to that effect, and listened to it.[70]

Hoover also knew the Democratic nominee. He and Joseph Kennedy had long been friends despite their partisan differences. One Kennedy son, Robert, had been a staffer on the Second Hoover Commission, and a second, Senator John F. Kennedy, now the Democratic nominee, had chaired a Senate subcommittee on the commission's legislative recommendations.

Hoover was not in any sense active in the campaign, although he was heard to abhor the attitude that Senator Kennedy was not fit for the presidency due to his Catholicism. When the results were in, he and Joe Kennedy brokered a postelection public peacemaking between the two combatants over the holidays in Palm Beach. Hoover had boarded a plane to attend John Fitzgerald Kennedy's inauguration, but poor weather prevented it from landing and he missed the event.[71]

So great was JFK's regard for Hoover that he repeatedly tried to put him back in harness, first as honorary chair of the national advisory council for the new Peace Corps, and later as honorary chair of the advisory committee for the Food for Peace program run by White House aide George McGovern. Kennedy would have been Hoover's sixth president but he said no to both offers. Hoover supported Kennedy through the notorious Bay of Pigs invasion, although he thought the president should have used more force to "decimate the Cuban army," consistent with the Monroe Doctrine. The existence of a Communist regime on America's back porch was "an intolerable menace to the safety of our country."[72]

He was devastated by the assassination of the forty-six-year-old Kennedy on November 22, 1963. Hoover's son Allan spent the night with him at the Waldorf. A message from Lyndon Baines Johnson, sworn in as the nation's thirty-sixth president, reached the suite overnight to advise Hoover that Harry Truman and Dwight Eisenhower had been invited to Washington in a show of continuity and solidarity. Johnson said he wanted to touch base with Hoover as well. First thing in the morning, Hoover messaged the president at the White House: "I am ready to serve our government in any capacity from office boy up."[73]

President Johnson made an unscheduled visit to the Waldorf the following week, with New York mayor Robert Wagner and Chief Justice Earl Warren in tow. Robert Kennedy and Jacqueline Kennedy stopped by at a later date. "You were always wonderful to my husband and he admired you so much," she said. Hoover was pleased at the opportunity to give attention to her young son, John Kennedy Jr.[74]

Perhaps the most emotional farewell Hoover made in these years was to his rod and reel. He had fished incessantly since the end of his presidency, from coast to coast in the United States, in Canada, and off the shores of Mexico. A good year would include a dozen trips, usually in small, tight-knit parties of men who knew each other well enough to use firecrackers as morning alarm clocks and to share brandy and jokes about traveling salesmen and farmers' daughters around a roaring fire in the evenings.

It had become difficult, as Hoover progressed through his seventies, to wade around all day in an ice-cold stream, his knees stiffening and his legs turning blue with cold. He became increasingly devoted to the pursuit of bonefish in the shallow waters of the Florida Keys. His usual haunt was the Key Largo Anglers Club, an exclusive resort with a grand clubhouse, a broad veranda, a swimming pool, and a skeet range. Among its members were Richard Joshua Reynolds Jr., of the tobacco fortune, and James L. Knight, publisher of the *Miami Herald*. Hoover had his own six-room, six-bath cottage.

In 1947, during his first winter at the Anglers Club, he had met Calvin Albury, a tall, broad-shouldered guide with long legs, huge hands, and a baseball cap pulled low over his eyes. He was the picture of piscatorial competence, and a man, like Hoover, of serious purpose and precise habits. Hoover wanted to fish with Albury. The guide was not sure about taking on an elderly, sunburned man who fished in a suit, tie, black socks, and fedora, even if he was an ex-president. On their first day out, however, Hoover pulled in a twelve-pound bonefish, his largest to that date. Albury watched him closely and decided that his client, necktie or not, "was one of the tops."[75]

Usually in the range of eight to ten pounds, bonefish, or "bones," as Hoover called them, are elusive and skittish. "Think of the most nervous person you know," he said, "and multiply that behavior by twenty and that is the life of a bonefish." They are also crafty, able to nibble almost imperceptibly at a shrimp-baited hook. Once struck, they put up what Hoover considered the best fight, pound for pound, of any fish he had encountered. They ran at lightning speeds, charged the boat, cut figure eights, swirled around coral to catch the line, and circled the boat ten or twenty times before being landed.[76]

Hoover had developed his own techniques for registering a nibble and setting his hook. He often used double-rigged lines and once pulled in nine fish on five casts. He would sit patiently for fifteen minutes in any given flat or inlet. If he caught something, he stayed another fifteen minutes; if not, he moved on. Time was marked either by his pocket watch or the duration of a Lifesaver candy.

He and Albury became regular partners, starting out every morning after breakfast, with Hoover walking down to the boat carrying his brown canvas kit bag. The guide would ask him how he was. "Well, I'm happy to be alive and to be here," said Hoover. "If we catch something, that's just a little extra bonus. If we don't get anything, I'm not going to feel bad about it. I'm just happy to be alive and to be here."[77]

Hoover took the guide's advice on where to fish and responded to each suggested spot with clear memories of when he had fished there and what he had caught. At their best, the two men would sit out on the clear, smooth, cyan water for thirty consecutive days, eight hours a day, on a little skiff under the hot sun, lost in a hypnotic state known to Zane Grey as "bonefish oblivion."

For lunch, Hoover would open his kit bag and make sandwiches, with a piece of bread on each knee. His worst habit was cleaning his pipe with a knock to the side of the skiff, which never failed to scare the bones. He smoked constantly on the water. On one occasion, frustrated by the workings of his gold pipe lighter, he said good riddance and threw it to Albury. It turned out to have been a gift from Winston Churchill.

The pair soon became so close that Hoover would not fish with anyone but Albury. He would spend the day ashore if the guide was ill, refusing a replacement. "Calvin isn't going to be sick forever," he said. "He knows my ways and I know his, and I'll sit here and wait until he gets back." This was an enormous display of personal loyalty for a man who otherwise insisted on fishing even in gales.[78]

Still nimble enough to walk the gunwales through his mid-eighties, Hoover did make some concessions to age, taking the occasional day off and shortening his hours on the water. By the winter of 1962, at the age of eighty-seven, his doctors told him that his annual trip to Key Largo would probably be his last. It was a good trip. He was down on the club board for the largest tarpon and the largest bonefish of the season. Returning to the dock for the last time, he took off his wristwatch and handed it to Albury along with his rod and reel. "Here's a little memento for you," he said. "If I ever get back, I'll use the rod and reel. If I never get back, it's yours."[79]

The next morning, as he was preparing to leave, Hoover found Albury again, put his arm over his shoulder, and with tears streaming down his cheeks told him, "I regard you as being one of the best friends I have on earth."

"Thank you, Mr. Hoover," said the guide. "And I feel the same way."[80]


He was too old for politics, and he was too old to fish, but he was not too old to write. Hoover produced seven books in his last five years of existence, often working on several at a time, with a desk for each one. These late works ranged from a lighthearted essay on the joys of fishing to a four-volume set on his humanitarian adventures under the title *An American Epic*.

He published *On Growing Up*, a selection of his thousands of letters to and from American boys and girls. On one candid page, he acknowledged that "answering their letters . . . has been a great relief from the haunts of nights sleepless with public anxiety." His tone with the children is uniformly friendly, occasionally amusing, and he always does them the honor of answering their queries forthrightly. Asked by an eighth-grader how to keep peace in the world:

> Don't begin to worry about international affairs until after you go to college. There is nothing you can do about them at this time of your life.

Asked about his time in office:

> During my term the people were subjected to the great trial of a world-wide depression which swept over us from Europe.

We adopted measures to prevent suffering and laid the foundations for recovery. That recovery came alongside the recovery of the rest of the world but was somewhat delayed by some foolish legislation. Nevertheless . . .

In response to a prospective space traveler:

I am not worried about your ambition to go to either Mars or Saturn. Even at the speed of 17,545 miles per hour made by Colonel Glenn, it would take several hundred years to make that journey. You'd better choose a nearby planet. Two are named for me and you may use them. However, if you got there you would die as there is no oxygen or water. So, I suggest you stick to the earth for the present.[81]

The best of these late books is *The Ordeal of Woodrow Wilson*, a firsthand account of Wilson's pursuit of peace in the wake of the Great War, a story Hoover was uniquely positioned to tell. It has a vividness and narrative drive missing from his other efforts. With excellent reviews, it became a bestseller on its own merits. It remains the only book written by a former president about another former president, and one of an opposing party, at that.[82]

The book leaves little doubt that Wilson, of the five presidents he served, impressed Hoover most. He claims a kinship with the Virginian based on a shared faith in economic competition, equality of opportunity, small government, judicious regulation of business, international peace, democratic principles, and the independence of nations, as well as shared antipathies to small-minded partisans, great power politics, and socialism. He wrote elsewhere that he did not mind being called a reactionary because the label would have suited Wilson too.

Hoover claims that Wilson, had he lived longer, would have agreed with him on the folly of Roosevelt's alliance with the Soviet Union, and the need to purge the United Nations of dictatorships. "A steadfast concert for peace," he quotes Wilson as saying, "can never be maintained except by a partnership of democratic nations. No autocratic government could be trusted to keep faith within it or observe its covenants. It must be a league of honor."[83]

It is plain, if unsaid, in *The Ordeal of Woodrow Wilson* that Wilson's reputational journey also resonates for Hoover. Wilson died unpopular and disgraced—Hoover's original title was to be *The Crucifixion of Woodrow Wilson*—only to be redeemed over time by the clarity of his vision and the strength of his principles.

The most curious manuscript in the Hoover oeuvre, sometimes called by its author his "magnum opus," was not published until 2012. The first draft of *Freedom Betrayed* was begun at a personal nadir, in the autumn following Lou's death in 1944. It is a comprehensive critique of American foreign policy from the recognition of the Soviet Union until the end of the Second World War, with a special emphasis on Roosevelt's diplomatic errors. It went through so many drafts and revisions over such a long period of time that it has to be seen as an act of self-therapy as much as a literary endeavor. That is not to diminish either the effort or the final product.[84]

The effort was prodigious. Hoover reviewed some 350,000 documents, including the record of the Pearl Harbor Congressional Inquiry, transcripts of the Nuremberg trials, diplomatic archives at the Hoover Institution, and papers collected for him by Herbert Jr. during his employment at the State Department.[85]

The final product is both a summation of and an elaboration on Hoover's argument that Roosevelt, desperate to retain office, cynically backed America into an unnecessary European war with tragic consequences for the United States and the world. Worse still was FDR's support for the Soviets. "The greatest loss of statesmanship in all American history" was the "tacit American alliance" with Communist Russia after it had been attacked by Hitler in June 1941, wrote Hoover. "American aid to Russia meant victory for Stalin and the spread of communism to the world." By its date of publication, Hoover's critique was as far from mainstream opinion as ever.[86]

It was only in the last two years of his life that Hoover's magnificent health betrayed him. A growth on his large intestine required surgery in the autumn of 1962. He returned to the Waldorf on a strict diet and under orders to refuse telephone calls and visitors while he healed. He would not leave his suite again. He cut his work schedule back to six hours a day. He showed improvement in the early months of 1963 until an attack of gastrointestinal bleeding laid him low in June. He looked frail for the first time in his life. "I have had some bad luck this year," he wrote to Hulda Hoover McLean, Theodore's daughter, at the end of 1963. "Too much time in bed, six good nurses, five good doctors, 12 pills daily! We have been making some good progress against them, and I am promised I will defeat them before I pass the 100 mark, so that is my health report."[87]

He reopened his literary factory and continued to plan new books, an old man working like his next meal depended on it. He had the companionship of a Siamese kitten in his suite, and guests continued to stop by, sometimes finding him in his bath gown and with his teeth out, nevertheless ready for conversation. He accepted his last honorary degree, perhaps his ninetieth, in May 1964. Now that he was confined to a wheelchair much of the time, there was no question of his accepting in person, or of attending Bohemian Grove or the Republican convention that summer.

He put out a statement on his ninetieth birthday, predicting that the United Sates would continue to grow in freedom and prosperity, and insisting that the abundance of American life would always overshadow the nation's other difficulties:

> Deeply as I feel the lag in certain areas which denies equal chance to our Negro population, I cannot refrain from saying that our 19 million Negroes probably own more automobiles than all the 220 million Russians and the 200 million African Negroes put together.[88]

Not long after this he advised the Republican nominee, Senator Barry Goldwater, to attack the Democrats for being soft on Communism.

His last illness, manifest as massive internal hemorrhaging, struck at 3:55 p.m. on October 20, 1964, a Saturday. Doctors stabilized him with large transfusions of blood, but they could not save him. He slipped into a coma and died, officially of cancer, three days later at 11:35 a.m., with both Allan and Herbert Jr. at his side. John Adams was the only president to live a longer life, by 176 days.

# "I Admire a Lot in Hoover's Career"

Television networks preempted scheduled programming the evening of October 17 for half-hour tributes to the late president. The national election campaign was temporarily suspended. The next day, Presidents Johnson, Eisenhower, and Truman all released elegiac statements. The Supreme Court called a recess in honor of Hoover, its champion in that dangerous year, 1937. The bells tolled at noon in the tower of the Hoover Institution on War, Revolution and Peace at Stanford University. The nation's stock exchanges closed early in his memory.[1]

Hoover's body was taken to St. Bartholomew's Episcopal Church in New York for viewing, drawing tens of thousands of mourners a day. A funeral service was held on October 22 and attended by the presidential and vice-presidential candidates of both tickets, along with Richard and Patricia Nixon, Robert Kennedy, Bernard Baruch, and other eminences.

Hoover's remains were next transported in a sealed coffin to Washington's Union Station and met by President Johnson and a Coast Guard band playing "Hail to the Chief." Quiet crowds lined Delaware Avenue as a horse-drawn caisson made its way to the Capitol. The hush was broken only by a twenty-one-gun salute from a battery of cannon and, later, by fifty Air Force jets flying in formation overhead. Black Jack, the handsome stallion that had taken part in the funeral procession for President Kennedy, was a part of the cortege.

He was riderless, with cavalry boots reversed in the stirrups, emblematic of a fallen warrior. The coffin was borne to the Rotunda, where before an audience of legislators, civil servants, and the public, the Reverend Frederick B. Harris, chaplain of the Senate, remembered the late president's humanitarianism:

> The daring projects he assumed threw bridges across the gulf of misery—bridges of mercy and help . . . food, clothing and medicine for millions, including huddled armies of children who otherwise would have perished.
>
> And so it is ours today to gratefully salute one who brought sustenance to more starving humans than any other man who has ever walked this earth.[2]

Reverend Harris handled the Great Depression deftly, recalling the criticism and ridicule Hoover had endured and his faith in the long-term viability of the American economy: "In the midst of an economic hurricane, still he believed clouds were lies and the blue sky the truth." He credited Hoover's "strong, unbending, and unblemished character" for his ability to "come through the fires of criticism to adulation and coronation in the heart of the Nation he had served so faithfully."[3]

The chaplain can be excused the eulogistic license of "unblemished" and "adulation." He was making an important point. Hoover's boundless faith in the promise of American life, his conviction that "there will always be a frontier to conquer or to hold as long as men think, plan, and dare," had been sustained through two world wars, against the intellectuals who gave up on their country in the 1920s, and against Roosevelt, who declared the American party over in the '30s, right through to his final days. He died vindicated at the dawn of the space age, amid one of the greatest booms in U.S. history, having heard Democratic nominee Kennedy deliver one of the greatest acceptance speeches ever:

> Some would say . . . that all horizons have been explored, that all battles have been won, that there is no longer an American frontier. But I trust that no one in this assemblage would

agree with that sentiment; for the problems are not all solved and the battles are not all won; and we stand today on the edge of a New Frontier.

Hoover's unexampled record of national service was more or less unanimously praised in hundreds of printed and spoken eulogies. So sensitive to every criticism, he would have been pleased, on balance, had he somehow read his clippings. There were nevertheless strong hints at what would become a complicated legacy.

Walter Lippmann claimed Hoover for the left, remembering him as a "brilliant" and "fascinating" progressive, and the natural heir of Woodrow Wilson. He added that the late president was "in no way responsible" for "the disaster which engulfed him in the White House," and he dredged quotes from the 1932 campaign speeches to prove Hoover was responsible for "virtually all the main principles of the early years of Franklin Roosevelt's New Deal."[4]

"It is impossible to catalogue the achievements of this extraordinary man," wrote William F. Buckley, claiming Hoover for the right. His conception of public service "was about the purest thing to be seen in major national politics." His only failure had been "as a political dramatist." He had been unable to "communicate to the people the true meaning of the mechanized welfarism which is a great semantical and economic imposture: the chimera, which is the demagogic mainstay of Liberal politics, that it is possible for the majority of Americans a) to receive benefits from the federal government; without b) paying for them."[5]

The question of where Hoover belongs in American political traditions remains a loaded one to this day. While he clearly played important roles in the development of both the progressive and conservative traditions, neither side will embrace him for fear of contamination with the other. That one man can in one lifetime be a leader to opposed schools raises the inconvenient fact that they have more in common than not.

·   ·   ·

The newspapers, on the occasion of his death, generally credited Hoover with a sincere, dignified, scandal-free administration, and some of their assessments of his presidency hold up well through the years. The *Washington Post*, while faulting his weak political leadership during the Depression, wrote that the accusations of inaction and reaction leveled at Hoover were, like "the bitter hatred that accompanied them at the time," unfair. The paper also supported Hoover's view that recovery from the Depression had begun in the summer of 1932, and that the bank panic of March 1933 could have been avoided had Roosevelt cooperated with the defeated administration.

The frustrations of the Depression years, declared the *New York Times*, "have been put into better perspective by our increasing awareness of Herbert Hoover's total contribution to the age in which he lived. History has not credited him with being a great president; yet it is clear now that the weight of the burden he carried in a bitterly divided and frustrated United States, complicated by the devastating European financial collapse in 1931, was perhaps more than any human being could have borne with success."

Interestingly, Milton Friedman and Anna Schwartz published their landmark *A Monetary History of the United States* months before Hoover died. The book transformed discussion of the Great Depression, placing blame on the failure of the Federal Reserve to maintain an adequate supply of money from 1929 to 1933. It had not penetrated the popular understanding of that calamity by the time Hoover's eulogies were written, and it has hardly been the last word. The point is that our current consensus on the causes of the Depression emerged far too late to be of use to Hoover, and it remains to this day far from settled. (Indeed, recently the New Keynsian economist Christina Romer and the New Classical economist Robert Barro were each asked independently to list sources crucial to an understanding of the Great Depression: of the eight texts they cited, the oldest was Friedman and Schwartz.)[6]

Hoover's work on the executive branch commissions was well remembered, as was his success in the Commerce Department and his lifelong service to children. The *Times* noted that the United Nations Children's Fund (UNICEF) was a direct descendant of Hoover's Great War relief operations, just as the relief agency CARE was a child of his European Children's Fund. It recalled that he had been instrumental in the success of the 600,000-member Boys Clubs of America, and that he had served as "a sort of super-uncle" to the nation's children through his writings, letters, and speeches: "When talking to them or about them, or when replying to the thousands of youngers who wrote to him every year for advice, his shyness and reserve vanished."[7]

Receiving less attention was Hoover's magnificent four-year project, *Recent Social Trends in the United States* (1933), although it stood as one of the century's most important contributions to social science, serving as a resource and playbook for social reformers throughout the century. Likewise, the law-reform sections of the Wickersham report were largely overlooked despite their contributions to decades of improvement in the American legal system. Hoover's obsessions with the standardization of materials, devices, and other facets of American life, once so controversial, had by his death become so commonplace that they received little mention. Nor was much said of Hoover's conservationism and the 2 million acres of federal land he had placed within the national forest reserve (perhaps because FDR had outdone him on this score), or his consistent work for more and better housing. His business career, too, was underplayed. It was only by coincidence that a poll of seven thousand Columbia University engineering graduates conducted as part of the school's one hundredth anniversary celebrations was released by newspapers the day after Hoover's death. It named Hoover and Thomas Alva Edison as the two greatest engineers produced in the United States, ahead of Alexander Graham Bell and John A. Roebling, builder of the Brooklyn Bridge.[8]

Hoover's social vision of a bottom-up America rooted in individual freedom, public service, and strong self-sufficient communities, encouraged by a limited federal government, seemed by his death a relic of another era and was seldom discussed except as evidence of his supposedly reactionary temperament. Yet the late twentieth century would obsess over a well-documented decline in social capital, defined as the networks and shared values or understandings that enhance co-operation among people.[9] A vast literature would arise on the difficulty of maintaining social linkages in an age of big government, multinational corporations, and ex-burbs. Hoover's relevance to this conversation has yet to be discovered. The same can be said for his insistence on federal guardianship of equality of opportunity, an ideal that has deteriorated miserably over the years.

Perhaps the best tribute to Hoover, containing as it did a keen appreciation for the sheer magnitude of his life, came four years after his obituaries were printed. Months before he was assassinated, the leading candidate for the Democratic presidential nomination, Robert F. Kennedy, was asked by David Frost in a live television interview which historical character he admired most. The unexpected question left Kennedy scrambling. "Ah, let's see," he said, looking away from Frost and wringing his hands. "Well, most of the ones that I really think about just rapidly are Americans." He paused for a few seconds and as if to buy himself time threw out the name of Abraham Lincoln. Clearly dissatisfied with the obviousness of that choice, he paused again before venturing, without conviction, "Uh, I think Theodore Roosevelt I admire a great deal." He was still thinking. Frost, who knew his business, sat patiently as his guest shifted uncomfortably in his chair and the question hung in the air and an expectant audience looked on. Kennedy continued to search his mind until finally he found what he was looking for. He perked up and leaned forward, face shining, to say:

> I admire still a lot in Herbert Hoover's career. I thought that his career and his earlier career and what he did working in the mines and his career in China, what he did for Europe after the First World War and what he did during the 1950s, the Hoover Commission of the United States, were just marvelous contributions to our country and to his fellow man. Of course, the difficulties that he had in the nineteen twenties as part of the cabinet and while he was president of the United States, but when you consider his overall career there were some marvelous things that he did.[10]

Lou and Allan had purchased Hoover's birthplace cottage in West Branch at about the lowest point of his reputational slide. They refurbished it and decorated it with period furnishings, and eventually it was opened to the public. In 1962, the Herbert Hoover Presidential Library and Museum, a modest building with a sandstone face, was erected on adjacent land.

On October 25, under an Indian summer sky, Herbert Hoover was buried under a simple slab of Vermont white marble on a grassy hill overlooking his father Jesse's cottage and his own library. Lou would be moved to his side a week later.

Forty thousand people were on hand to hear Dr. D. Elton True-blood, a Quaker friend of the deceased, read from Paul's Epistle to the Corinthians:

> Behold I show you a mystery; we shall not all sleep, but
>     we shall all be changed.
> In a moment, in a twinkling of an eye, at the last trump:
>     for the trumpet shall sound and the dead shall be
>     raised incorruptible, and we shall be changed.
> O death, where is thy sting? O grave, where is thy
>     victory.[11]

# ACKNOWLEDGMENTS

Interstate 80 is one of the nation's great trucking routes, stretching from Teaneck, New Jersey, straight through the heartland to San Francisco, California. It approximates the route of the first transcontinental railroad, the first transcontinental highway (the Lincoln Highway), and the first transcontinental airmail route, which is to say it was built to move vast amounts of traffic efficiently from one end of the country to the other, not for scenery, not for dallying. The middle sections of the I-80 are particularly bereft of distractions unless you like corn. The road urges you forward, east or west, swiftly and conveniently, stopping only for gas or food at somewhere like the World's Largest Truckstop outside of Davenport, Iowa, an infinitely more popular landmark than the Herbert Hoover Presidential Library and Museum, thirty miles to the west.

The Hoover library is tucked into a well-groomed park at the edge of West Branch, Iowa, a town that feels smaller than its population of 2,322. The setting is pleasant, although from any part of the park you can hear the I-80 rumbling a few hundred yards away. Precious little of the traffic bothers to pause and pay its respect to the thirty-first president. When I made the first of my six visits, the library felt like the loneliest place in America. There were more staff than visitors in its corridors. Thankfully, that initial impression did not hold.

I love West Branch, in part because I enjoyed the twelve-hour drives from Toronto, in part because it is an island of presidential pomp in the middle of nowhere, in part because of Reid's Beans, a delightful little eatery on Main Street, in part because my researches there were far more fruitful than I had anticipated, but mostly because of the great assistance and fellowship I received from the library's wonderful staff.

Spencer Howard, my main contact at the library, and his colleague Matthew Schaefer, are incredibly knowledgeable and resourceful archivists. They steered me through their vast collections, introduced me to primary and secondary sources I might otherwise have missed, and answered innumerable questions about Hoover, Iowa, its corn, its weather, its politics, and its football. They are two of the most pleasant and interesting people I have ever met in the course of my book work. Spencer read this manuscript and saved me from at least a dozen embarrassing errors. Craig Wright, another archivist whom I came to know in my later visits to West Branch, also provided useful guidance.

Thomas Schwartz, a historian and the director of the Herbert Hoover Presidential Library and Museum, took me to lunch at Reid's and generously shared his profound views on Hoover's life and work. He also read a draft of my manuscript, asked searching questions, and made many comments that were of great benefit to the final product. I thank him with respect and admiration.

The critic, author, and editor David Staines read early chapters of this book and provided invaluable notes and advice, an act of friendship for which I am eternally grateful. Barry Eichengreen, professor of economics and political science at the University of California, Berkeley, and author of several groundbreaking works on the Great Depression, also read a portion of the manuscript and gave me constructive suggestions and wise counsel. The historian Tammy M. Proctor, now at Utah State University, joined me for a lunch at Reid's Beans, gave me the benefit of her deep knowledge of Hoover and the Great War, and directed me to the Mullendore papers, which were of considerable use to me. Julia Belluz, Kristen Chew, Chris Johnston, and Wesley Beck ably assisted with aspects of my research.

I want to thank my agent, Andrew Wylie, for convincing me to write a life of Hoover, a project I initially resisted, not being a fan of the genre of presidential biography. Andrew also led me to my publisher, Alfred A. Knopf, and in particular to my editor, Andrew Miller, whom he described as one of the great young talents in the business, and he was right. Andrew Miller had the chore of editing a writer who is also an editor and who thinks he knows more than he does about everything from telling a story to organizing a manuscript for production. His patience and professionalism is much appreciated. I could not be happier with his stewardship of this project, and I have enjoyed all of my interactions with him. Thanks also to his excellent assistant, Zakiya Harris.

I have never met George H. Nash, author of the first three volumes of the official Hoover biography, among other important books on Hoover and American conservatism, but I hold him in high esteem. He is peerless among Hoover scholars and his trenchant, trustworthy work was an incredible resource to me in this writing. I would also like to salute Hal Elliott Wert, David Burner, Kendrick Clements, Gary Dean Best, Glen Jeansonne, Eugene Lyons, Craig Lloyd, Ellis Hawley, Joan Hoff Wilson, William Leuchtenburg, and Richard Norton Smith for their salient contributions to the endless task of getting Hoover's biography right. I have benefited from all of their efforts.

Finally, and most importantly, my deepest gratitude to Tina Leino-Whyte and Thea Whyte for their love and support. Sooner or later I will get them to West Branch.

# NOTES

ABBREVIATIONS USED IN THE NOTES

HHPL   Herbert Hoover Presidential Library and Museum, West Branch, Iowa
  PPP   *Public Papers of the Presidents of the United States: Herbert Hoover.* 4 vols.
        (1929–1933). Washington, DC: U.S. Government Printing Office, 1974–
        1977.


PREFACE

1. *Saturday Evening Post,* April 14, 1928.
2. *Des Moines Capital,* April 26, 1925; *New York Times,* February 5, 1933.
3. *New York Times,* February 5, 1933.
4. Theodore G. Joslin Diaries, March 28, 1932, Theodore G. Joslin Papers,
   HHPL; President Hoover Address, June 15, 1931, *PPP,* vol. 3, p. 295.
5. Eric Hobsbawm, *The Age of Extremes: A History of the World, 1914–1991* (New
   York: Vintage Books, 1996).
6. *Palo Alto Times,* November 7, 1928.


CHAPTER 1   "A PRETTY STIFF TIME"

1. Hulda Hoover McLean, *Hulda's World: A Chronicle of Hulda Minthorn Hoover,
   1848–1884* (West Branch, IA: Herbert Hoover Presidential Library Associa-
   tion, 1989), pp. 30–31, 33. Also on Hoover's childhood, see the "Genealogy of
   the Herbert Hoover Family" in the Hulda Hoover McLean Papers at HHPL.
   There are more details in the *Cedar County Historical Review* (Cedar County
   Historical Society), August 1959, July 1965, July 1974, July 2002. See also
   George H. Nash, *The Life of Herbert Hoover: The Engineer, 1874–1914* (New
   York: Norton, 1983) and David Burner, *Herbert Hoover: A Public Life* (Newton,
   MA: American Political Biography Press, 1978) for Hoover's life in Iowa. Both
   are more reliable than Hoover, *The Memoirs of Herbert Hoover: Years of Adven-
   ture, 1874–1920* (New York: Macmillan, 1952).
2. Agnes Minthorn Miles to Harriette Miles Odell, January 21, 1920, "Genealogy," HHPL.

3. Ibid.
4. Ethel Rensch, "Herbert Hoover, the Son of a Pioneer People," Ethel Rensch Papers, HHPL; Frank Nye, *Doors of Opportunity: The Life and Legacy of Herbert Hoover* (West Branch, IA: Herbert Hoover Presidential Library Association, 1988), p. 13.
5. Ethel Rensch, "Dr. John Minthorn: Biographical," p. 2, Ethel Rensch Papers, HHPL.
6. Dorothy Schwieder, *Iowa: The Middle Land* (Iowa City: Iowa State University Press, 1996).
7. West Branch Little House file, unpublished manuscript by Lou Henry Hoover, and "Genealogy," HHPL.
8. Hulda Minthorn Hoover Correspondence, January 3, 1863, "Genealogy," HHPL.
9. Undated clipping, *Evening Bulletin* (Philadelphia), Accretions 1994–1999, McLean Papers, HHPL.
10. Ray Lyman Wilbur, "Herbert Hoover: A Personal Sketch," Correspondence, Pre-Commerce Papers, HHPL.
11. "Herbert Hoover: The Son of a Pioneer People," undated clipping, *Christian Science Monitor*, Hulda Minthorn Hoover Correspondence, "Genealogy," HHPL.
12. Burner, *Herbert Hoover*, p. 8.
13. Theodore J. Hoover, "Statement of an Engineer," Theodore J. Hoover Papers, HHPL.
14. McLean, *Hulda's World*, p. 79.
15. Ibid., p. 69; Jesse Clark Hoover, "Genealogy," HHPL; McLean, *Hulda's World*, p. 80.
16. McLean, *Hulda's World*, pp. 76–77.
17. *Des Moines Sunday Register*, March 5, 1931.
18. Rose Wilder Lane, *The Making of Herbert Hoover* (New York: Century, 1920), p. 42.
19. Obituaries in Jesse Clark Hoover file, "Genealogy," HHPL.
20. Ibid.
21. McLean, *Hulda's World*, pp. 76, 85; letter fragment, Hulda Minthorn Hoover Correspondence, "Genealogy," HHPL.
22. Interview with Theodore Hoover, January 6, 1919, Theodore Hoover file, "Genealogy," HHPL; McLean, *Hulda's World*, p. 91; David Hinshaw, *Herbert Hoover: American Quaker* (New York: Farrar, Straus, 1950), p. 6.
23. Nash, *Engineer*, pp. 5–6; Hoover, "Statement of an Engineer," p. 27.
24. *Detroit Free Press*, July 31, 1932.
25. Hoover, "Statement of an Engineer."
26. Hulda Minthorn Hoover to Agnes Minthorn Miles, October 24, 1883, Accretions 1994–1999, McLean Papers, HHPL.
27. Nash, *Engineer*, p. 9.
28. Eugene Lyons, *Herbert Hoover: A Biography* (Garden City, NY: Doubleday, 1964), p. 16.

29. Laban Miles file, "Genealogy," HHPL.

30. Will Irwin, *Herbert Hoover: A Reminiscent Biography* (New York: Century, 1928), p. 19.

31. Hulda Minthorn Hoover to Agnes Minthorn Miles, October 24, 1983, Accretions, McLean Papers, HHPL; McLean, *Hulda's World*, pp. 94–95.

32. Obituary, *West Branch Times*, Jesse Hoover file, "Genealogy," HHPL; Flora Clark Gardner, "Famous Mothers of Famous Men," May 9, 1929, unidentified clipping, Hulda Minthorn Hoover file, "Genealogy," HHPL; McLean, *Hulda's World*, p. 95; Nash, *Engineer*, p. 10.

33. Hoover, *Years of Adventure*, p. 4; Herbert Hoover, "Informal Address Before the Iowa Society of Washington," November 10, 1927, www.hooverassociation.org.

34. Hoover, "Statement of an Engineer," p. 35.

35. Hulda Hoover Estate file, Jesse Hoover Estate file, Hoover Legal Records 1880–1895, 1964, HHPL.

36. Herbert Hoover, *The New Day: Campaign Speeches of Herbert Hoover, 1928* (Palo Alto, CA: Stanford University Press, 1928), p. 50.

37. Lyons, *Herbert Hoover*, p. 17.

38. Burner, *Herbert Hoover*, p. 10.

39. Hulda Minthorn Hoover, McLean Papers, Accretions, HHPL, p 10.

40. John A. Timour to George H. Nash, September 4, 1978, Henry John Minthorn file, "Genealogy," HHPL.

41. Hoover, *Years of Adventure*, p. 11.

42. Alva W. Cook, October 22, 1928, addendum to Burt Barker Brown Oral History Interview, HHPL.

43. Henry John Minthorn to Theodore Hoover, March 8, 1920, Accretions, McLean Papers, HHPL.

44. *Pacific Historian* 8–9 (February 1964): 221.

45. Herbert Hoover, "Information for Biographers," Subject Files, Pre-Commerce Papers, HHPL.

46. *Sunday Oregonian*, October 30, 1932.

47. *Oregonian*, July 15, 1931.

48. John Henry Minthorn to Rose Wilder Lane, February 28, 1920, in Rose Wilder Lane, "Genealogy," HHPL.

49. Herbert Hoover to Daisy Trueblood, Addendum to Burt Brown Oral History Interview, HHPL.

CHAPTER 2  "A WHOLE JUG FULL OF EXPERIENCE"

1. H. J. Minthorn to Wm. F. Smith, August 1917, and "The Minthorn Family," in Henry John Minthorn file, "Genealogy of the Herbert Hoover Family," McLean Papers, HHPL; "Dr. John Minthorn" in Ethel Rensch Papers, HHPL.

2. *Capital Journal* (Salem), March 17, 1920, typescript in Oregon Collections, HHPL; Eugene Lyons, *Herbert Hoover: A Biography* (Garden City, NY: Doubleday, 1964), p. 19.

3. George H. Nash, *The Life of Herbert Hoover: The Engineer, 1874–1914* (New York: Norton, 1983), p. 19; Richard Norton Smith, *An Uncommon Man: The Triumph of Herbert Hoover* (New York: Simon and Schuster, 1984), p. 67.

4. David Burner, *Herbert Hoover: A Public Life* (Newton, MA: American Political Biography Press, 1978), p. 15.

5. *Capital Journal* typescript; William F. Smith to H. J. Minthorn, August 1917, Henry John Minthorn file, "Genealogy," HHPL.

6. Joslin Diaries, May 13, 1931, HHPL.

7. Elmer Edson Washburn, "Westward Across Four Frontiers," unpublished, Oregon Collections, Various Sources, HHPL.

8. Glen Jeansonne, *Herbert Hoover: A Life* (New York: New American Library, 2016), p. 21.

9. Bert Brown Barker Oral History, HHPL.

10. Ibid.

11. Ibid.; Herbert Hoover, "Information for Biographers," Subject Files, Pre-Commerce Papers, HHPL.

12. Bert Brown Barker Oral History.

13. "Thank You Miss Gray!" *Reader's Digest*, July 1959.

14. Bert Brown Barker Oral History.

15. Ibid.

16. Nash, *Engineer*, p. 23.

17. *Capital Journal* typescript.

18. "When 'Bertie' Hoover Came West," Lucia Ellis, clipping, Oregon Collections, HHPL.

19. George H. Nash, *Herbert Hoover and Stanford University* (Stanford: Hoover Press, 1988), p. 5.

20. Herbert Hoover to Nell May Hill, August 30, 1892, Correspondence, Pre-Commerce Papers, HHPL.

21. "Herbert Hoover: A Personal Sketch," Ray Lyman Wilbur, Correspondence, Pre-Commerce Papers, HHPL; Will Irwin, *Herbert Hoover: A Reminiscent Biography* (New York: Century, 1928), p. 45; Hoover, *The Memoirs of Herbert Hoover: Years of Adventure, 1874–1920* (New York: Macmillan, 1952), p. 17.

22. Irwin, *Reminiscent Biography*, p. 48.

23. Jackson Reynolds Oral History, HHPL; Nash, *Engineer*, p. 29.

24. Hoover, *Years of Adventure*, p. 18; Theodore J. Hoover, "Statement of an Engineer," Theodore J. Hoover Papers, HHPL, p. 91.

25. Jackson Reynolds Oral History, HHPL.

26. Herbert Hoover to Nell May Hill, November 9, 1894.

27. Irwin, *Reminiscent Biography*, pp. 58–59.

28. Ibid., p. 60.

29. Herbert Hoover to Nell May Hill, July 9, 1895.

30. Charles Dickens, *David Copperfield* (New York: Modern Library, 2000), p. 761.

31. Herbert Hoover to Nell May Hill, July 19, 1894.

32. Ibid., September 7, 1895.

33. Nash, *Engineer*, p. 34.
34. Herbert Hoover to Nell May Hill, July 19, 1894.
35. Ibid., July 19, 1895.
36. Herbert Hoover to May Hoover, November 7, 1894, August 4, 1895, September 7, 1895.
37. Ibid.; Herbert Hoover to Nell May Hill, September 7, 1895, November 7, 1894.
38. Ibid., November 7, 1894.
39. Ibid.
40. Dale C. Mayer, *Lou Henry Hoover: A Prototype for First Ladies* (New York: Nova History Publications, 2004); Nancy Beck Young, *Lou Henry Hoover: Activist First Lady* (Lawrence: University of Kansas Press, 2004).
41. Stanford file, Pre-Commerce Subject Files, HHPL; Jackson Reynolds Oral History, HHPL.
42. "Herbert Hoover as an Educational Illustration," John C. Branner, Correspondence, Pre-Commerce Papers, HHPL.

CHAPTER 3 "I AM THE DEVIL"

1. Hoover, Information for Biographers, HHPL.
2. Rose Wilder Lane, *The Making of Herbert Hoover* (New York: Century, 1920), pp. 180–81.
3. Ibid., p. 183.
4. Hoover, *The Memoirs of Herbert Hoover: Years of Adventure, 1874–1920* (New York: Macmillan, 1952), p. 26.
5. *San Francisco Call*, February 1896; Carson City Gold & Silver Min. Co. v. North Star Min. Co., 83 F. 341 (9th Cir., October 18, 1897) at 658–69.
6. Walter W. Liggett, *The Rise of Herbert Hoover* (New York: H. K. Fry, 1932), p. 49; Herbert Hoover, "Some Notes on 'Crossings,'" *Mining and Scientific Press* 72 (1896).
7. Liggett, *Rise of Herbert Hoover*, pp. 49–50; George H. Nash, *The Life of Herbert Hoover: The Engineer, 1874–1914* (New York: Norton, 1983), p. 49; Ron Limbaugh, "Pragmatic Professional: Herbert Hoover's Formative Years as a Mining Engineer, 1895–1908," *Mining History Journal* 11 (2004): 43–58; Julie Sweetkind-Singer, "Herbert Hoover: A Geologist in Training," *Journal of Map & Geography Libraries* 6 (2010): 129–39.
8. Herbert Hoover, "Information for Biographers," Subject Files, Pre-Commerce Papers, HHPL; Nash, *Engineer*, p. 50; Herbert Hoover to Lester Hinsdale, April 14, 1897, September 11, 1897, Correspondence, Pre-Commerce Papers, HHPL.
9. Lane, *Making of Herbert Hoover*, p. 201; Herbert Hoover to Lester Hinsdale, April 14, 1897.
10. "Hoover in the Nineties: An Interview with Caspar W. Hodgson," *Woman Republican*, July 1928.
11. Burner, *Herbert Hoover*, p. 26.

12. Herbert Hoover to Theodore Hoover, April 16, 1897, Theodore Hoover Papers, HHPL.

13. Ibid., April 24, 1897.

14. Ibid.

15. Ibid.

16. Herbert Hoover to Theodore and May Hoover, undated, Theodore Hoover Papers, HHPL; Herbert Hoover to Lester Hinsdale, September 11, 1897, Correspondence, Pre-Commerce Papers, HHPL.

17. Liggett, *Rise of Herbert Hoover*, p. 58.

18. Nash, *Engineer*, pp. 68–69, 291.

19. J. W. Kirwan, "Hoover in Western Australia," Subject Files, Pre-Commerce Papers, HHPL; Nash, *Engineer*, p. 67.

20. Herbert Hoover to Lester Hinsdale, September 11, 1897, Lester J. Hinsdale Papers, HHPL.

21. Hoover to Theodore and May Hoover, undated, Correspondence, Theodore Hoover Papers, HHPL.

22. Herbert Hoover to Lester Hinsdale, November 22, 1897, Lester J. Hinsdale Papers, HHPL.

23. Herbert Hoover to Theodore Hoover, August 1897 (undated), September 27, 1897, Theodore Hoover Papers, HHPL.

24. See photograph, Herbert Hoover 1898, Kalgoorie, Scrapbooks, HHPL.

25. Herbert Hoover to Theodore Hoover, August 1897, Theodore Hoover Papers, HHPL.

26. Ibid., February 15, 1898.

27. Ibid.

28. Ibid.; George Wilson to Lester Hinsdale, October 8, 1898, Correspondence, Pre-Commerce Papers, HHPL.

29. Herbert Hoover to Theodore Hoover, Coolgardie, 1898, Theodore Hoover Papers, HHPL.

30. Herbert Hoover to Theodore Hoover, undated, Theodore Hoover Papers, HHPL.

31. Herbert Hoover to Lester Hinsdale, December 13, 1897, March 23, 1898, Lester J. Hinsdale Papers, HHPL.

32. Herbert Hoover to Theodore Hoover, August 1897, Theodore Hoover Papers, HHPL.

33. Herbert Hoover to Theodore Hoover, September 27, 1897, HHPL.

34. Ibid.; Herbert Hoover to Theodore Hoover, February 15, 1898, HHPL.

35. Herbert Hoover to Theodore Hoover, September 27, 1897, HHPL.

36. Ibid.

37. Herbert Hoover to Theodore Hoover, June 6, 1897, February 15, 1898, HHPL.

38. Herbert Hoover to Theodore Hoover, August 1897, HHPL.

39. Herbert Hoover to Theodore Hoover, June 1897, and undated, HHPL.

40. Theodore Hoover, "Statement of an Engineer," Theodore J. Hoover Papers, HHPL.

41. George Wilson to Lester Hinsdale, April 10, 1898, August 6, 1898, October 8, 1898.

42. Statement of W. J. Loring, Walter William Liggett Papers, New York Public Library.

43. Ibid.

CHAPTER 4   THE ADVENTURES OF HU-HUA AND HOO LOO

1. Scrapbooks, HHPL.

2. Nancy Beck Young, *Lou Henry Hoover: Activist First Lady* (Lawrence: University of Kansas Press, 2004), pp. 8–9.

3. Ibid., p. 11.

4. Ibid.

5. Hal Elliott Wert, *Hoover, The Fishing President: Portrait of the Private Man and His Life Outdoors* (Mechanicsburg, PA: Stackpole Books, 2005), p. 54.

6. Dale C. Mayer, *Lou Henry Hoover: A Prototype for First Ladies* (New York: Nova History Publications, 2004), p. 46.

7. Herbert Hoover to Harriette Miles, January 5, 1899, Mining-Australia, Pre-Commerce Papers, HHPL; Herbert Hoover to Theodore Hoover, November 2, 1898, Theodore Hoover Papers, HHPL.

8. Herbert Hoover to Nell May Hill, July 9, 1895, Pre-Commerce Correspondence, HHPL.

9. Mrs. Henry to Mrs. Mason, March 12, 1898, Lou Henry Hoover, Biographical, Allan Hoover Papers, HHPL.

10. Diana Preston, *The Boxer Rebellion* (New York: Berkley Publishing, 1999), p. 15.

11. Herbert Hoover to Theodore Hoover, November 2, 1899, Theodore Hoover Papers, HHPL.

12. Lou Henry Hoover, Diaries, Subject Files, Lou Henry Hoover Papers, HHPL.

13. George Wilson to Lester Hinsdale, March 19, 1899, Correspondence, Pre-Commerce Papers, HHPL.

14. Nash, *Engineer*, p. 104.

15. Lou Henry Hoover to Ray Lyman Wilbur, May 23, 1899, Correspondence, Pre-Commerce Papers, HHPL.

16. Herbert Hoover to Theodore Hoover, undated, 1899, Theodore Hoover Papers, HHPL.

17. Herbert Hoover, "The Kaiping Coal Mines and Coal Field, Chihle Province, North China," *Transactions of the Institution of Mining and Metallurgy* 10 (1901–2): 419–43.

18. George Wilson to Lester Hinsdale, September 8, 1899, Correspondence, Pre-Commerce Papers, HHPL.

19. *Milwaukee Journal*, October 9, 1914, p. 14; Scrapbooks, HHPL.

20. Herbert Hoover to Theodore Hoover, August 21, 1899, Theodore Hoover Papers, HHPL; Young, *Lou Henry Hoover*, p. 14.

21. Lou Henry Hoover to Mrs. Henry, July 13, 1899, Personal Correspondence, Lou Henry Hoover Papers, HHPL.

22. Stephen C. Thomas, *Foreign Intervention and China's Industrial Development, 1870–1911* (Boulder, CO: Westview Press, 1984), p. 91; Walter W. Liggett, *The Rise of Herbert Hoover* (New York: H. K. Fry), p. 75.

23. Herbert Hoover to R. A. F. Penrose, July 9, 1899, Hoover Institution.

24. Will Irwin, *Herbert Hoover: A Reminiscent Biography* (New York: Century, 1928), p. 88.

25. Ian Phimister, "Foreign Devils, Finance and Informal Empire: Britain and China c. 1900–1912," *Modern Asian Studies* 40, no. 3 (2006): 737–59.

26. Diana Preston, *The Boxer Rebellion* (New York: Berkley Publishing, 1999), pp. 75–76.

27. George Wilson to Lester Hinsdale, December 2, 1900, Correspondence, Pre-Commerce Papers, HHPL.

28. *Evening News* (San Jose), July 6, 1900.

29. Elssworth Carlson, *The Kaiping Mines* (Cambridge: Harvard University Press, 1971), p. 55ff.

30. Nash, *Engineer,* p. 129.

31. Frederick Palmer, "Mrs. Hoover Knows," *Ladies' Home Journal,* March 1929; Rosemary Carroll, "Lou Henry Hoover: The Emergence of a Leader, 1874–1916," in Dale C. Mayer, ed., *Lou Henry Hoover: Essays on a Busy Life* (Worland, WY: High Plains Publishing, 1994), p. 20.

32. Herbert Hoover, *Years of Adventure,* p. 53.

33. Nash, *Engineer,* p. 134; Burner, *Herbert Hoover,* p. 137.

34. Nash, *Engineer,* pp. 136–38.

35. *New York Times,* November 19, 1900.

36. Nash, *Engineer,* p. 152.

37. Ibid., p. 153.

38. Carlson, *Kaiping Mines,* p. 76; Liggett, *Rise of Herbert Hoover,* pp. 94–95; Nash, *Engineer,* p. 166.

39. William E. Leuchtenburg, *Herbert Hoover* (New York: Times Books, 2009), pp. 14–15.

40. Herbert Hoover to Theodore Hoover, April 10, 1901, Theodore Hoover Papers, HHPL.

41. Ibid., July 15, 1901.

42. *San Francisco Chronicle,* October 24, 1901.

43. Herbert Hoover to Theodore Hoover, April 10, 1901, Theodore Hoover Papers, HHPL.

CHAPTER 5    "THE LATE JAR RATHER SMASHED MY NERVES"

1. George H. Nash, *The Life of Herbert Hoover: The Engineer, 1874–1914* (New York: Norton, 1983), p. 48.

2. Will Irwin, *Herbert Hoover: A Reminiscent Biography* (New York: Century, 1928), p. 109.

3. Lou Henry Hoover to Family, undated, LHH Personal Correspondence, Henry Family Correspondence, HHPL.

4. Herbert Hoover, *The Memoirs of Herbert Hoover: Years of Adventure* (New York: Macmillan, 1952), p. 76.

5. Ibid., pp. 83–85.

6. A. S. Rowe to Herbert Hoover, December 28, 1902, Rowe Defalcation Correspondence, Subject Files, Pre-Commerce Papers, HHPL.

7. Ibid.; Nash, *Engineer*, pp. 245–51.

8. Hoover, *Years of Adventure*, pp. 83–85.

9. Ibid., p. 84; Hoover and Mr. Wellsted to Moreing, December 31, 1902, Rowe Defalcation Correspondence, Subject Files, Pre-Commerce Papers, HHPL.

10. Hoover to Moreing, December 30, 1902, Rowe Defalcation Correspondence, Subject Files, Pre-Commerce Papers, HHPL; Nash, *Engineer*, pp. 245–51.

11. Nash, *Engineer*, p. 257; Jean Henry to Mr. and Mrs. Henry, February 1, 1903, Lou Henry Hoover, Personal Correspondence, Henry Family Correspondence, Lou Henry Hoover Papers, HHPL.

12. Hoover to Theodore Hoover, undated, Correspondence, Theodore Hoover Papers, HHPL.

13. Nash, *Engineer*, pp. 263–71.

14. Ellsworth Carlson, *The Kaiping Mines* (Cambridge: Harvard University Press, 1971), p. 84ff; Nash, *Engineer*, p. 202.

15. Nash, *Engineer*, p. 198; Liggett, *Rise of Herbert Hoover*, p. 98.

16. Herbert Hoover to Theodore Hoover, July 15, 1903, Pre-Commerce Correspondence, HHPL.

17. Ibid.

18. Lou Henry Hoover to Mr. Henry, undated, and Lou Henry Hoover to Mrs. Henry, May 6, 1903, Personal Correspondence, Lou Henry Hoover Papers, HHPL.

19. Lou Henry Hoover to Mr. and Mrs. Henry, June 7, 1903, HHPL.

20. Liggett, *Rise of Herbert Hoover*, p. 129.

21. *Daily Mail*, November 8, 1903; Miss F. Rowe to Hoover, July 2, 1909, Rowe Defalcation Correspondence, Subject Files, Pre-Commerce Papers, HHPL.

22. Herbert Hoover to A. S. Rowe, May 18, 1911, Rowe Defalcation Correspondence, Subject Files, Pre-Commerce Papers, HHPL.

23. Hoover, *Years of Adventure*, p. 75; Herbert Hoover, "Thank You Miss Gray," *Reader's Digest*, July 1959, pp. 118–20.

24. Nash, *Engineer*, p. 283.

25. T. A. Rickard, Walter Benton Ingalls, Herbert Hoover, and R. Gilman Brown, *The Economics of Mining* (New York: Engineering and Mining Journal, 1905), pp. 191, 192; Nash, *Engineer*, p. 288.

26. Richard Hartley, "Bewick, Moreing in Western Australian Gold Mining, 1897–1904," *Labour History* 65 (November 1993): 11–12.
27. Herbert Hoover to Theodore Hoover, July 21, 1904, Hoover Scrapbooks, Album 42, HHPL.
28. Ibid.
29. George W. Nash, *The Life of Herbert Hoover: The Humanitarian 1914–1917* (New York: Norton, 1988), p. 372.
30. Hartley, "Bewick, Moreing," pp. 8–12.
31. James J. O'Brien, *Hoover's Millions and How He Made Them* (New York: James J. O'Brien Publishing, 1932), plate 10.
32. *The Times*, January 8, 1905; Hoover, *Years of Adventure*, p. 90; Nash, *Engineer*, p. 205.
33. Carlson, *Kaiping Mines*, p. 104.
34. *Pall Mall Gazette*, February 2, 1903.
35. E. J. Nathan papers, Bodleian Library, MS. Eng. hist.c. 454; Liggett, *Rise of Herbert Hoover*, pp. 95, 121.
36. Ibid., p. 121.
37. *Dixon Evening Telegraph*, October 25, 1928.
38. Herbert Hoover, "Information for Biographers," Subject Files, Pre-Commerce Papers, HHPL.
39. Burner, *Herbert Hoover*, p. 52.
40. Bewick Moreing Papers, 1910–1942, 1910 Lawsuit file, HHPL.
41. Nash, *Engineer*, p. 185.

CHAPTER 6    WHAT LIES BEYOND WEALTH

1. Herbert Hoover, *The Memoirs of Herbert Hoover: Years of Adventure, 1874–1920* (New York: Macmillan, 1952), p. 124.
2. George H. Nash, *The Life of Herbert Hoover: The Engineer, 1874–1914* (New York: Norton, 1983), p. 500.
3. Mary Austin, *Earth Horizon* (Santa Fe, NM: Sunstone Press, 2007), p. 312.
4. George H. Nash, *The Life of Herbert Hoover: Humanitarian* (New York: Norton, 1988), pp. 369, 371.
5. J. W. Kirwan, "Hoover in Western Australia," Subject Files, Pre-Commerce Papers, Mining, HHPL.
6. Statement by Mary Austin, Walter William Liggett Papers, New York Public Library; "Tell Me What's She Really Like," anonymous, Lou Henry Biographical Data file, Subject Files, Lou Henry Hoover Papers, HHPL.
7. Statement by Anne Martin, Walter William Liggett Papers, New York Public Library.
8. Jackson Reynolds Oral History, HHPL.
9. Theodore J. Hoover, "Statement of an Engineer," Theodore J. Hoover Papers, HHPL.

10. Hal Elliott Wert, *Hoover, The Fishing President: Portrait of the Private Man and His Life Outdoors* (Mechanicsburg, PA: Stackpole Books, 2005), p. 83.

11. Austin, *Earth Horizon*, p. 312; Nash, *Engineer*, p. 497.

12. Hoover, *Years of Adventure*, p. 123.

13. *New York Sun*, November 9, 1928.

14. Rosemary Carroll, "Lou Henry Hoover: The Emergence of a Leader, 1874–1916," in *Lou Henry Hoover: Essays on a Busy Life*, edited by Dale C. Mayer (Worland, WY: High Plains Publishing, 1994), pp. 26–28; "Tell Me What's She Really Like," anonymous, Lou Henry Biographical Data file, Subject Files, Lou Henry Hoover Papers, HHPL.

15. Hoover, *Years of Adventure*, p. 121.

16. Mary Austin to Lou Hoover, December 3, 1911, January 28, 1912, Personal Correspondence, Lou Henry Hoover Papers, HHPL; Austin, *Earth Horizon*, p. 312.

17. Herbert Hoover to Mary Austin, undated, Pre-Commerce Correspondence, HHPL.

18. Ibid.; Mary Austin to Lou Henry Hoover, October 3, 1910, Personal Correspondence, Lou Henry Hoover Papers, HHPL; Mary Austin to Herbert Hoover, April 26, 1912, Subject Files: Mining Correspondence, Pre-Commerce Papers, HHPL.

19. Austin, *Earth Horizon*, p. 323.

20. Mary Austin Statement, Liggett Papers, New York Public Library; Mary Austin, *A Woman of Genius* (Garden City, NY: Doubleday, 1912).

21. Theodore Hoover, "Statement of an Engineer," p. 123.

22. Hoover, *Years of Adventure*, p. 100; Walter W. Liggett, *The Rise of Herbert Hoover* (New York: H. K. Fry, 1932), p. 172.

23. Liggett, *Hoover*, pp. 153–54.

24. Ibid., pp. 169, 195.

25. Ibid., p. 172.

26. Ibid., p. 169.

27. Herbert Hoover to Theodore Hoover, August 30, 1909, Correspondence, Theodore Hoover Papers, HHPL; Herbert Hoover, "Economics of a Boom," *Mining Magazine*, May 1912; Nash, *Engineer*, pp. 388–90; Burner, *Herbert Hoover*, pp. 65–66.

28. Hoover, *Years of Adventure*, p. 88; Geoffrey Blainey, *The Rush That Never Ended* (Carlton: Melbourne University Press, 1993), p. 254ff.; Nash, *Engineer*, pp. 353–70.

29. Hoover, *Years of Adventure*, pp. 90–96, 101; Hoover, "Statement of an Engineer"; Eugene Lyons, *Hoover: A Biography* (Garden City, NY: Doubleday, 1964), p. 66; Wert, *Fishing President*, p. 85; Nash, *Engineer*, pp. 414–25.

30. Nash, *Engineer*, pp. 421–25.

31. Blainey, *Rush That Never Ended*, p. 69.

32. Bewick Moreing Papers, 1910–1942, 1910 Lawsuit file, HHPL; Burner, *Herbert Hoover*, p. 53; Nash, *Engineer*, pp. 446, 568–69.

33. Herbert Hoover, *The Principles of Mining* (New York: Hill Publishing, 1909), p. 168.
34. Ibid., pp. 185–86.
35. William E. Leuchtenburg, *Herbert Hoover* (New York: Times Books, 2009), p. 19.
36. Herbert Hoover to Mary Austin, undated, Correspondence, Pre-Commerce Papers, HHPL; Hoover, *Principles of Mining*, p. 193.
37. Nash, *Humanitarian*, p. 300; Leuchtenburg, *Herbert Hoover*, p. 19.
38. Hoover, "Statement of an Engineer"; Georgius Agricola, *De Re Metallica*, ed. Herbert Hoover and Lou Henry Hoover (New York: Dover, 1912).
39. Hoover, *Years of Adventure*, p. 117; Nash, *Engineer*, pp. 490–93; *American Historical Review* 19, no. 3 (April 1914): 598.
40. Hoover, *Years of Adventure*, p. 134; Burner, *Herbert Hoover*, pp. 67–68.
41. Herbert Hoover, "Information for Biographers," Subject Files, Pre-Commerce Papers, HHPL; Nash, *Engineer*, p. 384; Austin, *Earth Horizon*, p. 323.
42. Burner, *Herbert Hoover*, p. 46; Ron Limbaugh, "Pragmatic Professional: Herbert Hoover's Formative Years as a Mining Engineer, 1895–1908," *Mining History Journal* 11 (2004): 50.
43. Leuchtenburg, *Herbert Hoover*, p. 21.
44. Will Irwin, *The Making of a Reporter* (New York: G. P. Putnam's Sons, 1942), pp. 182–83.
45. Henry F. Pringle, *The Life & Times of William Howard Taft* (Newton, MA: American Political Biography Press, 1998), p. 614.
46. "When 'Bertie' Hoover Came West," Ellis Lucia, clipping in Oregon Collections, HHPL; Nash, *Engineer*, p. 521.
47. Gabriel Abend, *The Moral Background: An Inquiry into the History of Business Ethics* (Princeton, NJ: Princeton University Press, 2014), p. 109.
48. Hoover, "Statement of an Engineer," p. 267.
49. Nash, *Engineer*, p. 521.
50. Memorandum, January 2, 1913, Stanford Academic and Financial Positions, Subject Files, Pre-Commerce Papers, HHPL.
51. Nash, *Engineer*, pp. 527–40.
52. Sir Edward Grey to Herbert Hoover, June 9, 1914, Mining Correspondence, Subject Files, Pre-Commerce Papers, HHPL; Craig Lloyd, *Aggressive Introvert: A Study of Herbert Hoover and Public Relations Management, 1912–1932* (Columbus: Ohio State University Press, 1972), p. 27; Nash, *Engineer*, p. 549.

CHAPTER 7   "HARD TO STATE WITHOUT BECOMING HYSTERICAL"

1. Herbert Hoover, *The Memoirs of Herbert Hoover: Years of Adventure* (New York: Macmillan, 1952), p. 137; see also George H. Nash, *The Life of Herbert Hoover: The Humanitarian 1914–1917* (New York: Norton, 1988), the most comprehensive work on Hoover's activities during the Great War.
2. Hoover, *Years of Adventure*, p. 138.

3. Herbert Hoover to J. A. Agnew, July 16, 1914, Correspondence, Pre-Commerce Papers, HHPL.

4. Hoover, *Years of Adventure*, p. 139.

5. Ibid., p. 140.

6. George H. Nash, *The Life of Herbert Hoover: The Engineer, 1874–1914* (New York: Norton, 1983), p. 575.

7. Herbert Hoover to R. L. Wilbur, August 4, 1914, Correspondence, Pre-Commerce Papers, HHPL; Nash, *Engineer*, p. 576.

8. Herbert Hoover to Ambassador Walter Hines Page, September 23, 1914, Correspondence, Pre-Commerce Papers, HHPL, contains a thorough report on the activities of the Citizens' Committee.

9. Hoover, *Years of Adventure*, p. 141.

10. Nash, *Humanitarian*, p. 9.

11. Ibid., p. 10.

12. Ibid., p. 11.

13. Ibid.

14. Ibid., p. 12.

15. Nash, *Humanitarian*, pp. 13, 59.

16. Martin Gilbert, *The First World War: A Complete History* (New York: Henry Holt, 1994); Hew Strachan, *The First World War*, vol. 1, *To Arms* (Oxford: Oxford University Press, 2003); John Keegan, *The First World War* (Toronto: Key Porter Books, 1998).

17. Brand Whitlock, *Belgium: A Personal Narrative*, vol. 1 (New York: D. Appleton, 1919), p. 53; Keegan, *First World War*, p. 80.

18. Keegan, *First World War*, pp. 132–37; Alan Kramer, *Dynamic of Destruction* (Oxford: Oxford University Press, 2007), p. 34.

19. Herbert Hoover to A. H. Ackerman, October 7, 1914, Mining Correspondence, Subject Files, Pre-Commerce Papers, HHPL; Hoover, *Years of Adventure*, p. 145; Nash, *Humanitarian*, p. 16.

20. Nash, *Humanitarian*, p. 15.

21. Hoover, *Years of Adventure*, p. 143.

22. Ibid.

23. Whitlock, *Belgium*, p. 3.

24. Keegan, *First World War*, pp. 82–83; Kramer, *Dynamic of Destruction*, p. 22.

25. Whitlock, *Belgium*, pp. 119–25.

26. Nash, *Humanitarian*, p. 17.

27. Whitlock, *Belgium*, p. 239.

28. Nash, *Humanitarian*, p. 19.

29. Ibid., pp. 20, 22; George I. Gay, *Public Relations of the Commission for Relief in Belgium*, vol. 1 (Palo Alto, CA: Stanford University Press, 1929), p. 10.

30. Whitlock, *Belgium*, p. 346.

31. Brand Whitlock, *The Letters and Journal of Brand Whitlock: The Journal*, ed. Allan Nevins (New York: D. Appleton-Century, 1936), p. 77; Kramer, *Dynamic of Destruction*, p. 42; Whitlock, *Belgium*, p. 546.

32. Brand Whitlock, *The Letters and Journal of Brand Whitlock: The Letters*, ed. Allan Nevins (New York: D. Appleton-Century, 1936), p. 181.

33. Gay, *Public Relations*, p. 13; Nash, *Humanitarian*, pp. 26, 34.

34. Merle Curti, *American Philanthropy Abroad* (New Brunswick, NJ: Transaction Books, 1988).

35. Whitlock, *Belgium*, p. 537.

36. Nash, *Humanitarian*, p. 33.

37. Ibid., pp. 37, 38; *Boston Daily Globe*, February 28, 1915.

38. Herbert Hoover to Lou Henry Hoover, October 26, 1914, Correspondence, Pre-Commerce Papers, HHPL.

39. Ibid.

40. Herbert Hoover to Lou Henry Hoover, November 6, 1914, and Lou Henry Hoover to Herbert Hoover, undated, Personal Correspondence, Lou Henry Hoover Papers, HHPL.

41. Lou Henry Hoover to Herbert Hoover, undated, Personal Correspondence, Lou Henry Hoover Papers, HHPL.

42. Whitlock, *Belgium*, p. 344.

43. Nash, *Humanitarian*, pp. 44–48.

44. Ibid., pp. 35, 41.

45. Ibid., p. 28.

46. Ibid., p. 18; Hoover, *Years of Adventure*, p. 159.

47. Whitlock, *Belgium*, p. 398.

48. Ibid., p. 400; Whitlock, *Journal*, pp. 69–70.

49. Whitlock, *Belgium*, pp. 403–4.

50. George H. Nash, *The Life of Herbert Hoover: Master of Emergencies, 1917–1918* (New York: Norton, 1996), p. 23.

51. Nash, *Humanitarian*, pp. 70, 253.

CHAPTER 8    A PIRATE STATE ORGANIZED FOR BENEVOLENCE

1. George W. Nash, *The Life of Herbert Hoover: The Humanitarian 1914–1917* (New York: Norton, 1988), p. 69.

2. Ibid.

3. Brand Whitlock, *The Letters and Journal of Brand Whitlock: The Journal*, ed. Allan Nevins (New York: D. Appleton-Century, 1936), p. 78.

4. Ibid.

5. Nash, *Humanitarian*, p. 83.

6. Lou Henry Hoover to Jackson Reynolds, November 24, 1914, Personal Correspondence, Lou Henry Hoover Papers, HHPL.

7. Ibid.

8. Ibid.

9. Lou Henry Hoover to Herbert Hoover Jr., November 25, 1914, Personal Correspondence, Lou Henry Hoover Papers, HHPL.

10. Lou Henry Hoover to Allan Hoover, November 24, 1914, Personal Correspondence, Lou Henry Hoover Papers, HHPL.

11. Allan Hoover to Lou Henry Hoover, undated, 1914, HHPL.

12. George I. Gay, *Public Relations of the Commission for Relief in Belgium*, vol. 1 (Palo Alto, CA: Stanford University Press, 1929), p. 44; Whitlock, *Journal*, p. 81.

13. Gay, *Public Relations*, pp. 232–35.

14. Ibid.

15. Ibid., pp. 231–32.

16. Ibid., pp. 236–37.

17. Hoover, *Years of Adventure*, p. 165.

18. Gay, *Public Relations*, pp. 252–55; Isabel V. Hull, *A Scrap of Paper: Breaking and Making International Law during the Great War* (Ithaca, NY: Cornell University Press, 2014), p. 16; Nash, *Humanitarian*, p. 87.

19. Hoover, *Years of Adventure*, p. 166.

20. Nash, *Humanitarian*, pp. 285–86.

21. Hoover, *Years of Adventure*, p. 193.

22. Herbert Hoover, *An American Epic: Introduction, The Relief of Belgium and Northern France, 1914–1930*, vol. 1 (Chicago: Regnery, 1959), p. 132.

23. Tracy Barrett Kittredge, *The History of the Commission for Relief in Belgium, 1914–1917* (LaVergne, TN: General Books, 2010), p. 136; Gay, *Public Relations*, p. 262; Nash, *Humanitarian*, p. 88.

24. Gay, *Public Relations*, pp. 263–64; Nash, *Humanitarian*, p. 88.

25. Gay, *Public Relations*, p. 266.

26. Gay, pp. 258, 260; Nash, *Humanitarian*, p. 90.

27. Nash, *Humanitarian*, p. 93.

28. Ibid., pp. 94, 303.

29. Herbert Hoover to Lou Henry Hoover, October 2, 1915, Correspondence, Pre-Commerce Papers, HHPL; Statement by Lou Henry Hoover, October 3, 1915, Correspondence, Pre-Commerce Papers, HHPL; Nash, *Humanitarian*, p. 39.

30. Nash, *Humanitarian*, p. 59.

31. Brand Whitlock, *Belgium: A Personal Narrative*, vol. 1 (New York: D. Appleton, 1919), p. 393.

32. Ibid., p. 563.

33. Alan Kramer, *Dynamic of Destruction* (Oxford: Oxford University Press, 2007), p. 44.

34. Whitlock, *Journal*, p. 246; Gay, *Public Relations*, pp. 128, 134.

35. Nash, *Humanitarian*, p. 176.

36. Ibid., pp. 91, 242–49.

37. Ibid., p. 240.

38. Ibid., pp. 247–49.

39. Ibid., p. 140.

40. Herbert Hoover to Lou Henry Hoover, October 14, 1915, Correspondence, Pre-Commerce Papers, HHPL.

41. Lou Henry Hoover to Miss Anderson, November 26, 1915, Correspondence, Lou Henry Hoover Papers, HHPL.

42. Nash, *Humanitarian*, p. 150.

43. Arthur S. Link (ed.), *The Papers of Woodrow Wilson*, vol. 31 (Princeton, NJ: Princeton University Press, 1979), p. 331.

44. John Milton Cooper Jr., *Woodrow Wilson: A Biography* (New York: Knopf, 2009), pp. 266, 299.

45. David Pietrusza, *1920: The Year of the Six Presidents* (New York: Basic Books, 2008), p. 61; *New York Times*, April 8, 1912; Cooper, *Woodrow Wilson*, p. 162.

46. Cooper, *Wilson*, p. 268; Arthur S. Link (ed.), *The Papers of Woodrow Wilson*, vol. 35 (Princeton, NJ: Princeton University Press, 1980), pp. 164–65.

47. Lou Henry Hoover to Allan Hoover and Herbert Hoover Jr., undated, July 1932, Correspondence, Allan Hoover Papers, HHPL.

48. *World's Work*, April 1920.

49. Burton Hendrick, *The Life and Letters of Walter H. Page, 1885–1918* (Garden City, Garden City Publishing, 1926), p. 216.

50. Walter Hines Page to Woodrow Wilson, January 12, 1915, Hendrick, *Walter H. Page*, p. 215.

51. Nash, *Humanitarian*, p. 121.

52. Craig Lloyd, *Aggressive Introvert: A Study of Herbert Hoover and Public Relations Management, 1912–1932* (Columbus: Ohio State University Press, 1972), p. 27.

53. *Bulletin of the American Institute of Mining and Metallurgical Engineers*, no. 154, October 1919.

54. Kittredge, *Commission for Relief in Belgium*, p. 16.

55. Nash, *Humanitarian*, p. 362; Hoover, *American Epic*, pp. 165, 416.

56. Kramer, *Dynamic of Destruction*, pp. 58, 154.

57. *New York Times*, January 31, 1917.

CHAPTER 9     MAKE WAY FOR THE ALMONER OF STARVING BELGIUM

1. George W. Nash, *The Life of Herbert Hoover: The Humanitarian 1914–1917* (New York: Norton, 1988), p. 278.

2. John Milton Cooper Jr., *Woodrow Wilson: A Biography* (New York: Vintage Books, 2011), p. 143.

3. Joan Hoff Wilson, *Herbert Hoover: Forgotten Progressive* (Long Grove, IL: Waveland Press, 1992), p. 282.

4. John Milton Cooper Jr., *Woodrow Wilson: A Biography* (New York: Knopf, 2009), p. 400; Stuart Joseph Woolf (ed.), *Nationalism in Europe: 1815 to the Present* (London: Routledge, 1996), p. 109.

5. Erik Larson, *Dead Wake: The Last Crossing of the Lusitania* (New York: Crown, 2015), p. 300; Nash, *Humanitarian*, p. 291; Francis William O'Brien, *The Hoover-Wilson Wartime Correspondence* (Ames: Iowa State University Press, 1974), p. 7.

6. O'Brien, *Hoover-Wilson Wartime Correspondence*, pp. 11–12.

7. Eugene Lyons, *Herbert Hoover: A Biography* (Garden City, NY: Doubleday, 1964), p. 21.

8. "Not Hoover, He's Too Busy," *Harper's Weekly*, April 3, 1916.

9. Cooper, *Woodrow Wilson*, p. 342; Hugh Gibson to Lou Henry Hoover, March 21, 1917, May 31, 1917, Hugh Gibson Collection, HHPL.

10. *New York Times*, February 1, 1917; *High Point Enterprise* (North Carolina), February 1, 1917; Nash, *Humanitarian*, p. 313.

11. *New York Tribune*, February 1, 1917; *New York Herald*, February 4, 1917.

12. Nash, *Humanitarian*, pp. 293, 345.

13. Herbert Hoover, *The Ordeal of Woodrow Wilson* (Washington, DC: Woodrow Wilson Center Press, 1992), p. 6.

14. *New York Times*, April 2, 1917.

15. David Kennedy, *Over Here: The First World War and American Society* (Oxford: Oxford University Press, 2004), p. 20.

16. O'Brien, *Hoover-Wilson Wartime Correspondence*, p. 20.

17. Nash, *Humanitarian*, p. 350.

18. *New York Times*, April 12, 1917, April 21, 1917.

19. Ibid., April 3, 1917.

20. U.S. Food Administration, *Bulletin No. 2* (Washington, DC: U.S. Government Printing Office, 1917).

21. Woodrow Wilson, Second Inaugural Address, March 5, 1917.

22. Lou Henry Hoover to Herbert Hoover, April 28, 1917, Correspondence, Pre-Commerce Papers, HHPL.

23. *New York Times*, May 3, 1917; *New York Tribune*, May 3, 1917.

24. George H. Nash, *The Life of Herbert Hoover: Master of Emergencies, 1917–1918* (New York; Norton, 1996), pp. 72–73.

25. Ibid., p. 15; *New York Times*, May 14, 1917; *Lincoln County News*, May 7, 1917.

26. *New York Times*, May 4, 1917; *New York Herald*, May 4, 1917.

27. Edward House Diaries, vol. 5, May 3, 1917, Edward Mandell House Papers, Series 2, Yale University Library.

28. Ibid.

29. Ibid.

30. E. M. House to Woodrow Wilson, May 4, 1917, as quoted in Charles Seymour (ed.), *The Intimate Papers of Colonel House: Into the World War* (Boston: Houghton Mifflin, 1928), p. 17.

31. Ibid., pp. 16–17.

32. *New York Times*, May 10, 1917; *Indianapolis News*, May 11, 1917.

33. Nash, *Master of Emergencies*, pp. 17, 409.

34. Herbert Hoover to Lou Henry Hoover, May 11, 1917, Correspondence, Pre-Commerce Papers, HHPL.

35. Lou Henry Hoover to Herbert Hoover, May 14, 1917, HHPL.

36. Herbert Hoover to Lou Henry Hoover, May 15, 1917, HHPL.

37. *New York Times*, May 17, 1917.

CHAPTER 10    A HERO IN THE HOUSE OF TRUTH

1. *Time*, October 24, 1927; George H. Nash, *The Life of Herbert Hoover: Master of Emergencies, 1917–1918* (New York: Norton, 1996), p. 59.

2. *St. Louis Post-Dispatch*, June 19, 1917.

3. Nash, *Master of Emergencies*, pp. 49, 55.

4. Ibid., pp. 39, 59.

5. Herbert Hoover, *The Memoirs of Herbert Hoover: Years of Adventure, 1874–1920* (New York: Macmillan, 1952), p. 261.

6. Nash, *Master of Emergencies*, pp. 30–31; Lewis Strauss Oral History, HHPL.

7. *New York Times*, July 1, 1917, August 18, 1917; Donald W. Whisenhunt, *President Herbert Hoover* (New York: Nova Science Publishers, 2007), p. 40; William E. Leuchtenburg, *Herbert Hoover* (New York: Times Books, 2009), p. 34; Nash, *Master of Emergencies*, p. 229.

8. Leuchtenburg, *Herbert Hoover*, p. 35; Jennifer Keene and Michael Neiberg, *Finding Common Ground: New Directions in First World War Studies* (Leiden, the Netherlands: Brill, 2007), p. 156; Hannah Marshall, "Voluntary Food Conservation: The United States Home Front in WWI," senior seminar paper, WOU, 2010. www.wou.edu/history/files/2015/08/Hannah-Marshall1.pdf. Western Oregon University.

9. Nash, *Master of Emergencies*, p. 66.

10. Ibid., pp. 39–40, 59–63; *New York Times*, June 22, 1917, July 11, 1917, July 20, 1917; *Washington Times*, August 15, 1917.

11. Nash, *Master of Emergencies*, pp. 44, 61.

12. Ibid., pp. 58, 59.

13. *Pittsburgh Press*, July 16, 1917.

14. Nash, *Master of Emergencies*, pp. 63–64.

15. John Milton Cooper Jr., *Woodrow Wilson: A Biography* (New York: Knopf, 2009), pp. 204, 332, 383.

16. Francis William O'Brien, *The Hoover-Wilson Wartime Correspondence* (Ames: Iowa State University Press, 1974), p. 53.

17. Nash, *Master of Emergencies*, p. 74; *New York Times*, August 9, 1917.

18. Nash, *Master of Emergencies*, p. 74.

19. Ibid., p. 72.

20. Ibid., pp. 79–92, 95, 101.

21. Ibid., p. 110.

22. Francis William O'Brien, *Two Peacemakers in Paris* (College Station: Texas A&M University Press, 1978), p. xlii.

23. Mark Requa Diary, Mark Requa Collection, Hoover Institution.

24. Nash, *Master of Emergencies*, p. 137.

25. Josephus Daniels, *The Cabinet Diaries of Josephus Daniels: 1913–1921*, ed. David E. Cronon (Lincoln: University of Nebraska Press, 1963), pp. 267, 276, 281, 282; David Kennedy, *Over Here: The First World War and American Society*

(Oxford: Oxford University Press, 2004), p. 99; Nash, *Master of Emergencies*, pp. 213–24.

26. Nash, *Master of Emergencies*, p. 223.

27. Ibid., p. 224.

28. "Report on R," April 20, 1918, Senator James A. Reed file, Pre-Commerce Papers, HHPL.

29. House Diaries, vol. 6, February 10, 1918.

30. Ibid., December 30, 1917.

31. *Indianapolis News*, March 1, 1920.

32. Hugh Gibson to his mother, February 24, 1916, Hugh Gibson Collection, HHPL.

33. Ibid., November 25, 1917, December 10, 1917, HHPL.

34. Ibid., September 30, 1917, HHPL.

35. Ibid., December 10, 1917, HHPL.

36. Clay Risen, "The House of Truth," *Morning News*, July 19, 2006.

37. Nash, *Master of Emergencies*, p. 43; Kennedy, *Over Here*, p. 132.

38. Ronald Steel, *Walter Lippmann and the American Century* (Boston: Atlantic Monthly Press, 1980), p. 121.

39. Ibid., p. 123; *San Bernardino County Sun*, October 24, 1964.

40. Leuchtenburg, *Herbert Hoover*, p. 35; *Fort Wayne Gazette*, May 28, 1918; *Collier's*, October 12, 1918.

41. Nash, *Master of Emergencies*, pp. 431–32.

42. Edgar Rickard to Lou Henry Hoover, undated, 1917, Personal Correspondence, Lou Henry Hoover Papers, HHPL.

43. Alice Dickson to Lou Henry Hoover, May 4, 1917, May 22, 1917, Personal Correspondence, Lou Henry Hoover Papers, HHPL.

44. Alice Dickson to Lou Henry Hoover, August 5, 1917, November 17, 1917, February 2, 1918, HHPL.

45. Hugh Gibson to Lou Henry Hoover, February 25, 1919, Correspondence, Pre-Commerce papers, HHPL.

46. House Diaries, June 17, 1918.

47. Lewis Strauss Diary, July 10–July 28, 1918, Hoover Institution.

48. Ibid.

49. Ibid.; Nash, *Master of Emergencies*, p. 350.

50. Strauss Diary, July 10–July 28, 1918.

51. John A. Agnew to Lou Henry Hoover, August 14, 1918, Correspondence, Lou Henry Hoover Papers, HHPL; R.W. Boyden to K.W. Boyden, August 1918, Pre-Commerce Papers, HHPL; Strauss Diary, July 10–July 28, 1918; Lewis Strauss, *Men and Decisions* (Garden City, NY: Doubleday, 1962), pp. 16–17.

52. Hugh Gibson Diaries, August 4, 1918, Hugh Gibson Collection, HHPL; Nash, *Master of Emergencies*, p. 357.

53. R. W. Boyden to K. W. Boyden, August 1918, Pre-Commerce Papers, HHPL.

54. Ibid.; Nash, *Master of Emergencies*, pp. 462–63.

CHAPTER 11  INCONSOLABLE IN THE HALL OF MIRRORS

1. Witold Sworakowski, "Herbert Hoover, Launching the American Food Administration, 1917," in Lawrence Emerson Gelfand (ed.), *Herbert Hoover: The Great War and Its Aftermath, 1914–1923* (Iowa City: University of Iowa Press, 1979), p. 60, n. 39.

2. George H. Nash, *The Life of Herbert Hoover: Master of Emergencies* (New York: Norton, 1996), p. 460.

3. David Kennedy, *Over Here: The First World War and American Society* (Oxford: Oxford University Press, 2004), p. 262.

4. Gibson Diaries, August 1918, HHPL; Lewis Strauss Diary, August 1918, Hoover Institution; Nash, *Master of Emergencies*, pp. 357–58.

5. Margaret MacMillan, *Paris, 1919* (New York: Random House, 2003), p. 61.

6. John Milton Cooper Jr., *Wilson: A Biography* (New York: Knopf, 2009), p. 417.

7. Gary Dean Best, *The Politics of American Individualism: Herbert Hoover in Transition, 1918–1921* (Westport, CT: Greenwood Press, 1975), p. 16.

8. Herbert Hoover, *The Ordeal of Woodrow Wilson* (Washington, DC: Woodrow Wilson Center Press, 1992), p. 88.

9. Francis William O'Brien, *Two Peacemakers in Paris* (College Station: Texas A&M University Press, 1978), p. xxx.

10. MacMillan, *Paris, 1919*, p. 33; O'Brien, *Two Peacemakers*, p. xxvii.

11. O'Brien, *Two Peacemakers*, pp. xxxv–xxxvi; David Burner, *Herbert Hoover: A Public Life* (Newton, MA: American Political Biography Press, 1978), pp. 116–20; Kendrick A. Clements, *The Life of Herbert Hoover: Imperfect Visionary, 1918–1928* (New York: Palgrave Macmillan, 2010), p. 17.

12. Hugh Gibson to Edgar Rickard, March 20, 1919, Personal Correspondence, Lou Henry Hoover Papers, HHPL.

13. Edgar Rickard to Lou Henry Hoover, February 18, 1919, Personal Correspondence, Lou Henry Hoover Papers, HHPL; "Overseas Trip—Reports," Pre-Commerce Papers, HHPL.

14. O'Brien, *Two Peacemakers*, p. 136.

15. MacMillan, *Paris, 1919*, p. 14; Bernard M. Baruch, *The Public Years* (New York: Rinehart and Winston, 1960), p. 100; Burner, *Herbert Hoover*, pp. 126–29; Lewis Strauss, *Men and Decisions* (Garden City, NY: Doubleday, 1962), pp. 43–46.

16. Thomas J. Fleming, *The Illusion of Victory: America in World War I* (New York: Basic Books, 2003), p. 323.

17. Clements, *Imperfect Visionary*, pp. 10, 24.

18. Robert F. Himmelberg, "Hoover's Public Image, 1919–1920," in Lawrence Emerson Gelfand (ed.), *Herbert Hoover: The Great War and Its Aftermath, 1914–1923* (Iowa City: University of Iowa Press, 1979), p. 208n.

19. Nash, *Master of Emergencies*, p. 266; House Diaries, vol. 7, May 18, 1919, June 21, 1919, House Papers, Yale; Clements, *Imperfect Visionary*, p. 12.

20. Edgar Rickard to Lou Henry Hoover, February 18, 1919, Lou Henry Hoover Papers, HHPL; Julius Barnes to Gertrude, December 17, 1918, Pre-Commerce

Papers, HHPL; Hugh Gibson to Lou Henry Hoover, April 19, 1919, Hugh Gibson Papers, HHPL.

21. Adaline Fuller Oral History, HHPL; Hugh Gibson to Lou Henry Hoover, April 19, 1919, Hugh Gibson Papers, HHPL.

22. Hoover, *Ordeal of Woodrow Wilson*, pp. 72, 234.

23. O'Brien, *Two Peacemakers*, pp. 114–15.

24. Hoover, *Ordeal of Woodrow Wilson*, p. 231; Cooper, *Woodrow Wilson*, p. 500; David Pietrusza, *1920: The Year of the Six Presidents* (New York: Basic Books, 2008), pp. 31–33.

25. O'Brien, *Two Peacemakers*, pp. 112–15.

26. Herbert Hoover, *The Memoirs of Herbert Hoover: Years of Adventure, 1874–1920* (New York: Macmillan, 1952), p. 467.

27. Royal Schmidt, "Hoover's Reflections on the Versailles Treaty," in Lawrence Emerson Gelfand (ed.), *Herbert Hoover: The Great War and Its Aftermath, 1914–1923* (Iowa City: University of Iowa Press, 1979), p. 66.

28. Harry Hansen, June 28, 1919, in Charles Horne (ed.), *Source Records of the Great War*, vol. 7 (Washington, DC: National Alumni, 1923).

29. Ibid.; Schmidt, "Hoover's Reflections," p. 67.

30. House Diaries, vol. 8, August 3, 1919.

31. O'Brien, *Two Peacemakers*, p. 173; Clements, *Imperfect Visionary*, p. 23.

32. O'Brien, *Two Peacemakers*, pp. 221–22.

33. Herbert Hoover to Lewis Strauss, August 7, 1919, Lewis L. Strauss Papers, HHPL.

34. *New York Times*, September 14, 1919, December 13, 1920; John Maynard Keynes, *The Economic Consequences of the Peace* (New Brunswick, NJ: Transaction Publishers, 2009), pp. 273–74.

35. *New York Times*, December 13, 1920.

36. George W. Nash, *The Life of Herbert Hoover: The Humanitarian 1914–1917* (New York: Norton, 1988), p. 95.

CHAPTER 12    AN ENGINEER AT THE OPERA

1. *Bulletin of the American Institute of Mining and Metallurgical Engineers*, no. 154, October 1919.

2. Ibid.; *Boston Globe*, September 18, 1919; *New York Times*, September 18, 1919; *New York Sun*, September 17, 1919.

3. *Indianapolis News*, November 13, 1919.

4. Ibid.

5. *Pittsburgh Post-Gazette*, September 17, 1919.

6. *New York Sun*, September 17, 1919; *Indianapolis Star*, October 1, 1919.

7. *Indianapolis Star*, October 1, 1919; Robert F. Himmelberg, "Hoover's Public Image, 1919–1920," in Lawrence Emerson Gelfand (ed.), *Herbert Hoover: The Great War and Its Aftermath, 1914–1923* (Iowa City: University of Iowa Press, 1979), p. 222.

8. *Boston Globe*, April 14, 1920.

9. *St. Louis Post-Dispatch*, September 30, 1919.

10. Francis William O'Brien, *The Hoover-Wilson Wartime Correspondence* (Ames: Iowa State University Press, 1974), pp. 282–83.

11. William Leuchtenburg, *Herbert Hoover* (New York: Times Books, 2009), p. 45.

12. House Diaries, vol. 8, February 18, 1920, House Papers, Yale; Rose Wilder Lane, *The Making of Herbert Hoover* (New York: Century, 1920).

13. Pietrusza, *1920: The Year of the Six Presidents* (New York: Basic Books, 2008), p. 118.

14. Ibid., p. 117.

15. Hugh Gibson Diaries, April 22, 1920, HHPL.

16. Lou Henry Hoover to Allan Hoover, undated, Correspondence, Allan Hoover Papers, HHPL.

17. Henry John Minthorn to Theodore Hoover, March 8, 1920, Accretions, Hulda Hoover McLean Papers, HHPL; Vernon Kellogg, "The Story of Hoover," *Everybody's Magazine*, February–April, 1920.

18. David Burner, *Herbert Hoover: A Public Life* (Newton, MA: American Political Biography Press, 1978), p. 153; Pietrusza, *1920*, pp. 219, 234.

19. Gary Dean Best, *The Politics of American Individualism: Herbert Hoover in Transition, 1918–1921* (Westport, CT: Greenwood Press, 1975), p. 118.

20. Ralph Arnold, "Laying Foundation Stones," *Historical Society of Southern California Quarterly* 37, no. 2 (June 1955): 122.

21. Herbert Hoover to Theodore Hoover, March 3, 1917, Correspondence, Pre-Commerce Papers; Herbert Hoover, "Information for Biographers," Subject Files, Pre-Commerce Papers, HHPL.

22. Mark Requa to Herbert Hoover, October 21, 1921, Correspondence, Commerce Papers, HHPL.

23. Alice King to Lou Henry Hoover, December 21, 1920, Alice King file, Pre-Commerce Papers, HHPL.

24. Hoover, *The Ordeal of Woodrow Wilson* (Washington, DC: Woodrow Wilson Center Press, 1992), p. 19.

25. Edgar Rickard to Lou Henry Hoover, January 27, 1921, Correspondence, Lou Henry Hoover Papers, HHPL.

26. Lou Henry Hoover to Edgar Rickard, July 25, 1921, HHPL.

27. Herbert Hoover to Lou Henry Hoover, August 23, 1921, Lou Henry Hoover to Philippi Harding, August 24, 1921, both in Correspondence, Lou Henry Hoover Papers, HHPL.

28. Herbert Hoover to Allan Hoover, December 24, 1920, Correspondence, Allan Hoover Papers, HHPL.

29. Lou Henry Hoover to Allan Hoover, undated, 1921, HHPL.

30. Ibid.

31. Herbert Hoover to Warren Harding, June 26, 1920, Warren Harding file, Pre-Commerce Papers, HHPL.

32. Robert K. Murray, *The Harding Era: Warren G. Harding and His Administration* (Newtown, CT: American Political Biography Press, 2008), pp. 11–12.

33. *Charlotte Observer*, September 5, 1920.

34. Pietrusza, *1920*, p. 110.

35. Murray, *Harding Era*, p. 71.

36. Nathan Miller, *New World Coming: The 1920s and the Making of Modern America* (Cambridge, MA: Da Capo Press, 2003), p. 60.

37. John W. Dean, *Warren G. Harding* (New York: Times Books, 2004), pp. 57, 73, 148; James David Barber, *The Pulse of Politics* (New Brunswick, NJ: Transaction Publishers, 2007), pp. 225–26; Frances Russell, *The Shadow of Blooming Grove* (New York: McGraw Hill, 1969), p. 453.

38. Russell, *Blooming Grove*, p. 487.

39. Ibid., p. 418; Herbert Hoover to Warren Harding, November 8, 1920, Warren Harding file, Pre-Commerce Papers, HHPL.

40. *New York Times*, December 13, 1920.

41. Warren F. Kuehl and Lynne Dunn, *Keeping the Covenant: American Internationalists and the League of Nations, 1920–1939* (Kent, OH: Kent State University Press, 1997), p. 10.

42. Russell, *Blooming Grove*, p. 408; Herbert Hoover to Senator Harding, August 3, 1920, September 29, 1920, Correspondence, Pre-Commerce Papers, HHPL.

43. Herbert Hoover to Senator Harding, December 22, 1920, HHPL.

44. Martin Fausold, *The Presidency of Herbert C. Hoover* (Lawrence: University Press of Kansas, 1985), p. 94.

45. Senator Harding to Herbert Hoover, September 21, 1920, Correspondence, Pre-Commerce Papers, HHPL.

46. Robert K. Murray, "Herbert Hoover and the Harding Cabinet," in Ellis Wayne Hawley (ed.), *Herbert Hoover as Secretary of Commerce* (Iowa City: University of Iowa Press, 1981), p. 34.

47. House Diaries, vol. 8, January 30, 1921.

48. Senator Harding to Herbert Hoover, February 22, 1921, Correspondence, Pre-Commerce Papers, HHPL.

49. *New York Times*, February 23, 1921.

50. Eugene Lyons, *Herbert Hoover: A Biography* (Garden City, NY: Doubleday, 1964), pp. 139, 144.

51. Ibid.

52. Ibid., February 21, 1921, February 23, 1921; *New York American*, February 26, 1921.

53. House Diaries, vol. 8, March 4, 1921.

54. *New York Times*, February 24, 1921.

55. Ibid., February 25, 1921.

56. Franklin Lane to Herbert Hoover, March 21, 1921, Correspondence, Commerce Papers, HHPL.

57. Franklin Lane to Herbert Hoover, March 21, 1921, HHPL.

58. Herbert Hoover to Franklin Lane, March 8, 1921, HHPL.

CHAPTER 13   MEDDLING WITH GOD'S ECONOMY

1. *Saturday Evening Post*, June 6, 1925; Hal Elliott Wert, *Hoover, The Fishing President: Portrait of the Private Man and His Life Outdoors* (Mechanicsburg, PA: Stackpole Books, 2005), p. 112.
2. *New York Times*, March 9, 1921.
3. Ibid., March 11, 1921.
4. R. D. Cuff, "We Band of Brothers, Woodrow Wilson's War Managers," *Canadian Review of American Studies* 5, no. 2, September 1974.
5. *New York Times*, May 9, 1923.
6. *Washington Sunday Star*, December 25, 1921; Robert K. Murray, *The Harding Era: Warren G. Harding and His Administration* (Newtown, CT: American Political Biography Press, 2008), p. 125; Kendrick A. Clements, *The Life of Herbert Hoover: Imperfect Visionary, 1918–1928* (New York: Palgrave Macmillan, 2010), p. 109.
7. *New York Times*, May 29, 1921.
8. Gabriel Abend, *The Moral Background: An Inquiry into the History of Business Ethics* (Princeton, NJ: Princeton University Press, 2014), p. 179.
9. Clements, *Imperfect Visionary*, pp. 101–26.
10. Leuchtenburg, *Herbert Hoover*, p. 55; Clements, *Imperfect Visionary*, p. 111.
11. Liaquat Ahamed, *Lords of Finance* (New York: Penguin, 2009), p. 14.
12. Clements, *Imperfect Visionary*, p. 132.
13. Murray, *Harding Era*, p. 171.
14. Clements, *Imperfect Visionary*, p. 131; *Report of the President's Conference on Unemployment* (Washington, DC: U.S. Government Printing Office, 1921), p. 27.
15. *Report of the President's Conference on Unemployment* (Washington, DC: U.S. Government Printing Office, 1921), p. 15.
16. Ibid., p. 28.
17. Ibid., pp. 29, 30.
18. *New York Times*, September 28, 1921.
19. *Journal Gazette* (Fort Wayne), September 27, 1921.
20. William J. Barber, *From New Era to New Deal* (Cambridge, UK: Cambridge University Press), pp. 16–22; Burner, *Herbert Hoover*, pp. 164–67.
21. Clements, *Imperfect Visionary*, p. 143; *St. Louis Post-Dispatch*, May 29, 1922.
22. *Report of the President's Conference on Unemployment* (Washington, DC: U.S. Government Printing Office, 1921), p. 28.
23. Ibid., pp. 157, 169.
24. Amy Sterling Casil, *The Department of Labor* (New York: Rosen Publishing Group), p. 9.

CHAPTER 14   HOOVER VERSUS A BOTCHED CIVILIZATION

1. Francis Russell, *The Shadow of Blooming Grove* (New York: McGraw-Hill, 1968), p. 470.

2. Isaac F. Marcosson, *Caravans of Commerce* (New York: Harper and Bros., 1926), pp. 2–3.

3. Ibid., p. 31.

4. Kendrick A. Clements, *The Life of Herbert Hoover: Imperfect Visionary, 1918–1928* (New York: Palgrave Macmillan, 2010), pp. 259–60.

5. David Burner, *Herbert Hoover: A Public Life* (Newton, MA: American Political Biography Press, 1978), p. 174; Clements, *Imperfect Visionary*, pp. 220–21.

6. Burner, *Herbert Hoover*, p. 180.

7. Clements, *Imperfect Visionary*, p. 226.

8. Ibid., p. 296.

9. Burner, *Herbert Hoover*, pp. 118–22.

10. Hearings before the Committee on Foreign Affairs, House of Representatives, 67th Congress, 2nd Session, on H.R. 9459 and H.R. 9548 for the Relief of the Distressed People of Russia, December 13–14, 1921.

11. Leuchtenburg, *Herbert Hoover*, p. 58.

12. Ibid.

13. Wert, *Fishing President*, p. 112; Clements, *Imperfect Visionary*, p. 47.

14. Leuchtenburg, *Herbert Hoover*, p. 54.

15. Clements, *Imperfect Visionary*, pp. 255–56.

16. Leuchtenburg, *Herbert Hoover*, p. 56.

17. Herbert Hoover, "Our Goal: The Normal Child," May 18, 1926, Child Health file, Commerce Papers, HHPL.

18. Clements, *Imperfect Visionary*, pp. 82, 165.

19. Hoover, "Normal Child."

20. Ibid.

21. Vincent Barnett, *John Maynard Keynes* (London: Routledge, 2013), p. 88; J. J. Wilhelm, *Ezra Pound in London and Paris, 1908–1925* (University Park: Pennsylvania State University Press, 1990), p. 252; Ruth Prigozy, *The Cambridge Guide to F. Scott Fitzgerald* (London: Cambridge University Press, 2002), p. 33; and especially Michael E. Parrish, *Anxious Decades: America in Prosperity and Depression, 1920–1941* (New York: Norton, 1994), pp. 183–99.

22. Howard E. Stearns (ed.), *Civilization in the United States, An Inquiry by Thirty Americans* (New York: Harcourt, Brace, 1922), p. vii.

23. Sinclair Lewis, *Babbitt* (London: Jonathan Cape, 1922), pp. 18, 23, 99.

24. Parrish, *Anxious Decades*, p. 199; Lewis, *Babbitt*, p. 116.

25. Herbert Hoover, *American Individualism* (New York: Doubleday, 1922).

26. Ibid., p. 9.

27. Ibid., p. 8.

28. Ibid., pp. 31, 55.

29. Ibid., pp. 9, 71.

30. Ibid., p. 64.

31. Abraham Lincoln, "Speech to the One Hundred Sixty-sixth Ohio Regiment," *The Collected Works of Abraham Lincoln*, vol. 7, ed. Roy P. Basler (New Brunswick, NJ: Rutgers University Press, 1953), p. 512; Thomas Jefferson, *The Works*

*of Thomas Jefferson*, vol. 8, ed. Paul Leicester Ford (New York: G. P. Putnam's Sons, 1904), p. 258.

32. Robert K. Murray, *The Harding Era: Warren G. Harding and His Administration* (Newtown, CT: American Political Biography Press, 2008), p. 445.

33. *New York Times*, June 22, 1923, June 25, 1923.

34. Clements, *Imperfect Visionary*, p. 266.

35. Murray, *Harding Era*, p. 436.

36. Clements, *Imperfect Visionary*, p. 266.

37. *New York Times*, June 22, 1923.

38. Wert, *Fishing President*, p. 121; Clements, *Imperfect Visionary*, p. 184.

39. Henry John Minthorn to Herbert Hoover, May 17, 1922, Herbert Hoover to Henry John Minthorn, May 29, 1922, both in Minthorn file, Commerce Papers, HHPL.

40. Herbert Hoover to Dr. W. B. Holden, September 27, 1922, Dr. W. B. Holden to Herbert Hoover, September 28, 1922, both in Minthorn file, Commerce Papers, HHPL.

41. Hoover Statement, September 29, 1922; Herbert Hoover to Mrs. John Minthorn, November 11, 1922; both in Minthorn file, Commerce Papers, HHPL.

42. Herbert Hoover, "President Harding's Last Illness and Death," August 25, 1923, President Harding file, Commerce Papers, HHPL.

43. Ibid.

44. Herbert Hoover Statement, August 3, 1923, President Harding file, Commerce Papers, HHPL.

CHAPTER 15   SCANDAL, EMBARRASSMENT, AND THE LITTLE FELLER

1. *New York Times*, July 4, 1923.

2. Nathan Miller, *New World Coming: The 1920s and the Making of Modern America* (Cambridge, MA: Da Capo Press, 2003), p. 78; Paul Johnson, *Modern Times* (London: Orion, 1992), p. 219.

3. Robert K. Murray, *The Harding Era: Warren G. Harding and His Administration* (Newtown, CT: American Political Biography Press, 2008), pp. 456–58.

4. Ibid., pp. 471–72.

5. Ibid., pp. 473–85.

6. Nan Britton, *The President's Daughter* (Elizabeth Ann Guild, 1927).

7. *New York Times*, April 13, 1924.

8. Lewis Strauss to Christopher Herter, February 4, 1924, Lewis Strauss file, Commerce Papers, HHPL.

9. Arthur M. Schlesinger Jr., *The Crisis of the Old Order: 1919–1933* (Boston: Houghton Mifflin, 2003), p. 55.

10. Lou Henry Hoover to Allan Hoover and Herbert Hoover Jr., undated, 1924, Correspondence with Lou Henry Hoover, Allan Hoover Papers, HHPL.

11. *New York Times*, January 17, 1924; Lou Henry Hoover to William C. Mul-

lendore, January 18, 1924, Correspondence, William C. Mullendore Papers, HHPL.

12. Lou Henry Hoover to William C. Mullendore, January 18, 1924, HHPL.

13. Lou Henry Hoover to William C. Mullendore, February 13, 1924, William C. Mullendore to Lou Henry Hoover, February 21, 1924, March 3, 1924, P. G. Harding to William C. Mullendore, May 23, 1924, William C. Mullendore to Mrs. P. G. Harding, May 15, 1924; all in HHPL.

14. Lou Henry Hoover to William C. Mullendore, June 30, 1924, William C. Mullendore to Lou Henry Hoover, July 7, 1924; both in HHPL.

15. Joslin Diaries, July 27, 1931, HHPL.

16. *New York Times*, January 26, 1921; Edgar Rickard Diaries, January 7, 1925, April 11, 1925, December 26, 1925, End of Year Summary, 1925, January 12, 1932, Edgar Rickard Papers, HHPL; Richard Roberts, *Schroders: Merchants & Bankers* (London: Macmillan Press, 1992), pp. 219–20.

17. Rickard Diaries, February 3, 1925, December 15, 1925, March 25, 1926, May 18, 1926, October 15–16, 1927, December 10, 1929, November 26, 1930.

18. Belle Livingstone, "They Called Me the Most Dangerous Woman in Europe," *Hearst's International-Cosmopolitan*, July 1924, Belle Livingstone file, Commerce Papers, HHPL.

19. Ibid.

20. Ibid.

21. Edgar Rickard to George Barr Baker, undated, Belle Livingstone file, Commerce Papers, HHPL

22. Livingstone file, Commerce Papers, HHPL.

23. Herbert Hoover, telegram, June 25, 1925, Livingstone file, Commerce Papers, HHPL.

24. "The Secretariat," *American Mercury*, December 1929.

25. William Allen White, *A Puritan in Babylon* (New York: Macmillan, 1958).

26. Amity Shlaes, *Coolidge* (New York: Harper Perennial, 2014).

27. Lou Henry Hoover, Personal Correspondence, Grace Coolidge file, Lou Henry Hoover Papers, HHPL; Bascom Slemp to Herbert Hoover, October 19, 1923, President Coolidge file, Commerce Papers, HHPL.

28. *Good Housekeeping*, May 1924; White, *Puritan in Babylon*, pp. 294–96.

29. *New York Times*, June 14, 1924.

30. Shlaes, *Coolidge*, pp. 318–19; George H. Nash, "The 'Great Enigma' and the 'Great Engineer'" in John Earl Haynes (ed.), *Calvin Coolidge and the Coolidge Era* (Washington, DC: Library of Congress, 1998), p. 156.

31. Nash, "'Great Enigma'"; Rickard Diaries, January 23, 1925.

32. Calvin Coolidge, Inaugural Address, March 4, 1925; Herbert Hoover to Calvin Coolidge, April 21, 1924, President Coolidge, Commerce Papers, HHPL.

33. *Bulletin*, San Francisco, April 7, 1924; Nash, "'Great Enigma.'"

34. *NEA Service*, July 27, 1927, Articles and Speeches, Commerce Papers, HHPL.

35. *Christian Science Monitor*, April 29, 1927; ibid.

36. Bradley Nash Oral History, HHPL.
37. *Minneapolis Tribune*, September 3, 1927; *Time*, November 16, 1925; *New York Times*, September 19, 1926.
38. William E. Leuchtenburg, *Herbert Hoover* (New York: Times Books, 2009), p. 63.
39. *Des Moines Capital*, September 26, 1925; *Chicago Tribune*, October 4, 1925.
40. Michael E. Parrish, *Anxious Decades: America in Prosperity and Depression, 1920–1941* (New York: Norton, 1994), p. 48; David Greenberg, *Calvin Coolidge* (New York: Times Books, 2006), pp. 9, 60; Herbert Hoover, *The Memoirs of Herbert Hoover: The Cabinet and the Presidency, 1920–1933* (New York: Macmillan, 1952), p. 55.
41. Hoover, *Cabinet and the Presidency*, p. 56.
42. Robert E. Gilbert, *The Tormented President: Calvin Coolidge, Death, and Clinical Depression* (Westport, CT: Praeger, 2003), p. 268.
43. David Cannadine, *Mellon: An American Life* (New York: Vintage Books, 2008), p. 293.
44. Ibid.
45. Ibid., pp. 213, 303.
46. Parrish, *Anxious Decades*, pp. 16–18; Cannadine, *Mellon*, pp. 266–74, 313–15.
47. Shlaes, *Coolidge*, p. 288; Parrish, *Anxious Decades*, pp. 16–18.
48. Cannadine, *Mellon*, pp. 315–16; Shlaes, *Coolidge*, pp. 281, 338–39.
49. Cannadine, *Mellon*, pp. 321–22, 343, 396.
50. Clements, *Imperfect Visionary*, p. 309; Liaquat Ahamed, *Lords of Finance* (New York: Penguin, 2009), p. 309; Parrish, *Anxious Decades*, p. 30; Geoffrey Perrett, *America in the Twenties: A History* (New York: Touchstone Books, 1983), p. 337; Barry Eichengreen, *Hall of Mirrors: The Great Depression, the Great Recession, and the Uses—and Misuses—of History* (New York: Oxford University Press, 2015), p. 20.
51. Parrish, *Anxious Decades*, pp. 29–31.
52. Colin Gordon, "Growing Apart: A Political History of American Inequality," Inequality.org, 2016, http://scalar.usc.edu/works/growing-apart-a-political -history-of-american-inequality/index.

CHAPTER 16    SLEEPLESS IN GOOD TIMES

1. Hal Elliott Wert, *Hoover, The Fishing President: Portrait of the Private Man and His Life Outdoors* (Mechanicsburg, PA: Stackpole Books, 2005).
2. Ibid., p. 127.
3. Ibid., p. 128.
4. Ibid., p. 129.
5. Lou Henry Hoover to Allan Hoover and Herbert Hoover Jr., February 22, 1925, Correspondence, Allan Hoover Papers, HHPL.
6. Ibid.

7. Wert, *Fishing President*, pp. xi–xiv.

8. Lou Henry Hoover to Allan Hoover and Herbert Hoover Jr., February 22, 1925, Correspondence, Allan Hoover Papers, HHPL.

9. Wert, *Fishing President*, pp. 131–33.

10. Ibid.

11. Michael Kazin, *A Godly Hero: The Life of William Jennings Bryan* (New York: Anchor Books, 2006), p. 208; Lawrence W. Levine, *Defender of the Faith: William Jennings Bryan, The Last Decade, 1915–1925* (Cambridge, MA: Harvard University Press, 1987), p. 93.

12. Wert, *Fishing President*, pp. 131–33.

13. Ibid.

14. Lou Henry Hoover to Charles Henry, July 13, 1925, July 30, 1927, Personal Correspondence, Lou Henry Hoover Papers, HHPL.

15. Lou Henry Hoover to Herbert Hoover, May 21, 1924, Personal Correspondence, Lou Henry Hoover Papers, HHPL.

16. Allan Hoover to Lou Henry Hoover, March 23, 1925, Correspondence, Allan Hoover Papers, HHPL.

17. Lou Henry Hoover to Allan Hoover, undated, Correspondence, Allan Hoover Papers, HHPL; Lou Henry Hoover to Herbert Hoover, September 25, 1923, Personal Correspondence, Lou Henry Hoover Papers, HHPL.

18. Louisetta Losh to Lou Henry Hoover, July 5, 1924, August 15, 1924, Personal Correspondence, Lou Henry Hoover Papers, HHPL.

19. Kendrick A. Clements, *The Life of Herbert Hoover: Imperfect Visionary* (New York: Palgrave Macmillan, 2010), pp. 91–94.

20. Clements, *Imperfect Visionary*, p. 174; Dale C. Mayer, *Lou Henry Hoover: A Prototype for First Ladies* (New York: Nova History Publications, 2005), pp. 182–87.

21. Mayer, *Lou Henry Hoover*, p. 219.

22. Anonymous, *Boudoir Mirrors of Washington* (Philadelphia: John. C. Winston, 1923), pp. 251–55.

23. *New York Times*, May 9, 1923.

24. Silvano A. Wueschner, *Charting Twentieth-Century Monetary Policy: Herbert Hoover and Benjamin Strong, 1917–1927* (Westport, CT: Greenwood Press, 1999), p. 23.

25. Ibid., pp. 34–35.

26. Ibid., pp. 32–33; Clements, *Imperfect Visionary*, pp. 242–45.

27. Wueschner, *Monetary Policy*, pp. 46–47.

28. Ibid., p. 50.

29. Ibid., p. 52.

30. Ibid., p. 53.

31. *New York Times*, May 9, 1923.

32. Wueschner, *Monetary Policy*, p. 76; Liaquat Ahamed, *Lords of Finance* (New York: Penguin, 2009), p. 272.

33. Wueschner, *Monetary Policy*, p. 91; Ahamed, *Lords of Finance*, p. 275.

34. Wueschner, *Monetary Policy*, p. 92; Irvine Lenroot to D. R. Crissinger, November 23, 1925, Irvine Lenroot file, Commerce Papers, HHPL.

35. Wueschner, *Monetary Policy*, p. 78.

36. Ibid., p. 95.

37. Ibid., p. 85.

38. Eichengreen, *Mirrors*, p. 30.

39. Ibid., p. 105.

40. Rickard Diaries, December 15, 1925, May 18, 1926, December 6, 1926, HHPL.

41. Ibid., End of Year Summary, 1925.

42. *Boston Herald*, January 1926.

43. Amity Shlaes, *Coolidge* (New York: Harper Perennial, 2014), p. 267; Robert E. Gilbert, *The Tormented President: Calvin Coolidge, Death, and Clinical Depression* (Westport, CT: Praeger, 2003), p. 38.

44. H. L. Mencken, *On Politics: A Carnival of Buncombe* (Baltimore: Johns Hopkins University Press, 2006), p. 139.

45. Rickard Diaries, June 29, 1926, June 30, 1926, September 25, 1926.

46. Mark Requa to Herbert Hoover, September 10, 1925, November 15, 1926, March 18, 1927, Mark Requa file, Commerce Papers, HHPL; Rickard Diaries, December 2, 1926, February 13, 1927.

47. *New York Times*, April 8, 1927.

48. Ibid.

49. Rickard Diaries, April 15, 1927.

50. *New York Times*, April 16, 1927.

51. Ibid.

52. Ibid.

53. *Courier-Journal*, Louisville, April 18, 1927.

54. Ibid.

55. Lou Henry Hoover to Allan Hoover and Herbert Hoover Jr., undated, April 1927, Correspondence, Allan Hoover Papers, HHPL.

56. Ibid.

57. *New York Times*, April 19, 1927, April 20, 1927.

58. Ibid., April 17, 1927.

59. John M. Barry, *Rising Tide: The Great Mississippi Flood of 1927 and How It Changed America* (New York: Simon & Schuster, 1997).

60. Clements, *Imperfect Visionary*, pp. 372–73.

61. Ibid., pp. 13, 205.

62. Ibid., pp. 240, 347.

63. Barry, *Rising Tide*, pp. 368–69.

64. Clements, *Imperfect Visionary*, p. 398.

65. Ibid., pp. 376–77.

66. *New York Times*, May 15, 1927.

67. Barry, *Rising Tide*, p. 375; *New York Times*, April 28, 1927.

68. *New York Times*, May 1, 1927.

69. Ibid.
70. Ibid.
71. Ibid.; Clements, *Imperfect Visionary*, p. 297.
72. *New York Times*, May 15, 1927.
73. *Scribner's*, September 1927.
74. Calvin Coolidge to Herbert Hoover, June 20, 1927, President Coolidge file, Commerce Papers, HHPL.
75. William Allen White, *A Puritan in Babylon* (New York: Macmillan, 1958), p. 353.

CHAPTER 17 "THE WONDER BOY"

1. John M. Barry, *Rising Tide: The Great Mississippi Flood of 1927 and How It Changed America* (New York: Simon & Schuster, 1997), p. 289.
2. Lou Henry Hoover to Charles Henry, July 30, 1927, Correspondence, Lou Henry Hoover Papers, HHPL.
3. Amity Shlaes, *Coolidge* (New York: Harper Perennial, 2014), p. 381.
4. Hall Elliott Wert, *Hoover, The Fishing President: Portrait of the Private Man and His Life Outdoors* (Mechanicsburg, PA: Stackpole Books, 2005), pp. 106–9; Michael Rosenthal, *Nicholas Miraculous* (New York: Columbia University Press, 2015), p. 268.
5. Herbert Hoover to Mark Sullivan, May 2, 1925, Mark Sullivan file, Commerce Papers, HHPL; *The Stanford Daily*, August 15, 1933.
6. Rickard Diaries, August 2, 1927, HHPL.
7. Shlaes, *Coolidge*, p. 402.
8. William Allen White, *A Puritan in Babylon* (New York: Macmillan, 1958), p. 363; Rickard Diaries, February 12, 1928.
9. Rickard Diaries, August 28, 1927; Lou Henry Hoover to Allan Hoover, undated, 1928, Correspondence, Allan Hoover Papers, HHPL.
10. George H. Nash, "The 'Great Enigma' and the 'Great Engineer,'" in John Earl Haynes (ed.), *Calvin Coolidge and the Coolidge Era* (Washington, DC: Library of Congress, 1998), pp. 168–69.
11. *New York Times*, December 7, 1927.
12. Nash, "'Great Enigma,'" p. 169; *Chicago Tribune*, February 13, 1928.
13. Robert E. Gilbert, *The Tormented President: Calvin Coolidge, Death, and Clinical Depression* (Westport, CT: Praeger, 2003), p. 221; Nash, "'Great Enigma,'" p. 170; William E. Leuchtenburg, *Herbert Hoover* (New York: Times Books, 2009), p. 64.
14. Rickard Diaries, April 27, 1928.
15. *Saturday Evening Post*, April 14, 1928.
16. Kendrick A. Clements, *The Life of Herbert Hoover: Imperfect Visionary, 1918–1928* (New York: Palgrave Macmillan, 2010), p. 402; *Baltimore Sun*, June 7, 1928; Lou Henry Hoover to Allan Hoover, June 5, 1928, Correspondence, Allan Hoover Papers, HHPL.

17. Rickard Diaries, June 8, 1928.

18. Mrs. James MacLafferty "Dear Folks" letter, June 22, 1928, James MacLafferty Papers, HHPL.

19. Clements, *Imperfect Visionary*, pp. 408–11.

20. Rickard Diaries, June 14, 1928.

21. Ibid.; Bradley Nash Oral History, HHPL.

22. Clements, *Imperfect Visionary*, pp. 411–12.

23. Leuchtenburg, *Herbert Hoover*, p. 72.

24. Robert A. Slayton, *Empire Statesman: The Rise and Redemption of Al Smith* (New York: Free Press, 2001), p. 166.

25. Ibid.

26. Clements, *Imperfect Visionary*, p. 417.

27. Slayton, *Empire Statesman*, pp. 209, 273; Clements, *Imperfect Visionary*, p. 413.

28. David Greenberg, "Beyond the Bully Pulpit," *Wilson Quarterly* 35, no. 3 (Summer 2011): 27; Alonzo Hamby, *Man of Destiny: FDR and the Making of the American Century* (New York: Basic Books, 2015), p. 172.

29. Leuchtenburg, *Herbert Hoover*, p. 79; Nathan Miller, *New World Coming: The 1920s and the Making of Modern America* (Cambridge, MA: Da Capo Press, 2003), p. 89.

30. Slayton, *Empire Statesman*, p. 272.

31. Ibid., p. 156.

32. Daniel Okrent, *Last Call: The Rise and Fall of Prohibition* (New York: Simon & Schuster, 2011).

33. Ibid., p. 129.

34. Ibid., p. 256.

35. Leuchtenburg, *Herbert Hoover*, p. 96; Lou Henry Hoover to Allan Hoover, June 29, 1929, Correspondence, Allan Hoover Papers, HHPL.

36. Glen Jeansonne, *The Life of Herbert Hoover: Fighting Quaker, 1928–1933* (New York: Palgrave Macmillan, 2012), p. 22.

37. Joseph George Jr., "The Lincoln Writings of Charles P.T. Chiniquy," *Journal of the Illinois State Historical Society* 69 (February 1976): 17–25; Christopher M. Finan, *Alfred E. Smith, the Happy Warrior* (New York: Hill & Wang, 2002), p. 182.

38. Herbert Hoover, *The New Day: Campaign Speeches of Herbert Hoover, 1928* (Palo Alto, CA: Stanford University Press, 1928), p. 36.

39. Ibid., p. 3; Jeansonne, *Fighting Quaker*, p. 198.

40. Allan J. Lichtman, *Prejudice and the Old Politics: The Presidential Election of 1928* (Lanham, MD: Lexington Books, 1979), p. 62.

41. Alfred E. Smith, "Campaign Address of Governor Alfred E. Smith, Oklahoma City, September 20, 1928," *Campaign Addresses of Governor Alfred E. Smith* (Washington, DC: Democratic National Committee, 1929).

42. Lichtman, *Prejudice and the Old Politics*, p. 62; *The Brooklyn Daily Eagle*, June 17, 1928.

43. Lenroot Opinion, Irvine Lenroot file, Commerce Papers, HHPL.

44. Hoover, *New Day*, p. 70.

45. Ibid., p. 3.

46. Liaquat Ahamed, *Lords of Finance* (New York: Penguin, 2009), p. 299; Richard Norton Smith, *An Uncommon Man: The Triumph of Herbert Hoover* (New York: Simon & Schuster, 1984), p. 42.

47. Ahamed, *Lords of Finance*, p. 299; White, *Puritan in Babylon*, pp. 338–90.

48. "Automobile Production," "Passenger Cars, Factory Production for United States," and "Number of Private Nonfarm Housing Units Started for United States" in Federal Reserve Economic Data, https://fred.stlouisfed.org.

49. Claudius O. Johnson, *Borah of Idaho* (New York: Longmans, Green, 1936), p. 430; Walter Lippmann, *Men of Destiny* (New Brunswick, NJ: Transaction Publishers, 2003), p. 141; Shlaes, *Coolidge*, p. 324.

50. Johnson, *Borah of Idaho*, p. 426.

51. Ibid., p. 435.

52. *New York Times*, October 27, 1928.

53. White, *Puritan in Babylon*, p. 262.

54. *New York Times*, October 28, 1928.

55. Ibid., November 6, 1928.

56. Ibid., November 7, 1928.

57. *New York American*, November 7, 1928.

58. *San Francisco News*, November 7, 1928.

59. Clements, *Imperfect Visionary*, p. 423; Wert, *Fishing President*, pp. 172–73; *San Francisco Chronicle*, November 7, 1928; *San Francisco News*, November 7, 1928.

60. *San Francisco Chronicle*, November 7, 1928; *San Francisco News*, November 7, 1928.

CHAPTER 18 "GIVING GENIUS ITS CHANCE"

1. Alexander DeConde, *Herbert Hoover's Latin-American Policy* (Stanford, CA: Stanford University Press, 1951), p. 14.

2. *Washington Post*, March 4, 1929; *New York Times*, March 4, 1929, March 5, 1929.

3. Glen Jeansonne, *The Life of Herbert Hoover: Fighting Quaker, 1928–1933* (New York: Palgrave Macmillan, 2012), pp. 47–49; David Burner, *Herbert Hoover: A Public Life* (Newton, MA: American Political Biography Press, 1978), pp. 208–10.

4. H. L. Mencken, *On Politics: A Carnival of Buncombe* (Baltimore: Johns Hopkins University Press, 2006), p. 256.

5. *Good Housekeeping*, June 1928.

6. President Hoover to William O. Thompson, January 12, 1930, *PPP*, vol. 2, p. 15.

7. *New York Times*, November 18, 1928, December 28, 1928, February 26, 1929.

8. Ibid., March 4, 1929; *Washington Post*, March 4, 1929; *New York World*, March 4, 1929.

9. *Palo Alto Times*, November 7, 1928; *San Francisco Chronicle*, November 7, 1928; *New York Times*, March 2, 1930.

10. *Christian Science Monitor,* November 27, 1932.

11. *New York World,* March 5, 1929; *San Francisco Chronicle,* March 4, 1929; *New York Herald-Tribune,* March 4, 1929.

12. Unidentified clipping, Clippings files, Inaugural, 1929, HHPL.

13. William Allen White, *A Puritan in Babylon* (New York: Macmillan, 1958), p. 417.

14. *New York Times,* March 5, 1929.

15. Ibid.

16. Herbert Hoover, President Hoover Inaugural Address, March 4, 1929, *PPP,* vol. 1.

17. Ibid.

18. Ibid., p. 2.

19. *Washington Post,* March 5, 1929.

20. Hoover, Inaugural Address, pp. 7–9.

21. Ibid., p. 12.

22. MacLafferty Memorandum, March 4, 1929, James MacLafferty Papers, HHPL.

23. *Washington Post,* March 5, 1929; *Washington Herald,* March 5, 1929.

24. Joslin Diaries, October 12, 1932, HHPL; President Hoover News Conference, March 5, 1929, *PPP,* vol. 1, p. 14.

25. Hoover, News Conference, March 22, 1929, p. 33.

26. Ibid., March 12, 1929, p. 21.

27. Rickard Diaries, April 14, 1929, April 14, 1929, May 22, 1929.

28. Executive Order 5079, March 14, 1929, A. W. Mellon to President Hoover, March 14, 1929; both in *PPP,* vol. 1, pp. 24–25.

29. William E. Leuchtenburg, *Herbert Hoover* (New York: Times Books, 2009), p. 82.

30. President Hoover Address, April 22, 1929, *PPP,* vol. 1, p. 101; President Hoover Remarks, May 28, 1929, p. 159, *PPP,* vol. 1.

31. President Hoover Proclamation, March 25, 1929, *PPP,* vol. 1, p. 41.

32. David M. Kennedy, *Freedom from Fear: The American People in Depression* (New York: Oxford University Press, 1999), p. 12.

33. Kathleen Dalton, *Theodore Roosevelt: A Strenuous Life* (New York: First Vintage Books, 2004), p. 299.

34. *New York Times,* February 3, 1929, December 27, 1929.

35. President Hoover Press Conference, April 9, 1929, *PPP,* vol. 1, p. 63.

36. Joel T. Boone Memoir, pp. 154–157, Joel T. Boone Collection, HHPL; President Hoover Address to the Gridiron Club, April 13, 1929, *PPP,* vol. 1, p. 111.

37. Lou Henry Hoover to Allan Hoover, May 25, 1929, Correspondence, Allan Hoover Papers, HHPL.

38. *New York Times,* April 24, 1932.

39. William Hard, "Hoover the President," *World's Work,* September 1929; Boone Memoir, p. 1060.

40. *New York Times,* March 2, 1930.

41. Boone Memoir, pp. 51–55.

42. Ibid., p. 161.

43. Ibid., pp. 55-58.

44. Ibid., pp. 119-23.

45. Ibid., pp. 36, 117.

46. Ibid., p. 36.

47. Ibid., p. 217; Robert E. Gilbert, *The Tormented President: Calvin Coolidge, Death, and Clinical Depression* (Westport, CT: Praeger, 2003), p. 220.

48. President Hoover to Dr. Julius Klein, September 10, 1929; T. F. Murtha, Cigar Dept., Ritz-Carlton Hotel to Lawrence Richey, September 27, 1929; President Hoover Cigars file, Presidential Papers, HHPL.

CHAPTER 19 "HE DIDN'T KNOW WHERE THE VOTES CAME FROM"

1. *Daily Chronicle* (De Kalb, IL), April 22, 1929; Loretta Kehoe, "The Relation of Herbert Hoover to Congress, 1929-1933" (master's thesis, Loyola University, 1949); Douglas A. Irwin, *Peddling Protectionism: Smoot-Hawley and the Great Depression* (Princeton, NJ: Princeton University Press, 2011).

2. *New York Times*, April 28, 1929.

3. Ibid., March 14, 1929.

4. Ibid., February 3, 1929, February 7, 1929, February 21, 1929, April 14, 1929, April 15, 1929, April 16, 1929.

5. *New York World*, March 5, 1929.

6. President Hoover Message, April 16, 1929, *PPP*, vol. 1, p. 75.

7. Kehoe, "Relation of Herbert Hoover to Congress," p. 25.

8. President Hoover Statement, June 15, 1929, *PPP*, vol. 1, p. 186.

9. Conrad Black, *Franklin Delano Roosevelt: Champion of Freedom* (New York: Public Affairs, 2003), p. 202.

10. President Hoover, State of the Union, December 3, 1929, *PPP*, vol. 1, p. 404ff.

11. President Hoover, Message to the Special Session, April 16, 1929, *Public Papers*, vol. 1, p. 74; *New York Times*, May 19, 1929; *Tariff Act of 1930 on Imports into the United States* (Washington, DC: U.S. Government Printing Office, 1930); Irwin, *Peddling Protectionism*, p. 31.

12. *New York Times*, May 5, 1929, May 6, 1929; Irwin, *Peddling Protectionism*, p. 36.

13. *New York Times*, May 5, 1929, May 6, 1929, May 8, 1929, May 9, 1929, May 12, 1929, May 13, 1929.

14. *Economist*, May 18, 1929.

15. Irwin, *Peddling Protectionism*, p. 40.

16. Ibid., p. 4; *New York Times*, April 29, 1929.

17. *New York Times*, May 19, 1929.

18. Lou Henry Hoover to Allan Hoover, November 10, 1929, Correspondence, Allan Hoover Papers, HHPL; Boone Memoir, pp. 65-69, HHPL.

19. Robert S. Allen clipping, Drew Pearson Collection, HHPL; David Burner, *Herbert Hoover: A Public Life* (Newton, MA: American Political Biography Press, 1978), p. 254.

20. Rickard Diaries, August 3, 1930, HHPL.

21. Boone Memoir, pp. 142–46; Letter from Thomas Schwartz, director of the HHPL, to the author, January 30, 2017.

22. *New York Times*, July 29, 1929, August 3, 1929; *Chicago Tribune*, August 3, 1929; Martin Fausold, *The Presidency of Herbert C. Hoover* (Lawrence: University Press of Kansas, 1985), p. 56.

23. President Hoover Statement, August 6, 1929, *PPP*, vol. 1, p. 245.

24. *New York Times*, July 2, 1929.

25. Irwin, *Peddling Protectionism*, p. 47.

26. *New York Times*, August 29, 1929, August 30, 1929, August 31, 1929.

27. Ibid., August 26, 1929.

28. Kehoe, "Relation of Herbert Hoover to Congress," pp. 42–45; *New York Times*, September 13–16, 1929; Irwin, *Peddling Protectionism*, p. 48.

29. *New York Times*, September 14, 1929, September 21, 1929, September 22, 1929; Irwin, *Peddling Protectionism*, pp. 48–49.

30. White House Statement, September 21, 1929, *PPP*, vol. 1, p. 299; President Hoover Statement, September 24, 1929, *PPP*, vol. 1, p. 301.

31. *New York Times*, September 27, 1929.

32. President Hoover Statement, September 24, 1929, *PPP*, vol. 1, p. 301; Irwin, *Peddling Protectionism*, p. 52.

33. *New York Times*, November 23, 1929.

34. Ibid., November 2, 1929, November 3, 1929.

35. Ibid., October 29, 1929.

36. Ibid., September 15, 1929.

37. Fausold, *Presidency of Herbert C. Hoover*, p. 70; *New York Times*, February 1, 1930.

38. Fausold, *Presidency of Herbert C. Hoover*, p. 93.

CHAPTER 20    NOTHING TO FEAR BUT FEAR ITSELF

1. Herbert Hoover, *The Memoirs of Herbert Hoover: The Great Depression, 1929–1941* (New York: Macmillan, 1952), p. 18; Martin Fausold, *The Presidency of Herbert C. Hoover* (Lawrence: University Press of Kansas, 1985), p. 71.

2. Barry Eichengreen, *Hall of Mirrors: The Great Depression, the Great Recession, and the Uses—and Misuses—of History* (New York: Oxford University Press, 2015), p. 109; William J. Barber, *From New Era to New Deal* (Cambridge, UK: Cambridge University Press), p. 71.

3. Christina D. Romer, "The Great Crash and the Onset of the Great Depression," *Quarterly Journal of Economics* 105, no. 3 (1990): 597–98.

4. Frederick Lewis Allen, *Since Yesterday* (New York: Harper & Row, 1939), p. 2; Liaquat Ahamed, *Lords of Finance* (New York: Penguin, 2009), p. 350.

5. Edward M. Lamont, *The Ambassador from Wall Street* (Lanham, MD: Madison Books, 1994), p. 266; Ahamed, *Lords of Finance*, p. 354; Eichengreen, *Hall of Mirrors*, p. 106.

6. *New York Times*, October 22, 1929.

7. President Hoover Statement, October 21, 1929, *PPP*, vol. 1, p. 337; *Washington Star*, October 21, 1929; *New York Herald-Tribune*, October 21, 1929.

8. *New York Times*, October 24, 1929; Ahamed, *Lords of Finance*, p. 354.

9. *New York Times*, October 24, 1929, to October 31, 1929; Ahamed, *Lords of Finance*, pp. 354–60; Eichengreen, *Hall of Mirrors*, pp. 106–8; Kennedy, *Freedom from Fear: The American People in Depression and War, 1929–1945* (New York: Oxford University Press, 1999), pp. 37–39.

10. Hoover, *Great Depression*, p. 30; David Burner, *Herbert Hoover: A Public Life* (Newton, MA: American Political Biography Press, 1978), p. 252.

11. President Hoover Statement, October 25, 1929, President Hoover News Conference, November 5, 1929, *PPP*, vol. 1, pp. 356, 366; *New York Times*, October 24, 1929, October 26, 1929.

12. Eichengreen, *Hall of Mirrors*, pp. 114–15.

13. President Hoover News Conference, November 19, 1929, *PPP*, vol. 1, p. 384.

14. Burner, *Hoover*, pp. 248–52.

15. President Hoover Statement, November 15, 1929, *PPP*, vol. 1, p. 382.

16. President Hoover, State of the Union, December 3, 1929, *PPP*, vol. 1, p. 404.

17. *New York Times*, November 20, 1929, November 21, 1929.

18. President Hoover, State of the Union, December 3, 1929, *PPP*, vol. 1, p. 404.

19. President Hoover Remarks, December 5, 1929, *PPP*, vol. 1, p. 426.

20. *New York Herald-Tribune*, November 23, 1929.

21. *New York Herald-Tribune*, December 31, 1929; *New York Times*, March 2, 1930.

22. *New York Evening Post*, November 23, 1929.

23. Kennedy, *Freedom from Fear*, pp. 55–57; President Hoover Remarks, December 5, 1929, *PPP*, vol. 1, p. 453.

24. *New York Times*, November 23, 1929.

25. Summary of editorial opinion, *Washington Star*, November 23, 1929; Foster and Catchings, *Review of Reviews* 81 (1930): 50.

26. Ahamed, *Lords of Finance*, pp. 358, 375.

27. *New York Times*, December 3, 1929; Ahamed, *Lords of Finance*, pp. 361–62.

28. Eichengreen, *Hall of Mirrors*, p. 117; Ahamed, *Lords of Finance*, pp. 361–62.

29. *New York Herald-Tribune*, December 25, 1929, December 26, 1929; *New York World*, December 26, 1929; *New York Times*, December 25, 1929, December 26, 1929.

30. Douglas A. Irwin, *Peddling Protectionism: Smoot-Hawley and the Great Depression* (Princeton, NJ: Princeton University Press, 2011), pp. 67, 72, 86; *New York Times*, May 14, 1930.

31. Irwin, *Peddling Protectionism*, pp. 82, 84, 86.

32. Ibid., p. 84.

33. President Hoover Statement, June 16, 1930, *PPP*, vol. 2, p. 230.

34. Irwin, *Peddling Protectionism*, pp. 105–11.

35. Ibid., pp. 89–90.

36. Kennedy, *Freedom from Fear*, pp. 58, 59; Eichengreen, *Hall of Mirrors*, p. 118; Ahamed, *Lords of Finance*, p. 362; Gross National Product, Federal Reserve Economic Data, https://fred.stlouisfed.org.
37. President Hoover News Conference, March 7, 1930, *PPP*, vol. 2, p. 78; Ahamed, *Lords of Finance*, p. 363; Eichengreen, *Hall of Mirrors*, pp. 118–19.
38. President Hoover Address, May 1, 1930, *PPP*, vol. 2, p. 171.
39. Ibid.
40. John Kenneth Galbraith, *The Great Crash of 1929* (Boston: Houghton Mifflin, 1988), pp. 144–45; *New York Times*, March 29, 1930, May 4, 1930; Robert Sobel, *Herbert Hoover at the Onset of the Great Depression* (Philadelphia: Lippincott, 1975), p. 60.
41. Robert Cowley, "The Drought and the Dole," *American Heritage*, February 1972.
42. President Hoover Statements, August 8, 1930, August 14, 1930, *PPP*, vol. 2, pp. 323, 336.
43. MacLafferty Diaries, June 10, 1930, James MacLafferty Papers, HHPL; Frank R. Kent, "Charley Michelson," *Scribner's Magazine*, September 1930.
44. *New York Times*, November 12, 1930.
45. MacLafferty Diaries, September 6, 1930, September 8, 1930.
46. President Hoover Address, May 30, 1930, *PPP*, vol. 2, p. 208; President Hoover Address, December 14, 1929, *PPP*, vol. 1, p. 473.
47. Stimson Diaries, November 4, 1930, Henry Lewis Stimson Papers, Yale University.
48. Kennedy, *Freedom from Fear*, p. 60.
49. MacLafferty Diaries, November 5, 1930.
50. Ibid.

CHAPTER 21   JUST WHEN WE THOUGHT IT WAS OVER

1. *New York Times*, November 16, 1930.
2. President Hoover Statements, November 5, 1930, November 15, 1930, *PPP*, vol. 2, pp. 366, 384.
3. Elmus Wicker, *The Banking Panics of the Great Depression* (Cambridge, UK: Cambridge University Press, 1996), p. 33; Barry Eichengreen, *Hall of Mirrors: The Great Depression, the Great Recession, and the Uses—and Misuses—of History* (New York: Oxford University Press, 2015), pp. 127–29.
4. Kennedy, *Freedom from Fear: The American People in Depression and War, 1929-1945* (New York: Oxford University Press, 1999), p. 67; Eichengreen, *Hall of Mirrors*, pp. 129–32.
5. Kennedy, *Freedom from Fear*, p. 66; President Hoover, State of the Union, December 3, 1929, *PPP*, vol. 1, p. 404.
6. Herbert Stein, *The Fiscal Revolution in America* (Washington, DC: AEI Press, 1996), p. 21; *Harvard Economic Society Weekly Letter*, vol. 9 (Cambridge, MA: Harvard Economic Society, 1930), p. 282.

7. President Hoover, State of the Union, December 2, 1930, *PPP*, vol. 2, p. 509.

8. President Hoover Address, *PPP*, vol. 2, pp. 575, 577.

9. President Hoover Veto Statement, March 3, 1931, *PPP*, vol. 3, p. 120.

10. Ibid.; MacLafferty Diaries, January 8, 1931.

11. President Hoover Veto Statements, March 3, 1931, February 26, 1931, *PPP*, vol. 3, pp. 103, 120.

12. President Hoover Veto Statement, February 26, 1931, *PPP*, vol. 3, p. 103; Stimson Diaries, February 17, 1931, Yale University.

13. President Hoover Statement, March 8, 1931, *PPP*, vol. 3, p. 132.

14. *New York Times*, February 1, 1931.

15. Ibid., March 11, 1931; Stimson Diaries, November 25, 1930.

16. President Hoover Statement, February 3, 1931, *PPP*, vol. 3, p. 54.

17. President Hoover Radio Address, February 12, 1931, *PPP*, vol. 3, p. 71.

18. Ibid.

19. Ibid.

20. Stimson Diaries, November 30, 1930.

21. *Christian Science Monitor*, December 3, 1980; National Commission on Law Observance and Enforcement, *Report on the Enforcement of the Prohibition Laws of the United States* (Washington, DC: U.S. Government Printing Office, 1931).

22. Stimson Diaries, January 20, 1931.

23. Ibid.

24. Martin Fausold, *The Presidency of Herbert C. Hoover* (Lawrence: University Press of Kansas, 1985), p. 125; *New York Times*, January 18, 1931; National Commission on Law Observance, *Report on the Enforcement*, p. 37.

25. Rickard Diaries, February 5, 1931, HHPL; Stimson Diaries, November 25, 1930, December 28, 1930; MacLafferty Diaries, December 17, 1930.

26. President Hoover Message to Congress, January 20, 1931, *PPP*, vol. 3, p. 69.

27. Kennedy, *Freedom from Fear*, p. 68.

28. Stimson Diaries, April 3, 1931; Burner, *Hoover*, p. 264.

29. Edward Eyre Hunt Memoranda, March 14, 1931, Economics, Subject Files, Presidential Papers, HHPL.

30. Stimson Diaries, October 24, 1930, October 28, 1930.

31. Eichengreen, *Hall of Mirrors*, pp. 144–45; Kennedy, *Freedom from Fear*, p. 72.

32. President Hoover Address, May 4, 1931, *PPP*, vol. 3, p. 255.

33. President Hoover News Conference, April 11, 1930, *PPP*, vol. 2, p. 165.

34. President Hoover Address, May 4, 1931, *PPP*, vol. 3, p. 255; The President's Diary of Developments of the Moratorium, May 6–July 22, 1931, *PPP*, vol. 3, p. 636.

35. Kennedy, *Freedom from Fear*, p. 72.

36. The President's Diary of Developments, May 6–July 22, 1931, *PPP*, vol. 3, p. 636.

37. Ibid.

38. Joslin Diaries, May 27, 1931.

39. Stimson Diaries, June 5, 1931; The President's Diary of Developments, *PPP*, vol. 3.

40. Ibid.
41. Joslin Diaries, June 5, 1931.
42. Stimson Diaries, June 12, 1931.
43. Ibid., November 25, 1931, December 4–5, 1930, February 2, 1931.
44. Ibid., June 13, 1931.


CHAPTER 22   "IT SEEMED LIKE THE END OF THE WORLD"

1. *New York Times*, June 16, 1931.
2. President Hoover Address, June 15, 1931, *PPP*, vol. 3, p. 295.
3. Ibid.
4. Ibid.; *New Republic*, March 4, 1931; *Harper's*, June 1931; *Forum*, July 1931.
5. President Hoover Address, June 15, 1931, *PPP*, vol. 3, p. 295.
6. *New York Times*, June 16, 1931.
7. President Hoover Address, June 16, 1931, *PPP*, vol. 3, p. 308.
8. *New York Times*, June 18, 1931; President Hoover Address, June 17, 1931, *PPP*, vol. 3, p. 315.
9. *New York Times*, June 17, 1931, June 18, 1931.
10. Joslin Diaries, June 19, 1931, HHPL.
11. President Hoover Press Conference, June 20, 1931, *PPP*, vol. 3, p. 321; Stimson Diaries, June 20, 1931, Yale University; Joslin Diaries, June 20, 1931.
12. *New York Times*, June 20, 1931, June 21, 1931, June 22, 1931, June 23, 1931, June 24, 1931; H. C. Johnson, *Gold, France and the Great Depression* (New Haven, CT: Yale University Press, 1997), p. 146; Carmen M. Reinhart and Christoph Trebesch, "Sovereign Debt Relief and Its Aftermath," Harvard Kennedy School Faculty Research Working Paper Series RWP15-028, June 2015.
13. Joslin Diaries, June 23, 1931.
14. *New York Times*, June 23, 1931.
15. Stimson Diaries, June 18, 1931; Barry Eichengreen, *Hall of Mirrors: The Great Depression, the Great Recession, and the Uses—and Misuses—of History* (New York: Oxford University Press, 2015), p. 114.
16. President Hoover Address, May 4, 1931, *PPP*, vol. 3, p. 232.
17. David M. Kennedy, *Freedom from Fear: The American People in Depression and War, 1929–1945* (New York: Oxford University Press, 1999), p. 93; Joslin Diaries, July 2, 1931, September 14, 1931.
18. Joslin Diaries, August 25, 1931, September 14, 1931.
19. Stimson Diaries, September 15, 1931.
20. Ibid., May 19, 1931.
21. David Cannadine, *Mellon: An American Life* (New York, Vintage Books, 2008), pp. 396, 402, 414–27.
22. Joslin Diaries, July 23, 1931.
23. Stimson Diaries, June 18, 1931.
24. Ibid., November 1, 1930, November 3, 1930; Joslin Diaries, July 23, 1931.
25. Stimson Diaries, November 1, 1930.

26. Stimson Diaries, September 12, 1931, September 13, 1931.

27. Margo J. Anderson, *The American Census: A Social History* (New Haven, CT: Yale University Press, 1988), pp. 168–69; Herbert Hoover News Conference, September 11, 1931, *PPP,* vol. 3, p. 417.

28. Herbert Hoover, *The Memoirs of Herbert Hoover: The Great Depression, 1929–1941* (New York: Macmillan, 1952), p. 83; Martin Fausold, *The Presidency of Herbert C. Hoover* (Lawrence: University Press of Kansas, 1985), pp. 141, 147; gross national product for 1929 and 1931, Federal Reserve Economic Data, https://fred.stlouisfed.org.

29. Stimson Diaries, September 12, 1931.

30. President Hoover Statement, July 31, 1931, President Hoover News Conference, September 11, 1931, *PPP,* vol. 3, pp. 366, 417.

31. President Hoover Letter, August 21, 1931, *PPP,* vol. 3, p. 392.

32. Ibid.; David Burner, *Herbert Hoover: A Public Life* (Newton, MA: American Political Biography Press, 1978), p. 268.

33. White House Statement, August 12, 1931, *PPP,* vol. 3, p. 384; President Hoover Press Conference, September 1, 1931, *PPP,* vol. 3, p. 401.

34. Joslin Diaries, August 21, 1931.

35. *New York Times,* September 6, 1931.

36. Ibid., September 8, 1931.

37. President Hoover Statement, August 7, 1931, *PPP,* vol. 3, p. 378.

38. Robert S. McElvaine, *Encyclopedia of the Great Depression,* vol. 2 (New York: Macmillan Reference, 2004), p. 770.

39. Kennedy, *Freedom from Fear,* p. 90.

40. Ibid., p. 88; Glen Jeansonne, *The Life of Herbert Hoover: Fighting Quaker, 1928–1933* (New York: Palgrave Macmillan, 2012), p. 257.

41. Cowley, "The Drought and the Dole," *American Heritage,* February 1972.

42. Joslin Diaries, November 30, 1931.

43. MacLafferty Diaries, November 25, 1931.

44. Ibid.

45. Ibid.

46. *New York Times,* September 16, 1931.

47. President Hoover Press Conference, September 4, 1931, *PPP,* vol. 3, p. 406.

48. Jackson Reynolds Oral History, HHPL.

49. Eichengreen, *Hall of Mirrors,* pp. 152–53; *New York Times,* September 23, 1931.

50. President Hoover News Conference, September 22, 1931, *PPP,* vol. 3, p. 434.

51. Hoover, *Great Depression,* p. 83.

52. Kennedy, *Freedom from Fear,* pp. 77–78.

53. Ibid., p. 78.

54. Eichengreen, *Hall of Mirrors,* p. 155; Kennedy, *Freedom from Fear,* p. 77.

55. Stimson Diaries, September 22, 1931; Cannadine, *Mellon,* p. 440.

56. Ibid., October 5, 1931; Joslin Diaries, October 4, 1931; President Hoover Statement, October 4, 1931, *PPP,* vol. 3, p. 451.

57. President Hoover Statement, October 4, 1931, *PPP,* vol. 3, p. 451.

58. Ibid.

59. Stimson Diaries, October 5, 1931; Hoover, *Great Depression*, p. 86.

60. Hoover, *Great Depression*, p. 86.

61. Dean A. Sullivan (ed.), *Middle Innings: A Documentary History of Baseball, 1900–1948*, pp. 144–47; *New York Times*, October 4, 1931, October 5, 1931, October 6, 1931.

62. *New York Times*, October 6, 1931; Joslin Diaries, October 6, 1931.

63. Hoover, *Great Depression*, p. 89.

64. Ibid., p. 90.

65. Joslin Diaries, October 6, 1931; *New York Times*, October 6, 1931, October 7, 1931; Herbert Hoover Statement, October 7, 1931, *PPP*, vol. 3, p. 465.

CHAPTER 23   THE PRESIDENT IN HIS FIGHTING CLOTHES

1. *New York Times*, October 8, 1931; *New York Herald-Tribune*, October 8, 1931.

2. *New York Times*, October 18, 1931.

3. Stimson Diaries, October 20, 1931, Yale University.

4. David M. Kennedy, *Freedom from Fear: The American People in Depression and War, 1929–1945* (New York: Oxford University Press, 1999), p. 58; Herbert Stein, *The Fiscal Revolution in America* (Washington, DC: AEI Press, 1996), p. 26.

5. Kennedy, *Freedom from Fear*, pp. 78–81; Stein, *Fiscal Revolution*, pp. 27–38.

6. President Hoover, State of the Union, December 8, 1931, *PPP*, vol. 3, p. 580.

7. Kennedy, *Freedom from Fear*, p. 81.

8. Herbert Hoover, *The Memoirs of Herbert Hoover: The Cabinet and the Presidency, 1920–1933* (New York: Macmillan, 1952), pp. 365–79.

9. Stimson Diaries, October 9, 1931, October 27, 1931.

10. Ibid., November 6, 1931; Hoover, *Cabinet and the Presidency*, p. 369.

11. Stimson Diaries, November 27, 1931.

12. Stimson Diaries, November 9, 1931; Hoover, *Cabinet and the Presidency*, p. 373.

13. *New York Times*, August 6, 1931.

14. John Hamill, *The Strange Career of Mr. Hoover Under Two Flags* (New York: W. Faro, 1931).

15. Walter W. Liggett, *The Rise of Herbert Hoover* (New York: H. K. Fry, 1932).

16. John Knox, *The Great Mistake* (Washington, DC: National Foundation Press, 1930); James J. O'Brien, *Hoover's Millions and How He Made Them* (New York: James J. O'Brien Publishing, 1932).

17. Rickard Diaries, October 14, 1931, HHPL; Rosanne Sizer, "Herbert Hoover and the Smear Books," *Annals of Iowa* 47, no. 4 (Spring 1984); Joslin Diaries, September 15, 1931, January 4, 1932, HHPL; MacLafferty Diaries, December 24, 1931; Rickard Diaries, October 14, 1931, October 24, 1931, January 9, 1932, January 23, 1932.

18. *New York Times*, February 7, 1932; Joslin Diaries, January 8, 1932; Boone Memoir, pp. 1000–1005, HHPL.

19. Herbert Hoover State of the Union, December 8, 1931, *PPP*, vol. 3, p. 580; Stimson Diaries, October 20, 1931; Joslin Diaries, November 3, 1931.

20. Joslin Diaries, December 6, 1931.

21. MacLafferty Diaries, December 5, 1931; Martin Fausold, *The Presidency of Herbert C. Hoover* (Lawrence: University Press of Kansas, 1985), p. 148.

22. President Hoover State of the Union, December 8, 1931, *PPP*, vol. 3, p. 580.

23. *New York Times*, December 9, 1931, December 17, 1931.

24. Kennedy, *Freedom from Fear*, p. 84.

25. Ibid.

26. President Hoover Radio Remarks, October 25, 1931, *PPP*, vol. 3, p. 503.

27. *Hearings Before a Subcommittee of the Committee on Manufactures, United States Senate, 72d Congress, First Session, S. 174, S. 262* (Washington, DC: U.S. Government Printing Office, 1932).

28. Ibid., p. 156.

29. Ibid., p. 59.

30. Ibid., pp. 188, 344.

31. John Kenneth Galbraith, *The Great Crash of 1929* (Boston: Houghton Mifflin, 1988), p. 146.

32. Loretta Kehoe, "The Relation of Herbert Hoover to Congress, 1929–1933," master's thesis, Loyola University, Chicago, 1949, p. 115.

33. Kehoe, "Relation of Herbert Hoover," pp. 122–23; Joslin Diaries, January 22, 1932, January 27, 1932.

34. Kehoe, "Relation of Herbert Hoover," p. 124.

35. President Hoover Radio Address, March 6, 1932, *PPP*, vol. 4, p. 93.

36. *New York Times*, February 17, 1932.

37. Undated clipping, 1932, Drew Pearson Collection, Presidential Documents File, HHPL; Joslin Diaries, February 17, 1932.

38. Joslin Diaries, January 3, 1932.

39. Ibid., January 20, 1932, January 26, 1932, February 3, 1932, February 4, 1932.

40. Ibid., February 10, 1932.

41. Ibid., January 13, 1932, January 25, 1932, February 27, 1932.

42. MacLafferty Diaries, March 16, 1932.

43. Joslin Diaries, January 18, 1932, February 3, 1932; White House Statement, February 9, 1932, *PPP*, vol. 4, p. 48.

44. Joslin Diaries, January 23, 1932.

45. Ibid., February 25, 1932.

46. L. Edward Purcell (ed.), *The Vice Presidents: A Biographical Dictionary* (New York: Facts on File, 2010), p. 311.

47. Herbert Hoover News Conference, January 8, 1932, *PPP*, vol. 4, p. 11.

48. Steven Horwitz, "Hoover's Economic Policies," in *The Concise Encyclopedia of Economics*, 2nd ed., http://www.econlib.org.

49. Special Message to Congress, May 5, 1932, *PPP*, vol. 4, p. 193; Joslin Diaries, May 9, 1932; Burner, *Herbert Hoover*, p. 281.

50. Horwitz, "Hoover's Economic Policies."

51. Radio Address, March 6, 1932, *PPP*, vol. 4, p. 93; Mark Sullivan memo, February 28, 1932, Presidential Subject Files, Presidential Papers, HHPL.
52. William E. Leuchtenburg, *Herbert Hoover* (New York: Times Books, 2009), p. 132; Letter from Thomas F. Schwartz, director of HHPL, to the author, January 30, 2017.
53. *New York Times*, April 28, 1932; Joslin Diaries, March 29, 1932; MacLafferty Diaries, April 16, 1932.
54. *New York Times*, June 14, 1932.
55. *Public Ledger* (Philadelphia), undated clipping, 1932, in Boone Memoir, p. 1010, HHPL.

CHAPTER 24   "A HUMAN CREATURE DESPERATELY HURT AND PAINED"

1. Lou Henry Hoover to Allan Hoover, January 6, 1932, Correspondence, Allan Hoover Papers, HHPL.
2. Joslin Diaries, June 7, 1932, HHPL.
3. Rickard Diaries, May 21, 1932, May 22, 1932, HHPL; Stimson Diaries, June 7, 1932, June 8, 1932, June 10, 1932, Yale University; Joslin Diaries, June 13, 1932.
4. Joslin Diaries, June 13–16, 1932.
5. *New York Times*, June 16, 1932.
6. Joslin Diaries, June 16, 1932.
7. *New York Times*, June 13, 1932; Joslin Diaries, May 1–3, 1932, June 11, 1932.
8. H. W. Brands, *Traitor to His Class* (New York: Doubleday, 2008); Jean Edward Smith, *FDR* (Random House: New York: 2008); Conrad Black, *Franklin Delano Roosevelt: Champion of Freedom* (New York: Public Affairs, 2003).
9. Mark Sullivan to Herbert Hoover, January 16, 1932, Presidential Subject Files, Presidential Papers, HHPL.
10. Lou Henry Hoover to Allan Hoover, undated, 1932, Correspondence, Allan Hoover Papers, HHPL.
11. Joslin Diaries, June 24, 1932, June 28, 1932.
12. Scripps-Howard, September 2, 1932, Clippings Files, HHPL.
13. Stephanie Fitzgerald, *The New Deal: Rebuilding America* (Minneapolis: Compass Point Books, 2007), p. 31; Susan Dunn, *Roosevelt's Purge* (Cambridge, MA: Belknap Press, 2010), p. 35; *New York Times*, July 3, 1932; *Literary Digest*, July 9, 1932.
14. Franklin D. Roosevelt Speech at Oglethorpe University, *Public Papers of the Presidents of the United States, Franklin D. Roosevelt, 1940*, vol. 9 (Washington, DC: U.S. Government Printing Office, 1940), p. 645.
15. Ibid., p. 811.
16. Black, *Franklin Delano Roosevelt*, p. 238.
17. Franklin D. Roosevelt, "Address Accepting the Presidential Nomination," July 2, 1932, p. 647, and Campaign Address at Columbus Ohio, August 20, 1932, p. 669, both in *Public Papers of the Presidents of the United States, Franklin*

D. *Roosevelt, 1940*, vol. 9 (Washington, DC: U.S. Government Printing Office, 1940), p. 647.

18. Roosevelt, "Address Accepting the Presidential Nomination"; David Burner, *Herbert Hoover: A Public Life* (Newton, MA: American Political Biography Press, 1978), p. 314.

19. *New York Herald-Tribune*, January 8, 1932.

20. Joslin Diaries, July 2, 1932, September 7, 1932; Stimson Diaries, July 19, 1932.

21. President Hoover News Conference, June 24, 1932, *PPP*, vol. 4, p. 276.

22. *New York Times*, July 17, 1932.

23. Ibid.

24. Donald J. Lisio, *The President and Protest: Hoover, MacArthur, and the Bonus Riot* (New York: Fordham University Press, 1994); Stimson Diaries, June 7, 1932.

25. Joslin Diaries, June 10, 1932; Lisio, *President and Protest*, pp. 59–60, 74.

26. Lisio, *President and Protest*, p. 193; William Manchester, *American Caesar* (New York: Dell, 1983), p. 166; *New York Times*, August 4, 1932.

27. Roger Daniels, *Franklin D. Roosevelt: Road to the New Deal, 1882–1939* (Champaign: University of Illinois Press, 2015), p. 108; Lisio, *President and Protest*, p. 285.

28. *New York Times*, July 29, 1932; *Literary Digest*, August 6, 1932.

29. *New York Times*, October 30, 1932.

30. Campaign Addresses of Franklin Roosevelt, *Public Papers of the Presidents of the United States, Franklin D. Roosevelt, 1940*, vol. 9 (Washington, DC: U.S. Government Printing Office, 1940), pp. 418, 698, 709; Martin Fausold, *The Presidency of Herbert C. Hoover* (Lawrence: University Press of Kansas, 1985), p. 193; gross national product, Federal Reserve Economic Data, digital database.

31. *New York Times*, July 17, 1932.

32. Lou Henry Hoover to Allan Hoover and Herbert Hoover Jr., undated, July 1932, Correspondence, Allan Hoover Papers, HHPL.

33. Lou Henry Hoover to Allan Hoover, August 22, 1932, HHPL.

34. Joslin Diaries, February 12, 1932, April 23, 1932; Stimson Diaries, March 2, 1932.

35. Stimson Diaries, July 26, 1932.

36. Ibid., August 11, 1932.

37. Joslin Diaries, August 20, 1932.

38. Stimson Diaries, September 22, 1932, September 27, 1932; *New York World*, September 2, 1932.

39. Lou Henry Hoover to Allan Hoover, July 7, 1932, Correspondence, Allan Hoover Papers, HHPL; production, capital expenditure, price, employment, and GNP data from Federal Reserve Economic Data, https://fred.stlouisfed.org.

40. *Literary Digest*, September 24, 1932; Joslin Diaries, September 13, 1932; Hearst Presidential Poll and Houser Poll in Polls, Presidential Subject Files: Press Releases, Presidential Papers, HHPL.

41. Joslin Diaries, September 24, 1932, September 28, 1932, September 30, 1932.

42. Ibid., October 3, 1932; President Hoover Address, October 4, 1932, *PPP,* vol. 4, p. 452.

43. President Hoover Address, October 4, 1932.

44. Ibid.

45. Ibid.

46. *New York Times,* October 5, 1932, October 11, 1932.

47. Joslin Diaries, October 4, 1932.

48. Ibid., October 5, 1932.

49. *New York Times,* October 5, 1932.

50. *Washington Evening Star,* September 27, 1932; Joslin Diaries, October 13, 1932, October 18, 1932.

51. Boone Memoir, pp. 1279, 1280, HHPL.

52. Joslin Diaries, October 17, 1932.

53. Boone Memoir, pp. 1304–5.

54. Herbert Hoover Campaign Speeches, *PPP,* vol. 4, pp. 609, 656, 716.

55. Ibid., p. 716.

56. Rickard Diaries, November 5, 1932; Joslin Diaries, November 5, 1932.

57. Boone Memoir, pp. 1310–11.

58. Joslin Diaries, November 7, 1932.

59. Boone Memoir, p. 1314.

60. Houser Poll, in Polls, Press Releases, Presidential Subject Files, Presidential Papers, HHPL.

61. Ibid.

62. Ibid.

63. Ibid.

64. Ibid.

65. Ibid.

66. Ibid.

67. Ruth Fesler Lipman to Rachel, November 8, 1932, Ruth Fesler Lipman Papers, HHPL.

68. Library of Congress U.S. Election Statistics digital database, https://www.loc .gov/rr/program/bib/elections/statistics.html.

69. *New York Times,* November 9, 1932.

70. Herbert Hoover, *The Memoirs of Herbert Hoover: The Cabinet and the Presidency, 1920–1933* (New York: Macmillan, 1952), p. 4.

71. *New York Times,* November 10, 1932, November 15, 1932; Herbert Hoover, *The Memoirs of Herbert Hoover: The Cabinet and the Presidency, 1920–1933* (New York: Macmillan, 1952), p. 4.

72. Raymond Moley, *After Seven Years* (New York: Harper & Brothers, 1939), pp. 68–70.

73. Ibid., p. 73.

74. Stimson Diaries, November 22, 1932.

75. *New York Times,* November 24, 1932, December 20, 1932, January 1, 1933;

Glen Jeansonne, *The Life of Herbert Hoover: Fighting Quaker, 1928–1933* (New York: Palgrave Macmillan, 2012), p. 430.

76. Barry Eichengreen, *Hall of Mirrors: The Great Depression, the Great Recession, and the Uses—and Misuses—of History* (New York: Oxford University Press, 2015), pp. 161–66.

77. *New York Times*, January 1, 1933; Susan Estabrook Kennedy, *The Banking Crisis of 1933* (Lexington: University Press of Kentucky, 1973), p. 71.

78. *New York Times*, December 8, 1932, January 10, 1933, February 5, 1933, February 6, 1933, February 10, 1933, February 14, 1933; Jeansonne, *Fighting Quaker*, pp. 438–42.

79. *New York Times*, February 21, 1933.

80. *Recent Social Trends in the United States*, 2 vols. (New York: McGraw-Hill, 1933), p. v.

81. Eichengreen, *Hall of Mirrors*, pp. 164–66.

82. Lou Henry Hoover to Allan Hoover, undated, 1933, Correspondence, Allan Hoover Papers, HHPL; Rickard Diaries, February 14, 1932.

83. Eichengreen, *Hall of Mirrors*, p. 166; Liaquat Ahamed, *Lords of Finance* (New York: Penguin, 2009), p. 444.

84. John S. West to W. H. Moran, February 27, 1933, *PPP*, vol. 4, p. 1033.

85. President Hoover to Governor Roosevelt, February 18, 1933, *PPP*, vol. 4, p. 1030.

86. Ibid.; Kennedy, *Banking Crisis of 1933*, p. 59.

87. David M. Kennedy, *Freedom from Fear: The American People in Depression and War, 1929–1945* (New York: Oxford University Press, 1999), pp. 110, 324.

88. Raymond Moley, *After Seven Years* (New York: Harper & Brothers, 1939), pp. 139, 143; Kennedy, *Freedom from Fear*, p. 111.

89. Franklin Roosevelt, *The Public Papers and Addresses of Franklin D. Roosevelt*, vol. 2 (New York: Random House, 1938), p. 11; Boone Memoir, p. 1471, HHPL.

CHAPTER 25    THROUGH THE ABYSS IN A BUICK

1. Gary Dean Best, *The Life of Herbert Hoover: Keeper of the Torch, 1933–1964* (New York: Palgrave Macmillan, 2013), p. 1.

2. Ibid., pp. 4, 24.

3. Ibid., pp. 4, 8–9; Rickard Diaries, April 14, 1933, HHPL.

4. Franklin Lane to Herbert Hoover, March 21, 1921, Correspondence, Commerce Papers, HHPL.

5. Rickard Diaries, January 22, 1933.

6. Lou Henry Hoover to Allan Hoover, January 19, 1933, Correspondence, Allan Hoover Papers, HHPL.

7. Rickard Diaries, August 4, 1933, January 25, 1935, January 28, 1935.

8. Ibid., April 6, 1933, and enclosed 1933 letter from Dare Stark McMullin.

9. George W. Nash, *The Life of Herbert Hoover: The Engineer, 1874–1914* (New York: Norton, 1983), p. 34; Hal Elliott Wert, *Hoover, The Fishing President: Por-*

*trait of the Private Man and His Life Outdoors* (Mechanicsburg, PA: Stackpole Books, 2005), p. 221.

10. Wert, *Fishing President,* pp. 222–24.

11. Ibid., p. 225.

12. Ibid., pp. 225–26.

13. Ibid., p. 227.

14. Best, *Keeper of the Torch,* p. 16.

15. Rickard Diaries, January 27–29, 1934, February 23, 1934, April 1–5, 1934; Best, *Keeper of the Torch,* p. 17; Lou Henry Hoover to Allan Hoover, undated, Correspondence, Allan Hoover Papers, HHPL.

16. Best, *Keeper of the Torch,* pp. 40–41.

17. David M. Kennedy, *Freedom from Fear: The American People in Depression and War, 1929–1945* (New York: Oxford University Press, 1999), p. 363ff.

18. Glen Jeansonne, *The Life of Herbert Hoover: Fighting Quaker, 1928–1933* (New York: Palgrave Macmillan, 2012), p. 94.

19. Barry Eichengreen, *Hall of Mirrors: The Great Depression, the Great Recession, and the Uses—and Misuses—of History* (New York: Oxford University Press, 2015), pp. 229–30; Kennedy, *Freedom from Fear,* pp. 135–36.

20. Eichengreen, *Hall of Mirrors,* pp. 229–30; Kennedy, *Freedom from Fear,* p. 137.

21. Davis W. Houck, *Rhetoric as Currency: Hoover, Roosevelt and the Great Depression* (College Station: Texas A&M University Press, 2001), p. 9; Kennedy, *Freedom from Fear,* p. 176.

22. Raymond Moley, "Reappraising Hoover," *Newsweek,* June 14, 1948; Amity Shlaes, *The Forgotten Man: A New History of the Great Depression* (New York: HarperCollins, 2007), p. 149.

23. Kennedy, *Freedom from Fear,* pp. 175, 205.

24. *New York Times,* November 24, 1933; Kennedy, *Freedom from Fear,* p. 179; Best, *Keeper of the Torch,* p. 28.

25. Stimson Diaries, October 23, 1931; Kennedy, *Freedom from Fear,* p. 155.

26. Kennedy, *Freedom from Fear,* p. 155.

27. Ibid., p. 143.

28. President Hoover Address, February 13, 1933, *PPP,* vol. 4, p. 985.

29. Kennedy, *Freedom from Fear,* pp. 157–58.

30. Best, *Keeper of the Torch,* p. 40.

31. *St. Louis Post-Dispatch,* September 30, 1919.

32. President Hoover Address, October 31, 1932, *PPP,* vol. 4, p. 656.

33. Best, *Keeper of the Torch,* p. 45; Herbert Hoover, *The Memoirs of Herbert Hoover: The Great Depression, 1929–1941* (New York: Macmillan, 1952), p. 355.

34. Herbert Hoover, *The Challenge to Liberty* (New York: Charles Scribner's Sons, 1934).

35. Ibid.

36. Richard Norton Smith, *An Uncommon Man: The Triumph of Herbert Hoover* (New York: Simon & Schuster, 1984), p. 202.

37. Best, *Keeper of the Torch,* pp. 20, 22.

38. Ibid., p. 14; National Bureau of Economic Research, "Unemployment Rate for United States, 1929–1942," Federal Reserve Economic Data digital database.

39. Rickard Diaries, June 5, 1933.

40. Ibid., September 25, 1935.

41. Ibid., August 15, 1935, September 25, 1925.

42. Ibid., June 12, 1935.

43. Best, *Keeper of the Torch*, pp. 44–45; Rickard Diaries, March 18, 1936.

44. Best, *Keeper of the Torch*, p. 37.

45. Ibid., p. 48; Rickard Diaries, May 14, 1936.

46. *New York Times*, June 11, 1936.

47. Herbert Hoover, *Addresses Upon the American Road, 1933–1938* (New York: Charles Scribner's Sons, 1938), p. 173ff.

48. Ibid.

49. *New York Times*, June 11, 1936.

50. Hoover, *American Road, 1933–1938*, p. 183.

51. *New York Times*, June 11, 1936.

52. Best, *Keeper of the Torch*, pp. 48–49; Smith, *Uncommon Man*, p. 206.

53. Rickard Diaries, June 9–13, 1936, August 14–15, 1936, September 25, 1936, October 10, 1936; Best, *Keeper of the Torch*, pp. 52–56.

54. Library of Congress U.S. Election Statistics digital database, https://www.loc .gov/rr/program/bib/elections/statistics.html.

55. Best, *Keeper of the Torch*, p. 74.

CHAPTER 26    FATHER OF THE NEW CONSERVATISM

1. David M. Kennedy, *Freedom from Fear: The American People in Depression and War, 1929–1945* (New York: Oxford University Press, 1999), pp. 324–27.

2. Ibid., p. 327; Conrad Black, *Franklin Delano Roosevelt: Champion of Freedom* (New York: Public Affairs, 2003), p. 411.

3. Gary Dean Best, *The Life of Herbert Hoover: Keeper of the Torch, 1933–1964* (New York: Palgrave Macmillan, 2013), p. 58.

4. Ibid., p. 58.

5. Ronald Steel, *Walter Lippmann and the American Century* (Boston: Atlantic Monthly Press, 1980), p. 319.

6. Best, *Keeper of the Torch*, pp. 87–88; National Bureau of Economic Research, "Unemployment Rate for United States, 1929–1942, Federal Reserve Economic Data digital database.

7. Richard Norton Smith, *An Uncommon Man: The Triumph of Herbert Hoover* (New York: Simon & Schuster, 1984), p. 205.

8. Best, *Keeper of the Torch*, pp. 87–88; Smith, *Uncommon Man*, p. 228.

9. Kennedy, *Freedom from Fear*, pp. 308–13.

10. Ibid., pp. 318–19.

11. Ibid., pp. 319–22.

12. Will Irwin, *Liberty Magazine*, July 16, 1938; Best, *Keeper of the Torch*, p. 90; Her-

bert Hoover, *Addresses Upon the American Road, 1933–1938* (New York: Charles Scribner's Sons, 1938), p. 287ff.

13. Hoover, *American Road, 1933–1938*, p. 295.
14. Ibid., pp. 291–92.
15. Ibid., pp. 293, 295.
16. Best, *Keeper of the Torch*, p. 55; Hoover, *American Road, 1933–1938*, p. 260.
17. Hoover, *American Road, 1933–1938*, p. 294.
18. *New York Times*, December 17, 1937.
19. Ibid., December 16, 1937.
20. Ibid.
21. Donald W. Whisenhunt, *President Herbert Hoover* (New York: Nova Science Publishers, 2007), p. 122.
22. Best, *Keeper of the Torch*, pp. 79–80.
23. *Life*, April 11, 1938.
24. Best, *Keeper of the Torch*, pp. 80–81; Notes from 1938 European Trip, March 23–29, 1938, Post-Presidential Papers, HHPL.
25. Best, *Keeper of the Torch*, pp. 80–81; Notes from 1938 European Trip, March 23–29, 1938, Post-Presidential Papers, HHPL.
26. Smith, *Uncommon Man*, p. 255.
27. Notes from 1938 European Trip, March 23–29, 1938, Post-Presidential Papers, HHPL.
28. Ibid.
29. Ibid.
30. Adam Tooze, *The Wages of Destruction* (New York: Viking, 2006), pp. 268–69, 287.
31. Smith, *Uncommon Man*, p. 258.
32. Ibid., p. 258; Herbert Hoover, *Freedom Betrayed: Herbert Hoover's Secret History of the Second World War*, ed. George H. Nash (Stanford, CA: Hoover Institution Press, 2011), p. xxi, 93; Hoover, *American Road, 1933–38*, p. 313.
33. Gary Dean Best, "Herbert Hoover, 1933–1941: A Reassessment," in Arthur S. Link and Mark O. Hatfield, *Herbert Hoover Reassessed* (Honolulu, HI: University Press of the Pacific, 2002), p. 260.
34. Franklin Roosevelt, *The Public Papers and Addresses of Franklin D. Roosevelt*, vol. 6 (New York: Macmillan, 1941), pp. 407–8.
35. Ibid., pp. 408–10.
36. Ibid.; Hoover, *Addresses Upon the American Road, 1933–1938*, p. 318.
37. Hoover, *Freedom Betrayed*, pp. xix, xxxii; Hoover, *American Road, 1938–1940*, p. 89.
38. Hoover, *American Road, 1933–1938*, pp. 318–19; *New York Times*, April 1, 1938; Hoover, *American Road, 1938–1940*, p. 112.
39. Hoover, *American Road, 1938–1940*, p. 89; *Life*, April 11, 1938.
40. Kennedy, *Freedom from Fear*, p. 386.
41. Ibid., pp. 393–94, 415.

42. Best, *Keeper of the Torch*, pp. 83, 97.

43. Ibid., pp. 86, 124–25.

44. Hoover, *Freedom Betrayed*, p. xxx.

45. *New York Times*, November 1, 1936.

46. *Fortune*, September 1932; Morris Dickstein, *Dancing in the Dark: A Cultural History of the Great Depression* (New York: Norton, 2009), pp. 8–11.

47. Best, *Keeper of the Torch*, p. 131.

48. Ibid., p. 118.

49. David McCullough, Harvard Business Review, January/February, 2013, http://hbr.org/2013/01/david-mccullough. Best, *Keeper of the Torch*, p. 146.

50. Library of Congress U.S. Election Statistics digital database, https://www.loc.gov/rr/program/bib/elections/statistics.html.

51. Kennedy, *Freedom from Fear*, p. 364ff.

52. Ibid., p. 476.

53. Hoover, *Freedom Betrayed*, pp. xvi, li, 232.

54. Ibid., pp. lv, 286; Best, *Keeper of the Torch*, p. 184.

55. Best, *Keeper of the Torch*, p. 190.

56. Tooze, *Wages of Destruction*, pp. 287, 306–7; Smith, *Uncommon Man*, pp. 307, 308.

57. Best, *Keeper of the Torch*, pp. 179, 191–92.

58. Hoover, *Freedom Betrayed*, p. 541.

59. Rickard Diaries, October 10, 1942, April 19, 1943, September 29, 1944, End of Year Summary, 1943.

60. Best, *Keeper of the Torch*, p. 249.

61. Kirk Elise, "First Lady in the Arts," and Richard Norton Smith, "Carrying On: Lou Henry Hoover as a Former First Lady," in Dale C. Mayer (ed.), *Lou Henry Hoover: Essays on a Busy Life* (Worland, WY: High Plains Publishing, 1994).

62. Nancy Beck Young, *Lou Henry Hoover: Activist First Lady* (Lawrence: University Press of Kansas, 2004), p. 183.

63. Rickard Diaries, January 7, 1944.

64. Ibid., End of Year Summary, 1944.

CHAPTER 27     REBORN IN A DARKER WORLD

1. David M. Kennedy, *Freedom from Fear: The American People in Depression and War, 1929–1945* (New York: Oxford University Press, 1999), p. 801; Gary Dean Best, *The Life of Hoover: Keeper of the Torch* (New York: Palgrave Macmillan, 2013), p. 255.

2. Best, *Keeper of the Torch*, p. 252.

3. Ibid., p. 255.

4. Ibid., p. 259.

5. Ibid.

6. *New York Times*, May 9, 1945, May 17, 1945.

7. Best, *Keeper of the Torch*, p. 262.

8. Timothy Walch and Dwight M. Miller (eds.), *Herbert Hoover and Harry Truman: A Documentary History* (Worland, WY: High Plains Publishing, 1992), p. 35.

9. Ibid.

10. David McCullough, *Truman* (New York: Simon & Schuster, 1992).

11. Walch and Miller, *Herbert Hoover and Harry Truman*, pp. 37–42.

12. Ibid., p. 53.

13. *New York Times*, May 27, 1945; Walch and Miller, *Herbert Hoover and Harry Truman*, p. 53.

14. Best, *Keeper of the Torch*, p. 270.

15. Ibid.; Walch and Miller, *Herbert Hoover and Harry Truman*, pp. 8–9.

16. Best, *Keeper of the Torch*, p. 274; Herbert Hoover, *Addresses Upon the American Road, 1945–1948* (New York: D. Van Nostrand, 1949), p. 21.

17. Best, *Keeper of the Torch*, p. 274.

18. Ibid., pp. 274–75.

19. Hoover, *American Road, 1938–1940*, p. 20.

20. Ibid.

21. Hoover, *American Road, 1945–1948*, pp. 37, 38, 39.

22. Herbert Hoover, *Addresses Upon the American Road, 1940–1941* (New York: Charles Scribner's Sons, 1941), p. 234.

23. George Orwell, *1984* (London: Penguin, 1954); Jeffrey Meyers, *George Orwell* (London: Routledge, 1975), p. 24.

24. Walch and Miller, *Herbert Hoover and Harry Truman*, p. 68; Best, *Keeper of the Torch*, p. 278.

25. Best, *Keeper of the Torch*, p. 280.

26. Ibid., p. 281.

27. Ibid., pp. 280–87.

28. Ibid.

29. Rickard Diaries, End of Year Summary, 1946, HHPL.

30. Best, *Keeper of the Torch*, p. 85.

31. Walch and Miller, *Herbert Hoover and Harry Truman*, p. 131; Best, *Keeper of the Torch*, p. 385; Richard Norton Smith, *An Uncommon Man: The Triumph of Herbert Hoover* (New York, Simon & Schuster, 1984), p. 374.

32. Hoover, *American Road, 1945–1948*, p. 68.

33. Ibid., p. 71.

34. *New York Times*, October 28, 1948.

35. Herbert Hoover, "People I have Known," Topic File, Allan Hoover Papers, HHPL; Best, *Keeper of the Torch*, p. 334.

36. Ibid.

37. Robert H. Ferrell, *Harry S. Truman: A Life* (Columbia: University of Missouri Press, 1994), p. 195.

38. Best, *Keeper of the Torch*, p. 338.

39. Ibid., pp. 126, 381.

40. Smith, *Uncommon Man*, p. 15.

41. Ibid., p. 371.

42. Best, *Keeper of the Torch*, p. 458.

43. Ibid., p. 434.

44. Smith, *An Uncommon Man*, p. 22; Hal Elliott Wert, *Hoover, The Fishing President: Portrait of the Private Man and His Life Outdoors* (Mechanicsburg, PA: Stackpole Books, 2005), p. 328.

45. Rickard Diaries, End of Year Summary, 1941.

46. Smith, *Uncommon Man*, p. 393.

47. Ibid., p. 364; David Hinshaw, *Herbert Hoover: American Quaker* (New York: Farrar, Straus, 1950), p. 369.

48. Best, *Keeper of the Torch*, p. 343.

49. Ibid., pp. 403–4.

50. Walch and Miller, *Herbert Hoover and Harry Truman*, p. 201.

51. Best, *Keeper of the Torch*, pp. 271, 398.

52. Ibid.

53. Ibid., pp. 352, 353.

54. Ibid., pp. 360, 401.

55. Smith, *Uncommon Man*, p. 409.

56. Best, *Keeper of the Torch*, p. 386.

57. Ibid.

58. Ibid., p. 394.

59. Ibid., p. 398.

60. Ibid., p. 389.

61. Ibid., pp. 395, 398.

62. Ibid., pp. 379, 390.

63. *New York Times*, November 2, 1958; Best, *Keeper of the Torch*, p. 416; http://www.lhc.ca.gov/.

64. Walch and Miller, *Herbert Hoover and Harry Truman*, p. 237.

65. Best, *Keeper of the Torch*, p. 402–3.

66. Timothy Walch (ed.), *Herbert Hoover and Dwight D. Eisenhower: A Documentary History* (New York: Palgrave Macmillan, 2013), p. 175.

67. Herbert Hoover, 1960 Republican convention address, C-Span Video, http://www.c-spanvideo.org/event/169735.

68. Ibid.

69. Ibid.; *New York Times*, July 26, 1960.

70. Best, *Keeper of the Torch*, pp. 447–48.

71. Ibid., p. 447.

72. Ibid., p. 449.

73. Nancy Gibbs and Michael Duffy, *The Presidents Club: Inside the World's Most Exclusive Fraternity* (New York: Simon & Schuster, 2012), p. 154.

74. Smith, *Uncommon Man*, p. 426.

75. Wert, *Fishing President*, pp. 298–345.

76. Ibid.

77. Ibid.

78. Ibid.
79. Ibid.
80. Ibid.
81. Herbert Hoover, *On Growing Up* (New York: William Morrow, 1962), pp. 29, 74, 82, 117.
82. Herbert Hoover, *The Ordeal of Woodrow Wilson* (Washington, DC: Woodrow Wilson Center Press, 1992).
83. Ibid., pp. 18–19.
84. Herbert Hoover, *Freedom Betrayed: Herbert Hoover's Secret History of the Second World War*, ed. George H. Nash (Stanford, CA: Hoover Institution Press, 2011), xvi.
85. Ibid., p. lxiii.
86. Ibid., p. xvi.
87. Herbert Hoover to Hulda McLean, December 10, 1963, Hulda Hoover McLean Papers, HHPL
88. *Life*, August 21, 1964.


EPILOGUE

1. *Washington Post*, October 21, 1964; *New York Times*, October 21–23, 1964.
2. *Washington Post*, October 24, 1964.
3. Ibid.
4. *San Bernardino County Sun*, October 24, 1964.
5. *Leavenworth Times*, October 22, 1964.
6. *Washington Post*, October 21, 1964; *New York Times*, October 21, 1964; Milton Friedman and Anna Schwartz, *A Monetary History of the United States* (Princeton, NJ: Princeton University Press, 1963); http://fivebooks .com/interview/robert-barro-on-the-lessons-of-the-great-depression/; https:// mostlyeconomics.wordpress.com/2012/02/21/christy-romer-picks-books-to -read-on-great-depression/.
7. *New York Times*, October 21, 1964.
8. Ibid.
9. Glossary of Statistical Terms, OECD, https://stats.oecd.org/glossary/detail .asp?ID=3560.
10. David Frost interview of Robert F. Kennedy, "The Next President," June 4, 1968, MR 93–4, John Fitzgerald Kennedy Presidential Library.
11. *Washington Post*, October 26, 1964.

# SELECTED BIBLIOGRAPHY

### A NOTE ON SOURCES

Most of the primary documents used in this study can be found at the Herbert Hoover Presidential Library and Museum in West Branch, Iowa, including the papers of Herbert Hoover, Lou Henry Hoover, Allan Hoover, Theodore Hoover, Hulda Hoover McLean, and numerous other family members as cited in the endnotes. The HHPL also holds the invaluable diaries of Theodore Joslin, Edgar Rickard, James MacLafferty, and Ruth Fesler Lipman, as well as copies of the Joel T. Boone memoir and an extensive oral history collection.

More papers related to Hoover and his activities, including the invaluable records of Hugh Gibson, were accessed at the Hoover Institution on War, Revolution, and Peace at Stanford University.

My thanks to both institutions for permission to quote from their materials, and specifically to the HHPL for permission to quote from the diary of Edgar Rickard.

Other archives for whose permissions I am grateful include:

Calvin Coolidge Papers, Library of Congress
Edward Mandell House Papers, Yale University Library
E. J. Nathan Papers, Bodleian Libraries, University of Oxford
Federal Reserve Economic Data (online), Federal Reserve Bank of St. Louis
Franklin Delano Roosevelt Presidential Library and Museum, Hyde Park, New York
Joel T. Boone Papers, Library of Congress
John F. Kennedy Presidential Library and Museum, Boston
U.S. Election Statistics Resource Guide (online), Library of Congress
Walter William Liggett Papers, New York Public Library
Warren G. Harding Papers, Library of Congress

### BOOKS AND ARTICLES

Abend, Gabriel. *The Moral Background: An Inquiry into the History of Business Ethics.* Princeton, NJ: Princeton University Press, 2014.
Ahamed, Liaquat. *Lords of Finance.* New York: Penguin, 2009.

Allen, Anne Beiser. *An Independent Woman: The Life of Lou Henry Hoover*. Westport, CT: Greenwood Press, 2002.

Allen, Frederick Lewis. *Since Yesterday*. New York: Harper & Row, 1939.

Anonymous. *Boudoir Mirrors of Washington*. Philadelphia: John C. Winston, 1923.

Armytage, W. H. G. *A Social History of Engineering*. Cambridge, MA: M.I.T. Press, 1961.

Austin, Mary. *Earth Horizon*. Santa Fe, NM: Sunstone Press, 2007.

———. *A Woman of Genius*. Garden City, NY: Doubleday, 1912.

Barber, James David. *The Pulse of Politics*. New Brunswick, NJ: Transaction Publishers, 2007.

Barber, William J. *From New Era to New Deal*. Cambridge, UK: Cambridge University Press.

Barry, John M. *Rising Tide: The Great Mississippi Flood of 1927 and How It Changed America*. New York: Simon & Schuster, 1997.

Baruch, Bernard M. *The Public Years*. New York: Rinehart & Winston, 1960.

Bernanke, Ben S. *Essays on the Great Depression*. Princeton, NJ: Princeton University Press, 2000.

Bernstein, Michael A. *A Perilous Progress: Economists and Public Purpose in Twentieth-Century America*. Princeton, NJ: Princeton University Press, 2001.

Best, Gary Dean. "Herbert Hoover, 1933–1941: A Reassessment," in *Herbert Hoover Reassessed*. Honolulu, HI: University Press of the Pacific, 2002.

———. *The Life of Herbert Hoover: Keeper of the Torch, 1933–1964*. New York: Palgrave Macmillan, 2013.

———. *The Politics of American Individualism: Herbert Hoover in Transition, 1918–1921*. Westport, CT: Greenwood Press, 1975.

Black, Conrad. *Franklin Delano Roosevelt: Champion of Freedom*. New York: Public Affairs, 2003.

Blainey, Geoffrey. *The Rush That Never Ended*. Carlton, Australia: Melbourne University Press, 1993.

———. "Herbert Hoover's Forgotten Years." *Business Archives and History* 3, no. 1 (February 1963): 53–70.

Blom, Philipp. *The Vertigo Years: Europe, 1900–1914*. New York: Basic Books, 2006.

Brandes, Joseph. *Herbert Hoover and Economic Diplomacy*. Pittsburgh, PA: University of Pittsburgh Press, 1962.

Brands, H. W. *Traitor to His Class: The Privileged Life and Radical Presidency of Franklin Delano Roosevelt*. New York: Doubleday, 2008.

Bremner, Robert H. *American Philanthropy*. Chicago: University of Chicago Press, 1988.

Brinkley, Alan. *The End of Reform: New Deal Liberalism in Recession and War*. New York: Knopf, 1995.

Britton, Nan. *The President's Daughter*. New York: Elizabeth Ann Guild, 1927.

Brooks, David. *The Age of Upheaval: Edwardian Politics, 1899–1913*. Manchester, UK: Manchester University Press, 1995.

Burner, David. *Herbert Hoover: A Public Life*. Newton, MA: American Political Biography Press, 1978.

Burns, Richard D. *Herbert Hoover: A Bibliography of His Times and Presidency*. Wilmington, DE: Scholarly Resources, 1991.

Cannadine, David. *Mellon: An American Life*. New York: Vintage Books, 2008.

Carlson, Ellsworth. *The Kaiping Mines*. Cambridge, MA: Harvard University Press, 1971.

Cashman, Sean Dennis. *America in the Twenties and Thirties: The Olympian Age of Franklin Delano Roosevelt*. New York: New York University Press, 1989.

Chickering, Roger. *Imperial Germany and the Great War, 1914–1918*. Cambridge, UK: Cambridge University Press, 2004.

Clements, Kendrick A. *Hoover, Conservation, and Consumerism: Engineering the Good Life*. Lawrence: University Press of Kansas, 2000.

———. *The Life of Herbert Hoover: Imperfect Visionary, 1918–1928*. New York: Palgrave Macmillan, 2010.

Cohen, Paul A. *History in Three Keys: The Boxers as Event, Experience, and Myth*. New York: Columbia University Press, 1997.

Cohrs, Patrick O. *The Unfinished Peace after World War I: America, Britain and the Stabilization of Europe, 1919–1932*. Cambridge, UK: Cambridge University Press, 2008.

Cole, Harold L., and Lee E. Ohanian. "The Great Depression in the United States from a Neoclassical Perspective." *Federal Reserve Bank of Minneapolis Quarterly Review* 23, no. 1 (Winter 1999): 2–24.

Cooper, John Milton, Jr. *Woodrow Wilson: A Biography*. New York: Knopf, 2009.

Croly, Herbert. *The Promise of American Life*. Cambridge, MA: Belknap Press, 1965.

Curti, Merle. *American Philanthropy Abroad*. New Brunswick, NJ: Transaction Books.

Dalton, Kathleen. *Theodore Roosevelt: A Strenuous Life*. New York: First Vintage Books, 2004.

Daniels, Josephus. *The Cabinet Diaries of Josephus Daniels: 1913–1921*. Edited by David E. Cronon. Lincoln: University of Nebraska Press, 1963.

Daniels, Roger. *Franklin D. Roosevelt: Road to the New Deal, 1882–1939*. Champaign: University of Illinois Press, 2015.

Dawley, Alan. *Changing the World: American Progressives in War and Revolution*.

Dean, John W. *Warren G. Harding*. New York: Times Books, 2004.

DeConde, Alexander. *Herbert Hoover's Latin-American Policy*. Stanford, CA: Stanford University Press, 1951.

DeLong, Bradford. "Fiscal Policy in the Shadow of the Great Depression," in *The Defining Moment: The Great Depression and the American Economy in the Twentieth Century*, edited by Michael D. Bordo et al. Chicago: University of Chicago Press, 1998.

Dennis, Ruth. *The Homes of the Hoovers*. West Branch, IA: Herbert Hoover Presidential Library Association, 1986.

Dickens, Charles. *David Copperfield*. New York: Modern Library, 2000.

Dickstein, Morris. *Dancing in the Dark: A Cultural History of the Great Depression*. New York: Norton, 2009.

Dumenil, Lynn. *The Modern Temper: American Culture and Society in the 1920s*. New York: Hill & Wang, 1995.

Eichengreen, Barry. *Golden Fetters: The Gold Standard and the Great Depression, 1919–1939*. New York: Oxford University Press, 1995.

———. *Hall of Mirrors: The Great Depression, the Great Recession, and the Uses—and Misuses—of History*. New York: Oxford University Press, 2015.

———. "The Political Economy of the Smoot-Hawley Tariff." Working Paper No. 2001, National Bureau of Economic Research, August 1986.

Ellis, L. Ethan. *Republican Foreign Policy, 1921–1933*. New Brunswick, NJ: Rutgers University Press, 1968.

Fausold, Martin. *The Presidency of Herbert C. Hoover*. Lawrence: University Press of Kansas, 1985.

Ferguson, Niall. *The Pity of War: Explaining World War I*. New York: Basic Books, 1998.

Ferrell, Robert H. *Harry S. Truman: A Life*. Columbia: University of Missouri Press, 1994.

———. *Peace in Their Time: The Origins of the Kellogg-Briand Pact*. New York: Norton, 1969.

———. *The Presidency of Calvin Coolidge*. Lawrence: University Press of Kansas, 1998.

Finan, Christopher M. *Alfred E. Smith, the Happy Warrior*. New York: Hill & Wang, 2002.

Fishback, Price V. "U.S. Monetary and Fiscal Policy in the 1930s." Working Paper No. 16477, National Bureau of Economic Research, October 2010.

Fleming, Thomas J. *The Illusion of Victory: America in World War I*. New York: Basic Books, 2003.

Friedman, Milton, and Anna Schwartz. *A Monetary History of the United States*. Princeton, NJ: Princeton University Press, 1963.

Friedman, Walter A. *Fortune Tellers*. Princeton, NJ: Princeton University Press, 2014.

Fromkin, David. *Europe's Last Summer: Who Started the Great War in 1914?* New York: Vintage Books, 2005.

Gaddis, John Lewis. *The Cold War: A New History*. New York: Penguin, 2007.

Galbraith, John Kenneth. *The Great Crash of 1929*. Boston: Houghton Mifflin, 1988.

Gay, George I. *Public Relations of the Commission for Relief in Belgium*, vol. 1. Palo Alto, CA: Stanford University Press, 1929.

Gelfand, Lawrence Emerson, ed. *Herbert Hoover: The Great War and Its Aftermath, 1914–1923*. Iowa City: University of Iowa Press, 1979.

Gibbs, Nancy, and Michael Duffy. *The President's Club: Inside the World's Most Exclusive Fraternity*. New York: Simon & Schuster, 2012.

Gibson, Hugh. *A Journal from Our Legation in Belgium*. New York: Doubleday, Page, 1917.

Gilbert, Martin. *The First World War: A Complete History*. New York: Henry Holt, 1994.

Gilbert, Robert E. *The Tormented President: Calvin Coolidge, Death, and Clinical Depression*. Westport, CT: Praeger, 2003.

Gordon, John Steele. *An Empire of Wealth: The Epic History of American Economic Power*. New York: Harper Perennial, 2005.

Gordon, Robert J. *The Rise and Fall of American Growth*. Princeton, NJ: Princeton University Press, 2016.

Greenberg, David. *Calvin Coolidge*. New York: Times Books, 2006.

Gregory, Ross. *Walter Hines Page: Ambassador to the Court of St. James's*. Lexington: University Press of Kentucky, 1970.

Grierson, Miss. *Pierre and His Family, Or, a Story of the Waldenses*. Philadelphia: American Sunday School Union, 1827.

Hamby, Alonzo. *Man of Destiny: FDR and the Making of the American Century*. New York: Basic Books, 2015.

Hamill, John. *The Strange Career of Mr. Hoover Under Two Flags*. New York: W. Faro, 1931.

Hartley, Richard. "Bewick, Moreing in West Australia Gold Mining, 1897–1904." *Labour History*, no. 65 (November 1993): 1–18.

Hawley, Ellis W., ed. *Herbert Hoover and the Historians*. West Branch, IA: Herbert Hoover Presidential Association, 1989.

———, ed. *Herbert Hoover as Secretary of Commerce*. Iowa City: University of Iowa Press, 1981.

Haynes, John Earl, ed. *Calvin Coolidge and the Coolidge Era*. Washington, DC: Library of Congress, 1998.

Hendrick, Burton. *The Life and Letters of Walter H. Page, 1885–1918*. Garden City, NY: Garden City Publishing, 1926.

Hiltzik, Michael. *Colossus: Hoover Dam and the Making of the American Century*. New York: Free Press, 2010.

Hinshaw, David. *Herbert Hoover: American Quaker*. New York: Farrar, Straus, 1950.

Hodgson, Godfrey. *Woodrow Wilson's Right Hand: The Life of Colonel Edward M. House*. New Haven, CT: Yale University Press, 2006.

Hoover, Herbert. *Addresses Upon the American Road, 1933–1938*. New York: Charles Scribner's Sons, 1938.

———. *Addresses Upon the American Road, 1940–1941*. New York: Charles Scribner's Sons, 1941.

———. *Addresses Upon the American Road, 1945–1948*. New York: D. Van Nostrand, 1949.

———. *An American Epic: Introduction, The Relief of Belgium and Northern France, 1914–1930*, vol. 1. Chicago: Henry Regnery, 1959.

———. *American Individualism*. New York: Doubleday, 1922.

———. *The Challenge to Liberty*. New York: Charles Scribner's Sons, 1934.

———. *Fishing for Fun and to Wash Your Soul*. West Branch, IA: Herbert Hoover Presidential Library, 1990.

———. *Freedom Betrayed: Herbert Hoover's Secret History of the Second World War*. Edited by George H. Nash. Stanford, CA: Hoover Institution Press, 2011.

———. *Further Addresses Upon the American Road, 1938–1940*. New York: Charles Scribner's Sons, 1940.

———. *The Memoirs of Herbert Hoover: Years of Adventure, 1874–1920*. New York: Macmillan, 1952.

———. *The Memoirs of Herbert Hoover: The Great Depression, 1929–1941*. New York: Macmillan, 1952.

———. *The Memoirs of Herbert Hoover: The Cabinet and the Presidency, 1920–1933*. New York: Macmillan, 1952.

———. *The New Day: Campaign Speeches of Herbert Hoover, 1928*. Palo Alto, CA: Stanford University Press, 1928.

———. *The Ordeal of Woodrow Wilson*. Washington, DC: Woodrow Wilson Center Press, 1992.

———. *The Principles of Mining*. New York: Hill Publishing, 1909.

Horwitz, Steven. "Herbert Hoover: Father of the New Deal." The Cato Institute Briefing Paper No. 122 (September 29, 2011).

Houck, Davis W. *Rhetoric as Currency: Hoover, Roosevelt and the Great Depression*. College Station: Texas A&M University Press, 2001.

Hughes, Thomas P. *American Genesis: A Century of Invention and Technological Enthusiasm, 1870–1970*. Chicago: University of Chicago Press, 2004.

Hull, Isabel V. *A Scrap of Paper: Breaking and Making International Law During the Great War*. Ithaca, NY: Cornell University Press, 2014.

Hunt, Edward Eyre. *War Bread: A Personal Narrative of the War and Relief in Belgium*. New York: Henry Holt, 1916.

Irwin, Douglas A. *Peddling Protectionism: Smoot-Hawley and the Great Depression*. Princeton, NJ: Princeton University Press, 2011.

Irwin, Will. *Herbert Hoover: A Reminiscent Biography*. New York: Century Co., 1928.

———. *The Making of a Reporter*. New York: G. P. Putnam's Sons, 1942.

Jeansonne, Glen. *The Life of Herbert Hoover: Fighting Quaker, 1928–1933*. New York: Palgrave Macmillan, 2012.

Jenkins, Roy. *Asquith*. London: Collins, 1964.

Johnson, Claudius O. *Borah of Idaho*. New York: Longmans, Green, 1936.

Johnson, Paul. *Modern Times*. London: Orion, 1992.

Joslin, Theodore. *Hoover off the Record*. Garden City, NY: Doubleday, Doran, 1934.

Keegan, John. *The First World War*. Toronto: Key Porter Books, 1998.

Keene, Jennifer, and Michael Neiberg. *Finding Common Ground: New Directions in First World War Studies*. Leiden, the Netherlands: Brill, 2007.

Kehoe, Loretta. "The Relation of Herbert Hoover to Congress, 1929–1933." Master's thesis, Loyola University, 1949. http://ecommons.luc.edu/luc_theses/768.

Kellogg, Vernon. *Headquarter Nights: A Record of Conversations and Experiences at the Headquarters of the German Army in France and Belgium*. Boston: Atlantic Monthly Press, 1917.

Kennedy, David M. *Freedom from Fear: The American People in Depression*. New York: Oxford University Press, 1999.

———. *Over Here: The First World War and American Society*. Oxford, UK: Oxford University Press, 2004.

Kennedy, Susan Estabrook. *The Banking Crisis of 1933*. Lexington: University Press of Kentucky, 1973.

Keynes, John Maynard. *The Economic Consequences of the Peace*. New Brunswick, NJ: Transaction Publishers, 2009.

Kittredge, Tracy Barrett. *The History of the Commission for Relief in Belgium, 1914–1917*. LaVergne, TN: General Books, 2010.

Kramer, Alan. *Dynamic of Destruction*. Oxford, UK: Oxford University Press, 2007.

Kuehl, Warren F., and Lynne Dunn. *Keeping the Covenant: American Internationalists and the League of Nations, 1920–1939*. Kent, OH: Kent State University Press, 1997.

Lamont, Edward M. *The Ambassador from Wall Street*. Lanham, MD: Madison Books, 1994.

Lane, Rose Wilder. *The Making of Herbert Hoover*. New York: Century Co., 1920.

Larson, Erik. *Dead Wake: The Last Crossing of the Lusitania*. New York: Crown, 2015.

Lears, Jackson. *Rebirth of a Nation: The Making of Modern America, 1877–1920*. New York: HarperCollins, 2009.

Leuchtenburg, William E. *Herbert Hoover*. New York: Times Books, 2009.

———. *The Perils of Prosperity: 1914–1932*. Chicago: University of Chicago Press, 1958.

Lewis, Sinclair. *Babbitt*. London: Jonathan Cape, 1922.

Lewis, Tom. *Empire of the Air*. New York: Harper Perennial, 1993.

Lichtman, Allan J. *Prejudice and the Old Politics: The Presidential Election of 1928*. Lanham, MD: Lexington Books, 1979.

Liggett, Walter W. *The Rise of Herbert Hoover*. New York: H. K. Fry, 1932.

Limbaugh, Ron. "Pragmatic Professional: Herbert Hoover's Formative Years as a Mining Engineer, 1895–1908." *Mining History Journal* 11 (2004): 43–58.

Link, Arthur S., ed. *The Papers of Woodrow Wilson*, vol. 31. Princeton, NJ: Princeton University Press, 1979.

———, and Mark O. Hatfield, eds. *Herbert Hoover Reassessed: Essays Commemorating the Fiftieth Anniversary of Our Thirty-First President*. Honolulu, HI: University Press of the Pacific, 2002.

Lippmann, Walter. *Men of Destiny*. New Brunswick, NJ: Transaction Publishers, 2003.

Lisio, Donald J. *The President and Protest: Hoover, Conspiracy and the Bonus Riot*. Columbia: University of Missouri Press.

Lloyd, Craig. *Aggressive Introvert: A Study of Herbert Hoover and Public Relations Management, 1912–1932*. Columbus: Ohio State University Press, 1972.

Lloyd, Gordon, and David Davenport. *The New Deal and Modern American Conservatism: A Defining Rivalry*. Stanford, CA: Hoover Institution Press, 2013.

Longworth, Alice Roosevelt. *Crowded Hours*. New York: Charles Scribner's Sons, 1933.

Lukas, John. "Herbert Hoover Meets Adolf Hitler." *The American Scholar* 62, no. 2 (Spring 1993): 235–38.

———. *The Last European War, September 1939–December 1941*. New Haven, CT: Yale University Press, 1976.

Lyons, Eugene. *Herbert Hoover: A Biography*. Garden City, NY: Doubleday, 1964.

MacMillan, Margaret. *Paris, 1919*. New York: Random House, 2003.

Manchester, William. *American Caesar: Douglas MacArthur, 1880–1964*. New York: Back Bay Books, 1978.

Marcosson, Isaac F. *Caravans of Commerce*. New York: Harper and Bros., 1926.

Mason, Robert. *The Republican Party and American Politics from Hoover to Reagan*. Cambridge, UK: Cambridge University Press, 2012.

Mayer, Dale C. *Dining with the Hoover Family*. West Branch, IA: Herbert Hoover Presidential Library Association, 1991.

———. *Lou Henry Hoover: Essays on a Busy Life*. Worland, WY: High Plains Publishing, 1994.

———. *Lou Henry Hoover: A Prototype for First Ladies*. New York: Nova History Publications, 2004.

McCullough, David. *Truman*. New York: Simon & Schuster, 1992.

McDougall, Walter A. *Promised Land, Crusader State: The American Encounter with the World Since 1776*. Boston: Mariner Books, 1997.

McLean, Hulda Hoover. *Hulda's World: A Chronicle of Hulda Minthorn Hoover, 1848–1884*. West Branch, IA: Herbert Hoover Presidential Library Association, 1989.

Meltzer, Allan H. *A History of the Federal Reserve*, vol. 1, 1913–1951. Chicago: University of Chicago Press, 2003.

Mencken, H. L. *On Politics: A Carnival of Buncombe*. Baltimore: Johns Hopkins University Press, 2006.

Meyers, Jeffrey. *George Orwell*. London: Routledge, 1975.

Michelson, Charles. *The Ghost Talks*. New York: G. P. Putnam's Sons, 1944.

Miller, Nathan. *New World Coming: The 1920s and the Making of Modern America*. Cambridge, MA: Da Capo Press, 2003.

Moley, Raymond. *After Seven Years*. New York: Harper & Bros., 1939.

Morris, Edmund. *The Rise of Theodore Roosevelt*. New York: Ballantine Books, 1980.

———. *Theodore Rex*. New York: Random House, 2001.

Murray, Robert K. *The Harding Era: Warren G. Harding and His Administration*. Newtown, CT: American Political Biography Press, 2008.

Myers, William Starr, and Walter H. Newton. *The Foreign Policies of Herbert Hoover, 1929–1933*. New York: Charles Scribner's Sons, 1940.

———. *The Hoover Administration: A Documented Narrative*. New York: Charles Scribner's Sons, 1936.

Nash, George H. "The 'Great Enigma' and the Great Engineer," in *Calvin Coolidge and the Coolidge Era*, edited by John Earl Haynes. Washington, DC: Library of Congress, 1998.

————. *Herbert Hoover and Stanford University*. Stanford, CA: Hoover Press, 1988.

————. *The Life of Herbert Hoover: The Engineer, 1874–1914*. New York: Norton, 1983.

————. *The Life of Herbert Hoover: The Humanitarian 1914–1917*. New York: Norton, 1988.

————. *The Life of Herbert Hoover: Master of Emergencies, 1917–1918*. New York: Norton, 1996.

————. *Reappraising the Right*. Wilmington, DE: ISI Books, 2009.

Nash, Lee. *Herbert Hoover and World Peace*. Lanham, MD: University Press of America, 2010.

————, ed. *Understanding Herbert Hoover: Ten Perspectives*. Stanford, CA: Hoover Institution Press, 1987.

Nye, Frank. *Doors of Opportunity: The Life and Legacy of Herbert Hoover*. West Branch, IA: Herbert Hoover Presidential Library Association, 1988.

O'Brien, Francis William. *The Hoover-Wilson Wartime Correspondence*. Ames: Iowa State University Press, 1974.

————. *Two Peacemakers in Paris*. College Station: Texas A&M University Press, 1978.

O'Brien, James J. *Hoover's Millions and How He Made Them*. New York: James J. O'Brien Publishing Co., 1932.

Okrent, Daniel. *Last Call: The Rise and Fall of Prohibition*. New York: Simon & Schuster, 2011.

Olson, James Stuart. *Herbert Hoover and the Reconstruction Finance Corporation, 1931–1933*. Ames: Iowa State University Press, 1977.

Parrish, Michael E. *Anxious Decades: America in Prosperity and Depression, 1920–1941*. New York: Norton, 1994.

Percy, Eustace. *Some Memories*. London: Eyre & Spottiswoode, 1958.

Perrett, Geoffrey. *America in the Twenties: A History*. New York: Touchstone Books, 1983.

Phimister, Ian. "Foreign Devils, Finance and Informal Empire: Britain and China, c. 1900–1912." *Modern Asian Studies* 40, no. 3 (2006): 737–59.

————, and Jeremy Mouat. "Mining Engineers and Risk Management: British Overseas Investment, 1894–1914." *South African Historical Journal* 49 (November 2003): 1–26.

Pietrusza, David. *1920: The Year of the Six Presidents*. New York: Basic Books, 2008.

Preston, Diana. *The Boxer Rebellion*. New York: Berkley, 1999.

Pringle, Henry F. *The Life & Times of William Howard Taft*. Newton, MA: American Political Biography Press, 1998.

*Public Papers of the Presidents of the United States: Franklin D. Roosevelt*, vol. 9. Washington, DC: U.S. Government Printing Office, 1940.

*Public Papers of the Presidents of the United States: Herbert Hoover*, 4 vols., 1929–1933. Washington, DC: U.S. Government Printing Office, 1974–77.

Rickard, T. A. Walter Benton Ingalls, Herbert Hoover, and R. Gilman Brown. *The Economics of Mining*. New York: Engineering and Mining Journal, 1905.

Ritchie, Donald A. *Electing FDR: The New Deal Campaign of 1932.* Lawrence: University Press of Kansas, 2007.

Romasco, Albert U. *The Poverty of Abundance.* New York: Oxford University Press, 1965.

Romer, Christina D. "The Great Crash and the Onset of the Great Depression." *The Quarterly Journal of Economics* 105, no. 3 (August 1990): 597–624.

———. "What Ended the Great Depression?" *The Journal of Economic History* 52, no. 4 (December 1992): 757–84.

Roosevelt, Franklin D. *The Public Papers and Addresses of Franklin D. Roosevelt,* vol. 2. Edited by Samuel Irving Rosenman. New York: Random House, 1938.

———. *The Public Papers and Addresses of Franklin D. Roosevelt,* vol. 6. Edited by Samuel Irving Rosenman. New York: Macmillan, 1941.

Rosen, Elliot A. *Hoover, Roosevelt and the Brains Trust.* New York: Columbia University Press, 1977.

Russell, Francis. *The Shadow of Blooming Grove.* New York: McGraw Hill, 1969.

Schlesinger, Arthur M., Jr. *The Age of Roosevelt: The Politics of Upheaval.* Boston: Houghton Mifflin, 1988.

Schwarz, Jordan A. *The Interregnum of Despair: Hoover, Congress, and the Depression.* Urbana: University of Illinois Press, 1970.

———. *The Crisis of the Old Order: 1919–1933.* Boston: Houghton Mifflin, 2003.

Schwieder, Dorothy. *Iowa: The Middle Land.* Iowa City: Iowa State University Press, 1996.

Seymour, Charles, ed. *The Intimate Papers of Colonel House,* 2 vols. Boston: Houghton Mifflin, 1926–28.

Sheffield, Gary. *Forgotten Victory: The First World War, Myths and Realities.* London: Headline Review, 2002.

Shlaes, Amity. *Coolidge.* New York: Harper Perennial, 2014.

———. *The Forgotten Man: A New History of the Great Depression.* New York: HarperCollins, 2007.

Sizer, Rosanne. "Herbert Hoover and the Smear Books." *The Annals of Iowa* 47, no. 4 (Spring 1984): 343–61.

Slayton, Robert A. *Empire Statesman: The Rise and Redemption of Al Smith.* New York: Free Press, 2001.

Smith, Alfred E. *Campaign Addresses of Governor Alfred E. Smith.* Washington, DC: Democratic National Committee, 1929.

Smith, Gene. *The Shattered Dream: Herbert Hoover and the Great Depression.* New York: William Morrow, 1970.

Smith, Jean Edward. *FDR.* New York: Random House, 2008.

Smith, Richard Norton. *An Uncommon Man: The Triumph of Herbert Hoover.* New York: Simon & Schuster, 1984.

Snyder, Richard J. "Hoover and the Hawley-Smoot Tariff." *The Annals of Iowa* 41, no. 7 (Winter 1973): 1173–89.

Sobel, Robert. *Herbert Hoover at the Onset of the Great Depression.* Philadelphia: Lippincott, 1975.

Stearns, Howard E., ed. *Civilization in the United States, An Inquiry by Thirty Americans*. New York: Harcourt, Brace, 1922.

Steel, Ronald. *Walter Lippmann and the American Century*. Boston: Atlantic Monthly Press, 1980.

Stein, Herbert. *The Fiscal Revolution in America*. Washington, DC: AEI Press, 1996.

Stevenson, David. *Cataclysm: The First World War as Political Tragedy*. New York: Basic Books, 2004.

———. *The First World War and International Politics*. Oxford, UK: Clarendon Press, 1988.

Strachan, Hew. *The First World War*. Vol. 1, *To Arms*. Oxford, UK: Oxford University Press, 2003.

Stratton, Maud. *Herbert Hoover's Home Town: Early History and Environment of the First President Born West of the Mississippi River*. West Branch, IA: West Branch Times, 1938.

Strauss, Lewis. *Men and Decisions*. Garden City, NY: Doubleday, 1962.

Susman, Warren I., and Joseph J. Huthmacher, eds. *Herbert Hoover and the Crisis of American Capitalism*. Cambridge, MA: Schenkman Publishing, 1973.

Sweetkind-Singer, Julie. "Herbert Hoover: A Geologist in Training." *Journal of Map and Geography Libraries* 6 (2010): 129–39.

Temin, Peter. *Did Money Forces Cause the Great Depression?* New York: W. W. Norton, 1976.

Thomas, Stephen C. *Foreign Intervention and China's Industrial Development, 1870–1911*. Boulder, CO: Westview Press, 1984.

Tooze, Adam. *The Wages of Destruction*. New York: Viking, 2006.

Tracey, Kathleen. *Herbert Hoover—A Bibliography, His Writings and Addresses*. Stanford, CA: Hoover Institution Press, 1977.

Traxel, David. *Crusader Nation: The United States in Peace and the Great War, 1898–1920*. New York: Vintage Books, 2007.

Walch, Timothy, ed. *Herbert Hoover and Dwight D. Eisenhower: A Documentary History*. New York: Palgrave Macmillan, 2013.

———. *Uncommon Americans: The Lives and Legacies of Herbert and Lou Henry Hoover*. Westport, CT: Praeger, 2003.

———, and Dwight M. Miller, eds. *Herbert Hoover and Franklin D. Roosevelt: A Documentary History*. Westport, CT: Greenwood Press, 1998.

———, and Dwight M. Miller, eds. *Herbert Hoover and Harry Truman: A Documentary History*. Worland, WY: High Plains Publishing, 1992.

Walworth, Arthur. *Woodrow Wilson*. New York: Norton, 1978.

Warren, Harris Gaylord. *Herbert Hoover and the Great Depression*. New York: Norton, 1967.

Wert, Hal Elliott. *Hoover, The Fishing President: Portrait of the Private Man and His Life Outdoors*. Mechanicsburg, PA: Stackpole Books, 2005.

Whisenhunt, Donald W. *President Herbert Hoover*. New York: Nova Science Publishers, 2007.

White, William Allen. *Masks in a Pageant*. New York: Macmillan, 1928.

———. *A Puritan in Babylon*. New York: Macmillan, 1958.

Whitlock, Brand. *Belgium: A Personal Narrative*, vol. 1. New York: D. Appleton, 1919.

———, and Allan Nevins, eds. *The Letters and Journal of Brand Whitlock: The Journal*. New York: D. Appleton-Century, 1936.

———, and Allan Nevins, eds. *The Letters and Journal of Brand Whitlock: The Letters*. New York: D. Appleton-Century, 1936.

Wicker, Elmus. *The Banking Panics of the Great Depression*. Cambridge, UK: Cambridge University Press, 1996.

Wilbur, Ray Lyman. *Memories, 1875–1949*. Stanford, CA: Stanford University Press, 1960.

Willmott, H. P. *The Great Crusade: A New Complete History of the Second World War*. New York: Free Press, 1990.

Wilson, Joan Hoff. *Herbert Hoover: Forgotten Progressive*. Long Grove, IL: Waveland Press, 1992.

Woolf, Stuart Joseph, ed. *Nationalism in Europe: 1815 to the Present*. London: Routledge, 1996.

Wueschner, Silvano A. *Charting Twentieth-Century Monetary Policy: Herbert Hoover and Benjamin Strong, 1917–1927*. Westport, CT: Greenwood Press, 1999.

Young, Nancy Beck. *Lou Henry Hoover: Activist First Lady*. Lawrence: University of Kansas Press, 2004.

Zuckerman, Larry. *The Rape of Belgium*. New York: New York University Press, 2004.

# INDEX

Hoover, Herbert (*continued*)
  as skillful negotiator, 114
  smear books and, 475–6
  social aspirations of, 107–8, 121
  social graces lacked by, 106–7
  in vicious counterattacks on critics,
    168, 171, 202
  as voracious reader, 31, 96, 99,
    102–3, 108, 273, 306, 531
  World War I financial losses of, 139
Hoover, Herbert Charles, Jr., 96, 97,
    139, 140, 146, 147, 152–5, 169,
    186, 190, 209, 240–1, 242, 290,
    309, 310, 311–12, 326, 339, 358,
    368, 530–1, 534, 573, 606, 607
  birth of, 95
  camping and fishing trips of, 335–6
  Lou's long letters to, 154–5
  at Stanford, 240
Hoover, Herbert, childhood and
    youth of
  on Allen Hoover farm, 18–19
  at Stanford, 34–9
  attention craved by, 13, 24
  Bible reading by, 14, 22
  bicycle of, 29
  birth of, 3, 4–5
  croup contracted by, 5–6
  entrepreneurialism of, 28, 29
  evening courses taken by, 32
  father's death in, 12–13
  geology degree of, 44
  industriousness of, 22, 27, 36
  jobs held by, 22, 35–6, 37, 40–2
  lifelong reading habit developed
    in, 31
  Lindgren as role model for, 40–1
  with Minthorn family, 20–5, 26–34
  mother's absences in, 16
  mother's death and, 17

  Oregon Land Company job of,
    27–9, 32
  Quaker faith of, 29
  schooling of, 13–14, 23
  serious demeanor of, 30
  in train trip to Oregon, 19–20
  in West Branch, 8–9, 11–19
Hoover, Herbert, III, 358, 359, 368
Hoover, Herbert, political career of
  aversion to campaigning of, 234, 344,
    346
  as Commerce secretary, *see*
    Commerce Department, U.S.,
    under Hoover
  Economic Club speech of, 553–7
  European intervention opposed by,
    562–3, 565, 570–1
  FDR's death and, 575–6
  and FDR's Supreme Court packing
    attempt, 551
  foreign policy writings and speeches
    of, 593–5, 606
  Harding scandals and, 289–90, 291–2
  as Hoover Commission chair, *see*
    Hoover Commission
  internationalism of, 231
  laissez-faire economics rejected by,
    230–1, 256–7, 479–80
  New Deal equated with despotism
    by, 540–3, 546
  1920 election and, 234–8, 239
  1927 Mississippi floods and, 328–33,
    334, 341, 354
  1936 convention speech of, 545–7
  and 1936 election, 544–5
  overtures from Truman
    administration rejected by, 576–7
  post-1932 hostility toward, 544–5
  presidential ambitions of, 322, 323,
    337, 340

PHOTOGRAPHY CREDITS

*page 1, top and bottom:* Courtesy of the National Archives & Records Administration—Hoover Presidential Library

*page 2:* Courtesy of the National Archives & Records Administration—Hoover Presidential Library

*page 3:* Courtesy of the National Archives & Records Administration—Hoover Presidential Library

*page 4, top and bottom:* Courtesy of the National Archives & Records Administration—Hoover Presidential Library

*page 5, top and bottom:* Courtesy of the National Archives & Records Administration—Hoover Presidential Library

*page 6, top and bottom:* Courtesy of the National Archives & Records Administration—Hoover Presidential Library

*page 7:* Courtesy of the National Archives & Records Administration—Hoover Presidential Library

*page 8, top and bottom:* Courtesy of the National Archives & Records Administration—Hoover Presidential Library

*page 9:* Courtesy of the National Archives & Records Administration—Hoover Presidential Library

*page 10, top and bottom:* Courtesy of the National Archives & Records Administration—Hoover Presidential Library

*page 11, top:* Courtesy of Clifton R. Adams / National Geographic Creative; *bottom:* Courtesy of the National Archives & Records Administration—Hoover Presidential Library

*page 12, top and bottom:* Courtesy of the National Archives & Records Administration—Hoover Presidential Library

*page 13:* Courtesy of Bettmann / Getty Images

*page 14, top:* Courtesy of Imagno / Getty Images; *bottom:* Courtesy of Underwood Archives, from the Library of Congress, Prints & Photographs Division, LC-USZ62-131801 *page 15, top:* Courtesy of Imagno / Getty Images; *bottom:* Courtesy of the Library of Congress, Prints & Photographs Division, FSA / OWI Collection, LC-DIG-fsa-8b27057

*page 16, top and bottom:* Courtesy of AP Photo; center: Courtesy of the Truman Library

A NOTE ABOUT THE AUTHOR

Kenneth Whyte is the author of *The Uncrowned King: The Sensational Rise of William Randolph Hearst*, a *Washington Post* and *Toronto Globe and Mail* book of the year, and a nominee for four major Canadian and American book awards. He is a publishing and telecommunications executive and chairman of the Donner Canada Foundation. He was formerly editor in chief of *Maclean's* magazine, editor of the monthly *Saturday Night* magazine, and founding editor of the *National Post*. He lives in Toronto.

A NOTE ON THE TYPE

This book was set in Janson, a typeface long thought to have been made by
the Dutchman Anton Janson, who was a practicing typefounder in Leipzig
during the years 1668–1687. However, it has been conclusively demonstrated that these types are actually the work of Nicholas Kis (1650–1702),
a Hungarian, who most probably learned his trade from the master Dutch
typefounder Dirk Voskens. The type is an excellent example of the influential and sturdy Dutch types that prevailed in England up to the time
William Caslon (1692–1766) developed his own incomparable designs
from them.

Composed by North Market Street Graphics,
Lancaster, Pennsylvania

Printed and bound by Berryville Graphics,
Berryville, Virginia

Designed by Soonyoung Kwon